Wolf and Stanley on Environmental Law

Sixth edition

Written with real clarity by authors teaching and researching in the field, *Wolf and Stanley on Environmental Law* offers an excellent starting point for both law and non-law students encountering this diverse and controversial subject for the first time. Topics covered include elements of environmental law, law enforcement, water pollution, EU environmental law, waste management, environmental permitting, contaminated land, environmental torts and air pollution.

The book is supported by a range of learning features designed to help students:

- **Consolidate your learning:** Chapter learning objectives and detailed summaries clarify and highlight key points
- **Understand how the law works in practice:** 'Law in Action' features demonstrate the application of environmental law
- **Plan your research:** Detailed end of chapter further reading sections outline articles, books and online resources that provide next steps for your research.

This sixth edition has been updated and revised to take into account recent developments in the subject, including coverage of the Environmental Permitting (England and Wales) Regulations 2010, as well as developments in Environment Agency enforcement and sanctions policy guidance and updates relating to the defence of statutory authority in the tort of private nuisance.

Suitable for students of environmental law and the wider environmental studies, *Wolf and Stanley on Environmental Law* is a valuable guide to this wide-ranging subject.

Susan Wolf is Principal Lecturer in Law at the University of Northumbria.

Neil Stanley is Lecturer in Law at the University of Leeds.

Routledge
Taylor & Francis Group

LONDON AND NEW YORK

Sixth edition published 2014
by Routledge
2 Park Square, Milton Park, Abingdon, Oxon OX14 4RN

and by Routledge
711 Third Avenue, New York, NY 10017

Routledge is an imprint of the Taylor & Francis Group, an informa business

First edition published by Cavendish Publishing 1995
Fifth edition published by Routledge 2011

British Library Cataloguing in Publication Data
A catalogue record for this book is available from the British Library

Library of Congress Cataloging in Publication Data
A catolog record for this book has been requested.

ISBN: 978-0-415-68514-6 (hbk)
ISBN: 978-0-415-68516-0 (pbk)
ISBN: 978-1-315-88569-8 (ebk)

Typeset in Joanna
by RefineCatch Limited, Bungay, Suffolk

MIX
Paper from
responsible sources
FSC® C013604
www.fsc.org

Printed and bound in Great Britain by CPI Group (UK) Ltd, Croydon, CR0 4YY

Outline Contents

Detailed Contents

For
Rebecca and Jules,
Alex and Carla

Preface

The authors' objectives in writing this text are as follows:

- to provide the reader with a succinct and accessible account of the core features of pollution control law in England and Wales;
- to design and write a book with the needs of both law and non-law students, at both undergraduate and postgraduate levels, firmly in mind. The authors teach a variety of law modules to undergraduate students (on law, environmental science, environmental management and other degree programmes) and to students who have included employees of the regulators (e.g. the Environment Agency, local authorities and Defra) and the regulated (e.g. waste and water industries);
- to focus on the topics which feature most often and are therefore of most relevance to students on environmental law courses offered by higher education institutions in England and Wales;
- to set the law in its policy and practical context;
- to provide illustrations of common pollution failures which result in prosecution;
- to provide the reader with research assistance through links to key sources of further information; and
- to provide non-lawyers with basic advice on how to access case reports, journal articles, etc, either in a law library or via online databases/websites.

We provide the reader with a simple framework to guide him or her through this text. We have arranged the material from the perspectives of the regulators (who 'police' compliance with the law), the regulated (those who are subject to the law), and those legal persons (individuals, NGOs and companies) and groups who wish either to challenge decisions made by government or the regulators, or claim compensation for pollution-related damage.

We recommend that the reader reads Chapter 1 followed by Chapter 6, prior to reading the remaining chapters. Much of the content of this book concerns the regulation of polluting discharges and the importance of an environmental permit-based approach to pollution control. Chapter 6 explains the environmental permitting regime introduced by the Environmental Permitting (England and Wales) Regulations 2010.

In Chapter 1, we introduce the reader to the legal framework which controls polluting emissions in England and Wales against the backcloth of EU environmental and international environmental law. We also examine the sources of environmental law, the ethical underpinning of the law, relevant legal principles and the emergence of alternative methods (to the basic 'Command and Control' regulatory system) to control polluting activity. In Chapter 2, we outline the administrative (e.g. dealing with applications for environmental permits) and enforcement roles of the regulators and the role of the courts. In Chapter 3, we consider the impact of the UK's membership of the EU on the rapid development of environmental law and policy. In Chapters 4–10, we describe and analyse the main pollution control regimes, largely from the perspective of the regulator: water pollution, waste management, environmental permitting, contaminated land, air pollution, statutory nuisance and noise. In Chapters 11 and 12, we discuss the use of environmental law by individuals and others to protect property interests, human health and the environment, and how the law may be used as a tool to oversee the activities of the regulators and to mount private prosecutions. Chapter 11 addresses the 'environmental torts' of nuisance, negligence, trespass and the rule in *Rylands v Fletcher*, whilst Chapter 12 covers access to environmental information, human rights, public concern, judicial review and private prosecutions. Neil was responsible for updating Chapters 1, 2, 4, 5, 8, and 11, whilst Susan has updated Chapters 3, 6, 7, 9, 10 and 12.

This textbook focuses on those laws in England and Wales which are concerned with the regulation of polluting substances discharged into the environment from industrial, commercial, agricultural and domestic premises. Whilst we concede that environmental law extends well beyond pollution control, we have been guided in the selection of content by the needs of our primary readership. We concentrate on an analysis of the main vehicle which is used by the government to control polluting emissions in the UK: the series of 'Command and Control' laws (that is, legislation, enacted by Parliament which 'commands' the UK subject (legal person) to do, or refrain from doing, something—usually obtaining a permit to authorise an activity—and thereby the legislation 'controls' the UK subject's activities) which address specific environmental problems. Whilst we do discuss EU law and international law, we discuss developments at these levels in terms of how they impact upon national regulation, often by driving the development of our law forward.

Since this is a textbook, and reasons of space require us to be selective, we recognise that we run the risk of generalising at the expense of accuracy in some cases. Short of writing an encyclopaedia, this problem is inescapable. We would therefore recommend any reader who has a specific environmental problem to resolve should seek professional advice for, in a fast moving field such as environmental law, total accuracy is a challenge.

We would like to thank our publishers for their help in writing this book. Special thanks go to our editorial team comprising Emma Nugent and Rebekah Jenkins for supporting us as we endeavoured to meet production targets. We have endeavoured to strike the right balance between broad structure and detailed analysis. If we have disappointed the reader in any way then we would urge him or her to contact us at n.k.stanley@leeds.ac.uk and susan.wolf@northumbria.ac.uk. We will endeavour to update, amend and correct any errors in the text via the online resources. We are committed to continuous improvement of this text and value all constructive comments.

Table of Cases

Table of Statutes

Table of Statutory Instruments

Chapter 1

Elements of Environmental Law

Chapter Contents

> ### Learning Objectives
>
> By the end of this chapter you should have acquired an understanding of:
>
> - the legal framework which controls (regulates) polluting emissions to the three environmental media (air, land and water) in England and Wales;
>
> - the fact that national law incorporates aspects of European environmental and international environmental law;
>
> - the sources of environmental law;
>
> - the relevant legal and policy principles;
>
> - the legal definitions of key terms (e.g. 'pollution' and 'environment');
>
> - the relationship between environmental law and environmental policy;
>
> - the emergence of alternative methods (to the basic legal framework) to control polluting activities.

1.1 Introduction

In this chapter, we introduce the reader to the legal framework which controls polluting emissions to the three environmental media (air, land and water) in England and Wales. The relevant national law is set in the context of European environmental and international environmental law. We examine the sources of environmental law, the relevant legal and policy principles, and the emergence of alternative methods (to the basic legal framework) to control polluting activities. Throughout this textbook we aim to provide the reader with a practical perspective in regard to how the law in England and Wales controls polluting substances discharged into the environment.

1.2 What is environmental law?

Before embarking on an explanation of the legal framework which regulates polluting emissions in England and Wales, we suggest that the reader spends a few minutes thinking about his or her answers to the following seven questions which are designed to provide the reader with a 'mindset' (orientation) which will help him or her grasp much of what follows:

(a) What is 'pollution' and what is the 'environment'?
(b) What is environmental law? (What does it comprise?)
(c) What is environmental law for? (What are its functions?)
(d) What are the main features of environmental law?
(e) Who uses environmental law and for what purpose(s)?
(f) What are the main driving forces behind the changes in and development of environmental law?
(g) Is the use of legal devices, such as legislation, the only available means to control pollution?

1.3 Environmental law: an overview

In this introductory chapter, we provide an outline of environmental law as it relates to the regulation of polluting activities in England and Wales.[1] At 1.4.1, we consider some preliminary issues, especially the difficulties associated with the concepts of 'pollution' and 'environment', before moving on to discuss the components or elements of environmental law. At 1.4.2, we refer to the persons who frequently use environmental law and their respective objectives. At 1.4.3, we consider the primary functions of environmental law before referring to the forces which are driving its rapid development. At 1.5, we map out the structure of the public regulation of private polluting activities. By this we mean to refer to the regulation of the polluting activities of private legal persons, such as companies and individuals, by public regulatory bodies (such as the Environment Agency and the local authorities). As much of this textbook concerns an explanation of how the Environment Agency regulates polluting emissions via environmental permitting, we recommend readers to read Chapter 6 prior to referring to Chapters 4, 5, 7, 8, 9 and 10. At 1.6, we outline the use of environmental law by private persons to protect private interests, to prosecute and to oversee the fairness and legality of decisions made by public regulators. At 1.7, we summarise the sources of environmental law and at 1.8 the principles which guide its development. Finally, at 1.9, we refer to the emergence of new pollution control tools to supplement the basic Command and Control framework.[2]

1.4 Preliminary issues

1.4.1 'Pollution' and the 'environment'

Most of us think of 'pollution' in terms of something which is contaminated, unclean, spoilt or irreparably damaged. For example, we may be outraged by the damage to our health caused by atmospheric pollution from a nearby factory, or we may be saddened that the pristine beauty of a local beach has been marred by an oil spill. Implicit in the term 'pollution' is the existence of some element of risk, threat, danger or hazard to ourselves, or some other object such as an important wildlife habitat, which is important to us. We place a high value on the maintenance of a healthy environment. 'Pollution' is therefore a relative term. The level of threat or damage to humans, or some part of the wider environment perceived as important to humans, must be significant enough to trigger a recognition that 'pollution' has occurred. However, what is perceived as pollution by one person (or group or society) may not be perceived as pollution by another. The assessment of what constitutes pollution, in any given set of circumstances, will therefore vary with the values and risk perception of the relevant individual, group or society.

1.4.1.1 Pollution

In environmental law, there is no single, accepted definition of pollution; however, the Royal Commission on Environmental Pollution (RCEP)[3] has provided the following helpful definition:

> The introduction by man into the environment of substances or energy liable to cause hazards to human health, harm to living resources and ecological systems, damage to structure or amenity or interference with the legitimate uses of the environment.

---

1 At the end of the chapter, we provide references to texts which address the law in Scotland and Northern Ireland.
2 See 1.5 below for an explanation of 'Command and Control'.
3 *Pollution in Some British Estuaries and Coastal Waters*, Third Report, Cmnd 5054, 1972.

Pollution is associated with risks to human health and property, plants, animals, habitats and ecological systems. Pollution is not restricted to the impact of chemical substances upon man or the environment, but may extend to the introduction of energy into the environment, such as the 'hot' cooling water discharged from a power station into a river, or electro-magnetic fields emitted by electrical apparatus, such as power lines.

In an environmental law context, chemical substances and/or energy may be introduced into the environment in any of the following ways:

(a)   a legal person (for example, an individual or a company) discharges chemicals and/or energy into the environment in accordance with the conditions of a permit issued by a regulator;

(b)   a legal person discharges chemicals and/or energy into the environment in breach of permit conditions;

(c)   a legal person discharges chemicals and/or energy into the environment without the benefit of a permit issued by a regulator authorising the discharge.

In the first scenario, there is no pollution within the meaning of the relevant legislation under which the permit was issued. The permit holder will have a defence against regulatory criminal offences alleging pollution of the environment. In the second scenario, the permit holder has caused pollution to occur by exceeding the terms of its permit. A criminal offence has been committed: breach of permit conditions. Readers should note that it is not necessary for the prosecution to prove that environmental harm has occurred as a result of the breach of permit conditions. If the breach is minor, the regulator is likely to exercise its discretion not to prosecute, but may nevertheless ensure future compliance with environmental law, for example, by serving the polluter with an enforcement notice.

In regard to permitted discharges, Keith Hawkins observed that: 'Pollution is an administrative creation.'[4] This is a reference to the fact that, because the regulator controls the permitting process, especially the conditions attached to permits, it has the power to determine which discharges will, or will not, amount to pollution because they exceed permit conditions and are therefore unlawful.

1.4.1.2 Environment

In its most general sense, 'the environment' refers to our surroundings. It is often understood to include not only land, air and water, but also the built environment and the condition of the local neighbourhood. The environment can, for others, mean something more specific and refer to the conservation of natural habitats and ecology.

In an environmental law context, s 1(2) of the Environmental Protection Act 1990 (EPA 1990) contains the following definition of the environment which provides a useful guide regarding the issues addressed in this text:

> The 'environment' consists of all, or any of the following media, namely, the air, water and land; and the medium of air includes the air within buildings and the air within other natural or man-made structures above or below ground.

---

4   K Hawkins, *Environment and Enforcement* (Clarendon, Oxford 1984).

1.4.2 What is environmental law, who is using it and for what purpose or purposes?

Environmental law is primarily a mix of primary legislation,[5] secondary legislation,[6] judicial decisions reported in law reports, common law principles developed by the judiciary, European Union (EU) legislation[7] which is transposed into national law,[8] and international law.[9]

The study of environmental law is not confined to a study of the law which is written down in legislation (so-called 'black letter' law), but it is also concerned with how the law is used to achieve the objectives of the key environmental stakeholders: the regulators, the regulated industry (i.e. businesses which require a permit), central government, local government, industry associations, pressure groups, local amenity societies, NGOs and the public. The government and its agencies issue policy documents to public officials and the public, in the form of official guidance, in a never-ending stream of White Papers, Green Papers, consultation documents, guidance notes and circulars. Although this guidance is not law, it is nevertheless important because it guides how the regulators (such as the Environment Agency) will use the law to achieve the regulator's statutory objectives.[10]

It may therefore be helpful to conceive of environmental law not as a collection of separate pieces of legislation and policy documents, but as a 'toolbox' containing a range of legal and policy instruments. Only those legal and policy tools which will achieve the objectives of the specific user will be applied to the problem in hand. Thus, a regulator will use the powers available to it, and which are built into the specific regulatory regime it administers, to enforce the compliance of regulated businesses (and all other legal persons) with the relevant pollution control law. An individual who has sustained pollution damage to his or her property may resort to the common law, for example, using the tort of nuisance, to obtain compensation or other means of redress. An amenity group or society, such as Greenpeace, may mount a private prosecution against a polluter in circumstances where a regulator has exercised its discretion not to prosecute.

Alternatively, an amenity group, such as Friends of the Earth, may challenge by way of a judicial review application[11] a regulator's decision to grant a pollution permit to an applicant. In this way, an amenity society may seek to bring a regulator to account for an allegedly unlawful decision. Environmental law is therefore not a simple application of the contents of legislation to particular facts. To understand environmental law properly, we need to be aware of not only the contents of the relevant law and policy, but also how the law and policy will be applied by the regulator, the private litigator or the courts to resolve an environmental problem.

1.4.3 The function of environmental law

Much of environmental law concerns the *regulation* of polluting emissions discharged into the three environmental media: air, water and land. The primary function of environmental law is *not* to eliminate pollution, except in the case of a relatively few highly toxic pollutants, but to *balance* the polluting emissions generated by economic activity against the demands of society for a tolerably healthy environment. Polluting emissions must therefore be set, in most cases, by government (or its regulators) at levels which are acceptable to its two major stakeholders: regulated businesses and the public.[12] This balancing task is performed on behalf of government by regulatory agencies such

---

5 Acts of Parliament.
6 Regulations otherwise known as statutory instruments.
7 Mainly in the form of directives.
8 Usually in the form of regulations.
9 Found in treaties, conventions and protocols.
10 See 2.4.
11 Subject to 'standing' restrictions, discussed in Chapter 12.
12 But subject to European environmental law and international environmental law to which the state is a party.

as the Environment Agency and the local authorities. Environmental law also has subsidiary preventive, remedial (clean-up) and compensatory functions.

1.4.4 What is driving the development of environmental law?

The early history of environmental law in England and Wales was characterised by a parochial focus on localised pollution problems. Reliance on the common law, especially the law of torts, to resolve individual disputes over pollution-related property damage was overtaken by the need for legislation to address the gross, and widespread, pollution problems caused by the Industrial Revolution. A series of legislative enactments followed, addressing specific problems: atmospheric pollution from the chemical industry, water pollution controls to prevent rivers becoming effluent channels and the regulation of statutory nuisances.

See Chapter 11 →

In the last three decades of the twentieth century and the first decade of the twenty-first century, the UK's membership of the European Union (EU), together with the recognition of global pollution problems, has marked a turning point in the pace of environmental legal change. Over 200 pieces of European legislation have been passed to date which relate in various ways to the environment. Recent developments in international environmental law, especially regarding 'sustainable development', have helped to influence EU pollution policy and the development of new controls which are then transposed into the legislative systems of the EU's Member States. In addition, the public is both better informed of and is more sensitive to environmental risks. As we have seen, especially in regard to the genetically modified crop protests, the public may be a powerful influence upon the regulation of environmental risks.[13] The pattern of environmental pollution control, with its reliance on Command and Control regulatory regimes, has begun to change. The almost total reliance on the Command and Control regulatory model is giving way to a mixed approach to pollution control incorporating Command and Control and other tools such as eco-taxes, market mechanisms, environmental management systems and self-regulation.[14]

1.5 The public regulation of private pollution

Pollution regulation is primarily concerned with the *public regulation of private pollution*. In other words, the State is tasked with the job of setting limits on the polluting activities of private enterprise.[15] The chief method employed by the state to regulate polluting emissions is the creation of a series of *Command and Control* regulatory frameworks. 'Command and Control pollution regulation' involves 'the "command" of the law and the legal authority of the state'.[16] It is an approach to regulation which is characterised by several distinguishing features, which are summarised below.

1.5.1 Primary legislation

Command and Control regulatory regimes are dependent upon legislation. Parliament passes an Act of Parliament[17] which creates a broad framework for the control of various types of polluting activity. Implementation of an Act of Parliament is often phased in over an extended period of time and it is the Secretary of State who controls how quickly the individual sections of each statute

---

13 See 1.5.
14 See 1.9.
15 Companies, firms and individuals.
16 B Hutter, *A Reader in Environmental Law* (OUP, Oxford 1999).
17 Also referred to as a statute, enactment or piece of legislation.

come into force. Acts of Parliament are scrutinised by both Houses of Parliament prior to their becoming law. The public is not directly consulted in the drafting of new legislation.

1.5.2 Secondary legislation

Secondary legislation[18] supplements primary legislation by providing the more detailed and technical content of the relevant regulatory regime. Regulations are generally prepared by the Secretary of State under the authority delegated to him by Parliament. There is little parliamentary scrutiny of the content of secondary legislation as the regulation is merely placed before Parliament for a limited period. The public may comment upon secondary legislation proposals where these are issued as consultation papers by the government. Secondary legislation is frequently used to provide greater detail with regard to the general definitions contained in primary legislation and to provide data on the regulatory standards which are crucial to the setting of individual permits. European environmental legislation is invariably transposed into national law via secondary legislation.

1.5.3 Separate and integrated regulation of air, water and land pollution

Command and Control regulatory regimes are often environmentally media-specific responses to problems caused by polluting discharges. For example, the Water Resources Act 1991 (WRA) established a regulatory framework to control the discharge of polluting substances and energy into the aquatic environment only. In contrast, the Integrated Pollution Prevention and Control (IPPC) regime regulates all discharges emitted from a limited number of highly polluting activities into all three environmental media.

In 2007 the government introduced a standardised system of environmental permits to regulate polluting emissions. Initially this covered IPPC and waste management facilities but the environmental permitting system was extended in 2010 to cover polluting discharges to surface waters and groundwaters. Chapter 6 contains detailed analysis of environmental permitting.

1.5.4 The administrative and 'policing' functions of the regulator

Each Command and Control regime has its own regulatory agency which has the day-to-day responsibility for administering the relevant controls and policing compliance of regulated businesses with the law. Following the creation of the Environment Agency in 1996, the number of regulatory agencies in the UK was reduced.[19] The Environment Agency, the local authorities and the large, privatised, water and sewage services companies are the main regulatory agencies which we encounter in this textbook.

1.5.5 Permits authorising the discharge of polluting substances into the environment

Many Command and Control pollution statutes compel legal persons, especially businesses, who wish to discharge polluting substances into the environment to obtain a permit authorising such emissions. Pollution permits may be divided into two groups: permits which authorise

---

18 In the form of regulations/statutory instruments, e.g. the Environmental Permitting (England and Wales) Regulations 2010.
19 In consequence of the Environment Agency taking over the functions of the National Rivers Authority, the Waste Regulation Authorities and Her Majesty's Inspectorate of Pollution.

the discharge of waste products into the environment;[20] and permits which authorise the operational activities of an applicant.[21] Permits may also be categorised according to whether they are 'anticipatory'[22] or 'operational'.[23] Readers should refer to Chapter 6 for a detailed analysis of the permit-based system of pollution regulation which applies in England and Wales.

See Chapter 6 →

1.5.6 Notice-based and other Command and Control regulatory regimes

Not all Command and Control regulatory regimes require prior permit-based authorisation of polluting activity. Legislation may, as in the case of statutory nuisance, noise and contaminated land controls, impose a dual duty on the regulator to identify pollution problems in its area and ensure the rectification of the pollution problems so identified. After a statutory nuisance, noise or contaminated land problem has been identified, the regulator serves the person responsible for the problem with a notice specifying the necessary remedial works. In the case of air pollution control under the Clean Air Act 1993, where regulatory control is neither permit-based nor notice-based, the 1993 Act lays down strict limits on smoke (and similar) emissions. If these limits are breached, the local authority may prosecute.

1.5.7 Permit conditions

In the water, waste and IPPC pollution control regimes regulated under the Environmental Permitting (England and Wales) Regulations 2010, each permit issued by the regulator is subject to detailed conditions which apply at the level of the individual polluting plant. The regulator has a wide discretion as to the conditions which it can include in each permit in order to achieve the objectives of the particular Command and Control regime. In addition, the regulator has the power to vary permit conditions. This power ensures that pollution control keeps pace with developments in technology and any new European or international obligations.

1.5.8 Permit conditions and environmental standards

Permit conditions are set by reference to standards. An increasing number of standards emanate from the EU in the form of directives which are then transposed into national legislation (as regulations). Standards may be set by reference to specific 'objects' which require protection from the adverse impacts of pollution. These object-based or target-based standards are designed to maintain the quality of the three environmental media upon which the relevant objects[24] depend for a tolerably healthy existence. The standards set limits for the presence of various chemical substances in the relevant environmental media—air, water or soil.[25] The required environmental quality to sustain life is taken into account when the regulator sets the conditions of individual pollution permits. Alternatively, and more commonly, standards are set by reference to the activity which is

---

20 E.g., a water pollution permit authorising the discharge of wastes into the aquatic environment.
21 E.g., a waste management permit or an IPPC permit authorising both the relevant process and the emission of wastes generated by that process.
22 E.g., the grant of a planning permission permitting the construction of a waste incinerator.
23 E.g., an environmental permit regulating the day-to-day operational activities of a waste incinerator once it is constructed.
24 Humans, animals, birds, fish, plants, habitats or ecosystems.
25 E.g., the Air Quality (England) Regulations 2000, the Bathing Waters Regulations 1991 and the Water Supply (Water Quality) Regulations 1989, as amended.

responsible for generating pollution. These activity- or 'source'-based standards can either be in the form of emission standards[26] or product standards,[27] or process standards.[28]

1.5.9 Command and Control regulatory systems are underpinned by criminal law offences

In the case of the permit-based regulatory regimes, failure to apply for a permit, or failure to abide by the terms of a permit once granted, will result in breach of the criminal laws contained in the legislation establishing the regulatory regime. In the case of non-permit-based Command and Control regimes, failure to comply with the relevant remedial notice, or the exceeding of emission limits specified in the legislation, constitutes a criminal law offence. The regulator has a wide discretion as to the enforcement action it may take in these circumstances to bring the polluter back into compliance with the law.[29] The regulator is not obliged to prosecute each and every breach of the law which comes to its attention. In fact, prosecution is the exception rather than the rule.

See Chapter 2

1.5.10 Permits and legal compliance

Compliance with the terms of a permit entitles the permit holder to discharge substances and energy into the environment in compliance with the law and without fear of prosecution. Possession of and compliance with a permit provides the holder with a defence to any criminal charge relating to the emissions authorised by the permit.

1.5.11 Discretion

Regulatory agencies, such as the Environment Agency, local authorities and the large privatised water service companies, are given a wide discretion with regard to how they ensure compliance with the law. For example, a regulator may choose whether or not to prosecute an offending person (usually a business) in order to bring that person's activities back into compliance with the law. Alternatively, a regulator may use its administrative powers[30] to secure the compliance of a regulated business with the terms of its permit, without recourse to mounting a criminal prosecution.

1.5.12 The regulator's powers of investigation

Regulatory agencies are given wide powers to enable them to fulfil their functions. These powers are detailed in the relevant Command and Control framework or other legislation. In particular, the regulator has the following investigatory powers: entry onto premises, examination, investigation, inspection, measurement, testing, recording, photography, removal of items and/or evidence, sampling, installation and operation of monitoring equipment.

---

26 Limits on specific chemical substances discharged, via pipe or chimney, from an industrial process.
27 E.g., the installation of catalytic converters in all new vehicles or the requirement that vehicle engines be able to run on lead-free petrol.
28 E.g., the use of a particular pollution abatement technology in a manufacturing process, or simply specifying the height of a plant chimney discharging pollutants into the atmosphere.
29 See 2.4.15.
30 E.g., an enforcement notice.

1.5.13 Administrative powers

Regulatory agencies are given a range of administrative powers to enable them to fulfil their statutory obligations. These powers are especially important in ensuring that permit holders continue to comply with the terms of their permits. To secure compliance with environmental law, the regulator relies heavily upon the use of a wide range of notices including: Enforcement Notice (EN); Variation Notice (VN); Suspension Notice (SN); Revocation Notice (RN); Works Notice (WN); and Prohibition Notice (PN). The Environment Agency has the power, in appropriate circumstances, to impose a civil financial penalty.[31]

1.5.14 Definition of key legislative terms

The primary legislation establishing the relevant Command and Control regulatory framework uses wide flexible terms, for example, 'pollution' in the WRA 1991 and 'contamination' in the Environment Act 1995 (EA 1995). The definitions of these terms are subsequently interpreted by the regulator, via guidance notes, and by the courts in litigation.

1.5.15 Official guidance

A large volume of policy, in the form of official guidance notes, is issued by government departments and regulatory agencies for the guidance of public decision-making bodies and regulated legal persons.[32] This is used to fill out the details of each pollution regulatory regime. This guidance does not have legal force, in the way in which primary and secondary legislation does, but is important in guiding regulatory decision making. For example, guidance notes may set out 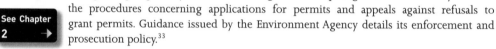 the procedures concerning applications for permits and appeals against refusals to grant permits. Guidance issued by the Environment Agency details its enforcement and prosecution policy.[33]

See Chapter 2 →

1.5.16 Judicial review

A regulator's use of discretion, for example, with regard to the decision to set permit conditions for an industrial plant, or with regard to a decision not to prosecute a polluter, is subject to the supervisory jurisdiction of the courts. The courts, upon a judicial review action by an 'aggrieved person', may strike down a decision arrived at in breach of established procedure, but the court cannot substitute its own decision for that of the regulator (the relevant decision is remitted to the regulator for a fresh decision). The courts therefore have a 'supervisory' jurisdiction over the decision-making activities of the regulators. Judicial review is used by persons with 'standing' (a sufficient interest in the decision challenged) to ensure the accountability of regulators for their decisions. The courts scrutinise decisions for errors in procedure or unreasonableness in the outcome of the decision process. Thus, the regulatory agency is responsible for arriving at a decision on the merits of the case taking care to observe the correct procedure.

---

31 See 2.4.17 and the Regulatory Enforcement and Sanctions Act 2008.
32 E.g. permitted companies.
33 See 2.4.15.

1.5.17 Appeals

Command and Control regulation is characterised by the right of regulated legal persons[34] to appeal against a wide range of regulatory decisions, such as the refusal to grant a permit, the conditions attached to a permit, the service of an administrative notice such as an Abatement Notice and the service of an Enforcement Notice.

1.5.18 Public registers

Publicly accessible registers of information are a further facet of Command and Control regulation. Registers contain information on the operation of the relevant pollution control regime including: applications for permits, the identity of permit holders, relevant permit conditions, notices served on permit holders, sampling, details of any notices applied for or served in regard to variation, revocation, enforcement, works, etc., appeals, convictions and directions given by the Secretary of State.

1.5.19 Continuous control

Command and Control regulation is the primary tool used by the government to regulate environmental pollution. It provides regulators, in the case of permit-based regimes, with a coherent set of continuous controls which are capable of being tailored to the circumstances of each permit holder. The site permit is the main vehicle through which the government attempts to deliver its environmental policy targets.

1.5.20 The main Command and Control regimes

The main pollution Command and Control statutes addressed in this textbook are: the EPA 1990,[35] the WRA 1991,[36] the Water Industry Acts of 1991 and 1999,[37] the Pollution Prevention and Control Act (PPCA) 1999,[38] the EA 1995,[39] and the Control of Pollution Act 1974.[40] These Command and Control regimes are discussed in detail in Chapters 4–10. The primary legislation establishing the framework of controls is supplemented by detailed secondary legislation.[41] Of particular importance, in environmental permit based pollution 'Command and Control' regulatory regimes, are the Environmental Permitting (England and Wales) Regulations 2010. These regulations are explored in Chapter 6.

> **See Chapters ◄ 4 and 10**

> **See Chapter ◄ 6**

1.5.21 Pollution control, planning control, nature conservation, the historic built environment and contaminated land

The permit-based or 'permitting' approach to regulation, evident in water pollution, waste management and IPPC regulation, is similar in structure to the control of building development, the central feature of which is the issue of a planning permission. In contrast, the protection of animal species,

---

34 E.g. businesses.
35 Pt II of which contains waste management and Pt III statutory nuisance.
36 Water pollution controls.
37 The regulation of discharges to sewers.
38 Containing the IPPC regime which replaces the IPC regime.
39 Introducing the contaminated land regime which forms Pt IIA of the EPA 1990.
40 Noise.
41 I.e. regulations.

habitat,[42] landscape[43] and the historic built environment[44] are achieved through a 'listing' process. This form of regulation[45] has some similarity to contaminated land control. Once the regulator has identified contaminated land, the details of the contaminated site are placed on a public register. In this way contaminated land is, in effect, 'listed'.

1.6 Private law: the role of the individual, companies and non-governmental organisations in the regulation of pollution

In contrast to Command and Control regulatory regimes,[46] legal persons, especially individuals and companies, also have a role to play in the regulation of pollution. Any person may find it necessary to utilise environmental law in any of the following ways:

(a)   to protect property and property-related interests from the threat of environmental damage;
(b)   to protect humans from the threat of environmental injury;
(c)   to obtain compensation for damage to property and property-related interests;
(d)   to obtain compensation for personal injury caused by pollution;
(e)   to challenge the decision of a regulator via a judicial review action;
(f)   to mount a private prosecution against a polluter.

The reference to 'private law' is intended to convey to the reader the distinction between the role of private persons and the role of 'public' regulators. In the main, private persons are only concerned to advance their own private interests. They do not generally engage in environmental litigation for the greater good of society. Thus, we note that private persons resort to the common law in order to resolve 'one on one' disputes concerning damage to person or property caused by the polluting activities of a neighbouring property owner. The law therefore attempts to balance the competing interests of individual persons. In contrast, Command and Control regulation focuses upon 'the bigger picture'. The polluting emissions of entire industries are regulated in order to safeguard public health and the wider environment. Regulatory law therefore attempts to achieve a balance between the needs of industry to be competitive (and not over-regulated) and the need of society for a tolerably clean environment.

Private persons seeking redress, often in the form of financial compensation, for damage caused to property or person (personal injury) will often resort to civil litigation to achieve their objectives. Such actions will often be based upon common law principles, especially those contained in the law of torts. The outcome of an individual common law action, whilst resolving the dispute between the parties to the litigation, may also set important legal precedents which have wide-spread application. One such example is the case of *Cambridge Water Co Ltd v Eastern Counties Leather plc* (1994),[47] which drew widespread industry attention to the increased risk of civil liability for damage caused by the escape of polluting substances from land and business premises.

Private persons who wish to challenge the lawfulness of regulatory decisions, such as a decision to issue a permit to an applicant or a decision not to prosecute a polluter, may mount a

---

42   E.g., Sites of Special Scientific Interest.
43   E.g., Areas of Outstanding Natural Beauty.
44   Listed Buildings, Conservation Areas and Ancient Monuments.
45   Listing the 'objects' of the legislation and requiring specific permission for works which may affect or damage their intrinsic importance.
46   Such as the PPCA 1999, which create bureaucracies to regulate whole industries in the public interest.
47   *Cambridge Water Co Ltd v Eastern Counties Leather plc* [1994] 2 AC 264; [1994] 2 WLR 53; [1994] 1 All ER.

judicial review challenge in the High Court. The objective of such proceedings is to persuade the court to strike down an unlawful decision which has been arrived at in breach of established procedure or is otherwise unreasonable. The judicial review process is only open to applicants with a sufficient interest ('standing') in the decision which is the subject of the complaint. Private persons may also mount a private prosecution against a polluter, provided the legislation specifying the relevant offence does not exclude the right to launch such a private prosecution.

1.7 The sources of environmental law

1.7.1 The evolution of environmental legislation

Early pollution control legislation in the UK was characterised by: (a) a narrow UK focus; (b) an environmental media focus (air, water and land); (c) reactive creation (especially following industrialisation); and (d) limited scientific input. In the late twentieth and early twenty-first centuries, the identification of inter-state (transboundary) and global pollution problems[48] has forced all states to adopt a wider focus in their use of environmental law to address the adverse impacts of a rapidly rising population, the consequential pressure on global resources and the resultant pollution problems which occur at national, EU (regional) and global levels.

1.7.2 National sources of UK environmental law

The principal sources of pollution control law in the UK are domestic legislation, EU directives (which are transposed into UK law), the common law and international agreements. Domestic legislation comprises primary legislation[49] and secondary legislation[50] which establish the pollution control regimes considered in Chapters 4–10 of this text. The common law provides the principles which enable pollution victims to obtain redress (often compensation) from the polluters and the means to challenge, via judicial review, the actions and decisions of government and its agencies.[51]

See Chapters
◀ 4 and 10

1.7.3 European Union (EU) sources of UK environmental law

Much environmental legislation in the UK[52] arises out of the transposition (conversion) of EU legislation (directives) into UK law. As a Member State of the EU, the UK is bound to implement in national law the content of EU directives. EU environmental law comprises the treaties which establish the EU's remit, the legislation (especially directives) passed by the EU institutions, the judgments and principles of the European Court of Justice (ECJ) and the international treaties and agreements to which the EU is a party and which are binding on Member States.

1.7.4 International sources of UK environmental law

International environmental law comprises the body of rules derived both from international agreements and customary international law to which sovereign states have expressly or impliedly (via state practice) consented. Other sources of international environmental law are general legal

---

48 Climate change, sea level rise, rapid consumption of resources and ozone depletion in the upper atmosphere.
49 E.g., the EPA 1990.
50 E.g., the Environmental Permiting (England and Wales) Regulations 2010.
51 E.g., the Environment Agency.
52 As much as 80%—Royal Commission on Environmental Pollution (RCEP) Report No 21.

principles, international case law, and the written analysis and comments of eminent academics and judges.

The principal sources of UK environmental law derived from international law are the treaties or other agreements entered into by states on a bilateral or multi-lateral basis. States only incur obligations under international environmental law when they have consented (signing and ratifying treaties and conventions) to them. All states that are recognised under international law are sovereign and equal in their relations with one another. States are, however, not the only participants in the development and use of international law. International organisations, inter-governmental organisations, non-governmental organisations (NGOs), multinational companies and individuals may also be the subjects of international law. Increasingly, international agreements are characterised by the following features: they are problem-specific; their provisions are detailed and require the taking of adequate enforcement action; the content of the agreements may be amended in the light of new information;[53] and there are state requirements regarding identifica-tion/delimitation of the relevant problem or issue, monitoring, preventive action and compliance measures.

1.8 Legal and policy principles

1.8.1 Principles of environmental law

A number of influential legal and policy principles have emerged from international environmental law and EU environmental law which have important roles to play in guiding the future develop-ment of environmental law. These principles relate to both the maintenance of an appropriate balance between development/production on the one hand and conservation of a healthy environ-ment/resources on the other, as well as the allocation of liability for environmental damage.

1.8.2 Sustainable development

International environmental law is important in the following respects:

(a)   it focuses attention on the existence of global problems and the need for international solutions to those problems; and

(b)   it has pioneered and developed important legal and policy principles[54] which are so influen-tial that they have been incorporated into the national environmental law and policy of indi-vidual nation states and regional communities of states, such as the EU. The UK's participation in the 1992 Rio 'Earth Summit' (the UN Conference on Environment and Development) and the conclusion of 'Agenda 21' led to the emergence of 'sustainable development' as a key component of UK national environmental policy. Several important policy documents were subsequently prepared including: the 1990 White Paper, *This Common Inheritance*;[55] *Sustainable Development: The UK Strategy* in 1994;[56] and *A Better Quality of Life: A Strategy for Sustainable Development for the United Kingdom* in 1999.[57] In turn, national policy has led to the incorporation of sustainable development policies at the local level, for example, the appearance of sustainable develop-ment policies in local authority town and country planning local development frameworks and in waste management planning.

---

53 E.g. scientific.
54 E.g., sustainable development.
55 Cm 1200.
56 Cm 2426.
57 Cm 4345.

The most commonly cited expression of the Sustainable Development Principle is to be found in a 1987 United Nations conference on 'Our Common Future' (the Brundtland Report): 'Development that meets the needs of the present without compromising the ability of future generations to meet their own needs.' The principle is clearly anthropocentric—viewing the environment from a human-centred, human needs perspective. It also exhibits elements of equality and fairness in its concern for the rights of present-day societies, both rich and poor, and for the right of future generations to be able to develop the earth's available resources. The principle has, to a certain extent, moved beyond the status of a pure policy tool and has become incorporated into a number of documents as a legal principle. It forms part of the Signatory States' 'Agenda 21' Earth Summit requirements and, more importantly, is incorporated into Art 3 of the Treaty on European Union[58] as a fundamental principle. Thus, the EU now has the task of working for sustainable development and also a high level of protection and improvement of the quality of the environment. The principle has also made an appearance in a UK context, for example, in s 1 of the Natural Heritage (Scotland) Act 1991 and s 4 of the Environment Act 1995 (applying to the Environment Agency). References to sustainable development in UK legislation generally require regard to be had to the principle but do not go so far as to impose any legal obligation to ensure that sustainable development is achieved. The Environment Agency's statutory duties are worded in such a way that the principle is merely a guide to the way in which the Environment Agency should exercise its functions. The importance of sustainable development concerns its impact upon government and regulatory policy by providing targets and tools to monitor progress. These developments in turn affect the Command and Control regulatory regimes discussed in Chapters 4–10. Pollution permit conditions may be tightened to give effect to international agreements.

See Chapters 4–10

The concept of 'sustainable development' comprises four subsidiary principles:

(a) inter-generational equity;[59]
(b) sustainable use;[60]
(c) intra-generational equity;[61] and
(d) integration.[62]

The sustainable development principle is important in that it displays an ethical dimension to the future development of environmental law. What is the value of natural resources from a human-centred (anthropocentric) perspective? Should we, in our economic/development-related decisions, value and preserve nature only if it has some utility, especially economic, relevant to humans? What weight should be given to these resources in development-related decisions? What weight does the law require us to give to important natural habitats?[63] There is a wide spectrum of human perspectives on these issues ranging from the extreme preservationist stance of the 'deep greens' and becoming progressively more pro-development-orientated as we encounter the proponents of land ethics, eco-centrism, bio-centrism, animal welfare, non-anthropocentric individualism, extended anthropocentrism, enlightened anthropocentrism and ultimately anthropocentric utilitarianism. These alternative ethical perspectives on the intrinsic value of flora and fauna are discussed in Alder and Wilkinson, 1999.[64] Perhaps to a large extent our own ethical perspectives reflect our

---

58 Following amendments made by the Treaty of Lisbon 2009.
59 Conservation of natural resources for the use of future generations.
60 Prudent use of natural resources.
61 Use of resources by one state taking into account the needs of other states.
62 Integration of environmental considerations into development projects, plans and programmes.
63 E.g. Sites of Specific Scientific Interest.
64 J Alder and D Wilkinson, *Environmental Law and Ethics* (Macmillan, Basingstoke 1999).

'hierarchy of needs' (Abraham Maslow)[65] so that a father of a hungry family in Africa will have few, if any, qualms about killing apes for food, whereas a well-fed citizen in the developed world has less pressing needs and more time to consider the ethical dimension of the plight of the apes.[66]

1.8.3 The preventive principle

This principle advocates the taking of timely action to eliminate or minimise environmental damage. The principle may be used to prohibit damaging activities, for example, Art 194 of the UN Convention on the Law of the Sea (UNCLOS) of 1984 obliges states to prevent, reduce or control pollution of the marine environment whether within or outside their national waters.

1.8.4 The precautionary principle

This principle enables or requires states to take action where a risk to human health or the environment exists,[67] but there is evidential uncertainty as to the existence or extent (magnitude) of the risk. A number of versions of the principle include a cost/benefit test[68] designed to limit the potentially far-reaching consequences of a strict application of the principle.[69]

Principle 15 of the Rio Declaration provides that:

> . . . where there are threats of serious or irreversible damage lack of full scientific certainty shall not be used as a reason for postponing cost effective measures to prevent environmental degradation.

This definition may be compared with those in Art 2(2)(a) of the Paris Convention and Art 3(3) of the Climate Change Convention of 1992.

From a UK perspective, it is important to note that EU environmental policy and ultimately EU law incorporates the precautionary principle.[70] The principle has been applied in both EU and UK contexts. In *UK v Commission*,[71] the ECJ upheld the Commission's decision to impose an export ban on UK beef in order to reduce the risk of transmitting BSE to cattle in other countries.

The UK case of *R v Secretary of State for Trade and Industry ex p Duddridge and Others* (1995)[72] concerned the possible link between the exposure of children to electro-magnetic field radiation, via high voltage electricity power cables, and the development of leukaemia. The applicants unsuccessfully argued that the Secretary of State should take precautionary action (lowering the voltage) to prevent the risk arising. It seems that the mere possibility of serious harm occurring is not sufficient to justify the government taking precautionary action.

It is clear that the UK government will be minded to take precautionary action only if: (a) the risk is serious; (b) there is good reason to believe that prompt action at comparatively low cost will avoid the greater expense of remedying the damage at a later stage; and (c) irreversible damage is likely if timely action is not taken.[73]

---

65 AH Maslow, *Motivation and Personality* (Harper Row, London 1954).
66 See *Sustainable Development: The UK Strategy*, Cm 2426, 1994.
67 See the Environmental Impact Assessment Directive 85/337/EEC and restrictions on hazardous waste transport.
68 Principle 15 of the Rio Declaration of 1992.
69 E.g., a prohibition on an activity until such time as the persons engaging in the activity can prove that it poses no threat to man or the environment.
70 Art 174(2) of the EC Treaty (as amended).
71 *UK v Commission* (Cases C-157/96 and C-180/99) [1998] ECR 1–2265; [1998] ECR 1–221.
72 *R v Secretary of State for Trade and Industry ex p Duddridge and Others* (1995) *The Times*, 26 October; [1995] Env LR 151; [1995] JEL 224; [1996] Env LR 325.
73 See paras 1.17 and 1.18 of *This Common Inheritance*, 1990.

1.8.5 The polluter pays principle

This principle envisages that polluters[74] should internalise the costs of the pollution which they generate so that the cost of their goods and services reflects the true cost of the measures which primarily the state adopts to eliminate, reduce and treat the polluters' emissions. An alternative, and more limited, version of the principle is that it enables the state to charge the cost of rectifying environmental damage to the relevant polluter, provided the polluter can be identified, prosecuted and convicted of a pollution offence.[75] The UK policy-based interpretation of the principle contained in *This Common Inheritance*, 1990, refers to the government's aim to make those responsible for causing environmental damage responsible for 'the costs of control in full without subsidy'.[76]

1.9 Alternatives to the Command and Control approach to pollution regulation

1.9.1 Emerging regulatory mechanisms

Recognition of the fact that Command and Control permit-based pollution controls are never going to be the complete answer to environmental pollution regulation has led to greater interest in using the market to provide incentive-based pollution controls. Market mechanisms (otherwise referred to as economic instruments) are not generally thought to be as expensive to set up and run as a standard Command and Control regulatory regime.[77] A 'market mechanism' is any tool which uses fiscal incentives or deterrents in order to achieve environmental objectives. These mechanisms do not involve the use of the law to compel companies or individuals to act in a particular way. They are persuasive rather than coercive.

The government, in resorting to market mechanisms, aims to send a 'signal' to consumers and manufacturers encouraging them to behave in ways which will reduce the environmental damage they cause. Thus, a motorist may be faced with progressive rises in petrol prices designed to encourage him or her to use public transport or a less polluting motor vehicle. Similarly, a manufacturing company may be faced with increased waste disposal costs, due to the landfill tax, designed to encourage waste minimisation through recycling. Annex A to the 1990 White Paper *This Common Inheritance* lists the government's preferred pollution control tools: charging schemes, subsidies, deposit/refund schemes, enforcement incentives and markets in pollution credits.

1.9.2 Eco-taxes

The objective of eco-taxes is to persuade businesses to reduce the environmental impact of their activities via the use of financial incentives. Such 'economic instruments' not only save businesses money but they are also attractive to the government because they are perceived as a more economically efficient and cheaper tool than the creation of Command and Control pollution control regimes.[78]

Currently, the best example in the UK of an eco-tax is the landfill tax. The Finance Act 1996, supplemented by the Landfill Tax Regulations 1996, created this eco-tax regime under the control of HM Customs and Excise with effect from October 1996. The tax is paid by operators of landfill sites on the waste deposited in the relevant landfills. The tax paid by the landfill site operators is

---

74 E.g., the manufacturing and service sectors.
75 E.g. reg 38 of the Environmental Permitting (England and Wales) Regulations 2010.
76 At para 1.25.
77 See 1.5.
78 They do not require the establishment of a regulatory agency such as the EA.

recovered from waste depositors via 'gate' fees[79] (at the entrance to the landfill). There is a differential rate of tax payable: a lower fee for inert wastes[80] and a higher figure for active waste.[81]

The substances which qualify as waste, and are therefore subject to the tax, are not subject to quite the same degree of problems as the legal definition of waste. The tax applies to materials in transport to the landfill as well as when it is actually tipped (finally disposed of) at the landfill site.[82]

The tax is subject to exemptions,[83] including dredged materials, mining and quarry wastes and reclaimed material from contaminated land sites. In regard to the contaminated land exemption, the power in s 46 of the 1996 Act was used by the Treasury to amend the original scheme to provide exemption for reclaimed deposits from contaminated sites.[84] In addition, the Landfill Tax (Site Restoration and Quarries) Order 1999[85] exempts inert wastes used to infill a quarry or restore a landfill.[86]

In the late 1990s, the House of Commons Environment Select Committee undertook an investigation into the operation of the landfill tax.[87] Overall, the Report was favourable, although the Committee noted an increase in fly-tipping (the illegal dumping of waste) since the introduction of the tax.

Other forms of tax-related economic instrument include the aggregate levy, the tax/price differentials between unleaded and more polluting fuels, and the reduced level of Vehicle Excise Duty (the road fund licence fee) on vehicles of up to 1400cc engine capacity.

The Aggregates Levy has been set up by virtue of the Aggregates Levy (Registration and Miscellaneous Provisions) Regulations 2001[88] and the Aggregates Levy (General) Regulations 2002.[89] The levy aims to address, via an eco-tax, the environmental costs of quarrying.[90]

1.9.3 Tradeable pollution permits (emissions trading)

This regulatory mechanism is designed to create a market in pollution credits. Such schemes are operational in the USA, Canada and in the EU (Directive 2003/87/EC). Currently, emissions trading is focused on creating markets in 'greenhouse' gas emissions from power-generating plants burning fossil fuels. Such schemes fix an upper ceiling for emissions of specified chemical substances (for example, carbon dioxide) and firms operating in the industries emitting these substances bid for pollution credits. Over time, the regulator reduces the number of credits in circulation and this results in an increase in the price of the credits. This provides a financial incentive for participating firms to reduce their need for credits by developing less polluting methods of production.

Section 3(5) of the EPA 1990 enables the Secretary of State for the Environment to establish tradeable pollution permit schemes in the UK.

An emissions trading scheme was introduced into the UK in 2002. The voluntary scheme was intended to reduce emissions of greenhouse gases via the setting-up of a market to trade in[91] emission allowances. The scheme was superseded in 2006 by a European (EU) scheme created by

---

79 See page 239.
80 E.g., construction waste.
81 E.g., waste which produces methane, a potent 'greenhouse gas' associated with climate change.
82 See *Customs and Excise Commissioners v Darfish Ltd* [2001] Env LR 3 and *Customs and Excise Commissioners v Parkwood Landfill Ltd* [2002] EWHC Ch 47; [2002] STC 417.
83 See ss 43–46 of the Finance Act 1996.
84 See ss 43A and 43B.
85 SI 1999/2075.
86 See ss 43A and 43C.
87 *The Operation of the Landfill Tax*, HC 150 (1998–99).
88 SI 2001/4027.
89 SI 2002/761.
90 Noise, dust, visual intrusion, loss of amenity and damage to biodiversity.
91 I.e. buying and selling.

Directive 2003/87/EC and transposed into national law by the Greenhouse Gas Emissions Trading Scheme Regulations 2005 (as amended by the Greenhouse Gas Emissions Trading Scheme Regulations 2012).

1.9.4 Charging schemes

This approach to pollution regulation involves the recovery of the costs of operating a Command and Control regulatory regime. Permit fees charged by the regulator may be designed to recover all or part of the regulator's operational costs, such as the administrative costs involved in processing permit applications, pollution monitoring and enforcement action. Higher fees may be charged to polluters whose emissions cost more to process, treat and monitor. The fees currently charged for waste, water and IPPC permits are examples of this approach. The Environment Agency has tested an 'enforced self-regulation' scheme in the waste management industry called 'OPRA' (operator pollution risk appraisal). Permit holders who score consistently well in Environment Agency risk assessment visits will be visited less frequently and the savings in monitoring costs made by the Environment Agency will be reflected in reduced annual permit fees. Permit holders who have an accredited environmental management scheme in place, such as ISO 14001, will find that their environmental risk 'score' is reduced. The lower the score, the less often the Environment Agency will visit the permit holder's premises.

1.9.5 Enforcement incentives

Regulators, such as the Environment Agency, may use their enforcement powers in ways that encourage permit holders to comply with the terms of their permits. The threat of prosecution offers a dual incentive: not only the financial penalties and legal costs which a court may impose upon conviction of an environmental offence, but also the damage to a permit holder's reputation as an environmentally responsible business as the progress of a court case is reported in the media. Large companies are more likely to comply with the law, not in consequence of the financial impact of a fine, but as a result of the damage which adverse media coverage may have on sales and company image. The Environment Agency publishes details of companies it wishes to 'name and shame' on its website. The regulator may also use its powers of remediation, for example, s 161 of the WRA 1991 and s 59 of the EPA 1990, to recover the cost of clean-up from the polluter. The use of these powers is not dependent upon a linked criminal prosecution and the costs of remediation may far exceed any fine imposed by a court for breach of environmental law. In addition, the regulator has administrative powers, for example, Anti-Pollution Works Notices,[92] to compel permit holders to install water pollution prevention devices.

Polluters must also have regard to the risk of civil actions commenced by individuals whose property or health has been damaged by the polluters' activities. Victims of pollution incidents may use the torts of negligence, nuisance, trespass and the rule in *Rylands v Fletcher*[93] to recover compensation for their losses. For example, the *Cambridge Water Co*[94] case involved a claim of £1 million.

1.9.6 Subsidies and grants

Grants may be made available by government departments as an incentive towards the cost of installation of pollution prevention devices. For example, grants are available for the construction

---

92 See WRA 1991 s 161A.
93 *Rylands v Fletcher* (1868) LR 3HL 330.
94 (1994) 2 AC 264.

of plant to treat silage effluent and management agreements provide for payments to farmers who agree, by contract, to certain restrictions on their farming methods in environmentally sensitive areas such as Sites of Special Scientific Interest and nitrate-sensitive areas.

1.9.7 Deposit and refund schemes

Perhaps the most famous of these schemes was established by a Danish law[95] requiring beer and soft drinks containers to be returnable.[96] The ECJ upheld the relevant law, even though it interfered with the operation of the common market, because the scheme was justifiable on environmental protection grounds.

1.9.8 Environmental contracts (environmental covenants)

Governments, whether national, regional or local, and industry associations may enter into contracts with one another to regulate pollution. Several countries, but not as yet the UK, have made use of this tool. For example, the Rotterdam municipality (local authority) in the Netherlands has concluded an environmental contract with the German chemical industry relating to the pollution of the mouth of the River Rhine. The mouth of the Rhine has been contaminated with heavy metals. These contaminants form part of the silt lying on the river bed of the estuary. When the Rotterdam municipality dredges the navigation channels in the river, the silt it collects is too contaminated to dump at sea. A special containment facility (the *schlufter*) has therefore been built to store the contaminated silt. The environmental contract provides that the German chemical industry would reduce heavy metal discharges to agreed limits by 2005. If the terms of the agreement are breached, the Rotterdam municipality will sue the German chemical industry for the costs involved in constructing the *schlufter* and any future extension of that facility.[97]

1.10 Summary of key points

Chapter 1 has covered the following topics and issues:

- the basic 'Command and Control' framework of pollution control requiring a primary Act of Parliament supported by more detailed secondary legislation (regulations);
- a consideration of national environmental law in its European and international context;
- the definition of key terms, e.g. 'pollution';
- the main vehicle used to regulate polluting emissions from static sources: the permit;
- the need for government to create one or more regulatory bodies charged with responsibility to issue permits and police the compliance of holders with the relevant permit conditions;
- the important relationship between environmental law and environmental policy (and key legal principles and policy principles);
- methods of pollution regulation which are not based upon the standard 'Command and Control' framework;
- the use of environmental law as a 'tool' which can be used by a range of stakeholders to achieve their individual objectives.

---

95 The full details of which are examined in *Commission v Denmark* (*Danish Bottles*) (Case 302/86) [1988] ECR 460; [1989] 1 CMLR 619.
96 *Commission v Denmark* (n 94 above).
97 See ENDS 1992 205 and 211 and 1993 224.

1.11 Further reading

Environmental encyclopaedias

Encyclopaedia of International Environmental Law (Kluwer, London).
Garner's Environmental Law (Butterworths, London).
Payne, S (ed), *Commercial Environmental Law and Liability* (Longman, London).
Slater, J (ed), *EC Environmental Law* (Sweet & Maxwell, London).
Tromans, S (ed), *Encyclopaedia of Environmental Law* (Sweet & Maxwell, London).

Casebooks

Lee, M and Holder, J, *Environmental Protection: Text and Materials* (2nd edn Butterworths, London 1997).
Sunkin, M, Ong, D and Wight, R, *Sourcebook on Environmental Law* (2nd edn, Cavendish Publishing, London 2001).

Books

Alder, J and Wilkinson, D, *Environmental Law and Ethics* (Macmillan, Basingstoke 1999).
Dobson, A, *Fairness and Futurity: Essays on Environmental Sustainability and Social Justice* (OUP, Oxford 2000).
Dobson, A, *Green Political Thought* (3rd edn, Routledge, Abingdon 2000).
Dobson, A, *Justice and the Environment: Conceptions of Environmental Sustainability and Theories of Distributive Justice* (OUP, Oxford 1998).
Markham, A, *A Brief History of Pollution* (Earthscan, London 1994).
Maslow, AH, *Motivation and Personality* (Harper Row, London 1954).
O'Riordan, T, *Environmental Science for Environmental Management* (Longman, Harlow 1999).
Sagoff, M, *The Economy of the Earth: Philosophy, Law and the Environment* (CUP, Cambridge 1998).
World Commission on Environment and Development, *Our Common Future* (OUP, Oxford 1987).

Books covering Scotland and Northern Ireland

Reid, C, *Green's Guide to Environmental Law in Scotland* (W Green and Son, Edinburgh 1997).
Smith, C, Collar, N and Poustie, M, *Pollution Control: The Law in Scotland* (2nd edn, T&T Clark, Edinburgh, 1997).
Turner, S and Morrow, K, *Northern Ireland Environmental Issues* (Gill and Martin, Belfast 1996).

Statute collections

Annotated Statutes (a yearly chronological record of all primary legislation in England and Wales with explanatory notes for each section) (Sweet & Maxwell, London).
Halsbury's Statutes (Butterworths, London).

Journal articles and government papers

Bailey, PM, 'The creation and enforcement of environmental agreements' (1999) EELR 170.
Biekart, JW, 'Environmental covenants between government and industry: a Dutch NGO's experience' (1995) RECIEL 141.

Commission (EC), 'Environmental Agreements' (Communication) COM/96/500.

Commission (EC), 'Environmental Taxes and Charges in the Single European Market' COM/97/9.

Commission (EC), 'The Precautionary Principle' COM/2000/1.

Commission (EC), 'The Sixth Action Programme of the European Community, Environment 2010: Our Future, Our Choice' COM/2001/31.

Department of the Environment, 'A Better Quality of Life' (Cm 4345, 1999).

Department of the Environment, 'Economic Instruments in Relation to Water Abstraction' (DoE, 2000).

Department of the Environment, 'This Common Inheritance: Britain's Environmental Strategy' (Cm 1200, 1990).

Department of the Environment and Environmental Resources Ltd, *Market Mechanisms: Charging and Subsidies*, 1990.

European Environment Agency, *Environmental Taxes: Implementation and Environmental Effectiveness* (EEA, 1996).

European Environment Agency, *Environmental Taxes*, Environmental Issues Series Number 18 (EEA, 2000).

European Environmental Law Review.

European Foundation for the Improvement of Living and Working Conditions, 'Employment and Sustainability: The UK Landfill Tax', 1998.

HM Customs and Excise, 'Review of Landfill Tax', 1998.

House of Lords Select Committee on the European Communities, 'Paying for Pollution', 25th Report (1989–90).

House of Lords Select Committee on the European Communities, 'Carbon/Energy Tax', 8th Report (1991–92).

Jewell, T, 'Setting environmental standards' (1999) ELM 31.

Jewell, T and Steele, J, 'UK regulatory reform and the pursuit of sustainable development: the Environment Act 1995' [1996] JEL 283.

Organisation for Economic Co-operation and Development, *Economic Instruments for Environmental Protection* (OECD, Paris 1989).

Organisation for Economic Co-operation and Development, *Taxation and the Environment* (OECD, Paris 1993).

Organisation for Economic Co-operation and Development, *Environment and Taxation* (OECD, Paris 1994).

Organisation for Economic Co-operation and Development, *Managing the Environment: The Role of Economic Instruments* (OECD, Paris 1994).

Organisation for Economic Co-operation and Development, *Environmental Tax and Green Tax Reform* (OECD, Paris 1997).

Organisation for Economic Co-operation and Development, *Reforming Environmental Regulation* (OECD, Paris 1997).

Rose-Ackerman, S, 'Market models for water pollution control: their strengths and weaknesses' (1977) Public Policy 383.

Royal Commission on Environmental Pollution, 'Setting Environmental Standards', 21st Report (Cm 4053, 1998).

Stone, C, 'Should trees have standing?: towards legal rights for natural objects' (1972) Southern California Law Review 450.

Stone, C, 'Should trees have standing? revisited. How far will law and morals reach—a pluralist perspective' (1985) Southern California Law Review 1.

Tietenberg, T, 'Economic instruments for environmental regulation' (1990) Oxford Review of Economic Policy 17.

United Nations, 'Policy, Effectiveness and Multilateral Environmental Agreements', United Nations Environment Programme, Environment and Trade Paper 17, 1998, UNEP/98/6.

Law reports

Environmental Law Reports.
Environmental Health Law Reports.
European Environmental Law Reports.
Common Market Law Reports.

Useful websites

The Environment Agency
www.environment-agency.gov.uk

Statutes
www.hmso.gov.uk/legis.htm
UK Acts of Parliament from 1988 and statutory instruments from 1987.

Government policy papers
www.official-documents.co.uk
White and Green Papers.

Two of the main legal databases
www.westlaw.co.uk
www.lexisnexis.co.uk
These are databases of case reports, legislation and academic articles. Students will require the allocation of an Athens Password to access them.

www.bailli.org
A site operated by British and Irish lawyers containing cases and legislation.
www.lawtel.com
Site containing case summaries and other information.
www.casetrack.com
Casetrack site
www.venables.co.uk
Website containing environmental information.

Kent University Law Department website
http://library.ukc.ac.uk/library/lawlinks

The Department of Environment, Food and Rural Affairs
www.defra.gov.uk
An important government site for environmental information such as the GM crop debate.

The European Court of Human Rights
www.echr.coe.int

The Royal Commission for Environmental Pollution
www.rcep.org.uk
The RCEP has authored a number of highly influential reports on various aspects of the UK environment.

Europa
http://europa.eu/
The main website of the EU.

The European Environment Agency
http://www.eea.europa.eu/

The European Parliament
www.europarl.eu.int

United Nations Environment Programme
www.unep.org

Friends of the Earth (UK)
www.foe.co.uk

Greenpeace
www.greenpeace.org

Transport 2000
http://www.transport2000.org.uk/

The Sustainable Development Commission
http://www.sd-commission.org.uk/

The Environmental Law Foundation
www.elflaw.org.uk

The United Kingdom Environmental Law Association
www.ukela.org.uk

Chapter 2

The Administration and Enforcement of Environmental Law

Chapter Contents

Learning Objectives

By the end of this chapter you should have acquired an understanding of:

- the roles and responsibilities of the regulators who administer the main pollution control regimes;

- the functions, objectives and powers of the regulators;

- regulatory enforcement policy;

- the main stakeholders/organisations who play a part in developing environmental law and environmental policy.

2.1 Introduction

As we noted in the previous chapter, the main vehicle which the government uses to regulate pollution in the UK is the Command and Control regulatory model. To be effective, Command and Control regimes require the creation of administrative organisations capable of fulfilling two essential tasks: (a) the bureaucratic task of processing paperwork relating to the issue of permits to pollute[1] and notices to take action regarding pollution problems identified by the regulator;[2] and (b) 'policing' compliance with the relevant permits, notices and other regulatory controls. This latter role involves the regulator in monitoring and enforcement roles.

Because of the historically reactive nature of pollution regulation in the UK, where successive governments responded to pollution issues with the creation of layer on layer of Command and Control regimes in the period 1863–1972, UK pollution control laws presented a picture of a fragmented, complex and unwieldy patchwork of separate controls. The last three decades of the twentieth century and the first decade of the twenty-first century have witnessed concerted government efforts to achieve a more integrated and coherent set of regulatory controls. It is against this backdrop that we now turn to consider the role of the Environment Agency, and its forerunners, in the administration and enforcement of environmental law. In addition, we shall outline the role of the courts in the adjudication of disputes arising out of the administration and enforcement of environmental law and summarise the roles of other relevant bodies.

On 8 July 1991, the then Prime Minister John Major announced the government's intention to create a new authority with overall responsibility for the protection of the environment. The principal aim of the government was to create a unified body which would have responsibility for the protection of the environment as a whole, bringing together the key regulatory pollution control functions affecting air, land and water. In order to do this, the government enacted the Environment Act 1995 (EA 1995), which established the Environment Agency.[3] Prior to the establishment of the Environment Agency, responsibility for various aspects of environmental protection and pollution control was largely divided between Her Majesty's Inspectorate of Pollution (HMIP), the National Rivers Authority (NRA), the Waste Regulation Authorities (WRAs) and the local authorities, each exercising control under different statutory provisions.[4]

---

1 E.g. the water, sewage, waste and Integrated Pollution Prevention and Control (IPPC) regimes.
2 E.g. the statutory nuisance, noise and contaminated land controls.
3 Which became fully operational in April 1996.
4 The functions of HMIP, the NRA and the WRAs were transferred to the Environment Agency in April 1996 and each of these regulatory bodies ceased to exist from that date.

The fragmentary system of control which existed prior to the creation of the Environment Agency reflected the way in which environmental legislation had developed in this country, largely in a piecemeal fashion and often in response to pollution problems or incidents. The pre-Environment Agency system of control was often criticised because it did not respect the cross-media integrity and indivisibility of the environment and also because it was unnecessarily confusing to those subject to it. As a consequence, the government took the view that the time was right for the creation of a new unified body, which would effectively provide not only greater co-ordination of environmental protection but would also provide a 'one stop' approach to pollution control, thus simplifying the burdens on industry.

Despite the creation of the Environment Agency in 1996, regulatory control is not entirely unified and it is still the case that some controls are exercised by the local authorities and the large water and sewerage companies. Local authorities still play a key role in environmental protection, indirectly through the planning system and also more directly in relation to air pollution, hazardous substances, statutory nuisances and contaminated land.

Because of the creation of the Environment Agency, this chapter is broken down into four parts. First, it considers the system of regulatory control that was in operation prior to the Environment Act 1995. The next section considers the reasons behind the creation of the Environment Agency. The chapter will then consider the structure, role and powers of the Environment Agency, the local authorities and other bodies that play a role in environmental protection. Finally, the chapter will consider the role of the courts in the administration of environmental law.

2.2 The system of pollution control prior to the Environment Act 1995

Prior to the enactment of the Environment Act 1995 and the creation of the Environment Agency, the system of pollution control was exercised by the following regulatory bodies:

(a)   Her Majesty's Inspectorate of Pollution (HMIP);
(b)   the National Rivers Authority (NRA);
(c)   the Waste Regulation Authorities (WRAs);
(d)   the local authorities;
(e)   the water services companies responsible for the sewerage system.

2.2.1 Her Majesty's Inspectorate of Pollution (HMIP)

In a sense, HMIP was a forerunner of the Environment Agency in that it was established to provide a co-ordinated system of pollution control. Prior to its formation in 1987, control of pollution was the responsibility of a number of central government inspectorates: the Alkali Inspectorate;[5] the Radiochemical Inspectorate; the Hazardous Waste Inspectorate; and the Water Pollution Inspectorate.[6] HMIP was designed to provide a more co-ordinated system of pollution control, particularly through its administration of the system of Integrated Pollution Control (IPC) established by Pt I of the Environmental Protection Act 1990 (EPA).

HMIP, unlike the NRA, was part of the Department of the Environment (DoE). HMIP operated on a regional basis with seven regions although it had a central office based in the DoE in London.

---

5 The Alkali Inspectorate was formed in 1863 and was later called the Industrial Air Pollution Inspectorate.
6 The functions of the Water Pollution Inspectorate were transferred to the NRA by the Water Act 1989.

The Head of HMIP was the Chief Inspector. Regional responsibilities were handled through the regional offices, which employed in total over 430 staff. In addition, HMIP also contained a Technical Guidance Branch and a Monitoring Branch. In outline, HMIP was responsible for the following:

(a)   regulation of the most seriously polluting processes through the system of IPC introduced by Pt I of the EPA 1990;

(b)   regulation of sites which use, store or dispose of radioactive material under the Radioactive Substances Act 1993 (RSA 1993);

(c)   responsibilities under the Health and Safety at Work Act 1974 (HSWA 1974) in relation to the air emissions of IPC processes;

(d)   duties under the Water Industry Act 1991 (WIA 1991) to act on behalf of the Secretary of State with regard to special category effluents discharged into the sewers;

(e)   research on pollution control and also on radioactive waste disposal;

(f)   acting as a statutory consultee in environmental impact assessments;

(g)   oversight of the work of local WRAs;

(h)   maintenance of the public register regarding IPC authorised processes.

In carrying out these functions, it appeared that HMIP was meant to serve the government, industry and also the citizen. In addition to these various roles, HMIP provided expert advice and support to government departments on a wide range of environmental issues. HMIP officials were involved in European Community (EC) working groups and other international bodies.

HMIP drew its powers from a number of statutory provisions including:

(a)   the Alkali etc. Works Act 1906 (repealed);

(b)   the Health and Safety at Work etc. Act 1974;

(c)   the EPA 1990;

(d)   the WRA 1991;

(e)   the Radioactive Substances Act 1993.

HMIP's main activity was the administration and enforcement of the system of IPC established under Pt I of the EPA 1990. During its period of office, HMIP was responsible for regulating over 200 categories of industry, 5,000 major industrial plants and 8,000 premises storing radioactive material. Once an industrial process had been authorised by HMIP, the Inspectorate was responsible for ensuring compliance with the conditions and standards it had laid down in the authorisations (permits). Usually any authorisation granted would require the holder to carry out routine monitoring and to report the results to HMIP on a regular basis. These monitoring results, plus any obtained directly by HMIP inspectors, were placed on the public register. In addition to this, HMIP inspectors carried out their own site inspections, either on a regular or ad hoc basis or in response to any complaints received. In recognition of the significant role that monitoring played, a new monitoring branch of HMIP was established in August 1991.

In terms of enforcement, HMIP had the power to revoke authorisations granted and also to halt a process where there was an imminent risk of serious pollution. In addition, it had the power to bring prosecutions against offenders, which, if upheld in the magistrates' court, could lead to a fine of up to £20,000 or, on indictment in the Crown Court, to an unlimited fine and/or a period of up to two years' imprisonment. To assist HMIP in the process of enforcement, its inspectors enjoyed considerable powers of investigation, particularly under s 17 of the EPA 1990 to enter premises and take samples. However, HMIP was often criticised for its poor prosecution record, particularly in contrast with the NRA which appeared much more willing to prosecute offenders. The following statistics illustrate the number of HMIP prosecutions during the period 1987–92:

Year	HMIP prosecutions
1987–88	3
1988–89	2
1989–90	4
1990–91	1
1991–92	11

In its publicity material,[7] it was stated that 'breaches of authorisations are normally dealt with quickly and effectively with the co-operation of the operator. But where this does not produce the necessary results, HMIP uses its powers of enforcement and prosecution.' Most critics of HMIP's 'poor' prosecution record failed to take account of the extensive array of enforcement powers that were available to HMIP to ensure that regulated businesses complied with the terms of their pollution permits without recourse to prosecution.[8] These powers, such as Revocation Notices, were potentially so draconian that the threat of their use was more effective in achieving compliance than the comparable threat of prosecution.

In order to assist both operators of licensed facilities and regulatory staff, HMIP published a considerable amount of guidance material. Following the introduction of IPC, HMIP also began the process of publishing a series of guidance notes covering all IPC processes. These guidance notes gave advice on matters such as the best available technology for the particular process, pollution abatement techniques, operating procedures and, importantly, the emission standards to be achieved.

One of the government's stated ambitions for HMIP was that it should be self-financing, recovering its costs from charges made for authorisations, variations, etc. of IPC processes. This reflected the notion that the polluter should pay, not just for remedying pollution, but also for the costs of pollution control. A charging scheme was introduced in April 1990. HMIP was required by the EPA 1990 to set fees and charges so that income and relevant costs balance 'so far as practicable'. However, HMIP never managed to become completely self-financing.

The Environment Agency inherited responsibility for administering the system of IPC and the system of IPPC.[9] The IPPC system of control is largely the same although the powers of inspection are now to be found in s 108 of the EA 1995.

2.2.2 The National Rivers Authority (NRA)

The NRA was between 1989 and 1996 the main regulatory body with responsibility for controlling pollution of water, although it shared responsibility with HMIP in relation to those industrial processes subject to the IPC regime established under Pt I of the EPA 1990.

The NRA was set up by the Water Act 1989 (WA 1989), at the same time as water privatisation, to provide integrated management of river basins and the water environment in England and Wales. It took over the functions previously exercised by the Water Authorities. Although the NRA was established by the WA 1989, its constitution, function and powers were later to be governed by the WRA 1991 and the following references relate to the 1991 Act. The NRA exercised a range of functions beyond pollution control; for example, it was also responsible for flood protection. In the context of environmental protection, the record shows that the NRA was regarded by many as a strong regulator, willing to prosecute if necessary.

---

7 *Protecting Britain's Environment—The Work of HMIP*.
8 I.e. without the need to prosecute the polluter.
9 Integrated Pollution Prevent Control, which replaced IPC on or before 2007.

The NRA was established as an independent public body and did not enjoy Crown immunity. However, it was nevertheless accountable to the Secretary of State for the Environment. The Secretary of State had the power to issue directions to the NRA, although only after consultation with the authority, unless the direction was issued in an emergency situation. Details of any directions issued by the Secretary of State were published in the authority's annual report. The NRA was identified by the Department of the Environment (DoE) as the 'competent body' to implement the requirements of numerous EC directives concerning water quality.

Unlike HMIP, the NRA was a non-departmental body. The NRA had its national headquarters in Bristol, but was structured on a regional basis with the regions corresponding to the catchment boundaries of the former regional Water Authorities. In 1993, NRA Northumbria and NRA Yorkshire were amalgamated and NRA South West and NRA Wessex Regions were merged. The NRA was assisted by a number of regional advisory committees that were required to act in a consultative role to the authority, providing advice on those areas within their spheres of influence. These committees were established under s 7 of the WRA 1991. There were three main advisory committees that operated in each region:

(a)   Regional Rivers Advisory Committees;
(b)   Regional Flood Defence Committees;
(c)   Regional Fisheries Advisory Committees.

In addition, there was an Advisory Committee for Wales. The advisory committee structure still exists and supports the Environment Agency in its water pollution functions.

When the NRA was established in 1989, it inherited the functions of the Water Authorities relating to pollution control, water resource management, flood defence, fisheries, navigation and conservation and recreation. The functions of the NRA[10] were laid down in s 2 of the WRA 1991 and covered the following areas:

(a)   maintaining and improving water quality in controlled waters;
(b)   regulating discharges into controlled waters;
(c)   monitoring the extent of water pollution;
(d)   managing and safeguarding water resources (abstraction);
(e)   conserving amenity and promoting recreation;
(f)   flood defence and land drainage;
(g)   regulating fisheries (under the Salmon and Freshwater Fisheries Act 1975).

NRA inspectors, often referred to as the 'river police', enjoyed various powers by virtue of ss 169–173 of the WRA 1991.[11]

The WRA 1991 placed the NRA under a number of statutory duties which it was required to have regard to when exercising its various functions. The NRA was required by s 16 of the WRA 1991 to promote (to the extent that it considered desirable) the conservation and enhancement of the natural beauty and amenity of inland and coastal waters and of land associated with such waters; the conservation of flora and fauna which were dependent on the aquatic environment; and the use of such waters and land for recreational purposes. The NRA also had a duty to consider water supply issues and by virtue of s 15 of the WRA 1991 it had to have regard, when exercising any of its powers, to the duties imposed on water undertakers or sewerage undertakers by Pts II–IV

---

10   Which have now been transferred in full to the Environment Agency.
11   As in the case of HMIP, the Environment Agency's pollution control powers of inspection are now to be found in s 108 of the EA 1995 which repealed s 169 of the WRA 1991.

of the WIA 1991. The Environment Agency has similar duties in respect of its water-related functions.

The policy of the NRA was to provide strong effective regulation in order to secure real environmental improvements of controlled waters. However, it did not view regulation as the only means at its disposal to fulfil its functions. The NRA placed an emphasis on changing attitudes and behaviour. As part of its pollution prevention campaign, the NRA produced a short promotional video entitled *Pollution Prevention Pays*. The video was made widely available to businesses promoting the benefits of compliance and good practice. Nevertheless, since its creation in 1989, the NRA showed itself to be more willing to prosecute offenders than HMIP. Although prosecution figures are not conclusive of a strong enforcement policy, the statistics are telling. Between 1989 and the end of 1994 the NRA had made over 2,200 successful prosecutions. These resulted in over £5 million in fines.

2.2.3 The Waste Regulation Authorities (WRAs)

WRAs were created by Pt II of the EPA 1990 as part of the overall reform of waste regulation. The functions of the WRAs were carried out by the county councils, or in metropolitan areas the district councils. Special waste regulation authorities were created in Greater London, Greater Manchester and Merseyside. The WRAs were responsible for administering and enforcing the provisions under Pt II of the EPA 1990 relating to waste management and in particular the waste licensing system. WRAs were responsible for:

(a) preparation of waste disposal plans;
(b) control over the waste management licensing system;
(c) supervision of licensed activities;
(d) inspection of licensed sites;
(e) maintaining public registers;
(f) reporting to the Secretary of State.

The functions of the WRAs were transferred to the Environment Agency in 1996 and the WRAs ceased to exist.

2.3 Reasons for change

The government identified several reasons for change. It argued that there was a need to create a unified regulatory agency which would facilitate a more coherent approach to environmental control. Therefore, HMIP, as the body responsible for regulating processes subject to IPC, was responsible for authorising discharges made into controlled waters as well as air and land. However, the NRA was the body responsible generally for regulating water pollution and enforcing the water pollution control provisions under the WRA 1991. Consequently, HMIP was required to consult the NRA before it set any permit conditions relating to polluting discharges to water. This meant effectively that the NRA had the power indirectly to determine any conditions which should be attached. Clearly, bringing control of water pollution and IPC under the auspices of one unified agency negated the need for this consultation. The problem of overlap was not confined to water pollution. A further example relates to the WRAs, which were required also to consult closely with the NRA before setting any waste management permit conditions[12] in order to prevent any contamination of groundwaters from any leachate from a landfill site.

---

12 Under Pt II of the EPA 1990.

A further and very cogent reason for change was to simplify the system of control for those subject to it, namely the polluting industries and activities regulated under the various statutory provisions. It was not only the government that advocated the creation of a unified regulatory agency; the idea was supported by many quarters of industry. It is worth considering the way in which the system of regulation, pre-Environment Agency, operated in order to grasp what was perceived in some quarters as a regulatory maze.

2.3.1 The regulatory authority maze—pre-Environment Agency[13]

For any new or expanding industrial development, it is necessary to obtain planning permission from a local planning authority before the development can go ahead. However, the developer may also need to seek further authorisations from the local authority depending on the nature of the project. For example, it may be necessary for the developer to obtain a noise consent from the local authority for the noise generated during the construction period. An industrial development may need to obtain a waste management permit or register with the WRA, which would normally be the county council. It may also have needed to obtain Local Authority Air Pollution Control (LAAPC) authorisation if the development was a Part B prescribed process.[14] There may have been a need to obtain chimney height approval from the local authority or possibly even a hazardous substances consent.

In addition, an industrialist or industrial developer may need to obtain a permit from the NRA to discharge liquid waste into watercourses. Alternatively, if the process was prescribed for central control,[15] it would require IPC authorisation from HMIP. If there was a need to abstract water from a local river, NRA approval would be required. There may have been a need to discharge trade effluent into the drains and in these circumstances the consent of the sewerage undertaker must also have been obtained. In short, a business may have had to deal with several environmental protection bodies.

Such a hypothetical scenario illustrates that any industrial developer had to understand the statutory controls that regulated the relevant development and also be aware of which regulatory bodies were responsible for controlling the various aspects of the development. Failure to obtain the correct permissions could result in a criminal prosecution. Fines were unlimited in the Crown Court, which also had the power to impose a custodial sentence of up to two years. Reported cases suggest that the courts were becoming more willing to impose large fines and exercise the option of imprisonment. Additionally, both s 217 of the WRA 1991 and s 157 of the EPA 1990 provided that prosecutions could also be brought against company directors, managers, secretaries or other such officials if the offence (committed by the company) was committed with their consent, connivance or negligence.

In the light of the complexity of the regulatory system and the consequences of breaching the regulatory controls, it really came as no surprise that industry and business supported the government's call for the creation of a unified regulatory agency which would reduce the amount of bodies and bureaucracy that a business had to deal with.

2.3.2 The desire to achieve the best practicable environmental option

It is not only from the point of view of the industrialist that the picture was confusing. With so many organisations involved in various aspects of environmental protection, it was often difficult

---

13 This section relates to the variety of Command and Control regulatory regimes which were in existence prior to 1 April 1996.
14 Under Pt I of the EPA 1990.
15 A Part A IPC Process.

to establish an overview of what polluting activities were going on and more importantly, to be certain that each regulatory body was exercising its functions in a manner which would benefit the environment as a whole. This respect for the integrity and indivisibility of the environment was at the heart of the decision to create a unified Environment Agency. Although HMIP was established in 1987 with the aim of achieving a more coherent approach to pollution control through the system of IPC, there remained the need for a more integrated approach to pollution control. Whilst the authorities themselves were very active in publicising their work and increasing public awareness of their respective roles, the picture was still not entirely free of confusion.

The government therefore saw the Environment Agency as a means to develop a consistent and uniform approach to environmental protection, which would at the same time provide a more transparent system of control, more understandable to those subject to it. This desire to have a more co-ordinated approach to environmental protection was also generally supported by the environmentalists and pressure groups, many of whom believed that this unified approach would assist government in integrating environmental concerns into other government policies.

2.3.3 Options for change

The desire to establish a unified approach to environmental control is not entirely new and it is clear that the government was considering such an option as early as 1990 when it considered the possibility of creating an 'umbrella' organisation for overseeing the work of HMIP and NRA in *This Common Inheritance*, 1990. In July 1991, the then Prime Minister John Major made the first announcement that it was his government's intention to create an Environment Agency. The process of bringing together HMIP, NRA and the WRAs was a long-drawn-out and complex one, subject to much debate and consultation. In October 1991, the government issued a consultation paper, *Improving Environmental Quality: the Government Proposals for a New Independent Environment Agency*. This suggested four options and sought views from all interested parties. The options suggested were as follows:

(1)   The creation of an environment agency and the retention of the NRA. The Environment Agency would assume the responsibilities of the WRAs and HMIP. The NRA would exercise control over all aspects of water pollution including HMIP's water pollution functions. The main criticism of this option was that it still did not provide an integrated approach to pollution control.

(2)   The environment agency would be simply an umbrella organisation overseeing and co-ordinating HMIP and the NRA. Although this might secure a greater degree of co-ordination, it would still not provide a unified approach for industry.

(3)   The environment agency would take over the functions of HMIP, NRA and the WRAs.[16]

(4)   The environment agency would take over HMIP and the WRAs and would also assume the NRA's water pollution functions, but the NRA would continue to exist and exercise its remaining controls over matters such as fishing, flood defence and drainage.

The government invited consultation on all four options. Much of the debate centred on options 3 and 4 and the real issue was whether to retain the NRA, given its very wide-ranging functions. Interestingly, the NRA did not favour a separation of its functions and its preferred option was full integration into the environment agency.

---

16 The option finally selected.

2.4 The Environment Agency

In November 1994, the Environment Bill was introduced before Parliament, its principal purpose being the creation of an Environment Agency for England and Wales and a Scottish Environmental Protection Agency (SEPA).[17] The Environment Agency was established in July 1995 and became operational on 1 April 1996.

2.4.1 The structure of the Environment Agency

Section 1(1) of the EA 1995 established the Environment Agency as a body corporate. The Agency consists of between eight and 15 members, of whom three are appointed by the Minister for Agriculture, the remaining members being appointed by the Secretary of State. In appointing members, both the Minister and the Secretary of State must have regard to the desirability of appointing a person who has experience of, and has shown some capacity in, some matter relevant to the functions of the Environment Agency.

Like the former NRA, the Environment Agency is an independent body. HMIP, on the other hand, was part of the DoE. Although it is independent, the Environment Agency is accountable to Parliament through the Secretary of State. The Environment Agency does not have Crown immunity. In terms of staffing, most of the employees of the Environment Agency have been drawn from HMIP, NRA and the WRAs, thus retaining the expertise which had developed in those bodies.

2.4.2 Regional structure and regional environmental protection advisory committees

The Environment Agency is based upon a regional structure and this is augmented by the regional advisory committees under s 12 of the EA 1995 and the Welsh Advisory Committee under s 11 of the EA 1995. The regional boundaries are complicated. In terms of water management purposes, the regional boundaries correspond exactly with the eight regional boundaries of the NRA, which were drawn up on a river catchment basis. As far as pollution control functions are concerned, the regional boundaries are those eight regions, modified to fit the local authority boundary which is closest to the water management boundary.

The Welsh Advisory Committee, which must meet at least once a year, is made up of members appointed by the Secretary of State. Its function is to advise the Secretary of State on matters affecting or connected with the carrying-out of the Environment Agency's functions in Wales.[18] During the passage of the Environment Bill, there were calls for a separate Environment Agency for Wales similar to the Scottish Environmental Protection Agency for Scotland. These calls were, however, dismissed, largely on the grounds that this would be an inefficient and wasteful use of resources.

Section 12 of the EA 1995 provides for the establishment of regional environmental protection advisory committees in both England and Wales.[19] By virtue of s 12(2) of the EA 1995, the Environment Agency is required to consult the relevant advisory committee as to any proposals relating generally to the manner in which the Agency carries out its functions in that region and also to consider any representations made to it by the advisory committee. The committee consists of a chairman appointed by the Secretary of State and other members appointed by the Agency. In addition to the regional environmental protection advisory committees, s 13 of the EA 1995 provides for the establishment of regional and local fisheries advisory committees on a similar basis.

---

17 In addition, the EA 1995 introduced new provisions relating to contaminated land, abandoned mines and national parks.
18 S 11(1).
19 Therefore, note that in Wales there is a Welsh Advisory Committee and a regional environmental protection committee.

The Environment Agency is under a duty to consult the relevant committee on any proposals relating generally to the manner in which it carries out its functions in that region.

2.4.3 Transfer of functions

On 1 April 1996, the Environment Agency became fully operational. Section 2 of the EA 1995 provides specifically for the transfer to the Environment Agency of the following:

(a) the functions exercised by the NRA under the WRA 1991 and the Land Drainage Act 1991 and various other statutory provisions such as the Salmon and Freshwater Fisheries Act 1975. As a consequence, the NRA was abolished. Thus, the Environment Agency has inherited the NRA's water resource management functions, pollution control functions and also its operational functions relating to flood defence, land drainage, navigation and fisheries;

(b) the waste management functions exercised by the WRAs under Pt II of the EPA 1990 and the Control of Pollution (Amendment) Act 1989;

(c) HMIP's responsibilities under Pt I of the EPA 1990;[20]

(d) HMIP's functions relating to radioactive substances under the RSA 1993;

(e) certain enforcement functions under Pt I of the HSWA 1974;

(f) certain functions of the Secretary of State.[21]

As a consequence of this transfer of functions, Sched 22 to the EA 1995 has made a large number of amendments to most of the environmental protection legislation discussed in this book, notably the EPA 1990 and WRA 1991, in order that the legislation now refers to the Environment Agency rather than the NRA, HMIP or the WRAs. Section 3 of the EA 1995 makes provisions for the transfer of property rights and liabilities.[22]

In addition to the transfer of functions, the EA 1995 conferred new functions on the Environment Agency arising out of new provisions introduced in the Act. These are:

(a) functions relating to contaminated land under s 57 of the EA 1995. The Agency has specific powers relating to certain contaminated sites which have been designated as 'special sites' by a local authority. In addition, the Agency has the power to give guidance to local authorities in respect of the latter's role in relation to contaminated land;

(b) functions relating to air quality under Pt IV of the EA 1995. The Agency acts as a statutory consultee in relation to the Secretary of State's proposals for a national air quality strategy and also in relation to any regulations which he or she issues relating to air quality.

2.4.4 Aims of the Environment Agency

The principal aims and objectives of the Environment Agency are laid down in s 4 of the EA 1995. Section 4(1) states that it shall be the 'principal aim of the EA[23] in discharging its functions so as to protect or enhance the environment, taken as a whole, as to make a contribution towards attaining the objective of achieving sustainable development'. It is clear from this, therefore, that

---

20 The LAAPC controls exercised by local authorities under Pt I were retained by the local authorities.
21 These are listed in s 2(2) of the EA 1995.
22 Specifically those of the NRA and the WRAs.
23 Subject to and in accordance with the provisions of [the] Act or any other enactment and taking into account any likely costs.

the government envisaged that the Environment Agency should be guided by the objective of achieving sustainability. However, it is also very clear that this is not an absolute objective in so far as the principal aim of the Environment Agency is qualified in two ways. First, the aim is subject to and in accordance with any other provisions of the EA 1995 or any other enactment. Therefore, in situations where the EA 1995 or any other enactment places the Environment Agency under a duty to have regard to particular considerations, or instructs the Environment Agency to fulfil actions, then these other provisions will overrule the principal aim. Secondly, the Environment Agency is required to take into account any likely costs of discharging its functions in the attainment of this aim. This includes the likely costs to any person and to the environment.[24]

The Secretary of State can issue guidance to the Environment Agency on any further objectives which are considered to be appropriate for the Environment Agency to pursue[25] and in particular the guidance must include advice on how, having regard to the Environment Agency's responsibilities and resources, it is to attain the objective of sustainable development.[26] Once again, the reference to resources appears in the guidance given to the Environment Agency. Before issuing this guidance, the Secretary of State must consult with the Environment Agency and any other appropriate bodies or persons.[27]

2.4.5 Sustainable development

Given that the principal aim of the Environment Agency is to use its powers to attain the objective of sustainable development, it is worth considering how the government defined this all-important concept. A widely accepted definition of sustainable development is to be found in the 1987 Brundtland Report:[28]

> development that meets the needs of the present without compromising the ability of future generations to meet their own needs.

The EA 1995, however, fails to provide a definition and sustainable development remains to be defined in the guidance notes referred to above.

The concept of sustainable development, considered at 1.8.2 above, seems to place an important emphasis on the education of stakeholders[29] in order to minimise the damaging impacts of human activity upon the planet. The Environment Agency perceives itself, in part, as an educator and advocator of current best environmental practice. Permit holders and others are provided with guidance,[30] pollution prevention campaign information and NETREGS[31] to enable them to comply with the law.

2.4.6 General functions of the Environment Agency with respect to pollution control

The general functions of the Environment Agency are defined in s 5 of the EA 1995. Section 5(1) states that the Environment Agency's pollution control functions shall be exercisable for the purpose

---

24 S 56(1) of the EA 1995. This latter qualification is considered more fully at 2.4.11 below.
25 S 4(2) of the EA 1995.
26 S 4(3) of the EA 1995.
27 S 4(5) of the EA 1995.
28 *Report of the World Commission on Environment and Development*, 1987.
29 Government, regulators, companies, NGOs and individuals.
30 For example, Pollution Prevention Guidance Notes.
31 See www.environment-agency.gov.uk/netregs.

of preventing or minimising, or remedying or mitigating, the effects of pollution of the environment. The EA 1995 does not, however, provide a definition of 'pollution of the environment' and it has been suggested that the definition as provided in the EPA 1990[32] should be used. In order to carry out these functions, or to establish a general picture about the state of the environment, the Environment Agency must compile information which it has either gathered itself or which has been obtained from some other source. Section 5 goes on to list several other functions of the EA, including:

(a) carrying out assessments of the environmental effect or likely effect of existing levels of pollution of the environment;

(b) reporting to the Secretary of State on the ways in which the Environment Agency considers it can prevent, minimise, remedy or mitigate the effects of pollution and reporting on the costs and benefits of such options;[33]

(c) following developments in technology and techniques for preventing, minimising, remedying or mitigating the effects of pollution of the environment. This clearly relates to the Environment Agency's functions in respect of IPPC under the Pollution Prevention and Control Act 1999.

2.4.7 Duties of the new Environment Agency

The Environment Agency is placed under certain statutory duties which it must have regard to when exercising any of its functions. Section 6 of the EA 1995 deals specifically with those duties pertaining to water, s 7 of the EA 1995 deals with the Agency's general environmental and recreational duties and s 8 of the EA 1995 deals with its duties with respect to sites of special interest. Section 39 of the EA 1995 provides that the Environment Agency is under a general duty to have regard to the costs and benefits in exercising its powers. This has already been referred to in relation to the general aims of the Environment Agency and is considered more fully at 2.4.11 below.

2.4.8 Section 6—duties in respect of water

In the same way that the NRA was under a similar duty under the WRA 1991, the Environment Agency has specific duties regarding water. The EA is obliged, to the extent that it considers desirable, generally to promote:

(a) the conservation and enhancement of the natural beauty and amenity of inland and coastal waters and land surrounding them;

(b) the conservation of flora and fauna which are dependent upon the aquatic environment;

(c) the use of such waters and land for recreational purposes, taking into account the needs of the chronically sick or disabled.

In regard to water resources, the Environment Agency is also obliged to take all such action, as it may from time to time consider necessary in accordance with any directions issued by the Secretary of State, to be necessary or expedient to conserve, redistribute or generally augment water resources in England and Wales and also to secure the proper use of water resources. These duties are described as being 'without prejudice' to the Environment Agency's other duties under s 7 of the EA 1995.

---

32 Pt I, s 1(3) and Pt II, s 29(3).
33 S 5(3)(ii) of the EA 1995.

2.4.9 Section 7—general environmental duties

Section 7 of the EA 1995 deals with the general environmental duties placed upon the Secretary of State and the Environment Agency and in doing so draws a distinction between the Environment Agency's pollution control functions and non-pollution control functions.

When formulating or considering any proposals relating to any non-pollution control functions, the Secretary of State and the Environment Agency are under a duty to 'exercise any power' in respect of such proposals so as to further the conservation and enhancement of natural beauty and the conservation of flora, fauna and geological or physiographical features of special interest.[34] This duty applies to such proposals made by the EA so far as may be consistent:

(a)   with the purpose of any enactment relating to the functions of the Environment Agency;

(b)   with any guidance given under s 4 of the EA 1995. In the case of the Secretary of State, this duty applies to him or her so far as it is consistent:

    (i)   with the objective of sustainable development;

    (ii)   with his or her general duties regarding the water industry under the provisions of s 2 of the Water Industry Act 1991.

Where the proposals relate to the Environment Agency's pollution control functions, the duty is worded differently.[35] Here, the Secretary of State and the Environment Agency must 'have regard' to the desirability of conserving and enhancing natural beauty and of conserving flora, fauna and geological or physiographical features of special interest. Clearly, the duty to have regard to these matters is less onerous than in relation to s 7(1)(a) of the EA 1995 where the duty is to exercise any powers to further these matters. This difference was the subject of a great deal of criticism during the passage of the Environment Bill.

In addition, s 7(1)(c) of the EA 1995 requires the Secretary of State and the Environment Agency, when formulating or considering any proposals relating to any functions of the Environment Agency:

(a)   to have regard to the desirability of protecting and conserving buildings, sites and objects of archaeological, architectural, engineering or historic interest;

(b)   to take into account any effect which the proposals would have on the beauty or amenity of any rural or urban area or any such flora, fauna, features, buildings, sites or objects; and

(c)   to have regard to any effect which the proposal would have on the economic and social well-being of local communities in rural areas.

In addition to the above duties laid down in s 7(1), s 7(2) of the EA 1995 requires the Secretary of State and the Environment Agency, in formulating or considering proposals relating to any functions of the Environment Agency, to:

(a)   have regard to the desirability of preserving for the public any freedom of access to areas of woodland, mountains, moors, heathlands, downs, cliffs, the foreshore and other places of natural beauty;

(b)   have regard to the desirability of maintaining the availability to the public of any facility for visiting or inspecting any building, site or object of archaeological, engineering or historic interest; and

---

34 S 7(1)(a) of the EA 1995.
35 S 7(1)(b) of the EA 1995.

(c) take into account any effect which the proposals would have on any such freedom of access or on the availability of any such facility.

Section 7(3) of the EA 1995 applies the Environment Agency's duties[36] to water and sewerage undertakers.

2.4.10 Section 8—environmental duties with respect to sites of special interest

The provisions of s 8 of the EA 1995 are based on the provisions of s 17 of the WRA 1991 which were repealed by the EA 1995. Under s 8(1), the Nature Conservancy Council for England (Natural England) or the Countryside Council for Wales may designate land as being of 'special interest'[37] and notify the Environment Agency accordingly if it is its opinion that any area of land:

(a) is of special interest by reason of its flora, fauna or geological or physiographical features; and
(b) may at any time be affected by schemes, works, operations or activities of the Environment Agency or by an authorisation given by the EA.

The consequence of designating a site as being of special interest is that the Environment Agency is required to consult with the notifying body before carrying out or authorising certain works which are likely to affect the land. The requirement to consult does not operate in relation to anything done in an emergency.[38]

2.4.11 Section 39—duty to have regard to costs and benefits

One of the underlying features of the Environment Agency, and probably one of the most contentious issues surrounding it, is the obligation placed on it to have regard to the costs and benefits of exercising any of its powers. Section 39 of the EA 1995 provides that both the Scottish Environmental Protection Agency and the Environment Agency shall, in considering whether or not to exercise any power conferred upon it by any legislation, or even in deciding the manner in which to exercise any such power, take into account the likely costs and benefits of the exercise, non-exercise or manner of exercise in question. This duty does not apply if, or to the extent that, it is unreasonable in view of:

(a) the nature or purpose of the power; or
(b) in the circumstances of the particular case.

In addition, s 39(2) of the EA 1995 provides that the duty does not affect the Environment Agency's obligation to discharge any duties, comply with any requirements or pursue any objectives imposed upon it or given to it otherwise than under s 39. Reference to costs and benefits also appears in relation to the principal aims of the Environment Agency. It should be noted that s 56(1) of the EA 1995 provides that the definition of costs includes both costs to any person and also costs to the environment. The essence of this duty was described by the Secretary of State during the second reading stage of the Bill where he asserted that 'we cannot deliver on environmental demands

---

36 Ss 7(1) and 7(2) of the EA 1995.
37 E.g. Sites of Special Scientific Interest.
38 S 8(4) of the EA 1995.

unless we take into account the costs and ensure that they are proportionate to the benefits that we gain'. Hence, an evaluation of the costs and the benefits that accrue from taking a course of action must be assessed.

2.4.12 Codes of practice with respect to environmental duties

Section 9 of the EA 1995 empowers the Secretary of State and the Minister of Agriculture to approve codes of practice which have as their purpose the provision of practical guidance to the Environment Agency concerning any of the duties detailed in ss 6(1), 7 and 8 of the EA 1995 and also to promote other practices which the Minister considers desirable for the Environment Agency to carry out. The codes of practice are made by statutory instrument and may be modified or withdrawn. In carrying out its duties under ss 6(1), 7 and 8 of the EA 1995, the Environment Agency must have regard to any code of practice issued. In drafting any code, the Minister or Secretary of State must, however, first consult the Environment Agency, the Countryside Agency, Natural England or the Countryside Council for Wales, the Historic Buildings and Monuments Commission for England (English Heritage), the Sports Council and other such persons as he considers appropriate to consult.

2.4.13 Powers of inspectors

The powers of Environment Agency inspectors are set out in s 108 of the EA 1995.[39] The purpose of s 108 is to streamline the powers of entry and inspection across the range of pollution control functions now exercised by the Environment Agency.

It is essential that inspectors have adequate powers of entry and inspection in order to ensure compliance with the pollution permits and also to identify instances where processes are being carried on without the appropriate permit or otherwise in breach of environmental law. The powers listed in s 108 of the EA 1995 may be exercised for one or more of the following purposes:

(a) determining whether any pollution control legislation is being or has been complied with;
(b) exercising or performing pollution control functions;
(c) determining whether and, if so, how such a function should be exercised or performed.

Section 108 of the EA 1995 refers to persons authorised in writing. In practice, this will be the inspectors employed by the Environment Agency (or the relevant local authority officers). An inspector has the following powers of entry and inspection:

(a) to enter at any reasonable time premises which he or she has reason to believe it is necessary for him or her to enter. This should normally be at any reasonable time unless there is an emergency, in which case entry is permitted at any time and, if need be, by force;
(b) on entering premises, to take with him or her any other person duly authorised by the Environment Agency, and a policeman. The latter may be needed in situations where the inspector has reasonable cause to apprehend any serious obstruction in carrying out his or her duties;

---

39 Previously s 17 of the EPA 1990.

(c)   to take any equipment or materials required for any purpose for which the power of entry is being exercised;

(d)   to make such examination and investigation as may in any circumstances be necessary;

(e)   to instruct that the premises or any part of them, or anything in them, be left undisturbed. The inspector may require that the premises or the part of the premises under investigation are not disturbed for as long as is reasonably necessary to enable him or her to carry out any examination or investigation;

(f)   to take such measurements and photographs and make recordings as he or she considers necessary;

(g)   to take samples, or instruct samples to be taken, of any articles or substances found in or on the premises and also from the air, water or land in, on or in the vicinity of the premises. Specific provisions relate to the possession, safekeeping and use in evidence of such samples;

(h)   in the case of any article or substance found in or on premises which appears to him or her to be an article or substance which has caused or is likely to cause pollution of the environment, or harm to human health, to cause it to be dismantled or subjected to any process or test (but not so as to damage or destroy it unless that is necessary);

(i)   to require information from any person—the inspector can require any person whom he or she has reasonable cause to believe to be able to give any information relevant to any examination or investigation to answer such questions as the inspector thinks fit to ask. The person answering the questions will be required to sign a declaration of the truth of the answers given (note the application of the privilege against self-incrimination discussed below);

(j)   to inspect any information and to take copies—the inspector can require the production of any information that he or she considers necessary, including information held on computer. He or she also has the right to inspect and take copies of such information or any entry in the records;

(k)   to require facilities and assistance—here, the inspector can require any person to afford him or her such facilities and assistance with respect to any matters or things within that person's control or in relation to which that person has responsibilities. So, for example, the inspector can require an engineer on the premises to show him or her how the monitoring and testing equipment is working (or not working as the case may be);

(l)   any other powers conferred by regulation by the Secretary of State. Certain information can be withheld from the inspector if it is subject to legal professional privilege. This covers correspondence between clients and their solicitors or legal professional advisors.

It is an offence not to comply with the requirements of the inspector or to obstruct him or her in carrying out his or her duty. Save for offences involving hazardous waste, Environment Agency officials have no power of arrest.

2.4.14 Environmental criminal offences

Command and Control regulation uses the criminal law to help enforce compliance with the provisions of the relevant regulatory regime. A range of criminal offences is built into and forms an intrinsic part of the legislation which created the relevant Command and Control regulatory framework. These criminal law offences and the sanctions associated with them are designed to provide the regulator with the 'muscle' to secure compliance with the law.

Typically, these offences fall into the following categories:

Causing or knowingly permitting pollution	This is a widely drafted pollution offence which is applicable to both permit holders and non-permitted dischargers, e.g. reg 38 of the Environmental Permitting (England and Wales) Regulations 2010 (EP Regulations 2010).
Breach of permit conditions	Targeted at permit holders (reg 38(2) of the EP Regulations 2010).
Breach of statutory duty	For example, breaching the s 34 EPA 1990 duty of care with respect to waste.
Non-compliance with administrative notices issued by the regulator	Aimed at permit holders who are required to take action in response to an administrative notice served upon them by the regulator. Typically, the regulator will serve an Enforcement Notice requiring full compliance with permit conditions. Alternatively, this offence is relevant to offenders who fail to comply with the terms of an Abatement or similar Notice, such as an Anti-Pollution Works Notice (s 161A WRA 1991).
Personal liability of senior company officers such as directors and managers who consent to or connive in the commission of an offence by their employing company. Liability also extends to offences committed by the company which are attributable to the neglect of a senior company officer.	It is not possible to imprison a company or similar organisational entities (reg 41 EP Regulations 2010).

Most of these offences are offences of 'strict liability'. This phrase refers to the fact that the regulator does not need to establish that the polluter knew that what he or she was doing was wrong and would lead to a pollution incident.

Criminal prosecutions are, in practice, used sparingly by the Environment Agency.

2.4.15 Enforcement and prosecution policy

Enforcement is the process by which the regulator ensures that the law, as set out in the relevant Command and Control regulatory regime, is complied with. Enforcement primarily entails the regulator 'policing' the activities regulated by the relevant regime, be they compliance with the terms of a pollution permit or compliance with the terms of an administrative notice (e.g. an Enforcement Notice). Compliance activities also extend to controlling unpermitted polluting activities. Through regular monitoring and inspection visits, the regulator assures itself that the terms of permits and notices are being complied with. In contrast, unpermitted discharges are often identified as a result of information received from the public. These incidents are investigated and dealt with in ways appropriate to the particular circumstances.[40]

The regulator has a discretion[41] as to how it will enforce compliance with the relevant Command and Control regulatory regime. It has a range of 'tools' available to it to achieve the

---

40 For example, by issuing a warning, caution, prosecution or requiring the offender to apply for a permit.
41 I.e. a choice.

objectives of the relevant pollution control regime. It may prosecute any person who breaches environmental law or it may use its extensive range of administrative powers to achieve compliance with the law. It may not even have to resort to the use of criminal or administrative sanctions since the threat of prosecution and the attendant bad publicity, or the threat of the use of its administrative powers, may be sufficient of themselves to ensure the offender's future observance of the law.

The general public would undoubtedly find it surprising to learn that the regulator does not automatically prosecute each and every violation of environmental law it identifies. In fact, prosecution is the exception rather than the rule. However, the regulator's marked reluctance to prosecute should not be equated with a failure to perform its statutory duties. The regulator aims to ensure a tolerably clean[42] environment and in pursuance of that aim it will choose the tool which it believes is best suited to achieving that end.

Any person who is aggrieved that the regulator has exercised its discretion not to prosecute a polluter will, in most instances, have the option to mount a private prosecution. It is a feature of most UK environmental law that enforcement of the law is not the exclusive province of the regulator; however, relatively few private prosecutions are launched because of a number of practical considerations. Litigation is expensive: in addition to the costs involved in hiring lawyers must be added the cost of gathering evidence to prove the commission of an offence. Expert witnesses are often expensive. The scientific evidence required to prove a case may be complex and contested. If the private prosecutor loses his or her case, then the defendant's costs may be awarded against him or her. Even if the private prosecutor wins the case, the sanction imposed by the courts may be disappointing. In certain circumstances, the threat of mounting a private prosecution may exert sufficient pressure upon the regulator to persuade it to prosecute. It has been suggested that Friends of the Earth's inclination to mount a private prosecution was instrumental in persuading the Environment Agency to prosecute those responsible for the *Sea Empress* oil pollution.[43]

The apparent reluctance of regulators to use the formal apparatus of the law to prosecute a polluter may be due to a number of operational constraints. Regulators have limited financial and human resources at their disposal.[44] The regulator may perceive that its resources are better spent in preventive monitoring and the provision of advice and guidance to regulated businesses than in litigation. The regulator may be reluctant to hand over control of the outcome of the case to the courts. This will inevitably happen if a prosecution is launched. Until relatively recently, the courts[45] tended to be lenient in the sanctions which they meted out to polluters. Litigation may also damage the ongoing, co-operational relationship which the regulator has built up, over time, with the permit holder. Finally, regulators possess an increasingly powerful armoury of administrative powers which it is open to them to use to secure the resolution of cases on terms which they, rather than the courts, deem appropriate. Administrative powers such as the service of a Suspension Notice or a Revocation Notice are draconian and have the effect of stopping a business dead in its tracks temporarily or permanently. The use of these powers provides the regulator with flexible tools to control the environmentally damaging impacts of polluters without recourse to the courts.

2.4.15.1 Enforcement styles

Regulators in the UK have traditionally adopted a 'compliance' enforcement policy. The seminal work on compliance enforcement was written by Keith Hawkins in the mid-1980s. In *Environment*

---

42 The EA cannot eliminate all pollution, since this would result in the closing-down of a large proportion of manufacturers. The EA therefore aims to use its powers to attain a tolerably clean environment.
43 See *Environment Agency v Milford Haven Port Authority and Andrews* [1999] 1 Lloyd's Rep 673.
44 See Environment Agency annual reports.
45 Especially the magistrates' courts.

and Enforcement,[46] Hawkins explored the foundations of the compliance style of enforcement. Compliance was based on negotiation, conciliation, co-operation and compromise. The regulator, in recognition of the fact that enforcement is an ongoing process, bargained with the polluter to arrive at a solution which 'fixed' the problem which had caused the polluter to breach environmental law in the first place. The objective of the enforcement process was to prevent harm rather than punish wrongdoing. Compliance enforcement is therefore remedial in nature and is chiefly concerned with the attainment of a tolerably clean environment at least cost. Compliance is incremental and recognises that enforcement is not a once and for all response to a breach of environmental law. Over a period of time, the regulator is able to persuade the permit holder to introduce operational improvements which are designed to bring it back into compliance with the conditions of its discharge or operating permit.

Compliance enforcement tends to work precisely because the regulator rarely resorts to prosecution. As Hawkins observed:

> The polluter has goodwill, co-operation and most important, conformity to offer. The enforcement agent may offer in return two important commodities: forbearance and advice.[47]

Generally, only blameworthy breaches of the law result in prosecution. The relevant breach is set in its social context and the blameworthiness of the polluter's conduct is the key to understanding the likely outcome of the enforcement process. Hawkins asserts:

> Pollution control is done in a moral, not a technological world.[48]

Hawkins identified that a zealous reliance on prosecution could be counter-productive. The regulator was likely to make better progress if it was able to demonstrate an understanding of the polluter's problems and adopted a patient and reasonable stance. In direct contrast to the compliance style of enforcement is the sanctioning, deterrence or penal style of enforcement. The focus here is on coercing the polluter to comply with its legal obligations under threat of prosecution. The law is used to prohibit unacceptable conduct and punish transgressors. Typically, the regulator adopts a confrontational stance in its dealings with offenders. This style of enforcement is common in ordinary policing activities where the prosecutor and offender are unlikely to have an ongoing relationship. In Hawkins' account of compliance enforcement in the water industry, he records a telling comment from a regulatory pollution inspector:

> You can get so much more done by not upsetting people.[49]

In recent years, a 'third way' enforcement style has emerged which advocates the selection of enforcement tools from both the compliance and sanctioning schools. This enforcement style is captured in Ayres and Braithwaite's *Responsive Regulation*.[50] This approach is based upon a compliance pyramid. At the base of the pyramid are the co-operational tools such as advice and verbal warnings. In the event that the regulator encounters a difficult polluter, it will, over time, increase the pressure on the polluter to comply with its legal obligations by moving up the 'compliance pyramid'. At the apex of the pyramid are criminal prosecutions and the use of administrative

---

46 K Hawkins, *Environment and Enforcement: Regulation and the Social Definition of Pollution* (Clarendon, Oxford 1984).
47 Ibid, 122.
48 Ibid.
49 Ibid.
50 I Ayres and J Braithwaite, *Responsive Regulation: Transcending the Deregulation Debate* (OUP, Oxford 1992).

notices, such as a Revocation Notice, which will shut the offender down and put him or her out of business.

2.4.15.2 Environment Agency enforcement and prosecution policy

Since 1998 the Environment Agency has published a publicly accessible enforcement and sanctions policy. The publication of enforcement guidance is designed to standardise the EA's approach to enforcement of environmental law in all the EA's regional offices in England and Wales. Whilst the contents of the policy documents guide the EA's enforcement decisions it cannot fetter them and the EA is free to decide how best to enforce the law in an individual case.

The three core enforcement and sanctions guidance documents are:

(i)   Enforcement and sanctions: statement www.environment-agency.gov.uk/business/regulation/31851.aspx

(ii) Enforcement and sanctions: guidance www.environment-agency.gov.uk/business/regulation/36419.aspx

(iii) Enforcement and sanctions: offence response options www.environment-agency.gov.uk/static/documents/Business/1430_10_External.pdf

In deciding the appropriate enforcement action, the EA is guided by four principles: (a) action will be proportionate to the environmental risks and the seriousness of the breach; (b) whilst like cases should be treated alike (in the interests of consistency), EA staff will continue to exercise discretion; (c) enforcement action will be targeted at those activities which pose the greatest threat to the environment; and (d) transparency with regard to how the Environment Agency operates and what it expects others to do. Readers should refer to the EA's enforcement and sanctions statement and enforcement and sanctions guidance documents for a detailed account of the principled basis upon which enforcement action is taken.

In deciding whether to prosecute, the EA adopts a two-stage test: (a) is the evidence sufficient?; and (b) is a prosecution in the public interest? In regard to the latter limb of the test, the EA will have regard to the aggravating and mitigating circumstances surrounding the alleged breach. In particular, it will have regard to: the environmental impact of the incident; the foreseeability of the incident; the intent of the offender; the previous history of offending; the attitude of the offender; the deterrent effect of prosecution; and the personal circumstances of the offender, amongst other factors. The EA's enforcement and sanctions guidance document, referred to above, contains a list of public interest factors which the EA has regard to when selecting the appropriate enforcement response.

In regard to offences committed by companies, the EA's practice, in most cases, provided it exercises its discretion to prosecute, is to prosecute the company rather than any company employee who was the immediate cause of the offence. Where there is evidence that the offence was committed with the consent of a senior company officer, or the offence was due to a senior officer's neglect, or the senior officer connived at the commission of the offence, then the EA may also prosecute the senior company officer. Readers should note that the EA may choose to prosecute all legal persons who are a cause of a pollution incident (there may be several causes of a single pollution incident).

It is probable that the EA will prosecute in any of the following circumstances: incidents or breaches of the law with serious environmental consequences; operating without a permit; excessive or persistent breaches of the law (especially non-compliance with environmental permit conditions); failure to comply with remedial measures; reckless disregard for management or quality standards; failure to supply information without reasonable excuse or supplying false information to the EA; obstructing EA staff; and impersonating EA staff. The Environment, Transport and Regional Affairs Select Committee of the House of Commons criticised the Environment Agency in

2000 for its alleged bias in prosecuting smaller companies rather than larger company polluters. In smaller companies the senior officers (e.g. directors) are likely to have an intimate knowledge of the day-to-day running of the business and its attendant pollution risks, whereas senior officers of large companies are rather insulated from the day-to-day activities of the company.

Environmental permits contain two types of conditions: (a) those controlling the amount (that is, numeric limit) of substances that may be discharged into the environment; and (b) other conditions (for example, conditions relating to the operation of the process). The EA aims to target its enforcement resources on environmentally risky activities rather than instances of trivial non-compliance presenting little or no risk to the environment. Only those instances of non-compliance which cause actual harm (for example, fishkill or detectable smell) will be classified as pollution incidents. Enforcement action will then be guided by the contents of the EA's published enforcement policy.

2.4.15.3 Key considerations in enforcement practice

The enforcement style adopted by the regulator in any given case will, to a large extent, depend upon the following factors:

(a) the circumstances surrounding the breach of the law, in particular, the extent of environmental damage, its visibility and the culpability of the polluter. Visible and serious pollution incidents will be observed by the public and will be reported to the regulator and the media. As regulators function in a political environment, they will be alive to the fact that they need to be perceived as doing their job[51] and they will probably prosecute. The more culpable the offender, the more likely it will be that the regulator may have to adopt a sanctioning style of enforcement to punish and deter the offender and others from future transgressions;

(b) the compliance 'history' of the polluter will be taken into account by the regulator in deciding which enforcement tool or tools to use to bring the polluter back into compliance with the law. If the offender is a problem polluter and shows no inclination to respond to the regulator's previous attempts to help it, the regulator is likely to move up the enforcement pyramid;

(c) the contents of the regulator's publicly available enforcement policy documents will shape its response to a polluting incident. However, the existence of such policy can never fetter a regulator's discretion to choose which enforcement tool it prefers to use;

(d) the range and content of the criminal charges available to the regulator is also relevant. The greater the range of offences, the more likely it will be that the regulator will be able to fit the offence to the pollution incident. In addition, as most environmental offences are 'strict liability' offences, the regulator will find it easier to establish liability. Once the regulator has decided to prosecute the polluter, there will be little chance of the polluter successfully mounting a defence.[52] Thus, the threat of prosecution will be a credible threat;

(e) in considering what action to take, especially a prosecution, the regulator will pay attention to the probable consequences of passing the control over the outcome of the case to the courts. Will the sanctions and sentencing options open to the courts have the desired deterrent effect? Are the sanctions available a credible deterrent? Assuming that the regulator has the evidence to establish the offence, it will consider what the outcome of a prosecution is likely to be. It will be unlikely to prosecute if, on conviction, the offender is likely to receive only a minimal fine. Compliance enforcement and the threat of prosecution works better when penalties are credible. Until relatively recently, maximum fines in magistrates' courts

---

51 As this is perceived by the public—prosecuting polluters.
52 The regulator is unlikely to prosecute if it is unsure that it will get a conviction.

(where most cases are heard) were limited. These have been increased, for most offences, to £50,000, but the regulator will also bear in mind whether the courts tend to restrict themselves to imposing lower levels of the available maximum. The regulator's view of what would be an appropriate sanction might not reflect the court's view. In addition, the regulator will be influenced by its impressions of the 'environmental awareness' of the courts. Do the courts perceive environmental pollution as morally unacceptable and will they reflect that opprobrium in the sanctions they impose? Too often in the past, the punishment has appeared to the regulator not to fit the crime;

(f) the regulator will have regard to other enforcement tools. The regulator will usually have an extensive range of administrative powers available to it. The impact of an Anti-Pollution Works Notice can be significant—forcing the polluter to acquire and install pollution abatement technology or safeguards. The financial impact of these notices upon the polluter may outstrip the financial impact of the financial sanctions/penalties imposed by the courts. The use of a Notice has certain advantages: (i) the regulator is able to maintain control of the outcome of the case; and (ii) the polluter avoids adverse publicity and is given time to phase in the required improvement. Use of these powers also extends to proactive preventive measures such as a Works Notice, and remedial powers such as the use of remediation ('clean-up') powers;

(g) there are constraints on the regulator's ability to adopt a sanctioning style of enforcement. Regulators have limited financial and staffing resources which restrict their ability to opt for litigation. Regulators are partly funded from government grants and in the current funding climate increases in budgets are likely to be minimal. Regulators which adopted a sanctioning enforcement style would soon feel the backlash of industry pressure on government to reign them in;

(h) the extent to which the public, the media and political parties perceive pollution as a pressing problem impacts upon the regulator's mission. The media report on what concerns the public. Increasingly, pollution is a matter of public concern. The more the media reports the adverse impacts of pollution, the more the public becomes sensitised to the issue. This process impacts upon political and legislative processes. Accompanying increases in the public understanding of the causes of pollution are calls for tighter regulation, both at national and EU level. Pollution is no longer perceived as a morally neutral 'quasi-crime' committed by high status white-collar criminals. These days, pollution is a crime which attracts just as much opprobrium as street crime. From time to time, the Environment Agency will attempt to harness the damaging impact on businesses of adverse publicity by including the 'worst' polluters in its 'Hall of Shame';[53]

(i) the Environment Agency tends to charge the defendant with no more than six offences, unless the circumstances warrant more.

2.4.15.4 The elements of criminal offences and case law

If a regulator, such as the Environment Agency, decides to prosecute a polluter, it must select the relevant offence or offences with care. In order to secure a conviction the EA must establish that all the elements of the relevant offence are present. This will require the EA to link the elements (i.e. the key words and phrases) of the relevant offence to the facts of the alleged breach of the law. For an example of how an offence may be broken down into its elements, see the analysis of section 33 of the Environmental Protection Act 1990 in 5.17.2.

See Chapter 5 ◄

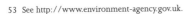

53 See http://www.environment-agency.gov.uk.

Each Command and Control regulatory regime generates a body of case law, some of which is concerned with the interpretation of words and phrases which appear in the primary and secondary legislation establishing the regulatory framework. Great care should therefore be exercised in embarking upon any attempt to apply the judicial reasoning in regard to the meaning of a word or phrase, as it appears in the case law appertaining to one regime, to that of another. Similarly, any word or phrase appearing in a criminal case does not necessarily have the same meaning when the same word appears in a civil case. In the case of the Environmental Permitting (England and Wales) Regulations 2010, the Regulations themselves provide definitions of some key words and phrases but in some instances, for example the word 'causing', reference must be made to court decisions (i.e. reported case law) which help to interpret the meaning of the relevant word.

2.4.16 Criticisms of the Environment Agency

Most criticisms of the Environment Agency appear to relate to the comparatively small number of prosecutions commenced each year by the Agency against polluters. This could be explained by the fact that many people do not understand the method by which the Agency achieves improvements in environmental quality. As we discussed at 2.4.15.1, the Agency adopts a 'compliance' enforcement policy which views prosecution as a last resort. This is little understood by the general public, which expects the Agency to adopt a penal style of enforcement, using the relevant pollution offences to coerce polluters to comply with environmental law in all pollution incidents investigated.

A number of reports have been critical of the Environment Agency in the following respects: the Agency's poor prosecution record allegedly sending the wrong signal to regulated businesses; the lack of expertise (of staff) in some areas of the Agency's remit; selecting 'easy' targets for prosecution (that is, the smaller companies) rather than the large company polluters with the legal and financial resources to 'take on' the Agency; the failure of the Agency to become the public's environmental champion; and the reluctance of the Agency to enter into debate with the government, business and the public with regard to important environmental debates (for example, the genetically modified organisms (GMO) debate).[54]

A more balanced view of the House of Commons Environment Select Committee would have been obtained by paying attention to the improvements in environmental quality recorded in the Agency's annual report and other corporate documentation.

2.4.17 The Regulatory Enforcement and Sanctions Act 2008

The Regulatory Enforcement and Sanctions Act 2008 came into force on 1 October 2008. The Act provides a range of civil powers for use by a number of regulatory agencies including the Environment Agency. The civil powers include:

(a)   a fixed monetary penalty—a low financial penalty used in the case of minor breaches;
(b)   a variable monetary penalty—for use in regard to more serious breaches;
(c)   a compliance notice—requiring compliance with the relevant law;
(d)   a restoration notice—requiring remedial works within a specified time period;
(e)   an enforcement undertaking—a voluntary agreement to do or refrain from doing something;
(f)   an enforcement notice;

---

54 See House of Commons Select Committee on the Environment, Transport and Regions, *Inquiry into the Workings of the Environment Agency*, 6th Report, HC 484 (1997–98) and House of Commons Environment Select Committee, *The Environmental Impact of Cement Manufacture*, HC 124 (1996–97).

(g)   a stop notice;

(h)   a regulatory cost recovery notice—requiring payment of the regulator's costs in regard to imposing a variable monetary penalty, a restoration notice, compliance notice or stop notice.

Regulators which use a fixed monetary penalty or variable monetary penalty will be prevented from bringing subsequent criminal proceedings in respect of the breach which gave rise to service of the relevant notice. The remainder of the civil penalties are not punitive and therefore a regulator may still decide to bring criminal proceedings. It remains to be seen whether and to what extent the Environment Agency uses the new civil penalties. The EA's enforcement and sanctions guidance policy (referred to in 2.4.15.2 above) provides a helpful insight into the circumstances in which the EA considers the use of its RESA 2008 powers (especially the fixed monetary penalty, the variable monetary penalty and the enforcement undertaking) appropriate.

2.5 The local authorities

Despite the creation of the Environment Agency, local authorities continue to play a key role in environmental protection. The provisions of the EA 1995 have, however, transferred the functions of the WRAs, previously carried out by the local authorities, to the Environment Agency. Other than that significant transfer of responsibilities, the EA 1995 has done little to affect the overall functions of the local authorities.[55]

Local authorities are involved in various aspects of environmental protection, which are described more fully in other parts of this book. This section intends only to provide a brief overview of the main environmental protection functions carried out by local authorities:

(a)   local authorities are responsible for the planning control system,[56] which requires local planning authorities to take environmental considerations into account in the preparation of development plans and also in respect of determining the outcome of planning applications;

(b)   district councils are responsible for investigating and abating statutory nuisances under Pt III of the EPA 1990. For many, the statutory nuisance provisions represent the very localised aspect of pollution control, where polluting incidents in their very widest sense (noise, smells, animals) are controlled by the local authorities responding to complaints;

(c)   local authorities are responsible under the Clean Air Act 1993 (CAA 1993) for controlling emissions of dark smoke and they also have the power to control smoke emissions through the creation of Smoke Control Areas;

(d)   local authorities are responsible for permitting the environmental impacts of Integrated Pollution and Prevention Control Part A2 installations and atmospheric emissions of Part B installations under the Pollution and Prevention Control Act 1999;

(e)   local authorities are responsible for identifying areas of contaminated land under the provisions of Pt IIA of the EPA 1990.[57] Sites which are designated as contaminated under the provisions of the Act fall under the regulatory control of the local authority unless the authority determines that the site is a special site, in which case the Environment Agency is the relevant enforcing authority. Part IIA of the EPA 1990 empowers local authorities and the Environment Agency to serve Remediation Notices on appropriate persons in order to secure the clean-up of contaminated sites;

---

55 Save that local authorities play a key part in the regulation of contaminated land.
56 Under the town and country planning legislation.
57 Inserted into the EPA 1990 by s 57 of the EA 1995.

(f)   county councils, or in the metropolitan areas the district councils or London borough councils, have responsibilities as Hazardous Substances Authorities under the provisions of the Planning (Hazardous Substances) Act 1990.

2.6 Other bodies concerned with environmental protection

In addition to the Environment Agency, the large privatised water and sewerage companies, and the local authorities, a number of other stakeholders including governmental, statutory and non-governmental organisations[58] play a role in relation to environmental protection either in terms of promoting new legislation, acting in an advisory capacity or dealing with environmental regulation more indirectly. We now consider the role of these organisations.

2.6.1 The Department for Environment, Food and Rural Affairs (Defra)

Defra[59] has principal responsibility for environmental legislation and policy and also for promoting new environmental legislation. It is responsible for drafting many of the regulations which provide the detailed mechanisms for environmental control. The Department also issues various guidance notes and circulars which are intended to assist either the regulatory authorities or applicants seeking permits from the various bodies.

Organisationally, Defra has a number of specialist divisions dealing with the various aspects of environmental law.[60] These are:

(a)   the Directorate of Environmental Policy and Analysis, which is responsible for environmental policy and also provides the main interface with the EU;

(b)   the Directorate of Pollution Control and Wastes, which deals with all aspects relating to waste policy and law. The directorate is responsible, in particular, for overseeing the waste management permitting system and provides guidance to the agency and the waste industry;

(c)   the Directorate of Air, Climate and Toxic Substances, which is responsible for a wide range of activities, including air pollution[61] and chemical safety;

(d)   the Water Directorate, which is responsible for overseeing all aspects of water supply and water quality;

(e)   the Rural Affairs Directorate, which deals with wildlife and habitat conservation, National Parks, access to the countryside and Sites of Special Scientific Interest.

The Department's stated aims for environmental protection are to:

(a)   promote sustainable development;

(b)   ensure prudent use of natural resources and to minimise waste;

(c)   prevent and minimise pollution of air, land and water in cost-effective ways;

(d)   increase informed public participation in environmental decision making and the involvement of all sectors, especially business;

---

58 E.g. Friends of the Earth.
59 Formerly the DoE.
60 Readers should access the Defra website to note changes to Defra's organisational structure.
61 It supervises the activities of the local authorities in respect of their air pollution control activities.

(e)   ensure environmental concerns are reflected in all the government's work both at the national and international level;

(f)   reduce the burden of regulation and make markets work for the environment;

(g)   protect the environment, and save money, by encouraging better management methods and by promoting the cost-effective use of energy.

2.6.2 The Secretary of State for the Environment, Food and Rural Affairs

A glance through most of the chapters of this book will show that the Secretary of State for the Environment, Food and Rural Affairs plays a key role in regulating environmental protection. This involves, inter alia:

(a)   dealing with appeals against decisions of enforcement agencies;

(b)   issuing directions, for example, to the Environment Agency concerning applications or to meet various EU legal obligations;

(c)   exercising various discretionary powers, for example, in the designation of Special Protection Areas under the Habitats Directive;

(d)   reviewing waste disposal plans and waste recycling plans. Following the re-election of the Labour government in 2001, the government restructured a number of government departments. The Department of Environment, Transport and the Regions (DETR) was amalgamated with the Ministry of Agriculture, Fisheries and Food (MAFF) to form the Department of Environment, Food and Rural Affairs (Defra). This resulted in the separation of environmental protection and the planning system.

2.6.3 Other government departments

Although Defra is the lead department for environmental policy, other government departments have a significant role to play. It is established government policy that all government departments are under a duty to ensure that environmental considerations are taken into account in the development of all policies and programmes.

2.6.4 The Royal Commission on Environmental Pollution

The Royal Commission on Environmental Pollution (RCEP) was established in February 1970 as a standing body to 'advise on matters, both national and international, concerning the pollution of the environment; on the adequacy of research in this field; and the future possibilities of danger to the environment'. It is a permanent body made up of experts in environmental matters who are appointed on the advice of the Prime Minister.

The Royal Commission has played an extremely important role in the development of current environmental legislation, not least because of its expert advice and also because it has had the opportunity to give objective advice on different choices to be made/actions to be taken. The Royal Commission has published a number of reports that provide a valuable insight into a variety of environmental problems and invariably set the agenda for debate and consultation. The reports are intended to give advice to government but, in fact, they have been very influential on UK environmental policy.[62]

---

62 All the reports can be accessed via the RCEP's website.

2.6.5 Sewerage undertakers

The sewerage network is operated by the privatised water and sewerage services companies, known as sewerage undertakers. Notwithstanding the fact that they operate as private companies, the sewerage undertakers are responsible for licensing discharges into public sewers through the system of trade effluent consents.[63] The disposal of trade effluent into a sewer (through a drain or sewer) requires a consent under s 118 of the WIA 1991. A consent must be obtained by serving a notice on the sewerage undertaker.

2.6.6 The Office of Water Services

The Office of Water Services (OFWAT) was established in 1989 following privatisation of the water supply industry. Its principal function was to regulate the water supply industry in 'the public interest'. OFWAT was required to ensure that the water undertakers have regard to their general environmental duties as laid down in the WIA 1991. OFWAT[64] has been replaced by a Regulation Authority.

2.6.7 The Health and Safety Executive

The Health and Safety Executive (HSE) is responsible for the administration of the HSWA 1974. However, the boundaries between health and safety of workers and protection of the environment are not always clear and the HSE in fact fulfils a number of functions related to environmental protection. In particular, the HSE is involved in the regulation of certain activities in the workplace which, if not carried out properly, could have serious environmental consequences. These include the regulation of installations handling hazardous substances such as asbestos. In addition, the HSE acts as a statutory consultee in relation to applications for IPPC permits.

2.6.8 Natural England and the Countryside Council for Wales

Part VII of the EPA 1990 created the Nature Conservancy Council for England, now known as Natural England, and the Countryside Council for Wales out of the former Nature Conservancy Council. Natural England (NE) operates in England and the Countryside Council operates in Wales. NE does not have any pollution control powers or means of enforcement. Instead, it acts as the government's statutory scientific advisory body on nature conservation and is responsible for promoting nature conservation generally.[65] The powers of NE are mainly contained in the Wildlife and Countryside Act 1981 as amended and the Countryside and Rights of Way Act 2000.

2.6.9 The European Environment Agency

The European Environment Agency (EEA) was set up in 1994 following the adoption by the Council of Ministers in May 1990 of Council Regulation 1210/90 EEC. After considerable debate as to where it should be located, it was eventually decided that it should be based in Copenhagen. The functions of the Agency are as follows:

(a) to provide the Member States with objective, reliable and comparable information about the environment;

(b) to ensure that the public is properly informed about the state of the environment.

---

63 See the WIA 1991.
64 See page 124.
65 Especially the designation and regulation of Sites of Special Scientific Interest.

The Management Board of the EEA is made up of one representative from each Member State, two representatives from the European Commission and a further two designated by the European Parliament. However, membership of the EEA is not confined to Member States of the European Union (EU) and other non-EU countries may join.

The main criticism of the EEA, as it currently exists, is that it has no role to play in the enforcement of environmental law. Its role is limited essentially to that of gathering and disseminating information on the state of the environment. The EEA is assisted by the European Environment Information and Observation Network, which was set up to assist in the collection of information throughout the Member States and effectively links the environmental networks of the Member States into a Community-wide network.

2.6.10 Parliamentary select committees (of both the House of Commons and House of Lords)

The primary select committee with an environmental remit is the House of Commons Select Committee on Environment, Food and Rural Affairs. Its function is to scrutinise draft legislation and government environmental policy, and to audit the performance (plus expenditure) of relevant government departments and regulators. Although each select committee controls its own agenda, some criticism has been levelled at them because membership of select committees is controlled by the government.

2.6.11 The Advisory Committee on Business and the Environment

Created in 1991, the Committee informs the government on industry's views on environmental issues, especially where these issues impact upon business performance.[66] Members of the Committee are appointed by the government.[67]

2.6.12 Commission on Sustainable Development

The Commission was created in 2000 and comprises 22 members drawn from the government, industry, NGOs and the university sector. It replaces the Round Table on Sustainable Development and the UK Panel on Sustainable Development, and its functions are: (a) to review progress 'across all relevant fields' in regard to the attainment of sustainable development; (b) to promote awareness of sustainable development; (c) to promote agreement amongst stakeholders on sustainability-related issues; and (d) to identify government policies which undermine sustainability and suggest necessary remedial action.

2.7 The role of the courts in the administration and enforcement of environmental law

2.7.1 The principal functions

The courts have four principal functions with regard to environmental law and litigation:

(a)   an adjudicatory role;
(b)   sentencing;

---

66   For example, the impact of new EU directives.
67   By the Secretary of State for Trade and Industry and the Deputy Prime Minister.

(c)   an interpretative role; and

(d)   a supervisory role.

2.7.2 Adjudication

The chief function of the courts is to reach decisions on the merits of the cases which come before them. As we endeavour to explain in this book, much of environmental law is about the regulation of human activity and the principal vehicle which is used to regulate activities such as the discharge of polluting emissions and the use of resources[68] is the Command and Control regulatory regime. Each regulatory regime is underpinned by criminal law offences and, to a lesser degree, civil powers to remediate environmental damage.

The courts are called upon to adjudicate on disputes involving the operation of regulatory regimes, be they prosecutions commenced by the regulators for criminal law offences or the use of civil powers by regulators to force those persons responsible for environmental damage to engage in 'clean-up' operations. The courts also adjudicate upon actions commenced by private persons. These actions may be civil actions, based on the common law, whose function is to compensate the claimant for damage to person or property, or they may comprise challenges to the decisions of regulators. In addition, private persons may take advantage of the criminal laws contained in the legislation establishing regulatory Command and Control regimes to mount their own prosecutions of polluters.

Once the courts have adjudicated upon an environmental dispute, be it a criminal prosecution by the Environment Agency or a civil action brought by a private individual, it will, on conviction in a criminal prosecution, impose a penalty or, in the case of a civil action, make an award of compensation or other relief. The sentencing policy of the courts plays an important part in ensuring compliance with Command and Control regulation and it is to a consideration of this that we now turn.

2.7.3 Sentencing

Criticism has, for many years, been levelled at the minimal penalties imposed on defendants in criminal prosecutions arising out of breaches of environmental law. It is only relatively recently that significant financial penalties have been imposed on some defendants; nevertheless, the perception persists that the courts, especially the magistrates' courts, are too lenient.

2.7.3.1 Judicial guidance

In 1998, the Court of Appeal decision in R v F Howe & Son (Engineers) Ltd (1999)[69] shed some light on sentencing policy. In Howe, the defendant appealed against a fine of £42,000 imposed upon it by the Crown Court on conviction of breaches of s 2(1) of the HSWA 1974 and reg 4(2) of the Electricity at Work Regulations 1989, which caused the death of a workman. The Court of Appeal observed that the level of fines imposed in health and safety cases was generally too low and it went on to set out a number of sentencing guidelines. In particular, the court identified a number of factors which were relevant to fixing an appropriate penalty:

(a)   although it is often a matter of chance, in a health and safety incident, whether death or injury results from breach of the law, where death is the consequence, courts should regard

---

68 Such as land for building purposes.
69 R v Howe (F) & Son (Engineers) Ltd [1999] 2 Cr App R(S) 37.

death as an aggravating feature of the offence and the penalty imposed on the defendant should reflect public concern at the unnecessary loss of life;

(b) a deliberate breach of health and safety legislation with a view to cutting costs or maximising profits will seriously aggravate the offence charged;

(c) a failure to heed warnings is a seriously aggravating feature of an offence;

(d) mitigating features include a prompt admission of responsibility and guilty plea, prompt action to remedy deficiencies after they are brought to the attention of the defendant, and a good safety record.

The court indicated that the same standards would be expected to be attained regardless of the size and resources of a defendant company. It would also be open to the defendant to make submissions to the court with regard to the level of the financial penalty to be imposed upon conviction and its ability to pay, provided it produced its accounts well before the hearing. Although the Howe case is a health and safety case, it is likely to be an influential guideline in the sentencing of environmental crimes.

In R v Yorkshire Water Services Ltd (2001),[70] the Court of Appeal refined our understanding of the level of appropriate sanctions in the context of a breach of the law which affected a large number of people. Yorkshire Water had been fined £119,000 by Leeds Crown Court on 17 counts of supplying water unfit for human consumption (smelly and discoloured water) contrary to s 70(1) of the WIA 1991. The court affirmed the use of the sentencing principles in Howe. The fine was reduced to £80,000 because the Crown Court should not have used the number of complainants (by affected water customers) as a factor in multiplying the penalty imposed. Thus, a single incident, such as supplying unfit water (or a single pollution incident) may give rise to many breaches of the law,[71] but the number of breaches may not be aggregated to produce a fine which is, in the circumstances, inappropriate.

R v Friskies Petcare UK Ltd (2000)[72] establishes important guidelines as to the appropriate penalty to impose in the event of a 'guilty' plea. The important facts of the case, including aggravating and mitigating circumstances, are to be agreed by the prosecution and the defence and then presented to the court for sentence in the form of schedules. This clarifies the basis upon which the court imposes the relevant penalty and therefore assists the higher courts in the event that there is an appeal against sentence. In addition, it will assist the magistrates' court in deciding whether to commit the case to the Crown Court for sentence.

The Health and Safety Executive has published a document detailing its policy with regard to the prosecution of individuals. This document is likely to be influential in an environmental context. The document is not yet available on the HSE's website but is available via the website of the Centre for Corporate Accountability.[73]

2.7.3.2 Sentencing Advisory Panel guidance

It is also significant that the Sentencing Advisory Panel has been actively investigating sentencing policy with regard to a number of pollution offences. These include: polluting controlled waters (see references to 'water discharge activity' in the Environmental Permitting (England and Wales) Regulations 2010); treating, depositing or disposing of waste without a waste management permit; carrying out an IPPC process without a permit or in breach of permit conditions; and breach of the

---

70 R v Yorkshire Water Services Ltd (2001) The Times, 12 December.
71 For example, unfit water supplied to many individual households or a pollution exceeding several conditions of an operating permit.
72 R v Friskies Petcare UK Ltd [2000] 2 Cr App R (S) 401.
73 http://www.corporateaccountability.org/press_releases/2003/Aug18.htm.

packaging recycling and recovery obligations. The Sentencing Advisory Panel recommends that a distinction in sentencing be made between individual defendants and companies. It proposes that the starting point for the sentencing of individuals should be the fine, in recognition of the fact that pollution offences are generally non-violent and often result from the failure to devote adequate resources to preventing a breach of the law. The Panel recommends that the culpability of the defendant be assessed on the basis of how far the defendant's conduct fell below the requisite standard. In determining the culpability of the defendant, it is recommended that the court have regard to: whether the offence was deliberate; whether the defendant broke the law in order to make a commercial profit; whether the relevant breach of the law is part of a pattern of offending; whether the defendant has ignored advice provided by the regulator; whether the defendant ignored concerns expressed by its employees; and whether the defendant has special knowledge of the risks posed by its activities.

The Panel has proposed that the fine should reflect the ability of the defendant to pay:

> The fine should be substantial enough to have real economic impact which, together with the attendant bad publicity resulting from prosecution, will create sufficient pressure on management and shareholders to tighten regulatory compliance and change company policy.

With regard to smaller companies, the panel noted that a large fine might have a crippling effect on the company, an adverse impact on the local economy, and might interfere with the company's attempts to bring itself back into compliance with the law. With regard to companies which commit pollution offences, the courts are limited in the sentences they can impose (since a non-human legal person cannot be sentenced to a gaol term). In virtually all cases, a fine is imposed. In the case of human offenders, in addition to the ubiquitous fine, the courts have a number of other sentencing options at their disposal, including the following: absolute discharge, conditional discharge, community service, probation, suspended sentence, disqualification under the Disqualification of Directors Act 1986 (with regard to company directors) and imprisonment. The use of disqualification is rare.

2.7.3.3 Magistrates' courts sentencing guidelines

The Magistrates' Association issued guidance to all magistrates in May 2001 entitled 'Fining Companies for Environmental and Health and Safety Offences'. This guidance is significant as the vast majority of environmental incidents which the courts encounter are dealt with in the magistrates' courts. The guidance draws the attention of magistrates to the much higher public profile of environmental and health and safety offences. This increased level of public concern is reflected in the 'greatly increased' fines which may be imposed on a convicted offender. Magistrates are reminded that their aim should be to ensure that any fine imposed should have equal impact on the convicted offender, bearing in mind the relative financial positions of multinational companies with huge annual turnovers and individuals. The public must feel confident that convicted companies receive proper and meaningful penalties. Public disquiet at the low level of penalties led the Lord Chancellor to remind magistrates in 1998 that they 'should not flinch' from using maximum penalties if magistrates believed that they were deserved in the particular circumstances. The guidance refers to the sentencing guidance provided by the higher courts in the cases of R v Howe and Son (Engineers) Ltd and R v Friskies Petcare UK Ltd,[74] and also to the Sentencing Advisory Panel's advice on sentencing in environmental cases.

If the offence before the magistrates' court is an 'either way' offence (that is, it can be tried in either the magistrates' court or the Crown Court), magistrates must consider whether their sentencing powers are adequate and, if not, the case should be committed to the Crown Court. If

---

74 R v Howe (n 69 above); R v Friskies Petcare (n 72 above).

the matter is dealt with by the magistrates, the sanction on conviction will usually be a fine. Although environmental offences can cause or risk death, serious injury or ill health, they are 'non-violent' and will generally not pose a continuing threat because the Environment Agency will have used its administrative powers to address these issues. Offences dealt with in the magistrates' court will often be committed in circumstances in which the offender failed to devote adequate resources to prevent a breach of the law and, in such cases, a financial penalty is appropriate.

In assessing an appropriate penalty, magistrates will pay particular attention to the seriousness of the offence. This is 'calculated' by weighing up the aggravating and mitigating features of the offence. The main aggravating factors are: deliberate or reckless breach of the law; action or inaction prompted by financial considerations (profit or cost saving); disregard of Environment Agency warnings or warnings by employees; awareness of the risk leading to a breach of the law; non-co-operation with the Environment Agency; the extent of environmental damage; a previous history of offending; adverse human impacts—death, injury or ill health; adverse impacts on flora and fauna; expensive clean-up works required; activities causing unpermitted pollution; and interference with the lawful activities of others. Mitigating factors include: isolated incident/lapse; genuine lack of awareness of wrongdoing (for example, the regulations); the offender playing a minor role in the incident and having little personal responsibility; prompt reporting of the incident to the Environment Agency; co-operating with the Environment Agency; a good previous record; and a timely plea of 'guilty'.

In imposing a fine, magistrates, in line with the principles of the Criminal Justice Act 1991, must have regard to the seriousness of the offence and the defendant's financial circumstances.[75] The fine should reflect the culpability of the offender and a high fine is justified even where the damage which actually occurred was less than was the probable result of the offence. The fine will reflect any economic advantage enjoyed by the offender.[76] Where the offender is a company, the finances of the company should receive careful consideration. Turnover, profitability and liquidity should all be considered and the use of expert accountancy evidence may be necessary in order to determine the appropriate penalty. It is essential that companies provide their financial accounts. If they fail to do so, the court is entitled to assume that the offender can pay whatever fine is imposed. With regard to small companies, fines may be paid by instalments if this is necessary to avoid unduly burdening the company. Magistrates are cautioned not to impose a fine which will result in the offending company going into liquidation, with consequent loss of employment.

Whatever the size of the company, the fine should be large enough to make a financial impact on the company. Magistrates may also have regard to the effects of bad publicity upon the company which may pressurise the management and shareholders to improve compliance with the law. In the case of larger companies, magistrates should 'fix' a penalty near the maximum before considering aggravating and mitigating factors.

Other sentencing options include an absolute or conditional discharge, a compensation order of up to £5,000 if a victim of the offence has suffered loss or damage, personal liability of senior company officers,[77] and disqualification of directors under the Company Directors Disqualification Act 1986.

In addition to the impact of a fine, the offender will, in most cases, be ordered to pay the prosecution's costs. These costs may be very significant, especially if the offence has involved the Environment Agency in extensive investigation and remediation works. An order of costs must not be disproportionate to the fine imposed. If the fine, compensation (if any) and costs exceed the ability of the offender to pay, the level of costs is to be reduced rather than the fine.

---

75 Plus any advice sought from the court clerk.
76 For example, by failing to expend resources on preventive measures.
77 See, for example, reg 41 of the EP Regiulations 2010.

2.7.4 Interpretative role

The courts have an important role in the interpretation of words and phrases which appear in primary and secondary legislation. In addition, they have a similar role with regard to the interpretation and application of common law principles in civil actions. For example, the House of Lords has given the meaning of 'causing' in s 85 of the WRA 1991 a very strict interpretation in the context of a criminal offence whose purpose is to punish any person who causes pollution of controlled waters.[78] Similarly, in *Cambridge Water Co Ltd v Eastern Counties Leather plc* (1994),[79] the House of Lords gave detailed consideration to the application of a civil claim, relating to pollution of an aquifer, based on the common law torts of nuisance and the rule in *Rylands v Fletcher* (1868).[80]

2.7.5 Supervisory role

The High Court, Court of Appeal and the Supreme Court (formerly the House of Lords) exercise, with regard to public bodies such as regulators, a supervisory jurisdiction. This entails the consideration of judicial review challenges by persons who are aggrieved by the outcome of decisions made by public bodies. In a judicial review action, the court reviews the process by which the decision was made in order to confirm that it was not made in an unlawful manner. In other words, the court supervises how the relevant administrative decision was arrived at. In an environmental context, judicial review challenges often relate to the granting of permits, such as water pollution permits, or decisions relating to the enforcement of the law.[81] Applications for judicial review are usually based on one or more of the following grounds.

2.7.5.1 Illegality

Under this heading, it is alleged that a public body, such as the Environment Agency, has not acted in accordance with its legal powers, either because it has misunderstood them or because it has deliberately ignored them.

2.7.5.2 Procedural flaw

The public body fails to follow the correct procedure in reaching a decision.

2.7.5.3 Relevant and irrelevant considerations

The public body takes into account something which it should have disregarded or it fails to take into account something which it was required to take into account. This applies only where the matters considered or ignored are set out in or implied by statute.

2.7.5.4 Irrationality

This ground applies where no reasonable public body, which understood the relevant law and faced the same set of circumstances, could have acted in the way in which the public body in question has acted.

2.7.5.5 Procedural unfairness

Under this heading, it is alleged that the process by which a decision has been reached by a public body is unfair. This could include failing to allow someone who has a 'legitimate expectation', arising either from an express promise by a public authority or from the existence of a regular

---

78 See *Empress Car Co (Abertillery) Ltd v National Rivers Authority* [1998] 1 All ER 481; [1998] Env LR 396.
79 *Cambridge Water Co v Eastern Counties Leather plc* [1994] 2 AC 264; [1994] 2 WLR 53; [1994] 1 All ER 53.
80 *Rylands v Fletcher* (1868) LR 3HL 330.
81 Such as the Environment Agency choosing not to prosecute a polluter.

practice which the applicant can reasonably expect to continue, to participate in the decision-making process, for example, by giving him or her an opportunity to make representations to the public body before it reaches its decision.

2.7.5.6 Improper delegation of powers

The public body has purported to delegate powers to someone which only it can exercise. For example, this might involve the attempted delegation of authority to make decisions relating to the grant or refusal of pollution permits.

2.7.6 Who can bring a judicial review action?

In order to bring a judicial review action, a person[82] must demonstrate that he or she has locus standi or, in other words, the right to bring the action. The test laid down for 'standing', as it is referred to, appears in Pt 54 of the Civil Procedure Rules.[83] The applicant must show 'sufficient interest in the matter to which the application relates'. An applicant whose direct personal interests have been affected by the decision of a public body will have standing to challenge the decision. In addition, the court may also allow a challenge by a person, group or organisation acting in the public interest. Whether such a person, group or organisation has standing depends upon a variety of factors, including the importance of the legal issues at stake, the absence of any other responsible challenger, the nature of the alleged breach of duty against which the challenge is made, and the previous involvement and reputation of the applicant with regard to the issue which forms the basis of the challenge. The High Court has shown an increased willingness to grant standing to environmental organisations to enable them to challenge the decisions of regulators. In R v HM Inspectorate of Pollution and Another ex p Greenpeace Ltd (No 2) (1994),[84] the court granted Greenpeace standing to challenge the decision of HMIP to grant a permit authorising the operational activities of a nuclear reprocessing plant because Greenpeace was 'an entirely responsible and respected body with a genuine concern for the environment … who, with its particular experience in environmental matters, its access to experts in the relevant realms of science and technology not to mention law, is able to mount a carefully selected, focused, relevant, and well argued challenge'.

2.7.7 Speed

Applications for judicial review must be made 'promptly'. This requirement means, in most cases, that the application must be lodged with the court within three months of the decision or activity which forms the basis of the complaint. The use of strict time limits enables developments with environmental impacts to proceed without the constant threat of challenge at a late stage in the project's completion. In R v Secretary of State for Trade and Industry ex p Greenpeace Ltd (1998),[85] leave to commence a judicial review action was refused because of undue delay. Laws J observed that 'the courts have very firmly stated that a judicial review applicant must proceed with particular urgency where third party interests are involved'.

2.7.8 Relief

Upon a successful challenge, the court may make any of the following orders:

---

82 Individual, company, etc.
83 Formerly Ord 53, r 3(7) of the Rules of the Supreme Court.
84 R v HM Inspector of Pollution ex p Greenpeace (No 2) [1994] 4 All ER 329; [1994] Env LR 76.
85 R v Secretary of State for Trade and Industry ex p Greenpeace Ltd [1998] Env LR 415.

(a)   An order of certiorari cancels a decision of a public body which is invalid or has been made improperly. The court may order the matter to be sent back to the body which made the original decision so that the matter may be reconsidered using the correct procedure.

(b)   An order of mandamus compels a public body to carry out specified actions in accordance with the legal duties to which it is subject.

(c)   An order of prohibition restrains a public body from acting in a particular way. The court may also make a declaration of the correct legal position and may award damages.

2.8 A specialist environmental court?

There has been some debate with regard to the establishment of a specialist court to deal with environmental cases based on the model of the environmental courts which operate in New Zealand and some Australian states. The government appointed Professor Malcolm Grant in the late 1990s to investigate the case for such a court. The Grant Report was published in 2000, since which time the government has shown no desire to take the idea further. This may, to some extent, be due to the fact that most environmental prosecutions are dealt with in magistrates' courts and steps have been taken to bring magistrates up to speed on environmental issues and appropriate penalties to impose on conviction. The Defra-funded research report, *Modernising Environmental Justice: Regulation and the Role of an Environmental Tribunal*, has now been published. The report recommended the establishment of a specialist tribunal to hear environmental appeals,[86] but there have been no further developments to establish a specialist environmental court.

2.9 Online resource centre

We recommend that the reader regularly refers to the section of the online resources corresponding to this chapter for information relating to updates, amendments and corrections.

2.10 Summary of key points

Chapter 2 has covered the following topics and issues:

●   the considerations which led to the creation of the Environment Agency;
●   the statutory duties, functions and powers of the EA;
●   an insight into how the EA ensures compliance with environmental law (i.e. enforcement and prosecution policy);
●   the range of other organisations involved in using the law to achieve their individual objectives or helping to develop new law;
●   the important functions of the courts especially in a sanctioning context.

2.11 Further reading

Books

Ayres, I and Braithwaite, J, *Responsive Regulation: Transcending the Deregulation Debate* (OUP, Oxford 1992).

---

86 See www.ucl.ac.uk/laws/environment and also the 23rd Report of the RCEP—*Environmental Planning*.

Baldwin, R and Cave, M, *Understanding Regulation* (OUP, Oxford 1999).

Bardach, E and Kagan, R, *Going by the Book: The Problem of Regulatory Unreasonableness* (Temple UP, Philadelphia 1982).

Braithwaite, J, *To Punish or Persuade: Enforcement of Coal Mine Safety* (New York UP 1985).

Dimento, J, *Environmental Law and American Business: Dilemmas of Compliance* (Plenum Press, New York 1986).

Gouldson, A and Murphy, J, *Regulatory Realities: The Implementation and Impact of Industrial Environmental Regulation* (Earthscan, London 1998).

Grant, M, *Environmental Court Project: Final Report* (DETR, London 2000).

Gunningham, N and Grobosky, P (eds), *Smart Regulation: Designing Environmental Policy* (Clarendon, Oxford 1998).

Hawkins, K, *Environment and Enforcement: Regulation and the Social Definition of Pollution* (Clarendon, Oxford 1984).

Hawkins, K, *Law as Last Resort* (OUP, Oxford 2001).

Hawkins, K and Tomas, J, *Enforcing Regulation* (Kluwer-Nijhoff, Dordrecht 1984).

Hilson, C, *Regulating Pollution: A UK and EC Perspective* (Hart, Oxford 2000).

Hutter, B, *A Reader in Environmental Law* (OUP, Oxford 1997).

Hutter, B, *The Reasonable Arm of the Law* (Clarendon, Oxford 1988).

Ogus, A, *Regulation* (OUP, Oxford 1994).

Richardson, G, Ogus, A and Burrows, P, *Policing Pollution: A Study of Regulation and Enforcement* (Clarendon, Oxford 1982).

Ricketts, M and Peacock, A, *The Regulation Game: How British and West German Companies Bargain with Government* (Blackwell, Oxford 1984).

Vogel, D, *National Styles of Regulation* (Cornell UP, Ithaca 1986).

Wilson, W, *Making Environmental Laws Work* (Hart, Oxford 1999).

Journal articles and government papers

De Prez, P, 'Excuses, excuses: the ritual trivialisation of environmental prosecutions' (2001) JEL 65.

House of Commons Environment, Transport and Rural Affairs Committee, 'The Environment Agency', 6th Report (1999–2000).

House of Lords Select Committee on the European Communities, 'Implementation and Enforcement of Environmental Legislation', 9th Report (1991–92).

Rowan-Robinson J and Ross, A, 'The enforcement of environmental regulation in Britain' (1984) JPL 200.

Sandhovel, A, 'What can be achieved by using instruments of self-regulation in environmental policy-making?' (1998) EELR 83.

Steinzor, R, 'Reinventing regulation: the dangerous journey from command to self-control' (1998) Harvard Environmental Law Review 103.

Sinclair, D, 'Self-regulation versus command and control? Beyond false dichotomies' (1997) Law and Policy 529.

Useful websites

The Environment Agency

http://www.environment-agency.gov.uk/business/regulation/31851.aspx

Department of Environment, Food and Rural Affairs

www.defra.gov.uk

Royal Commission on Environmental Pollution

www.rcep.org.uk

Chapter 3

European Union Environmental Law

Chapter Contents

> ## Learning Objectives
>
> By the end of this chapter you should have acquired an understanding of:
>
> - the historical development of the European Union from its inception in 1957 and the extent to which the protection of the environment has become a key policy priority for the European Union;
>
> - the institutions of the EU, the sources of EU law and their effect within the domestic legal system; the mechanisms for securing the enforcement of EU environmental law;
>
> - the types of measures that the EU has adopted to achieve its environmental protection aims;
>
> - the extent to which membership of the EU has constrained the capacity of the Member States to legislate higher environmental standards than those prescribed by the EU;
>
> - the tensions between the desire on the part of the EU to secure the free movement of goods and also environmental protection and the impact that this tension has on the capacity of Member States to take unilateral national action to protect the environment.

3.1 Introduction

No textbook on English environmental law would be complete without some discussion of the role played by the European Union in shaping both domestic law and policy. The impact of EU law in the field of environmental protection is hugely significant. Arguably its significance is masked because most EU legislative environmental measures take the form of directives which are transposed into domestic law by means of statutory instruments.[1] According to the European Commission, 'EU legislation lies behind some 80 per cent of national environmental legislation'.[2] Without doubt, the EU is driving the development of UK environmental law. The sheer volume of EU environmental legislation makes it impossible for this book to provide anything like a complete discussion of the range of measures that have been adopted. Instead this chapter seeks to examine the way in which EU environmental policy has evolved, and to look at the types of legislative measures that have been adopted, focusing on just a few of the key legislative provisions impacting on topics covered elsewhere in this book.

By way of introduction to this topic the chapter commences with some general discussion about the European Union and EU law. It includes a brief introduction to the institutions of the EU commenting on their respective roles regarding the development of environmental law and policy including the role of the Commission and the European Court of Justice in ensuring that EU environmental law is enforced. The chapter also provides a brief explanation of the sources of EU law and the way in which EU law takes effect in the domestic legal system. Although these issues are

---

1 Although it should be noted that directives may be transposed into national law by means of statute, for example see the Pollution Prevention Control Act 1999 which transposed Council Directive 96/61/EC concerning integrated pollution prevention and control.

2 Communication from the Commission to the European Parliament, the Council, the European Economic and Social Committee and the Committee of the Regions on the Mid-term Review of the Sixth Community Environment Action Programme COM (2007) 225 Final.

important it is not appropriate in a textbook on environmental law to include lengthy discussion of all of the issues involved. Readers are recommended to consult an appropriate EU law textbook for further detailed analysis. In addition the chapter briefly examines the history of the EU, reflecting on the extent to which the environmental policy is now one of the most important EU policy areas.

Before embarking on this discussion, a short word about terminology. As will be seen below, the EU has evolved from the European Economic Community (EEC), to the European Community (EC) and eventually to the European Union (EU). During this evolution it was appropriate to refer to EEC law and then EC law. However since the Treaty of Lisbon came into force in December 2009 it is now technically correct to refer to EU law. With effect from 1 January 2010 the term 'EC law' is no longer used. In order to eliminate confusion (in so far as this is possible), this chapter will use the term EU law throughout, although technically any references to the law predating the Lisbon Treaty should be EC law. However where necessary the term EC law will be retained if the discussion or context demands it.

3.2 The development of the European Union (EU): from EEC to EU

3.2.1 Enlargement

The European Economic Community (EEC) was established by the Treaty of Rome in 1957. Since then, the EU has grown from an initial membership of six (Belgium, France, West Germany, the Netherlands, Luxembourg and Italy) to 27. By 1995 membership had increased from six to 15, with the accession of the UK, Denmark and Ireland in 1973, Greece in 1979, Spain and Portugal in 1986 and Austria, Finland and Sweden in January 1995. Following German reunification in 1989, East Germany was absorbed into the Community, subject to certain special transitional arrangements. It was anticipated that Norway would join at the same time as Austria, Finland and Sweden, but following a 'no' vote in the Norwegian referendum, the Norwegian government was unable to proceed to membership.

After successfully growing from six to 15 members, the EU saw the biggest single expansion on 1 May 2004, with a further 10 states joining.[3] Romania and Bulgaria joined in 2007, bringing the membership to 27 Member States. Croatia became the 28th Member State to accede to the EU in July 2013. The term used to describe this process is enlargement. It should be noted that before a state can be accepted for membership, it must fulfil certain conditions: it must demonstrate that its institutions are democratic and guarantee the rule of law and protect human rights. It must also show that it operates a market economy that is capable of surviving within the single market, and it must show that it is able to adopt and comply with the common rules, standards and policies that comprise EU law.[4]

3.2.2 From EEC to EC to EU

Not only did the EEC grow in size, it evolved from European Economic Community to Economic Community (EC) and finally to European Union (EU). It also evolved significantly in scope; originally the EEC was concerned with the creation of a common market in which goods, services, persons and capital could move freely throughout the EEC. The EU of 2010 has much broader social goals including respect for human rights, equality and of course environmental protection. It can

---

3 Cyprus, the Czech Republic, Estonia, Hungary, Latvia, Lithuania, Malta, Poland, the Slovak Republic and Slovenia.
4 Known as 'the acquis'.

no longer be categorised as an association of States pursuing economic goals. The EU can now legitimately take action in a broad range of areas, including environmental protection, which were never envisaged as 'Community' interests in its formative years. This evolution has been achieved by means of successive amendments to the original Treaty of Rome 1957 (referred to as the EC Treaty). This process culminated in December 2009 with the ratification of the Lisbon Treaty 2007. The Treaty of Lisbon renamed the EC Treaty; it is now referred to as the Treaty on the Functioning of the European Union (TFEU). Throughout the TFEU the word 'Community' has been replaced with the word 'Union' and, as noted earlier, the law of the EU is now accurately referred to as EU law.

3.2.3 The Treaty of Rome

When the Treaty of Rome was signed in 1957 the principal aim of the newly formed European Economic Community was to secure lasting peace in Europe by establishing a common market in which goods, services, persons and capital could move freely. The EEC, like the European Coal and Steel Community (ECSC),[5] adopted a functional approach to European integration. The Treaty of Rome enumerated a number of principal aims and transferred legislative power to the Community institutions in order to achieve those aims. The aims were laid down in Art 2 EC, which alongside the Preamble to the Treaty and Art 3 EC set out the aims and objectives of the six Member States. Article 2 EC in particular was pivotal; it laid down those areas in which the Union institutions could act; in short it defined the legal competencies of the then EEC. Originally, Art 2 EC was limited in scope to the establishment of the common market and the progressive approximation of the Member States' economic policies in order to promote throughout the EC a 'harmonious development of economic activities, a continuous and balanced expansion, an increase in stability, an accelerated raising of the standard of living and closer relations between the states belonging to it'.

The Treaty of Rome 1957 made no reference to environmental protection. However, as a result of the substantive amendments made to the EC Treaty by successive Treaties (which are discussed below), Art 2 EC was amended to significantly broaden the objectives of the Union:

> The Community shall have as its task, by establishing a common market and an economic and monetary union and by implementing common policies or activities referred to in Arts 3 and 4, to promote throughout the Community a harmonious, balanced and sustainable development of economic activities, a high level of employment and social protection, equality between men and women, sustainable and non-inflationary growth, a high degree of competitiveness and convergence of economic performance, a high level of protection and improvement of the quality of the environment, the raising of the standard of living and quality of life, and economic and social cohesion and solidarity among Member States.

The Treaty of Rome, as amended, was referred to as the EC Treaty.

3.2.4 The progressive amendment of the EC Treaty

As noted above, the original Treaty of Rome 1957 was amended on a number of occasions. In very general terms the amendments focussed on expanding the scope (competence) of the European Union, democratising the law making processes and making the institutional changes necessitated by the growing membership of the Union. The first amendment came with the Single European Act (SEA) 1986. Despite its rather modest title the SEA is a Treaty. The aim of the SEA was to make changes to the law-making procedures so that a programme of some 280 measures could be

---

5 Established by the Treaty of Paris 1951.

enacted to create the Single European Market by the self-imposed deadline of 31 December 1992. The SEA 1986 also established for the first time that the Union could legitimately take action in the field of environmental protection by including environmental protection as one of the Union's aims. This amendment was made in growing recognition of the reality of the situation; the protection of the environment had become a global concern and the EU had already developed its first environmental action programme.[6] The next key stage in the development of the EU was the Treaty on European Union (TEU) 1992.[7] The TEU was an altogether more complex Treaty in that it amended the EC Treaty and it also created the European Union, which was governed by a standalone TEU. The Union, as it was then, was made up of three so called 'pillars'. The central pillar was the European Community. The two flanking pillars allowed the Member States of the Union to cooperate at intergovernmental level in the fields of Common Foreign and Security Policy and also Co-operation in Justice and Home Affairs. Post 1992 there were two Treaties; the EC Treaty and the TEU. Broadly speaking, from an environmental lawyer's perspective only the EC Treaty was of relevance because only the European Community could enact legally binding legislation. Article G of the TEU introduced significant amendments to the EC Treaty. First it renamed the EEC to the EC in recognition of the fact that the tasks of the Community went well beyond those of a purely economic nature. The tasks of the EC were extended to include political and social goals including 'sustainable and non-inflationary growth respecting the environment'.[8] The TEU also introduced further changes to the law-making procedures, the main one being the creation of a new legislative procedure which strengthened the power of the Parliament. Citizenship of the Union was also established by the TEU.

The Treaty of Amsterdam (ToA) (1997) was supposed to address the issues facing the EU as a result of impending enlargement; however, in reality the ToA did relatively little to address the required institutional reform. It did however result in a further broadening of the aims of the EU to include wider social aims, such as the prevention of discrimination on the grounds of ethnicity, age and sexual orientation. In many respects the Amsterdam Treaty was a consolidating exercise removing some obsolete articles.[9] In 2001 the Treaty of Nice was signed although it did not come into force until 2003 because of the difficulties of ratification in Ireland. The principal purpose of the Nice Treaty was to make the institutional changes required for an enlarged Union of 27 Member States. A limited number of new policies were introduced, but nothing directly of relevance to environmental protection.

3.2.5 The Constitutional Treaty and the Treaty of Lisbon

The Amsterdam and Nice Treaties largely concentrated on addressing the difficulties of enlargement and the impact that a membership of 27 would have upon the institutional infrastructure of the EU. However, only one year after the Treaty of Nice was signed the 'Declaration of the Future of the European Union' was adopted by the European Council in Laeken, which committed the Union to becoming more democratic, transparent and effective.[10] There was recognition of the need for the EU to have a Constitution that would, inter alia, bring together, in a single document, all of the existing Treaties.[11] In October 2004 a draft Constitution was agreed by the Member States subject

---

6 See below at 3.12.
7 Frequently referred to as the Maastricht Treaty.
8 Art 2 EC Treaty.
9 Which resulted in the renumbering of most of the Treaty article numbers. However, the Treaty of Lisbon has resulted in a further renumbering exercise.
10 Declaration on the Future of the Union (SN 300101).
11 This would have removed the need for an EC Treaty and a Treaty on European Union.

to it being ratified by all Member States. The ratification process proved to be problematic, with some Member States requiring a referendum before ratification was possible. The Constitution was rejected by voters in France (May 2005) and the Netherlands (June 2005) resulting in the collapse of the Constitutional Treaty. Following a period of self-imposed reflection, the European Council took up the mantle once again in 2007 and called for a further intergovernmental conference to agree a new Treaty. The Lisbon Treaty (known as the Reform Treaty) was signed on 13 December 2007, and like its predecessor required ratification by all of the 27 Member States. In June 2008 the Irish held a referendum, with 53.4 per cent of those voting rejecting the Treaty. However, a second referendum was held in October 2009, this time returning 67 per cent in favour of the Treaty. The only other Member State that posed a problem for ratification was the Czech Republic, where a legal challenge was mounted through the Czech courts. In December 2008 the Czech Republic's highest court ruled that the Treaty of Lisbon was consistent with the Czech Constitution and in November 2009 the Czech Prime Minister finally signed the Treaty. With full ratification secured, the Treaty came into force in December 2009. Unlike the Constitutional Treaty, which would have replaced the EC Treaty and TEU into a single consolidated Treaty, the Treaty of Lisbon retains but amends the dual Treaty structure. The EC Treaty is renamed the Treaty on the Functioning of the European Union (TFEU). The TEU retains its name. The TFEU and the TEU constitute the Treaties on which the Union is founded.[12] Once again, from an environmental lawyer's perspective we are primarily interested in the TFEU. However, as we shall note later, the TEU now contains provisions relating to the Union's involvement in international matters relating to the environment and it also includes some common provisions discussed below.[13] The provisions of the TFEU and TEU relating to environmental protection are considered below at 3.10.

3.3 Sources of EU law

3.3.1 The Treaties

The TFEU and TEU are the primary source of EU law since it is from these Treaties that the EU institutions derive their power to enact secondary legislation. The TFEU can be described as *traité cadre*, which means that it sets out broad general principles and aims, but leaves the institutions to 'flesh out' and implement these aims by means of secondary legislation. However, the institutions can only act within the limits of the powers conferred upon them by the Treaties. In order to exercise the Union's competences the institutions are empowered to adopt legally binding measures. Previously these were defined in Art 249 EC Treaty, which is now Art 288 TFEU. The TFEU also defines the legislative procedures that are to be used when the institutions legislate in particular areas. Article 288 TFEU defines the types of legal instruments available to the EU institutions. Because these legislative Acts derive from the TFEU, they are regarded as secondary legislation and are hierarchically inferior to the Treaties, which are the primary source of EU law. It is important to be familiar with the distinctions between the types of secondary legislation.

3.3.2 Regulations

Regulations have general application, are binding in their entirety and are directly applicable in all Member States. Regulations apply equally to all Member States and can therefore be used to ensure that the law is uniform throughout the EU. For this reason, regulations take effect within Member States either on the date specified in the Official Journal of the European Union or, in the absence

---

12 Art 1 TEU.
13 Notably Arts 2 TEU and 5 TEU.

of a specified date, the regulation takes effect 20 days after publication.[14] Since regulations are binding in their entirety and directly applicable, there is no need for a Member State to implement the regulation in order for it to take effect. In fact, in Case 93/71, *Leonesio v Ministero dell'Agricoltura e delle Forests* (1971) it was held that national rules which sought to transpose regulations into national law would be incompatible with the aims of regulations.[15] By the end of 2011 there were a total of 8,862 regulations.[16] Although directives have been the preferred legal instrument of choice the EU is increasingly using regulations to deliver its environmental policy.

3.3.3 Directives

Directives differ from regulations in a number of respects. Article 288 TFEU states that:

> A Directive shall be binding as to the results to be achieved, upon each Member State to which it is addressed, but shall leave to the national authorities the choice and form of methods.

Directives state the 'aim to be achieved', which is binding upon the Member State, but leave the choice and means of implementation to the discretion of the Member State. Therefore, directives provide a timeframe which gives the Member State the time to enact national legislation that transposes the requirements of the directive into national law and to establish the necessary administrative procedures to ensure effective implementation.

Law in Action

The Waste Framework Directive 2008/98[17] includes the following provisions relating to transposition.

Article 40

1. Member States shall bring into force the laws, regulations and administrative provisions necessary to comply with this Directive by 12 December 2010.

When Member States adopt these measures, they shall contain a reference to this Directive or shall be accompanied by such reference on the occasion of their official publication. The methods of making such reference shall be laid down by Member States.

2. Member States shall communicate to the Commission the text of the main provisions of national law which they adopt in the field covered by this Directive.

The deadline or deadlines prescribed in a directive are binding and Member States are obliged to ensure that there is effective implementation of the directive by those dates. It should be noted from the example above that Member States are also required to provide the Commission with the text of the national legislation that has been adopted. This enables the Commission to monitor compliance and also to examine the national legislation to ensure that it fulfils the obligations laid down in the directive. Implementation must be in a legally certain manner. In the UK, implementation is

---

14 All regulations and directives are published in the Official Journal.
15 Case 93/71, *Leonesio v Ministero dell'Agricoltura e delle Forests* [1972] ECR 287.
16 Report from the Commission, 29th Annual Report on Monitoring the Application of EU Law 2011.
17 Directive 2008/98/EC of the European Parliament and of the Council of 19 November 2008 on waste and repealing certain Directives Text with EEA relevance OJ L 312, 22/11/2008 pp 3–30.

usually (but not exclusively) achieved by means of statutory instrument. The European Communities Act 1972 (as amended) provides powers for ministers to introduce delegated legislation giving effect to EU directives.

The majority of EU environmental 'acts' take the form of directives rather than regulations. This means that Member States play a large part in the implementation of EU environmental law by exercising discretion in terms of how to achieve the aims laid down by the EU. By leaving the choice and form of implementation to the Member States, there will automatically be divergences of approach. However, directives provide a flexible means of ensuring harmonised standards whilst taking account of the differing legal and administrative systems within the Member States and, to some extent, reflect the principle of subsidiarity which is so central to the Treaties.[18] However, the use of directives rather than regulations raises a number of problems. What happens when a Member State fails to transpose the directive into national law, or transposition is delayed or flawed? The first obvious thing to note is that the failure to transpose a directive into national law constitutes a breach of EU law. For example, in Case C-42/89, *Commission v Belgium* (1990),[19] the Commission brought an action against Belgium in respect of its failure to adopt legislation necessary to comply with the provisions of a directive. The ECJ held in respect of this infringement action that a Member State may not plead practical or administrative difficulties in order to justify non-compliance with the obligations and time limits laid down in directives. The same holds true for financial difficulties, which it is for the Member State to overcome by adopting appropriate measures. The fact that a Member State may argue that it already conforms to the directive in practice does not constitute a reason for not transposing that directive into the national legal system. The ECJ held in Case C-361/88, *Commission v Germany* (1991)[20] that legal transposition is necessary to enable individuals to ascertain their rights and obligations. In order to secure the full implementation of directives it isn't sufficient that the Member State merely introduces national legislation; it is also essential that it achieves the environmental objectives prescribed in the directive. In Case C-337/89, *Commission v UK (re the Drinking Water Directive)*,[21] Advocate General Lenz said there were two obligations under the drinking water directive: first, to transpose the directive into national law and, secondly, a further absolute obligation to bring about physical changes to the environment. The ECJ has stated that a failure in practice to achieve standards will be equated with a failure at law. In Case C-214/97, *Commission v Portugal* (1998),[22] the Portuguese authorities had argued that they had made 'serious efforts' to implement Art 4 of Directive 75/44/EEC, which required them to draw up a systematic plan of action including a timetable for the improvement of surface water. The ECJ held that this was not sufficient. This emphasis on full implementation can be seen in Case C-56/90, *Commission v UK (Bathing Water)* (1993),[23] where the ECJ unequivocally rejected the UK's argument that the Bathing Water Directive did not impose an obligation to achieve a result, but merely required Member States to take all necessary steps in order to comply with the directive. Observing closely the words of the directive and its permitted derogations, the ECJ held that the directive required the Member States to take all the steps necessary to ensure that certain results are attained and, apart from those derogations, they cannot rely on particular circumstances to justify a failure to fulfil that obligation.

The EU recognises that there have been significant implementation failures in certain areas of environmental law. The Sixth Environmental Action Programme states that the full application,

---

18 Art 5 TEU.
19 Case C-42/89, *Commission v Belgium* [1990] ECR I-2821.
20 Case C-361/88, *Commission v Germany* [1991] ECR I-2567.
21 Case C-337/89 *Commission v UK (Drinking Water Directive)* [1992] ECR I-6103.
22 Case C-214/97 *Commission v Portugal* [1998] ECR I-3839.
23 Case C 56/90 *Commission v UK (Bathing Water)* [1993] ECR I-4109.

implementation and enforcement of existing EU environmental legislation is a strategic priority for the Union in the current decade.[24] Given that directives are prone to such problems, it is reasonable to wonder why they remain the prominent means of enacting EU environmental legislation but they continue to be the principal vehicle by which the EU rolls out its environmental policy. By the end of 2011 the EU had adopted a total of 1885 directives.[25] For a further discussion of the problems associated with directives, see 3.5.2 in relation to direct actions against Member States for non-implementation.

3.3.4 Decisions

A decision is an individual act binding in its entirety. Article 288 TFEU makes it clear that a decision which specifies those to whom it is addressed shall be binding only on them. Decisions can be addressed to Member States but can equally be addressed to individuals and companies. Because it is a binding act, a decision has the force of law and does not require any implementation. Decisions are frequently used by the Commission in the field of competition law but are rarely used in environmental law.

3.3.5 Recommendations and opinions

In addition to regulations, directives and decisions, the TFEU also makes provision for recommendations and opinions, which are not legally binding. However, the ECJ held in Case 322/88, *Grimaldi v Fonds des Maladies Professionnelles* (1988)[26] that recommendations and opinions should be of persuasive influence in the decisions of national courts.

3.3.6 Case law of the Court of Justice of the European Union (ECJ)

The jurisprudence of the European Court of Justice (ECJ) and also the General Court (previously the European Court of First Instance) is a major source of EU law, not least in the field of environment law. The ECJ, sometimes accused of judicial law making, has played a pivotal role in the development of EU law, through the development of key principles, such as direct effect and state liability. National courts are bound to follow rulings of the ECJ by virtue of Art 4 (3) TEU,[27] which provides that Member States are bound to ensure fulfilment of the obligations arising out of the Treaty, or resulting from actions taken by the institutions of the EU.[28] Moreover, s 3(2) of the European Communities Act 1972 requires national courts to take judicial notice of any decision of the ECJ.

3.4 The institutional framework

To understand how environmental policy and legislation has developed in the EU, it is necessary to have at least a basic understanding of the role of the respective EU institutions. This is particularly the case when one considers the volume of environmental legislation that the EU has enacted and the way in which influence can be brought to bear to affect its content (or, indeed, existence). It is

---

24 Decision No 1600/2002/EC of the European Parliament and of the Council of 22 July 2002 laying down the Sixth Community Environment Action Programme OJ L 242, 10/9/2002, pp 1–15.
25 Report from the Commission, 29th Annual Report on Monitoring the Application of EU Law 2011.
26 Case 322/88, *Grimaldi v Fonds des Maladies Professionnelles* [1989] ECR 4407.
27 Previously Art 10 EC Treaty.
28 Which includes the decisions of the European Court of Justice.

also important to understand the role of the respective institutions in the enforcement of EU environmental law and the actions that they can take in the event of a breach of the legal obligations arising under EU environmental law. The issue of enforcement is of particular importance in the light of what has already been said about the use of directives in the field of environmental law. Since the implementation of most EU environmental law rests with the Member States themselves, the EU must have the means available to ensure that such implementation is both effective and uniformly applied. It is not however the intention of this chapter to provide a detailed or comprehensive examination of the composition, functions and powers of the respective EU institutions. Instead the chapter will include a very short description of the institution with some commentary about the role that it plays in relation to the development of EU environmental policy and law. At the outset it should be noted that within the EU, no one institution is solely responsible for passing legislation; the law-making process involves the Council, the Commission, and the Parliament.[29]

3.4.1 The European Council

The European Council was not 'created' by the original EC Treaty in 1957. It came into being in 1974 and was formally 'recognised' by the SEA in 1986. However, the Treaty of Lisbon now confers on to the European Council the full status of an EU institution. At the outset it should be carefully noted that the European Council is not to be confused with the Council of Ministers, which exists as a separate institution. The European Council is made up of the Heads of State or Government of the 28 Member States, a President and the President of the Commission. Its role is to provide the Union with the necessary impetus for its development and also to define the general political guidelines and priorities of the Union. To that extent the Council could be instrumental in determining the priority to be accorded to environmental protection. Prior to the ratification of the Lisbon Treaty the presidency of the European Council rotated on a six-monthly basis. However, in November 2009 the European Council met to elect its new President, Herman Van Rompuy, who will serve for a renewable term of two years and six months.

3.4.2 The Council of the European Union (Council of Ministers)

The Council of the European Union, or Council of Ministers as it is frequently referred to, is made up of 28 representatives from the Member States. The representatives must be Ministers of State who are authorised to commit their respective governments and cast their vote. When Ministers attend Council meetings, they represent their governments and generally pursue national interests. The composition of the Council alters, depending on the subject under discussion: General Council meetings are usually attended by Foreign Affairs Ministers, environment meetings are attended by Environment Ministers and so on. These are referred to as configurations. With the ratification of the Treaty of Lisbon the Council will now have a president for each configuration. The environment configuration, which comprises environment ministers, meets about four times a year.

The duty of the Council is to act jointly with the European Parliament in the exercise of legislative and budgetary functions. In addition it is required to carry out policy-making and coordinating functions as laid down in the Treaties.[30] In relation to environmental protection measures the majority of legislative decisions are taken jointly with the European Parliament under a legislative procedure called the ordinary legislative procedure. When this procedure is used the Council uses a qualified majority voting (QMV) system. However, where the proposed measure concerns town

---

29 And, in some instances, the Economic and Social Affairs Committee and the Committee of the Regions, neither of which are discussed in this chapter.
30 Art 16(1) TEU.

and country planning, quantitative management of water resources land use (with the exception of waste management) and energy sources and supply, the Council is required to act unanimously. Where a unanimous vote is required, there is a much greater likelihood that the proposals will be delayed for lengthy periods until a compromise can be reached which satisfies all the Member States. Where qualified majority voting is required each Member State has a weighted vote; the weight depending roughly on the size of population. As from 2007 the 28 Member States were accorded a total of 352 votes; the larger Member States,[31] each having 29 votes, Poland 27 and Latvia and Cyprus only four each. Acts of the Council that require a QMV require at least 260 votes in favour cast by a majority of the Member States. As from 1 November 2014, a qualified majority shall be defined as at least 55 per cent of the members of the Council, comprising at least 15 of them and representing Member States comprising at least 65 per cent of the population of the Union. A blocking minority must include at least four Council members, failing which the qualified majority shall be deemed attained. In certain limited circumstances, the Treaty still requires that decisions are agreed unanimously. However, the requirement for unanimity generally only applies to the more politically sensitive areas of policy making, for example, the accession of new Member States to the Union, legislation concerning citizenship or where the Council is seeking to override the proposals/opinions of the other institutions involved in the law-making process.

3.4.3 The European Commission

The European Commission is made up of 28 Commissioners. Commissioners are appointed by the governments of the Member States. From November 2014, the Commission will reduce in size to corresponding to two thirds of the number of Member States.[32] However, the Treaty provides that the European Council, acting unanimously, may decide to alter this number.[33]

Commissioners are nominated by the Member States on the basis of their competency; they are not elected. When appointed Commissioners must refrain from any action incompatible with their duties and Member States must respect their independence. In particular Member States should not seek to influence Commissioners in the performance of their duties. This means that Commissioners must act in the interests of the EU, and must not take instructions from any national government. The Commissioners are appointed for five years and during that time they are not permitted to engage in any other occupation whether paid or not. The TFEU requires Commissioners to solemnly undertake to comply with their duties and behave with integrity. The Commission works under the political guidance of its President who plays a considerable political role within the Commission. In particular the President determines the guidelines within which the Commission should work, decides on the internal organisation of the Commission and is responsible for appointing Vice Presidents. The European Commission, made up of 28 Commissioners, should not be confused with the Commission Services. The Commission Services, which is the civil service of the EU, employs over 20,000 employees, mostly in Brussels. The service is divided into over 30 departments which are known as Directorates General (DGs). Each DG is led by an administrative and permanent Director General, who reports to a specific Commissioner. Each Commissioner is given a specific portfolio of responsibilities.

The role of the Commission is set out in Art 17 TEU.[34] The Commission is tasked with promoting the general interests of the Union and must take appropriate initiatives to that end. To this end Art 17(2) TEU provides that the power of legislative initiative rests with the Commission unless the

---

31 Germany, France, Italy, UK.
32 This will include its President and the High Representative of the Union for Foreign Affairs and Security Policy.
33 Art 17 TEU.
34 Previously in Art 211 EC Treaty.

Treaty provides otherwise. This means that the Commission is responsible for drafting the EU environmental legislation. Invariably it will be subject to lobbying from a range of interested stakeholders including environmental NGOs. In addition the Commission plays a continuing role in the law-making processes as provided for by the Treaties. The Commission draws up an annual work programme which sets out its principal objectives for the coming year. The Commission also exercises considerable powers in relation to the enforcement of EU law, having the right to bring Member States before the ECJ under Art 258 TFEU. In this respect, the Commission is regarded as the 'watchdog' of the Union or is sometimes referred to as the 'guardian of the Treaties'.

3.4.4 The Environment DG and the Climate Change DG

The Commissioner with responsibility for the Environment (at the time of writing) is Janez Potočnik. The objective of the Environment DG is 'to protect, preserve and improve the environment for present and future generations'. To achieve this it proposes policies that ensure a high level of environmental protection in the European Union and that preserve the quality of life of EU citizens.[35] The Environment DG is currently working to fulfil the four priorities that it identified in the Sixth Environmental Action Programme[36] for the period 2002–2012, these being climate change; nature and biodiversity; environment, health and quality of life; and natural resources and waste. The DG Environment also represents the EU at international environmental meetings such as the United Nations Framework Convention on Climate Change. In addition the Environment DG fulfils an enforcement role and is responsible for investigating any complaints about breaches of environmental law in the Member States.

In recognition of the importance that the EU accords to climate change as a major issue facing the EU (and the globe) it took the decision to establish a wholly new Directorate General for Climate Action (DG CLIMA). This new DG was established on 17 February 2010. DG CLIMA develops and implements the EU Emissions Trading Scheme. It is also responsible for ensuring the EU meets its targets under the 20:20:20 agreement. Under this agreement, which was adopted by the European Council in 2008, the EU has set a target of reducing carbon emissions by 20 per cent (of 1990 levels) by 2020.

3.4.5 The European Parliament

The European Parliament was originally called the European Assembly and was made up of representatives from national parliaments. However, in 1979, direct elections to the Parliament were held for the first time and the Assembly changed its name to the European Parliament as required by the SEA 1986. The Parliament is made up of 766 directly elected representatives, known as Members of the European Parliament or MEPs.[37] MEPs are elected for a five-year term of office. The Parliament sits in plenary session at the Parliament in Strasbourg but it will also convene meetings at its offices in Brussels.

The Parliament's functions and powers have grown significantly since 1957. Prior to the SEA 1986, the Parliament acted largely in an advisory and supervisory capacity. Its involvement in the legislative procedure was limited to giving an opinion on proposed legislation, but only in relation to those areas of legislation where the EU Treaty specifically provided that the Parliament should be consulted. In some areas of legislation, the Council could take decisions without the need for any

---

35 See http://eceuropaeu/dgs/environment/index_enhtm, accessed March 2013.
36 Decision No 1600/2002/EC of the European Parliament and of the Council of 22 July 2002 laying down the Sixth Community Environment Action Programme OJ L 242, 10/9/2002, pp 1–15.
37 The UK elects 78 MEPs.

consultation with the Parliament. The Parliament, as befitting the only directly elected Union institution, pressed for greater powers and in particular a greater involvement in the legislative process.
Its powers were increased by the SEA 1986, which gave it the right in certain circumstances to be
consulted twice in relation to certain proposals. This procedure was referred to as the co-operation
procedure. When the Treaty of Lisbon came into force this procedure was discontinued. In 1992 the
TEU 1992 introduced a new decision-making procedure.[38] The procedure was called co-decision
and was very complex.[39] Suffice to note that this procedure gave substantial new powers of amendment and ultimately veto to the Parliament. The current position under the TFEU (Art 289) is that
a legislative act can now be adopted by either the 'ordinary procedure' or the 'special legislative
procedure'.[40] The ordinary legislative procedure is almost identical to the co-decision procedure
and is the procedure that must be adopted in the vast majority of cases.[41] The way in which the
Parliament votes in relation to proposals before it is specified in the TFEU. Unless otherwise provided
by the TFEU, the normal voting arrangement would be by a simple majority of votes cast. However,
in the ordinary legislative procedure referred to above the TFEU does specify that at certain times
the Parliament must secure an absolute majority of its membership.[42]

The Parliament currently exercises a range of functions. It participates in the legislative process
as discussed briefly above. In addition the Parliament plays a significant role in the Union's budgetary
process. Article 314(4) TFEU enables the Parliament to amend any part of the Union's draft budget.
It also acts in a supervisory capacity in relation to the Commission. Before the Commission starts its
term of office it is subject to a vote of approval by the Parliament and the Parliament has the power
to dismiss the whole of the Commission with a vote of censure.[43] The Parliament has never exercised
this power but the threat of exercising it resulted in the resignation, in March 1999, of the European
Commission then led by Commission President Jacques Santer. The Parliament also conducts its own
version of question time when it requires Commissioners to answer Parliamentary questions, either
verbally to the Parliament or in writing. The Commissioners are obliged by Art 230 TFEU to respond
to any questions put to them by the Parliament. It is in this way that the Parliament exercises a degree
of control over the Commission, and this reflects the checks and balances that are built into the institutional framework. The Council of Ministers also reports to the Parliament. At the end of each
Presidency period, the outgoing President of the Council reports to the Parliament on the Council's
achievements during that period. Since the TEU 1993, the Parliament has had the power to set up a
Committee of Inquiry to investigate alleged contraventions or maladministration in the implementation of EU law and has also been required to appoint an Ombudsman for Maladministration.

3.4.6 The Parliament and the environment

The political composition of the Parliament is wide-ranging, with large representations from both
the left and right of the political spectrum. Although MEPs stand as members of national political
parties they sit within the European Parliament within broad political groups (rather than national
groups). Following the June 2009 European Parliamentary elections there are 43 MEPs from the
Greens/European Free Alliance;[44] in addition there is a political grouping which embraces the
Nordic Green Left.

---

38 Under what was Art 251 EC Treaty.
39 Its fine detail falls well outside the scope of this book.
40 I.e. directive or regulation.
41 The ordinary procedure is defined and elaborated in Art 294 TFEU.
42 I.e. 369 votes.
43 Art 17 (8) TEU and Art 234 TFEU.
44 See http://wwwgreens-efaorg/cms/default/rubrik/6/6270htm, accessed March 2013.

The Parliament has some 20 policy committees which meet in Brussels, one of which includes Environment, Public Health and Food Safety.[45] Most of the Parliament's legislative work is conducted in these committees. The Parliament receives a number of petitions from environmental pressure groups and these are usually passed on to the Commission to deal with under the Art 258 TFEU proceedings.[46] The value of petitioning Parliament is that it can lend a political impetus to the process, which may be persuasive when the Commission decides upon enforcement proceedings.

3.4.7 The Court of Justice of the European Union (ECJ)

Although the Court is now called the Court of Justice of the European Union it has always been referred to as the European Court of Justice (or ECJ). Article 19 TEU provides that the role of the ECJ is to 'ensure that in the interpretation and application of this Treaty the law is observed'. The precise jurisdiction of the Court, however, is defined within Arts 251–281 TFEU. Of particular note, in the context of this book, is Art 258 TFEU, which gives the ECJ jurisdiction to hear infringement actions brought by the European Commission against Member States. This will be discussed more fully below in relation to the enforcement of EC law.

The ECJ itself is currently made up of 28 judges.[47] The judges of the ECJ are chosen from people whose independence is beyond doubt and who possess the qualifications required for appointment to the highest judicial offices in their respective countries or who are jurisconsults of recognised competence. Judges are appointed by the common accord of the governments of the Member States. However, the appointments must also be vetted by a special panel which comprises former ECJ judges and members of the national supreme courts.[48] Judges are appointed for a period of six years, but in an attempt to achieve some continuity the Treaty requires that there must be a partial replacement of the judges every three years. The ECJ is assisted by eight Advocate Generals who help it by presenting an analysis of the cases before it and also, importantly, their recommendations in the form of an opinion. The ECJ reaches its decisions in private and presents a single judgment known as a collegiate judgment. This means that there is no record of any dissenting judgment. It is often very useful when reading judgments of the ECJ to also read the opinion of the Advocate General. Whilst the judges are not bound to follow the Advocate General's recommendations, where they do, the opinion provides a very useful indication of the ECJ's reasoning.

In addition to the ECJ, there is also the General Court. This was previously called the European Court of First Instance (CFI), and was created in 1988 to alleviate some of the workload of the ECJ. The General Court consists of 28 judges whose qualifications, appointment and legal status are subject to the same requirements as judges of the ECJ. Its jurisdiction is set down in Art 256 TFEU and includes direct judicial review actions brought by natural and legal persons and also by Member States.[49] Originally the General Court had no jurisdiction to give preliminary rulings. However, as an attempt to address the serious workload issues of the ECJ the Treaty of Nice (ToN) conferred on the General Court the jurisdiction to hear and determine questions referred for a preliminary ruling in specific areas laid down by the Statute of the Court. At the time of writing, these areas had not been determined. In addition, the ToN allowed the establishment of judicial panels to hear and determine at first instance certain classes of action or proceedings brought in specific areas. These are attached to the General Court and the TFEU now refers to them as 'specialised courts'. Again, at the time of writing the only specialised court to have been established deals with EU patents law.

---

45 See http://wwweuroparleuropaeu/activities/committees/committeesListdo?language=EN, accessed 1 March 2013.
46 Formerly Art 226 EC.
47 One from each Member State.
48 See Art 255 TFEU.
49 Under Arts 263 and 265 TFEU.

The General Court has jurisdiction to hear and determine actions or proceedings brought against decisions of the specialised courts.

3.4.8 The European Environment Agency

The European Environment Agency (EEA) is not formally an institution of the EU in that it was not established by the Treaties. The EEA was established in 1993 by an EU regulation (Regulation 1210/90).[50] The regulation also established the European environment information and observation network (Eionet). The EEA is based in Copenhagen, Denmark and employs about 185 employees.

The EEA is responsible for helping the EU and its Member States to make informed decisions about improving the environment, integrating environmental considerations into economic policies and moving towards sustainability. It seeks to do this by providing environmental data, assessments and thematic analyses. The EEA is required to publish a report on the state of the environment every three years and these are accessible to the public via the EEA's website.[51] In addition the EEA has produced a number of significant documents, most particularly the European Pollutant Emission Register (EPER) which is compiled using data collected from the monitoring of the Integrated Pollution Prevention Control Directive.[52] The EPER is a web-based register, which enables the public to view data on emissions to water and air of 50 key pollutants from large and medium-sized industrial point sources in the European Union. In addition the EEA also coordinates the European environment information and observation network (Eion). The membership of the EEA, in addition to the 28 Member States, also includes Iceland, Liechtenstein, Norway, Switzerland and Turkey.

3.5 The enforcement of EU law: direct actions against Member States

3.5.1 The obligation to comply with EU law

Member States are obliged to fulfil their EU law obligations and not do anything which would jeopardise the attainment of the objectives of the Treaties. This obligation was previously to be found in Art 10 EC but is now stated in Art 4(3) TEU. The Member States are specifically required to take all appropriate measures, whether general or particular, to ensure fulfilment of the obligations arising out of the Treaties, or resulting from action taken by the institutions. Such 'action' includes both EU policy, secondary legislation and decisions of the ECJ and General Court. In addition, Member States must not take any measures which could jeopardise the attainment of the Union's objectives.

Failure to fulfil obligations can take many forms:

(a)   Introducing legislation in contravention of the Treaties. A good example of this happening, albeit not in the environmental law field, is the enactment by the English Parliament of Merchant Shipping Act 1988, which contravened the basic principle of non-discrimination on the grounds of nationality and resulted in the *Factortame* litigation.[53]

---

50 Council Regulation (EEC) No 1210/90 of 7 May 1990 on the establishment of the European Environment Agency and the European Environment Information and Observation Network OJ L 120, 11/5/1990, pp 1–6.
51 See http://wwweeaeuropaeu/.
52 Directive 2008/1/EC of the European Parliament and of the Council of 15 January 2008 concerning integrated pollution prevention and control (Codified version) 2008/1/EC OJL 24, 29/1/2008, p 8.
53 Case C48/93 R v *Secretary of State for Transport, ex p Factortame Ltd and others* [1996] ECR I-1029.

(b) Failure to implement directives either at all, or on time: during 2011 Member States were required to transpose 131 directives (not all environmental) into national law. During that year the Commission launched 1,185 late transposition actions, which represented a significant increase from previous years (885 in 2010 and 531 in 2009). As at end December 2011 there were 36 late transposition actions open against the UK.[54]

(c) Partial or flawed implementation of a directive.

(d) Inadequate enforcement of a directive. For example see Case C-340/96, *Commission v UK* in respect of the Secretary of State for the Environment's failure to take enforcement actions against water companies.[55]

3.5.2 Infraction proceedings

The main direct sanction against Member States is provided for by Art 258 TFEU.[56] This enables the European Commission to commence legal proceedings against Member States before the ECJ. If the Commission believes that a Member State is in breach of its obligations, it can inform the Member State in question by means of a letter of formal notice, which sets out the nature of the infringement and the course of action to be taken. This only usually happens after informal negotiations have been exhausted. The letter must state all the grounds for complaint. Member States must then be given an adequate time period to make their observations on the alleged breach. If the Commission is still not satisfied that the Member State is complying with its obligations, then it can take the next step of issuing a 'reasoned opinion'. This formally records the infringement and requires the Member State to take the necessary action to bring the infringement to an end. Normally the Member State will be given a deadline by which it must take appropriate action. Following this pre-litigation stage, the Commission can, if it chooses, commence legal proceedings against the Member State before the ECJ.

A number of points need to be made in relation to Art 258 TFEU proceedings:

(a) The Commission often acts on the basis of complaints made by aggrieved citizens or pressure groups. In addition, the Commission also receives numerous petitions from pressure groups, trade unions and so on. It is in this respect that individuals and pressure groups can exert pressure on the Commission to deal with breaches of environmental law. Complainants do not have to satisfy any legal or sufficient interest in the matter complained of. Therefore, Art 258 provides an inexpensive means by which interested parties can seek to enforce EU environmental law. In 2011 the three Member States against which the most complaints were filed were Italy (386 complaints), Spain (306) and Germany (263).[57]

(b) The Commission is not bound to investigate or follow through all complaints nor is it bound to commence Art 258 proceedings.

(c) Member States have raised various mitigating factors and defences but these have rarely succeeded. For example, in Case C-337/89 *Commission v UK* (*Drinking Water Directive*)[58] the Commission argued that the UK had failed to meet the required standards of the Drinking water Directive 80/778/EC, which set maximum acceptable nitrate levels for water used in food production. In this case the UK government argued that most food production was carried out using water from the domestic supply and that the legislation was unnecessary.

---

54 Report from the Commission, 29th Annual Report on Monitoring the Application of EU Law 2011.
55 Case C-340/96, *Commission v UK* [1999] ECR I-2023.
56 Previously Art 226 EC.
57 Report from the Commission, 29th Annual Report on Monitoring the Application of EU Law 2011.
58 Case C-337/89 *Commission v UK* (*Drinking Water Directive*) [1992] ECR I-6103.

However, this defence was rejected by the ECJ, which held that the UK could only rely on specific derogations contained in the directive. A Member State may not plead provisions, practices or circumstances existing in its internal legal system in order to justify a failure to comply with obligations resulting from EU directives.

In addition to Art 258 TFEU, Art 259 provides for a similar procedure enabling one Member State to bring an action against another Member State. It is very rare for Member States to resort to inter-state litigation. Member States are, in fact, required to notify the Commission of the alleged infringement and the Commission is required to issue a reasoned opinion to the state concerned before the complaining Member State can commence proceedings.

3.5.3 Fines

Where a Member State is found to be in breach of its EU law obligations, the ECJ will issue a declaration to that effect.[59] Failure to comply with the declaration and remedy the situation will result in the Member State being in breach of both Art 260 TFEU and Art 4(3) TEU. Prior to the TEU 1992, the ECJ's powers were limited to issuing a declaration. However, its powers were increased in 1992 to enable the ECJ to impose a fine where a Member State continues to breach its obligations after an ECJ declaration. The fine is not automatic; the Commission is required to recommence proceedings against the defaulting Member State before a fine can be imposed and the Commission is required to specify the amount of the lump sum or penalty payment to be paid by the Member State concerned which it considers appropriate in the circumstances. The ECJ cannot impose a fine in excess of the recommended fine. Interestingly, the first occasion in which the ECJ exercised its power to fine a Member State came in an environmental law case (Case C-387/97, *Commission v Hellenic Republic (Greece)* (2000)[60]) concerning the repeated failure by the Greek authorities to comply with the provisions of two waste directives.[61] The ECJ ruled that the breaches had been very serious and imposed a fine of 20,000 euros daily from the date of service of the judgment.

The Treaty of Lisbon incorporated an amendment to Art 258 which states that when the Commission brings a case before the Court pursuant to Art 258 on the grounds that the Member State concerned has failed to fulfil its obligation to notify measures transposing a directive it may, when it deems appropriate, specify the amount of the lump sum or penalty payment to be paid by the Member State concerned which it considers appropriate in the circumstances. Member States usually take the necessary measures to comply with the judgment of the Court in a timely manner. However, at the end of 2011, the Commission still had to continue 77 infringement procedures under Art 260(2) TFEU where Member States had failed to comply with the Court's judgment. Significantly almost half of the Art 260(2) TFEU infringements related to environment cases (36).[62]

Although the UK has never been fined by the ECJ it is worthy of note that in 2012 the Department for Communities and Local Government (DCLG) published a proposed policy statement under s 49 of the Localism Act 2011 relating to the liability of local authorities and devolved administrations in respect of any penalty payment. The consultation noted that financial sanctions for the UK could be significant, with a minimum lump sum of 8.992 million euros, based on the UK's GDP, and potential additional daily or periodic penalty payments.[63]

---

59 Art 260 TFEU.
60 Case C-387/97, *Commission v Hellenic Republic (Greece)* (2000) ECR-I 5047.
61 Directives 75/442/EEC and 78/319/EEC.
62 Report from the Commission, 29th Annual Report on Monitoring the Application of EU Law 2011.
63 Consultation on proposed policy statement on EU financial sanctions under the Localism Act 2011.

3.5.4 Infringement actions in relation to environmental directives

Following the Seveso accident[64] the European Parliament was highly critical of the European Commission alleging that it had failed to fully and properly perform its role as Guardian of the Treaty.[65] Perhaps as a result of this the Commission subsequently became more active in monitoring the enforcement of EU environmental law and bringing direct actions against the Member States. The non-implementation of environmental directives has given rise to a significant number of direct actions before the ECJ. One well-known example is Case C-337/89, Commission v UK (1993)[66] concerning non-implementation by the UK of Directive 80/778/EC[67] on drinking water intended for human consumption. This was the first case in which the UK was found to be in breach of an environmental directive. Another example of a direct action against the UK can be found in Case 56/90, Commission v UK (1993),[68] where the UK was found to be in breach of its obligation under EC law in respect of the Bathing Water Directive 76/160/EC.[69] More recently the UK was found to have breached its obligations under the Urban Waste Water Treatment Directive 91/271/EEC in case C-301/10 Commission v United Kingdom (Re storm water overflows) [2013].[70] The case came about as a result of complaints about excessive storm water overflows in parts of the UK and specifically at the Whitburn Sunderland steel pumping station and also in respect of untreated waste water being discharged into the Thames. One of the alarming features of this case is the time it took to get to court. The Commission sent its first letter of formal notice to the UK in April 2003. After seven years of protracted correspondence and negotiation, the Commission eventually commenced legal proceedings in 2010. The judgment in the case was handed down in October 2012, over nine years after the letter of formal notice. In this case the Commission argued that the UK was in breach of various provisions in Directive 91/271/EEC on Urban Waste Water Treatment.[71] Essentially the case concerned disagreements between the UK and the Commission over the interpretation of certain provisions within the directive. The Commission argued, inter alia, that the collecting systems for waste water had to be able to take into account natural climatic conditions as well as seasonal variations, and that 'storm water overflows' referred to in Annex I(A) to the directive were a part of such systems. The UK submitted that the concept of 'unusually heavy rainfall' referred to in Annex I(A) expressly acknowledged that it would not be possible to avoid discharges in particular circumstances. Additionally the Commission argued that the concept of 'best technical knowledge not entailing excessive costs' prescribed in Annex I(A) of the directive allowed Member States to choose between several solutions that promoted compliance with the objectives of the directive, such as building new or increased storage facilities or diverting rainwater before it can enter the collecting system. The UK disagreed with this interpretation and argued that the directive must be interpreted as leaving it to Member States to determine the manner in which urban waste water should be collected and treated in order to realise the directive's objective, which is to protect the environment from the adverse effects of waste water discharges. After a lengthy discussion of the various arguments the Court came to the conclusion that the UK had failed to fulfil its obligations under the directive.

There are of course numerous cases in relation to all areas of EU environmental law, some of which have been discussed in other chapters throughout this book. The European Commission, in reviewing the achievements of the Sixth Environmental Action Programme has noted that 'After 35 years of legal development a common environment policy framework is now in place. However, the

---

64 This was an industrial accident in a small chemical manufacturing plant in Italy in 1976.
65 See Resolution of the European Parliament on the treatment of Waste in the EC [1984] OJC 127/67.
66 Case C-337/89 Commission v UK (Drinking Water Directive) [1992] ECR I-6103.
67 Council Directive 80/778/EEC of 15 July 1980 relating to the quality of water intended for human consumption OJ L 229, 30/8/1980, pp 11–29 (now repealed).
68 Case 56/90, Commission v UK [1993] ECR I-4109.
69 Council Directive 76/160/EEC of 8 December 1975 concerning the quality of bathing water OJ L 31, 5/2/1976, pp 1–7.
70 C-301/10 Commission v United Kingdom (Re storm water overflows) [2013] 1 CMLR 24.
71 Council Directive 91/271/EEC of 21 May 1991 concerning urban waste-water treatment OJ L 135, 30/5/1991 p 40.

high number of complaints and infringement procedures are a sign that the implementation of environmental legislation remains far from satisfactory. Only by ensuring the correct implementation of the *acquis* will it be possible to realise environmental objectives.'[72] This is borne out by recent statistics. At the end of 2011, 1,775 infringement cases were open. Although overall the number of infringement cases has been falling year on year (2,100 cases in 2010 and nearly 2,900 cases in 2009) 17 per cent of the cases concerned environmental measures (followed by transport (15 per cent); internal market (15 per cent) and taxation (12 per cent)).[73] Most of the active infringement cases in 2011 (299) were in the environment field.

- During 2011 the Commission received 604 complaints on environmental matters with the majority of complaints concerning nature protection, waste and water.
- In 2011 of the 299 active infringement actions relating to environmental directives 174 were commenced on the Commission's own initiative; 84 arose from complaints from civil society and 41 concerned late transposition of directives.
- During 2011 the Commission opened 114 new environmental infringement actions; of these 58 were in respect of late transposition of environmental directives, most notably the Waste Framework Directive.
- 18 cases were referred to the Court of Justice including referrals for the late adoption of river basin management plans as required by the Water Framework Directive[74] and three referrals relating to the lack of Integrated Pollution Prevention and control (IPPC) permits for factories under the IPPC Directive.[75]
- By the end of 2011 56 ECJ judgements still required full implementation by the Member States concerned.

Law in Action

UK implementation of EU law[76]

- At the end of 2011 there were 76 open infringements against the UK. This is the eighth-highest number of infringements among the then EU-27. However, the UK's performance (along with that of Germany) is the best in its reference group (France and Poland had 95 open infringements each, Spain 99, and Italy 135.)

- The UK closed the year with more infringements than in 2010 (72) but fewer than in 2009 (98).

- Of the 77 infringement open cases, nine concerned the environment.

- During 2011 the Commission opened 57 infringement actions against the UK for late transposition of directives. This represents a significant increase from 2010 when only 35 infringement actions were opened. This figure puts the UK as the 23rd worst performing Member state re late transposition of directives in 2011.

---

72 Communication from the Commission to the European Parliament, the Council, the European Economic and Social Committee and the Committee of the Regions on the Mid-term Review of the Sixth Community Environment Action Programme COM (2007) 225 Final.
73 Report from the Commission, 29th Annual Report on Monitoring the Application of EU Law 2011.
74 Ibid.
75 Ibid.
76 Ibid, Annex 1.

- During 2011 the Commission received 192 complaints against the UK. Complaints in the environmental field notably included inadequate environmental assessment of fishing and wind farm developments.

- The Commission brought two Court cases against the UK during 2011 (compared to only one in 2010). Case C-530/11 relates to the alleged breach of Directive 2003/35/EC[77] and will be discussed further in Chapter 12. The case is still pending. The second case (Case 86/11), which is also pending, concerns a failure to comply with the Vat Directive 2006/112/EEC.

See Chapter
◀ 12

3.6 Judicial review of EU law

The TFEU also gives the ECJ the jurisdiction to review the acts of the EU institutions and to annul them on specific grounds. The power of the ECJ in this respect is important, because it acts as a check on the other EU institutions which have been given significant powers under the Treaties. Article 263 TFEU[78] specifies which 'acts' are reviewable, who may bring judicial review proceedings, the grounds on which review proceedings may be brought and the time limits for bringing such actions. The ECJ can review the legality of acts adopted by the European Parliament and the Council, of acts of the Council, of the Commission and of the European Central Bank other than recommendations and opinions. Actions may be brought by the institutions or the Member States (privileged applicants). In addition judicial review actions may be brought by natural and legal persons, such as environmental pressure groups (non-privileged applicants). However, the reality is that it is very difficult for such persons and groups to satisfy the ECJ that they have the requisite standing to embark on a judicial review of Union law. In essence there are only three situations where a non-privileged person can bring actions for judicial review and the applicant must show that the challenged measure is of direct and individual concern to them. The case law that has developed in relation to standing for non-privileged applicants is very complex and any discussion of it falls outside the scope of this book. However, from the perspective of environmental protection the following cases merit some discussion.

In Case C-321/95P *Stichting Greenpeace Council and others v Commission of the European Communities* (1998)[79] Greenpeace challenged a decision of the Commission to provide financial assistance (a grant under the European Regional Development Fund) to Spain for the construction of two power stations in the Canary Islands. Greenpeace (supported by a number of Canary Islands residents) challenged the decision on the grounds that there had been a failure to conduct an Environmental Impact Assessment in accordance with the Environmental Impact Assessment Directive 85/337/EEC.[80] The ECJ ruled that none of the applicants was individually concerned by the decision, and therefore the action was struck out as inadmissible. As far as the ECJ was concerned it was the decision taken by the Spanish authorities to build the two power stations which was liable to affect the environmental rights arising under Directive 85/337/EEC and it was this decision (the national

---

77 Directive 2003/35/EC of the European Parliament and of the Council of 26 May 2003 providing for public participation in respect of the drawing up of certain plans and programmes relating to the environment and amending with regard to public participation and access to justice Council Directives 85/337/EEC and 96/61/EC (OJ 2003 L 156, p 17).

78 Formerly Art 230 EC.

79 Case C-321/95P *Stichting Greenpeace Council and others v Commission of the European Communities* [1998] ECR I-1651; [1998] All ER (EC) 620; [1998] 3 CMLR 1; [1999] Env LR 181.

80 Council Directive 85/337/EEC of 27 June 1985 on the assessment of the effects of certain public and private projects on the environment OJ L 175, 5/7/1985, pp 40–48.

decision) that should have been challenged in the Spanish courts. The Court felt that in the circumstances, the contested decision, which concerned the Union financing of those power stations, could not directly affect such rights. The Court took this view notwithstanding the fact that it accepted that the protection of the environment has inherently a public dimension which constitutes a general Union interest.[81] As the Court stated:

> The fact that legality must be observed *per se* within the [Union], including the obligation to protect the environment, does not automatically confer on a natural or legal person a right or right interest enforceable by an action under the fourth paragraph of Article [263 TFEU]. The [Union] legal order does not recognise an *actio popularis* in environmental matters either.

In the *Greenpeace* case the court also rejected the Greenpeace argument that they should be granted standing on the basis that Greenpeace represented the general interests of the local residents on the islands. The ECJ concluded that since the residents were not individually concerned, it followed that neither was Greenpeace. In Case C-50/00 P *Union de Pequenos Agricultores v Council of the European Union* (2002),[82] Advocate General Jacobs put forward a far more liberal suggestion regarding the standing of individuals. The case concerned a challenge brought by a trade association seeking annulment of an EU regulation concerned with the common organisation of the market for olive oil.[83] Advocate General Jacobs thought:

> There are no compelling reasons that an individual applicant seeking to challenge a general measure must be differentiated from all others affected by it in the same way as an addressee. On that reading, the greater the number of persons affected by a measure the less likely it is that judicial review under the fourth paragraph of Article [263 TFEU] will be made available. The fact that a measure adversely affects a large number of individuals, causing wide-spread rather than limited harm, provides however to my mind a positive reason for accepting a direct challenge by one or more of those individuals.

Instead AG Jacobs favoured an approach whereby a person is to be regarded as individually concerned by a Union measure where, by reason of his particular circumstances, the measure has, or is liable to have, a substantial adverse effect on his interests. Clearly such an approach would be applicable in the environmental context where decisions affecting the environment necessarily impact on the community at large. However, the ECJ was not prepared to relax its stance on standing in these cases and held that the test remained the same as it was, namely that to demonstrate individual concern an applicant must prove that he is part of a closed class of applicants.

Despite the Court maintaining its strict stance on the standing of individuals a number of NGOs have argued that the requirement for individual concern in cases which fall within the scope of the UNECE Aarhus Convention constitutes a breach of the Convention.[84] The Convention provides, inter alia, for public participation in environmental decision making in relation to certain specified activities that are likely to have a significant effect on the environment. The Aarhus Convention has been implemented into EU law by the so-called Aarhus Regulation 1367/2006.[85]

---

81 At paras 51 and 52.
82 Case C-50/00 P *Union de Pequenos Agricultores v Council of the European Union* [2002] ECR I-6677; [2003] 2 WLR 795; [2002] All ER (EC) 893; [2002] 3 CMLR 1.
83 It was not an environmental law case but the principles as they relate to environmental pressure groups are applicable.
84 United Nations Economic Commission for Europe Convention on Access to Information, Public Participation in Decision-making and Access to Justice in Environmental Matters (1998).
85 Regulation (EC) No 1367/2006 of the European Parliament and of the Council of 6 September 2006 on the application of the provisions of the Aarhus Convention on Access to Information, Public Participation in Decision-making and Access to Justice in Environmental Matters to Community institutions and bodies, OJ L 264, 25/9/2006 pp 13–19.

Under Art 9(2) of the Convention the public concerned should have access to judicial review procedures which allow them to challenge breaches of Art 6. Moreover Art 9(3) of the Convention states that the Parties to the Convention must ensure that members of the public have access to administrative or judicial procedures to challenge acts and omissions by private parties which contravene national environmental law. Article 10 of the Aarhus Regulation implements this by providing first that any non-governmental organisation (which meets the criteria set out in Art 11) is entitled to make a request for internal review to the Union institution that has adopted an 'administrative act' under environmental law or, in case of an alleged administrative omission, should have adopted such an act. Article 11 lays down four criteria that must be met by the NGO; it must be an independent and non-profit-making legal person; its primary stated objective must be promoting environmental protection in the context of environmental law; it must have existed for more than two years and is actively pursuing its environmental protection objectives; and the subject matter of the internal review is covered by its objective and activities. Providing the NGO can satisfy these requirements it can request an internal review of any administrative act or omission on the part of an EU institution that the NGO considers breaches environmental law. At face value this would appear to give NGOs the right to challenge a wide range of acts which breach environmental law without having to go through judicial review proceedings. However, the Aarhus Regulation defines administrative acts narrowly as 'any measure of individual scope under environmental law, taken by a Union institution or body, and having legally binding and external effects'. This narrow definition has been successfully challenged before the General Court in Case T-396/09, *Vereniging Milieudefensie & Stichting Stop Luchtverontreiniging Utrecht v The Commission*.[86] In 2008 the Dutch government notified the Commission that it had postponed the attainment deadline for the annual limit for nitrogen dioxide under the Ambient Air Quality Directive 2008/50 EC. The Commission took a decision that it raised no objections to this postponement, and allowed the Dutch authorities until December 2014. The Commission's Decision was challenged by two Dutch NGOs whose objects included the improvement of air quality and campaigning against air pollution. The NGOs sought an internal review of the decision as permitted by Art 10 of the Aarhus Regulation but the Commission refused on the grounds that the contested decision was not an administrative measure since it was not of individual scope. The NGOs brought an action for annulment of the Commission's decision arguing first that it was a measure of individual scope. In the alternative the NGOs argued that if the first claim was to be rejected the Court should consider whether Art 10 of the Aarhus Regulation contravenes Art 9(3) of the Convention in so far as limits the concept of 'acts' for the purposes of Art 9(3) of the Convention to 'administrative act[s]', which are defined as 'measure[s] of individual scope'. The first argument was rejected by the General Court in the light of settled case law concerning Decisions addressed to Member States. However, the NGOs were successful in the alternate claim. The General Court held that the term 'acts' is not defined by Art 9(3) of the Convention but must be construed in the light of the objectives of the Convention. In the light of these objectives the Court decided that that an internal review procedure which covered only measures of individual scope would be very limited, since acts adopted in the field of the environment are mostly acts of general application. In the light of the objectives and purpose of the Aarhus Convention, such limitation is not justified and consequently Art 9(3) of the Aarhus Convention cannot be construed as referring only to measures of individual scope. The Council, Commission and Parliament have all appealed the General Court's ruling.[87]

---

86 Case T-396/09 *Vereniging Milieudefensie and Stichting Stop Luchtverontreiniging Utrecht v Commission* [2012] See also T-338/08 *Stichting Natuur en Milieu, Pesticide Action Network Europe v Commission* [2012].

87 Joined Cases C 401/12, 402/12 and 403/12, currently pending.

3.7 The preliminary rulings procedure

Given that Art 258 TFEU infringement proceedings can only be brought by the Commission and that individuals have in practice limited access to the ECJ under Art 263 TFEU, it is important for the student of environmental law to understand how EU law can be enforced by the domestic courts within the national legal system. As noted above in the *Stichting*[88] case the ECJ considered that the case should have been brought before the Spanish courts. The ECJ has established through its rulings that individuals can raise issues of EU law in the context of domestic legal proceedings in order to secure rights under EU law. So, for example, it is possible to use EU law to establish legal rights.[89] EU law can also be used to assert a defence in criminal prosecutions.[90]

In order to ensure that EU law is applied by national courts in a uniform manner, Art 267 TFEU[91] provides that the domestic courts can refer matters of interpretation and validity of EU law provisions to the ECJ in order to obtain a ruling. This is known as the preliminary rulings procedure.

The ECJ has jurisdiction to give preliminary rulings concerning the interpretation of the Treaties, the validity and interpretation of acts of the institutions, bodies, offices or agencies of the Union.[92] It is worth emphasising that the ECJ can only interpret the Treaties; it cannot, as is the case with secondary legislation, question its validity.

If a question regarding the interpretation of a provision of EU law arises in the context of national court proceedings then the national court or tribunal may, if it considers that decision is necessary to enable it to give judgment, request the ECJ to give a ruling. This is known as the preliminary rulings procedure. Once the ECJ gives its preliminary ruling, the national court is bound by it and must apply it to the facts of the case. The ECJ is not deciding on the facts or the outcome of the national court case, neither is it acting as an appeal court. Instead, it is essentially co-operating with the national court in order that the EU law provisions be interpreted uniformly and correctly. The ECJ is well placed to give this authoritative interpretation of EU law given its 'panoramic view' of the Union and of its institutions (per Lord Bingham in *Customs and Excise Comrs v Aps Samex* (1983)[93]). When the national court seeks a preliminary ruling from the ECJ, the court proceedings are suspended until the ECJ has given its ruling.

The ECJ cannot pass judgment on the compatibility of domestic law with EU law. In circumstances where the ECJ has been asked to do this, it will sometimes rephrase the question from the national court in order to provide the interpretation of the relevant EU law provision.[94]

The preliminary rulings procedure has provided the main vehicle for the ECJ to develop the principles of direct effect, supremacy and state liability, dealt with, briefly, in the following section. In the UK, the first reference in relation to an environmental law matter was made by the House of Lords in the case of *R v Secretary of State for the Environment ex p RSPB* (1995).[95] The RSPB challenged the decision of the Secretary of State's decision relating to the designation of the Medway Estuary and Marshes as a special protection area for birds (SPA) under the Wild Birds Directive (79/409/EEC[96]) in relation to the conservation of wild birds. The basis of the challenge was that the SoS had

---

88 Case C-321/95P *Stichting Greenpeace Council and others v Commission of the European Communities* [1998] ECR I-1651; [1998] All ER (EC) 620; [1998] 3 CMLR 1; [1999] Env LR 181.

89 A very good example of this in the field of sex discrimination is Case 152/84, *Marshall v Southampton and South West Hampshire AHA* [1986] ECR 723.

90 Case 148/78 *Criminal proceedings against Tullio Ratti* [1979] ECR 1629.

91 Formerly Art 234 EC.

92 For the purposes of this book the principal acts are directives and regulations.

93 *Customs and Excise Commissioners v ApS Samex* [1983] 1 All ER 1042; [1983] Com LR 72; [1983] 3 CMLR 194.

94 Since it is often in cases involving a conflict between domestic and EU law that questions of interpretation are raised.

95 The ruling was given in case C-44/95 *R v Secretary of State for the Environment Ex p Royal Society for the Protection of Birds (RSPB)* (C-44/95) [1997] QB 206; [1997] 2 WLR 123; [1996] ECR I-3805; [1996] 3 CMLR 411; [1997] Env LR 442.

96 Council Directive 79/409/EEC of 2 April 1979 on the conservation of wild birds OJ L 103, 25/4/1979, pp 1–18. Repealed and replaced by Directive 2009/147/EC of the European Parliament and of the Council of 30 November 2009 on the conservation of wild birds OJ L 20, 26/1/2010, pp 7–25.

excluded an area of mudflats from the SPA. The Port of Sheerness had planning permission to reclaim parts of the estuary, which formed part of Lappel Bank, in order to facilitate expansion without which the commercial viability of the port would be inhibited. It was common ground that the need for such expansion and the economic contribution which the port made to the area were strong economic considerations which could justify the decision to exclude the Lappel Bank area from the SPA designation, provided that it was lawful to take economic considerations into account. The House of Lords asked the ECJ whether the directive entitled the SoS to take account of economic considerations when excluding the Lappel Bank. The ECJ held in relation to Art 2 of the Directive that Member States must have regard to ecological, cultural and scientific requirements whilst taking into account economic and recreational factors. However, the criteria for defining the boundaries of protection areas laid down in Art 4(1) were specifically ornithological considerations, unlike the general conservation measures in Art 3, so that the economic requirements specified in Art 2 did not apply.

More recently in R (on the application of Edwards) v Environment Agency [2010][97] the Supreme Court referred a question to the Court of Justice regarding the interpretation of the phrase 'prohibitively expensive' in Directive 85/337/EEC as amended. The Directive requires that judicial review proceedings that concern certain environmental matters shall not be prohibitively expensive. The Supreme Court considered that the test that a court had to apply to ensure that proceedings were not prohibitively expensive remained in a state of uncertainty. Although it had been suggested in earlier cases that the approach should be an objective one the Supreme Court considered that the question should be referred to the Court of Justice.[98] The preliminary ruling is still pending.

> See Chapter
> ◀ 12

3.8 The effect of EU law on the domestic legal system

The relationship between EU law and national law is one which has dominated many articles and textbooks and which is usually covered within the context of most EU, Constitutional or Public law courses. Therefore, it is not the intention of this text to cover this subject in great detail.[99] However, in view of the problems of transposition it is necessary to consider the situation where a Member State has failed to implement or not adequately implemented a directive into national law, particularly in circumstances where the directive confers rights on individuals.

3.8.1 The supremacy of EU law

The EC Treaty did not specifically make reference to the issue of supremacy or the relationship between EU law and national law. However, Declaration 17 of the Lisbon Treaty states that 'in accordance with the settled case law of the Court of Justice of the European Union, the Treaties and the law adopted by the Union on the basis of the Treaties have primacy over the law of the Member States'. The Declaration refers to the case law of the ECJ, and indeed it is the ECJ that has been instrumental in developing the supremacy of European Union law. In a number of landmark decisions the ECJ has held that priority is to be accorded to EU law and that it should prevail over conflicting national provisions. To allow otherwise would undermine the very rationale of the EU and its

---

97 R (on the application of Edwards) v Environment Agency [2010] [2010] UKSC 57; [2011] 1 WLR 79; [2011] 1 All ER 785; [2011] Env LR 13.

98 C-260/11: Reference for a preliminary ruling from Supreme Court of the United Kingdom (United Kingdom) made on 25 May 2011, R on the application of David Edwards, Lilian Pallikaropoulos v Environment Agency, First Secretary of State, Secretary of State for Environment, Food and Rural Affairs OJ 2011 C226/16.

99 Readers should consult an appropriate text on EU law.

fundamental objective of creating a single market. As early as 1962, in the case of *Van Gend en Loos* (1962),[100] it was established by the ECJ that the Member States had limited their sovereign rights and that the EC constituted a new legal order. The ECJ went further in Case 6/64, *Costa v ENEL* (1964)[101] when it stated that:

> the transfer by the States ... to the Community legal system of the rights and obligations arising under the Treaty carries with it a permanent limitation of their sovereign rights against which a subsequent unilateral act incompatible with the concept of the Community cannot prevail.

National courts are required to apply provisions of EU law and to give full effect to those provisions and, if necessary, to set aside any conflicting provisions of national legislation, even if adopted after the relevant Community law provision (Case 106/77, *Amministrazione delle Finanze dello Stato v Simmenthal* (1978)[102]).

3.8.2 Direct effect of EU law

European Union law is unique in international law terms, largely because of the extent to which it permeates the domestic legal systems of the Member States and confers enforceable legal rights upon individuals. The ECJ has itself stated that the EU:

> constitutes a new legal order of international law for the benefit of which the states have limited their sovereign rights, albeit within limited fields and the subjects of which comprise not only Member States but also their nationals.[103]

The case of *Van Gend en Loos* established, for the first time, that the law contained in the Treaties was capable of conferring, on individuals, legally enforceable rights that must be upheld by the national courts. This is known as the principle of direct effect. The ECJ laid down three conditions which must be satisfied in order for a provision to be directly effective:

(a)   the content of the relevant provision must be both clear and precise;
(b)   the relevant provision must be unconditional; and
(c)   the provision must leave no room for the exercise of discretion by the Member State.

Following the *Van Gend en Loos* case, the ECJ has held a large number of Treaty articles to be directly effective. The criteria laid down have been applied generously and, as a result, even measures which are not particularly clear or precise have been deemed to be capable of direct effect. In addition to Treaty articles, the ECJ has established that EU secondary legislation is also capable of direct effect. Regulations which are described in Art 288 TFEU as 'directly applicable' may also be directly effective if they can satisfy the test laid down by the Court. However, since most EU environmental legislation is enacted in the form of directives it becomes necessary to consider the extent to which directives are capable of direct effect. Or to put it another way, the extent to which directives are capable of conferring legal rights on individuals which must be enforced by the national courts.

---

100 Case 26/62 *Van Gend en Loos v Nederlandse Administratie der Belastingen* [1963] ECR 1.
101 Case 6/64, *Costa v ENEL* [1964] ECR 585.
102 Case 106/77, *Amministrazione delle Finanze dello Stato v Simmenthal* [1978] ECR 629.
103 Case 26/62 *Van Gend en Loos v Nederlandse Administratie der Belastingen* [1963] ECR 1.

3.8.3 Direct effect of directives

It was thought that directives, by their nature, could not be capable of direct effect because they could not satisfy the requirement that they leave no room for the exercise of discretion by the Member State. However, the existence of discretion concerning the means of implementation of directives has not prevented them from being directly effective. The ECJ in Case 41/74, *Van Duyn v Home Office* (1974)[104] established conclusively that directives were capable of direct effect and therefore could be enforceable at the suit of individuals in the national courts, providing the provisions of the directive could satisfy the requirements laid down in *Van Gend en Loos*.[105] It follows therefore that directives are only capable of direct effect after the period for implementation by the Member State has expired (Case 148/78, *Publico Ministero v Ratti* (1979)[106]). Until expiry of the implementation period, Member States are free to rely on existing national law, even if it conflicts with the requirements of a directive which is not yet due for implementation.

As far as directives are concerned, it is well established[107] that litigants in national proceedings can only rely on the provisions of a directive as against the state or an emanation of the state. The ECJ has consistently maintained that directives, because they are addressed to Member States, cannot be relied upon against individuals. To use the jargon that has been adopted, directives are only capable of vertical direct effect. Because of this limitation in relation to the direct effect of directives, it becomes necessary to define what is meant by the state or an emanation of the state. The ECJ has interpreted the phrase widely. In Case C-188/89, *Foster v British Gas* (1991),[108] it was held that bodies responsible for the provision of public services and which have greater powers than are normally accorded to individuals or corporations are to be construed as emanations of the state.

Law in Action

Griffin v South West Water Services Ltd (1995)[109]
This case is of particular importance in environmental law because it involved the question of whether South West Water, a privatised water company, could be construed as an emanation of the state. The action concerned a directive relating to employment issues but the decision of the court is of wider significance. Blackburn J held that South West Water was an emanation of the state. He asserted that the relevant question was not whether the body in question is under the control of the state, but rather whether the public service in question is under the control of the state. The fact that the overall control of water services is exercised by the state was the relevant factor, not the legal form of the body, nor the fact that the body was a commercial concern. Blackburn J went on to say:

> It is also irrelevant that the body does not carry out any of the traditional functions of the state. It is irrelevant too that the state does not possess day-to-day control over the activities of the body.

---

104 Case 41/74, *Van Duyn v Home Office* [1974] ECR 1337; [1975] 1 CMLR 1.
105 Case 26/62 *Van Gend en Loos v Nederlandse Administratie der Belastingen* [1963] ECR 1. It should be noted that these tests are applied not to a directive as a whole but to the relevant provision that is being considered, such as an article of a directive or a particular paragraph.
106 Case 148/78, *Publico Ministero v Ratti* [1979] ECR 1629.
107 Case 152/84 *Marshall v Southampton & South West Hampshire Area Health Authority (Teaching)* [1986] ECR 723.
108 Case C-188/89, *Foster v British Gas* [1990] ECR I-3313.
109 *Griffin v South West Water Services Ltd* [1995] IRLR 15.

The judgment is of particular significance since it potentially paves the way for other directives in the field of environmental law to be directly effective against the water companies, as emanations of the state. See also Cases C-243–58/96, *Kampelmann v Landschaftsverband Westfalen-Lippe* (1997)[110] in which Advocate General Tesauro pointed out that:

> the Court has substantially widened the scope of 'vertical' direct effect, extending the possibility of relying on a directive against decentralised authorities or against public authorities and, in general, against 'organisations or bodies . . . subject to the authority or control of the state or having special powers beyond those which result from the normal rules applicable to relations between individuals' whatever the legal form of the body in question.[111]

3.8.4 Direct effect of environmental directives?

Not all EU environmental measures are capable of direct effect and in fact there are some who have argued that 'pure' environmental protection measures do not confer rights on individuals and are not capable of direct effect.[112] Many are simply not concerned with the conferral of 'rights' for individuals; they do not necessarily all adopt such an anthropocentric approach. Furthermore many are couched in very vague and uncertain terms and others are dependent on certain criteria being satisfied and will not satisfy the requirement that the provisions are unconditional. For example, in Case C-236/92 *Comitato di Coordinamento per la Difesa della Cava v Regione Lombardio* (1984)[113] the Italian court asked the ECJ whether Art 4 of Council Directive 75/422/EEC[114] was capable of granting to individuals 'subjective rights' which the national court is required to protect. The ECJ, referring back to the criteria for direct effect, held that Art 4 of the Waste Framework Directive was neither unconditional nor sufficiently clear or precise to be capable of direct effect:

> The provision at issue must be regarded as defining the framework for the action to be taken by the Member States regarding the treatment of waste and not as requiring, in itself, the adoption of specific measures or a particular method of waste disposal. It is therefore neither unconditional nor sufficiently precise and thus is not capable of conferring rights on which individuals may rely as against the state.[115]

However, other EU environmental directives which lay down specific maximum values for permissible discharges,[116] or specify procedures to be followed,[117] are capable of direct effect. For example, in relation to the Environmental Impact Assessment Directive 85/337/EEC[118] the Court of Justice in Case C-72/95 *Kraaijevald*[119] held that:

---

110 Cases C-243–58/96, *Kampelmann v Landschaftsverband Westfalen-Lippe* [1997] ECR I-6907.
111 Ibid para 16.
112 See Hilson, C, 'Community Rights in Environmental Law: Rhetoric or Reality' in Holder J (ed) *The Impact of EC Environmental Law in the United Kingdom.*
113 Case C-236/92 *Comitato di Coordinamento per la Difesa della Cava v Regione Lombardio* [1984] ECR I 483.
114 Council Directive 75/442/EEC of 15 July 1975 on waste OJ L 194, 25/7/1975, pp 39–41.
115 Case C-236/92 *Comitato di Coordinamento per la Difesa della Cava v Regione Lombardio* [1984] ECR I 483, para 14.
116 Such as Council Directive 80/778/EEC of 15 July 1980 relating to the quality of water intended for human consumption OJ L 229, 30/8/1980, pp 11–29.
117 Such as Council Directive 85/337/EEC of 27 June 1985 on the assessment of the effects of certain public and private projects on the environment OJ L 175, 5/7/1985, pp 40–48.
118 Ibid.
119 Case C-72/95 *Kraaijevald* [1996] ECR I-5403.

As regards the right of an individual to invoke a directive . . . it would be incompatible with the binding effect attributed to a directive by Article [288 TFEU] to exclude, in principle, the possibility that the obligation which it imposes may be invoked by those concerned. In particular, where the [Union] authorities have, by directive, imposed on Member States the obligation to pursue a particular course of conduct, the useful effect of such an act would be weakened if individuals were prevented from relying on it before their national courts.[120]

Law in Action

In Case C-337/89, *Commission v UK* (1993)[121] the Commission brought an action against the UK in respect of the Drinking Water Directive 80/778/EEC. The Directive required Member States to set drinking water quality standards not exceeding 'maximum admissible concentrations' (MACs). Member states had to implement the directive by 18 July 1982 and had to meet the water standards by 18 July 1985. The UK had taken no steps to implement the Directive by 1987 and so the Commission commenced infringement proceedings under Art 258 TFEU.[122] In 1989, the UK implemented the Water Supply (Water Quality) Regulations 1989,[123] but the Commission continued with the proceedings, arguing that the UK had not fully met the standards set in the directive in all parts of the UK.[124] The ECJ found that the UK was in breach of its obligations under the directive. By way of defence, the UK argued that it had taken all practical steps to secure compliance with the directive but the ECJ held that this argument could not justify the UK's failure to implement it. The ECJ held that the UK had formally breached the directive by failing to pass domestic legislation to implement it and that the UK had also substantively breached the directive by failing to achieve the MACs specified with regard to nitrates. The ECJ held that the MACs were enforceable obligations and implied as such that they were capable of direct effect, the consequence of direct effect being that the provisions may create legally enforceable rights in the national courts.[125]

The decision in the above case gave rise to further litigation in R v *Secretary of State for the Environment ex p Friends of the Earth and Another* (1995),[126] in which Roch LJ in the Court of Appeal was:

prepared to assume for the purposes of this appeal that the assertion of the appellants that this Directive created rights for the benefit of individuals and that includes the appellants. However, I would observe that these points are not free from difficulty. They beg the question of the precise rights and duties the Directive creates, and which individuals are to have the benefit and the burden of those rights and duties.[127]

---

120 Ibid para 56.
121 Case C-337/89 Commission v UK (Drinking Water Directive) [1992] ECR I-6103.
122 At the time Art 226 EC Treaty.
123 Water Supply (Water Quality) Regulations 1989 (SI 1989/1147).
124 Specifically that 28 supply zones in England and 17 supply zones in Scotland did not comply with MACs relating to nitrates and lead, and that there had been no formal implementation of the Directive in Northern Ireland.
125 Case 41/74, Van Duyn v Home Office [1974] ECR 1337; [1975] 1 CMLR 1.
126 R v Secretary of State for the Environment ex p Friends of the Earth and Another [1996] 1 CMLR 117; [1996] Env LR 198.
127 Ibid at 224.

3.8.5 The duty of sympathetic interpretation approach

Whilst the direct effect doctrine may assist individuals to enforce their rights in actions against the state or emanations of the state, it will not assist individuals bringing actions against other individuals. This creates a clear anomaly, but the lack of horizontal direct effect of directives has been justified by the ECJ on the grounds that, because directives are addressed to Member States, they may not of themselves impose obligations on individuals. However, the ECJ has sought to mitigate against this anomaly by developing principles which further enhance the enforceability of directives. The first of these principles/approaches is sometimes called 'indirect effect', but a more appropriate way of describing it is the 'duty of sympathetic interpretation'. The approach was first put forward in Case 14/83, *Von Colson v Land Nordrhein-Westfalen* (1983)[128] and later extended in Case C106/89, *Marleasing SA v La Commercial Internacional de Alimentación SA* (1989).[129] In *Von Colson*, the ECJ held that national courts (as emanations of the state) are under a duty to interpret national law, as far as possible, in the light of the purpose and the wording of the directive which generated the national legislation. In other words, the national legislation should be construed to give effect to the purpose of the directive. The judgment in *Marleasing*, which affirmed the position in *Von Colson*, was really quite remarkable in that the ECJ came to the view that the duty of interpretation also extended to national provisions whether they were introduced before or after a directive. The ECJ stated that in applying national law:

> whether the provisions in question [that is, the national provisions] were adopted before or after the Directive, the national court called upon to interpret it is required to do so, as far as possible, in the light of the wording and the purpose of the Directive in order to achieve the result pursued by the latter.

The response of the English courts has been mixed. In *Webb v EMO Air Cargo (UK) Ltd* (1993),[130] Lord Keith stated that the ECJ had, in the *Marleasing* decision, required national courts to construe national legislation to give effect to a directive only if it was possible to do so. He went on to say that it would only be possible to do so where a domestic law was 'open to an interpretation consistent with the directive whether or not it is also open to an interpretation inconsistent with it'. However, in the case of *Wychavon DC v Secretary of State and Others* (1994),[131] the High Court showed itself to be very unwilling to apply this principle.[132]

Law in Action

The Environmental Information Regulations (EIR) 2004[133] transpose the provisions of the Environmental Information Directive 2003/4/EC into domestic law.[134] The EIR came into force on the same day as the Freedom of Information Act (FOIA) 2000 and since both regimes are concerned with access to information there has been a tendency for public authorities to use the FOIA as a benchmark for the interpretation of the EIR. However in *R (on the application of*

---

128 Case 14/83, *Von Colson v Land Nordrhein-Westfalen* [1984] ECR 1891.

129 Case C-106/89, *Marleasing SA v La Commercial Internacional de Alimentación SA* [1990] ECR I-4135.

130 *Webb v EMO Air Cargo (UK) Ltd* [1995] 1 WLR 1454; [1995] 4 All ER 577; [1996] 2 CMLR 990.

131 *Wychavon DC v Secretary of State and Others* [1994] Env LR 239.

132 See also *R v Secretary of State for the Environment ex p Greenpeace* [1994] 4 All ER 352; [1994] 3 CMLR 737; [1994] Env LR 401.

133 Environmental Information Regulations 2004 SO 2004/3391.

134 Directive 2003/4/EC of the European Parliament and of the Council of 28 January 2003 on public access to environmental information and repealing Council Directive 90/313/EEC OJ L 41, 14/2/2003, pp 26–32.

Office of Communications) v Information Commissioner [2008],[135] Law LJ cautioned against such an approach:

> The EIR, giving effect to the Directive, provides for a right of access to environmental information held by public authorities. They came into force at the same time as the 2000 Act. Both measures promote increased openness in the public sector; but as seems to me one would have to be very cautious in using either as a guide to the interpretation of the other since the EIR are, and are only, a measure to implement European legislation. If their interpretation is to be coloured by anything it must be by the Directive.

On appeal the Supreme Court decided that the interpretation of the provisions of the directive were uncertain and therefore sought a preliminary ruling from the Court of Justice.[136]

See Chapter ◄ 12

3.8.6 The principle of state liability

In Cases C-6 and 9/90, *Francovich and Bonifaci v Italian State* (1991),[137] the ECJ extended yet further the impact of directives. The case is important in that it lays down the principle that Member States may be sued for damages as a result of their failure to implement a directive. The ECJ, in its previous judgments, had been clear that Member States should not be able to benefit from their failure to implement directives. Francovich was owed 6 million lire by his insolvent employers; however, because he was unable to enforce a judgment against them, he brought an action against the Italian government for compensation. Italy had failed to implement the provisions of a directive which required Member States to establish a wage guarantee scheme for employees in the event of their employers' insolvency. Francovich, however, could not rely on the direct effect of the directive since it was not sufficiently clear and precise. However, the ECJ held that, subject to three conditions, damages are available against the state for failure to implement directives.

The conditions for state liability laid down in *Francovich* were:

(a) the result prescribed by the directive should be the grant of rights to individuals;
(b) it must be possible to identify those rights on the basis of the provisions of the directive; and
(c) there must be a causal link between the breach of the state's obligation and the loss and damage suffered by the injured parties.

Despite previous assertions in the past that EU law did not require the introduction of specific legal remedies, this new principle was seen by many as the creation of a new 'EU law' remedy. However, the decision in *Francovich* left a number of questions unanswered. First, the judgment related specifically to the failure to implement directives; it remained unclear whether the principle would apply to a wider range of breaches. Secondly, the ECJ simply required that there be a 'breach' of EU law (in this case, the failure to implement the directive), but the ECJ did not provide particular guidance on the nature of this breach: whether it should be strict or fault-based. However, it was not long before the ECJ was given the opportunity to examine this principle further in the joined Cases C-46

---

135 *R (on the application of Office of Communications) v Information Commissioner* [2008] EWHC 1445 (Admin); [2009] Env LR 1.
136 *Office of Communications v the Information Commissioner* [2010] [2010] UKSC 3; [2010] Env LR 20.
137 Cases C-6 and 9/90, *Francovich and Bonifaci v Italian State* [1991] ECR I 5357(1991).

and C-48/93, *Brasserie du Pêcheur SA v Germany and R v Secretary of State for Transport ex p Factortame Ltd and Others* (1996).[138] These cases concerned the application of the *Francovich* decision to breaches of Treaty provisions rather than directives. The ECJ held that EU law confers a right to reparation where three conditions are met: the rule of law infringed must be intended to confer rights on individuals; the breach must be *sufficiently serious*; and there must be a direct causal link between the breach of the obligation by the state and the damage sustained by the injured parties. The decisive test for finding that a breach of EU law is sufficiently serious is whether the Member State 'manifestly and gravely disregarded the limits of its discretion'. In terms of division of responsibilities, the ECJ laid down the test for state liability but the decision in each case will rest with the national courts. However, the ECJ laid down a number of factors that the national court should take into account in reaching a decision on liability, including the clarity and precision of the rule breached, the degree of discretion imparted by that rule, whether the infringement and the damage caused were intentional or voluntary, and whether the error of law was excusable or not.

The *Brasserie du Pêcheur/Factortame* case thus established that, as a matter of principle, a State may be liable in damages for a wider range of breaches than was previously thought under *Francovich*. The judgment also clarified that only sufficiently serious breaches would give rise to such liability. In relation to the non-implementation of directives, the ECJ subsequently held that the failure to implement a directive within the prescribed period would always constitute a sufficiently serious breach because of the mandatory nature of Art 288 TFEU.[139] However, in circumstances where the implementation is flawed the national court will need to consider whether this improper implementation constitutes a sufficiently serious breach, having regard to the factors laid down by the ECJ.

The principle of state liability is not restricted to the acts or omissions of the state; the Court of Justice has held that a state may be liable in respect of breaches of EU law by all state authorities such as local government or the police.[140] This broad approach was further extended by the ECJ in 2003 in the case of *Kobler v Austria* (2003)[141] in what is now often referred to as 'Kobler liability'. The Court of Justice held that a Member State could be liable for damages for a breach of EU law on the part of a national court of final appeal. In order for such liability to arise the three conditions laid down in *Brasserie du Pêcheur/Factortame* must be satisfied. However, in order to determine whether the infringement is sufficiently serious when the infringement at issue stems from a national court of final appeal, the national court hearing the case must determine whether the infringement is 'manifest'.

In the context of environmental law a claimant would need to establish that an environmental law directive confers individual rights. This is likely to be the most significant obstacle to overcome because most environmental protection directives are concerned with measures which are in the public interest and for the collective good of society or are specifically aimed at protecting some aspect of the environment, for example the Habitats Directive 92/43/EC. In these circumstances it is very difficult to see how an individual could make a claim under the principle of state liability. On the other hand some directives, most notably the Environmental Impact Assessment Directive 85/337/EEC and the Environmental Information Directive 2003/4/EC, confer certain 'procedural rights' on individuals. In 2010 the Court of Appeal was faced with an action for damages under the Kobler liability principle in *Cooper v Attorney General* (2010).[142] The claims were based on two decisions of the Court of Appeal in 2000 and 2001 which concerned judicial review claims against the

138 Cases C-46 and C-48/93, *Brasserie du Pêcheur SA v Germany and R v Secretary of State for Transport ex p Factortame Ltd and Others* [1996] ECR I-1029.
139 Cases C-178 et al 94 *Dillenkofer and Others v Germany* [1996] ECR I-4845.
140 See e.g. Case C-424/97 *Haim* [2000] ECR I-512.
141 Case C-224/01 *Kobler v Austria* [2003] ECR I-10239.
142 *Cooper v Attorney General* [2010] EWCA Civ 464; [2011] QB 976 (CA (Civ Div)).

London Borough of Hammersmith and Fulham for granting planning permission for the White City Development in London. The judicial review claims concerned the Environmental Impact Assessment Directive but both claims were rejected by the Court of Appeal, which was the national court of final appeal in respect of those decisions. Consequently Cooper commenced the state liability claim before the High Court where he argued the Court of Appeal had erred in EU law and the conditions for liability laid down in *Kobler* were satisfied. The High Court held that the Court of Appeal had been wrong in the first case by confining the term 'development consent' in the Directive to outline planning permission and it had erred on the meaning of development consent, but the errors were not sufficiently serious to give rise to liability. The decision of the High Court was upheld on appeal by the Court of Appeal.

3.9 The development of EU environmental law and policy

3.9.1 Introduction

When the EEC was created in 1957 by the Treaty of Rome the principal objective of the founding members was the creation of a common market throughout the six Member States. The EC Treaty concentrated primarily on economic issues and there was no specific reference to the environment. It was not until the Single European Act (SEA) 1986 that Title VII 'Environment' was incorporated into the Treaty, giving the then EEC a legal competence in the field of environmental protection for the first time. However, despite the lack of an explicit legal basis, the EEC had in the intervening years taken numerous measures to protect the environment. It had also managed to develop its own interventionist environmental policy using other powers under the Treaty, namely Arts 94 and 308 EC Treaty.[143]

3.9.2 Environmental policy and law before the SEA 1986 (1957–86)

Article 2 of the original 1957 Treaty stated the aims of the Community as:

> establishing a common market and progressively approximating the economic policies of Member States, to promote throughout the Community a harmonious development of economic activities, a continuous and balanced expansion, an increase in stability, an accelerated raising of the standard of living and closer relations between the States belonging to it.

Given that the institutions of the EU can only legally act within the limits of the powers conferred upon them by the Treaties, legislation in the early days was largely concerned with market regulation. Nevertheless, despite the absence of any specific powers, the EU did in fact introduce a large number of directives which impacted either directly or indirectly upon the environment. As early as 1967, there was a directive on the classification, packaging and labelling of dangerous substances.[144] This directive was not specifically aimed at protecting the environment; its principal aim was to secure harmonised standards in relation to the packaging and labelling of dangerous substances. However the directive arguably had indirect implications for the environment.

The 'early' (pre-SEA 1986) environmental legislation was introduced under Arts 94 and 308 EC Treaty. (Following the Treaty of Lisbon, Art 94 was renumbered Art 114 TFEU and Art 308 was renumbered Art 352 TFEU; however, since the discussion relates to these pre-Treaty of Lisbon

---

143 Now Arts 114 and 352 TFEU.
144 Council Directive 67/548/EEC on the classification, packaging and labelling of dangerous substances [1967] OJ Spec Ed 234.

articles, the discussion will use the 'old' EC Treaty article numbers for ease of reference.) Article 94 EC provided for legislative measures to be introduced in order to secure the approximation of laws affecting the functioning of the internal market. Environmental measures enacted on the basis of Art 94 EC were justified on the basis that different levels and standards of environmental protection in the different Member States would interfere with the creation of an internal market by distorting competition. In other words, if the standards of environmental protection are low in one Member State compared to another with more rigorous standards, then industrialists in the former state spend less on meeting environmental protection standards than industrialists in the latter Member State. This disparity may give the industrialist in the Member State with the lower standards a competitive edge, in that they will be benefiting from a form of hidden subsidy and this could distort the patterns of trade. An example of a directive enacted under Art 94 is Directive 78/659/ EEC[145] on the quality of fresh waters needing protection or improvement in order to support fish life. Although it is clear that this directive serves environmental protection goals, the preamble to the directive states that:

> differences between the provisions . . . in the various Member States as regards the quality of waters capable of supporting the life of freshwater fish may create unequal conditions of competition and thus directly affect the functioning of the common market.

Article 308 EC Treaty[146] on the other hand provided a residual power which enabled action to be taken by the institutions even where the Treaty had not provided the necessary powers, but where it is 'necessary to attain, in the course of the operation of the common market, one of the objectives of the Community'. For example, Council Directive 79/409/EEC on the Conservation of Wild Birds[147] was adopted under Art 308. The justification for the Wild Birds Directive in particular was that the conservation of wild birds was necessary to attain the Union's objective of improving living conditions throughout the Common Market. The measure was justified rather tentatively by reference to Art 2 EC Treaty.

3.9.3 The Stockholm Conference and the emergence of EU Environmental Action Programmes

These early 'environmental' measures were not introduced as part of a coherent strategy on the environment which, at this stage, the Union did not have. However, the early 1970s saw a groundswell in public opinion about the environment and also marked the beginning of the Union's environmental policy. In 1972, a United Nations Conference was held in Stockholm[148] to consider the human environment. The Conference was significant because it marked the beginnings of international co-operation in the field of the environment, and it is from this date that environmental law has become a legitimate and important area of international law. It is also important because it was followed by the Paris Summit in October 1972,[149] when the Heads of State and governments of the Member States of the Union declared:

---

145 Council Directive 78/659/EEC of 18 July 1978 on the quality of fresh waters needing protection or improvement in order to support fish life OJ L 222, 14/8/1978, pp 1–10.
146 Now Art 352 TFEU.
147 Council Directive 79/409/EEC of 2 April 1979 on the conservation of wild birds OJ L 103, 25/4/1979, pp 1–18.
148 United Nations Conference on the Human Environment 1972 Stockholm.
149 The Heads of State of the nine Member States of the European Community met at the Paris Summit 19–21 October 1972.

Economic expansion is not an end in itself. Its firm aim should be to enable disparities in living conditions to be reduced. It must take place with the participation of all the social partners. It should result in an improvement in the quality of life as well as in standards of living. As befits the genius of Europe, particular attention will be given to intangible values and to protecting the environment, so that progress may really be put at the service of mankind.

Following this recognition of the importance of protecting the environment, the Commission was requested to draw up an Action Programme on the environment. This first Action Programme for the period 1973–76 was adopted in 1973. Since that time, the EU has produced six Action Programmes:

Action Programmes	Period	Official Journal Citation
First	1973–76	C112, 20.12.73
Second	1977–81	C139, 13.5.77
Third	1982–86	C46, 17.2.83
Fourth	1987–92	C328, 7.12.87
Fifth	1993–2000	C138, 17.5.93
Sixth	2001–10	L242, 10.9.2002

The Action Programmes are essentially political statements, which outline the Union's policy and legislative aspirations in the years ahead. The First Action Programme started with a general statement of the objectives and principles of an EU environmental policy and then went on to list the actions that the Commission would bring forward. This action was largely reactive, focussing on the urgent pollution problems which the EU considered had to be addressed. However, the first action programme listed 11 principles which are still largely applicable today; in particular, the polluter pays principle. The Sixth Environmental Action Programme will be discussed more fully at 3.12 below.

Although the EU had begun to develop an environmental policy as early as 1973, it still faced the problem that there was no real constitutional basis for that policy or for that matter 'pure' environmental law. Legislation was still largely enacted on the basis that different standards of environmental protection throughout the EU would distort competition, would hamper the establishment of a common market and had to be justified accordingly. However, the SEA 1986 provided for the first time a specific legal basis upon which the EU could legislate in the field of environmental protection. Nevertheless it is important to note that even before the SEA 1986 was amended to incorporate legal competence in the field of the environment, the ECJ had recognised that the environmental protection was an 'essential' component of EU policy, even to the extent that protection of the environment could hinder the free movement of goods, one of the fundamental principles of EU law. In Case 240/83, *Procureur de la République v ADBHU* (1983),[150] the ECJ stated that the protection of the environment constituted one of the Union's essential objectives. The case involved an action in the French courts to dissolve the *Association de défense de brûleurs d'huiles usagées*, an association established in 1980 to defend the interests of manufacturers, dealers and users of heating appliances designed to burn fuel oil and waste oils. In their defence, the Association contested the validity of Directive 75/439/EEC,[151] which aims to protect the environment against the risks from waste oils.

---

150 Case 240/83, *Procureur de la République v ADBHU* [1985] ECR 531.
151 Council Directive 75/439/EEC of 16 June 1975 on the disposal of waste oils OJ L 194, 25/7/1975, pp 23–25.

The Association contested that the directive was contrary to the principles of freedom of trade, free movement of goods and freedom of competition. The French court sought a preliminary ruling from the ECJ on the interpretation and validity of the directive. The ECJ held that: 'The Directive must be seen in the perspective of environmental protection, which is one of the Community's essential objectives.' One of the significant features of the ECJ's judgment in this case is that it came to this conclusion at a time when the Treaty did not provide any specific explicit legal basis for environmental action. The case predated the introduction of Arts 174–176. The view that environmental protection could constitute one of the Union's essential objectives was reinforced and developed in Case 302/86, *Commission v Denmark* (1988)[152] (usually referred to as the *Danish Bottles* case). For a further discussion of this case see below at 3.11.

3.9.4 The Environment Title and subsequent Treaty amendments

The SEA 1986 marked a key stage in the development of the Union's environmental protection policy. It resulted in the incorporation of a new 'Environment' Title into the EC Treaty, specifically Arts 174–176 EC.[153] In addition, Art 94 EC Treaty was also amended by the SEA 1986 and a new Art 95 was introduced, which provided that qualified majority voting in the Council of Ministers would be the normal voting procedure in relation to the harmonising measures pursued under this article. This change was introduced essentially to speed up the decision-making process in relation to harmonising measures needed to complete the internal market by the self-imposed deadline of 1992. Art 95 provided that the Commission would, when making proposals which concerned environmental protection, take as a base a high level of protection. This was significant because it was recognition in the Treaty itself that approximation measures enacted under this article could legitimately be concerned with environmental protection.

In 1992 the TEU resulted in a number of significant amendments relating to environmental law. These can be briefly stated as follows:

(a)   the EEC became the EC, in recognition that it was more than just an economic community;
(b)   Art 2 EC Treaty was amended to include reference to sustainable and non-inflationary growth regarding the environment;
(c)   Art 3 EC Treaty established that there should be a policy in the sphere of the environment;
(d)   Art 95 EC Treaty was amended so that the procedure used for harmonising legislation is the co-decision procedure, thus allowing the Parliament the right of veto in relation to such legislation;
(e)   Art 174 EC was amended and, in particular, changed the legislative procedure so that, with certain exceptions, environmental legislation could now be enacted using the co-operation procedure, thus giving the European Parliament a greater degree of control than it had previously. The amended Article also built in the requirement that Union environmental policy should aim at a high level of protection.

The significant change brought about by the ToA was the insertion of the 'integration principle' into the more prominent position of Art 6 EC instead of being included in the Environment Title. The integration principle requires that environmental protection requirements must be integrated into the definition and implementation of the Union policies and activities, in particular with a view to promoting sustainable development. This more prominent positioning of the requirement reflected

---

152   Case 302/86, *Commission v Denmark* [1988] ECR 4607.
153   The reader should however note that pre-Amsterdam Treaty Arts 174–176 were numbered as Arts 130r-t EC Treaty. Post-Lisbon Treaty the articles are now to be found at Arts 191–193 TFEU.

the importance which the Union placed on environmental protection as an all-pervading issue. In addition, the ToA further amended Art 2 EC to provide a new goal of 'promoting a harmonious and balanced and sustainable development of economic activities' as well as 'a high level of protection and improvement of the quality of the environment'. Amendments made by the ToN were more limited, in that they refined those areas of law making which would be subject to the consultation procedures under Art 175(2) EC.

Year	Development/Treaty amendment
1957	Treaty of Rome (EC Treaty). This concentrated on the creation of a common market and made no reference to the environment or environmental protection.
1972	United Nations Stockholm Conference.
October 1972, Paris Summit	Heads of State declare: 'Economic expansion is not an end in itself. Its firm aim should be to enable disparities in living conditions to be reduced. It must take place with the participation of all the social partners. It should result in an improvement in the quality of life as well as in standards of living. As befits the genius of Europe, particular attention will be given to intangible values and to protecting the environment, so that progress may really be put at the service of mankind.'
1973	UK joins the EEC.
1973–1976	First Environmental Action Programme.
1977–1981	Second Environmental Action Programme.
1982–1986	Third Environmental Action Programme.
1983	ECJ states that protection of the environment constitutes one of the Union's essential objectives (Case 240/83).
1986	Single European Act: incorporation of Environment Title (then Arts 130r–t EC Treaty). Environment Title defines objectives and principles of environmental policy.
1987–1992	Fourth Environmental Action Programme.
1992	Treaty on the European Union (Maastricht Treaty): Establish dual Treaty system, the EC Treaty and the Treaty on European Union. The EEC became the EC. Article 3 EC Treaty established that the EC should have a policy on the environment.
1993–2000	Fifth Environmental Action Programme.
1993	European Environment Agency established.
1997	Treaty of Amsterdam: Art 6 EC Treaty requires environmental protection to be integrated into the definition and implementation of all Community policies with a view to promoting sustainable development (the integration principle). Article 2 amended to include the goal of promoting a harmonious, balanced and sustainable development of economic activities. The Treaty articles are renumbered and Arts 130r-t become Arts 174–176 EC.
2000	The Treaty of Nice: no significant changes, largely concerned with preparing for enlargement.
2001–2010	Sixth Environmental Action Programme.
2009	Treaty of Lisbon: retains dual treaty structure (Treaty on the Functioning of the European Union and the Treaty on European Union). Articles 174–176 renumbered Arts 191–193 TFEU.

3.10 The environmental provisions of the TEU and TFEU

Before examining the specific provisions of the Treaties relating to environmental protection it is important to understand the relationship between the EU and the Member States in the formulation of environmental law.

3.10.1 Shared competence in the field of environmental protection

The TEU limits the competence of the Union on the basis of the principle of conferral. Under this principle the Union can only act within the limits of the competences *conferred* upon it by the Member States in the Treaties to attain the objectives set out in the Treaties.[154] In turn the TFEU seeks to address the issue of Union competence by defining which areas fall within the Union's exclusive competence and those which are shared with the Member States. When the Treaties confer on the Union exclusive competence in a specific area, only the Union may legislate and adopt legally binding acts, the Member States being able to do so themselves only if empowered by the Union or for the implementation of Union acts.[155] The EU has exclusive competence in respect of the conservation of marine biological resources under the common fisheries policy.[156] On the other hand when the Treaties confer on the Union a competence shared with the Member States in a specific area, the Union and the Member States may legislate and adopt legally binding acts in that area. Environmental protection and energy are both areas of shared competence. The capacity of the Union to act in areas of shared competence are subject to the principle of subsidiarity. This means that the Union 'shall act only if and in so far as the objectives of the proposed action cannot be sufficiently achieved by the Member States, either at central and local level, but can rather, by reason of the scale or effects of the proposed action, be better achieved at Union level'.[157] However, the flip side of this shared competence is that Member States can only exercise their competence to the extent that the Union has not exercised its competence or to the extent that the Union has decided to cease exercising its competence.

3.10.2 The Environment Title (Arts 191–193 TFEU)

Article 191 TFEU identifies the aims of EU environmental policy and the fundamental principles upon which EU legislative action should be taken:

(1) Union policy on the environment shall contribute to pursuit of the following objectives:

— preserving, protecting and improving the quality of the environment,
— protecting human health,
— prudent and rational utilisation of natural resources,
— promoting measures at international level to deal with regional or worldwide environmental problems, and in particular combating climate change.

(2) Union policy on the environment shall aim at a high level of protection taking into account the diversity of situations in the various regions of the Union. It shall be based on the precautionary principle and on the principles that preventive action should be taken, that environmental damage should as a priority be rectified at source and that the polluter should pay.

---

154 See Art 5 TEU.
155 Art 2 (1) TFEU.
156 Art 3 (d) TFEU.
157 Art 5 TEU.

These provisions pose several interpretative difficulties. For example, it is not clear what is exactly meant by a 'high' level of protection. According to Kramer,[158] the benchmark for determining 'high' would be the environmental standard of those Member States which seek a high level of environmental protection, such as Denmark or Germany. Clearly, the attempt here is to ensure that Union policy does not aim for the 'lowest common denominator'. However, environmental policy must take into account the diversity of situations in the regions—an implicit recognition that the Member States have different problems and will in fact go at different speeds in pursuance of environmental goals. This recognition has even more resonance given the expansion of the Union to include 28 very diverse states. Similarly the principles listed in Art 191(2) are not defined. However, careful attention to the wording of Art 191 TFEU shows that Union policy shall be based on these principles. It does not say that EU legislation has to be so based. Nevertheless, one would expect that any environmental legislation developed in pursuance of this policy should also be based upon these principles, and may be subject to challenge if these principles are thwarted in some way. Therefore it is important to understand what each principle means. Some guidance as to the nature of these principles can be ascertained from Commission communications. For example, in 2000, the Commission issued a communication on the precautionary principle.[159] This outlines the Commission's approach to using the precautionary principle and suggests that the precautionary principle may inform certain Union actions, but there is nothing in this to suggest that action must be based on the principle. Similarly in R v Secretary of State for Trade and Industry, ex p Duddridge and Others[160] it was held that at the national level, the Secretary of State was not required to apply the precautionary principle when enacting domestic legislation.

See Chapter
◄ 1

In preparing its policy on the environment the Union must take into account:

- available scientific and technical data;
- environmental conditions in the various regions of the Union;
- the potential benefits and costs of action or lack of action;
- the economic and social development of the Union as a whole and the balanced development of its regions.[161]

3.10.3 The Integration principle

One of unique features about the EU's environmental policy is its status in relation to other policy areas. By virtue of Art 11 TFEU[162] environmental protection requirements must be integrated into the definition and implementation of the Union's policies and activities, in particular with a view to promoting sustainable development. In 1998, the European Council met in Cardiff, launching the Cardiff Integration Process. By this, the various Council formations responsible for developing Union policy across the span of Union competences were required to integrate environmental considerations into their respective activities. Each Council formation[163] was required to produce its own strategies for integrating the environment into its work. The importance of the integration principle was further substantiated in the Sixth Environmental Action Programme, which stipulates that 'integration of environmental concerns into other policies must be deepened' in order to move towards sustainable development.

---

158 Kramer, L EC Treaty and Environmental Law (Sweet & Maxwell, London 1995, 2nd edn).
159 Communication from the Commission on the precautionary principle (COM(00)1).
160 R v Secretary of state for Trade and Industry, ex p Duddridge and Others [1996] Env LR 325.
161 Art 19 (3) TFEU.
162 Formerly Art 6 EC Treaty.
163 E.g., in relation to agriculture, transport, the internal market.

3.10.4 International relations

Article 2 TEU states that the Union shall define and pursue common policies and actions, and shall work for a high degree of cooperation in all fields of international relations, in order to, inter alia:

● foster the sustainable economic, social and environmental development of developing countries;
● help develop international measures to preserve and improve the quality of the environment and the sustainable management of global natural resources, in order to ensure sustainable development.

In addition to which Art 191(4) TFEU provides that, within their respective spheres of competence, the Union and the Member States must cooperate with third countries and the competent international organisations such as the United Nations.

3.10.5 Environmental legislation under the TEU and TFEU

The Union can enact environmental protection measures under Title 20 (Arts 191–193 TFEU) or under Art 114.

Arts 191–193 TFEU allow the EU to adopt legislation specifically to achieve the specific environmental protection objectives defined in Art 191 TFEU (see above). These articles specify, inter alia, the objectives of EU environmental policy, the principles upon which such policy should be based, the factors to be taken into account by the Union and the manner in which such legislation should be adopted. Article 192 requires the use of the ordinary legislative procedure. However, Art 192(2) TFEU requires the use of the special legislative procedure when the Union is adopting legislation primarily of a fiscal nature; measures affecting town and country planning, quantitative management of water resources or the availability of those resources, and also legislation concerned with land use, with the exception of waste management. Article 114 allows the Union to adopt measures designed to secure the harmonisation of national laws in order to secure the proper functioning of the internal market. Article 114 requires the use of the ordinary legislative procedure.

3.11 Stricter environmental rules in Member States

The most significant difference between the two Treaty articles discussed above is the extent to which Member States can introduce stricter environmental protection rules than the EU-wide rules or standards. This is an issue of twofold importance. On the one hand, it is a matter of concern to those Member States that place a particularly strong emphasis upon environmental protection and wish to secure the highest levels of protection. For some Member States, harmonisation suggests harmonising down rather than up, and this may be wholly unsatisfactory to them. On the other hand, the second and inextricably related issue is the extent to which stricter environmental protection rules can be permitted where they hamper or restrict the free movement of goods required by Art 34 TFEU.[164] The trade versus environment debate has generated considerable academic debate

---

164 Formerly Art 28 EC Treaty.

because it takes place against the backdrop of the shared responsibility for environmental protection between the Member States and the EU.

3.11.1 The relationship between environmental protection and the free movement of goods

The free movement of goods throughout the EU is regarded as one of the fundamental cornerstones of EU law. Article 34 TFEU prohibits Member States from introducing quantitative restrictions and measures having equivalent effect to quantitative restrictions (MEQRs). Measures which are introduced by Member States which have the effect of hindering the free circulation of goods across borders are therefore prohibited. Even where a measure applies equally to domestic and imported goods,[165] the measure may still breach Art 34 TFEU where it affects inter-state trade. The types of measures which have been held to breach Art 34 TFEU range from more obvious measures such as import bans and import quotas to 'buy national' campaigns which have the effect of discriminating against imports. Article 34 TFEU has been used widely in litigation and its scope has been widely defined by the ECJ. In environmental terms, it is easy to see how measures taken at the national level to preserve and protect the environment or to encourage recycling might fall within the wide scope of Art 34 TFEU. For example, in Case C-389/96, *Aher-Waggon GmbH v Germany* (1998),[166] German legislation designed to limit noise from aircraft was held to amount to a measure having equivalent effect to a quantitative restriction, contrary to Art 234 TFEU.

There are of course circumstances in which national rules which prima facie breach Art 34 TFEU may be justified in the wider public interest. These 'justifications' take the form of specific derogations in Art 36 TFEU[167] and also under the growing number of so-called mandatory requirements laid down by the ECJ in the famous *Cassis* case.[168] Each of these is considered below.

Article 36 TFEU provides a list of six derogations from Art 34 TFEU; the list is exhaustive. Breaches of Art 34 TFEU may be justified on the grounds of public morality; public policy or public security; the protection of health and life of humans, animals or plants; the protection of national treasures possessing artistic, historic or archaeological value; or the protection of industrial or commercial property. However, Art 36 TFEU stipulates that measures cannot be justified if they constitute a means of arbitrary discrimination or a disguised restriction on trade between Member States. The ECJ has tended to treat the derogations under Art 36 TFEU with a great deal of circumspection by placing a very narrow construction on each derogation. The ECJ has consistently emphasised the need to preserve as far as possible the fundamental freedom conferred by Art 34 TFEU by narrowly interpreting the exceptions to it under Art 36 TFEU. This is particularly the case where the national measure in question is inherently discriminatory, for example, in relation to an import ban. The burden of proof falls squarely on the Member State pleading the justification to demonstrate the need to adopt such restrictive measures to achieve the stated objective. In relation to national measures of an environmental protection nature, the obvious justification is the 'protection of health and life of humans, animals or plants'.

---

165 Known as indistinctly applicable measures.
166 Case C-389/96, *Aher-Waggon GmbH v Germany* [1998] ECR I 44731998.
167 Formerly Art 36 EC Treaty.
168 Case 120/78, *Cassis de Dijon (Rewe-Zentral v Bundesmonopolver-wältung für Branntwein)* [1979] ECR 649.

Law in Action

Case C-67/97, *Criminal Proceedings against Bluhme* (1998)[169]
The case concerned Danish legislation which was enacted in order to secure the survival of the Læsø brown bee, a bee native to the island of Læsø. The legislation prohibited the keeping of any bees other than the Læsø brown bee. The case involved a criminal prosecution in respect of a breach of this prohibition by B, who argued in his defence that the Danish rule was contrary to Art 34 TFEU. The ECJ accepted that the rule did breach Art 34 TFEU but then went on to consider whether it could fall within the Art 36 TFEU derogation. Presented with various arguments about the importance of maintaining biodiversity, the ECJ accepted that 'measures to preserve an indigenous animal population with distinct characteristics contribute to the maintenance of biodiversity by ensuring the survival of the population concerned. By doing so they are aimed at protecting the life of those animals and are capable of being justified under Article [36] of the Treaty.'

Whether a measure may be justified under Art 36 TFEU also requires a consideration of the type of rule adopted and, in particular, whether it is proportionate to the aims. This was evidenced in Case C-131/93, *Commission v Germany*,[170] in which Germany introduced a total ban on the import of live freshwater crayfish, in order to protect native crayfish from disease. Although the ECJ did not challenge the purported aims of the measure, it did accept the Commission's argument that an outright ban was disproportionate and that Germany could have employed less restrictive measures, such as health checks on crayfish coming from other Member States, to achieve the same aim. Thus, this case fell at the proportionality hurdle. However, in practice, it is very difficult for Member States to pass the proportionality test in relation to import bans of this nature.

In addition to the specific heads of derogation under Art 36 TFEU, the ECJ has developed the so-called 'rule of reason' in Case 120/78, *Cassis de Dijon (Rewe-Zentral v Bundesmonopolver-wältung für Branntwein)* (1979).[171] Essentially, the rule of reason operates to 'save' certain national rules/measures which, whilst being capable of hindering trade, are to be 'accepted' in so far as they are necessary to satisfy some overriding wider public interest. These overriding public interests are referred to as 'mandatory requirements':

> Obstacles to movement in the Community resulting from disparities between the national laws relating to the marketing of the products in question must be accepted in so far as those provisions may be recognised as being necessary in order to satisfy mandatory requirements relating in particular to the effectiveness of fiscal supervision, the protection of public health, the fairness of commercial transaction and the defence of the consumer.

The effect of this is that national rules which are introduced to satisfy these mandatory requirements are 'acceptable' and do not breach Art 34 TFEU. In the *Cassis* case, the ECJ listed only four mandatory requirements, but this list is not exhaustive and has been expanded through further case law to include, inter alia, environmental protection in Case 302/86, *Commission v Denmark (Disposable Cans and Bottles)*,[172] in which the Court held that:

---

169 Case C-67/97, *Criminal Proceedings against Bluhme* [1998] ECR I-8033.
170 Case C-131/93, *Commission v Germany* [1994] ECR I 3303.
171 Case 120/78, *Cassis de Dijon (Rewe-Zentral v Bundesmonopolver-wältung für Branntwein)* [1979] ECR 649.
172 Case 302/86 *Commission v Denmark (Danish Bottles)* [1988] ECR 4607.

the protection of the environment is one of the Community's essential objectives, which may justify certain limitations of the principle of the free movement of goods . . . it must therefore be stated that the protection of the environment is a mandatory requirement which may limit the application of [Art 34] of the Treaty.

Law in Action

The Danish Bottles case
In 1981, the Danish government, concerned about the environmental consequences of litter and waste from discarded metal cans, instituted a system requiring beer and soft drinks to be marketed only in containers that could be reused. The use of metal cans was forbidden. Containers had to meet the requirements laid down and be approved by the Danish National Agency for the Protection of the Environment. In 1984, the legislation was amended so that non-approved containers were permitted subject to very strict limits and also to a deposit and return system. Although the object of the system was to reduce the numbers of discarded metal tins, it had as an effect a potential restriction on competition. Manufacturers of beers and soft drinks outside Denmark could sell their products throughout the EU but not in Denmark unless they could comply with the Danish deposit and return system. Therefore, the Danish manufacturers were in effect protected from external competition.

The European Commission commenced proceedings against the Danish government under Art 258 TFEU.[173] The Commission alleged that the introduction of a system, under which all containers for beers and soft drinks must be returnable, was contrary to Art 34 TFEU.

The Danish government argued that the compulsory deposit and return system was justified by a mandatory requirement, namely the protection of the environment. The ECJ accepted that the protection of the environment could constitute a mandatory requirement, given the ECJ's previous decision in *Procureur de la République*[174] that the protection of the environment is one of the Union's essential objectives. The question which remained for the ECJ to decide was whether the Danish rules were necessary in order to satisfy the mandatory requirement, or whether the environment could be protected in ways which were less restrictive to trade. In other words, the ECJ had to apply a test of proportionality. The ECJ accepted that the deposit and return system for empty containers was an 'indispensable element of a system intended to ensure the re-use of containers and therefore appears necessary to achieve the aims pursued by the contested rules'. Turning to the system for non-approved containers and the strict limit on the amount of containers that could be imported in non-approved containers,[175] the ECJ held that the Danish rules were disproportionate. The reasoning was that the system for non-approved containers was also capable of protecting the environment and, since the quantity of imports was limited, the limitation to 3,000 hecti-litres was excessive.

---

173 Formerly Art 226 EC Treaty.
174 Case 240/83, *Procureur de la République v ADBHU* [1985] ECR 531.
175 Non-approved containers could be used where the quantity of marketed drinks did not exceed 3,000 hecti-litres per year per producer.

The ECJ applied the same reasoning in Case C-2/90, *Commission v Belgium* (*Walloon Waste*) (1992)[176] and Case C-389/96, *Aher-Waggon*,[177] where, in relation to German legislation governing the noise levels of aircraft registered in Germany, the ECJ stated that:

> National legislation of the kind at issue . . . restricts infra-Community trade since it makes the first registration in national territory of aircraft previously registered in [another] Member State conditional upon compliance with stricter noise standards . . . Such a barrier may, however, be justified by considerations of public health and environmental protection.

The fact that a national measure is introduced in order to protect the environment will not necessarily mean that it is acceptable under this rule. Some important limitations need be considered. First, the rule of reason only operates to save national rules in the absence of EU measures. Thus, where the EU has already enacted a directive, for example, in relation to the level of chemicals acceptable in a given product, then that becomes the norm and Member States may not be able to deviate from this unless, as in Case C-389/96, *Aher-Waggon*, the directive only specifies a minimum acceptable standard. Secondly, national measures must satisfy a proportionality test. The ECJ has made it clear that any national rules which have the effect of hindering trade must be *necessary* to satisfy a mandatory requirement and must not go beyond that which is necessary. As with Art 36 TFEU, the national measure must be proportionate and will fail if it can be shown that there are other less restrictive ways of achieving the same objective.

Finally, one further limitation of the rule of reason needs to be considered. The traditional position of the ECJ is that the rule of reason is only available when national legislation is 'indistinctly applicable'.[178] However, this view has been cast into some doubt following two cases concerning Art 35 TFEU.[179] Article 35 TFEU prohibits Member States from introducing quantitative restrictions or measures having equivalent effect to a quantitative restriction on exports. The ECJ's earlier position was that the rule of reason should never be available in Art 35 TFEU cases, because national legislation only breaches Art 35 TFEU if it is 'distinctly applicable'.[180] However, in Case C-203/96, *Dusseldorp BV* (1998),[181] the ECJ appears to concede that it would be prepared to accept a rule of reason argument in cases where the national legislation is not 'indistinctly applicable' after all.

In *Dusseldorp*, Dutch legislation prohibited the export of waste oil filters unless it could be shown that they would be subject to a waste recovery treatment of a higher quality than that available in the Netherlands. The aim of the legislation was to promote the principles of self-sufficiency in waste. On a preliminary ruling, the ECJ held that the ban was contrary to Art 35 TFEU, but then went on to consider possible justifications for it. Despite the fact that the measure was discriminatory, the ECJ explored the possibility that it could be acceptable under the rule of reason. On the facts, the ECJ held that the 'justifications' in fact were purely economic and thus held that the Dutch rules were incompatible with Art 35 TFEU. Nevertheless, the ECJ appears to have considered using the rule of reason in respect of a distinctly applicable measure. Thus, the ECJ appears to have blurred the distinction between distinctly and indistinctly applicable measures. Various commentators[182] have argued that, specifically in relation to the environmental protection mandatory requirements, the ECJ should allow the mandatory requirement to be used to save distinctly applicable measures as well as indistinctly applicable measures because, in most cases, it is not possible to distinguish

176 Case C-2/90, *Commission v Belgium* (*Walloon Waste*) [1992] ECR I-4431.
177 Case C-389/96, *Aher-Waggon v Germany* [1998] ECR I 4473.
178 See Case 788/79, *Gilli & Andres* [1981] ECR 2071 and Case 113/80, *Commission v Ireland* (*Souvenir Jewellery*) [1981] ECR 1625.
179 Formerly Art 29 EC Treaty.
180 See Case 53/76, *Bouhelier* [1977] ECR 197 and Case 15/79 *PB Groenveld BV* [1979] ECR 3409.
181 Case C-203/96, *Dusseldorp BV* [1988] ECR I-4075.
182 See e.g., Notaro, N, 'The New Generation Case law on Trade and Environment' (2000) 25 ELR 467.

between justifications based on the 'protection of the health and life of humans, animals or plants' under Art 36 TFEU and those based on the 'environmental protection' mandatory requirement. The ECJ appeared to do this in Case C-2/90, *Commission v Belgium (Walloon Waste)*,[183] in relation to a ban on waste imports imposed by the Wallonia region of Belgium. Although the ban was to all intents and purposes discriminatory, because it discriminated against imported non-hazardous waste, the ECJ employed some interesting reasoning to reach the conclusion that it was not distinctly applicable 'having regard to the differences between waste produced in one place and that in another and its connection with the place that it is produced the measures cannot be considered to be discriminatory'. Thus, in consideration of the 'special' character of waste, the ECJ concluded that this ban was not discriminatory and was acceptable to serve the mandatory requirement of environmental protection.

3.11.2 Stricter national environmental protection measures

Where the EU has enacted an environmental directive, the extent to which Member States may maintain or even introduce more stringent environmental protection measures than those laid down in the directive will be determined by the legal basis on which the directive was enacted, namely Art 192 TFEU or Art 114 TFEU. Where legislation is adopted under Art 192 TFEU the position is clarified in Art 193 which states that the environmental protection measures adopted under Art 192 shall not prevent any Member State from maintaining or introducing more stringent protective measures. However, it also warns that such measures must be compatible with the Treaties (most particularly Art 34 TFEU, discussed above) and that the Member State must notify the Commission of the national measure. Where EU measures have been adopted under Art 114 TFEU the situation is slightly different. As noted above the principal aim of legislation adopted under Art 114 TFEU is to achieve approximation of standards so as not to distort the functioning of the internal market. Hence any deviation from the EU wide standards necessarily causes a problem in terms of approximation/harmonisation. Notwithstanding that observation, Art 114 TFEU does allow, in limited circumstances, for Member States to maintain and introduce stricter national measures.

3.11.2.1 Maintaining stricter standards

Article 114(4) TFEU refers specifically to the situation where a Member State wishes to maintain existing national measures. Specifically the Member State must 'deem it necessary'; on the grounds of the protection of the environment or the working environment and also of the major needs referred to in Art 36 TFEU. The Member State must notify the Commission and must justify their reasons for wishing to maintain the measure.[184]

3.11.2.2 Introducing stricter standards

Article 114(5) TFEU allows Member States to introduce national measures relating to the protection of the environment but this right is circumscribed. First, the Member State must 'deem it necessary' to introduce the rule based on 'new scientific evidence' relating to need, and the national measure must address a problem that is specific to that Member State, the problem having arisen after the adoption of the EU harmonising measure. Clearly, this will have limited application. Once again, the Member State must notify the Commission, which has the power to confirm or accept the national provision. Moreover, where this occurs, the Commission is bound to examine immediately whether to propose an adaptation to the harmonising measure.

---

183 Case C-389/96, *Aher-Waggon v Germany* [1998] ECR I 4473.
184 See Case C-41/93, *France v The Commission of the EC* [1994] ECR I-1829.

In reaching a decision on either of the above the Commission must verify that the national measures in question are not a means of arbitrary discrimination or a disguised restriction of trade between the Member States. The Commission has six months to do this. If the Commission fails to do this within six months then the national measure is deemed to have been approved.

3.12 Environmental Action Programmes

The First Action Programme for the Environment was adopted by the Council of Ministers on 22 December 1973. It set EU-wide objectives to resolve urgent pollution problems concerning water, air and soil. More importantly, it also established 11 principles upon which the Union's environmental policy is based. The Second, Third and Fourth Action Programmes continued in much the same vein as the first, only providing refinements to the objectives. They concentrated upon specific environmental media: air, water and waste. In particular, many of the policy aims, subsequently translated into directives, were concerned with setting emission limits. They were seen largely as 'end of pipe' solutions or 'fire fighting' measures. However, they were not entirely reactive in nature and over the subsequent programmes there was a growing emphasis on prevention rather than cure. The Fifth Action Programme represented a departure and change in thinking. On 26 June 1990, the Heads of State of the Member States called for the Fifth Action Programme to be drawn up on the principles of sustainable development, preventive and precautionary action and shared responsibility. The programme covered the period 1993 to 2000 and, to that extent, differed from the previous programmes in that it covered a seven-year period rather than five. More significantly the programme also marked a more important departure from previous programmes in its approach. Entitled *Towards Sustainability*, the programme did not specifically concern itself with the protection of environmental media, such as air, water or land. Instead, the programme concentrated on five key sectors of activity which have significant impacts on the state of the environment. The five sectors were: industry, energy, transport, agriculture and tourism. In the field of transport, for example, the Commission had produced a Green Paper on transport entitled *Sustainable Mobility*. This recommended the transfer from private transport use to more public transport and considered using fiscal measures such as road pricing and higher fuel prices to reduce demand. Agriculture, as another key sector, is responsible for a significant amount of environmental damage and there was recognition that the Common Agricultural Policy had been responsible for a negative impact on the environment. The aims of the Fifth Action Programme in this regard were to reduce the impact of agriculture on the environment by encouraging farmers to see themselves as 'guardians of the countryside' and to reduce in particular the pollution from nitrates and phosphates. Another feature of the Fifth Environmental Action Programme was the emphasis that it placed on 'shared responsibility'. Inherent in the programme was the belief that everyone shares a responsibility towards the environment and that there must be an 'optimum involvement of all sectors of society'. In order to change patterns of behaviour of producers, consumers, government and citizens, the Action Programme called for information campaigns to raise public awareness. Access to environmental information was also seen as a key element in enabling citizens to assist with the monitoring of pollution throughout the Community and also as a means of exercising consumer preferences for 'green' products and producers. The Action Programmes provide the broad policy framework from which the Commission can initiate legislative proposals. However, the Fifth Action Programme recognised that environmental protection could not be secured entirely by legal and regulatory measures. In a review of the measures available to improve the environment, the Commission stated that future environmental policy would be based on regulatory instruments; market-based measures; support measures, such as education, information and research; and financial support mechanisms. This theme of using different measures is continued in the current Sixth Action Programme.

3.12.1 The Sixth Environmental Action Programme

The Sixth Environmental Action Programme proposals were set out in 'Environment 2010: Our Future, Our Choice'. The programme focuses on the following four priority areas: climate change; nature and bio-diversity; environment and health; and sustainable use of natural resources and sustainable management of wastes coupled with seven thematic strategies: air, pesticides, waste prevention and recycling, natural resources, soil, marine environment, urban environment. The programme sets objectives for each priority area. In line with Kyoto Protocol commitments, the action programme includes a target of an 8 per cent reduction in greenhouse gases, based on 1990 levels of the six main gases, during 2008–12. The programme also sets a target for noise reduction: 10 per cent fewer people suffering from long-term high levels of noise by 2010, rising to 20 per cent by 2020. Efforts are to be made to 'protect and restore the functioning of natural systems and halt the loss of biodiversity' and to protect soils against erosion and pollution. Also of note are the following objectives: 12 per cent of total energy use to be derived from renewable sources by 2010; loss of biodiversity to be halted by 2010; only chemicals which do not have significant adverse impacts on man and the environment to be produced and used by 2020; fossil fuel subsidies to be phased out; and economic growth de-coupled from resource usage. As well as the priority areas, the Sixth Action Programme details four 'approaches' to be taken in regard to environmental issues. These approaches relate to:

(1) effective implementation and enforcement of environmental legislation in order to set a common baseline for all EU countries;

(2) integration of environmental concerns into other policy areas;

(3) use of a range of instruments including legal instruments alongside fiscal and educational measures;

(4) the stimulation of participation and action of all actors from business to citizens, NGOs and social partners through better and more accessible information on the environment.

3.12.2 Review of the Sixth Environmental Action Programme

In 2007 the European Commission published a mid-term review of the Sixth Action Programme[185] and this was followed by the Final Review in 2011.[186] The final assessment makes rather gloomy reading. On a positive note the Sixth EAP appears to have kept the environment firmly on the EU agenda by providing an over-arching environmental policy. The report also claims that the use of the ordinary legislative procedure in the adoption of EU environmental legislation gave the legislation more legitimacy. However, the report includes more negative points. In particular it notes that the programme's capacity to lever specific environmental instruments has not been compelling and the fact that a policy objective is included in the programme is no guarantee that Member States are actually committed to those objectives. Although the 10-year programme was long enough to cover policy formulation and the early stages of implementation in some areas (for example waste) it was too short to deliver specific legal instruments in other areas such as air and the urban environment. Perhaps more worryingly the report concludes that the absence of a longer-term vision

185 Communication from the Commission to the European Parliament, the Council, the European Economic and Social Committee and the Committee of the Regions on the Mid-term review of the Sixth Community Environment Action Programme COM (2007) 225 Final.

186 COM/2011/0531 final, Communication from the Commission to the European Parliament, the Council, the European Economic and Social Committee and the Committee of the Regions, The Sixth Community Environment Action Programme Final Assessment.

compromised the programme's capacity to deliver a clear message, which would have helped to maintain its profile more effectively throughout its lifespan. The overall achievement of the Sixth EAP has been compromised by a lack of implementation of environmental directives in the areas of air pollution, water and waste management treatment, waste and nature conservation.

3.12.3 Proposals for a Seventh Action Programme

At the end of 2010, the European Environment Agency published 'The European Environment – State and Outlook 2010',[187] which provided an in-depth and comprehensive analysis of the state and trends of the European environment. Like the Final Assessment of the Sixth EAP, this report noted that more needed to be done to ensure implementation of EU policy objectives. Both reports formed the basis of the Commission's public consultation on the formulation of the Seventh Environmental Action Programme. In November 2012 the European Commission published its Proposal for a Decision on the Seventh Environmental Action Programme, to be entitled 'Living well, within the limits of our planet'.[188] The proposal for the Seventh EAP is to build upon, inter alia, the European Union's 2020 Strategy for Smart, Sustainable and Inclusive Growth;[189] the EU climate and energy package;[190] and the EU's Biodiversity Strategy to 2020.[191] Very specifically the new programme aims to 'step up the contribution of environment policy to the transition towards a resource-efficient, low-carbon economy in which natural capital is protected and enhanced, and the health and well-being of citizens is safeguarded'.[192] The programme covers the period 2013 to 2020 but it is set within the context of a longer term vision for 2050.

The Seventh EAP identifies nine priority objectives for the EU and its Member States to attain:

1.   to protect, conserve and enhance the Union's natural capital;
2.   to turn the Union into a resource-efficient, green and competitive low-carbon economy;
3.   to safeguard the Union's citizens from environment-related pressures and risks to health and wellbeing;
4.   to maximise the benefits of the Union's environment legislation;
5.   to improve the evidence base for environment policy;
6.   to secure investment for environment and climate policy and get the prices right;
7.   to improve environmental integration and policy coherence;
8.   to enhance the sustainability of the Union's cities;
9.   to increase the Union's effectiveness in confronting regional and global environmental challenges.

Specific plans and targets for each of these nine priority objectives are included in the annex to the Proposal. As far as the fourth objective is concerned the EAP includes a number of broadly stated proposals but provides little in the way of detail. For example it proposes that the way in which knowledge about implementation of directives is collected and disseminated will be improved to help the public and environmental professionals fully understand how Member State authorities

---

187 SEC(2011) 1067; The European Environment – State and Outlook 2010: Assessment of Global Megatrends (EEA, 2010).
188 Proposal for a Decision of the European Parliament and of the Council on a General Union Environment Action Programme to 2020, 'Living well, within the limits of our planet' COM (2012) 710 final.
189 COM(2010) 2020, OJ C 88 of 19/3/2011.
190 Regulation (EC) No 443/2009, Directive 2009/28/EC, Directive 2009/29/EC, Directive 2009/30/EC, Directive 2009/31/EC, Decision No 406/2009/EC, all in OJ L 140 of 5/6/2009.
191 COM(2011) 244, OJ C 264 of 8/9/2011.
192 Proposal for a Decision of the European Parliament and of the Council on a General Union Environment Action Programme to 2020, 'Living well, within the limits of our planet' COM (2012) 710 final, p 2.

put Union commitments into effect. Presumably this could result in more reporting requirements in directives and greater emphasis on active dissemination of information. The EU will also extend requirements on inspections and surveillance to the wider body of EU environment law, complementing these with an EU-level capacity that can address situations where there is due reason for concern. It is also proposed that the way in which complaints about implementation of EU environment law are handled and remedied at national level will be improved but again no details are provided. However, what is particularly interesting is that there will be a shift away from the use of directives in favour of regulations where the legal obligations are 'sufficiently clear and precise'. It is asserted that regulations have direct and measurable effects and lead to fewer inconsistencies in implementation. This move towards the use of regulations is discussed below at 3.13. The proposal for the Seventh EAP needs to be adopted by the Parliament and the Council during 2013.

3.13 EU environmental legislation

The EU has enacted over 300 directives which are either directly or indirectly concerned with environmental protection. It is clearly not possible within the scope of this book to cover all of this legislation, the majority of which has been incorporated into UK law and is rightly regarded now as domestic law. In any event several of the key directives are considered elsewhere in this book in relation to specific topics such as waste and water and environmental remediation. Much of the legislation has been amended over time and so it is very welcome that the European Commission has embarked on a programme of codifying, consolidating or recasting legislation as part of the EU's Smart Regulation Agenda.[193] For example, Directive 2010/75 on industrial emissions (integrated pollution prevention and control) reforms the twice-amended consolidated EU Directive on Integrated Pollution Prevention Control. The new directive seeks to implement a holistic, integrated approach to pollution control for a range of major industrial activities. More interestingly the European Commission has replaced a number of directives with regulations. Notably some 24 directives on vehicle emissions have been repealed and replaced with a single Regulation.[194] This trend is likely to continue under the framework of the Seventh EAP, which states: 'As a general rule, legal obligations which are sufficiently clear and precise will be enshrined in Regulations, which have direct and measurable effects and lead to fewer inconsistencies in implementation.'

It is important to note that the EU's environmental policy is not delivered purely by means of Command and Control legal instruments. For many years now the EU has sought to develop a mix of market-based measures including incentives, financial instruments, and voluntary schemes. For example, in key policy areas such as agriculture, the Commission has proposed to enhance incentives for farmers to provide environmentally beneficial public goods and services, matched by environment-related conditions. The proposal for the Seventh EAP notes that an appropriate mix of policy instruments will continue to be needed to enable businesses and consumers to improve their understanding of the impact of their activities on the environment and to manage the impact. As far as legislation is concerned the EU has, over time, developed a number of different approaches ranging from laying down maximum admissible concentrations of substances that can be present in specific media, to regulating the levels of polluting substances in products (such as lead in petrol) to establishing frameworks for regulatory control by national competent authorities. The

---

193 COM/2010/0543 final, Communication from the Commission to the European Parliament, the Council, the European Economic and Social Committee and the Committee of the Regions, Smart Regulation in the European Union.

194 Regulation (EC) No 715/2007 of the European Parliament and of the Council of 20 June 2007 on type approval of motor vehicles with respect to emissions from light passenger and commercial vehicles (Euro 5 and Euro 6) and on access to vehicle repair and maintenance information OJ L 171, 29/06/2007, pp 1–16.

following section aims to provide a brief description of the different approaches that have been adopted with some examples. In addition the section will comment on some further developments that have not been considered elsewhere in this book. The discussion is not intended to be exhaustive, but further reading has been suggested in the reading list at the end of the chapter.

3.13.1 Framework directives

The EU has adopted a number of 'framework directives'. They are categorised as such because they provide a broad framework for action and outline general rules and basic requirements. Framework directives are useful in establishing a broad regulatory framework and are then usually followed by 'daughter directives' which deal with detailed specific issues. Classic examples are the Waste Framework Directive[195] and the Water Framework Directive.[196] The Water Framework Directive 2000/60 typifies this approach. Although the EU had previously adopted a range of measures in relation to water pollution there was a growing recognition of the fragmented nature of these measures both in terms of objectives and means. As a result of calls for the need for a more global and combined approach to water pollution, the Water Framework Directive was adopted. The Water Framework Directive sets out in a single piece of legislation a range of measures and a framework for developing future controls. The Water Framework Directive has a number of objectives, for example preventing and reducing pollution, promoting sustainable water usage, environmental protection, improving aquatic ecosystems and mitigating the effects of floods and droughts. Its ultimate objective is to achieve 'good ecological and chemical status' for all EU waters by 2015. Member States are required to identify all river basins lying within their national territory and to assign them to individual river basin districts. Additionally the Member State must designate a competent authority for implementing the provisions of the Directive within each river basin district. Under Art 4 the Water Framework Directive Member States are required to implement the necessary measures laid down in subsequent EU measures, with the aim of progressively reducing pollution from priority substances and ceasing or phasing out emissions, discharges of priority hazardous substances. Subsequent directives are often referred to as daughter directives. As far as the Water Framework Directive is concerned the various EQS that Member States must achieve are listed in Directive 2008/105/EC on environmental quality standards in the field of water policy.[197] It should be noted that this is a good example of the consolidating exercise referred to above because Directive 2008/105/EC repeals some five earlier directives on water quality. The first list of 33 substances that the EU has prioritised for action were listed in Decision 2455/2001/EC and the respective EQS are to be found in the annex to Directive 2008/105/EC. In 2012 the Commission put forward a proposal for amending the Water Framework Directive.[198]

3.13.2 Environmental quality standards

It was noted above that Directive 2008/105 lays down certain environmental quality standards in the field of water policy. An Environmental Quality Standard is a value, which is normally prescribed by legislation which specifies the maximum permissible concentration of a potentially hazardous chemical in an environmental sample. It may also be referred to as an ambient standard. An EQS

---

195 Directive 2008/98/EC of the European Parliament and of the Council of 19 November 2008 on waste and repealing certain Directives Text with EEA relevance OJ L 312, 22/11/2008, pp 3–30.
196 Directive 2000/60/EC of the European Parliament and of the Council of 23 October 2000 establishing a framework for Community action in the field of water policy OJ L 327, 22/12/2000, pp 1–73.
197 Directive 2008/105/EC of the European Parliament and of the Council of 16 December 2008 on environmental quality standards in the field of water policy, amending and subsequently repealing Council Directives 82/176/EEC, 83/513/EEC, 84/156/EEC, 84/491/EEC, 86/280/EEC and amending Directive 2000/60/EC of the European Parliament and of the Council.
198 COM 2011 (876).

may be specified generally or in relation to particular classifications of water, for example depending on whether the water is intended for human consumption. In relation to water a number of directives have been adopted which establish water quality objectives for different uses of water. Directive 98/83/EEC,[199] sets standards for water intended for human consumption; 2006/44/EC[200] for quality of fresh waters needing protection or improvement in order to support fish life. Directive 2006/13/EC[201] makes a similar provision for shellfish, and note also Directive 76/160/EEC,[202] which sets standards for water used for bathing purposes. This will be repealed from December 2014 by Directive 2006/7/EC.

3.13.3 Control of dangerous substances

Another approach that the EU has adopted is to control the use, discharge or emission of dangerous substances. Framework Directive 2006/11/EC[203] is particularly important in this regard since it is concerned with the control of certain dangerous substances discharged into the aquatic environment. This Directive provides a list of dangerous substances which are either to be eliminated (List I substances) or to be progressively reduced (List II substances). Subsequent daughter directives have since been adopted relating to specific discharges of dangerous substances from industrial discharges. However, this Directive will be repealed with effect from December 2013 by the Water Framework Directive, which will continue to control the release of hazardous substances into the water environment as discussed above.

3.13.4 Vehicle emission standards and product quality standards

Directive 70/220/EEC[204] was first introduced to minimise air pollution from car exhaust fumes, and did this by prescribing limit values for certain gaseous emissions. This was followed by a similar Directive 72/306/EEC,[205] in relation to diesel engines, and further directives relating to vehicle emissions, such as Directive 91/441/EEC[206] which required that all new petrol engine cars must be fitted with a three-way catalytic converter. These were amended by subsequent legislation, increasing the stringency of the controls.[207] However, all three were repealed in 2007 and replaced with Regulation 715/2007[208] and the Member States were required to repeal all the corresponding

---

199 Council Directive 98/83/EC of 3 November 1998 on the quality of water intended for human consumption.
200 Directive 2006/44/EC of the European Parliament and of the Council of 6 September 2006 on the quality of fresh waters needing protection or improvement in order to support fish life OJ L 264, 2592006, pp 20–31.
201 Directive 2006/113/EC of the European Parliament and of the Council of 12 December 2006 on the quality required of shellfish waters (codified version) OJ L 376, 27122006, pp 14–20.
202 Council Directive 76/160/EEC of 8 December 1975 concerning the quality of bathing water OJ L 31, 521976, pp 1–7.
203 Directive 2006/11/EC of the European Parliament and of the Council of 15 February 2006 on pollution caused by certain dangerous substances discharged into the aquatic environment of the Community (Codified version) OJ L 64, 432006, pp 52–59.
204 Council Directive 70/220/EEC of 20 March 1970 on the approximation of the laws of the Member States relating to measures to be taken against air pollution by gases from positive-ignition engines of motor vehicles OJ L 76, 6/4/1970, pp 1–22. Now repealed.
205 Council Directive 72/306/EEC of 2 August 1972 on the approximation of the laws of the Member States relating to the measures to be taken against the emission of pollutants from diesel engines for use in vehicles OJ L 190, 20/8/1972, pp 1–23. Now repealed.
206 Council Directive 91/441/EEC of 26 June 1991 amending Directive 70/220/EEC on the approximation of the laws of the Member States relating to measures to be taken against air pollution by emissions from motor vehicles OJ L 242, 30/8/1991, pp 1–106.
207 Regulation (EC) No 715/2007 of the European Parliament and of the Council of 20 June 2007 on type approval of motor vehicles with respect to emissions from light passenger and commercial vehicles (Euro 5 and Euro 6) and on access to vehicle repair and maintenance information (Text with EEA relevance) OJ L 171, 29/6/2007, p 1.
208 Regulation (EC) No 715/2007 of the European Parliament and of the Council of 20 June 2007 on type approval of motor vehicles with respect to emissions from light passenger and commercial vehicles (Euro 5 and Euro 6) and on access to vehicle repair and maintenance information Official Journal L 171, 29/06/2007, pp 1–16.

national legislation. The preamble to the regulation, which replaces some 24 directives, is that a regulation will ensure that the detailed technical provisions are directly applicable to manufacturers, approval authorities and technical services and that they can be updated in a much faster and more efficient way. Certain directives aim to restrict the level of polluting substances in products. For example, Directive 85/210/EEC[209] set the maximum content of lead in petrol.

3.13.5 Horizontal and vertical directives

In addition directives are often categorised as either horizontal or vertical measures. A vertical measure is one that applies to a specific field of activity or topic. For example a directive on water quality or fishing is a vertical measure. In contrast, so-called horizontal measures apply widely across various fields or activities. Horizontal measures tend not to focus on a specific environmental medium or polluting substance but usually seek to lay down a procedure or regulatory system. The Integrated Pollution Prevention Control Directive,[210] which is discussed in Chapter 6, falls into this category, as do the Environmental Impact Assessment Directive[211] and the Environmental Information Directive.[212] In addition a very important horizontal directive is the Environmental Liability Directive (Directive 2004/35/EC), which is discussed in Chapter 7.[213]

3.13.6 The REACH package

A chapter on EU environmental law would not be complete without some discussion of the REACH package, which was adopted in 2006. The REACH package comprises the REACH Regulation 1907/2006 concerning the Registration, Evaluation, Authorisation and Restriction of Chemicals and Directive 2006/121/EC on the approximation of laws, regulations and administrative provisions relating to the classification, packaging and labelling of dangerous substances. The purpose of the directive is to adapt national provisions to the requirements of the REACH Regulation. The REACH package has replaced the former patchwork of earlier legislation which comprised many different directives and regulations and which had developed in a rather piecemeal fashion.

The REACH Regulation seeks to provide a high level of protection of human health and the environment from the use of chemicals by making the people who place chemicals on the market responsible for understanding and managing the risks associated with their use. It applies to manufacturers and importers who manufacture or import into the EU in quantities of 1 tonne or more per year, subject to some specific exemptions. Manufacturers and importers are required to register a dossier of certain information with the European Chemicals Agency (ECA), which was established by the REACH Regulation. If a company fails to register a substance it means that this company is no longer allowed to manufacture or import this substance. Manufacturers and importers of substances are required to obtain information on the substances they manufacture or import and use this information to assess the risks arising from the uses and to ensure that the risks which the

209 Council Directive 85/210/EEC of 20 March 1985 on the approximation of the laws of the Member States concerning the lead content of petrol OJ L 96, 341985, pp 25–29.
210 Directive 2010/75/EU of the European Parliament and of the Council of 24 November 2010 on industrial emissions (integrated pollution prevention and control) Text with EEA relevance OJ L 334, 17/12/2001, pp 17–119.
211 Council Directive 85/337/EEC of 27 June 1985 on the assessment of the effects of certain public and private projects on the environment OJ L 175, 5/7/1985, as amended.
212 Directive 2003/4/EC of the European Parliament and of the Council of 28 January 2003 on public access to environmental information and repealing Council Directive 90/313/EEC OJ L 41, 14/2/2003, pp 26–32.
213 Directive 2004/35/CE of the European Parliament and of the Council of 21 April 2004 on environmental liability with regard to the prevention and remedying of environmental damage OJ L143, 30/4/2004, pp 56–75.

substances may present are properly managed. The ECA is responsible for the management of the data supplied and also for co-ordinating the evaluation of suspicious chemicals.

The REACH Regulation also contains important provisions about data sharing and making certain information available to 'downstream users', such as customers who can use the information in order to use the chemicals safely. Information relating to health, safety and environmental properties, risks and risk management measures is required to be passed both down and up the supply chain. Commercially sensitive information is not required to be exchanged.

The REACH Regulation also provides for the progressive substitution of the most dangerous chemicals when suitable alternatives have been identified. REACH is based on the idea that industry itself is best placed to ensure that the chemicals it manufactures and puts on the market in the EU do not adversely affect human health or the environment. This requires that industry has certain knowledge of the properties of its substances and manages potential risks. The enforcement authorities in the Member States therefore should focus their resources on ensuring industry are meeting their obligations and taking action on substances of very high concern or where there is a need for EU action. For a fuller examination of the REACH programme, see the European Commission's briefing note on REACH.[214]

3.14 Online resource centre

We recommend that the reader regularly refers to the section of the online resources corresponding to this chapter for information relating to updates, amendments and corrections.

3.15 Summary of key points

The aim of this chapter was to provide a general overview of EU law and the evolution of the Treaties and to provide the reader with a basic understanding of the importance of EU environmental law and policy within the domestic legal order. To this end Chapter 3 has covered the following topics and issues:

- the evolution of the European Union from the EEC in 1957, with six Member States, to a Union of 28 Member States and how, over time, the Treaties have been amended to incorporate environmental protection as a key policy area;
- the institutional arrangement of the EU and the roles played by the respective institutions;
- the development of EU environmental law and the way in which the EU was able to legislate in the field of environmental protection despite the absence, before 1986, of a specific legal base;
- the enforcement of EU law with a particular focus on EU environmental law;
- an overview of the environmental protection provisions of the TEU and TFEU;
- the differences between Arts 114 and 192 TFEU in terms of the adoption of environmental legislation;
- the extent to which EU law fetters the rights of Member States to maintain or introduce stricter environmental standards than those laid down by EU law;
- the relationship between the free trade goals of the EU and environmental protection;
- the range of different types of measures that the EU has adopted in the field of environmental protection.

---

214 Available at http://eceuropaeu/environment/chemicals/reach/pdf/2007_02_reach_in_briefpdf.

3.16 Further reading

Books

Holder J (ed), *The Impact of EC Environmental Law in the United Kingdom.*
Krämer, K, *EC Environmental Law*, 5th edn, Sweet & Maxwell, London 2003.
Wallace, H, Pollack, M, Young, A, *Policy Making in the European Union* 2010 Oxford University Press—in particular Chapters 12 and 13.

Articles

Doolittle, I, 'After implementation, enforcement? The next challenge for European environmental law' (1999) 11(3) Env Law Management 101–02.

This considers a survey carried out by specialist environmental law firms in EU Member States questioning the implementation and enforcement of EU law throughout the European Union by reference to a number of issues, including the responsibilities of environmental enforcement agencies, the number of court actions concluded by the agencies and the penalties usually imposed. The article concludes with an analysis of the strengths and weaknesses of each environmental regime, and proposals for improvements.

Falkenberg, K, Director General of DG Environment at the European Commission, Brussels, 'Better EU regulation for a greener environment and sustainable economic activity in Europe', the United Kingdom Environmental Association annual Garner lecture 2012 Published in UKELA e Law, March 2012 Issue 75.

Notaro, N, 'The new generation case law on trade and environment' [2000] 25(5) EL Rev 467–91.

This provides an in-depth analysis of the trade and environment case law of the Court of Justice since the entry into force of the Treaty on European Union of 1992. In particular, the article considers the replacement of traditional necessity and proportionality tests with a single necessity test and replacement of extra-territorial application of national law with extra-jurisdictional application of national law.

Oliver, P, 'Some further reflections on the scope of Articles 28–30 EC' (1999) 26 CMLR 783.

This article examines the use of the environmental protection mandatory requirement in cases involving environmental law.

Stokes, E, 'Precautionary steps: the development of the precautionary principle in EU jurisprudence' (2003) 15(1) Env Law Management 8–15.

This gives a detailed examination of the approach of the European Court of Justice to the precautionary principle.

Usui, Y, 'Evolving environmental norms in the European Union' (2003) 9(1) ELJ 69–87.

This discusses the development of EU environmental law and how this law developed in the absence of a specific legal base. It also examines the rights of individuals to enforce EC environmental law.

Wasmeier, M, 'The integration of environmental protection as a general rule for interpreting Community law' [2001] 38(1) CMLR 159–77.

This examines the importance of the protection of the environment objective incorporated into EU law by Art 2 of the EC Treaty and the requirement that environmental protection be an integral part of EU law.

Williams, R, 'Commission's reasoned opinion in Danish Can ban—legal sense, environmental nonsense?' (1999) 11(1 and 2) Env Law Management 57–60.

This examines the provisions of the Packaging Waste Directive and their application by the Commission in infringement proceedings against Denmark.

Weblinks

The European Union online. The Europa portal provides access to the websites of the institutions of the EU, including the Commission and the Court of Justice.
http://europa.eu/

The official website of the European Court of Justice.
www.curia.eu.int

The official website of the European Environment Agency.
www.eea.eu.int

Chapter 4

Water Pollution

Chapter Contents

> ## Learning Objectives
>
> By the end of this chapter you should have acquired an understanding of:
>
> - how discharges of polluting emissions into surface waters, groundwaters, coastal waters and sewers are regulated under the relevant primary and secondary legislation;
>
> - the regulatory bodies which have roles to play in the control of water pollution;
>
> - permits to pollute—the key vehicle by which the Environment Agency/privatised water and sewerage companies control polluting discharges into the aquatic environment;
>
> - pollution offences which underpin the relevant legislative regimes—the separate elements of each offence, the regulator's discretion to prosecute, prosecution and enforcement policy, sanctions and defences;
>
> - the impact of the EU upon the regulation of water pollution in England and Wales;
>
> - the regulator's use of its regulatory or administrative powers to achieve compliance with water pollution control law and policy;
>
> - the role of individuals and environmental groups in water pollution control.

4.1 Introduction

This chapter is concerned with the regulation of water pollution and water quality. Without pollution controls, water would become grossly polluted and unusable for a wide range of human and non-human needs. Humans require clean water for drinking and other uses such as manufacturing, food production and agriculture. Once water has been used, it is returned to the aquatic environment as an effluent. These effluent discharges into surface waters and sewers must be regulated so as to maintain a sufficiently high quality of the receiving waters[1] to meet our needs. These needs vary according to the use which is made of the available surface and groundwaters. Thus, an industrial discharge of effluent into a river will be tightly controlled if there is a fishery downstream of the industrial plant, or water is abstracted from the river for human consumption.

The control of water pollution through Command and Control legislative regulation has a longer history than similar environmental controls over waste disposal or atmospheric pollution; nevertheless, it shares a basic and recognisable structure with other environmental media-based controls, especially as a result of the introduction of the Environmental Permitting (England and Wales) Regulations 2010. That structure is reflected in the arrangement of the material in this chapter, the majority of which concerns the public regulation of water pollution generated by businesses[2] and individuals.

---

1 Waters into which effluent is discharged.
2 E.g., legal persons such as companies, firms/partnerships, public sector organisations.

4.2 Control over water pollution: an overview

The Water Resources Act 1991 (WRA 1991), as amended by the Environment Act 1995 (EA 1995), the Environmental Permitting (England and Wales) Regulations 2010, the Water Industry Act 1991 (WIA 1991) and Water Industry Act 1999[3] provide the main regulatory control framework relating to the prevention and control of water pollution in England and Wales. The Environment Agency is responsible for controlling pollution of 'controlled waters'[4] and for achieving the improvements in water quality necessary to meet statutory water quality objectives.[5]

The control of water pollution is exercised by the Environment Agency through a system of permits. Any *polluting* discharge made into controlled waters must be authorised by the Environment Agency via the issue of a permit. The permit system enables the Environment Agency to control, by means of conditions, the nature and volume of contaminants discharged into surface and ground-waters in order to maintain water quality or achieve improvements in water quality. Discharges made without consent, or in breach of the conditions attached to a permit, constitute criminal offences[6] but prosecution does not automatically follow.[7] The Environment Agency employs inspectors who have wide-ranging administrative powers to secure compliance with the relevant law. In the event that there is a discharge into controlled waters which is not authorised by a permit or is in breach of permit conditions, the Environment Agency has the power to prosecute. Various statutory defences exist.[8] The fines for water pollution offences may be unlimited if a case is dealt with by the Crown Court and, indeed, some of the fines have been very high. In addition, under s 161 of the WRA 1991, the Environment Agency has a preventive power to take action to avoid pollution of controlled water and a remedial power to 'clean up' after an incident. It can then recover its reasonable costs from those responsible for the pollution. The costs of clean-up may well far exceed any fine imposed by a court. The pace of legislative change delivering improvements in water quality and water pollution reduction has been profoundly influenced by the UK's membership of the EU.

4.3 Polluting substances and polluting activities

In order to comprehend the development and 'shape' of regulatory water pollution controls, we need to develop some understanding of (1) the activities which are chiefly responsible for water pollution, and (2) the substances which are discharged by those activities into the aquatic environment and which have an *adverse* effect upon the aquatic environment. There are four key questions: (a) who (i.e. which activities) are the main polluters?; (b) what substances do these activities discharge into the aquatic environment?; (c) what properties do these substances possess which are problematic?; and (d) what factors will affect the impact of such pollutants upon the waters into which they are discharged?

The main water polluters are industry and commerce. According to various estimates, there are in excess of 100,000 water pollution discharge permits. In addition to these legitimate discharges, industrial activity is associated with a significant number of accidental spillages of chemical substances, such as oils and fuels. Every individual is also partly responsible for the discharge of

---

3 Plus the regulations which supplement these statutes listed in the Table of Statutory Instruments.
4 See 4.6.
5 See 4.8.8.2.
6 See 4.9.
7 The Environment Agency has a discretion whether to prosecute or not and it may choose to use other methods to secure compliance with environmental law.
8 See 4.10.

treated sewage, from the numerous sewage treatment works spread throughout the UK, into surface waters. Run-off from mining waste tips (slag heaps), which are rich in metals, also cause pollution. Pollutants may leach out and escape from the base of waste sites, especially old landfills, and cause contamination of groundwaters. Abandoned mines cause pollution when old mine workings fill up with water and the water becomes contaminated prior to its discharge into surface waters.

The contamination of groundwaters by farming-related activities[9] is also a significant cause of pollution of the aquatic environment.[10] It is not only the activities of man which are associated with water pollution incidents. Droughts will result in low flows of surface waters and an increase in the concentration of substances discharged into receiving waters. So what would not normally be polluting may become polluting due to a period of low rainfall.

The substances which, when discharged into the aquatic environment, cause pollution are those which have one or more of the following properties:

(a)   they deoxygenate water, for example, sewage, agricultural slurry[11] and milk;

(b)   they cause eutrophication, for example, fertilisers which accelerate algal growth;

(c)   they block out light which disrupts plant growth, for example, suspended solids, such as silty water pumped out of a construction site and discharged into a stream;

(d)   they are toxic to humans, plants and animals, for example, pesticides, fuel oils, chemicals and heavy metals;

(e)   they cause disease, for example, water-borne bacterial infections such as cryptosporidium;

(f)   they damage amenity, for example, dyes from the textile industry, detergents (causing foaming on surface waters), unsightly waste objects;[12] and

(g)   they have undergone change, due to the presence of energy, for example, water which is abstracted from a river in order to provide cooling water for a power station. The water is heated in the cooling (energy exchange) process and is then reintroduced into the river where it may have an adverse impact upon the ecology of the river system (e.g. deoxygenation).[13]

The objective of water pollution controls is to regulate the entry of any substance, even seemingly innocuous substances such as milk, which in sufficient quantities may have an adverse impact upon the aquatic environment (whether surface, ground or coastal waters). In deciding whether to regulate a particular substance the regulator will pay attention to the purpose for which the receiving waters (i.e. those waters into which the potentially polluting substance is discharged) are used, such as drinking, food production (e.g. fishing) and bathing. Pollution of the relevant receiving waters therefore occurs when the receiving waters become unusable for their intended use due to the presence of a damaging substance. With this in mind we can appreciate why the focus of water pollution regulation is upon maintaining the quality of receiving waters (the target-based statutory water quality approach to regulation favoured by the UK), rather than fixing strict limits on a range of substances at the point they are discharged into receiving waters (the emission standard/maximum allowable concentration approach to water pollution regulation favoured by the EU).

The following types of incidents are significant causes of water pollution:

---

9   E.g. fertiliser 'run-off' and pesticide use, particularly from sheep dips.

10   It is estimated that approximately 30% of the public drinking water supply is sourced from groundwaters.

11   For an assessment of the significance of agricultural activities as a water polluter see the report of the Policy Commission on the Future of Farming and Food (2002).

12   E.g. old tyres and shopping trolleys thrown into controlled waters.

13   Unless the water is cooled in cooling ponds before reintroduction into surface waters.

(a)   non-permitted discharges from sewage treatment plants;
(b)   accidental spillages, especially of fuels and oils during storage or transport;
(c)   leachate from landfill sites and contaminated land;
(d)   non-point/diffuse pollution primarily from agricultural run-off (of fertiliser and pesticide).

National water pollution policy and its relationship to the permit system is set out in government policy documents such as *River Quality:The Government's Proposals* (DoE 1992) and *Directing the Flow: Priorities for FutureWater Policy* (Defra 2002).

The impact of polluting substances and energy upon the waters into which they are discharged will vary with a variety of factors, including:

(a)   the rate of flow (to disperse and dilute the pollutant) of the receiving water system;
(b)   the volume of the receiving water system;
(c)   the geology and topography of the relevant area in which the river system is situated (for example, the impact of an agricultural spillage of slurry, which deoxygenates a river, will be mitigated by the presence of a downstream waterfall which reoxygenates the river);
(d)   upstream or downstream uses of a river system (for example, the presence of urban and industrial areas discharging pollutants into a river upstream of a polluter, or the presence of a sensitive area, such as a Site of Special Scientific Interest, downstream of a polluting activity);
(e)   the existing water quality (chemical composition) of the relevant water (e.g. oxygen content).[14]

Whilst the public regulatory apparatus of the WRA 1991, and supplementary regulations,[15] have the primary role to play in the control of water pollution, the private regulatory activities of individuals and environmental groups are also relevant. Such persons may use private prosecution, judicial review of regulatory decision making, and common law tortious actions to achieve their objectives. In the context of the 'private' regulation of pollution, it is important to bear in mind the differing aims of the criminal and civil law and the differing aims of the public regulators and ordinary individuals, non-governmental organisations (NGOs) or regulated dischargers (e.g. manufacturing companies and public sector bodies, e.g. the NHS Trusts). Private prosecutions, based on criminal law offences contained in the relevant primary and secondary legislation, are concerned with punishing the polluter and enforcing compliance with the law through the deterrent effect of prosecution. Civil actions are, in the context of environmental pollution, concerned with obtaining compensation for damage to property or person (personal injury) caused by pollution.[16] Regulatory agencies, such as the Environment Agency, the privatised water and sewerage companies and local authorities, 'police' compliance with the law laid down in Command and Control legislation.[17] The objectives of individuals, environmental groups and companies in their use of environmental law vary. Environmental groups may mount a private prosecution against a polluter if they disagree with the exercise of regulatory discretion not to prosecute or they may commence a civil action for judicial review of the Environment Agency's decision not to prosecute. An individual may commence an action against a polluter, using the tort of nuisance, to compensate him or her for pollution damage to his or her property. A regulated business may wish to challenge, by way of a judicial review action, a decision by the regulator to refuse an appeal against service of

---

14 Water quality is addressed in 4.8.8.
15 Especially the Environmental Permitting (England and Wales) Regulations 2010.
16 See 4.16.
17 E.g., the WRA 1991, the WIA 1991, the Environmental Protection Act (EPA) 1990 and the Pollution Prevention and Control Act 1999.

an Enforcement Notice. In a civil law context, possession of and compliance with the conditions of a water pollution permit will not provide a defence to a civil action brought by any person against the holder of a water pollution permit,[18] but will provide a defence in regard to a criminal prosecution, for example, an alleged breach of reg 38 of the Environmental Permitting (England and Wales) Regulations 2010.

4.4 The historical development of the public regulation of water pollution

Significant legislative attempts to prevent and control water pollution date back to the 1860s. Since that time, various governments have introduced new controls and have established new criminal offences. The following section is intended to provide a very brief overview of the history of those controls. The first Act of Parliament to attempt to control water pollution was the Rivers (Pollution Prevention) Act of 1876. Although there had been previous Acts which had dealt with water pollution, they were primarily aimed at improving public health[19] or the productivity of fishing.[20] The Rivers (Pollution Prevention) Act 1876 created several offences in relation to the discharge or dumping of specified solid matter into any stream; the discharge of solid or liquid sewage matter into any stream; and the discharge of poisonous, noxious or polluting liquid from any factory or manufacturing process into surface waters. The Rivers (Pollution Prevention) Act 1876 also introduced a number of defences, including the defence that the 'best practicable means' had been employed to render pollutants harmless. Despite the creation of these offences, the Act was regarded as ineffective.

The Rivers (Pollution Prevention) Act 1876 was replaced 75 years later by the Rivers (Prevention of Pollution) Act 1951. This Act created the offence of causing or knowingly permitting any poisonous, noxious or polluting matter to enter a stream and it also introduced the first system of discharge consents.[21] It required all new discharge outlets to be licensed. However, any existing discharge outlets were not required to be licensed unless they were altered, or the composition of the discharge itself was altered or increased.

The River Boards Act 1948 created 32 River Boards.[22] The regulators of any *new* industrial or sewage effluent discharges into surface waters were now the River Boards, whose regulatory remit was extended in 1960 by the Clean Rivers (Estuaries and Tidal Waters) Act 1960 to estuarine and tidal waters.

The Rivers (Prevention of Pollution) Act 1961 extended the consent procedure to cover certain types of discharges that were operational before the 1951 Act, thus extending the coverage of the licensing system of water pollution control. The 1961 Act also provided a much stricter regime in so far as it removed some defences which had been available under the 1951 Act. The Water Resources Act 1963 transferred regulatory control of water pollution responsibilities from the River Boards to 27 River Authorities. The new River Authorities extended their regulatory remit to underground waters and the licensing of water abstractions. Control of existing water supply and sewerage systems remained with local authorities.

The Control of Pollution Act 1974 repealed both the 1951 and 1961 Acts.

---

18 S 100(b) of the WRA 1991.
19 E.g. Public Health Act 1875.
20 E.g. The Salmon Fisheries Act 1861.
21 Now referred to as permits.
22 Whose regulatory remit was based on river basin catchments.

4.4.1 The 1991 Water Acts

The starting point in considering the current legislative controls is the Water Act 1989 (WA 1989) which, although superseded by consolidating legislation in 1991, was the Act which established the National Rivers Authority (NRA). It also led to the privatisation of water supplies and sewerage services. In 1991, Parliament passed five Acts which consolidated the various legislative provisions relating to all aspects of the water industry and control of water pollution. The main Acts were the Water Industry Act 1991 (WIA 1991) and the Water Resources Act 1991 (WRA 1991). The provisions of the WRA 1991 as amended by the Environmental Permitting (England and Wales) Regulations 2010 provide the main framework for control of water quality and quantity and are considered in detail below. The WIA 1991 contains provisions relating to water supply and sewerage services; however, some provisions are related to environmental protection, particularly in relation to the controls over the quality of drinking water. The Environment Act 1995 (EA 1995) transferred the NRA's water pollution functions to the Environment Agency.

4.4.2 Other statutory controls

In addition to the controls within the main water legislation, various other statutes contain provisions which relate to the control and prevention of water pollution or the maintenance of water quality standards. These include:

(a)   the EA 1995;
(b)   the EPA 1990;
(c)   the Salmon and Freshwater Fisheries Act (SFFA) 1975;
(d)   the Land Drainage Act 1994;
(e)   the Pollution Prevention and Control Act 1999; and
(f)   the Environmental Permitting (England and Wales) Regulations 2010.

Readers should also note the range of secondary legislation relating to water pollution and water quality: see the Table of Statutory Instruments.

4.5 The water industry and the Water Industry Act 1991

The water industry covers a wide range of diverse activities, all of which share a common involvement in the water cycle, ranging from the collection and treatment of water and its supply, to the provision of sewers and sewage treatment works. It also covers those bodies involved in the control of pollution, the regulation and control of fishing, navigation, flood defence, land drainage, water-related conservation and recreational activities.

The water industry has undergone many changes since the 1940s, primarily as a result of reorganisation and privatisation. Before 1948, the responsibility for water supply and also sewage disposal fell to the local authorities. In 1948, the River Boards Act established 32 River Boards which were organised on a catchment area basis. The River Boards acquired responsibility for most water industry activities, including water supply and sewage disposal. In 1963, the River Boards were taken over by 27 River Authorities.[23] The River Authorities had responsibility, among other things, for pollution control. However, it was not really until 1973 that there was any real attempt to achieve an integrated control of the industry. The Water Act 1973 (WA 1973) established 10 Regional Water Authorities which took charge of managing the various water functions in the

---

23 See the Water Resources Act 1963 (WRA 1963).

relevant river basin areas. The WA 1973, however, did permit the continued existence of a number of statutory private water companies.

Although the WA 1973 was intended to provide a more coherent framework for control, it did not tackle one of the main problems that had so far existed in the industry. The regional water authorities had responsibility for pollution control but were at the same time themselves major polluters in their capacity as operators of sewage disposal works. This 'gamekeeper and poacher' scenario (role conflict) gave rise to a great deal of criticism of the water industry. Consequently, the industry went through further reorganisation in 1989 with the Water Act 1989, which led to the privatisation of water supply and sewerage services and the creation of the National Rivers Authority. In 1991, the government consolidated the legislation controlling the water industry and now the WIA 1991 (plus the WIA 1999) provide for the regulation of water supply and sewerage.

The position today is that the supply of water and the provision of sewerage services rests with privatised water service companies (known as water undertakers and sewerage undertakers). In addition, there are also water companies which are only responsible for the supply of water and play no role in relation to sewerage services. The office of the Director General of Water Services was established to regulate the activities of the privatised water industry. Regulatory control of the water supply and sewerage services industry passed in 2006[24] from the Office of Water Services (OFWAT) to a Regulation Authority (comprising an independent regulatory panel).

4.6 Controlled waters

The pollution controls contained in the Water Resources Act (WRA 1991) apply only in respect of waters defined as 'controlled waters' and the Environment Agency *can only exercise its controls over pollution in relation to those waters*. Section 104 of the WRA 1991 provides a definition of controlled waters which includes:

(a) inland fresh waters—including lakes, ponds, canals, reservoirs, rivers or water courses above the fresh water limit[25] (including any inland fresh waters which are temporarily dry);

(b) ground waters—that is, waters contained in underground strata: wells, boreholes and aquifers;

(c) coastal waters—including all estuarine waters up to the fresh water limit of rivers and other water courses;

(d) territorial waters—the seas within the relevant territorial limit (the three mile limit).

These terms are defined much more fully in s 104 as follows:

● 'Inland fresh waters' means the waters of any relevant lake or pond or of so much of any relevant river or watercourse as is above the fresh water limit. 'Relevant lake or pond' means any lake or pond, including reservoirs, which, whether it is natural, artificial, above or below ground, discharges into a relevant river or watercourse or into another lake or pond which is itself a relevant lake or pond. The Secretary of State is empowered to provide by order that any lake or pond which does not discharge into a relevant river or watercourse or into a relevant lake or pond is to be treated as a relevant lake or pond, or to be treated as if it were not a relevant lake or pond as the case may be.

● A 'watercourse' includes all rivers, streams, ditches, drains, cuts, culverts, dikes, sluices, sewers and passages through which water flows, except mains and other pipes which belong to the

---

24 See the Water Act 2003.
25 See s 104 WRA (below).

authority or a water undertaker or are used by a water undertaker or any other person for the purpose only of providing a supply of water to any premises.

- 'Relevant river or watercourse' means any river or watercourse, including an underground river and an artificial river or watercourse, which is neither a public sewer nor a sewer or drain which drains into a public sewer. The Secretary of State has the power to provide by order that a watercourse of a specified description is to be treated for these purposes as if it were not a relevant river or watercourse.

- The 'fresh water limit', in relation to any river or watercourse, means the place for the time being shown as the fresh water limit of that river or watercourse in the latest map deposited by the Secretary of State with the authority for that purpose.

- 'Ground waters' are defined as any waters which are contained in underground strata. Underground strata means strata subjacent to the surface of any land.

- 'Coastal waters' means waters which are within the area which extends landward from the baselines of the territorial sea as far as the limit of the highest tide or, in the case of the waters of any relevant river or watercourse, as far as the fresh water limit of the river or watercourse, together with the waters of any enclosed dock which adjoins waters within that area. The relevant territorial waters are those waters which extend seaward for three miles from the baselines from which the breadth of the territorial sea adjacent to England and Wales is measured. This definition is subject to the power of the Secretary of State to provide by order that any particular area of territorial sea adjacent to England and Wales is to be treated as if it were an area of relevant territorial waters.

- The meaning of 'controlled waters' has been considered in a number of cases.[26]

- Discharge of polluting substances (industrial effluents and sewage) into sewers is regulated by the privatised water supply and sewerage services companies.[27]

4.7 The regulator's statutory water pollution responsibilities

4.7.1 The National Rivers Authority (NRA)

Between 1989 and 1 April 1996, the National Rivers Authority (NRA) was the main regulatory body with responsibility for controlling water pollution, although it shared responsibility with Her Majesty's Inspectorate of Pollution (HMIP) in relation to those industrial processes which were then governed by the Integrated Pollution Control (IPC) regime under Pt I of the Environmental Protection Act 1990 (EPA). By virtue of s 2(1)(a)(i) of the EA 1995, the water-related (including pollution control) functions of the NRA were transferred to the Environment Agency and the NRA ceased to exist, as did the IPC functions of HMIP which were also transferred to the Environment Agency. Consequently, the Environment Agency is now the primary regulatory body which is concerned with water pollution; nevertheless, it is useful to consider at this juncture the role of the NRA during the period 1989 to 1996.

The NRA was set up in 1989 by the WA 1989 to provide integrated management of river basins and the aquatic environment in England and Wales. The constitution, functions and powers of the NRA were prescribed by the WRA 1991. The NRA was a body corporate, unlike HMIP which was part of the Department of the Environment (DoE). When the NRA was established, it inherited the functions of the water authorities relating to pollution control, water resource management, flood

---

26 See 4.9.3.7.
27 See 4.17.

defence, fisheries, navigation and conservation and recreation. The responsibilities of the NRA as laid down in s 2 of the WRA 1991 were as follows:

(a)   water resources;[28]
(b)   water pollution;[29]
(c)   flood defence and land drainage;[30]
(d)   fisheries;[31]
(e)   navigation authority, harbour authority and conservancy authority which were transferred to the NRA by virtue of Chapter V of Pt III of the WA 1989 (and other provisions);
(f)   functions assigned to the NRA by any other enactment.

The NRA was required by s 16 of the WRA 1991 to promote the conservation and enhancement of the natural beauty and amenity of inland and coastal waters and of land associated with such waters; the conservation of flora and fauna which are dependent on the aquatic environment; and the use of such waters and land for recreational purposes. The way in which the NRA was required to carry out this duty was described in the Code of Practice on Conservation, Access and Recreation which was issued pursuant to s 18(1) of the WRA 1991, and also in the Water and Sewerage (Conservation and Recreation) (Code of Practice) Order 1989.[32] The NRA also had a duty to consider water supply issues and by virtue of s 15 it had to have regard, when exercising its powers, to the duties that are imposed on any water undertakers or sewerage undertakers by Pts II–IV of the WIA 1991. During its period of operation, the NRA established itself as a strong regulator, willing to prosecute offenders where circumstances warranted prosecution.

4.7.2 The Environment Agency

By virtue of s 2 of the Environment Act 1995 (EA), the functions of the NRA under the WRA 1991 and various other statutory provisions were transferred to the Environment Agency. In addition, the

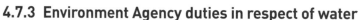 **See Chapter 2** ➡ water pollution control functions exercised by HMIP under the IPC regime[33] were also transferred to the Environment Agency, giving the Environment Agency overall control over water resources and water pollution.[34]

4.7.3 Environment Agency duties in respect of water

Section 6 of the EA 1995[35] obliges the Environment Agency, to the extent that it considers it desirable, to promote:

(a)   the conservation and enhancement of the natural beauty and amenity of inland and coastal waters and land surrounding them;
(b)   the conservation of flora and fauna which are dependent upon the aquatic environment;
(c)   the use of such waters and land for recreational purposes, taking into account the needs of the chronically sick or disabled.

---

28   Pt II of the WRA 1991.
29   Pt III of the WRA 1991.
30   Pt IV of the WRA 1991 and other enactments.
31   Pt V of the WRA 1991 and other enactments.
32   SI 1989/1152.
33   Pt I of the EPA 1990.
34   For a further discussion of the details of the transfer of functions and the reasons for the establishment of the Environment Agency, see Chapter 2.
35   See also s 19 of the WRA 1991.

With regard to water resources, the Environment Agency is also obliged[36] to take all such action as it may from time to time consider (in accordance with any directions issued by the Secretary of State) to be either necessary or expedient to conserve, redistribute or generally augment water resources in England and Wales and also to secure the proper use of water resources. This duty is described as being 'without prejudice' to the Agency's other environmental duties under s 7 of the EA 1995. The performance of the Agency's water resource management duties remains subject to its principal aims and objectives.[37] Sections 20–23 and Sched 5 to the WRA 1991 relate to the Agency's duty to devise, in conjunction with water undertakers, water resource management schemes. The Agency has the power to produce and submit draft statements to the Secretary of State for approval in respect of minimal acceptable flows of inland waters. Minimal acceptable flows are those which meet the needs of existing authorised users[38] as well as safeguarding public health. Schedule 5 contains the relevant provisions relating to publicity, consultation and procedure prior to obtaining the Secretary of State's approval of the draft statement (taking into account any representations received).

See Chapter ◀ 2

4.8 Permits

The permit is the primary vehicle through which the quality of the aquatic environment is regulated. A permit, issued by the Environment Agency,[39] is required to authorise the following activities:

(a)   a 'water discharge activity';[40]
(b)   a 'groundwater activity'.[41]

The permit system is underpinned by a range of administrative powers,[42] plus the criminal law offences contained in the Environmental Permitting (England and Wales) Regulations 2010.

Many permits relate to sewage treatment works. A person will not have committed an offence under the Environmental Permitting (England and Wales) Regulations 2010 if the discharge is carried out in accordance with the conditions included in the permit. The detailed provisions relating to the granting of permits are set out in the Environmental Permitting (England and Wales) Regulations 2010. The government, via the Secretary of State for the Environment, Food and Rural Affairs, retains a significant degree of policy control over the Environment Agency's water pollution functions. Section 40 EA 1995 provides the SoS with a wide power to issue directions to the Environment Agency (including directions relating to the Environment Agency's pollution regulation functions). Also of note to readers is the power in s 202 EA 1995 requiring the Environment Agency to make information available to the SoS, and the ss 40–41 'call in' decision-making power.[43]

---

36 S 20 of the WRA 1991.
37 See s 4 of the EA 1995 and Chapter 2.
38 Industry, agriculture and domestic (potable) consumption.
39 Also referred to as a 'discharge consent'.
40 See 4.9.1.3.
41 See 4.9.1.3.
42 See 4.14.
43 See page 130.

4.8.1 Applying for a permit

See Chapter
6.9 →

Applications for permits are made to the Environment Agency. Chapter 6 details the relevant procedure to be followed.

An application for a permit has to be made to the Environment Agency on the prescribed form accompanied by any such information that the Environment Agency may reasonably require or any information prescribed by the Secretary of State. The most important information contained in a water pollution permit application relates to the place where the polluting substances will be discharged into controlled waters, the temperature and chemical composition of the discharge, the volume, rate and timescale over which the discharge will be made. The Environment Agency has issued a Discharge Consents Manual to assist applicants and has published a charging scheme.[44]

Supplying false information to the Environment Agency is a criminal offence.[45] If the Environment Agency requires any further information from the applicant, it can serve a notice on the applicant.

4.8.2 Consultation and publicity requirements

See Chapter
6 →

The relevant consultation and publicity requirements are detailed in Chapter 6.

The Environment Agency has a discretion to dispense with publicity where it appears that the discharge will have 'no appreciable effect' on the controlled waters into which the substance or substances are to be discharged. DoE Circular 17/84 provides guidance on the circumstances in which a discharge will have no appreciable effect on the receiving waters. The Environment Agency has to allow a period of six weeks for consultees to submit their representations to the Agency, which is then required to consider any representations made, including any made by the public. The Secretary of State has the power to exempt any class of application from these consultation requirements.[46]

4.8.3 Permit conditions

On receipt of an application for an environmental permit the Environment Agency considers whether the application should be granted subject to conditions, or refused. The decision should normally be made within four months. The Environment Agency may refuse to deal with an application if the applicant has not provided all the required information or if the application is not accompanied by the appropriate fee. As far as fees are concerned, a charge is made in respect of each discharge (with the exception of minor discharges below certain thresholds).[47] Fees, based on charging schemes devised by the Environment Agency and approved by the Secretary of State, are designed to reimburse the agency's administrative costs (in particular, relating to application and monitoring). Such costs vary with the intrinsic polluting quality of the substances discharged and the quality of the receiving waters. Permits may be granted subject to such conditions as the Environment Agency thinks fit.

Conditions[48] may relate to:

44 Scheme of Charges in Respect of Applications and Consents for Discharges to Controlled Waters.
45 S 206 of the WRA 1991.
46 The consultation and publicity requirements are now contained in the Environmental Permitting (England and Wales) Regulations 2010.
47 See ss 41–42.
48 See chapter 2 of the Environmental Permitting (England and Wales) Regulations 2010.

(a) the composition of the proposed discharge, especially in regard to Biochemical Oxygen Demand (BOD), toxicity and suspended solids;

(b) volume;

(c) rate of flow;

(d) times at which discharges take place;

(e) means adopted to minimise the polluting impact of discharges;

(f) position and design of discharge pipe/outlet;

(g) provision of monitoring and metering equipment;

(h) sampling and recording, and provision of that information to the Environment Agency.

The conditions contained in each permit will reflect the quality of the waters into which the effluent is discharged. Therefore, conditions will be strict if there is a fishery or drinking water abstraction point downstream of the discharge point.

Currently, permit conditions tend to fix maximum numerical limits on the substances which make up the effluent discharge; however, at some point in the future, permits may be based on the toxicity[49] of the discharge. Any breach of the numerical limits[50] detailed in the permit conditions will be an offence,[51] but it is unlikely that the Environment Agency will prosecute isolated, 'technical' breaches of permit conditions. It is possible for the Environment Agency to specify, via a condition, the installation of abatement technology to pretreat effluent before it is discharged into controlled waters. The use of permit conditions to compel pretreatment of the discharge is rare, but note the biological pretreatment required by the Urban Waste Water Treatment Directive, and the policy preference for the discharger to have 'ownership' and control of the technology employed to meet permit conditions.

In reaching a decision upon whether or not to grant a permit, and the conditions to be included in the permit, the Environment Agency must have regard to all relevant considerations. If the Environment Agency fails to do this, its decision may be challenged by way of a judicial review application although, in practice, an appeal is more likely and is cheaper. The considerations which the Environment Agency must have regard to include:

(a) any relevant water quality standards and water quality objectives, with regard to the waters into which substances are to be discharged;

(b) the impact of the discharge on downstream users;[52]

(c) the 'cocktail' effect of the discharge when combined with upstream and downstream discharges;

(d) the Environment Agency's general and specific (water pollution) environmental duties contained in the EA 1995[53] and the WRA 1991;

(e) the responses received by the Environment Agency from consultees and members of the public in regard to the permit application;

(f) any relevant EU standards relating to both the nature of the proposed discharge and the quality of the receiving waters;

(g) any relevant EU directive, such as the Hazardous Substance Directive 76/464/EEC and the Water Framework Directive 2000/60/EC, concerning the elimination or minimisation of certain substances discharged into the aquatic environment.

---

49 That is, the toxic impact of the discharge on the receiving waters.

50 In regard to discharges from industrial premises it is common practice for the Environment Agency to set numerical limits or parameters on each substance discharged.

51 Reg 38(2) of the Environmental Permitting (England and Wales) Regulations 2010.

52 E.g., a water company abstraction point where water is abstracted for drinking use, agricultural uses such as irrigation, fisheries and any sensitive ecological sites such as Sites of Special Scientific Interest. See s 8 EA 1995.

53 Especially s 6 EA 1995.

Discharges, made by permit holders, which are made 'under and in accordance with' the relevant consent are lawful.[54] However, if any discharge contains substances not specified in the permit, this will constitute a breach of reg 38(2) of the Environmental Permitting (England and Wales) Regulations 2010.

Sections 41–42 WRA 1991 provide the Secretary of State with a 'call in' power enabling him (whether or not in response to a representation made by the applicant or the Environment Agency) to call in an application for his own determination. The Secretary of State may order a local inquiry or hearing to be held regarding the application (and must do so if requested by the applicant or the Environment Agency). At the conclusion of the inquiry or hearing, the Secretary of State may refuse the application, grant it with or without conditions, or grant it subject to the conditions which he deems appropriate.

4.8.4 Appeals

Appeals against Environment Agency permitting decisions[55] are made to the Secretary of State.[56] Appeals are generally heard by Planning Inspectors[57] and the Secretary of State is only personally involved in important appeals. An applicant can appeal to the Secretary of State against the Environment Agency's refusal to grant a permit, the conditions in the permit, a variation or revocation. The Secretary of State has four months within which to determine the appeal and failure to make a decision within that period will mean that the appeal is deemed to have been refused. Appeals are complete rehearings of the original Environment Agency decision. The relevant appeal procedures are detailed in the Environmental Permitting (England and Wales) Regulations 2010.

As to the outcome of an appeal, the Secretary of State may affirm the Environment Agency's decision on the original application or, in the case of a refusal to grant or vary a permit, he can direct the Agency to grant or vary the permit. Where the appeal relates to permit conditions, the Secretary of State can quash (cancel) as many of the conditions as he considers appropriate. Where the Environment Agency has revoked a permit, he may quash or vary the revocation. During the time it takes to conclude an appeal relating to a revocation, or a variation of conditions, the original decision of the Environment Agency is suspended pending the conclusion or withdrawal of the appeal.[58] However, no suspension will occur if the Agency reasonably believes that its original decision on the application is necessary: (a) to prevent/minimise the entry of poisonous, noxious or polluting matter and solid waste into controlled waters; and (b) to prevent harm to human health.[59] If the Agency's belief is challenged by a permit holder and is found by the Secretary of State to be unreasonable, the suspension will immediately take effect and the Agency must then compensate the permit holder for any loss sustained whilst the suspension was not effective.[60]

4.8.5 Reviewing permits

Regulation 34 of the Environmental Permitting (England and Wales) Regulations 2010 sets out the provisions relating to the review of an environmental permit. Where the Environment Agency has reviewed a permit, it has, if necessary, the power to vary the conditions of the permit or revoke the

---

54 See 4.10.
55 E.g. refusal to grant a permit, imposition of permit conditions which are unacceptable to the discharger, refusal to vary permit conditions or a decision to revoke an existing permit.
56 See reg 31 of the Environmental Permitting (England and Wales) Regulations 2010..
57 S 114 of the EA 1995.
58 See reg 31.
59 See reg 31.
60 See reg 31.

permit. The Environment Agency has used its power to review permits to tighten up permit conditions relating to sewage treatment works. Historically, the permit conditions relating to sewage treatment works were set not by reference to specific numerical limits for each substance discharged, but by reference to compliance with conditions 95 per cent of the time, averaged over a 12-month period and based on the results of sampled discharges into controlled waters. These outdated permits are gradually being varied and brought into line with all other permits which set numerical limits for each polluting substance discharged into controlled waters. The upshot of these changes is that enforcement action is made easier, since the Environment Agency may mount a prosecution based on a single discharge sample rather than a set of samples collected over a 12-month monitoring period.

4.8.6 Environment Agency compliance enforcement powers

The Environmental Permitting (England and Wales) Regulations 2010 provide the Environment Agency with a range of powers which it can use to bring environmental permit holders back into compliance with the conditions of the relevant permit. The more important of these powers are:

(i)   the power to serve an enforcement notice (reg 36);
(ii)   the power to serve a suspension notice (reg 37);
(iii)   the power to serve a revocation notice (regs 22 and 23);
(iv)   the power to serve a variation notice (reg 20).

These powers are discussed in detail in Chapter 6.

See Chapter
◀ **6**

4.8.7 Weaknesses in the permitting system

One of the main weaknesses of the permitting system of pollution control is that it only applies to specific identifiable discharges from a known spot, that is, through a pipe. Other diffuse sources of pollution such as agricultural run-off and accidental spillages cannot easily be controlled by the permit system, although criminal liability may occur in such circumstances (because a water discharge activity or groundwater activity has occurred).[61]

4.8.8 Water quality and permits

The ability to assess and classify (categorise) the quality of controlled waters is an important aspect of the WRA 1991 regulatory regime since it provides the Environment Agency with a baseline which will enable it to plan any necessary changes in discharge permit conditions either regionally or nationally.

The quality of the waters into which a polluting substance is discharged will form a key consideration with regard to the exact conditions incorporated into an individual water pollution permit. If the quality of the receiving waters is high and downstream users require that quality standard to be maintained, for example, because they own fishing rights, then the conditions attached to the permit will be strict.

In the late 1970s, the National Water Council (NWC) developed a non-statutory water classification scheme as a guide to the setting of river water quality objectives.[62] This scheme has been

---

61 See 4.9.1.3.
62 See 4.8.8.1.

superseded by a statutory scheme[63] but provides a useful insight into the link between water quality and water usage.

4.8.8.1 The NWC water classification system

The NWC water classification system reflected potential uses of water and provided for the following broad classes:

(a) High Quality—class 1a—water of high quality suitable for potable (drinkable) supply abstractions with modest treatment; game or other high class fisheries; high amenity value.

(b) Good Quality—class 1b—water of less high quality than class 1a but usable for substantially the same purposes.

(c) Fair Quality—class 2—waters suitable for potable supply after advanced treatment; supporting reasonably good coarse fisheries; moderate amenity value.

(d) Poor Quality—class 3—waters which are polluted to an extent that fish are absent or only sporadically present; may be used for low grade industrial abstraction purposes; considerable potential for further use if cleaned up.

(e) Bad Quality—class 4—waters which are grossly polluted and are likely to cause nuisance.

The NWC classification was utilised by the regulators[64] in setting non-binding water quality objectives, but the advent of the EU necessitated that the process of setting water quality objectives was put on a statutory footing.[65]

4.8.8.2 Statutory water quality standards

It was in fact the WA 1989 which introduced a system for setting statutory water quality standards and objectives, but the relevant provisions are now to be found in ss 82–84 of the WRA 1991.

Section 82 of the WRA 1991 enables the Secretary of State to make regulations which classify controlled waters into categories which reflect the standard of quality and the uses to which the water can be put, for example, drinking, bathing and fishing. The regulations specify the standard the waters must attain in order to fall within each classification. In accordance with this power, and also to implement EU directives in this area, a number of regulations have already been made, but the system is by no means complete. The classification of water is necessary before water quality objectives[66] can be established. The criteria specified in regulations made under s 82 in relation to any classification of water must consist of one or more of the following requirements:

(a) general requirements as to the purpose for which the waters to which the classification is applied are to be suitable;[67]

(b) specific requirements as to the substances that are to be present in or absent from the water and as to the concentrations of substances which are or can be present in the water;

(c) specific requirements as to the other characteristics of those waters.

The classification regulations[68] set out the parameters which waters must meet if they are to fall within a particular classification.

---

63 See ss 82–84 of the WRA 1991.
64 Originally the River Authorities.
65 In regard to the classification of the quality of water bodies see the provisions of the Water Framework Directive 2000/60/EC; at 4.21.11.
66 Under s 83.
67 In other words, water may be classified according to the use to which it will be put.
68 Based upon the requirements of the range of EU directives referred to below.

The following regulations have been introduced under s 82:

(a) the Surface Waters (Classification) Regulations 1989[69] and the Surface Waters (Abstraction for Drinking Water) (Classification) Regulations 1996.[70] These regulations give effect to the EU Abstraction Directive 75/440/EEC and prescribe a system for classifying waters according to their suitability for abstraction as drinking water;[71]

(b) the Surface Waters (Dangerous Substances) (Classification) Regulations 1989, 1992, 1997 and 1998,[72] which give effect to the EU Dangerous Substances Directive 76/464/EEC and its daughter directives by prescribing a system for classifying inland, estuarine and coastal waters according to the presence in them of concentrations of certain dangerous substances.[73] The regulations list a number of dangerous substances and state the concentration of each which should not be exceeded in fresh or marine waters;

(c) the Bathing Waters (Classification) Regulations 1991,[74] which give effect to the Bathing Waters Directive 76/160/EEC and which prescribe a system for classifying relevant territorial waters, coastal waters and inland waters which are used as bathing waters;

(d) the Surface Waters (River Ecosystem) (Classification) Regulations 1994.[75] The regulations lay down a system of classifying inland freshwaters;[76]

(e) the Surface Waters (Fishlife) (Classification) Regulations 1997[77] and the Surface Waters (Shellfish) (Classification) Regulations 1997[78] which prescribe systems for classifying freshwater fish waters and shellfish waters. The Surface Waters (Fishlife) (Classification) (Amendment) Regulations 2003[79] have amended the Surface Waters (Fishlife) (Classification) Regulations 1997.

4.8.8.3 Statutory water quality objectives

Once a range of classifications has been established under s 82 of the WRA 1991, the Secretary of State will, as required by s 83, set a Statutory Water Quality Objective (SWQO) for the relevant stretch of controlled waters. The Secretary of State serves a notice on the Environment Agency detailing a SWQO and maintains a five-yearly review of progress. The Agency is given at least three months' notice of the proposed SWQO whilst other interested persons are made aware of the SWQO via publicity. All representations received are taken into account by the Secretary of State before he confirms or varies the SWQO. Section 84 obliges the Environment Agency and the Secretary of State to use their water pollution powers to achieve the relavant SWQO. Together, ss 82–84 and 102 (a power to make regulations) enable England and Wales to comply with its EU and international legal obligations relating to water quality and water pollution. The SWQO established for each body of controlled waters will incorporate a water classification[80] as a target to be attained by the Environment Agency. In turn, the Environment Agency is under a duty[81] to exercise its functions, especially in regard to discharge permits, to achieve and maintain SWQOs. The

---

69 SI 1989/1148.
70 SI 1996/3001.
71 Waters are classified into bands DW1–DW3.
72 SI 1989/2286, SI 1992/337, SI 1997/2560 and SI 1998/389.
73 Waters are classified into bands DS1–DS7.
74 SI 1991/1597.
75 SI 1994/1057.
76 Waters are classified into bands RE1–RE5.
77 SI 1997/1331.
78 SI 1997/1332.
79 SI 2003/1053.
80 And the water quality standards referred to in the classification regulations.
81 s 84 of the WRA 1991.

Environment Agency risks a judicial review challenge if it does not exercise its powers[82] in ways which will achieve the SWQOs as far as practicable.

4.8.8.4 River quality improvements

Inland water quality is monitored and measured by the Environment Agency based upon a General Quality Assessment (GQA). The GQA covers chemical status, biological status, nutrient status and aesthetic quality. Since 1990 there have been significant improvements in the overall quality of controlled waters especially rivers. The Environment Agency's annual reports contain information relating to improvements in the quality of surface waters and groundwaters. The Environment Agency acknowledges that improvements are largely due to significant investment by water companies. Other factors are the declining pollution loads in industrial discharges, tighter limits on permit conditions and a reduction in the number of pollution incidents.

4.8.8.5 Groundwater pollution

Groundwaters are at risk due to a range of pollution risks including: leachate from landfill sites, leaks from underground fuel tanks, leaks and spillages of polluting substances and agricultural risks—sheep dips, pesticide and fertiliser use. The provisions of the Groundwater Directive 80/68/EEC[83] have been implemented in England and Wales by the Groundwater Regulations 1988[84] as amended by the Groundwater Regulations 2009. The Regulations require the permit system to prevent the direct discharge of Black List (priority hazardous substances) and Grey List substances into the aquatic environment.[85] The Regulations also regulate indirect discharges of substances (e.g. deposit of listed waste substances in landfill). The Regulations also include offences comparable to reg 38 of the Environmental Permitting (England and Wales) Regulations 2010.

4.8.9 Powers of inspection

The powers of inspection and entry by Environment Agency staff are contained within s 108 of the EA 1995.[86] The powers listed in s 108 are exercisable in respect of the Environment Agency's water pollution functions and can be used for one or more of the following purposes:

(a) determining whether any pollution control legislation has been complied with;
(b) exercising or performing its pollution control functions;
(c) determining whether, and if so, how such a function should be exercised.

The powers include the following:

(a) to enter at any reasonable time (or in an emergency at any time) any premises which the inspector believes it is necessary for him or her to enter;
(b) to make such examination and investigation as may be necessary in the circumstances;
(c) to carry out inspections, measurements, tests;
(d) to take photographs and make recordings as necessary;
(e) to remove samples of water, effluent, land or articles;
(f) to carry out experimental borings;
(g) to install and operate monitoring equipment.

---

82 For example, in regard to the grant and variation of discharge permits.
83 Revised by Directives 86/280/EC and 2006/118/EC.
84 SI 1998 1998/2746.
85 See 4.21.1.
86 These powers are discussed in Chapter 2.

The original tripartite sampling procedure contained in s 209 of the WRA 1991[87] has been replaced by s 111 of the EA 1995. Information obtained by permit conditions[88] is admissible in evidence in proceedings brought against the permit holder or any other person. Information so obtained includes data from automatic effluent sampling equipment and therefore a permit holder will be convicted on evidence which the permit holder has itself supplied. Apparatus recording relevant data is presumed to be accurate and failure to record data is treated as admissible evidence of breach of permit conditions.

4.9 Water pollution offences

4.9.1 Criminal liability underpins the environmental permitting system

Prior to the extension of environmental permitting to discharges of polluting substances to surface waters and groundwaters in 2010 the Water Resources Act 1991 established and governed a framework of water pollution controls including the legal requirement to apply for a licence (permit) to discharge pollutants into controlled waters (controlled waters are defined in s 104 WRA 1991 but typically they comprise surface waters and groundwaters). These controls were underpinned by the offences set out in s 85 WRA 1991. Section 85 was repealed by the Environmental Permitting (England and Wales) Regulations 2010 and the equivalent offences to those in s 85 WRA 1991 are now to be found in reg 38 of the 2010 Regulations.

The environmental permitting regime, in a water pollution context, is based upon the premise that if polluting discharges are to be made into either surface waters or groundwaters, those discharges will be made in accordance with an environmental permit. If a permit is not in place the discharger will have committed an offence (see reg 38(1)). In addition if a permit is in place to authorise the polluting discharges to surface waters and groundwaters an offence is committed where any condition of an environmental permit is breached (see reg 38(2)).

Whilst the relevant offences are set out in reg 38 of the 2010 permitting regulations it is necessary to refer to other parts of the permitting regulations to enable the Environment Agency to establish in a court of law that a water pollution offence has been committed. The key regulations are as follows.

4.9.1.1 Who requires a permit?

Regulation 12 provides:

> 12—(1) A person must not, except under and to the extent authorised by an environmental permit—
>
> (a) operate a regulated facility; or
> (b) cause or knowingly permit a water discharge activity or groundwater activity.
>
> (2) Paragraph 1(b) does not apply if the water discharge activity or groundwater activity is an exempt facility

4.9.1.2 What is a regulated facility?

Regulation 8 defines a regulated facility as follows:

---

87 In which the sample was immediately divided into three parts—one part was given to the permit holder, one part was retained by the NRA and the final part was sent for analysis.
88 Requiring the installation of sampling equipment by the permit holder.

8—(1) In these Regulations 'regulated facility' means any of the following—

(a) installation;
(b) mobile plant;
(c) a waste operation;
(d) a mining waste operation;
(e) a radioactive substance activity;
(f) a water discharge activity;
(g) a groundwater activity.

4.9.1.3 What is a water discharge activity and what is a groundwater activity?

Part (1) of paragraph 3 of Schedule 21 of the Regulations provides:

3—(1) 'A water discharge activity' means any of the following—

(a) the discharge or entry to inland freshwaters, coastal waters or relevant territorial waters of any—

(i) poisonous, noxious or polluting matter;
(ii) waste matter; or
(iii) trade effluent or sewage effluent;

(b) the discharge from land through a pipe into the sea outside the seaward limits of relevant territorial waters of any trade effluent or sewage effluent.

Part (1) of paragraph 3 of Schedule 22 of the Regulations provides:

3—(1) Subject to sub-paragraphs (2) and (3), 'groundwater activity' means any of the following—

(a) the discharge of a pollutant that results in the direct input of that pollutant to groundwater;
(b) the discharge of a pollutant in circumstances that might lead to an indirect input of that pollutant to groundwater;
(c) any other discharge that might lead to the direct or indirect input of a pollutant to groundwater;
(d) an activity in respect of which a notice under paragraph (10) has been served and has taken effect;
(e) an activity that might lead to a discharge mentioned in paragraph (a), (b) or (c), where the activity is carried on as part of the operation of a regulated facility of another class.

4.9.1.4 What offences are contained in regulation 38?

38(1)—It is an offence for a person to—

(a) contravene regulation 12(1); or
(b) cause or knowingly permit the contravention of regulation 12(1)(a).

(2) It is an offence for a person to fail to comply with or contravene an environmental permit condition.

(3) It is an offence for a person to fail to comply with the requirements of an enforcement notice, or of a prohibition notice, suspension notice or landfill closure notice or mining facility closure notice.

(4) It is an offence to—

    (a) fail to contravene a notice, issued under regulation 60(1), regarding the supply of information;

    (b) make a false statement;

    (c) intentionally make a false entry in records required to be kept by a permit condition.[89]

The majority of these offences are offences of strict liability. This means that it is irrelevant whether the defendant intended to cause the offence. The defendant's state of mind is not one of the elements of the offence which the prosecution must establish. As long as the defendant did the act which was a cause of the pollution incident, he will be strictly liable. In contrast, the 'knowingly permitting' offence in reg 12(1)(b) requires the prosecution to prove that the defendant was aware that a pollution incident had taken place but took no action to bring the incident to an end. Each regulation containing the words 'causing' or 'knowingly permitting' in effect contain separate methods of committing the offence (see *McLeod v Buchanan* (1940)[90]).

In summary the main offences relating to water pollution consist of:

(i) discharging pollutants into surface waters or groundwaters in circumstances in which no environmental permit is in force authorising the discharge (reg 38(1));

(ii) breaching any condition of an environmental permit (reg 38(2));

(iii) non-compliance with a range of notices including Enforcement Notices, Prohibition Notices and Suspension Notices;

(iv) Supplying false or misleading information to the Environment Agency (regs 38 (4) and (5)).

4.9.2 Regulation 38 and water pollution offences

Regulation 38 of the Environmental Permitting (England and Wales) Regulations 2010, as amended, contains the main offences relating to polluting discharges to surface waters or groundwaters. The reg 38 offences supersede the offences set out in s 85 of the Water Resources Act 1991. Whilst the key offences are contained in reg 38, it is important to understand the interplay between reg 38 and other parts of the Environmental Permitting Regulations.

The permit-based system of water pollution control assumes that a permit is in place to authorise and legitimise any polluting discharge to surface or groundwaters. Thus reg 12(1) of the 2010 Regulations requires that:

A person must not, except under and to the extent authorised by an environmental permit:

    (a) operate a regulated facility; or

    (b) cause or knowingly permit a water discharge activity or groundwater activity.[91]

In order to understand whether the Environment Agency is able to prosecute an offender, using one or more of the offences contained in reg 38, we must turn our attention to the requirement, set out in reg 12(1)(b), that a permit must be in place authorising any water discharge activity or groundwater activity. What do the phrases 'water discharge activity' and 'groundwater activity' mean? These phrases are defined in Scheds 21 and 22 to the 2010 Regulations.

---

89 Reg 38(1)–(3) accurately reproduce the offences in subss (1), (2) and (3) but subs (4) is a summary of the relevant offences. There are other parts of reg 38 which are not reproduced here.

90 *McLeod v Buchanan* (1940) 2 All ER 179.

91 Reg 12(2) para 1(b) does not apply if the water discharge activity or groundwater activity is an exempt facility.

Paragraph 3(1) of Sched 21 defines 'Water discharge activity' as:

(a) the discharge or entry to inland fresh waters, coastal waters or relevant territorial waters of any–

  (i)   poisonous, noxious or polluting matter
  (ii) waste matter, or
  (iii) trade effluent or sewage effluent

(b) the discharge from land through a pipe into the sea outside the seaward limits of relevant territorial waters of any trade effluent or sewage effluent.[92]

Paragraph 3(1) of Sched 22 defines 'groundwater activity' as any of the following:

(a) the discharge of a pollutant that results in the direct input of that pollutant to groundwater;

(b) the discharge of a pollutant in circumstances that might lead to an indirect input of that pollutant to groundwater;

(c) any other discharge that might lead to the direct or indirect input of a pollutant to groundwater;

(d) an activity in respect of which a notice under paragraph 10 has been served and has taken effect;

(e) an activity that might lead to a discharge mentioned in paragraph (a), (b), or (c), where that activity is carried on as part of the operation of a registered facility of another class.[93]

The word 'pollution', in regard to a water discharge activity or groundwater activity, is defined in reg 2 as:

the direct or indirect introduction, as a result of human activity, of substances or heat into the air, water or land which may –

(a) be harmful to human health or the quality of aquatic ecosystems or terrestrial ecosystems directly depending on aquatic ecosystems

(b) result in damage to material property, or

(c) impair or interfere with amenities or other legitimate uses of the environment.

Having considered reg 12, reg 2 and Scheds 22 and 23, we can now turn our attention to reg 38. Regulation 38(1) states:

It is an offence for a person to–

(a) contravene regulation 12(1); or

(b) cause or knowingly permit the contravention of regulation 12(1)(a).

---

92 There are other subparas of para 3 of Sched 21 which are not reproduced here. In particular, para 3(2) contains exemptions relating to activities which will not fall within the definition of a water discharge activity.

93 Para 3(2) of Sched 22 contains exemptions relating to activities which will not fall within the definition of a groundwater activity. Para 10 of Sched 22 refers to a notice, served by the Environment Agency, requiring an environmental permit to be applied for to authorise the relevant activity.

Other offences, contained in reg 38, include:

(2) It is an offence for a person to fail to comply with or contravene an environmental permit condition.

(3) It is an offence for a person to fail to comply with the requirements of an enforcement notice, or of a prohibition notice, suspension notice or landfill closure notice or mining facility closure notice.

(4) It is an offence to –

(a) fail to contravene a notice, issued under regulation 60(1), regarding the supply of information;

(b) make a false statement;

(c) intentionally make a false entry in records required to be kept by a permit condition.[94]

All the elements (i.e. the key words and phrases) of each of the offences in reg 38 must be established if the polluter is to be successfully prosecuted and convicted of a reg 38 offence. The reg 38(1)(b) offence may be both 'caused' and 'knowingly permitted'. Thus there are two ways in which this offence may be committed. A person who 'causes' a reg 38(1)(b) offence does not need to be aware that what he is doing constitutes an offence. Simply engaging in the activity is enough to cause the offence and the defendant's state of mind is not one of the elements of the offence which the prosecution need establish. This type of offence is referred to as an offence of strict liability. In contrast a person who 'knowingly permits' an activity must be aware that what he is doing contravenes the law. Offences usually have two elements: the act itself (*actus reus*) and a mental element (*mens rea*). In offences of strict liability it is not necessary to establish the mental element. In contrast, in 'knowingly permitting' offences, the prosecution must establish both the *actus reus* and the *mens rea*.

4.9.3 Elements of the permitting offences

If the Environment Agency decides to prosecute an alleged polluter,[95] it must be able to establish that each element of the relevant offence is present before it can prove its case to the satisfaction of the court and obtain a conviction. A number of the key words or phrases which appear in reg 38 of the Environmental Permitting (England and Wales) Regulations 2010 require consideration in order to grasp the judicial interpretation of those words and phrases.[96]

4.9.3.1 Causing

The leading cases on the meaning of 'causing' water pollution are the House of Lords decisions in *Alphacell Ltd v Woodward* (1972)[97] and *Empress Car Company (Abertillery) Ltd v NRA* (1998).[98] In the *Alphacell* case, the defendant paper manufacturer was charged with an offence, under s 2 of the Rivers (Prevention of Pollution) Act 1951, of causing polluting matter to enter a river. This offence is

---

94 Reg 38(1), (2) and (3) accurately reproduce the relevant offences but reg 38(4) is a summary of the relevant offences. There are also other parts of reg 38 which are not reproduced here.

95 The Environment Agency has a discretion to mount a prosecution or it may use its powers to bring the polluter back into compliance with environmental law.

96 See the examples of common pollution problems resulting in prosecutions on page 151.

97 *Alphacell Ltd v Woodward* [1972] 2 WLR 1320; [1972] All ER 475.

98 *Empress Car Co (Abertillery) Ltd v National Rivers Authority* [1998] 1 All ER 481; [1998] Env LR 396.

similar to s 85(1) of the WRA 1991. Settling tanks in the defendant's paper factory overflowed when vegetation clogged up the pumps which maintained the level of effluent in the tanks. The tanks filled up and overflowed, causing polluting matter to enter a stream. An overflow channel led directly from the tanks to the stream. Although the factory had a permit, this could not save the defendant company from prosecution because the conditions attached to the permit were breached when the settling tank effluent entered the stream. Alphacell argued unsuccessfully that it had not caused the polluting matter to enter the stream; rather, the presence of vegetation (a natural cause or natural event) in its settling tanks was the real cause of the incident. Rejecting Alphacell's submission, the court held that the act of constructing and operating the effluent tanks was a positive and deliberate act which led to the overflow which caused the pollution of the stream. By constructing the settling tank overflow channel the defendant must have considered the possibility that the pump maintaining the level of effluent in the settling tanks might malfunction with the result that effluent would be discharged into the stream. Lord Wilberforce stated:

> In my opinion, 'causing' here must be given a common sense meaning and I deprecate the introduction of refinements such as *causa*, effective cause or *novus actus*. There may be difficulties where acts of third parties or natural forces are concerned but I find the present case comparatively simple. The appellants abstract water, pass it through their works where it becomes polluted, conduct it to a settling tank communicating directly with the stream, into which the polluted water will inevitably flow if the level rises over the overflow point.

The test set out in the *Alphacell* decision relating to the meaning of 'causing' water pollution simply requires the defendant to carry on an activity which gives rise to a pollution incident. Provided the defendant's activities could be said to be intentional (e.g. operating an industrial process), all that was necessary to prove liability was to establish a link between the defendant's activities and the pollution of controlled waters.

Alphacell has been applied in Scotland,[99] Australia,[100] and in a number of English cases, including *FJH Wrothwell v Yorkshire Water Authority* (1984)[101] and *Southern Water Authority v Pegrum* (1989).[102]

In the period 1975–95, some dilution of the original *Alphacell* interpretation of 'causing' water pollution occurred. In *Price v Cromack* (1975),[103] a farmer contracted with a company to allow the storage of liquid animal waste (slurry) in lagoons erected on the farmer's land. One lagoon wall failed and a serious water pollution incident occurred. The farmer was acquitted of causing water pollution as he had only permitted the accumulation of polluting matter and had done nothing positive to cause the pollution.

Eighteen years later, in *Wychavon District Council v NRA* (1993),[104] the defendant local authority successfully appealed against its conviction for causing water pollution.[105] The defendant had entered into a contract with Severn Trent Water Authority to operate and maintain part of Severn Trent's sewerage system. A blockage occurred in one of the pipes which the defendant did not promptly discover and rectify. This resulted in a pollution incident. The High Court refused to convict the defendant. The defendant had not caused the pollution, because what the defendant had done (failing to detect and repair a blockage) was not a positive act which was, in law, the cause of

---

99 *Lockhart v NCB* 1981 SLT 161.
100 *Marjury v Sunbeam Corp Ltd* (1974) 1 NSWLR 659.
101 *Wrothwell (FJH) v Yorkshire Water Authority* [1984] Crim LR 43.
102 *Southern Water Authority v Pegrum* [1989] Crim LR 442.
103 *Price v Cromack* [1975] 1 WLR 988; [1975] 2 All ER 113.
104 *Wychavon District Council v NRA* [1993] 2 All ER 440.
105 Contrary to s 107(1)(a) of the WA 1989.

the pollution. Similarly, in *NRA v Welsh Development Agency* (1993),[106] the defendant escaped liability because it was held not to have actively caused the pollution despite the fact that it had designed, constructed and maintained the industrial estate drainage system which conducted polluting substances (which had escaped from one of the units on the industrial estate) into controlled waters.

The tide in favour of a strict interpretation of 'causing' began to turn in the mid-1990s. In *NRA v Yorkshire Water Services Ltd* (1995),[107] the prosecution argued that the law had taken a wrong turning by insisting that a positive act by the defendant causing the pollution was an essential prerequisite of liability. Although the House of Lords did not overrule *Wychavon*, it confined it to its particular facts. In the same year, the Court of Appeal in *Attorney General's Reference (No 1 of 1994)* (1995) held that: (a) 'causing' offences could be committed by more than one person where each person's act had formed part of the causal chain; (b) a defendant (sewage treatment company) which, due to a defect in its pumping system, accepted and disposed of polluting matter into controlled waters had caused a pollution, since what it had done amounted to a chain of operations which was a cause of the pollution; and (c) the failure properly to maintain the sewage treatment system, despite the fact that someone else had undertaken responsibility for its day-to-day running, entitled a jury to find the defendant guilty of causing the relevant offence.

The return to *Alphacell*'s strict liability interpretation of causing pollution occurred three years later in the House of Lords in *Empress Car Company (Abertillery) Ltd v NRA* (1998).[108] The decision in *Empress Cars* concerned the prosecution of a car sales company for causing red diesel fuel to enter controlled waters contrary to s 85(1) of the WRA 1991. The defendants maintained a fuel storage tank on their site. The tank was protected by a bund (a barrier built around a tank to contain spillages) wall. Standing outside the bund was a small drum which was connected to the tank by a rubber hose. From time to time, the defendants would take fuel from the drum. The open/close valve on the tank was not lockable and site security was poor. A trespasser entered the site and opened the valve on the tank. Red diesel flowed from the tank, via the rubber hose, to the drum, which rapidly filled up and overflowed. The fuel oil escaping from the metal drum, which was standing outside the protection of the bund, flowed into a surface water drain and from there entered controlled waters. The defendant argued that it had not caused the resultant pollution but had merely created the circumstances whereby a trespasser could enter the site, open storage tank valve and cause the pollution. The defendant submitted that the act of the trespasser broke the chain of causation linking the defendant to the pollution and absolved it of liability. The House of Lords rejected this argument and found the defendant guilty.

Lord Hoffmann gave the leading judgment of the court in which he laid down five key guides for judges and magistrates who might be faced with determining the question who or what had caused a water pollution incident. First, the relevant court should require the prosecution to identify what it was that the defendant had done to cause pollution. If the defendant had not done anything at all, then the prosecution for 'causing' must fail. The prosecution need not prove that what the defendant did was the *immediate* cause of the pollution. Maintaining the storage tank was doing something, even if the immediate cause of the pollution was lack of maintenance, a natural event, or the act of a third party, such as a trespasser. Once it had been established that the defendant had done something, the court must then decide whether what the defendant had done was *a* cause of the pollution. It was quite conceivable that a single pollution incident would have several causes. If the defendant had done something which had produced a situation in which a polluting substance could escape into controlled waters, but a necessary precondition of that escape was the

---

106 *National Rivers Authority v Welsh Development Agency* [1993] Env LR 407; [1995] 1 All ER 225; [1994] Env LR 177.
107 *National Rivers Authority v Yorkshire Water Services Ltd* (1995) 1 AC 444.
108 *Empress Car Co (Abertillery) Ltd v National Rivers Authority*, n 94.

act of a third party or a natural event, then the court had to consider whether that act or event *was a normal fact of life or was something extraordinary*. If it was a matter of ordinary occurrence (something normal), it would not break the chain of causation and the defendant would be liable for causing the pollution. Only extraordinary or abnormal events act to break the chain of causation.

The *Empress Cars* case has important ramifications for defendants charged with causing water pollution. Liability has been extended to situations in which the defendant fails to take appropriate steps to guard against the actions of trespassers and other third parties (e.g. vandals), equipment failure or natural events. The Hoffmann test for events which operate to break or interrupt the causal chain has created a situation in which s 85(1) WRA 1991 creates almost absolute liability for escapes of pollutants into controlled waters. The prospect that a defendant will be able to establish that an extraordinary event has occurred is very slim indeed. It is also clear from the judgment of Lord Clyde that a failure to take precautions in relation to the risk of an escape of polluting substances will amount to 'doing something' for the purposes of establishing liability.

This very strict judicial approach to liability will be tempered by Environment Agency enforcement and prosecution policy limiting the number of prosecutions commenced. However, a very strict rule of liability may act as a disincentive to businesses which take their environmental management responsibilities seriously. They may be disinclined to invest in pollution prevention if the courts will hold them strictly liable for causing water pollution irrespective of the efforts they have made to control polluting emissions.[109]

The Hoffmann test may be difficult to apply in practice. A terrorist bomb which damages storage tanks and causes a pollution incident may well be an extraordinary event if it occurs in rural North Yorkshire but may not be extraordinary in Northern Ireland. The test is a 'fact and degree' test (that is, it depends on the particular circumstances). The *Empress* decision has been applied in subsequent decided cases. In *Environment Agency v Brock plc* (1998), the failure of a valve on a hose during a pumping operation caused leachate from a landfill site to spray out and enter controlled waters via a ditch. The defendant was convicted of the s 85(1) WRA 1991 offence, irrespective of the fact that the immediate cause of the pollution was defective equipment. There was no evidence that the defendant had been in any way negligent. The escape of polluting substances had occurred due to a latent defect (pipework seal failure). See the comparable cases of *CPC (UK) Ltd v NRA* (1995)[110] and *Express Dairies Distribution v Environment Agency* (2003),[111] confirming that a pollution incident caused by a tyre 'blowout' which damaged a milk tanker (and which in turn caused a pollution of surface waters) was not an extraordinary event absolving the defendant, although the defendant was able to take advantage of a statutory defence which covered such emergency situations.[112]

It is submitted that the defendant in *Environment Agency v Brock plc*[113] was rightly convicted because the design of the landfill leachate collection system was something which was under the defendant's control. The failure of the hose seal, although a rare occurrence, was not an extraordinary event. In *Environment Agency v British Steel plc* (1999),[114] the defendant was charged with causing polluting matter (mill coolant) to enter controlled waters contrary to s 85(1) WRA 1991. The defendant submitted that the combined failure of a hose, which had been poorly installed by one of its employees, and the failure of a sub-contractor's employee[115] to act appropriately in response to alarms (audible and visual alarms were ignored) warning of an impending pollution was an

---

109 See *CPC (UK) Ltd v NRA* (1995) Env LR 131 in which an undiscoverable latent defect in pipework did not absolve the defendant company of liability, but the strict liability nature of the offence was mitigated by the court when it imposed a minimal sanction.

110 n 109.

111 *Express Dairies Distribution v Environment Agency* [2003] EWHC 448. See 4.10.1.

112 See 4.10.2.

113 *Environment Agency v Brock plc* [1998] Env LR 607.

114 *Environment Agency v British Steel plc* (1999) 29 ENDS, December.

115 A security guard in the employ of RCO, a security company employed by British Steel.

extraordinary event absolving the defendant of liability. The stipendiary magistrate who heard the case applied the Hoffmann test and convicted the defendant. It is clear from this decision that the court was not diverted from a strict interpretation of 'causing' by the fact that the immediate cause of the pollution incident was the failure of the defendant's agent to respond to an alarm.

4.9.3.2 Intervening acts of third parties and vicarious liability

In the event of an escape of polluting substances from company premises or other land into controlled waters, a defendant company cannot escape conviction for causing a water pollution offence by blaming an employee who was the immediate cause of the pollution (provided the employee was acting within the terms of his employment contract). The defendant company is *vicariously* liable for the acts or omissions of its employees who are acting within the terms of their employment contracts and on the authority of *NRA v McAlpine Homes East Ltd* (1994),[116] it is not necessary for the prosecution to prove that the controlling officers of the company were directly involved in the incident. It is sufficient that an employee was responsible for the act or omission which caused the pollution.[117]

Prior to the *Empress Cars* decision, it was possible for a defendant to escape liability in circumstances in which a third party, such as a trespasser, vandal or independent contractor, had intervened to break the causal chain linking the defendant to the pollution. Such third party acts are not defences, but operate to negate the 'causing' element of the relevant offence. In such circumstances, the third party's act has supervened the defendant's act and relegated it to one of the background circumstances. In *Impress (Worcester) Ltd v Rees* (1971),[118] a vandal entered Impress's premises at night and opened a valve on an unbunded fuel tank which allowed fuel to escape from the site, enter and pollute a river. The defendant company's conviction was quashed (cancelled) by the High Court on the ground that the defendant's conduct (operating the premises) was not a cause at all, but was merely part of the surrounding circumstances.[119] The House of Lords in *Empress Cars* has overruled *Impress* and has drastically restricted the circumstances in which third party acts will operate as a supervening cause to absolve the defendant of legal liability.[120]

4.9.3.3 Knowingly permitting

Water pollution offences such as reg 38(1) of the Environmental Permitting (England and Wales) Regulations 2010 and s 4(1) of the Salmon and Freshwater Fisheries Act 1975 may be 'knowingly permitted'. Liability is established in circumstances in which the defendant has knowledge of ongoing pollution yet fails to act to put a stop to it. As it is necessary to establish the defendant's knowledge of water pollution, this offence is not an offence of strict liability. This may well explain the few prosecutions brought by the Environment Agency and its predecessors. In *Schulmans Inc v NRA* (1993),[121] Schulmans was charged with two 'knowingly permitting' offences.[122] Fuel oil from a tank standing on the defendant's premises escaped into a nearby brook. The defendant was acquitted of the charges because there was no proof that the defendant could have acted sooner than it did to prevent the pollution occurring. The prosecution could not establish all the elements of the offence and in particular that: (a) the defendant was aware of the spillage of fuel oil; (b) the polluting matter had entered the surface water drainage system which discharged into controlled waters;

---

116 *National Rivers Authority v McAlpine Homes East Ltd* [1994] 4 All ER 286.
117 In this case, two employees on a building site allowed concrete to enter and pollute a stream.
118 *Impress (Worcester) Ltd v Rees* (1971) 2 All ER 357.
119 See also *Welsh Water Authority v Williams Motors (Cymdu) Ltd* (1988) The Times, 5 December and *National Rivers Authority v Wright Engineering Co Ltd* [1994] 4 All ER 281.
120 See the discussion relating to Lord Hoffmann's distinction between normal and extraordinary acts or events on pages 141–142 above.
121 *Schulmans Inc v NRA* [1993] Env LR D 1.
122 Under s 107(1)(a) of the WA 1989 and s 4(1) of the SFFA 1975.

(c) unless prompt action was taken, a pollution would occur; and (d)[123] the defendant was aware of the extent of the pollution.

Price v Cromack (1975)[124] provides a useful illustration of the difference between the 'causing' offence and the offence of 'knowingly permitting'. A farmer was charged with 'causing' water pollution when a lagoon on his land failed and waste animal products were released into a river. The farmer had a contract with an animal products firm which allowed the firm to discharge animal waste products into the lagoons on the farmer's land. The farmer was acquitted of the 'causing' charge on the basis that he had not caused the pollution. Whilst he had permitted the build-up of the waste on his land, he could not be said to have caused the pollution. Had he been charged with knowingly permitting pollution, then the verdict would probably have been different. Following the Empress Cars decision, the courts would convict the defendant in Price v Cromack for causing a water pollution incident because constructing and maintaining effluent lagoons on your land is doing something and is therefore a cause of the resulting pollution incident.

4.9.3.4 Enter

The term 'enter', referred to in the definition of water discharge activity in para 3 of Sched 21 of the Environmental Permitting (England and Wales) Regulations 2010, refers to a wide range of circumstances in which polluting matter may enter surface waters. The term 'enter' covers situations in which polluting matter is deliberately introduced into controlled waters, such as the deliberate pouring of the contents of a drum of pesticides into a stream, accidental spillages of polluting matter into surface drains, leaky pipes and tanks which cause polluting matter to escape into surface waters and groundwaters, and 'run-off' from farmers' fields which enter a river over a wide area. 'Enter' covers the introduction of polluting substances into controlled waters from both point (pipe) and diffuse (run-off) sources.

4.9.3.5 Discharge

The term 'discharge', referred to in the definition of water discharge activity in para 3 of Sched 21, refers to discharges from pipes, channels, or similar features (e.g. conduits). It is possible that polluting matter from a single incident could both enter and be discharged into controlled waters. If an unprotected oil storage tank (for example, a tank with no protective surrounding barrier or bund) were to rupture on an industrial site situated adjacent to a river or canal, some of the escaping oil could flow into the surface drains of the industrial estate and be discharged (because the drains lead directly to the nearest stream) into controlled waters, whilst a further quantity of oil could flow down the river or canal bank (or spray out of the tank directly into a stream) and enter controlled waters.

4.9.3.6 Poisonous, noxious or polluting

This term, referred to in the definition of water discharge activity in para 3 of Sched 21, has a wide meaning which is not restricted to its impact upon human health. Poisonous matter entering or discharged into controlled waters is often associated with large fish kills and is therefore largely unproblematic from an evidentiary perspective. 'Polluting' may cover the discharge of dyes or detergents (also shopping trolleys and tyres) into controlled waters in quantities which may do little damage to the ecology of the receiving waters but are polluting in the sense that they damage the amenity of controlled waters. Streams will be discoloured by the presence of dyes and banks of foam (the latter caused by the presence of detergents) are unsightly (as are tyres, shopping trolleys, etc.). In NRA v Egger (UK) Ltd (1992),[125] the court held that the term 'polluting' requires the substance

---

123 With regard to s 4(1) of the SFFA only.
124 Price v Cromack (1975) 1 WLR 988.
125 National Rivers Authority v Egger (UK) Ltd [1992] Env LR 130.

which has entered controlled waters to have the likelihood or capability of causing harm to humans, animals and plants. In R v Dovermoss Ltd (1995),[126] the defendant argued that slurry which had contaminated a spring could only be 'polluting matter' if actual harm had resulted from its introduction into controlled waters. The Court of Appeal held that the definition of 'polluting' should be based on the Oxford English Dictionary's definition—'to make physically impure, foul or filthy; to dirty, stain, taint, befoul'. Polluting material was the 'sort of material which, if introduced into the water reduces the quality of the water'. On this basis, the court held that there was no need to prove actual harm. The question was whether the matter was capable of causing or likely to cause harm to controlled waters. Whether or not a substance has polluted water is a question of fact.

The Dovermoss case illustrates the fact that water pollution offences focus upon the release, whether deliberate or accidental, of poisonous, noxious or polluting matter into controlled waters. The focus is not on whether the release results in a pollution incident but on the discharge/entry of substances which have the capability to cause harm to the aquatic environment. If it were otherwise, a polluter might escape liability merely because he was fortunate to discharge substances into a river whilst it was in flood, thereby causing no harm to the receiving waters.

4.9.3.7 Controlled waters

The term 'controlled waters', defined in s 104 of the Water Resources Act 1991, establishes the geographical remit of the Environment Agency's water pollution authority. The term formed an important element of the offences (now repealed) contained in s 85 WRA 1991. There is a degree of overlap between the definition in s 104 WRA 1991 and the references in the environmental permitting regulations to inland fresh waters, coastal waters, groundwaters and territorial waters.

In R v Dovermoss Ltd (1995), the Court of Appeal was asked to interpret the meaning of the term 'controlled waters'. In this case, Welsh Water had received a number of taste complaints from consumers whose drinking water had been supplied from a spring. It was discovered, following investigations, that the water contained excessive amounts of ammonia which were traced back to two fields adjacent to the stream. The fields were owned by Dovermoss Ltd. Slurry had been spread on these fields. As a result of a heavy rainfall, the stream had deviated from its normal course (i.e. it was in flood) and ran over the slurry-covered fields into the spring, thus causing contamination. Dovermoss was charged and convicted causing polluting matter to enter controlled waters contrary to s 85 of the WRA 1991. Dovermoss appealed on a number of grounds. One of its arguments was that the water, which had been diverted from its normal course, was no longer controlled waters within the meaning of s 104 of the WRA 1991. The Court of Appeal held that the term 'controlled waters' included 'waters of any watercourse', not, as it was argued, water in any watercourse. The court went further and stated that the term 'watercourse' refers to the channel rather than the water itself. Consequently, waters from a watercourse (such as the stream) remain controlled waters even where the water has departed from its normal course (e.g. whilst in flood).

In Environment Agency v Brock plc (1998),[127] the court held that a man-made ditch could fall within the definition of controlled waters provided the ditch connected to and drained into controlled waters. In National Rivers Authority v Biffa Waste [1996][128] it was held that a river bed does form part of controlled waters. Readers should note that the media (pipes) which conduct drinking water and sewage effluent are not controlled waters.

---

126 R v Dovermoss Ltd [1995] Env LR 258; [1995] ELM 106.
127 Environment Agency v Brock plc, n 109.
128 National Rivers Authority v Biffa Waste [1996] Env LR 227.

4.9.3.8 Discharge

The term 'discharge' is synonymous with the entry of substances into controlled waters via a pipe, channel, or conduit from a point source. Arguably a 'discharge' would also include liquid poured from a drum or similar receptacle into controlled waters.

4.9.4 Regulation 38(2) of the Environmental Permitting (England and Wales) Regulations 2010

Breach of any of the conditions of a permit is an offence of strict liability. In the case of a minor breach, the Environment Agency is unlikely to prosecute, unless breaches are persistent. A separate reg 38(2) offence is committed on each occasion a breach of condition occurs.[129] Permits may contain a condition banning the discharge of any substances not specifically referred to in the permit. It is most unlikely, in view of the Court of Appeal's decision in R v Ettrick Trout Co Ltd v Baxter (1994),[130] that in a reg 38(2) prosecution the defendant will evade liability by challenging the validity of the permit conditions in the reg 38(2) criminal proceedings. In Ettrick, the defendants, who ran a fish farm, were alleged to have breached a condition of their permit by exceeding the volume of effluent which could be discharged into controlled waters in any 24-hour period. They attempted to challenge the validity of the relevant condition in the criminal proceedings.[131] They argued that the condition had been unlawfully imposed for water abstraction control purposes rather than pollution control. The Court of Appeal rejected this submission and held that this type of collateral challenge was clearly an attempt to bypass the judicial review and statutory appeal procedures, and was an abuse of process.[132]

4.9.5 Criminal personal liability of senior officers of companies and other similar organisations

Regulation 41 of the Environmental Permitting (England and Wales) Regulations 2010, which replaces s 217 of the Water Resources Act 1991 (and other similarly worded offences), enables senior officers of corporate bodies (i.e. directors and senior managers of companies and other organisations with legal personality) to be prosecuted in his/her personal capacity for offences committed by the corporate body.

Where a body corporate is guilty of an offence, for example breach of reg 38 of the Environmental Permitting (England and Wales) Regulations 2010, any of the corporate officers specified in reg 41 may be prosecuted in his/her personal capacity if he/she has consented to the offence committed by the corporate body or he/she has connived at the commission of an offence by the corporate body or the offence committed by the corporate body is attributable to the neglect of the relevant corporate officer.

Regulation 41 provides:

> Where a body corporate is guilty of an offence . . . and that offence is proved to have been committed with the consent or connivance of, or to be attributable to, any neglect on the part of any director, member of the committee of management, chief executive, manager, secretary, or other similar officer . . . or any person purporting to act in such a capacity then he, as well as the body corporate, shall be guilty of that offence.

---

129 *Severn Trent Water Authority v Express Foods Group Ltd* (1988) 153 JP 126.
130 R v Ettrick Trout Co Ltd v Baxter [1994] Env LR 165.
131 Prosecution for breach of s 85(6) WRA 1991.
132 See R v Wicks [1998] 2 AC 92 and Boddington v British Transport Police [1999] 2 AC 143.

Readers should be alerted to the fact that there are difficulties in successfully prosecuting a manager or director in a large company where the senior corporate officers are often 'shielded' from awareness of wrongdoing and/or poor practice by layers of middle management responsibility. A successful prosecution under reg 41 is much more likely in a small company in which the senior corporate officers, such as the managing director, are intimately concerned with the day-today running of the business.

Readers should also note the 'controlling officer' test (sometimes referred to as the identification doctrine), to establish who is a manager for the purposes of the reg 41 offence.

See Chapter
◀ 5.17.8

Regulation 41 is drafted in wider terms than s 217 of the Water Resources Act 1991 (now repealed). Regulation 41 includes references to a 'member of the committee of management' and the 'chief executive', terms that were not present in s 217 of the Water Resources Act 1991.

4.9.6 The Salmon and Freshwater Fisheries Act 1975 (SFFA 1975)

Section 4(1) of the SFFA 1975 provides that it is an offence where a person 'causes or knowingly permits to flow, or puts, or knowingly permits to be put, into waters containing fish or into any tributaries of waters containing fish, any liquid or solid matter to such an extent as to cause the waters to be poisonous or injurious to fish or the spawning grounds, spawn or food of fish'. A prosecution may be brought under s 4 of the SFFA 1975 where fish or their spawning grounds are damaged.

4.10 Defences

4.10.1 Authorised (permitted) discharges to surface waters and groundwaters

Any legal person who has applied for, been granted, and has complied with the conditions attached to an environmental permit will have a defence to any alleged offence relating to polluting discharges to surface waters or groundwaters. In addition it will also be a defence to a prosecution if the relevant discharge was made in accordance with:

(a) a licence granted by the Ministry of Agriculture (now Defra) under Pt II of the Food and Environment Protection Act 1985;[133]

(b) s 163 of the WRA 1991 or s 165 of the WIA 1991;[134]

(c) any local statutory provision or statutory order[135] which expressly confers power to discharge effluent into water; or

(d) any prescribed enactment.[136]

The primary defence to the offences contained in reg 38(1), (2) and (3) is detailed in reg 40, which provides in subs (1):

> 40—(1) It is a defence for a person charged with an offence under regulation 38 (1), (2) or (3) to prove that the acts alleged to constitute the contravention were done in an emergency to avoid danger to human health in a case where—

---

133 Authorising the deposit of waste at sea.
134 Concerned with discharges for works purposes.
135 E.g., a drought order.
136 Primary or secondary legislation.

(a) the person took all such steps as were reasonably practicable in the circumstances for minimising the pollution; and

(b) particulars of the acts were furnished to the regulator as soon as reasonably practicable after they were done.

This emergency defence is limited to acts which are designed to avoid danger to human health but not acts which would avoid damage to the environment. Regulation 40 corresponds to the former defence, to a s 85 WRA 1991 charge, contained in s 89(1)(a) of the Water Resources Act 1991.

In *Express Ltd t/a Express Dairies Distribution v Environment Agency* (2003),[137] the High Court considered the circumstances in which the statutory defence to a s 85 WRA 1991 prosecution could apply. Under s 89(1)(a) of the WRA 1991, it was a defence to a s 85 charge if the pollution is caused in order to avoid danger to life or health.

The defendant's milk tanker suffered a tyre 'blowout' on the M5 and the incident damaged a delivery pipe, causing 4,000 litres of milk to escape and enter controlled waters (when the driver pulled onto the hard shoulder and the milk entered surface drains). The driver took prompt action to stop the spillage and contacted the emergency services. The defendant was convicted of a s 85 WRA 1991 offence (an offence of strict liability) in the relevant magistrates' court. The magistrates rejected the defendant's submission that the driver had pulled onto the hard shoulder to avoid danger to life or health, preferring to view the cause of the pollution as the 'blowout'. The defendant appealed against its conviction to the High Court by way of case stated. The question the High Court was required to consider was:

> whether the s 89 statutory defence is available in circumstances in which the entry[138] is caused or permitted or the discharge is made as a result of an emergency in which a person acts so as to avoid danger to life or health or whether the statutory defence is limited to circumstances in which the entry or discharge is itself the emergency occasioned to avoid danger to life or health.

Hale LJ allowed the appeal. Although, in the opinion of the court, there was no break in the causal chain from the blowout to the pollution (that is, no 'extraordinary event' to break the causal chain), nevertheless, the defence applied. The court was entitled to focus on the latter part of the causal chain (that is, the driver's decision to pull onto the hard shoulder to reduce the risk of a road traffic accident caused by the presence of milk on the carriageway) rather than the immediate cause of the incident (the blowout)—which the magistrates had done. Thus, the driver's actions fell within the wording of the statutory defence.

4.11 Proving water pollution

In carrying out their investigations, Environment Agency inspectors have the power to take samples of water or effluent, which may later be used as evidence in court to substantiate a criminal case.[139] Evidence of pollution must be 'sufficient' if the Agency is to commence a criminal prosecution.

See Chapter 2.4.15.2→

Many permits include a condition requiring the discharger to (a) install monitoring equipment and (b) transmit those monitoring results to the Environment Agency. The monitoring results are admissible[140] in evidence in court proceedings. It is presumed that the defendant's monitoring

---

137 *Express Dairies Distribution v Environment Agency* [2003] EWHC 448.
138 Of the pollutant into controlled waters.
139 S 108 of the EA 1995.
140 S 111 EA 1995.

equipment is functioning properly, although a defendant may adduce evidence to establish that the equipment was not recording accurately.

4.12 Enforcement

4.12.1 Environment Agency enforcement powers

The Environment Agency has various powers (in particular the service of an Enforcement Notice)[141] at its disposal which enable it to ensure that permit holders comply with discharge permit conditions, to investigate any breaches of permits and also to detect and investigate pollution incidents. The Environment Agency can exercise control through the permit system, using its power to prohibit certain discharges or by varying or revoking a permit. The Environment Agency may also decide to bring criminal proceedings against a person who contravenes the relevant water-related legislation. In deciding what action to take, the Agency will be mindful of its s 39 EA 1995 cost/benefit duty and the contents of its published enforcement policy.

See Chapter ◀ 2

4.12.2 Enforcement policy

Whether the Environment Agency chooses to enforce compliance with environmental law by means of a prosecution will, to some extent, depend upon the Environment Agency's Enforcement and Prosecution Policy. Essentially, the Environment Agency bases its decision whether or not to prosecute upon the aggravating and mitigating circumstances surrounding the commission of the alleged relevant offence (plus sufficient evidence on which to base a prosecution). Of particular significance will be the severity of environmental damage resulting from the pollution incident.

See Chapter ◀ 2.4.15

The Environment Agency[142] has introduced a Common Incident Classification Scheme (CICS) to record and classify pollution incidents and provide guidance on the appropriate enforcement response.

The Environment Agency's CICS divides water pollution incidents into the following categories based upon their severity:

Category 1   major incidents resulting in any of the following impacts: extensive fish kill; major and/or frequent breach of permit conditions; closure of potable (drinkable) water abstraction point; extensive remediation required; actual and/or potential persistent effect on water quality and/or aquatic life; significant adverse affect on amenity; and significant effect on an important conservation site.

Category 2   significant incidents resulting in any of the following: significant fish kill; water abstractors notified (water companies, farms, industry, etc.); readily observable effect on aquatic invertebrates; stock watering ban necessary; watercourse bed contamination; and amenity value reduced (odour, appearance, etc.) to downstream users.

Category 3   minor incidents with localised impacts.

Category 4   incidents with no environmental impact.

Unfortunately the Environment Agency's published statistics on enforcement do not detail the number of breaches of water pollution permits. Prosecutions which are commenced tend to focus

---

141 See 4.14.3.
142 Access the Environment Agency's website (www.environment-agency.gov.uk) and search for the Common Incident Classification Scheme.

on serious (Categories 1 and 2) incidents which attract media attention rather than on persistent breaches of permit conditions.

Category 1 incidents, because of their severity, will often result in prosecution; however, the Environment Agency has a discretion whether to prosecute or deploy some other response to ensure that the polluter is brought back into compliance with environmental law. Readers are recommended to study the contents of the EA's enforcement and sanctions guidance document (which contains a range of public interest factors) and the EA's offence response options guidance, both of which the EA uses to guide its compliance enforcement response. A Category 2 incident usually results in prosecution or warning. A Category 3 incident usually entails a warning only.

The Environment Agency's water pollution statistics for 2007[143] reveal that there were 522 pollution incidents which had a serious impact on water quality. This was a decrease of 14 per cent on the figures for 2006.

The total number of reported incidents rose in 1999 and subsequent years because the Agency has changed its reporting methods. Before 1999, Category 4 incidents were not included in the total number of substantiated pollution incidents, but now Category 4 incidents are those which relate to substantiated pollution incidents (incidents with regard to which there is evidence of pollution) with no environmental impact.

In 2007, in regard to serious (Category 1 and 2) water pollution incidents, industry was responsible for 42 per cent of serious water pollution incidents, the sewerage industry 19 per cent, and farming 12 per cent. Sewage was the main pollutant affecting water quality arising out of sewer overflows, pipe failures or due to the failure of control measures.

The strict liability nature of many water pollution offences ensures that there is little prospect of the defendant being able to mount a successful defence. In the vast majority of cases (over 90 per cent), the Environment Agency secures a conviction. Readers should note the supplementary 'policing' role of NGOs who may use monitoring results as the basis of a private prosecution. We set out below, in our Law in Action section, some typical examples of pollution incidents which have ended in the Environment Agency commencing a prosecution.

We recommend readers to refer to the ENDS Report or the EA's annual report for current information on water pollution prosecutions and sanctions imposed by the courts on conviction.

4.12.3 Penalties for water pollution offences

The imposition of a financial penalty by the courts to punish and deter water polluters appears to be the rule in the criminal courts. Only rarely will a custodial penalty be imposed. Custodial penalties may not be imposed on companies and similar organisations. Whilst these are legal persons, they cannot be imprisoned.

The penalties for breach of s 33(1)(a), (b) and (c) EPA 1990 mirror those for breach of reg 38(1), (2) or (3) of the Environmental Permitting (England and Wales) Regulations 2010.

Under reg 39 of the Environmental Permitting (England and Wales) Regulations 2010, a person found guilty of an offence under reg 38(1), (2) or (3) is liable:

(i)   on summary conviction (i.e. in a magistrates' court) to a fine of up to £50,000 or a gaol term of up to 12 months or both;

(ii)   on conviction on indictment (i.e. in a Crown Court) to an unlimited fine or a term of imprisonment of up to five years or both.

Section 33(8) and (9) EPA 1990 set out the relevant penalties for breach of s 33(1)(a), (b) and (c) EPA 199.

---

143 See the Agency's website: www.environment-agency.gov.uk for current statistics.

Law in Action

As illustrations of (1) the Environment Agency's decision to prosecute polluters and (2) the sanctions imposed by the courts upon conviction, we set out below two typical water pollution incidents:

(a) A Huddersfield-based cleaning company and its director were fined £50,000 in 2007 after careless handling of detergent caused serious water pollution. Adam Khan, a director of Dr Clean (UK) Ltd, appeared before Bradford Crown Court in 2007 charged with causing polluting matter to enter controlled waters contrary to s 85(1) and also breach of permit conditions 85(6) of the Water Resources Act 1991. In 2005 Environment Agency officials found the River Holme covered in several feet of foam. The pollution was traced back to the defendants' premises. During a loading operation a large amount of detergent was spilt in the defendants' premises, and entered surface drains. The pollution incident killed 755 fish and affected a 2–3 km stretch of the River Holme. Both defendants pleaded guilty and Adam Khan was fined £50,000 and Dr Clean (UK) Ltd was fined one pound with costs of £5,000. Dr Clean ceased trading prior to its appearance in the Crown Court.

(b) On 21 February 2008 Anglian Water was convicted in Lowestoft Magistrates' Court of water pollution offences. Members of the public complained to the Environment Agency regarding the condition of the River Ore: the water was discoloured and there was a strong smell of sewage. The Environment Agency found that a 5 km stretch of the River Ore was polluted with sewage, resulting in the deaths of thousands of leeches, hundreds of sticklebacks and an unknown number of roach. The pollution was caused by a collapsed manhole cover which caused a blockage of the sewer, resulting in the back-up of sewage, which had entered the River Ore. There were a number of aggravating features relating to this pollution incident: the relevant manhole did not appear on Anglian's mapping system, the manhole was not maintained and there was no alarm system to alert Anglian that a leak of sewage had occurred. Anglian Water pleaded guilty to causing untreated sewage to enter controlled waters contrary to s 85(1) and also breach of permit conditions 85(6) WRA 1991. Anglian was fined £12,000 with £6,250 costs.

4.13 Preventive approaches to water pollution control

4.13.1 Introduction

The WRA 1991 contains provisions which enable the Environment Agency to take a more preventive approach to water pollution, whereby harm is prevented by means of anticipatory action. Section 161 of the WRA 1991 in particular empowers the Environment Agency to take action to avoid pollution of controlled waters. This section also equips the Environment Agency with extensive clean-up powers. In addition to s 161, ss 92–95 of the WRA 1991 contain provisions relating to the prevention of pollution. These provisions are particularly useful in relation to more diffuse sources of pollution such as run-off arising from agricultural activities. However, we begin our examination of the preventive role of the Environment Agency by reference to the advisory documents which it has produced.

4.13.2 Pollution prevention advice and information

The Environment Agency produces a range of documents and other media to educate and guide permit holders and others as to best environmental management practice to minimise the risk of substances escaping containment to pollute controlled waters.

Prior to the creation of the Environment Agency, the NRA produced, and issued on request, a free pack of information, comprising a leaflet and video, entitled *Pollution Prevention Pays*.[144] This initiative formed part of a campaign to highlight common errors in operational practice which were often the real causes of pollution incidents. The key features of the initiative are summarised below:

(a)   site drains—distinguish between surface drains (draining into controlled waters) and foul drains (draining to sewer); colour coded drainage systems; drainage plans should be accessible;

(b)   deliveries—label maximum content of storage tanks; gauges should be installed to give a visual display of tank levels; build bund walls; isolate delivery areas from drains; pipes should be above ground or placed in 'sleeves'; install automatic cut-off valves to prevent overfilling; install high level alarms in storage tanks; and ensure the supervision of unloading and loading operations;

(c)   storage—check bund walls in good repair with no valves in bund wall to drain rain water; drum storage areas should be bunded and roofed; use sturdy drums and label appropriately; install oil interceptor pits on surface drains to minimise the risk of pollution of controlled waters;

(d)   security—ensure adequate perimeter security through proper fencing; CCTV surveillance; and install locks on open/close tank valves;

(e)   training and emergency planning—ensure adequate staff training and prepare contingency plans.

This initiative demonstrates the link between poor environmental management practice and the increased probability that the Environment Agency will exercise its discretion to prosecute should a pollution incident occur on a poorly managed site.

The Environment Agency has also produced a range of Pollution Prevention Guidance notes (PPGs)[145] which are provided free on request to enquirers. Environment Agency staff will draw the attention of businesses to relevant PPGs as part of its rolling programme of routine site inspection visits. The PPGs cover the following topics:

PPG 1—general guide to the prevention of pollution;

PPG 2—above ground oil storage tanks;

PPG 3—use and design of oil separators in surface water drainage systems;

PPG 4—treatment and disposal of sewage where no foul sewer is available;

PPG 5—works and maintenance in or near water;

PPG 6—working at demolition and construction sites;

PPG 7—refuelling facilities;

PPG 8—safe storage and disposal of used oils;

PPG 9—pesticides (replaced by Defra Code of Practice for Using Plant Protection Products);

PPG 10—highway depots;

PPG 11—industrial sites (replaced by *Is Your Site Right?*);

---

144 A revised version of this document is available on the Environment Agency's website: www.environment-agency.gov.uk/business/topics/pollution/39083.aspx.

145 www.environment-agency.gov.uk/business/topics/pollution/39083.aspx.

PPG 12—sheep dip (replaced by Defra Groundwater Protection Code of Practice: Use and Disposal of Sheep Dip);

PPG 13—vehicle washing and cleaning;

PPG 14—marinas and crafts;

PPG 15—retail premises (replaced by *Is Your Site Right?*);

PPG 16—schools and other educational establishments (replaced by *Is Your Site Right?*);

PPG 17—dairies and other milk-handling operations;

PPG 18—managing fire, water and major spillages;

PPG 19—garages and vehicle service centres;

PPG 20—dewatering underground ducts and chambers;

PPG 21—pollution incident response planning;

PPG 22—dealing with spillages on highways;

PPG 24—stables, kennels and catteries;

PPG 25—hospitals and health care establishments;

PPG 26—storage and handling of drums and intermediate bulk containers;

PPG 27—installation, decommissioning and removal of underground storage tanks;

PPG 28—controlled burning.

Adherence by farmers to agricultural best practice with regard to the water pollution risks identified in *The Water Code Revised*, 1998 is an important factor which the Environment Agency takes into account when deciding whether to prosecute a farmer for causing a water pollution incident.

The government published in 2003 a strategic review of *Diffuse Water Pollution from Agriculture*.[146] The function of the review is to create an action plan to help reduce diffuse water pollution from agricultural sources. This type of pollution is a significant barrier to compliance with the terms of the Water Framework Directive 2000/60/EC by 2012–15. The publication of the strategy follows publication of *The Government's Strategic Review of Diffuse Water Pollution from Agriculture in England: Initial Thinking on the Problem and Solutions* in June 2002 and the *Strategy for Sustainable Farming and Food*.

The Environment Agency has placed on its website,[147] chiefly for the benefit of small and medium-sized enterprises, information relating to the primary and secondary legislation affecting business.[148]

4.13.3 Section 92 of the WRA 1991

Under s 92 of the WRA 1991, the Secretary of State has the power to make provisions (by means of regulations) for:

(a) prohibiting a person from having custody or control of any poisonous, noxious or polluting matter unless prescribed works and prescribed precautions and other steps have been taken for the purpose of preventing or controlling the entry of the matter into any controlled waters;

(b) requiring a person who already has custody or control of, or makes use of, poisonous, noxious or polluting matter to carry out such works for that purpose and to take precautions and other steps for the same purpose as may be prescribed.

These activities cannot be described as discharges and therefore cannot be regulated by the usual licence/permit application process.

---

146 See www.defra.gov.uk/environment/water/dwpa/index.htm.

147 www.environment-agency.gov.uk.

148 Access NETREGS via the search facility on the home page of the Agency's website.

Using these powers, the Control of Pollution (Silage, Slurry and Agricultural Fuel Oil) Regulations were introduced in 1991.[149] These Regulations, as amended by subsequent regulations in 1999,[150] require persons with custody of silage, livestock slurry or fuel oil to carry out works and take precautions, and other steps, for preventing pollution of controlled waters.

Essentially, s 92 and the regulations made under it are designed to minimise the risk of highly polluting substances escaping containment and causing water pollution. The regulations may specify, as a condition of being allowed to store and handle such substances, that farmers adhere to a range of controls and standards relating to the design, construction and operation of manufacturing and storage facilities, especially relating to silage making, slurry lagoons and agricultural fuel and oil stores. Regulations made pursuant to s 92 may create criminal offences and administrative remedies which will be similar to the water pollution permit system. These regulations may apply to existing facilities if the Environment Agency believes the relevant facility poses a significant water pollution risk.

The Control of Pollution (Oil Storage) (England) Regulations 2001[151] came into force in March 2002. The Regulations apply to persons having custody or control of oil (that is, storage) and require the taking of precautions to prevent oil-related water pollution incidents. The Regulations apply to and set technical standards for storage tanks, valves, pipes, gauges, drums and secondary containment (e.g. bunds).

The Regulations do not apply to private dwellings and below-ground tanks in view of the powers available to the Environment Agency in the Groundwater Regulations 1998[152] (amended by the Groundwater Regulations 2009) and the Anti-Pollution Works Notices Regulations 1999[153] (which apply only in England).

4.13.4 Water Protection Zones: general zoning control

A further mechanism for preventing water pollution is contained in s 93 of the WRA 1991 and allows for the designation of Water Protection Zones (WPZs) by the Secretary of State. Where, upon the application of the Environment Agency,[154] the Secretary of State, after consultation with the Minister of Agriculture, considers that it is appropriate to prohibit or restrict the carrying-on in a particular area of activities which he considers are likely to result in the pollution of any controlled waters, he may by order make provision:

(a) designating an area as a WPZ; and
(b) prohibiting or restricting the carrying-on in the designated area of such activities specified or described in the order.

Section 93 orders may themselves prohibit or restrict specific activities or alternatively they can establish a system under which the Environment Agency is empowered to decide which activities are prohibited or restricted. They are especially useful in controlling diffuse pollution such as agricultural run-off which falls outside the ambit of permit-based pollution controls.[155] Similar to the permitting system, s 93 orders can establish procedures for obtaining a permit to engage in restricted activities and provide for criminal offences for breach of the relevant provisions. The detailed procedure for making a s 93 order is contained in Sched 11 to the WRA 1991. An example

---

149 SI 1991/324.
150 SI 1999/547.
151 SI 2001/2954.
152 SI 1998/2746.
153 SI 1999/1006.
154 Sched 11 WEA 1991.
155 See page 153.

THE PREVENTION AND REMEDIATION OF POLLUTED CONTROLLED WATERS | 155

of a designated WPZ is the River Dee Water Protection Zone (River Dee Catchment) Designation Order 1999.[156] The special regulatory regime on the Dee controls the use and storage of a number of polluting substances in order to safeguard drinking water abstracted from the Dee. It is mainly applicable to industrial sites[157] and the content of each permit is dependent upon the outcome of a risk assessment. A s 93 Order cannot be used to require potential polluters to carry out works. Carrying out the activities specified in the relevant order without a permit or in breach of permit conditions is an offence.[158] A 'controlled activity' refers to the keeping or use of controlled substances within a site in the WPZ. 'Controlled substances' include: dangerous substances; fuels; lubricants; liquid industrial solvents and spirits; liquid (animal) food or feed; and inorganic fertiliser. The Water Protection Zone (River Dee Catchment) (Procedural and Other Provisions) Regulations 1999[159] set out the procedure to obtain a WPZ permit. In order to process the application, the Environment Agency requires: a site map, emergency plan, controlled substances location plan, information relating to controlled substances such as density, solubility and quantity, and details of storage (for example, in tanks). The Agency must consult downstream abstractors and affected local authorities before determining the application. The Secretary of State has a 'call in' power and the applicant has a right of appeal to him. A due diligence defence[160] is available as well as a defence based upon the defendant's ability to prove that he was not aware of the regulated activity itself or was not aware of the extent of the storage or use of regulated substances.

4.14 The prevention and remediation of polluted controlled waters

4.14.1 Anti-Pollution Works Notices and clean-up operations

Section 161 of the WRA 1991 provides the Environment Agency with an important set of powers which enable it to take (a) preventive action where it identifies a pollution risk, and (b) post-incident remedial action following a pollution.

Under s 161(1), where it appears to the Environment Agency that any poisonous, noxious or polluting matter or any solid waste matter is likely to enter or has entered any controlled waters, the Environment Agency is entitled to carry out remedial works to clean up the pollution. The section provides that the following works and operations may be carried out for the purpose of:

(a)   preventing any matter entering controlled waters;[161]
(b)   removing or disposing of polluting matter;
(c)   remedying or mitigating any pollution caused by the presence of the matter in the waters; or
(d)   so far as it is reasonably practicable to do so, restoring the waters, including any flora and fauna (e.g. fish restocking) dependent on the aquatic environment of the waters, to their state immediately before the matter became present in the waters.

The Environment Agency is entitled to carry out and recover the costs of any investigations in order to establish the source of the polluting matter and also the identity of the person who caused or knowingly permitted it to be present in controlled waters or at a place from which it is likely to enter controlled waters.

---

156 SI 1999/915.
157 IPPC sites, farms, retail premises and construction sites are exempt.
158 To cause or knowingly permit a contravention of a WPZ controlled activity.
159 SI 1999/916.
160 I.e. the defendant took all reasonable steps to avoid the commission of an offence.
161 E.g. preventing a spillage from entering controlled waters.

The EA 1995[162] inserted a new provision[163] which provides that the power to carry out works (not the power to carry out investigations) is only exercisable in cases where:

(a) the Environment Agency considers it necessary to carry out the works forthwith; or

(b) it appears to the Environment Agency, after carrying out a reasonable enquiry, that no person can be found on whom it could serve a Works Notice (WN) under s 161A.

Section 161(3) provides that where the Environment Agency carries out any such works or operations as are mentioned in s 161, it will be entitled to recover the expenses reasonably incurred in doing so. Expenses may be recovered from any person who caused or knowingly permitted the matter in question to be present at the place from which it was likely to enter any controlled waters or who caused or knowingly permitted the matter in question to be present in any controlled waters. In *Bruton and NRA v Clarke* (1993),[164] the NRA sought recovery of its costs under s 161(3) of the WRA 1991 in remediating the damage to the ecology of the River Sappiston caused by the entry of three million gallons of agricultural slurry. The High Court limited the recovery of costs to £90,000 because not all the NRA's surveys directly related to the remediation.

The Environment Agency can exercise its s 161 powers *independently* of any criminal proceedings which it has the power to initiate. The Environment Agency has issued guidance regarding the circumstances in which it will use its s 161 powers: *Environment Agency Policy and Guidance on the Use of Anti-Pollution Works Notices*. Section 161 may not be used by the Environment Agency to override the authority of a permit authorising the discharge of substances into controlled waters. In such circumstances, the Environment Agency must apply for a variation of the permit.

4.14.2 Works Notices

Section 161 of the WRA 1991 is a powerful enforcement tool in view of the fact that the cost of clean-up is likely to far exceed any penalty imposed by the courts with regard to any linked prosecution.[165] The Environment Agency now has the power to compel polluters to take (and bear the cost of) preventive or remedial action themselves, rather than relying upon the Environment Agency's power to undertake the clean-up works itself and then attempt to recover the relevant costs from the person responsible. Under s 161 as amended, the Environment Agency may serve a Works Notice (WN) on the polluter, or potential polluter, requiring it either to remedy the pollution or take specified preventive action to stop pollution occurring. The WN procedure is not applicable in circumstances where immediate action is required or where the polluter cannot be found.

The Environment Agency may serve a WN on any person who caused or knowingly permitted the poisonous, noxious or polluting matter, or solid waste matter in question to be present either in any controlled waters or at the place from which it is likely to enter any controlled waters. The WN is a legal notice which requires the person on whom it is served to carry out the works or operations specified in the notice. Typically, the WN will require the recipient of the notice to:

(a) remove and/or dispose of the relevant polluting matter;

(b) remedy and/or mitigate the effects of the polluting matter; or

(c) so far as reasonably practicable, restore the waters and flora and fauna to their pre-pollution state.

---

162 Sched 22.
163 S 161(1A) WRA.
164 *Bruton and NRA v Clarke* (1994) WLWA 145.
165 Ibid.

A WN must specify the time period within which the recipient of the notice must comply. Before serving a WN, the Environment Agency should endeavour to consult with the intended recipient of the notice concerning the works that are to be specified in the Notice. A WN may not be served on the person responsible for polluting matter which enters controlled waters from an abandoned or partly abandoned mine.[166] The Anti-Pollution Works Regulations 1999[167] detail the form and content of WNs and the requirements for consultation. With regard to preventive works, the Regulations require that the WN contains details of the risk, the controlled waters likely to be affected and the location of the land from which the polluting matter is likely to enter controlled waters. With regard to post-pollution remediation, the WN must detail the nature and extent of pollution, the controlled waters affected and the necessary remedial works. A WN will contain the Environment Agency's reasons for serving the notice, rights of appeal, the Environment Agency's entitlement to have its reasonable costs reimbursed and the consequences of failure to comply with the WN.

4.14.3 Enforcement Notices

In cases involving the regulation of water pollution point sources by the issue of a permit, the Environment Agency may serve an Enforcement Notice (EN) on the permit holder[168] if either there has been a breach of permit condition or breach of condition is threatened. ENs specify the work required to remedy the breach of condition or threatened breach of condition and the timescale to rectify the problem. Failure to carry out the works identified by the Environment Agency within the relevant timescale is an offence.

4.14.4 Economic instruments as a compliance tool

Whilst there has been some interest in using economic instruments in a water pollution and water quality context, currently there are no concrete proposals to utilise this method of pollution control. A consultation paper was issued by the DETR in 1998 (Economic Instruments for Water Pollution) which considered the possible application of economic instruments to discharge permit holders, but it seems more likely that if such instruments are deployed, they will be used to address diffuse pollution.[169] In regard to the Urban Waste Water Treatment Directive the European Environment Agency has produced a report examining the potential use of taxes and charges to meet the objectives of the Directive.[170]

4.15 Access to information

The publicly accessible database relating to the aquatic environment and water pollution is maintained by the Environment Agency. Part 2 of the Environmental Permitting (England and Wales) Regulations 2010 detail the relevant procedures relating to and contents of the register (see regs 45–56). The register contains details of applications for water pollution environmental permits; environmental permits granted (and the relevant conditions); information provided by the permit holder as a condition of its pollution permit; sampling information; applications for variation of conditions; appeals; Enforcement Notices; Revocation Notices; Works Notices; convictions of the permit holder for water pollution offences offences; directions given by the Secretary of State; and

---

166 Provided the abandonment occurred before 2000.
167 SI 1999/1006.
168 See reg 36 of the Environmental Permitting (England and Wales) Regulations 2010.
169 E.g. some form of pesticide or fertiliser tax.
170 *Effectiveness of Urban Waste Water Treatment Policies in Selected Countries: A European Environment Agency Pilot Study* (2005).

notices relating to water quality objectives. In relation to results of sampling activities the information contained in the register includes sampling information relating to the substances discharged into controlled waters (often required to be supplied by the permit holder as a condition of its permit), information relating to the quality of the receiving waters and information relating to the analysis of these samples. Information relating to samples must be added to the register within two months from the date when the sample was taken.

Application may be made by the permit holder to exclude information from the public register which (a) is commercially confidential, or (b) affects national security. Inspection of the registers at the Environment Agency's offices (currently there is no internet access facility) at reasonable times is free. Copies of register entries may be taken subject to payment of a reasonable fee. The contents of the register have, on occasion, been used as both evidence in criminal prosecutions and civil actions. In the case of *Wales v Thames Water Authority* (1987),[171] Thames Water was successfully prosecuted by a private individual in regard to evidence of sewage pollution of controlled waters which the defendant had itself recorded in the public register.

Sections 51–52 of the EA 1995 require the Environment Agency to prepare an annual report and to supply the Secretary of State with relevant information. In addition, s 202 obliges the Environment Agency to supply government ministers with advice and assistance regarding their water pollution functions. Both the Environment Agency and ministers may serve on any person a notice requiring the provision of water pollution-related information. Failure to comply with a request is an offence. Section 203 requires the Environment Agency and water companies, subject to the restrictions in s 204, to exchange information relating to water quality and water pollution incidents.

4.16 The private regulation of water pollution

Individuals with 'riparian rights'[172] are often well placed to take action against polluters who damage their property and property-related interests. They have the right to receive water in its natural state, subject only to reasonable use by upstream users for ordinary purposes.[173] Any interference with the quantity and quality of the water a riparian owner receives is actionable, based upon the tort of nuisance.

In this section we provide a flavour of the civil law actions (torts) and criminal law prosecutions which can be commenced by legal persons, especially private individuals and environmental NGOs, arising out of water pollution incidents.[174] In regard to civil law litigation (the torts of nuisance, trespass, negligence and the rule in *Rylands v Fletcher*[175]) the Anglers' Conservation Association has frequently employed the civil law to protect the interests of its members.

See Chapter 11 →

Claimants in civil law (torts) actions resort to litigation in order to obtain redress in the form of monetary compensation or an injunction to stop or restrict the polluting activities of others. Damages may include the cost of restocking a fishery, pollution clean-up costs, loss of amenity and commercial losses arising from a downturn in fees paid by anglers to the owners of a damaged fishery. Injunctions are rarely granted but are available in limited circumstances.[176]

Industrial and sewage treatment plants which possess water pollution permits are not immune to civil law actions,[177] despite the fact that they are complying with the conditions of their permits.

---

171 *Wales v Thames Water Authority* (1987) 1(3) Environmental Law 3.
172 That is, property owners whose land adjoins a watercourse and who therefore own the bed and banks of the relevant river or stream, but not the waters flowing in them.
173 *Chasemore v Richards* (1859) 7 HL Cas 349.
174 We consider the role of the civil law in pollution control in greater detail in Chapter 11.
175 *Rylands v Fletcher* (1868) LR 3HL 330.
176 *Pride of Derby and Derbyshire Angling Association Ltd v British Celanese Ltd* (1953) Ch 149.
177 S 100 (b) WRA 1991.

The register of information maintained by the Environment Agency, relating to controlled waters, may be an evidential boon for any would-be claimant especially in regard to discharge composition and quality of receiving waters (before and after a discharge or alleged pollution incident).

4.16.1 The common law and water pollution

The law relating to the rights of riparian owners appears to be well settled. A riparian owner is entitled to:

> have the water of the stream, on the banks of which his property lies, flow down as it has been accustomed to flow down to his property, subject to the ordinary use of flowing water by upper proprietors, and to such further use, if any, on their part in connection with their property as may be reasonable under the circumstances. Every riparian proprietor is thus entitled to the water of his stream, in its natural flow, without sensible diminution or increase and without sensible alteration in its character or quality.[178]

In the John Young case,[179] a whisky distillery company obtained an injunction against a mine owner, in an action based on private nuisance, because the activities of the upstream mine owner had changed the chemistry of the water and so had unreasonably interfered with the whisky manufacturer's riparian right to receive water in its natural state. A riparian owner can bring an action for damages or can seek an injunction. Interference with fishing rights can also give rise to an action in nuisance. In *Cook v South West Water plc* (1992),[180] the plaintiff, Cook, owned three-quarters of a mile of salmon and trout fishing rights. During 1990, South West Water, which operated three sewage works upstream from the plaintiff's stretch of river, discharged detergent and phosphates into the river which damaged the river's ecosystem and also seriously interfered with fishing. The plaintiff brought an action in nuisance against South West Water seeking both damages and a successful injunction.

Water pollution-based nuisance actions appear, on the basis of the decision in *John Young v Bankier Distillery Co*[181] to avoid the problem of the application of the 'locality doctrine' that would require the court to take into account the level of pollution to be expected in the locality where the nuisance is alleged to have occurred. In *John Young* the courts treated damage to the claimant's riparian right in the same manner as if there had been damage to land.

See Chapter ◀ 11.7.4.1

In addition to a claim in nuisance, it may be possible for a riparian owner to make a claim in trespass. The tort of trespass to the claimant's land has many functions and its application for environmental protection and compensation purposes is a more recent and limited development. Trespass involves the unjustifiable physical interference with the claimant's land, arising from intentional or negligent entry onto the land. The key issues which must be present in order for an action in trespass to be brought are that the trespass was direct, that the defendant's act was intentional or negligent and that there is a causal link between the directness of the defendant's act and the inevitability of the consequences. An example of a successful claim in trespass in relation to water pollution can be found in the case of *Jones v Llanrwst UDC* (1911)[182] in which it was held that sewage, which had been released into a river (a defined channel) and which had passed downstream and settled on the plaintiff's land, was a direct interference and amounted to trespass.

178 John Young & Co v Bankier Distillery Co [1893] AC 691; [1891] All ER 439.
179 Ibid.
180 Cook v South West Water plc [1992] 3(4) Water Law 103; (1992) ENDS 207.
181 John Young v Bankier Distillery Co [1983] AC 691.
182 Jones v Llanrwst Urban District Council [1911] 1 Ch 393; [1908] All ER 922. See 11.12.5.

The tort of negligence may also have application in water pollution cases. In *Scott-Whitehead v National Coal Board* (1987),[183] the defendant, a regional water authority, was found to be negligent in failing to advise a farmer that the water he was abstracting from a stream (in accordance with an abstraction licence granted by the water authority) to irrigate his crops contained a strong chlorinated solution. The farmer's potato crop was damaged as a consequence of using the chlorinated water and the court held that the water authority was liable in negligence.

See Chapter 11.8.2 → The case of *R v SouthWestWater Authority* (1991)[184] illustrates the relevance of the tort of public nuisance in a drinking water context. The case arose out of the Camelford disaster, when a large quantity of aluminium sulphate was accidentally introduced into the water supply system of a Cornish town. The defendant water company was slow to respond to customer complaints about the taste of the water and slow to take remedial action. Approximately 5,000 people suffered varying degrees of injury, including memory loss, vomiting and temporary changes in hair colour. The defendant was found guilty of causing a public nuisance and was fined £10,000 and ordered to pay £25,000 costs.

See Chapter 11.14 → The torts of nuisance and the rule in *Rylands v Fletcher*[185] formed the basis of a very significant water pollution case concerning damage to an aquifer (groundwater) from which the claimant abstracted drinking water and supplied it to its customers: *Cambridge Water Co Ltd v Eastern Counties Leather*.[186]

4.16.2 Private prosecutions

Unless specifically restricted by the relevant legislation, any individual has the right to commence a private prosecution to enforce the criminal law, including regulatory offences.[187] This right is useful where the regulator declines to prosecute a polluter. Early environmental legislation tended to restrict this right by requiring the private prosecutor to obtain the consent of the Attorney General (AG) or the Director of Public Prosecutions (DPP).[188] Some restrictions continue to apply.[189]

Evidence to support a prosecution may be based upon the information contained in the publicly accessible registers of information[190] maintained by the Environment Agency. Private prosecutions are usually commenced by the more litigious NGOs, such as Greenpeace; however, an unsuccessful private prosecution will carry a financial risk. In the mid-1990s, Greenpeace brought an unsuccessful action against ICI.[191] Greenpeace brought this private prosecution under s 85(1) of the WRA 1991. Greenpeace was required, following the failure of its prosecution, to pay over £28,000 towards ICI's legal costs. Clearly, only large environmental pressure groups such as Friends of the Earth or Greenpeace can afford to run the financial risks of losing legal actions. However, in addition to traditional environmental pressure groups, such as Friends of the Earth and Greenpeace, the Anglers Conservation Association have availed themselves of these rights as well as resorting to

 See Chapter 12 → common law actions to secure injunctions or obtain damages. Readers may wish to refer to Chapter 12 for general coverage of private prosecutions and access to evidence of breach of the law contained in public registers.[192]

---

183 *Scott-Whitehead v National Coal Board* [1987] 2 EGLR 227; (1987) 53 P & CR 263.
184 *R v SouthWestWater Authority* (1991) 3 LMELR 65.
185 *Rylands v Fletcher* (1868) LR 3 HL 330.
186 *Cambridge Water Co v Eastern Counties Leather plc* [1994] 2 AC 264; [1994] 2 WLR 53.
187 Such as a breach of reg 38 of the Environmental Permitting (England and Wales) Regulations 2010.
188 For example see s 6(3) of the Control of Pollution Act (COPA) 1974.
189 See s 211 of the Water Industry Act 1991 and s 7(4) of the WIA 1991.
190 See 4.15.
191 *Greenpeace v ICI* (1994) 234 ENDS, July.
192 Two examples of successful private prosecutions are *R v AnglianWater Services* (2004) Env LR 10 and *Wales v Thames Water Authority* (1987) 1(3) Environmental Law 3.

4.17 Disposal of wastes into sewers

The disposal of effluent (industrial effluent and human sewage) into sewers is inextricably linked to pollution of controlled waters. Industrial processes generate enormous quantities of waste which is either discharged on land as solid waste, emitted into the atmosphere or, in the case of liquid wastes, either discharged into controlled waters or released into the sewers. The discharge of trade effluent into sewers is regulated directly by the sewerage undertakers, exercising their powers under the WIA 1991, but also indirectly by the Environment Agency. Sewerage undertakers grant permits for the disposal of trade effluent into the sewers but they are then required to obtain a permit from the Environment Agency to release the final treated effluent into controlled waters (usually from sewage treatment plants). The WIA 1991 regulates the discharge of trade effluents into sewers and s 87 of the WRA 1991 deals with the discharge of treated sewage effluent into controlled waters. A good example of the interface between these two regulatory regimes is illustrated in the *NRA v YorkshireWater Services Ltd* case. Not all substances discharged into the sewers ends up back in controlled waters. Some wastes from the sewerage process are spread on land or are incinerated.

4.17.1 Discharges of treated sewage into surface waters, groundwaters and coastal waters

The 10 privatised water companies which operate as both water and sewerage undertakers are responsible for discharging large quantities of treated effluent from sewage treatment plants into controlled waters. The sewerage undertakers receive trade effluent through the sewers which they then treat and finally return, after treatment, into controlled waters. The sewerage undertakers are therefore effectively responsible for all discharges made from their sewers or treatment plants into controlled waters. The sewerage undertakers control the trade effluent disposed of into the sewers (by industrial facilities) by means of trade effluent consents (i.e. permits) which they grant under s 118 of the WIA 1991.

Sewerage undertakers discharge treated waste from their sewage treatment works into surface waters. Each sewerage treatment plant must therefore have an environmental permit in place to control, via conditions, the treated effluent which is returned to the water cycle.

4.17.2 Discharges of trade effluent into the sewers

Given that sewerage undertakers are subject to the same controls (regulated by the Environment Agency under the the Environmental Permitting (England and Wales) Regulations 2010 and WRA 1991) as any other discharger,[193] they are required to maintain a tight control on the effluent they are prepared to accept into the sewers and, for this reason, the disposal of trade effluent into a sewer requires a separate consent from the sewerage undertaker under s 118 of the WIA 1991.

4.17.3 Trade effluent consents (permits): s 118 of the WIA 1991

The disposal of trade effluent into a sewer requires a trade effluent consent (or permit) granted under s 118 of the WIA 1991 and it is an offence to discharge any trade effluent from trade premises otherwise than in accordance with the conditions of a consent (permit) obtained from

---

193 Subject to the availability of the special defence, available to sewerage undertakers, discussed in the case of *NRA v YorkshireWater Services Ltd* (1995) 1 All ER 225.

the sewerage undertaker. The definitions of 'trade effluent' and 'trade premises' are contained in s 141 of the WIA 1991. Trade effluent means any liquid, which is partly or wholly produced in the course of any trade or business, but does not include domestic sewage.[194] Trade premises include premises used for industry or any trade, research activity and agriculture. The Secretary of State has the power[195] to amend the definitions contained in s 141 WIA 1991 to bring within/exclude from the ambit of the WIA particular discharges. The setting of trade effluent consents (permits) involves little, if any, input by legal persons other than the sewerage undertaker and the licence/trade effluent consent (permit) applicant.

The application for a consent (permit) is made by means of serving a trade effluent notice on the sewerage undertaker. At least two months' notice must be given of an intention to discharge trade effluent and the notice has to provide details of the proposed discharge, including information about the proposed quantity and composition of the trade effluent and the maximum daily volume of the discharge. Section 119(2) (a) and (b) WIA 1991[196] requires the applicant to provide information relating to any pretreatment or other means adopted by the applicant to minimise the polluting impact of the discharge on the sewerage system and controlled waters. Following the service of a notice, the sewerage undertaker has to decide whether or not to grant the consent (permit) and the relevant conditions to attach. Failure to determine the notice within two months constitutes a deemed refusal enabling the applicant to appeal.

Section 121 of the WIA 1991 gives the sewerage undertaker wide discretion as to the conditions which can be imposed. Conditions may relate to the point of discharge (i.e. the position of a pipe connecting with the sewer system), the time of day during which effluent may be discharged into sewers, the composition of the effluent, the temperature of the effluent, the rate at which the effluent is intended to be discharged into the sewer, the acidity or alkalinity of the effluent, the method adopted of removing or controlling particular substances which form part of the effluent, inspection of sewers, testing and monitoring of effluent[197] and the keeping of records. When framing conditions of WIA 1991 consents (permits), the sewerage undertaker must have regard to the conditions in its own permit, issued by the Environment Agency, under the Environmental Permitting (England and Wales) Regulations 2010.[198] In addition, a condition will be imposed which sets out the amount payable to the sewerage undertaker for receiving the trade effluent.[199] Compliance with the standards detailed in the 1994 Regulations has led to increases in discharge consent (permit) charges (and possibly an increase in the number of dischargers who pretreat their effluent). In setting trade effluent consent (permit) conditions, sewerage undertakers should have regard to the criteria in Water UK's *Trade Effluent Discharged to the Sewer* (1986),[200] which specify the key objectives or purposes of trade effluent control. The main objectives are:

(1) To protect the sewerage system—in particular:

   (a) to protect the integrity of the sewage system (that is, the conducting pipes and the treatment process itself);
   (b) to protect personnel;
   (c) to protect sewage treatment works (from substances and objects which will cause damage);

---

194 E.g. liquid effluent from industry, commercial/retail premises, farms, etc.
195 See s 139 WIA 1991.
196 Inserted by the Water Act 2003.
197 E.g. the installation of meters to record the volume and composition of the effluent.
198 Relating to the relevant sewage plant which will treat the effluent before discharging it into controlled waters.
199 See Sched 4 Urban Waste Water Treatment Regulations 1994 (SI 1994/2841).
200 Water UK is the sewerage industry's trade association which revised the 1986 guidance in 2008—see www.water.org.uk.

(d)   to protect the environment from the impact of treated sewage (i.e. adverse impacts of treated effluent on water resources); and

(e)   to control storm-related effluent discharges.

(2)   To ensure that effluent dischargers pay a reasonable amount for effluent treatment.

(3)   To keep records.[201]

Consent (permit) conditions are set by reference to the ability of the sewer system to treat the proposed discharge.[202] Substances, such as metals or solvents, which the sewage treatment works cannot cope with will be excluded from the terms of the discharge consent (permit). In such circumstances, the discharger must pretreat its effluent to remove the banned substances or use another means of disposal. An application will be refused if the relevant sewage treatment process is operating at full capacity.

The sewerage undertaker has various powers in respect of trade effluent consents (permits). The original, or current, consent (permit) may be varied by the sewerage undertaker on two months' notice,[203] although the undertaker can only do so after two years from the grant of the original or current consent (permit). This power is essential so that the sewerage undertaker can respond to the tightening, by the Environment Agency, of the terms of the permit relating to its sewage treatment works. A variation of the consent (permit) is possible within the two-year period to provide protection for people likely to be affected by the relevant effluent discharge, but compensation will be payable unless the need for the variation has resulted from circumstances which were not foreseen when the consent (permit) was last varied.[204] Similarly a variation can be made in order to comply with the requirements of the Urban Waste Water Treatment Regulations 1994. In contrast to the Environmental Permitting (England and Wales) Regulations 2010, there is no provision in the WIA 1991 relating to the revocation of trade effluent discharge consents. A person aggrieved by a consent condition, a consent variation or a refusal of an application, has the right of appeal to the Water Services Regulation Authority under s 122 of the WIA 1991. No appeal is possible in regard to effluent charges. The discharger and sewerage undertaker may enter into an agreement under s 129 of the WIA 1991 as an alternative to the trade effluent permitting process. The terms of such an agreement enable the discharger to pay the capital costs involved in constructing a new sewage treatment plant where the existing works are already at maximum capacity.

4.17.4 Special consents (regarding so-called 'red list' substances)

Certain types of effluents, known as 'special category effluents', require a special consent (permit) because they are potentially harmful and are difficult to treat. The Trade Effluents (Prescribed Processes and Substances) Regulations 1989,[205] as amended,[206] prescribe the particular substances that fall into this category. The Regulations enable the government to comply with the provisions of the Dangerous Substances in Water Directive 2006/11/EC. The Secretary of State has the power to prescribe both substances[207] and processes[208] so that they are controlled under the Regulations. Most facilities discharging red list substances will be subject to IPPC permitting but will require a special consent in addition to an IPPC permit.

---

201   Effluent data is used for planning future provision, monitoring the operation of each treatment system, and assisting effluent dischargers to be more effective in controlling effluent discharges.

202   Taking into account the legal obligations of the sewerage undertaker.

203   S 124 WIA 1991.

204   S 125 WIA 1991.

205   SI 1989/1156.

206   By SI 1992/339.

207   Listed in Sched 1—the red list.

208   Listed in Sched 2.

In cases where the trade effluent is special category effluent, the sewerage undertaker must consult the Environment Agency and ask whether the discharge should be prohibited or, if not, whether the Agency requires any specific conditions to be imposed.[209] The sewerage undertaker commits a criminal offence if it fails to comply with any direction given by the Environment Agency. Special consents may be varied in similar fashion to a trade effluent consent (permit) save that a variation of the consent may occur within two years of the last variation for the following reasons: (1) breach of the consent or agreement, (2) to enable compliance with EU or international law, or (3) to protect health and/or the aquatic environment.

4.17.5 Sanctions

One aspect of the regulation of the trade effluent and sewage effluent system which does not fully correspond to the Environmental Permitting (England and Wales) Regulations 2010 is the maximum sanction which may be imposed by the magistrates' courts on conviction of a summary offence.[210] The maximum fine is a mere £5,000, although on conviction on indictment (i.e. in the Crown Court) the maximum sanction is an unlimited fine. The sewerage undertakers, as regulators of the effluent treatment systems in England and Wales, do not have a formal published enforcement and prosecution policy (as does the Environment Agency). The ENDS Report contains few examples of WIA 1991 prosecutions commenced by the privatised water and sewerage companies.[211]

4.18 Water abstraction

The quality of water is not simply determined by what is discharged into it. Water quality is inextricably linked to water quantity. If water levels are low, there is less water available to dilute waste and effluents and this may cause a reduction in water quality. Therefore, it is appropriate in a chapter on water pollution to consider the legal controls that exist in relation to the abstraction of water. The Environment Agency is under a statutory duty to secure the proper use of water resources. Under s 19 of the WRA 1991, the Environment Agency is under a duty to conserve and increase the available water resources. The Agency therefore has to assess the need for new developments and ensure that the most appropriate schemes are licensed (permitted), taking into account the environmental impact of new developments on existing users. The system of water abstraction licensing controls has been the subject of a major overhaul.[212]

Before legislation was enacted to control the use of water, the common law had developed various rules which determined the rights of riparian owners to abstract water. These have largely been superseded by the legislation but need to be considered.

4.18.1 Riparian rights

Owners of property adjoining a river, known as riparian owners or occupiers, have the right to what the courts refer to as the 'ordinary use of water flowing past their land'. In *Miner v Gilmore* (1859),[213] Lord Kingsdown stated that:

---

209 S 120(1) of the WIA 1991.
210 See s 118(5) WIA 1991.
211 See the online resources.
212 See the coverage of the Water Act 2003 in 4.19.2 below.
213 *Miner v Gilmore* (1859) 12 Moo PCC 131 and see 4.16.1.

> By the general law applicable to running streams, every riparian proprietor has a right to what
> may be called the ordinary use of water flowing past his land; for instance to the reasonable use
> of the water for his domestic purposes and for his cattle, and this without regard to the effect
> which such use may have, in case of a deficiency on a proprietor lower down the stream.

Not only does this view have potentially detrimental consequences for riparian owners further
downstream, it clearly takes no account of any environmental consequences of such actions.
However, the position is qualified to the extent that uses which may be regarded as extraordinary
can only be carried out if they do not cause harm to lower riparian occupiers. Therefore, if one
riparian owner wished to use water for what would be described as an extraordinary use, he or she
could only do so if it would not harm the rights of others. This was the view taken in the case of
Rugby Joint Water Board v Walters (1967),[214] where the court stated that the water removed must either
have no effect on the river or it must be returned to it substantially undiminished in quantity or
quality. This more recent decision appears to reflect the changing attitude to the environment in so
far as the decision is couched in terms of the quality of the river in its own right.

4.18.2 Statutory controls over water abstraction

Growing concern about the problems of over-abstraction, water shortages, rivers drying out and
the consequent loss of natural habitat led to the creation of legislative controls to regulate the
abstraction of water. The Water Act 1945 (WA 1945) provided some limited controls over water
abstraction. However, it was the Water Resources Act 1963 (WRA 1963) which provided the first
comprehensive control over water abstraction, prohibiting the abstraction of water without an
abstraction licence.[215]

When the requirement for an abstraction licence was first introduced, many industrial companies had already been abstracting water for use in their industrial processes for many years.
Section 33 of the WRA 1963 provided a special entitlement for such users, automatically granting
a Licence of Right to any person who was entitled to abstract water from a source or supply in a
river authority area at the date that s 33 came into force, or to a person who had a record of five
years' continuous abstraction. These Licences of Right are presumed to be lawful by the WRA 1991;
however, such licence holders are now required to pay for their abstraction rights.

Together, s 6 of the EA 1995 and s 19 of the WRA 1991[216] impose the following water resource
management duties on the Environment Agency: (a) the promotion of the conservation and
enhancement of the natural beauty of inland and coastal waters; (b) the promotion of the conservation of the flora and fauna which are dependent upon the aquatic environment; (c) the promotion
of inland and coastal waters for recreational purposes, taking into account the needs of the chronically sick and disabled; (d) to conserve, redistribute, manage and secure the proper use of water
resources in England and Wales; and (e) to make water resource management schemes in conjunction with the large privatised water companies in order to implement (d).

Under s 21 of the WRA 1991, the Environment Agency has the power to prepare and submit
to the Secretary of State for approval draft statements regarding the minimum acceptable flows of
inland waters.[217] In preparing each minimum acceptable flow statement, the Environment Agency
must have regard to statutory water quality objectives (SWQOs) and its general environmental

---

214 *Rugby Joint Water Board v Walters* [1967] Ch 397 166; *Rushmer v Polsue and Alfieri Ltd* [1906] Ch 234; [1907] AC 121 379.
215 The current regulatory regime is contained in the Water Act 2003; 4.19.2 below.
216 Subject to s 4 of the EA 1995.
217 The term 'Inland Waters' include rivers, streams, lakes, ponds, channels, creeks, bays, estuaries, docks and natural and
    man-made watercourses.

duties. Proposed flows must safeguard public health and meet the needs of current lawful users of inland waters. Schedule 5 to the WRA 1991 contains the relevant publicity and consultation[218] requirements. The Secretary of State may approve the draft flow statements[219] and he may, of his own volition, direct the Environment Agency to consider the minimum acceptable flow of any inland waters.[220]

Under s 23, WRA 1991, the Environment Agency has a power to consider the level or volume of inland waters in addition to or in substitution for the flow under consideration.

4.18.3 Abstraction licences authorised by the WRA 1991

Abstraction licences are granted by the Environment Agency. Abstraction without a licence is prohibited,[221] subject to limited exceptions, for example, land drainage.[222] To apply for an abstraction licence,[223] it is necessary to be either:

(a)   an occupier of the land adjacent to an inland water; or
(b)   an occupier of land above the underground strata from which the water is drawn.

The licence[224] is issued to the occupier of land. Once his or her occupation ceases, the licence will lapse and the new occupier must notify the Environment Agency if he or she wishes to take over the licence.[225] Water undertakers are required to apply for a licence for the water which they abstract from water courses. Sections 27 and 29 of the WRA 1991 provide various exceptions to the need to obtain an abstraction licence. Owners of the land through which water flows may use for domestic or agricultural purposes a maximum of 20 cubic metres each day without the need for a licence.[226]

An application for an abstraction licence is made to the Environment Agency in accordance with the Water Resources (Licences) Regulations 1965 (as amended).[227] The application must be accompanied by a fee. Notice of the application is publicised by the applicant in the London Gazette and a local newspaper.[228] The Environment Agency is required when considering an application for an abstraction licence to consider:

(a)   representations made in response to publicity;
(b)   representations made arising from consultation with bodies such as water undertakers, drainage boards and Natural England;
(c)   the effect of the proposed abstraction on other existing licence (permit) holders;
(d)   the effect on other users of the supply (exempt users);
(e)   the reasonable requirements of the applicant; and
(f)   the need to maintain a minimum acceptable flow irrespective of whether a minimum flow has been determined.

The form and content of licences are detailed in ss 46–47 WRA 1991.

---

218 With privatised water companies, drainage boards, harbour authorities and conservancy authorities.
219 S 21(7) and Sched 5.
220 S 22 WRA 1991.
221 S 24 WRA 1991.
222 S 28 WRA 1991.
223 S 34 WRA 1991.
224 Which confers a right on the holder; s 48 WRA 1991.
225 Succession rights are governed by ss 49–50 WRA 1991, as amended.
226 S 6 WA 2003.
227 S 38 WRA 1991.
228 S 37 WRA 1991.

4.18.4 Water abstraction licence conditions

The Environment Agency may attach conditions to abstraction licences which may require the abstractor to return the water to the relevant watercourse after use. Monitoring of the amounts of water abstracted will usually be required as a condition of the licence. When considering whether to grant a licence or the conditions to be attached to it, the Environment Agency must consider whether the grant of the licence will prevent another current licence holder, or someone extracting water for domestic or agricultural purposes, from abstracting their full entitlement. If the proposed abstraction will affect existing abstractors in this manner, the Environment Agency must refuse to grant a licence unless the person affected agrees to the grant of the new licence. The Secretary of State has the power[229] to 'call in' an application for his own decision.

An abstraction licence may be varied either by the Environment Agency acting on its own initiative or at the request of the licence holder.[230] If the Environment Agency decides that it intends to vary a licence, a licence holder has a right of appeal to the Secretary of State.[231] If the holder suffers damage as a result of the Secretary of State's decision, he or she may recover compensation from the Environment Agency.[232] Once a licence is granted, the Environment Agency is not able to derogate from the grant of the licence.

4.18.5 Drought-related powers

The serious drought affecting West Yorkshire in 1995 (see the Uff Report) provided a timely reminder of the vulnerability of water supplies and the utility of Drought Orders, Emergency Drought Orders and Drought Permits.[233] Schedule 8 to the WRA 1991 contains the procedural requirements regarding the making of these orders and permits. Under s 73(1) WRA 1991, the Secretary of State has the power to make an 'Ordinary Drought Order' upon receipt of an application from the Environment Agency or a water undertaker (large privatised water company). This type of Order is used where an exceptional shortage of rain has brought about or threatens to bring about a serious deficiency of water supply or deficiency in flow or level of inland waters, posing a serious threat to the flora and fauna dependent on the relevant inland water. Under s 73(2) WRA 1991, the Secretary of State has the power, subject to receipt of an application from the Environment Agency or a water undertaker, to make an 'Emergency Drought Order' to address serious supply deficiencies due to low rainfall which is likely to impair the economic or social well-being of the public. Emergency Drought Orders enable water companies to supply water via stand pipes and bowsers (water tanks). The terms of a drought order[234] may provide the Environment Agency or a water undertaker with the power to enter land to carry out works. Compensation is payable to 'injuriously affected' owners, occupiers and interested persons.[235] Under s 80, it is an offence either to take, abstract or use water in contravention of the terms of a drought order, or to discharge water except in accordance with the terms of a Drought Order. Under s 79A WRA 1991, the Environment Agency may issue Drought Permits upon the application of a water undertaker, authorising the applicant to take water from the sources specified in the permit. A Drought Permit suspends or restricts the operation of any Drought Order relating to the relevant inland waters. Drought Permits, intended for use when a drought exists or is pending, last for six months unless extended by application to the Environment Agency (subject to a maximum duration of

229 Ss 41–42 WRA 1991.
230 Ss 51–53 WRA 1991.
231 Ss 43–45 WRA 1991.
232 S 61 WRA 1991.
233 See Pt II, Chapter III of the WRA 1991.
234 S 78 WRA 1991.
235 S 79 and Sched 9 WRA 1991.

12 months). Section 79 and Scheds 8 and 9 of the WRA 1991 detail the relevant procedural, publicity and financial requirements regarding the making of a Drought Permit.

4.19 Controls relating to drinking water

The WIA 1991 provides the regulatory framework concerning water quality and sufficiency of water supplies. Under s 67, WIA 1991 the Secretary of State may make regulations specifying the criteria relating to 'wholesome water' (that is, water which is safe and pleasant to drink).[236]

The relevant regulations giving effect to the EU Drinking Water Directive 80/778/EEC are the Water Supply (Water Quality) Regulations 2000.[237] The Regulations specify the substances which may be present in water, the characteristics of the water (taste, odour, etc.), sampling, and the mandatory standards regarding water used for drinking, washing, cooking and food production. The Regulations make provision for the keeping of publicly accessible registers of water quality information and reporting requirements. A water undertaker may apply to the Secretary of State to relax the Regulations subject to the right of local authorities to make representations or objections.

The quality of private water supplies such as wells is regulated by the Private Water Supply Regulations 1991.[238] Private water supplies are divided into domestic supplies (Category 1) and food production (Category 2). Local authorities have a duty to sample these supplies and if they are found to be unwholesome or insufficient, the authority may by notice specify remedial works or other action to improve the supply.

Under s 68 of the WIA 1991 and the Drinking Water (Undertakings) (England and Wales) Regulations 2000,[239] water undertakers have a duty to ensure that water supplied to premises for domestic or food production purposes is wholesome at the time of supply and, so far as is reasonably practicable, to ensure that (with regard to each source of supply or combination of supplies) there is no deterioration in the quality of supply. The Secretary of State has the power[240] to enforce these drinking water-related duties.

4.19.1 Section 70 of the WIA 1991

It is an offence under s 70 WIA 1991 for a water undertaker to supply water which is unfit for human consumption. Only the Secretary of State or the DPP may prosecute for breach of this provision. In *Drinking Water Inspectorate v Severn Trent Water* (1995),[241] the Crown Court convicted Severn Trent of supplying unfit water. The court drew a distinction between 'fitness' and 'wholesomeness' and held that water could be unfit for human consumption, although it was wholesome within the meaning of the Drinking Water Supply Regulations and did not pose a public health risk.

The heightened concern with health risks[242] is apparent in the case of *Secretary of State for Wales v Dwr Cymru* (1995),[243] in which the defendant, Welsh Water, was convicted of breaching reg 28 of the Water Supply (Water Quality) Regulations 1989 (now superseded by the 2000 Regulations).[244] Although there was no evidence that the breach (consisting of failure

---

236 See *McColl v Strathclyde Regional Council* [1984] JPL 351.
237 SI 2000/3184.
238 SI 1991/2790.
239 SI 2000/1297.
240 S 18 of the WIA 1991.
241 *Drinking Water Inspectorate v Severn Trent Water* (1995) 243 ENDS 45.
242 See 'public concern' in Chapter 12.
243 *Secretary of State for Wales v Dwr Cymru* (1995) 242 ENDS 169.
244 See SI 2000/3184.

to obtain a permit to line water pipes with a particular material (epoxy resin)) had affected drinking water quality, the defendant was nevertheless convicted, for it was not certain that its actions had not exposed its customers to any risk.

In R v Yorkshire Water Services Ltd (2001),[245] the court set out sentencing guidelines relating to breach of s 70 WIA 1991. In assessing an appropriate fine, the court should have regard to the following factors: the severity of the damage, culpability, previous convictions, the attitude of the defendant, the defendant's post-incident response, and the balance between a censorial penalty and the impact of a large fine on the water company's water supply responsibilities.

See Chapter ◄ 2.7.3

4.19.2 The Water Act 2003

The Water Act reforms the licensing system which regulates the abstraction of water for drinking and other uses from both surface and groundwaters. The Act addresses the shortcomings of the previous system: (a) licences which were granted with insufficient thought to their environmental impacts; and (b) the large number of statutory exemptions from licensing control. The Act enables the UK to comply with the EU Water Framework Directive which requires the regulation of the abstraction of fresh surface waters and groundwaters, the regulation of the impoundment of fresh surface waters (e.g. reservoir operation), the prior authorisation (licensing) of abstractions, and the setting-up of abstraction registers (publicly accessible).

The main aims of the Act are fourfold: (1) to bring about improvements in the sustainable use of water resources,[246] (2) to increase competition, (3) to promote water conservation, and (4) to provide opportunities for greater consumer input into water resource management issues.

Whilst the Act introduces a range of controls we focus, in this section of the text, on the implications of the Act for water abstraction licensing. The Act creates three types of abstraction licence:[247] (a) temporary licences (for a maximum of 28 days' abstraction); (b) a transfer licence (e.g. authorising a switch from one source of supply to another source); and (c) a full licence applying to one source of supply (all licences which existed prior to the Act are full licences).[248] The licence transfer and temporary licences are devices designed to assist the Environment Agency in improving sustainable water resource management.

Section 6 of the Act replaces the previous licensing exemptions, based on water use, with an exemption threshold of 20 cubic litres of water per day (i.e. abstractions below this threshold are exempt from the need to obtain a licence authorising the relevant abstraction). All irrigation and dewatering exemptions (except spray irrigation) are terminated. All abstraction licences are time-limited and the Act removes a licence holder's entitlement to compensation if the Secretary of State directs that a non-time-limited licence should be curtailed[249] in order to avoid causing serious environmental damage.

The Environment Agency is given powers to revoke or vary abstraction licences without payment of compensation (provided the relevant licence has not been used for four years).

---

245 R v Yorkshire Water Services Ltd (2001) The Times, 12 December.
246 See the 1999 government report on water abstraction: Taking Water Responsibly.
247 See s 1.
248 See s 102(1).
249 After 15 July 2012.

4.20 The interface of the WRA 1991 and WIA 1991 with other statutory water pollution controls

Section 69 of the WIA 1991 empowers the Secretary of State to make regulations (for monitoring, recording, analysis, etc.) relating to the s 68 WIA 1991 duty of water undertakers to supply wholesome water.[250]

4.20.1 Offences

Under s 71 of the WIA, it is an offence to cause or permit any underground water to run to waste from any well, borehole or other work, and to abstract water from a well, borehole or other work in excess of requirements.

Under s 72 of the WIA, it is an offence to commit any act of neglect whereby water in any water works (to be used for domestic or food production purposes) is likely to be polluted. Note the provision of exemptions relating to agriculture (complying with best husbandry practice) and highway authorities (using tar on public roads).

Under s 73 of the WIA, it is an offence for an owner or occupier of premises to cause or permit, whether intentionally or negligently, any of his water fittings to be in disrepair or misused so as to result in contamination or waste of water.[251]

If, in the opinion of a water undertaker, a serious water deficiency exists or is threatened, it may introduce a hosepipe ban.[252]

4.20.2 Local authority functions regarding water supply

Under s 77 of the WIA 1991, local authorities must be provided with information regarding the wholesomeness and sufficiency of water supplies. Regulations[253] require water undertakers to provide local authorities and health authorities with information regarding threats to water supplies which may result in serious risks to health. The Secretary of State has power to make regulations regarding the provision of information.[254]

Section 78 of the WIA 1991 requires local authorities to inform water undertakers of anything which suggests that any water supply is, or has been, or is likely to be:

(a) unwholesome or insufficient for domestic use;
(b) so unwholesome or insufficient as to be likely to endanger life or health; and
(c) likely to lead to breach of the suppliers' duty to supply wholesome water.[255] Local authorities have no power to control the remedial action taken by water undertakers with regard to public water supplies. Any concerns which local authorities have with regard to remedial action must be referred to the Secretary of State.

Local authorities enjoy their most extensive powers with regard to private water supplies. If a local authority believes that a private water supply is unwholesome or insufficient, it may serve a notice (a private supply notice (PSN)) on the owners and occupiers of the relevant land detailing the

---

250 See the Water Supply (Water Quality) Regulations 2000 (SI 2000/3184).
251 The Secretary of State may make regulations addressing this issue under s 74 WIA 1991.
252 S 76 of the WIA.
253 SI 2000/3184.
254 S 77(3) WIA 1991.
255 See 4.21.7.

necessary remedial works.[256] The PSN may specify that the local authority will undertake the remedial works or that a water undertaker or some other person will provide a supply of wholesome water. Sections 81–85 WIA 1991 set out: (a) the Secretary of State's powers to hold a local inquiry and to confirm, vary, or quash a PSN; (b) the powers of local authorities to obtain information and enter premises; and (c) provisions relating to the variation and enforcement of PSNs.

4.20.3 Part I of the EPA 1990

In addition to the controls under the WRA 1991 and the WIA 1991 discussed above, Pt I of the EPA 1990 also provided controls which related to water pollution. Part I introduced IPC as a system for controlling pollution from the most seriously polluting processes which were prescribed by the Act. Processes which were subject to IPC were controlled by the Environment Agency with the aim of controlling pollution discharged into all environmental mediums, including water, in order to achieve the best practicable environmental option. In other words, for the most seriously polluting processes subject to IPC, the controls over water pollution were not seen in isolation but were dealt with by considering the impact of the prescribed activity on the environment as a whole. IPC licences were replaced, at the latest in 2007, by IPPC permits. The IPPC permitting process is now set out in the Environmental Permitting (England and Wales) Regulations 2010.

4.20.4 The PPCA 1999

The PPCA 1999 introduced IPPC, which replaced IPC control by 2007. The licences (permits) issued under the PPCA 1999 controlled all environmental impacts of licensed installations, including discharges to controlled waters. IPPC permits are now issued in accordance with the Environmental Permitting (England and Wales) Regulations 2010.

See Chapter 6

4.20.5 Part IIA of the EPA 1990

Part IIA of the EPA 1990 establishes the contaminated land regime. The pollution pathways regulated under Pt IIA of the EPA 1990 include contamination of groundwaters.

As regards the overlap between water pollution controls and contaminated land, the Water Act 2003 alters the test for determining when land is contaminated[257] so that less property is stigmatised for what is, in effect, minor pollution. Prior to the Water Act 2003 land was contaminated under Pt IIA of the EPA 1990 if it was in such a state that 'pollution of controlled waters is being or is likely to be caused'. The Water Act only triggers contaminated land remediation where 'significant pollution of controlled waters is being caused or there is a significant possibility of such pollution being caused'.

See Chapter 7

4.21 Water pollution: the European Union and the pace of regulatory change

The UK's membership of the European Union has had important consequences for the UK with regard to improvements in water quality and the regulation of water pollution. The European Commission has been very active in drawing up a series of water-related directives which, when passed by the European Parliament, must then be transposed into national law by Member States.

---

256 S 80 WIA 1991.
257 See s 86 WA 2003.

These directives have sought to set standards for the regulation of a wide range of activities, including:

(a)   discharges of dangerous substances into the aquatic environment (surface waters, ground-waters and coastal waters);
(b)   bathing water quality;
(c)   regulation of nitrate levels;
(d)   sewage effluent treatment processes;
(e)   drinking water quality;
(f)   water quality for freshwater fish and shellfish;
(g)   river basin-based water pollution and water quality regulation.

These directives establish clear parameters and objectives and their effects are channelled through to individual dischargers, principally by (primary and secondary legislation transposing the directives into UK law) the discharge consent licensing (i.e. permitting) system. Most water directives fall into four types:

(a)   those, such as the Dangerous Substances Directive,[258] which set emission limits (emission standards);
(b)   those, such as the Bathing Water Directive,[259] which set quality objectives linked to actual or intended use of the relevant waters (quality objectives of receiving waters);
(c)   those, such as the Titanium Dioxide Directive,[260] regulating specific polluting discharges (in this case paint industry waste); and
(d)   those, such as the Detergents Directives,[261] which regulate product standards (in the case of detergents, only detergents with a biodegradability of at least 90 per cent may be sold).

Europe has had, and continues to have, a major impact on water quality and water pollution control in the UK.[262] Over the last four decades, the European Parliament has passed a range of directives designed to prevent discharges of pollutants into the aquatic environment and also to establish quality standards for waters which are used for the following non-exhaustive list of purposes: drinking, bathing, irrigation, industrial/manufacturing and fishing. Often, the EU adopts a 'framework directive' to establish a specific control regime and then, over time, supplements this with 'daughter directives' which, whilst establishing detailed controls, sets limits for the presence of specific chemical substances in different types of waters (e.g. drinking, bathing and fishing). Member States are given a set period of time to transpose the relevant EU directive into national law and achieve actual compliance with the specific provisions of the directive.

Water directives have established a coherent system of control of water pollution and water quality. Directives are often characterised by the following features: Member States must set up regulatory bodies (e.g. the Environment Agency) to 'police' compliance with the obligations contained in each directive; some directives set quality standards—these may be of two types: mandatory 'I' guides or target 'G' guides; Member States have limited discretion as to the waters which are designated for different uses (and therefore the EU-based controls which apply to those

---

258 See 4.21.1.
259 See 4.21.4.
260 See 4.21.9.
261 See 4.21.8.
262 Especially in view of the contents of the Water Framework Directive 2000/60/EC, which extends the reach of European law to the regulation of all polluting substances in all types of regulated waters; see 4.21.11.

waters); and the original standards (and other contents of the Directive) may be tightened to keep pace with technological and scientific advances. The Water Framework Directive 2000/60/EC will by 2013 have consolidated many of the earlier water-related directives.[263]

4.21.1 The Dangerous Substances Directive (76/464/EEC) as consolidated by Directive 2006/11/EC

The Dangerous Substances Directive, as consolidated, provides a good example of the EU's emission standard approach to water pollution regulation. The objectives of this framework directive are: (a) to *eliminate* the discharge (and presence) of highly toxic substances (the 'Black List'—List I) in the aquatic environment; and (b) to *reduce* the discharge (and presence) of other chemical substances (the 'Grey List'—List II) in the aquatic environment (note the comparable lists of hazardous substances referred to in the 1974 Paris Convention on the Prevention of Marine Pollution from Land Based Sources).

Black List substances are hazardous because of their toxicity, persistence and their bio-accumulative and carcinogenic properties (for example, mercury, cadmium, organophosphorous, mineral oils, hydrocarbons, etc.).

The EU favours the use of daughter directives to set limit values (maximum allowable concentrations—MACs) for these substances. Few daughter directives setting MACs for Black List substances have been adopted by the European Parliament. Currently where there is no daughter directive in place to set a MAC in regard to a Black List substance, the substance is regulated as if it were a Grey List substance.

List II substances are those which have an adverse impact on the aquatic environment but the severity of the relevant impacts varies with the location and characteristics of the receiving waters. These substances[264] have adverse effects on receiving waters with regard to such matters as taste and odour of water sources used for human consumption or food production. In contrast to Black List substances, where the EU sets the relevant MAC, the water quality standards applicable to Grey List substances are set by each Member State. In England and Wales the government has implemented its Grey List obligations by the setting of Statutory Water Quality Objectives.[265] In addition to establishing SWQOs, each Member State is required to put in place a programme to reduce the presence of Grey List substances in its aquatic environment. Such reduction programmes utilise the water pollution licensing discharge consent (i.e. permitting) system which exists in each Member State.

The Dangerous Substances Directive requires Member States to set up 'competent authorities', for example, the Environment Agency, to oversee the elimination and/or reduction of Black and Grey List substances via licensing (permitting) systems. Authorisation of the discharge of substances on both lists must be obtained before discharges commence. Licence (permit) conditions must include provisions relating to duration and the quality and quantity of the substances discharged. The limit values (MACs) for some Black List substances are set by daughter directives, although Member States are allowed to set stricter standards. As an alternative to the limit value approach (the majority of EU Member States prefer the EU to set uniform standards in regard to each Black List substance) with regard to Black List substances, the EU allowed Member States (notably the UK) to achieve compliance with EU law by focusing on the quality of the receiving waters into which listed substances are discharged (the so-called parallel approach to compliance). The consolidating directive 2006/11/EC has amended this provision in regard to Black List substances so that all

---

263 See 4.21.11.
264 For example, lead, zinc, chromium, copper, etc. and some biocides, cyanides, ammonia, nitrites and fluorites.
265 E.g. the Water Supply (Water Quality) Regulations 2000 SI 2000/3184.

Member States comply with the uniform emission standards set by the EU. The UK sets SWQOs, taking into account listed substances discharged into the relevant waters. Discharges of many Black and Grey List substances are regulated in England and Wales via the IPPC licensing and the regulatory regime controlling discharges of prescribed substances to sewers. Black List substances are now referred to as 'priority hazardous substances'.[266]

The Dangerous Substances Directive will be phased out and replaced by the Water Framework Directive in 2013.

4.21.2 The Groundwater Directive (80/68/EEC) as amended by Directive 86/280 and consolidated by Directive 2000/118/EC

The objective of this 1980 directive (adopting an emissions-based approach to pollution regulation) is to prevent, reduce or eliminate pollution of groundwater (e.g. an aquifer) due to the presence of listed substances. The contents of Lists I and II of this directive are similar to the Dangerous Substances Directive. The Groundwater Directive regulates both direct and indirect (for example, percolation from landfill sites) discharges. Direct discharges of List I substances are banned.[267] 'Groundwater' is defined as water below the surface of the ground, in the saturation zone, and in direct contact with the ground or sub-soil. Pollution of groundwater occurs where a discharge of listed substances results in danger to human health, water supplies, harm to living resources or aquatic ecosystems and interference with legitimate water use.

Regulation of List I and List II substances is licence-based. Licences contain conditions relating to place of discharge, method of discharge, maximum quantity, monitoring arrangements and precautionary measures. Licences are subject to a mandatory four-yearly review. The Groundwater Directive will, in due course, be replaced by the Water Framework Directive.

4.21.3 The Surface Waters Directive (75/440/EEC)

This Directive aims to maintain and, via treatment, improve the quality of surface waters, especially those waters from which water is abstracted for human consumption. Surface waters are classified (A1–A3) according to the measures necessary to produce potable (drinkable) water. The Directive contains a mix of mandatory standards and guideline standards to regulate water quality.

4.21.4 The Bathing Waters Directive (76/160/EEC) amended by Directive 2006/7/EC

The Bathing Waters Directive provides an example of a quality objective approach to pollution regulation. This Directive is designed to protect public health by maintaining the quality of bathing waters (e.g. freshwater lakes and sea waters). The Directive specifies the necessary micro-biological and physio-chemical characteristics of bathing waters. Both waters authorised for bathing and those which, although not authorised, are used by large numbers of bathers fall within the ambit of the Directive. All Member States were required to identify the relevant waters and put the relevant standards in place by the end of 1985; however, the UK was held to be in breach of the Directive.[268] The 1976 Bathing Waters Directive based compliance with the standards laid down by the Directive

---

266 See Water Framework Directive; see 4.21.11.

267 I.e. they must be prevented from entering groundwaters via the deployment of the discharge consent system of each Member State.

268 Because of its failure to designate Blackpool, Southport and Formby as bathing waters which met the designation criteria in the Directive. See *Commission v UK (Bathing Water)* (Case 56/90) [1993] Water Law 168; [1993] Env LR 472.

upon sampling evidence which confirmed that mandatory (Imperative—I values) standards were achieved in 95 per cent of samples and guide standards (G values) were achieved in 90 per cent of samples. Compliance with the Bathing Waters Directive 2006 is now based on an average of the results of several years of samples.[269] All Member States are subject to reporting requirements (that is, reporting to the Commission). The original Bathing Waters Directive has been revised by the Bathing Waters Directive 2000/7/EC, which came into force in March 2008. This directive brings the original directive into line with the requirements of the Water Framework Directive. The revisions to the Bathing Waters Directive reflect a more risk-based approach to regulation by adopting a public health orientation and provide the public with better information regarding the quality of bathing waters in each Member State. Bathing waters are now graded: excellent, good, satisfactory and poor, whilst bathing water quality is now assessed by reference to a four-year average, rather than a single year's statistical performance.[270]

4.21.5 The Freshwater Fish Waters Directive (78/659/EEC), as amended by Directive 91/692/EEC and Directive 2006/44/EC

The dual objective of this Directive is to designate relevant waters and set quality objectives for waters capable of supporting freshwater fish. Designations may either be 'salmonid' (capable of supporting salmon and trout) or 'cyprinid' (capable of supporting coarse fish). The Directive (a) sets mandatory 'I' and guide 'G' standards, (b) requires Member States to set up pollution reduction programmes with the aim that designated waters achieve 'I' and 'G' standards within five years of the date of designation, and (c) sets out sampling and reporting (three-yearly) obligations.

4.21.6 The Shellfish Waters Directive (79/923/EEC) amended by Directive 2006/113/EC

This Directive has the same objectives as the Freshwater Fish Water Directive, save that it sets water quality objectives for waters which support shellfish (bivalve and gastropod molluscs, e.g. oysters). Designated waters include coastal and brackish waters.

4.21.7 The Drinking Water Directive (80/778/EEC) replaced by Directive 98/83/EC

This Directive sets quality standards for drinking waters and waters used in cooking. The relevant standards (mandatory and guide) are located in Annex 1. Mandatory standards, whether maximum allowable concentrations (MACs) or minimum required concentrations (MRCs), must be achieved, but Member States have some flexibility in the actions they may take to achieve guide value (i.e. target) standards. Derogations (permitted delays in achieving the target standards) may be permitted due to exceptional climatic conditions (e.g. floods and droughts), the condition of the ground which is the source of water supply (e.g. aquifer contamination), the existence of an emergency, and in circumstances in which a state experiences compliance problems.[271] In 2003 the 1998 Directive was transposed into UK law by the Water Supply (Water Quality) Regulations 2000.[272] In England and Wales s 67 Water Industry Act 1991 requires drinking water to be 'wholesome'—a term which is defined in the 2000 Water Quality Regulations.

---

269 Directive 2006/11/EC.
270 See www.defra.gov.uk/environment/quality/bathing/revision.htm.
271 See Arts 9, 10 and 20.
272 SI 2000/3184.

4.21.8 The Detergents Directives (73/404/EEC) and (73/405/EEC), amended by Directives 82/242/EEC, 82/243/EEC and 86/94/EEC

The purpose of these Directives is to protect water quality from the adverse impacts, including photosynthesis, oxidation, and damage to sewage treatment processes, of detergents. The Directives set biodegradability standards (banning the sale of detergents which are less than 90 per cent biodegradable) and provides examples of a product-standard approach to pollution regulation.

4.21.9 The Titanium Dioxide Directive (78/176/EEC), amended by Directives 82/883/EEC and 83/29/EEC

Whilst titanium dioxide is an important constituent of paints, the waste from the manufacturing process poses problems when dumped, stored or injected into the earth. The Directive requires Member States to license the disposal of waste from the industry. Before granting permission to discharge, dump, store or inject waste in England and Wales, the Environment Agency will: (a) in the case of existing plants, undertake an assessment of the method of waste disposal. The Environment Agency must be satisfied that the method of disposal adopted poses no adverse aquatic consequences and there is no better way of dealing with the waste; and (b) in the case of a new plant, require an environmental impact assessment and undertakings from the operator to use the least damaging environmental techniques and raw materials. The Directive contains provisions relating to the establishment of waste reduction programmes, monitoring and reporting. Directive 89/428/EEC bans the dumping of wastes, including titanium dioxide wastes, into inland waters and marine waters.

4.21.10 The Urban Waste Water Treatment Directive (91/271/EEC)

This Directive sets minimum standards for the treatment of waste waters, such as industrial effluent and domestic sewage (by sewage treatment systems) generated by urban centres large enough to require sewage collection and treatment systems. The extent to which waste waters require treatment before their reintroduction into the waters of a Member State varies with the size of the relevant urban centre; however, biological treatment of waste waters is required for urban centres with a population of at least 15,000. Stricter standards apply to 'sensitive areas'. Member States are free to define these sensitive areas, but typically they are: (a) coastal waters and freshwaters prone to eutrophication (algal blooms associated with high nitrate content of coastal or inland waters); and (b) surface waters from which drinking water is abstracted, which are at risk of exceeding the nitrate levels in Directive 75/440/EEC. Less sensitive areas enjoy more relaxed standards. From 1998, the disposal of sewage sludge, whether by dumping or pumping, into surface waters (including coastal waters) has been banned. This has resulted in major sewerage infrastructure expenditure by the 10 large privatised water and sewerage companies in England and Wales. The Directive was implemented in England and Wales by the Urban Waste Water Treatment (England and Wales) Regulations 1994.

4.21.11 The Water Framework Directive (2000/60/EC)

This Directive, which came into force in December 2000, provides a framework for the protection of inland surface waters, groundwaters and transitional waters (river mouth/estuary waters which change from fresh to saline). In contrast to previous aquatic directives, the remit of the Water Framework Directive extends to the full range of water bodies including surface, ground, coastal and estuarine waters. The Directive consolidates a range of directives so that, by 2013, the following directives will have been repealed: the Groundwater Directive, the Dangerous Substances Directive, the Freshwater Fish Waters Directive and the Shellfish Waters Directive. The following directives will, however, remain in force: the Urban Waste Water Treatment Directive, the Drinking Water Quality Directive, the Bathing Waters Directive and the Agricultural Nitrates Directive.

The Directive aims to: (a) halt deterioration in the quality of these waters; (b) improve the quality of aquatic ecosystems and terrestrial systems which depend upon water and wetlands; (c) promote sustainable water use in order to protect water resources in the longer term; (d) mitigate the impacts of floods and droughts; (e) eliminate 'priority' hazardous substances (i.e. 'Black List' substances); (f) contribute to reducing concentrations of substances in the marine environment to their naturally occurring background levels and eliminating the presence of synthetic (man-made) substances; (g) progressively reduce water pollution (especially groundwater pollution); and (h) contribute to the supply of 'good quality' surface and ground waters to achieve sustainable and equitable water use.

The Directive obliges Member States to aim to achieve (1) good surface water status, (2) good groundwater status, and (3) good ecological potential by the beginning of 2016. Good surface water status is measured by reference to chemical status and ecological status, whilst good ground-water status is measured by reference to water quantity and (chemical) water purity. The chemical status of surface waters is determined by the presence of 'priority hazardous substances' in concentrations which do not exceed the relevant EU water quality standards or relevant parameters contained in other European legislative provisions (e.g. directives). The ecological status criterion (applicable to surface waters) refers to any surface water body (significantly affected by human activity) which, irrespective of human impacts, achieves a balanced and sustainable aquatic ecosystem.

'High ecological status' is defined in the Directive by reference to pristine waters (there are no such waters in the UK), whilst 'good ecological status' represents a minor change in pristine status due to human impacts. In regard to 'good ecological potential' waters, Member States may take the costs of achieving improvements into account (so that expenditure is not disproportionate). Also Member States are given a discretion, when deciding which waters have been 'heavily modified' by human actions (so that they fall within the good ecological potential class of waters), and are allowed to take into account the benefits (to humans) of current uses of the relevant waters.

The Directive adopts a river basin (river catchment) focus regarding water resource management and pollution control. This will require Member States to co-operate with non-EU States and will lead to greater integration of resource management and water pollution control. The Directive imposes the following duties on Member States:

(a) to identify river basins (small basins are to be combined into a river basin district);
(b) to create a regulatory body (or assign regulatory responsibility to an existing regulatory body);
(c) to assign a river basin which is shared with two or more Member States to an international river basin district;
(d) to endeavour to co-operate with a non-EU state where a river basin in the Member State is shared with a non-EU state (to achieve compliance throughout the entire basin);
(e) to analyse each year the characteristics of the river basin, review human impacts on ground and surface waters, and carry out an economic analysis of water use;
(f) to prepare and publish a series of river basin management plans by 2009. These plans are to be updated every six years. Each river basin management plan provides a programme of improvements with a view to ensuring that all the waters in the river basin achieve good water quality status. In preparing river basin management plans Member States must ensure that measures are taken to: (1) regulate point source polluting discharges, (2) set environmental quality standards to regulate the cumulative impact of polluting discharges, and (3) eliminate priority hazardous substances. The Directive provides an opportunity for some degree of public participation in the preparation of river basin management plans;

(g) to progressively reduce water pollution; and

(h) to contribute to the supply of 'good quality' surface waters to achieve sustainable and equitable water use.

Member States must ensure that water pricing policies provide adequate incentives to ensure the
efficient use of water resources. This provision recognises the link between water quantity and
water quality and the need to reflect this in water policy pricing via the introduction of full cost
recovery pricing by 2010.

The Commission is compiling a list of 'priority' hazardous substances[273] to be phased out over
a 20-year period. Implementation of the Directive in the UK will involve some amendment to
existing legislation. The Water Framework Directive has begun to be implemented in England and
Wales via secondary legislation, the first of which is the Water Environment (Water Framework
Directive) (England and Wales) Regulations 2003.[274]

The House of Commons Environment, Food and Rural Affairs Select Committee published its
fourth Report, *The Water Framework Directive*, HC 130 I and II (2002–03) in 2003. The Report was
critical of the apparent lack of urgency on the part of the government to implement the Directive
properly within the relevant time limits (transposition into UK law was due on 21 December
2003). In addition, the Committee drew attention to: the amount of work yet to be completed to
finalise the relevant criteria and definitions regarding ecological water quality; the lack of information regarding the extent of UK waters which will comply with the Directive; and the current
threats to water quality posed by over-abstraction, flood defence works, drainage works and
eutrophication (algal blooms). The Committee recommended setting up a scientific steering group
to commission research, clarify of the roles of Defra and the Environment Agency, the provision of
adequate resources to the Environment Agency, and an assessment of the legislative impact of the
Directive on the current national legislative framework.

The Water Environment (Water Framework Directive) (England and Wales) Regulations 2003
implement the Water Framework Directive. The regulations put in place a strategic planning process
for managing, protecting and improving the quality of water resources applying a river basin
management approach.

4.21.12 The Agricultural Nitrates Directive (91/676/EEC)

This Directive controls agricultural nitrate pollution by requiring Member States to establish nitrate
vulnerable zones.[275]

4.22 Marine pollution

Coverage of water quality and water pollution in England and Wales would not be complete without
some mention of marine pollution. The main human-related marine environmental problems
appear to be: discharge of hazardous substances into the aquatic environment,[276] especially if such
substances are bioaccumulative and get into the food chain;[277] waste dumping; chemical 'run-off'

---

273 Based on risk assessments: see Regulation (EEC) 793/93, Directive 91/41/EEC and Directive 98/8/EC.
274 SI 2003/3242.
275 See 4.13.6.
276 For example, oil pollution discharges from oil tankers, pipelines or oil rigs, and the discharge of toxic substances from
manufacturing and other human activity into surface or coastal waters.
277 For example, fish and shellfish contaminated with mercury.

which flows from rivers into the seas and results in eutrophication in coastal zones (algal blooms); resource depletion (overfishing); and the impact of climate change on oceanic currents (such as El Niño). Bell and McGillivray estimate that 77 per cent of marine pollution is caused by land-based discharges into the aquatic environment either directly into waters or indirectly via atmospheric deposition (e.g. from vehicles and factories).[278]

For centuries, waste substances were poured into surface waters and found their way into the marine environment, where their effects were diluted; however, international recognition that the practice of treating oceans as 'free' dustbins must be regulated led, in the late twentieth century, to the conclusion of a series of important multilateral treaties (although customary international law is still highly relevant).[279] Many international treaties contain provisions which are 'preventive' in approach (i.e. banning the entry of substances into the marine environment);[280] however, some treaties[281] take a reactive approach. The Intervention Convention enables action to be taken where oil pollution occurs as a result of non-deliberate release of oil (due to a tanker disaster, for example).

One significant treaty is the UN Convention on the Law of the Sea (UNCLOS), which was concluded in 1982 and came into force in 1994.[282] Part XII of UNCLOS contains important obligations binding contracting parties regarding marine protection and preservation (preventing pollution, minimising/reducing pollution and regulating pollution) arising from land-based sources of pollution, sea-based sources of pollution (e.g. mining of the seabed and oil rig/drilling operations) and dumping of waste substances in the marine environment. Contracting states are subject to a general duty to protect the marine environment, plus obligations relating to monitoring, exchange of information, scientific and technical co-operation and enforcement.

In regard to oil pollution, the key international treaty is the International Convention for the Prevention of Pollution from Ships (MARPOL) of 1973.[283] MARPOL was drafted by the International Maritime Organisation (IMO)—a UN agency with responsibility for the safety of shipping and marine oil pollution. By 2001, the vast majority of the world states with large shipping fleets had ratified the Convention, which is designed to eliminate and/or minimise the pollution of international waters by oil or other harmful substances (i.e. operational polluting discharges). Annexes I (oil pollution provisions) and II (noxious liquids) are compulsory (that is, they automatically bind contracting states), whereas Annexes III–VI are optional.[284] MARPOL was amended in 1992, in regard to existing provisions controlling the design, construction and maintenance of tankers, by introducing a requirement to fit double hulls to oil tankers over 25 years of age (all new tankers are subject to the double hull obligation).

International treaties, conventions and agreements are concluded between contracting states but do not automatically bind the citizens of the contracting state, hence the need to enact domestic legislation (primary or secondary legislation) to give effect to the terms of the relevant international agreement. In the UK, the key provisions of MARPOL, contained in Annex I, are implemented by the Merchant Shipping (Prevention of Oil Pollution) Order 1983,[285] the Merchant Shipping (Prevention of Oil Pollution) Regulations 1996,[286] the Merchant Shipping (Prevention of Oil Pollution) (Amendment) Regulations 2000[287] and the Merchant Shipping (Reporting Requirements

---

278 S Bell and D McGillivray, *Environmental Law* (7th edn OUP, Oxford 2008) 586.
279 See *Nicaragua v United States* (Merits) (1986) ICJ 14, *Lake Lanoux Arbitration* (1957) and *The Trail Smelter Arbitration* (1940).
280 E.g. OSPAR. See page 181.
281 E.g. the Intervention Convention 1969.
282 Ratified by the UK in 1997.
283 Plus the London Protocol of 1978.
284 And relate to the regulation of packaged harmful substances, sewage and waste dumping from ships, and air pollution from ships.
285 SI 1983/1106.
286 SI 1996/2154.
287 SI 2000/483.

for Ships Carrying Dangerous or Polluting Goods) Regulations 1995.[288] The MARPOL obligations apply to both flag states and port states (where foreign vessels dock). Territorially MARPOL applies to vessels in both territorial seas and, in some cases, the exclusive economic zone of a contracting state. The 1996 Regulations contain the key provisions and apply to all ships in UK territorial waters and UK registered vessels wherever they are. The Regulations ban discharges of oil and oily water (most often routine discharges resulting from cleaning a tanker's cargo tanks), whether a deliberate disposal or an accidental escape. A number of exemptions apply. Any ship is exempt if it has embarked on a voyage, is not within a special marine area at the time the discharge takes place (for example, the Mediterranean or Baltic Seas), the oil content of the discharge does not exceed 15 parts per million (ppm), and the vessel is operating the oil filtering and monitoring equipment specified in the Regulations. Additional restrictions apply to UK tankers. UK tankers must be at least 50 miles from land at the time the discharge takes place, the rate and quantity of the discharge must comply with the Regulations and 'control systems' (that is, cleaning the oil tanks) must be in operation. Exemptions also apply: (a) if the discharge was necessary for ship safety or for saving life; (b) the discharge was due to damage to the ship or its equipment; and (c) the discharge was made to combat pollution.

UK tankers of over 150 gross registered tonnage (similar provisions relate to UK offshore installations) are required to undergo a full survey every five years and annual and intermediate surveys, following which, if satisfactory, an International Oil Pollution Prevention Certificate will be issued to the vessel. Accidents or incidents affecting the integrity of the vessel or its equipment must be reported without delay to the relevant UK marine authority. Records must be kept of the movements of oil and oil tank cleaning operations.

The Secretary of State has power to refuse entry to UK ports of non-compliant tankers which represent an unreasonable threat of harm to the marine environment. The Secretary of State also has the power to detain any vessel suspected of breaching the Regulations.

Under s 131 of the Merchant Shipping Act (MSA) 1995, it is an offence to discharge oil (crude oil, fuel oil, some diesel oils, etc.) into navigable territorial waters. A defence is available to dischargers if the escape of oil, or the delay in discovering the escape, was not caused by lack of reasonable care and remedial actions were taken as soon as practicable. Harbour Masters have the power[289] to detain vessels believed to have committed a s 131 offence.

Under s 136 of the MSA 1995, discharges or escapes of oil or oily water into any UK harbour must be reported to the Harbour Master. Failure to report, subject to certain exceptions, is an offence. The provision of 'reception facilities' (port disposal) for waste oil and oily water arising from cargo tank cleaning is governed by the Merchant Shipping (Port Waste Reception Facilities) Regulations 1997.[290] The provision of such facilities will clearly reduce the need to discharge wastes at sea.

In the event of a tanker accident which threatens to cause significant pollution of UK waters, the Secretary of State[291] is empowered to give a direction to any of the tanker owner, the master, the pilot or the salvor to prevent and/or minimise pollution.[292] A s 137 direction may, for example, order the moving of a tanker, the removal of its cargo and the carrying-out of salvage operations. Furthermore, if the Secretary of State believes that his powers are insufficient, he can order the destruction of the vessel. It is an offence to fail to comply with a s 137 direction subject to due

---

288 SI 1995/2498.
289 S 144.
290 SI 1997/3018.
291 See s 137 MSA.
292 S 138A MSA enables a s 137 direction to be given in the case of threatened pollution due to hazardous substances other than oil.

diligence and emergency action defences. Section 141 MSA enables the Secretary of State to give directions to non-UK vessels sailing in non-UK waters but in a UK pollution zone (for example, the area around a damaged UK oil tanker).

Section 100A MSA enables the Secretary of State to create a temporary exclusion zone around a wrecked or damaged tanker (or offshore oil/gas rig) in UK waters or outside UK waters but within a UK pollution zone. The direction will specify the restrictions applying within the zone. Exclusion zones may only be created where significant harm may be caused by the wreck and an exclusion zone is necessary to prevent/reduce the actual/potential harm.

The EU has introduced a Directive on Ship Source Pollution Dir 2005/35/EC. The EU Commission was concerned that, despite international law,[293] deliberate discharges of waste oil and cargo residues would continue to occur at an unacceptable rate. Whilst MARPOL focuses on the provision of compensation to victims of oil pollution, the Directive aims to deter and punish offenders. The Directive incorporates the relevant international legal rules relating to discharges of wastes and sets out criminal offences and guidance on the sanctions to impose on convicted offenders.

The Prevention of Oil Pollution Act 1971 regulates polluting discharges from marine oil pipelines and oil exploration operations irrespective of the location of the relevant pipeline.

The main agreements regulating and/or banning waste dumping at sea are the London Convention of 1972 and the 1998 OSPAR Convention. The Convention on the Prevention of Marine Pollution by Dumping of Wastes and Other Matter (the London Convention) came into force in August 1975. The key objectives of the Convention are: (a) to control all sources of pollution entering the marine environment; and (b) to take all practicable steps to prevent dumping-related pollution likely to create hazards to man and marine life, taking into account the capacity (technical, scientific and economic) of each contracting state to achieve the relevant objectives. The Convention bans the dumping of certain highly toxic wastes (for example, mercury and radioactive wastes) and the dumping of other wastes must be licensed. The regulatory bodies in each contracting state which license dumping must keep records of the waste dumped (type of waste, quantity, location, when dumped and ('how') method of dumping). The Convention was amended by an important Protocol in 1996 requiring contracting states to adopt a precautionary approach to wastes licensed to be dumped. Annex I of the Protocol lists the categories of wastes which may be dumped (including sewage sludge, fish processing waste, dredged material, inert inorganic material, natural organic material, iron, steel, concrete and other non-harmful materials from islands with no other disposal option) subject to the grant of a licence. Consequently, the disposal of all other wastes by dumping is banned.

The Convention for the Protection of the Marine Environment of the North East Atlantic (OSPAR) entered into force in early 1998. It is intended that OSPAR will supersede the Oslo and Paris Conventions. OSPAR regulates all land-based and other (that is, offshore) sources of marine pollution within the limited geographical remit of the Convention. The need for effective regional co-operation underpins the Convention. Contracting states bind themselves to take all possible steps to prevent and/or eliminate all sources of marine pollution (contrast the 'listing'-based regulatory approach of the Paris Convention). 'Pollution' is widely defined: the introduction by man, directly or indirectly, of substances or energy into the maritime area which results, or is likely to result, in hazards to human health, harm to living resources and marine eco-systems, damage to amenities or interference with other legitimate uses of the sea.

Part II of the Food and Environmental Protection Act (FEPA) 1985, as amended, implements the UK's obligations stemming from the London and OSPAR Conventions. Under s 5 of the FEPA

---

293 See MARPOL, rr 73/78.

1985, any waste deposition (dumping) in UK waters must be licensed. Licences are also required for UK vessels with regard to (a) waste dumping in any sea, and (b) waste incineration at sea. Under the FEPA 1985, it is the Fisheries Minister who is the licensing authority. In deciding whether to grant or refuse a licence application, the Minister must have regard to marine ecosystem needs, human health and legitimate uses of the sea.

The disposal of offshore rigs (oil and gas) such as the Brent Spar is, in international law, governed by a combination of the London Convention, the 1996 Protocol to the London Convention, the OSPAR Convention and the OSPAR Decision 98/3 concerning the disposal of redundant offshore installations. The OSPAR Decision prohibits the disposal of rigs by dumping at sea save that dumping may be permitted (licensed) following an assessment (as required by Annex 2 of the OSPAR Decision) if there are significant reasons why disposal at sea is preferable to re-use of the facility, recycling or disposal on land. In the UK, these obligations are implemented by Pt IV of the Petroleum Act 1998.

4.23 Online resource centre

We recommend that the reader regularly refers to the section of the online resources corresponding to this chapter for information relating to updates, amendments and corrections.

4.24 Summary of key points

Chapter 4 has covered the following topics and issues:

- Water pollution control is primarily a statutory-based (e.g. WRA 1991, the Environmental Permitting (England and Wales) Regulations 2010 and WIA 1991) regulatory regime based, although tort (civil law) continues to play a supplementary role.
- Water pollution regulation is largely a permit-based process (in regard to point source pollution from industrial and sewage treatment plants), save that diffuse pollution (e.g. run-off from farmers' fields) is not amenable to permit-based regulatory control.
- Permit holders are required to pay an annual fee for each discharge permit/licence for releasing substances into controlled waters or into the sewage/effluent treatment system.
- The Environment Agency is the regulator with primary responsibility to 'police' pollution of surface waters, groundwaters and coastal waters. The privatised water companies 'police' the sewage/industrial effluent treatment systems.
- The focus of water pollution control is on the release (whether deliberate or accidental) of substances into the aquatic environment.
- EU directives are increasingly important in determining the shape and content of the water pollution regulatory regimes, especially in forcing Member States to set water quality standards and in tightly controlling substances which are hazardous to the aquatic environment.
- The statutory regulatory frameworks set out in the WRA 1991, the Environmental Permitting (England and Wales) Regulations 2010 and WIA 1991 are underpinned by criminal offences. Most offences are offences of strict liability, with few opportunities for defendants to escape conviction by running successful defences. The individual elements of each offence require careful analysis and case law must be referred to in order to fully understand the meaning of words and phrases used in each offence.
- Regulators which encounter evidence of water pollution offences have a discretion whether to mount a prosecution or resolve the pollution incident by other means. In the case of the Environment Agency its discretion to prosecute is aided by its own enforcement and sanctions policy documents.

- Regulators have a range of administrative powers, in addition to prosecution, which they often deploy to resolve a pollution incident. These administrative powers, in the case of the Environment Agency, include a 'clean-up' power which may be used to force a polluter to remediate the damage which it has caused.

 ## 4.25 Further reading

Books

Howarth, W and McGillivray, D, *Water Pollution and Water Quality Law* (Shaw and Sons, London 2001).

Looseleaf publications

Bates, J, *Water and Drainage Law* (Sweet & Maxwell, London 1990) (looseleaf publication, updated annually).
Garner's Environmental Law (Butterworths, London).

Journal articles and government papers

McFarlane, S, 'The *Empress* case: a plea for common sense' (1998) WLAW 104.
Parpworth, N, 'Who may be liable for an offence contrary to s 85 of the Water Resources Act 1991?' (2009) JPL 294.
Stanley, N, 'The *Empress* decision and causing water pollution' (1999) WLAW 37.

Useful websites

Environment Agency
www.environment-agency.gov.uk

Drinking Water Inspectorate
www.dwi.gov.uk

Chapter 5

Waste Management

Chapter Contents

Learning Objectives

By the end of this chapter you should have acquired an understanding of:

- how the law regulates waste generated in England and Wales;

- the main features of the waste regulatory regime;

- the roles and responsibilities of the regulators and the regulated;

- the impact of EU law and policy and international law on national waste law and policy;

- the key waste legislation—both primary (e.g. Environmental Protection Act 1990) and secondary (e.g. Environmental Permitting (England and Wales) Regulations 2010);

- the volume of waste generated and the main producers of waste;

- the main methods of disposal, treatment and recycling;

- the historical development of waste regulation in England and Wales;

- the legal definition of waste (especially the ongoing problem of defining what substances and materials are waste);

- the system of permit-based waste management regulation;

- the criminal law offences underpinning the waste regulatory regime;

- the permit-related powers of the regulators (used to persuade and/or compel permit holders to comply with pollution control law);

- the s 34 EPA 1990 duty of care—imposing cradle-to-grave responsibility on all persons in the 'waste chain';

- regulatory enforcement and prosecution policy.

5.1 Introduction[1]

The main planks of the regulatory regime relating to the management of solid wastes arising in England and Wales comprise Part II of the Environmental Protection Act 1990 (EPA 1990), as amended by the Environment Act 1995 (EA 1995), the Controlled Waste (Registration of Carriers and Seizure of Vehicles) Regulations 1991, as amended, the Hazardous Waste Regulations 2005 and the Environmental Permitting (England and Wales) Regulations 2010.

The EPA 1990 introduced a stricter and more extensive regulatory framework than had previously existed under the Control of Pollution Act 1974 (COPA 1974). In particular, the EPA 1990 introduced a statutory duty of care which creates 'cradle-to-grave' responsibility applying to all persons in the waste chain who handle waste from the time it is created to the time it is finally disposed of (or recycled). The definition of 'waste' has been amended, as a result of European Community legislation, so that a greater range of wastes are now subject to regulatory control.

---

1   In this chapter, references to licence and permit are interchangeable.

Additional controls apply to wastes which are 'hazardous' because they are particularly dangerous or difficult to handle.

Waste management permitting controls have been transferred to the Environment Agency, which is equipped with a wide range of permit-related powers, criminal law offences and civil powers to enable it to enforce compliance with the terms of waste management permits and waste management law.

Progressive waste policy, largely driven by EU policy developments, has brought about a planned and proactive approach to solid waste regulation with an emphasis on waste reduction and recycling. In contrast to the Control of Pollution Act 1974 (COPA 1974), the EPA 1990 focuses upon the management of waste throughout its lifecycle (cradle to grave) rather than concentrating simply upon its disposal.

The EPA 1990 combined with the Environmental Permitting (England and Wales) Regulations 2010 is an example of a Command and Control regulatory regime which requires those persons (usually companies) who engage in waste management operations (waste treatment/recycling and waste disposal) to obtain waste management permits authorising, controlling and legitimising those activities. There are, however, a significant number of activities which are exempt from the legal obligation[2] to obtain a waste management environmental permit. These controls represent a coherent and integrated response to the problems associated with the high level of waste production in an industrialised society.

5.2 The problem of waste

Since the Industrial Revolution, pollution of the landscape has been associated with the accumulation of unwanted solid waste materials. England and Wales is estimated to generate around 300–400 million tonnes of waste, divided approximately as follows: 35 per cent industry and commerce; 25 per cent mining; 18 per cent agricultural; and 5 per cent household. Some of this waste is recycled, especially construction industry waste and household waste. Commercial waste and industrial waste streams were largely exempt from control; the main regulatory efforts were, historically, directed at managing municipal waste.[3]

Today the constant increase in waste has become a cause for major concern. The UK, Germany, France and Italy produce the majority of the total volume of wastes in the European Union. In addition to the increased volume of waste, there has been a significant change, since the 1950s, in the nature of waste generated. Although the volume of domestic waste has increased, weight and density has decreased. Domestic waste, most of which goes to landfill, is no longer largely cinders and ash, but contains more packaging materials, particularly plastics. This has resulted in the need for bigger dustbins and often more frequent collections.

In England and Wales waste regulation has traditionally focused upon the environmentally safe disposal of unwanted substances. Regulation of waste disposal facilities via permitting generally works well but efforts to encourage waste minimisation and recycling through legal mechanisms pose a significant challenge to waste producers who are used to the availability of cheap landfill. Membership of the EU is driving improvements in waste reduction and recycling.[4] Also of significance is the imposition of producer responsibility obligations upon product manufacturers.[5]

---

2 See Scheds 2 and 3 of the Environmental Permitting (England and Wales) Regulations 2010.
3 Largely household waste, which is increasing at around 3% per annum and is set to double in volume by 2020.
4 E.g. the Landfill Directive and the Packaging Waste Directive.
5 E.g. designing products so that they can be easily recycled or imposing an obligation to take back and recycle a product at the end of its lifetime.

The waste targets (reduction, recycling and recovery) set by the EU are forcing Member States to vastly increase the infrastructure (facilities) and markets to recycle waste[6] or recover value from it.[7]

5.2.1 Methods of disposal

In England and Wales waste continues to be disposed of by means of landfill.[8] Other means of disposal include incineration and chemical treatment. Only a small percentage of waste is currently incinerated. All methods of disposing of waste raise objections, either from environmental protection groups or from residents who object to the disposal of waste in their locality. The NIMBY[9] philosophy is one which causes problems especially for the development of waste incinerators and landfills.[10] Inevitably, the disposal of waste will become more and more problematic as the amount of waste increases and the land available for landfill decreases. Efforts to reduce the volume of waste by encouraging waste producers to recycle more of their waste have gained momentum in England and Wales. Other EU Member States have been more prepared to use financial incentives such as charging householders for the volume of waste produced or increasing the cost of landfill to encourage waste minimisation and/or recycling.[11]

See Chapter 12 →

5.2.2 Landfill and co-disposal

One of the particular problems faced in England and Wales arises out of the former practice of co-disposal of waste (the mixed disposal of active[12] and inert waste in the same landfill). England and Wales had a large number of landfill sites which historically, when operational, accepted a wide range of differing types of wastes including inert solids and chemical and organic wastes. Often, the exact composition of waste contained in landfill sites is unknown. Surface water and groundwater contamination by leachate (liquid which pools at the bottom of landfills and escapes containment) discharges is a particular problem. Equally, the effect that these sites have on the environment is not known. Modern landfills are monitored with regard to methane gas and leachate production and the offsite migration of these substances.

The predominance of landfill as the preferred waste disposal option reflects the fact that, in most parts of England and Wales, it is the cheapest method of disposal (but note the impact of the landfill tax). Landfilling does, however, have a number of disadvantages:

(a) even in well-engineered sites, contaminants may leach into the ground to cause pollution of groundwaters;

(b) it adversely impacts upon the amenity of people living nearby because of the smell, noise, traffic, vermin, flies and litter associated with the operation of a landfill;

(c) there is a risk of methane build-up and explosion;

(d) methane is a greenhouse gas which contributes to global warming;

(e) landfilling generates public concern with regard to its impacts upon people and the environment (odour, noise, dust, birds, flies, vermin, litter, vehicle movements and adverse impacts on property prices).

---

6 E.g. by composting.
7 E.g. via 'energy from waste' incinerators which produce electricity.
8 Approximately 50–60% of regulated waste is disposed of in landfill.
9 'Not in my back yard'.
10 See the discussion regarding 'public concern' in Chapter 12.
11 See the statistics produced by the government's Waste Not Want Not strategy unit—www.strategy-unit.gov.uk.
12 Active waste produces greenhouse gases.

The volume of waste currently landfilled is undergoing reduction as a result of the waste reduction targets contained in the Landfill Directive and the introduction of the landfill tax.[13]

5.2.3 Incineration and other methods of disposal

Incineration as a means of waste disposal is not widely practised in England and Wales when compared with other European countries. According to the 17th Report of the Royal Commission on Environmental Pollution, incinerators only account for the disposal of 7 per cent of wastes (in England and Wales). In 1991, there were over 200 incineration plants in England and Wales licensed by Waste Regulatory Authorities. Thirty of these were municipal incinerators; most of the remaining incinerators were for clinical waste or were privately owned. Clinical waste incinerators were exempt from pollution controls and waste licensing because they benefited from Crown immunity. This was removed in 1991 following recommendations by the Royal Commission on Environmental Pollution in its 11th Report. Incinerators are now strictly regulated under the IPPC regime.

See Chapter 6

There are considerable differences of opinion about the desirability of incineration as a means of waste disposal. Incineration has a number of advantages over landfill. Unlike landfill, it does not produce leachate and methane, and it is able to cope with the disposal of some hazardous wastes which are unsuitable for landfilling. Incineration greatly reduces the volume of solid waste (i.e. reduction to ash) requiring final disposal. The new breed of 'energy from waste' incinerators produce electricity as a by-product of the incineration process.

Conversely, incineration is more expensive than landfill. Incinerators have high capital costs and their construction may be considerably delayed by opposition to such developments encountered in the town and country planning process. Incinerators require a minimum throughput of waste in order to function properly. Disposal contracts, entered into by the local authority and the operator of the incinerator, generally have lifespans of approximately 30 years, thereby reducing flexibility in waste management policy. Whilst incinerators do reduce the volume of material which requires disposal on or in land, they produce residues, such as bottom ashes and liquid effluent from the gas scrubbers (which clean the gases discharged to air), which require careful disposal.

Air pollution is, however, the most significant problem associated with incineration of waste. Incineration may produce dioxins and other hazardous atmospheric pollutants which cause high levels of public concern. Although there are concerns about the polluting effects of incinerators, there are rigorous controls over their operation. Incinerators are controlled under the following regimes:

(a)   the town and country planning regime;[14]
(b)   Integrated Pollution Prevention and Control (IPPC) and the Environmental Permitting (England and Wales) Regulations 2010.

Incinerators must meet the standards laid down in Directives 89/369/EEC, 89/429/EEC, 94/67/EEC and 2000/76/EC which relate to the incineration of hazardous waste.

In addition to landfilling and incineration, waste may be disposed of by the following methods which fall outside the ambit of the EPA 1990 and Environmental Permitting (England and Wales) Regulations 2010:

---

13 See 5.19.4. and 5.2.1.
14 See *Gateshead Metropolitan BC v Secretary of State for the Environment and Northumbrian Water Group* [1995] Env LR 37; [1995] JPL 432.

(a) landraise—this form of solid waste disposal (for example, the construction of slag heaps) is usually associated with the disposal of mine or quarry wastes;

(b) discharge of waste to sewers;

(c) discharge of waste to controlled waters;

(d) landspreading of wastes to 'condition' agricultural land;

(e) burying wastes (such as radioactive wastes); and

(f) injecting wastes underground.

5.3 The historical development of statutory waste controls

5.3.1 Public health protection

The system of waste regulation in this country has its roots in public health controls. Before 1972, there was no legislation primarily concerned with waste production and disposal. There were some basic provisions in the Public Health Acts of 1848 and 1936 which enabled local authorities to remove household and trade refuse and to require removal of any 'accumulation of noxious matter'. The Public Health Act 1936 placed local authorities under a statutory duty to inspect their areas to detect 'statutory nuisances' including 'any accumulation or deposit which is prejudicial to health'.[15] However, the aim of this early legislation was to protect public health from the problems of disease and vermin associated with the Industrial Revolution (crowded towns, poor housing and poor sanitation) rather than dealing with the environmental problems associated with solid waste creation.

5.3.2 Town and country planning controls

The Town and Country Planning Act 1947 provided the first preventative legislation requiring new developments, including waste disposal sites, to obtain planning permission (that is, a planning permit or licence). The deposit of waste on land is 'development' within the terms of the town and country planning regime and requires planning permission. Certain waste facilities may now require an environmental assessment to be carried out as part of the planning process. Current planning controls relating to waste are now to be found in the Town and Country Planning Act 1990 as amended.

5.3.3 The Control of Pollution Act 1974 (COPA 1974)

Growing concern in the early 1970s about the detrimental environmental effects of waste led the government to set up two working groups on refuse disposal and toxic waste disposal. The reports of these two groups provided the impetus for the COPA 1974. However, prior to that legislation, the government introduced the Deposit of Poisonous Wastes Act 1972 in response to a series of incidents concerning indiscriminate dumping of toxic wastes.[16] The 1972 Act is now repealed, but it was the first attempt at statutory control of industrial waste disposal in England and Wales.

The COPA 1974 attempted to achieve a degree of *comprehensive* pollution control in England and Wales. It introduced the requirement for local authorities to make plans regarding waste generated in their areas and also introduced a system of licensing (now called permitting) to regulate sites where waste was deposited. The 1974 Act required all Waste Disposal Authorities (WDAs)[17] to draw

---

15 These provisions are now contained in ss 79–82 of the EPA 1990.
16 E.g. asbestos dumped in the grounds of a school.
17 Which were the county councils in England and the district councils in Wales.

up a plan for the disposal of all household, commercial and industrial waste generated in its area. These plans were to be reviewed and modified by the WDA where appropriate. The authorities were placed under a statutory duty to publicise the draft plans, and provide the public an opportunity to make representations. In addition, there was a requirement that the WDAs consult with the water authorities, other levels of local government and other relevant bodies. Waste plans had to include information on the types and quantities of waste estimated to arise in the area or to be brought into it during the period of the plan, the methods of disposal and the provision of waste sites. The WDAs were also under a statutory duty to consider what arrangements could reasonably be made for reclaiming waste materials.

5.3.4 The COPA 1974—site licensing (permitting)

The COPA 1974 introduced a comprehensive licensing system for the disposal of waste on land, over and above the existing planning controls. Planning controls were not designed to address the operational aspects of landfill and incinerator regulation.[18]

COPA made it an offence to deposit household, commercial or industrial waste on land, unless the land in question was licensed by a WDA. In May 1994, the site licence provisions of the COPA 1974 were superseded by the waste management licensing system[19] under Pt II of the EPA 1990. Existing COPA 1974 licences were automatically transferred into EPA 1990 waste management licences. As many existing licence holders obtained their licences under the COPA 1974 regime, it is helpful to compare the two systems of waste regulation.

5.3.5 Defects in the COPA 1974

The COPA 1974 was the first comprehensive piece of legislation to tackle environmental pollution in an integrated way, and regulated air pollution, noise nuisance and the deposit of waste on land. In fact, the COPA 1974 was used as a model for the EU Waste Framework Directive 75/442/EEC. However, the COPA 1974, despite its worthy aims, was defective in the following respects:

(a) the relevant regulatory bodies were responsible for both waste regulation and waste disposal operations and this gave rise to a conflict of interest (that is, the 'poacher turned gamekeeper' role conflict);

(b) the regulatory bodies had very limited powers to refuse a licence application or control the transfer of licences;

(c) only those licence conditions which related specifically to the licensed activity, that is, the deposit of waste, could be enforced. Conditions relating to the management of sites and monitoring, for example, were unenforceable;

(d) licences could be surrendered at will. Disreputable licence holders could surrender licences to avoid obligations and liabilities arising from the licensed site.

The shortcomings of COPA were the subject of a parliamentary investigation.[20]

Prior to COPA 1974 the carriage of wastes (e.g. by skip hire companies) was brought within the waste regulatory framework by the Control of Pollution (Amendment) Act 1989.[21]

---

18 E.g. conditions relating to the construction and operation and post-closure aftercare of landfill sites.
19 See Waste Management Licensing Regulations 1994 (SI 1994/1056).
20 See House of Commons Environment Committee Select Report: Toxic Waste (2nd report 1989/90 session).
21 See 5.8.5.

5.3.6 Part II of the EPA 1990

Waste management regulation in England and Wales has undergone substantial reorganisation in recent years. Part II of the EPA 1990 was enacted to provide a more effective and comprehensive regime for dealing with solid waste on land, and also to address some of the defects of the COPA 1974. The EPA 1990, as amended by the Environment Act (EA) 1995, created a regulatory framework which has been supplemented by detailed secondary legislation. In May 1994, the Waste Management Licensing Regulations were introduced, bringing into force the provisions relating to the licensing system. These regulations have now been superseded by the Environmental Permitting (England and Wales) Regulations 2010.

The EPA 1990 did far more than re-enact the provisions of the COPA 1974. It introduced a number of very significant changes in the whole of the waste chain. In particular, it shifted the focus from the concept of waste disposal upon which the provisions of the COPA 1974 were based to the concept of waste management. The imperative behind the 1990 Act was that the legislative controls should relate to waste at all points in the waste chain creating a 'cradle to grave' system of control. The main changes introduced by the EPA 1990 are summarised below:

(a)   it introduced a much stricter licensing system, particularly in relation to the qualifications of licence holders, licence conditions and surrender of licences;
(b)   it established a statutory duty of care applicable to anyone who imports, produces, carries, keeps, treats or disposes of controlled waste; and
(c)   it reorganised the functions of the regulatory authorities to avoid the 'poacher turned gamekeeper' scenario that existed under the COPA 1974.

The Waste Management Licensing Regulations 1994 brought the original EPA 1990 definition of waste into line with that contained in the EU Waste Framework Directive.[22] Regulatory control extended to waste storage, treatment[23] and disposal. The 1994 regulations, as amended, have been superseded by the Environmental Permitting (England and Wales) Regulations 2010.

5.3.7 The Environment Act 1995

The Environment Act (EA) 1995 (EA 1995) introduced a new definition of 'directive waste' to give effect to the EU Waste Framework Directive 75/442/EEC, as amended. The principal change brought about by the EA 1995 was the transfer of the waste regulatory functions of the Waste Regulation Authorities (WRAs) to the newly established Environment Agency. The EA 1995 also made a number of amendments to the waste management licensing system; for example, the Environment Agency's enforcement powers were strengthened. The EA 1995 repealed s 61 of the EPA 1990 (concerned with closed landfills). On a more strategic level, s 92 of the EA 1995 inserted s 44A into the EPA 1990 which empowered the Secretary of State with responsibility for producing a national waste strategy and ss 93–95 of the EA 1995 introduced new provisions concerning producer responsibility for waste.

5.3.8 Post-1995 developments

This section provides an overview of the main waste-related legislative changes in the period 1996–2010.

---

22 Directive 75/442/EEC as amended by Directive 91/156/EC.
23 E.g. recycling.

The Finance Act 1996 was the first piece of legislation to introduce an 'eco tax' into the regulatory waste management framework. The Act imposed a tax on waste going to landfill. There were different rates of tax for inert and active wastes (producing greenhouse gases). Tax rates relating to active wastes were increased year-on-year subject to a maximum rate of tax.

The Pollution Prevention and Control Act 1999 was passed to give effect to the Integrated Pollution Prevention Directive.[24] A number of large landfill sites therefore fell within IPPC regulatory control.[25] All emissions from PPCA-regulated sites are controlled in a single permit. The 2002 Landfill Regulations implement the Landfill Directive setting binding reduction targets for waste going to landfill.

The Waste and Emissions Trading Act 2003 introduced a waste quota system in regard to landfill waste. Local authorities are allocated landfill waste quotas, which they are able to trade. The Act also introduced producer responsibility obligations for motor manufacturers.

The Household Waste Recycling Act 2003 obliges Waste Collection Authorities to make separate arrangements for kerbside collection of a minimum of two types of waste by 2010.

The Clean Neighbourhoods and Environment Act 2005 makes important changes to the waste regulatory framework including (1) sanctions for waste offences, (2) the introduction of 'on the spot' fixed penalties for some waste offences, and (3) clean-up powers.

The Waste Management (England and Wales) Regulations 2006 updated the Waste Management Licensing Regulations 1994. Of particular note is the reduction in the number of waste substances which are classified as exempt from regulatory control.

The Environmental Permitting (England and Wales) Regulations 2007 replacing the waste management licensing regulations were introduced and these were amended in 2010 to extend permitting to polluting discharges to the aquatic environment.[26]

See Chapter 6

5.3.9 What is waste?

In order to grasp the following section explaining the definition of waste for legal purposes, the following observations may help orientate the reader. It is helpful to think of a waste substance, material or article from the perspective of the person who wishes to dispose of it. A substance, material or article will, as a general rule, be waste, and fall within the current legal definition of waste, if the intention of the person who produced it, or who is currently in possession of it, is to rid himself or herself of it. This will usually entail either depositing it in a landfill site or sending it to be subjected to a recycling process. In such circumstances the relevant substance, material or article is waste regardless of any residual commercial value it may have. For example, a sawmill will produce large quantities of sawdust as a by-product of its timber-cutting operations. This material may be of no further use to the sawmill and the owner of the sawmill will desire to rid himself of it. The sawdust is 'waste' and continues to be so despite the fact that it may be sold, as a raw material feedstock, to a fibreboard manufacturer. This aspect of the definition of waste is reflected in government policy guidance. Department of the Environment (DoE) Circular 11/94 draws attention to the critical issue: 'Has the substance or object been discarded so that it is no longer part of the normal commercial cycle or chain of utility? If, in the above scenario, the sawmill owner retained possession of the sawdust in order to manufacture fibreboard himself then the sawdust would not be perceived as a waste by-product and there would be no intention to discard (i.e. get rid of) the material.

---

24 Directive 96/61/EC.
25 See the Landfill (England and Wales) Regulations 2002 for details of how landfills are selected for PPCA control.
26 See Chapter 6 for a detailed account of the impact of these regulations. 26 See Chapter 6 for a detailed account of the impact of these regulations.

5.4 The legal definition of waste

5.4.1 Introduction

We begin the task of explaining the definition of waste for legal purposes by posing the question: why is it important to provide a legal definition of which substances, materials or articles are waste?

The answer to this question is crucial to determining the linked question of whether the keeping, treating or disposing of the relevant waste substance, article or material requires an environmental permit. Any unwanted substance, material or article which satisfies the legal definition of waste, the current definition of which is set out below, must be regulated, unless an exemption applies, by under the Environmental Permitting (England and Wales) Regulations 2010.

The legal definition of waste contained in 575 EPA 1990 defined waste by reference to the term 'controlled waste'.[27] The subsequent advent of the Waste Framework Directive 2006/12/EC, with its own definition of 'directive waste[28] necessitated amendments[29] to the s75 EPA definition so that references to controlled waste and directive waste are synonymous.[30]

5.4.2 Directive waste

The current legal definition of waste which is applicable to all Member States of the EU is set out in Article 3(1) of the Directive 2008/98/EC. This directive is the most recent version of the Waste Framework Directive. Article 3(1) states:

> waste means any substance or object which the holder discards or intends or is required to discard.

This definition of **directive waste** appears to be relatively simple, but in practice has given rise to a great deal of litigation both in the courts of Member States and in the European Court of Justice.

In the above Art 3(1) definition of waste the term 'discard' refers to (1) consigning waste for disposal (e.g. landfilling) or (2) consigning waste to a recovery operation (e.g. subjecting the waste to treatment in order to recycle it). Waste disposal activities are listed in Annex IIa of the 2008 Waste Framework Directive, whereas waste recovery operations are listed in Annex IIb of the 2008 Directive. The Art 3(1) definition is given effect to in England and Wales by the Environmental Permitting (England and Wales) Regulations 2010. Regulation 2 of the Environmental Permitting (England and Wales) Regulations 2010 defines 'waste' as:

> anything that:
>
> (a)   is waste within the meaning of Article 3(1) of the Waste Framework Directive; and
>
> (b)   is not excluded from the scope of that directive by Article 2(1), (2) or (3).

---

27 In s75 (4) 'controlled waste' means 'household, industrial and commercial waste or any such waste,' s75(2) as amended now defines 'waste' as 'anything that is waste within the meaning of Article 3(1) of Directive 2008/98/EC'.

28 The definition of directive waste in Directive 2006/12/EC was a two stage test. The first part of the test involved an assessment of whether the relevant substance, material or product fell within any of the categories set out in Annex 1 of the Directive. If the answer to this enquiry was 'yes' then the substance, material or product was waste if it had been discarded by the holder, or there was an intention or requirement to discard it.

29 The original EPA 1990 definition of controlled waste was amended by paragraph 88 of Schedule 22 of the Environment Act 1995 to include the list of substances, materials and products listed in Schedule 2B of the Environment Act 1995. Schedule 2B mirrored the contents of Annex 1 of Directive 2006/12/EC.

30 See regulation 3 of the Controlled Waste (England and Wales) Regulations 2012.

Despite the apparent simplicity of the Article 3(1) definition of directive waste, problems do arise when the definition is applied to a wide range of circumstances. Problems of definition tend to arise because the EU waste regulatory regime requires many types of disposal and recovery operations to be regulated and it is not always easy to determine when a substance or material is consigned to a regulated recovery operation or whether it is subjected to ordinary industrial processes which are not recovery operations and are therefore not subject to regulatory control (permitting). Also, at what point in time does a substance or material change its status and become waste? When the waste creator or holder resolves to discard it? What if the waste generator subjects the substance or material to a waste recovery process? Has the substance or material been discarded in these circumstances? Is the substance or material waste if it has been: (a) discarded by disposal (that is, sent to a landfill site or to an incinerator); or (b) consigned to a waste recovery operation? Does a substance or material handed over to a waste disposal or waste recovery process listed in the Waste Framework Directive automatically fall within the definition of 'waste'? Do waste substances, or materials which have been subjected to a waste recovery process, ever cease to be waste? What is the status of a household item which is still in perfect working order but which the owner wishes to throw away? Is it waste at the point when the householder places it in his/her waste bin? The case law of the ECJ and the UK courts is complex and answers to the questions which we have posed above are not always easy to decipher from the judgments of the relevant courts.

5.4.3 Case law

Substances which are capable of being recycled and have a commercial value may nevertheless be waste.[31]

In the *Tombesi* litigation (1998),[32] the ECJ held that the Waste Framework Directive, based on a 'purposive' (inclusive) interpretation of the directive, was intended to apply to all substances or objects discarded by the original waste creator or current holder (despite any commercial value the substance might have if recycled, reclaimed or reused) and consignment of a substance to a recovery operation could amount to discarding it; in those circumstances, the substance could be waste.

The *Tombesi* decision has been subject to further judicial consideration. In *Inter-Environment Wallonie ASBL v Regione Wallonie* (1998),[33] the court held that a substance consigned to a recovery operation could be distinguished from ordinary or normal industrial treatment of raw materials. Consigning a substance to an Annex IIB recovery operation would usually indicate that the substance was intended to be discarded. Thus, the Waste Framework Directive could still apply to waste recovery operations which were part of a larger process. The question, however, remained: what is the distinction between an ordinary industrial process and an Annex IIB recovery operation? This question was considered by the English High Court in *Mayer Parry Recycling Ltd v Environment Agency* (1999).[34] The issue before the court was whether scrap metals which were then smelted and reused were waste. Carnwath J stated that 'discard' is synonymous with 'get rid of' and, therefore, materials which had ceased to be required for their original purpose were waste (because they were no longer suitable for their original purpose, or were unwanted or were surplus). Conversely, substances or materials which may be reused without being subjected to a recovery operation were not waste. If such substances were subjected to a recovery operation, then the substance ceased to be waste at the end of the recovery process. The *Mayer Parry* decision was subsequently rejected by

---

31 See *R v Rotherham Metropolitan BC ex p Rankin* [1990] JPL 503, and *Vessoso v Ministere Public of Italy and Zanetti v Same* (Joined Cases C-206/88 and C-207/88) [1990] ECR 1–1462.
32 *Tombesi Litigation* [1997] All ER 639; [1998] Env LR 59.
33 *Inter-Environment Wallonie ASBL v Regione Wallonie* [1998] Env LR 625.
34 *Mayer Parry Recycling Ltd v Environment Agency* [1999] Env LR 489.

the Court of Appeal in *Attorney-General's Reference* (No 5 of 2000). This decision related to the spreading on land of a by-product (which had not been through a waste recovery process) from an animal rendering plant. The Court of Appeal held that the by-product was capable of being waste.

More recent guidance on this ongoing issue is provided by the ECJ in Case 418–19/97, *ARCO Chemie Nederland Ltd v Minister van Volkshuisvesting and EPON* (2000).[35] This case concerned the use of a manufacturing by-product (for example, waste solvent) as a fuel in a separate (for example, cement) manufacturing process. The ECJ was of the opinion, in regard to the definition of waste, that the key determinant was whether the by-product had been discarded and not whether the substance was consigned to an Annex IIB waste recovery process. The factors which the ECJ paid particular attention to in deciding that the substance had been 'discarded' were: whether the material was generally regarded as waste; whether the use of the by-product was considered to be 'recovery'; whether the substance or material was really a process by-product; whether there was no other use for the substance, except disposal; and the extra precautions necessary to use the substance as a fuel. This decision has added another layer of complexity to the definition of waste, for the decision means that: (a) it is not automatically the case that substances which may be reused without being subjected to a recovery process fall outside the definition of waste; and (b) the substance produced by a recovery process ceases to be waste.

The ARCO *Chemie* decision, when applied in an English and Welsh context, effectively reverses the *Mayer Parry* decision that by-products of industrial production processes which could be reused without having to be subjected to a recovery process could not be waste. Thus there is no simple test which can be applied to determine whether by-products are waste, but much will hinge on whether the substance has been discarded.

In Case C-114/01, *AvestaPolarit Chrome Oy* (2003),[36] the ECJ considered whether Art 2(1)(b) of the Waste Framework Directive (75/442/EEC) applied to waste sand and rock left over from ore extraction and ore dressing operations (quarrying) in Finland. Under Art 2(1)(b), mineral extraction waste is exempt from the definition of waste if it is 'already covered by other legislation'. The ECJ considered whether the reference to 'other legislation' included national legislation and, if so, (a) whether that legislation had to be in force at the time Directive 75/442/EEC entered into force; and/or (b) whether the legislation had to comply with the environmental protection requirements of the Directive. In the opinion of Advocate General Jacobs, the Directive envisaged the possibility of other EU legislation entering into force after Directive (75/442/EEC) (rather than national legislation) and whilst mining wastes were covered by Finnish legislation, these wastes were not excluded by Art 2(1)(b) because there was as yet no EU legislation specifically covering mining wastes.

Confusion with regard to the definition of waste in EC law continued. In Case C-9/00, *Palin Granit Oy v Vemassalon kansanterveystoyn kuntayhtyman hallitus* (2002),[37] a Municipal Board in Finland granted a licence to Palin Granit Oy (PGO) to operate a quarry. The licence relating to quarrying operations could not, under Finnish law, authorise landfilling; however, the operating management plan for the quarry contained a proposed use (a filling material) for the stone left over from the quarrying operations. The issue in this case was whether the left-over stone was 'waste'. A Finnish administrative court had ruled that the material was waste, but PGO challenged that ruling on the grounds that (a) the waste stone was identical in composition to the rock from which it had been quarried, and (b) it posed no threat to human health or the environment. PGO contended that the site where the left-over stone was stored was not a landfill site, but a deposit of reusable materials.

35 *ARCO Chemie Nederland Ltd v Minister van Volkshuisvesting and EPON* [2000] ECR I-4475.
36 *AvestaPolarit Chrome Oy* (Case C-114/01) (2003) unreported judgment of 11 September.
37 *Palin Granit Oy v Vemassalon kansanterveystoyn kuntayhtyman hallitus* (Case C-9/00) [2002] ECR I-3533.

The ECJ held that there was no definitive test to determine whether a substance was waste; there were only indicators. It was not decisive that the material was capable of economic use. More important was the fact that the material was a production residue. Advocate General Jacobs stated, 'According to its ordinary meaning, waste is what falls away when one processes a material or an object and is not the end product which the manufacturing system directly seeks to produce.' The ECJ held that, having regard to the principle established in earlier cases, 'waste' should be interpreted widely so as to limit the substance's inherent risks and pollution threat. In determining whether the material or substance was waste, the fact that the material was a production residue was significant, as was the likelihood that the material could be reused without reprocessing. If there was financial advantage in the operator reusing the material, so that reuse was highly likely, and the substance was not a burden for the operator so that the operator would not wish to discard it, then the material was to be regarded as a product. In the circumstances of the PGO case, the only foreseeable use of the leftover stone was in the construction of harbour walls and breakwaters. This would necessitate long-term storage, which would impose a burden on PGO, and could potentially cause the type of pollution which the Waste Framework Directive sought to avoid. Reuse of the leftover stone was not certain and only foreseeable in the long term. In these circumstances, the material was held to be waste. This case has implications for residues produced by other industries such as power generation and waste incineration. Surprisingly, the ECJ, in contrast to previous cases, took into account the economic value of the leftover stone as a factor in deciding whether this particular production by-product was waste. We recommend that readers refer to the online resources corresponding to this chapter for updates on case law relating to the definition of directive waste.

5.4.4 What is meant by 'discarded'?

DoE Circular 11/94[38] suggests a number of questions that should be answered in order to help determine whether something is waste or not. These are:

(a) Has the item been discarded so that it is no longer part of the normal commercial cycle or chain of utility? If the answer is no, the matter is probably not waste.
(b) Has the item been consigned to a disposal operation? If the answer is yes, it is almost certainly waste.
(c) Has the item been abandoned or dumped? If the answer is yes, it is probably waste.
(d) Has the item been consigned to a specialised recovery operation? If the answer is yes, it is probably waste.
(e) Can the item be used in its present form without being subjected to a specialised recovery operation? If the answer is yes, then the item may well not be waste.
(f) Does the owner have to pay for the item to be taken away? If the answer is yes, this would usually suggest the matter is waste, although there are exceptions.
(g) Will the person who receives the item regard it as something to be disposed of rather than a useful product? If the answer is that the item is a useful product, it may nevertheless be waste.
(h) Has the item been reprocessed such that it can now re-enter the commercial cycle? If the answer is yes, it is probably no longer waste.

The ECJ and national courts have largely refrained from attempting to set down simple guides regarding which substances are waste. Instead the courts take a range of matters into account in

---

38 A government policy document which does not have the force of law.

deciding, in any given set of circumstances, whether a substance falls within the legal definition of waste (i.e. directive waste). It is, however, possible to discern a number of important criteria the courts use to guide them in their deliberations. The criteria include: whether the relevant substance or object has been consigned either to a waste disposal or a waste recovery process; whether the substance is a by-product of a process as opposed to a product which has an alternative and subsequent use; whether the substance appears in the EU List of Wastes or Annex IIA and IIB of the Waste Framework Directive and is in most circumstances regarded as a waste substance; whether the substance can be reused without the need to subject it to some form of recovery process; the objectives of the Waste Framework Directive; the likelihood that the substance will be reused because it has an economic value to the current holder; the need for safeguards if reused and whether the substance poses environmental or health risks if left in situ or is intended to be subjected to a recovery process.

5.4.5 What constitutes a disposal operation and what constitutes a recovery operation?

Disposal operations include:

(a) landfill or land raising;
(b) land treatment of waste such as biodegradation of sludge in soil;
(c) deep injection;
(d) surface impoundment;
(e) incineration;
(f) permanent storage.

Recovery operations include:

(a) solvent recovery;
(b) recycling/recovery of organic substances which are not used as solvents;
(c) recycling/reclamation of metals and their compounds;
(d) recovery of waste oil;
(e) spreading waste on land for agricultural purposes.[39]

Substances consigned to a recovery operation will not automatically be waste. There is a distinction, however, between recovery operations and specialist recovery operations. Waste consigned to a specialist recovery operation will probably be waste. A specialist recovery operation is one in which waste materials are recovered or recycled for reuse in a way which removes or reduces the threat posed by the original waste and which results in a new raw material.

DoE Circular 11/94 gives various practical examples of waste; however, as stated earlier, the Circular is neither definitive nor legally binding.

In February 2003, the ECJ set out the principles to determine whether the operation of waste incinerators or cement kilns (both generating energy) constituted waste recovery or waste disposal operations. The relevant cases, Case C-458/00 *Commission v Luxembourg* (2003)[40] and Case C-228/00 *Commission v Germany* (2003)[41] related to transboundary shipments of waste for incineration with

---

39 In regard to the range of waste-related operations which require an environmental permit, see the Environmental Permitting (England and Wales) Regulations 2007, as amended. In particular see reg 4 of the 2007 Regulations.
40 *Commission v Luxembourg* (2003) Case C-458/00.
41 *Commission v Germany* (2003) Case C-228/00.

energy recovery in another state. The shipments were described as being for the purposes of waste recovery, but both Luxembourg and Germany were of the opinion that the processes to which the wastes were to be subjected were waste disposal operations. The Commission rejected these opinions and claimed that there had been a contravention of the Waste Shipments Regulation (EC) 259/93. The Luxembourg shipment comprised municipal waste which was to be incinerated (with energy recovery), whereas the German shipment comprised waste which was to be incinerated in cement kilns whilst the energy produced was to be used in the cement manufacturing process to replace (fully or partially) ordinary kiln fuel.

The ECJ relied on Case C-6/00 *ASA Abfall Service AG v Bundesminister für Umwelt, Jugend und Familie* (2002)[42] as authority for holding that the incineration of waste is a recovery operation if the principal objective of incineration is that the waste can fulfil a useful function (energy generation), replacing the need to use a primary source of energy (that is, normal fuel). Annexes IIA and IIB of the Waste Framework Directive (75/442/EEC) list the main categories of waste disposal and waste recovery operations. The Annexes refer to categories D10 'incineration on land' and R1 'use principally as a fuel or other means to generate energy', and the Commission argued that both shipments were R1 waste recovery operations. In determining whether the shipments were designed for R1 processes/operations, the ECJ had regard to the following criteria:

(a) the main purpose of an R1 process was to use waste to generate energy;
(b) there must be a reason to believe that the waste is to be used to generate energy (the energy generated by the process is greater than the energy consumed and part of the surplus energy is immediately used as heat or, after processing, as electricity); and
(c) the term 'principally' referred to the fact that the majority of the waste had to be consumed and the majority of the energy generated recovered and utilised. Thus, the use of the German waste in a cement kiln was an R1 waste recovery process, but the use of the Luxembourg waste was a waste disposal operation because the reclamation of heat was only a secondary effect of a process whose main function was waste disposal.

Approximately one month later, the ECJ in Case C-116/01 *SITA EcoService Nederland BV v Minister van Volkshuisvesting, Ruimtelijke Ordening en Milieubeheer* (2003)[43] gave further guidance on distinguishing between waste recovery and waste disposal operations. The issue in this case was whether a process comprising distinct stages was a waste recovery or waste disposal process for the purposes of the Waste Shipments Regulation 259/93. SITA intended to ship waste for use as fuel in cement kilns and the ash from the incineration of the fuel was to be used in the production of clinker. The Dutch courts asked the ECJ to rule on the matter. Should all the stages of the process be viewed as a single comprehensive process or should they be treated as separate? The ECJ had regard to the fact that it was not uncommon for a process to comprise several successive stages of recovery or disposal, and ECJ held that, for the purposes of the Waste Shipments Regulation, only the first operation that the waste was subjected to after shipment determined whether it was a waste recovery or waste disposal operation. In this case, the first operation was combustion of the waste. The Dutch court would therefore have to take into account the three criteria in Case C-228/00, *Commission v Germany*[44] in deciding the question: was a D10 disposal operation or an R1 recovery operation?

In the ECJ case (Case C 1/03) *Van De Walle and others* (2005),[45] the Court had to decide (1) whether petrol, which had escaped from an underground storage tank at a petrol filling station, was

---

42 *ASA Abfall Services AG v Bundesminister fur Umwelt, Jugend und Familie* (Case C-6/00) [2002] ECR I-1961.
43 *SITA EcoService Nederland BV v Minister van Volkshuisvesting, Ruimtelijke Ordening en Milieubeheer* (Case C-116/01) (2003) unreported, judgment of 3 April.
44 See note 46 above.
45 *Van De Walle and others* (Case C-1/03) [2005] Env LR 24.

waste and (2) was contaminated soil (i.e. contaminated with escaped fuel) waste. In reaching its decision that the escaped fuel and contaminated soil were waste, the Court focused on the key question of whether the substance had been discarded. The Court held (a) that such leaks, whilst involuntary, were substances discarded by the holder, (b) contaminated soil was also waste because it could not be disposed of or reused without being subjected to a decontamination process, and (c) the petrol manufacturer was the producer and holder of the waste substances for the purposes of the Waste Framework Directive.

5.5 Exceptions to materials and substances classified as directive waste and exemptions from the requirement to obtain an environmental permit

Substances which fall outside the definition of directive waste are not capable of being controlled under the relevant national legislation. There are other categories of substances which, whilst falling within the definition of directive waste, are exempted from waste management licensing/environmental permitting because they are already controlled under other legislation. These exemptions comprise: radioactive wastes regulated by the Radioactive Substances Act 1993; waste waters regulated by the WIA; decommissioned explosives regulated by the Explosives Act 1875 and secondary legislation comprising the Control of Explosive Regulations 1991,[46] the Road Traffic (Carriage of Explosives) Regulations 1989[47] and a range of regulations made under the Health and Safety at Work etc. Act 1974; and gaseous discharges to atmosphere[48] regulated under the Clean Air Act 1993 and the Pollution Prevention and Control Act 1999.[49] Agricultural wastes and wastes from mining and quarrying were, at one time, exempt from regulation but are now subject to control.

Exemptions from the requirement, in reg 12 of the Environmental Permitting (England and Wales) Regulations 2010, to obtain an environmental permit are set out in Scheds 2 and 3 of the 2010 regulations.

5.6 Hazardous waste

5.6.1 Introduction

Within the general definition of 'directive waste' exists a range of wastes which are hazardous, and, in consequence of their hazardous properties, these wastes are subjected to tighter regulation than ordinary directive waste. Hazardous wastes[50] are hazardous because they have dangerous properties[51] and/or they are difficult to dispose of. Historically hazardous wastes have been subject to regulatory control since 1972;[52] however, the process of subjecting hazardous wastes to more effective controls commenced with the introduction of (a) the Control of Pollution (Special Waste) Regulations 1980, followed by (b) the Special Waste Regulations 1996 and culminating in (c) the Hazardous Waste (England and Wales) Regulations 2005.[53] Those readers who wish to learn more about the former Special Waste Regulations should refer to Chapter 5 in the fourth edition of

---

46 SI 1991/1531.
47 SI 1989/615.
48 But not emissions to air from sites regulated by Part II of the EPA.
49 I.e. IPPC regulated sites.
50 E.g. acids, alkalis, asbestos, pesticides and flammable solvents.
51 E.g. they are flammable, cause irritation, are corrosive, toxic, infectious, mutagenic or carcinogenic.
52 Deposit of Poisonous Waste Act 1972.
53 SI 2005/894.

this text. In this edition we focus on the regulatory regime contained in the Hazardous Waste Regulations 2005.

5.6.2 Hazardous waste

The Special Waste regulatory regime has been replaced with 'hazardous waste' controls in order to fully implement the Hazardous Waste Directive (91/689). The hazardous waste regime comprises two sets of secondary legislation: (1) the Hazardous Waste (England and Wales) Regulations 2005[54] and (2) the List of Wastes (England) Regulations 2005.[55] These regulations mirror the definition of hazardous waste to be found in the Hazardous Waste Directive and the EU List of Wastes.

Hazardous Waste is defined[56] as any waste which is: (1) listed as hazardous in the List of Wastes Regulations; (2) classified by the Secretary of State or a National Executive[57] as hazardous; or (3) specified as hazardous by any regulation made pursuant to s 62 EPA 1990.

The regime extends control to a wider range of wastes than existed under the Special Waste control regime. Regulation 12(2) of the HW Regulations excludes 'domestic waste' (this term is not defined in the HW Regulations) which has hazardous properties from hazardous waste control. Hazardous waste, such as asbestos,[58] is not subject to the domestic hazardous waste exclusion. The mixing of hazardous wastes with other hazardous or non-hazardous wastes is prohibited[59] unless this is permitted by licence.[60] The HW Regulations[61] create a duty requiring the separation of different types of hazardous wastes (provided separation is practical).

The hazardous waste controls impose strict notification requirements upon both producers of hazardous wastes and legal persons[62] who remove hazardous wastes from premises. HW reg 21 requires the EA to be notified, whether by a hazardous waste producer or a hazardous waste remover/carrier, of all premises producing hazardous wastes or from which such wastes are removed. Separate annual notifications are required to ensure that the EA has an accurate picture of hazardous waste generated and transported. It is an offence[63] to remove hazardous wastes from any premises unless such premises have been the subject of a notification or the relevant hazardous waste has been fly-tipped[64] on those premises.[65] Exemptions apply to a range of premises[66] producing a maximum 200 kg of hazardous waste per year.

The hazardous waste controls, like directive waste controls, create a consignment note system to track the transport of hazardous wastes.[67] A consignment note accompanies each hazardous waste movement and records information which includes (1) waste description, (2) waste producer, (3) waste carrier and (4) the legal person responsible for final disposal or recovery. The system also applies to movements of hazardous wastes from premises which are not subject to the notification requirements outlined above. Record-keeping obligations[68] apply to producers, carriers, holders, disposers and recoverers/recyclers of hazardous waste in much the same way as those which apply

---

54 SI 2005/894, hereinafter referred to as the HW Regulations.
55 SI 2005/895, hereinafter referred to as the LoW Regulations.
56 Reg 6 HW Regulations.
57 E.g. National Assembly of Wales.
58 E.g. asbestos sheeting generated by the demolition of an old shed in a residential garden.
59 Reg 19 HW Regulations.
60 E.g. environmental permit.
61 Reg 20.
62 E.g. waste transport companies/waste carriers.
63 HW reg 22.
64 See s 33(5) EPA.
65 HW reg 23.
66 E.g. medical, educational, residential and commercial.
67 HW regs 35–38.
68 HW regs 49–51.

to directive waste. Records of hazardous waste consignments must be kept for three years (one year in the case of hazardous waste carriers). Operators of hazardous waste disposal or hazardous waste recovery/recycling plants are required to provide (1) for EA use, every three months, a detailed account of the hazardous wastes which they have received[69] and (2) similar information for use by hazardous waste producers (and hazardous waste holders) who consigned hazardous waste to them.[70] By virtue of HW regs 47–48 any legal person who (1) deposits hazardous waste in on or under land, or (2) recovers hazardous waste, is required to keep records of the deposit/recovery.

HW reg 65 contains a range of offences relating to the failure to comply with obligations set out in the HW Regulations. In summary the offences relate to breach of the following types of obligation: the banning of the mixing hazardous waste, notification of premises, hazardous waste consignment processes, appropriate action in an emergency, record keeping/information provision and supplying false or misleading information.

Following a prosecution and conviction for an offence under reg 65 the maximum sanction if the matter is dealt with in a magistrates' court is a fine of £50,000 for each offence and in the Crown Court an unlimited fine and/or a sentence of imprisonment of up to two years.[71] HW reg 70 enables the EA to impose fixed penalty notices[72] in regard to breaches of the HW Regulations. Section 41 of the Clean Neighbourhoods and Environment Act 2005 brings the sanctions for breach of s 33 of the EPA into line with the sanctions applicable to breach of the HW Regulations.

The HW Regulations provide for limited defences.[73] A defendant may escape conviction if the relevant failure to comply with the HW Regulations resulted from an emergency and every reasonable step was taken by the defendant to (1) minimise the danger to the public and/or the environment and (2) rectify the failure as soon as reasonably practicable.

5.7 Radioactive wastes

Section 62 of the EPA 1990 empowers the Secretary of State to make regulations which provide for the control of radioactive wastes under the hazardous waste control regime. Such controls will only apply to radioactive wastes which have harmful properties characteristic of hazardous wastes.

5.8 The system of waste regulation

By virtue of the EA 1995, the Environment Agency was tasked with the responsibility for the waste management licensing (permitting) system under Pt II of the EPA 1990. The Environment Agency not only has responsibility for waste management licensing (permitting),[74] but is also responsible for waste carrier licensing, hazardous waste licensing and 'policing' the s 34 EPA 1990 duty of care. Prior to the establishment of the Environment Agency, the system of waste regulation was administered by WRAs. The WRAs ceased to exist on 1 April 1996 when the Environment Agency took over their functions. Since the system of waste regulation has undergone significant change in recent years, it is useful at this point to consider briefly some of those changes and to comment on the role fulfilled by the WRAs during their period of operation between 1990 and 1996.

See Chapter 6 →

---

69 HW reg 53.
70 HW reg 54.
71 A term of imprisonment is only applicable to humans as opposed to legal persons such as companies or public organisations.
72 Maximum £300 penalty per breach.
73 Reg 66.
74 Now referred to as environmental permitting; see Chapter 6.

5.8.1 Part II of the EPA 1990 prior to the EA 1995 amendments and the creation of the Environment Agency

Part II of the EPA 1990 was introduced in part to address some of the deficiencies of the COPA 1974 and to introduce a much stronger licensing system and system of waste regulation. Under the regulatory system established by the COPA 1974, local authorities were placed in the position of being waste regulators, issuing waste disposal licences, and operating their own waste disposal sites. This type of situation is often referred to as a 'poacher turned gamekeeper' scenario and often gives rise to conflicts of interest. The reasoning behind the administrative changes in the EPA 1990 was that local authorities should no longer be able to act as both regulators and operators of waste facilities and the EPA 1990 sought to provide for a division of responsibilities. Another principal reason for change was to ensure that waste disposal operations were no longer subsidised but run on a proper economic basis with charges reflecting the full economic cost of running the operation. In other words, the intention was to make waste disposal operations more competitive, subject them to market forces and reflect the EU's 'polluter pays' principle. The EPA 1990 therefore created three different levels of waste authority, each with a different role in relation to waste management. These were defined in s 30 of the EPA 1990 as:

(a)   Waste Regulation Authorities (WRAs);

(b)   Waste Disposal Authorities (WDAs);

(c)   Waste Collection Authorities (WCAs).

WDAs and WCAs continue to operate, but the functions of the WRAs have been transferred in full to the Environment Agency. The waste-related functions of the Environment Agency comprise: waste licensing,[75] licensing exemption registration, waste carrier registration, 'policing' compliance of licensed (permitted) sites, enforcement, removing illegal waste deposits, monitoring the movement of hazardous wastes and 'policing' the s 34 of the EPA 1990 duty of care.

5.8.2 WRAs (functions transferred to the Environment Agency)

In non-metropolitan local authorities, the WRAs were the county councils. In metropolitan areas, the WRAs were the district councils, with special authorities established for Greater London, Greater Manchester and Merseyside. WRAs were intended to 'regulate' the waste industry and had no operational responsibilities. Where a local authority was both a WRA and a WDA, provisions in the EPA 1990 required the local authorities' WDA functions to be carried out 'at arm's length'. Section 30(7) of the EPA 1990 made it the duty of each authority which was both a WRA and a WDA to make administrative arrangements for keeping these functions separate. This meant that the actual operational functions of the WDA were not carried out by the authority itself but by a 'waste disposal contractor'. Section 30(5) of the EPA 1990 defines a 'waste disposal contractor' as a person who in the course of business collects, keeps, treats or disposes of waste, being either:

(a)   a company formed for all or any of these purposes by a waste disposal authority; or

(b)   a company, partnership or individual (sole trader).

5.8.3 WDAs

The WDA is normally the county council in non-metropolitan areas and the district council in metropolitan areas. Special arrangements exist in London, Manchester and Merseyside. The functions of the WDA are:

---

75 See Environmental Permitting (England and Wales) Regulations 2010.

(a) making arrangements for the disposal of controlled (directive) waste collected in the area by WCAs;

(b) formation of waste disposal companies;

(c) provision of municipal waste sites for household waste to be deposited by residents (civic amenity sites);

(d) provision of waste transfer stations;

(e) waste recycling.

Section 51 of the EPA 1990 obliges a WDA to dispose of the waste collected in the WDA's area. Facilities (civic amenity/waste sites) are provided for residents to dispose of household waste at no charge (typically items which the waste collection contractors refuse to take). Sections 32 and 51 and Sched 2 of the EPA 1990 enable WDAs to enter into contracts with waste disposal contractors for the disposal of waste collected. Contracts may be arranged with either private contractors or Local Authority Waste Disposal Contractors (LAWDCs).[76] Schedule 2 regulates the waste disposal contract competition (competitive tendering) which WDAs must conclude with a private contractor or LAWDC. Each contract is put out to tender, must be advertised widely and attract a minimum of four tenders (often by invitation). In appointing a waste disposal contractor, the WDA is subject to a number of duties: (a) to create a competitive market in which private companies and LAWDCs compete on equal terms; and (b) to have regard to environmental considerations in discharging its functions.[77] A WDA is not obliged to accept the cheapest tender and is entitled to have regard to all the relevant factors (especially environmental impacts) including the WDA's favoured disposal option.[78]

5.8.4 WCAs

WCAs are the district councils or London boroughs. Their functions are:

(a) to arrange for the collection of household waste in their area;

(b) to arrange for the collection of commercial or industrial waste on request;

(c) to provide bins/receptacles;

(d) to collect waste and to deliver for disposal as directed by the waste disposal authority;

(e) to investigate, draft plans and make arrangements for recycling.

WCAs are placed under a statutory duty[79] to collect household waste free of charge.[80] In certain circumstances, WCAs can charge for household waste collection.[81] They include large items, garden waste and other difficult wastes or waste produced from commercially run residential premises. The WCAs also have a duty, if requested by the occupier of premises in its area, to collect commercial waste, and may charge a reasonable sum for the collection and disposal of the waste unless the authority considers it inappropriate to do so. If requested by the occupier of premises, WCAs may collect, subject to the consent and reasonable charges of the WDA, industrial waste. WCAs also have a discretion to collect sewage waste from occupiers of premises equipped with septic tanks and similar apparatus. WCAs are required by ss 46–47 EPA to provide commercial and household waste bins.

---

76 WDA-owned waste disposal businesses operated at arm's length; see Annex C of DoE Circular 8/91.
77 See R v Avon CC ex p Terry Adams Ltd [1994] Env LR 442.
78 See R v Cardiff City Council ex p Gooding Investments Ltd (1995) 7 ELM 134.
79 S 45 EPA 1990.
80 Except where the waste is not reasonably accessible and acceptable alternative arrangements are made.
81 See Sched 2 to the Controlled Waste Regulations 1992.

The WCAs are required by s 48 of the EPA 1990 to deliver the waste collected to such places as directed by the WDAs unless the WCAs intend to recycle any household or commercial waste collected. If the WCAs keep the waste for recycling purposes, they will still need to secure the consent of the WDAs, since WDAs have the power to buy and sell waste for recycling purposes. A WDA may withhold its consent where it has contracted with a waste disposal contractor to recycle all or part of the waste.

WCAs are obliged[82] to prepare waste recycling plans regarding household and commercial waste collected.

The Waste and Emissions Trading Act 2003[83] obliges WCAs (in areas where a two-tier county/district administrative division exists) to prepare a joint municipal waste strategy with the object of meeting landfill reduction targets. WDAs and WCAs are required to co-operate in regard to waste minimisation and waste reduction schemes.

5.8.5 Waste carriers—the Control of Pollution (Amendment) Act 1989

The requirements of Art 12 of the Waste Framework Directive have been implemented in England and Wales by the Control of Pollution (Amendment) Act 1989 (COP(A)A 1989). Businesses which transport controlled (directive) waste in England and Wales are obliged to register with the Environment Agency (and re-register every three years). Transporting waste without being registered is an offence[84] and carries a maximum fine of £5,000 on conviction in a magistrates' court. A limited number of defences are available: (a) the transport of waste occurred in an emergency, provided the Environment Agency is informed; (b) the carrier (vehicle driver) did not know and had no reasonable grounds to suspect that he was transporting controlled (directive) waste and (i) was acting in accordance with his employer's instructions, or (ii) took reasonable steps to check what he was carrying; (c) the carrier was transporting waste (i) within the same premises, (ii) from the place of importation in England and Wales to the first point of arrival, and (iii) to the place from which the waste is to be exported.

The Environment Agency is required to carry out periodic checks on waste carriers.[85] The Environment Agency has the power[86] to carry out off-road inspections of carriers' vehicles whilst the police have off-road and on-road inspection powers. These 'stop and search' powers of inspection are exercisable only if the EA or the police have reasonable grounds to suspect that directive waste is being carried in a vehicle belonging to an unregistered carrier. It is an offence to obstruct the EA or the police whilst they are exercising these powers. A carrier may also be required by the EA or the police (i.e. following a vehicle stop and search) to produce its carrier's registration certificate. In addition, the Environment Agency has a power of vehicle seizure.[87]

The following are exempt from registration: the Environment Agency (as waste regulator), WCAs, WDAs, a waste producer carrying waste (except construction and demolition waste) in its own vehicles, and charities and voluntary organisations.[88] Registration as a waste carrier may be refused by the Environment Agency, applying a two-stage test, if: (a) the applicant, or one of its employees, has been convicted of a relevant offence; and (b) a company of which the applicant is or was an officer has been convicted of a relevant offence[89] and the Environment Agency considers

82 S 49 of the EPA 1990.
83 S 32.
84 S 1(1) COP(A) A 1989.
85 See the Controlled Waste (Registration of Carriers and Seizure of Vehicles) Regulations 1991 as amended in 1998.
86 See s 5 of the COP(A)A 1989.
87 See s 6 of the EPA, s 6 of the COP(A)A 1989, and regs 20–25 of the Controlled Waste (Regulation of Carriers and Seizure of Vehicles) Regulations 1991 (SI 1991/1624), as amended.
88 See s 1(3) of the COP(A)A 1989 and reg 2 of the 1991 Regulations.
89 Reg 1(2) of and Sched 1 to the 1991 Regulations.

it undesirable that the applicant be registered.[90] In deciding whether to register an applicant, the Environment Agency takes into account the circumstances surrounding the commission of the relevant offence.[91] Carriers may appeal against refusals to register or re-register. The EA may revoke[92] a carrier's registration if it considers that the carrier is no longer a 'desirable carrier'.[93] In line with most pollution control regimes, the EA is obliged to keep a register of registered carriers.[94]

5.8.6 Waste brokers

The activities of waste brokers[95] are regulated by the EA under the Environmental Permitting (England and Wales) Regulations 2010. It is an offence to arrange, as a waste broker, for the disposal/recovery of directive waste belonging to another person unless the broker is registered with the EA. The EA has a discretion to refuse registration, for example, based on the applicant having been convicted of waste-related offences. Registration lasts for three years and is renewable. Exemptions from the obligation to register apply to a range of legal persons, including waste management/environmental permit holders, charitable/voluntary organisations which transport waste, and WCAs and WDAs.

5.8.7 Recycling

WCAs play a major role in the promotion of waste recycling. Section 46(2) EPA enables WCAs to arrange for the separation of household waste, via separate bins, into recyclable and non-recyclable waste streams. WCAs are subject to the s 49 EPA duty to prepare waste recycling plans and publicise information relating to recycling facilities available in each WCAs area.

Section 55 EPA enables, but does not oblige, a WCA to acquire or purchase waste in order to recycle it. Since it is economically more efficient for WCAs to recyle waste rather than it be landfilled in WDA-licensed facilities, WCAs have a s 52 EPA entitlement to receive recycling credits from the WDA in regard to the amount of waste recycled. Following publication of the National Waste Strategy 2000,[96] the government introduced secondary legislation to set recycling 'performance' targets for local authorities.[97] The Local Government (Best Value) Performance Indicators and Performance Standards (England) Order 2003[98] set statutory recycling targets.

The Household Waste Recycling Act 2003 obliges all local authorities in England to provide householders with separate bins for recyclable and non-recyclable waste streams for collection by 2010. Limited exceptions apply.[99]

5.9 The waste management permitting system

5.9.1 Introduction

The requirement for a waste management permit[100] to legitimise directive waste disposal operations and directive waste recovery operations lies at the heart of the waste regulatory regime

---

90 Reg 5(1).
91 See *Scott v Berkshire CC* [1984] JPL 94.
92 Reg 10.
93 E.g. due to the carrier committing one of the offences listed in the 1991 Regulations.
94 Reg 3.
95 Businesses which arrange for the disposal/recovery of waste belonging to others.
96 Updated in 2007.
97 Readers will recall that WCAs are the district councils and the London boroughs whilst WDAs are mainly the county councils and the metropolitan authorities.
98 SI 2003/530.
99 E.g. rural areas linked to cost considerations and apartment blocks where waste is not individually collected.
100 See reg 12(1) of the Environmental Permitting (England and Wales) Regulations 2010.

established by the Environmental Permitting regulations. The acquisition of a waste management permit and compliance with its conditions will shield the permit holder from liability for s 33(1) (a) and (b) of the EPA 1990 offences and breach of reg 38 of the Environmental Permitting (England and Wales) Regulations 2010. Nevertheless, activities which are carried out in accordance with the terms of a waste management permit may still constitute a criminal offence under s 33(1) (c) of the EPA 1990.

The Environment Agency is responsible for regulating the waste management permitting regime and is equipped with a range of enforcement powers to ensure that permit holders comply with the conditions incorporated into their permits.

The system of waste management licences (permits) originally came into force in May 1994 by virtue of the Waste Management Licensing Regulations 1994,[101] as amended. COPA 1974-licensed sites automatically became EPA 1990-licensed sites on 1 May 1994. The licensing system was complex: all waste producers had to determine, by reference to the Waste Management Licensing Regulations 1994, whether or not they needed to obtain a waste management licence or whether they were exempt. In the latter case, they were still required to register with the Environment Agency. Not all waste management facilities were subject to Part II EPA 1990 licensing control. Large landfill sites (those with a capacity in excess of 25,000 tonnes), waste incinerators and some waste recovery facilities were subject to IPPC control. From early 2007 waste and IPPC facilities have both been subject to the licensing (permitting) regime contained in the Environmental Permitting (England and Wales) Regulations 2007, as amended (replaced by the Environmental Permitting (England and Wales) Regulations 2010).

See Chapter 6

The main changes in the licensing system introduced by Pt II of the EPA 1990, as amended, were as follows:

(a)   applicants for licences had to satisfy the 'fit and proper person test';[102]
(b)   all aspects of the licence had to be enforceable at all times, that is, not only when the disposal operations were in progress;
(c)   the Environment Agency had to agree any proposed licence transfer; and
(d)   arrangements had to be introduced in respect of surrender of licences.

The effectiveness of the waste management licensing regime was also improved by:

(a)   a range of widely drafted criminal offences (many of them offences of strict liability) to underpin Part II of the EPA 1990;
(b)   a range of administrative enforcement powers which provided the Environment Agency with an alternative mechanism (to prosecution) to enforce compliance with the terms of licences; and
(c)   a duty of care, breach of which constituted a criminal offence, applying to everyone in the 'waste chain', and which ensured that directive waste was properly handled from 'cradle to grave'.

The Environment Agency targeted its enforcement activities on applicants at the point of application for a licence. Licences were unlikely to be granted to applicants with criminal records causing the Environment Agency serious concern unless the application was accompanied by a credible post-conviction plan setting out measures to improve the applicants' performance.[103] The licensing

---

101 SI 1994/1056.
102 S 74 EPA 1990. Repealed by reg 73 and Sched 21, para 17 of SI 2007/3538.
103 See www.environment-agency.gov.uk/commondata/105385/relevant_convictions.pdf.

or permitting system is now to be found in the Environmental Permitting (England and Wales) Regulations 2010.

5.9.2 The requirement to obtain an environmental permit to operate a regulated facility

All waste-related businesses which treat (e.g. recycle), keep (e.g. store) or dispose of (e.g. to landfill or incinerate) waste require an environmental permit, unless an exemption applies. The need for an environmental permit is set out in reg 12 of the Environmental Permitting (England and Wales) Regulations 2010:

> 12 (1) A person must not, except under and to the extent authorised by an environmental permit –
>
> (a) operate a regulated facility; or
> (b) cause or knowingly permit a water discharge activity or groundwater activity.

A range of waste-related activities or operations fall within the definition of 'regulated facility'. Regulation 8 of the Environmental Permitting (England and Wales) Regulations 2010 defines a regulated facility:

> 8—(1) In these Regulations 'regulated facility' means any of the following –
>
> (a) installation;
> (b) mobile plant;
> (c) a waste operation;
> (d) a mining waste operation;
> (e) a radioactive substance activity;
> (f) a water discharge activity;
> (g) a groundwater activity.

5.9.3 Exemptions and exclusions from licensing/permitting

The Environmental Permitting (England and Wales) Regulations 2007 as amended (replaced by the Environmental Permitting (England and Wales) Regulations 2010) exempt a range of activities from waste licensing/environmental permitting control. Sites operating exempt activities are nevertheless required to register with the Environment Agency, and supply details of the activity, the place where it is being carried on, and the exemption relied upon. It is an offence to carry on an exempt activity without registration, save that this requirement does not apply to private individuals. Exemptions granted by Member States' legislation must be compatible with the need to attain the objectives of the Waste Framework Directive. Except in very limited circumstances, there is no exemption from licensing in the case of hazardous waste.

The main exempt activities[104] are:

(a) temporary storage (for example, in a skip) of directive waste at the place of production pending disposal or recovery. 'Temporary' is not defined and will depend upon the particular circumstances;

---

104 See Scheds 2 and 3 of the Environmental Permitting (England and Wales) Regulations 2010.

(b)   temporary storage of hazardous waste by the waste producer at the place of production, subject to limitations, including quantity and security arrangements;

(c)   activities related to recovery and reuse such as baling, compacting and shredding;

(d)   the storage or deposit of demolition and construction waste for construction-related use at the place of demolition/construction;

(e)   the deposit of organic materials to 'condition' land; and

(f)   a wide range of recycling activities including the collection of metals, paper, cardboard, plastics, glass, textiles and drink cans.

Also exempt is the disposal of waste within the curtilage (that is, the small area of land around a building) of a dwelling house.[105] Exempt activities, except for the household waste exemption, are still subject to the prohibition contained in s 33(1)(c) of the EPA 1990 but are free of the requirements of s 33(1)(a) and (b).

The power to exclude certain activities from the licensing/permitting regime is given to the Secretary of State by s 33(3) and (4) of the EPA 1990. The Secretary of State can make regulations, excluding certain activities involving the deposit, keeping, treatment or disposal of waste from the need to obtain a licence/permit. Council Directive 91/156/EEC permits exemptions from the licensing system provided there are other adequate controls in place. This is reflected in s 33(4) EPA, which states that the Secretary of State when exercising his or her powers in respect of exemptions should have regard to the expediency of excluding from the controls imposed by the waste management licensing/environmental permitting system:

(a)   any deposits which are small enough or of such a temporary nature that they may be so excluded;

(b)   any means of treatment or disposal which are innocuous enough to be excluded;

(c)   cases for which adequate controls are provided by other legislation.[106]

The High Court case of *Environment Agency v Newcomb and Son Ltd and Another* (2002)[107] examined the powers of the Environment Agency with regard to waste management licensing exemptions. The case related to the carrying out of waste management and disposal activities on land owned by Newcomb and Son Ltd consisting of the deposit of inert waste,[108] as part of the construction of a football pitch and car park. The Environment Agency agreed to the carrying-out of the exempt activities provided at least 95 per cent of the waste imported onto the development was block waste destined for use in the development's foundations. The Agency stressed that the deposit of biodegradable waste was to be avoided. Evidence emerged that biodegradable waste had been deposited, and the company and one of its directors were charged by the Environment Agency with knowingly causing or permitting the deposit of controlled (directive) waste on land (where no waste deposit licence was in force) contrary to s 33 of the EPA 1990. In the magistrates' court, the defendants were acquitted on the ground that, although there was waste on the development which fell outside the exemptions in the 1994 Regulations, that waste was within the 5 per cent specified by the Environment Agency as acceptable. Subsequently, in the High Court, Newman J, allowing the Environment Agency's appeal, held that the Agency had no power to vary the exemptions detailed in the 1994 Regulations and the magistrates had been wrong to take the Agency's letter into account. Section 33 EPA 1990 banned the making of unauthorised waste deposits and, as each of

---

105 S 33(2) EPA 1990.

106 S 33(3) EPA 1990.

107 *Environment Agency v Newcomb and Son Ltd and Another* [2002] EWHC 2095.

108 Block-making and wood chipping wastes exempt from licensing under Sched 3 to the Waste Management Licensing Regulations 1994.

the charges related to a specific deposit made by the respondents, each deposit constituted a criminal act. The onus was on the prosecution to prove that the facts of the case established that the terms of the relevant exemption had been exceeded, resulting in a deposit or deposits prohibited by s 33.

5.9.4 The Environmental Permitting (England and Wales) Regulations 2007 and 2010

The Environmental Permitting (England and Wales) Regulations 2007 came into force on 6 April 2008, and existing waste management licences and pollution prevention and control permits were automatically transferred to the new permitting (licensing) regime. The 2007 Regulations were amended in 2010 to create a single set of controls[109] applying to activities previously regulated under the Waste Management Licensing Regulations 1994, the Pollution Prevention and Control Regulations 2000[110] and water pollution discharge consents regulated under the WRA 1991.

The permitting regulations are designed so that they impose no extra regulatory burdens upon operators. The permit application system includes provisions relating to monitoring and enforcement of permits. The permitting regulations impose a duty upon the regulator (i.e. the EA) to exercise its powers to achieve compliance with the following EU directives:

- 2008 Integrated Pollution Prevention and Control;
- 2006 Waste Framework Directive;
- 1993 Landfill Directive;
- 2001 Large Combustion Plant Directive;
- 2000 Waste Incineration Directive;
- 2002 Waste Electrical and Electronic Equipment Directive;
- 2000 End of Life Vehicles Directive;
- 1992 Titanium Dioxide Directive;
- 1987 Asbestos Directive;
- 1999 Solvent Emission Directive;
- 1994 Petrol Vapour Recovery Directive.

In contrast to the previous waste management licensing system, the holder of an environmental permit must be the 'operator' (the legal person controlling the regulated facility). The permitting regulations contain transitional provisions which address the situation where the holder of a waste management licence and the operator of the relevant 'regulated facility' are different legal persons. In this case the holder of the waste management licence is treated as the operator. A permit cannot be granted to more than one operator. In the case of two operators two permits will be required.

The principal regulator of the new permitting system is the Environment Agency,[111] whilst the local authorities have a subsidiary role.[112]

All 'regulated facilities' require a permit. These facilities include:[113]

---

109 With the object of simplifying the licensing system, reducing the administrative burden on the regulator and regulated alike but without adversely affecting the environmental and health standards set under the previous licensing regimes, and making the applications system simpler, cheaper and faster.
110 Some waste operations continue to be exempt under the new environmental permit application system.
111 Reg 32.
112 In regard to A2 and B IPPC regulated facilities.
113 Reg 8.

(a) Sched 1 installations regulated under the IPPC regime;[114]
(b) reg 4 waste operations—sites licensed/permitted for the disposal or recovery of directive waste excluding IPPC installations and any exempt or excluded sites;
(c) reg 2 mobile plant other than waste mobile plant;
(d) reg 4 waste mobile plant, unless exempt or excluded.

A single permit may cover several processes taking place on an operator's site.[115]

Many types of waste operation[116] are exempt from environmental permitting.[117] These include (1) waste storage at the place of production prior to its treatment/disposal elsewhere,[118] (2) the deposit of organic waste for fertilising/conditioning land, and (3) some waste reuse/recovery activities.[119] Exempt activities must be registered with the regulator. There are no exemptions in regard to facilities handling hazardous waste.

Only an operator may make an application for an environmental permit. The operator must supply the relevant regulator with all the relevant information and pay the relevant fee. The regulator must process the application within the relevant timescale: transfer within two months and surrender or variation or standard permit within three months. The Secretary of State may exercise his/her 'call in' power where the permit application relates to (1) regionally or nationally significant issues, (2) a controversial issue, (3) an issue of national security, or (4) an issue affecting the government of a foreign state. The Secretary of State issues a direction to the regulator (regarding the application decision).

In regard to public consultation the public have an opportunity to make their views heard in relation to a permit application. The permitting regulations oblige the regulator to provide 'public consultees'[120] with the opportunity to make representations.

The permitting system involves two types of environmental permit: standard and bespoke. The operator has a choice whether to apply for a standard or bespoke permit and advice may be sought from the Environment Agency.

In deciding whether to grant or refuse a permit application, a regulator who is minded to grant the application must have regard to whether the requirements of any relevant EU directive will be complied with. The regulator is under a legal duty to refuse an application if it considers that the operator will not be able to operate the regulated facility in accordance with the permit. The regulator, in assessing whether the operator will be able to comply with permit conditions, may take the following criteria into account:

(a) the relevant management system including accredited systems;[121]
(b) the level of technical competence assessed through management systems and/or certificates of technical competence;
(c) compliance history including convictions for relevant offences;
(d) financial provision designed to ensure adequate funding to operate the environmental permit.

---

114 E.g. power generation, metal processing, minerals, petrochemical, etc.
115 Reg 17.
116 Listed in Sched 3.
117 Reg 5 and Scheds 2 and 3 to the Environmental Permitting (England and Wales) Regulations 2010.
118 E.g. temporary waste storage in a skip awaiting collection by a waste carrier.
119 E.g. waste sorting by the waste producer, waste baling, waste shredding, waste compacting, and some waste recycling activities.
120 E.g. legal persons who will be affected or who are likely to be affected by or have an interest in the relevant application.
121 E.g. ISO and EMAS.

Standard permits contain only one condition referring to a fixed set of non-site-specific rules. Thus the Environment Agency does not have to get involved in setting site-specific conditions and also avoids the need for public consultation. If an operator wishes to carry out an activity which is covered by the standard rules (and the operator is satisfied that it can comply with those rules), it can apply for a standard environmental permit without the need for an environmental impact assessment or risk assessment. However, if a standard environmental permit is granted, the operator will not be able to appeal against any of the standard contents of the standard permit. There are 28 types of standard environmental permit which cover low- to medium-risk activities, such as waste transfer stations and recycling operations. The Secretary of State is empowered to make standard rules for permits relating to an industry sector. The regulated facility operator chooses whether to operate in accordance with standard rules or individually set permits.

Bespoke environmental permits are issued where any of the standard environmental permits will not apply. A bespoke environmental permit is normally required where the operator's activities pose a higher risk to the environment or require more complex controls, for example, landfill and waste to energy facilities.

The regulator is under a legal duty to regularly review permits in order to satisfy itself that the relevant permit conditions are up to date, reflect any change in the regulated facility, and incorporate any changes in the relevant EU environmental control regimes.

The environmental permitting regulations contain a range of offences relating to breach of the environmental permitting system.[122] The most serious offences are operating a regulated facility without a permit or in breach of permit conditions, and failing to comply with any statutory notice[123] served upon the operator. These offences are punishable in a magistrates' court with a maximum fine of £50,000 or imprisonment for a term of up to 12 months. The minor offences carry a maximum £5,000 fine. The most serious offences may be dealt with in the Crown Court, where the maximum penalty is an unlimited fine and/or imprisonment for a term of up to five years.

A court in sentencing a convicted offender[124] may order that the effects of the offence be remedied,[125] with the result that the offender bears the cost of remedial work.

Provided a regulator has exhausted other remedies, it may apply to the High Court for an injunction (in those cases in which the enforcement of the criminal law has failed to secure compliance).[126]

Should the regulator desire to keep control over the outcome of any enforcement action relating to breach of the permitting regime, it has a range of administrative powers (including enforcement notice, variation notice, suspension notice, and revocation notice) at its disposal to enforce compliance with the permitting regime (note the additional enforcement tools contained in the Regulatory Enforcement and Sanctions Act 2008) and thereby secure compliance with the terms of the relevant EU directives. The mandatory nature of this duty requires that the regulator take measures to ensure compliance with permit conditions. Any persistent breach of directive requirements, reflected in breach of permit conditions, is likely to result in formal enforcement action subject to the contents of EA enforcement policy. In regard to the regulator's duty to inspect regulated facilities regulators may impose conditions requiring the operator to self-monitor[127] and report any breaches. Any failure to report a breach of a permit condition to the regulator will be a further breach of the permitting regime.

---

122 Reg 38.
123 E.g. an enforcement notice.
124 E.g. for failure to comply with an enforcement or suspension notice.
125 Reg 44.
126 Reg 42.
127 E.g. using automated technology.

Operators have a right of appeal against (1) a decision to refuse or vary a permit, (2) the service of revocation, variation, enforcement, and suspension notices, or (3) the imposition of allegedly unreasonable permit conditions.[128]

The permitting regulations also make some changes to the defences available in relation to waste offences. Under the new regime there is a single statutory defence regarding breach of permitted activities, the so-called 'emergency defence', that the action which amounts to a breach of the regulations was taken in an emergency to avoid danger to human health.[129] Particulars of the emergency action must be supplied to the regulator as soon as reasonably practicable.[130]

No 'due diligence' defence is available under the permitting regulations. Under the previous waste management licensing system, operators charged with the offence of breaching a condition of a waste management licence could utilise this due diligence defence. The operator of a waste management facility could not be convicted of breach of licence conditions if the operator could satisfy the court that it took all reasonable precautions and exercised all due diligence to avoid the commission of the relevant offence.[131] The withdrawal of the defence[132] signals a more strict liability-based approach to the enforcement of the new permitting regime.

5.10 Permit conditions

5.10.1 Introduction

The objective of the environmental permitting system is to regulate the day-to-day operation of regulated facilities. This should be achieved by unambiguous conditions which leave the operator in no doubt as to what the required standards are and how they are to be met. Each condition should be necessary, comprehensive, unambiguous and enforceable, otherwise it will be unreasonable and challengeable. The Environmental Permitting (England and Wales) Regulations 2010 provide the EA with a wide discretion to attach conditions to the grant of a permit.

In *AG's Ref (No 2 of 1988) (1990)*, the Court of Appeal struck out a site licence (permit) condition requiring a waste site to be operated so as not to cause a nuisance to adjacent property owners. The condition did not relate to the purposes of the COPA 1974 (the forerunner to Pt II of the EPA 1990 and the Environmental Permitting (England and Wales) Regulations 2010) and was therefore unlawful. The main focus of permit conditions is the protection of the environment, human health and property. Guidance issued by the Secretary of State in Waste Management Papers[133] assists the Environment Agency with regard to the choice of appropriate conditions. Conditions attached to a permit should not duplicate planning conditions relating to the use of the site for waste management purposes.

The Environmental Permitting (England and Wales) Regulations 2010 provide that a permit will be granted on such terms and subject to such conditions as appear to the Environment Agency to be appropriate, and these conditions may relate to the activities authorised, the precautions to be taken and the works to be carried out. In practice, conditions will be set which cover fundamental issues such as the site infrastructure and site operation. They will also stipulate monitoring and record-keeping requirements and security. In practice, many of the conditions in the permit will primarily be the outcome of negotiation between the Environment Agency and the applicant.

---

128 Reg 31.
129 This defence was not available for pollution prevention and control permit-holders.
130 Reg 40.
131 E.g. breach of licence condition.
132 S 40 Clean Neighbourhoods and Environment Act 2005.
133 See Waste Management Paper 4.

Although the Environment Agency has a wide discretion as to the conditions it may include in a permit, its power to impose such conditions as it thinks fit is limited by the Waste Framework Directive, which obliges Member States to include conditions relating to 'technical matters' in permits. A permit may be set aside if it does not properly address these issues.[134]

The conditions that can be included in a permit can cover matters before the site becomes operational (that is, site preparation and insurance cover), during operation and, importantly, can include conditions after the operations have ceased (such as the monitoring of methane emissions and leachate production). The conditions will detail the types and quantities of waste that can be treated, kept or disposed of.

One condition which may be attached is particularly important: s 35(4) enables a condition to be set on a new application and also on a modification or suspension of an existing permit, requiring the operator to carry out works or do other things even though he or she is not generally entitled to do them. For example, a permit holder may be required to carry out sampling or monitoring on neighbouring land owned by another person. Section 35(4) further provides that any person whose consent would be required should grant or join in granting the holder of the permit such rights in relation to land as will enable the holder to comply with such a condition.[135] Waste Management Paper 4 suggests that this power will be used sparingly and only when absolutely necessary. Compensation is payable where conditions of this sort are imposed. Finally, it should be noted that the Secretary of State has the power to make regulations specifying conditions to be attached to permits.

5.10.2 EA's powers to enforce permit conditions

The Environment Agency has been granted significant administrative powers to 'police' permit holders' compliance with the terms of their waste management permits. These powers are important because they enable the Environment Agency to retain control of the outcome of the enforcement process without resorting to prosecution and thereby handing control over the outcome of the case to the courts. As we shall see, these powers are potentially draconian, because they enable the Environment Agency to put persistently poor operators out of business, either temporarily or permanently. Permit holders are not entitled to compensation when their operating permits are varied, suspended or revoked (unless the relevant notice is successfully appealed).

5.11 Permit-related powers

5.11.1 Operator and pollution risk appraisal (OPRA)

The Environment Agency has adopted a risk-based approach to regulation of waste and the IPPC regime. OPRA is a tool which the Agency uses to assess the environmental risks posed by waste (and other) sites and the competence of the site operator to manage those risks properly. Agency field staff visit sites and allocate scores for various aspects of the risks posed by the site and the performance of the operator (the lower the score, the better). The relevant scores are then used to help assess the number of compliance visits Agency staff will make in that year. The current OPRA methodology was first published in 2000 and is subject to continuous refinement.

OPRA comprises two types of appraisal: the Environmental Appraisal of the site and the Operator Performance Appraisal. The Environmental Appraisal focuses on the following factors: (a) the type of facility; (b) the type and quantity of waste received; (c) the control and containment

---

134 See *Guthrie v SEPA* [1998] Env LR 128.
135 Although, as noted above, a person has the right to be consulted and make representations under s 36A EPA 1990.

measures on site; (d) the sensitivity of 'receptors';[136] (e) groundwater sensitivity;[137] and (f) location of surface waters from the site and their sensitivity to contamination. The Operator Performance Appraisal comprises: (a) operator assessment—the operator's ability to manage the site in accordance with permit conditions. A zero score (for each criterion on the waste inspection score sheet) indicates full compliance with permit conditions, whereas the maximum score of 15 indicates an emergency situation; and (b) operator management—the level of management control. No control mechanism equals a score of 10, whereas a score of 1 equals an accredited management system in operation.[138]

5.11.2 Variation of permits (reg 20 Environmental Permitting (England and Wales) Regulations 2010)

Waste management environmental permits can, in contrast to planning permissions, be varied by means of a Variation Notice (VN) either by the Environment Agency or at the request of the permit holder (reg 20 of the Environmental Permitting (England and Wales) Regulations 2010).

A permit holder may seek a variation of the holder's permit, for example, to accommodate different types of waste. There is no restriction regarding the extent of a proposed variation. A permit holder must apply to the Environment Agency for a variation and pay the appropriate fee. Failure to determine an application to vary a permit within a period of two months, unless the period has been extended by agreement in writing, will result in the Environment Agency being deemed to have rejected the application. A permit holder can appeal to the Secretary of State against the decision of the Environment Agency to refuse the variation application.

5.11.3 Transfer of a permit (reg 21 Environmental Permitting (England and Wales) Regulations 2010)

Waste operations are businesses run on commercial lines. Many are very profitable. Like all businesses, the ownership and control of the business can change hands. It is therefore necessary in such circumstances for there to be a transfer of the permit to the new owner/operator. Regulation 21 of the Environmental Permitting (England and Wales) Regulations 2010 deals with the right of transfer. A permit must be transferred on the joint application of the present holder and of the present transferee using the prescribed form and on payment of the prescribed fee. However, the Environment Agency can only agree to the transfer if it is satisfied that the transferee is a 'competent operator'. As in the other provisions relating to permits, a right of appeal exists to the Secretary of State. If the Environment Agency fails to determine an application for transfer within a period of two months (unless applicants agree in writing to extend the period), the application will be deemed to have been rejected by the Environment Agency. Permits may be transferred even if they are subject to partial suspension or revocation.

See Chapter ◄ 6.9.3

5.11.4 Revocation of a permit (reg 22 Environmental Permitting (England and Wales) Regulations 2010)

The power to revoke a permit,[139] available to the Environment Agency, is dependent upon the existence of certain circumstances. A permit may be revoked in whole or in part, although it can only be partially revoked if the reason is the lack of technical competence of the management.

---

136 E.g. how close houses are to the site boundary.
137 Is the site in a groundwater protection zone?
138 For example, ISO 14001.
139 Provided in reg 37.

The partial revocation of the permit allows for continuing obligations[140] to be imposed on the permit holder even if operation of the site is no longer permitted. Partial revocation may occur where the Environment Agency revokes only that part of a permit which authorised the reception and management of hazardous waste. Complete revocation is unlikely, in most cases, because the Environment Agency will require aftercare permit conditions to remain in force.

5.11.5 Suspension of a permit (reg 37 Environmental Permitting (England and Wales) Regulations 2010)

The Environment Agency may suspend the permit in the following circumstances:[141]

(a) the permitted activities have caused or are about to cause serious pollution of the environment or serious harm to human health;

(b) continuation of the permitted activities will continue to cause serious pollution of the environment or serious harm to human health;

(c) the permit holder fails to comply with the terms of a condition of the environmental permit.[142]

The Environment Agency has a discretion whether to serve a Suspension Notice (SN). If it chooses to serve an SN, the Notice will specify the dates when the suspension will commence and cease. SNs will only suspend site activities and will not affect precautionary measures designed to prevent contaminants escaping from the site.

5.12 Surrender of permits (reg 25 Environmental Permitting (England and Wales) Regulations 2010)

A waste management mobile plant permit may be surrendered at any time by its holder but, in the case of a site permit, the permit can only be surrendered with the agreement of the Environment Agency. If the Environment Agency accepts the application for surrender, it will issue the permit holder with a 'certificate of completion'. However, the Environment Agency can only accept the surrender if it is satisfied that the condition of the relevant land whether or not permitted is unlikely to cause pollution of the environment or harm to human health.[143]

In order to reach a decision in regard to permit surrender, the Environment Agency must first inspect the land and consider any information provided by the permit holder about the state of the land. The information which the permit holder will be asked to supply includes: site location, details of all activities carried out on site and their respective locations, the times during which various activities were being carried out on site, the quantity of waste handled, hydrogeology, methane production and leachate production. In view of the fact that landfills, even those fitted with impermeable liners, create ongoing gas and leachate problems, it is unlikely that the Environment Agency will be keen to issue certificates of completion. It is safer to require permit holders of closed sites to continue monitoring and reporting the results to the Environment Agency.

The Environment Agency has three months to determine the application or a longer period if agreed in writing with the applicant. The Environment Agency may, however, determine within that period that it cannot accept the surrender until certain information is supplied about the site or

---

140 E.g. site aftercare, applying to a closed facility.
141 S 38(6).
142 S 42(6).
143 In which case the EA must accept the surrender of the environmental permit.

until the site has undergone remedial works. For this reason, the permit holder should always keep accurate and detailed records about the wastes that have been deposited in order to facilitate the process of surrender. The stricter EPA 1990 regime (permitting is now governed by the Environmental Permitting (England and Wales) Regulations 2010) is not completely watertight and problems have arisen in regard to the status of the licence/permit if the licence/permit holder dies or goes into liquidation (if a company). In *Official Receiver v Environment Agency, Re Celtic Extraction Ltd* (2000),[144] the Court of Appeal held that if a waste management company becomes insolvent, then the licence may qualify as 'onerous property' within the meaning of that term in the Insolvency Act 1986, and may be disclaimed by the Official Receiver. The court observed that there were no clear words in the EPA 1990 which were intended to exclude the effect of the Insolvency Act 1986. The Environment Agency conceded in the course of the proceedings that a licence ceases to have effect when a licence holder dies. Once a licence expires, the Environment Agency has no power to regulate; however, in such circumstances, the waste site may be subject to local authority control via the statutory nuisance or contaminated land regimes. In the event that the licence-holding company becomes insolvent but the licence is not disclaimed, the Environment Agency retains regulatory control. If the Environment Agency wishes to commence a prosecution against an insolvent licence holder, it must obtain the consent of the court before commencing any prosecution relating to breach of licence.[145] The fact that a financial penalty imposed on the insolvent company will adversely affect creditors will not necessarily lead to the Environment Agency refraining from prosecuting. In regard to landfill sites regulated under IPPC controls, the Landfill (England and Wales) Regulations 2002 set out the equivalent surrender procedure to s 39 EPA.

5.13 Rights of appeal

In all of the various provisions discussed above, it has been noted that the applicant (for a permit) or permit holder has a right of appeal. Regulation 31 of the Environmental Permitting (England and Wales) Regulations 2010 provides a right of appeal to the Secretary of State against a determination by the Environment Agency in the following instances:

(a) an application for a permit or a variation of the conditions of a licence/permit is rejected;
(b) a permit is granted subject to conditions which are unacceptable to the applicant;
(c) the conditions of the permit are varied;
(d) a permit is suspended;
(e) a permit is revoked;
(f) an application to surrender a permit is rejected;
(g) an application to surrender a permit is not decided upon within three months; or
(h) an application for the transfer of a permit is rejected.

An appeal must be made within six months of the relevant decision. There is no right of appeal where the Secretary of State has 'called in' the matter for his or her own determination. Nevertheless, the opportunity to make a judicial review application is available.[146]

The appellant and the Environment Agency may choose whether an appeal proceeds by way of a full hearing or by written representations (a paper-based appeal). Appeals are generally heard by inspectors appointed by the Secretary of State and drawn from the ranks of the planning

---

144 *Official Receiver v Environment Agency, Re Celtic Extraction Ltd* [2000] Env LR 86.
145 See *Environment Agency v Clarke, Re Rhondda Waste Disposal Ltd* [2000] Env LR 600.
146 *R v Vale of Glamorgan BC and ABP ex p James* [1996] 8 ELM 12; [1997] Env LR 195.

inspectorate. The Secretary of State will decide major or contentious appeals. There are no specific grounds of appeal, as in the case of statutory nuisance, but applicants are guided by Annex 10 of Circular 11/94.

5.14 Public registers

The Environment Agency maintains a publicly accessible register of information relating to regulated waste facilities.[147] Part 5 of the Environmental Permitting (England and Wales) Regulations 2010 requires 14 types of information to be noted on the register including the grant of a permit, permit conditions, monitoring data (whether collected by the Environment Agency or by the permit holder as a permit condition), permit applications, Variation, Suspension and Revocation Notices, and relevant convictions. Information may, by application to the Secretary of State, be excluded from the register due to commercial confidentiality and national security considerations,[148] subject to a right of appeal against a decision of the Secretary of State not to allow exclusion.[149]

5.15 Supervision and monitoring of permits (reg 34 Environmental Permitting (England and Wales) Regulations 2010)

5.15.1 Introduction

Under reg 34 of the Environmental Permitting (England and Wales) Regulations 2010 the Environment Agency is obliged to monitor and supervise the activities authorised by an environmental permit.[150] It must take the necessary steps to ensure that the permitted activities do not cause pollution of the environment, harm to human health or serious detriment to the amenities of the locality. The Environment Agency must also take steps to ensure that permit holders comply with permit conditions. In addition, the Environment Agency will also carry out inspections of its area to ensure that there are no unpermitted activities such as fly-tipping. Unlicensed waste disposal constitutes a breach of s 33 of the EPA 1990 and of reg 38 of the Environmental Permitting (England and Wales) Regulations 2010.

5.15.2 Powers of Environment Agency officials

In order to carry out its functions, the Environment Agency employs inspectors to inspect and monitor sites, thereby ensuring compliance with the relevant legislation.

The powers of inspection and entry, contained in ss 108–110 of the EA 1995, enable an Environment Agency inspector:

(a)   to enter at any reasonable time premises which he or she has reason to believe it is necessary for him or her to enter. This should normally be at any reasonable time unless there is an emergency, in which case entry is permitted at any time, and if need be, by force. Where an EA inspector has reason to believe that he or she will be refused entry by the person in occupation of the premises s/he desires to inspect, the inspector can obtain a court warrant;

---

147 S 64 EPA.
148 S 65.
149 S 65(5).
150 See reg 34.

(b) on entering premises to take with him or her any other person duly authorised by the Environment Agency, and a policeman. The latter may be needed in situations where the inspector has reasonable cause to apprehend any serious obstruction in carrying out his or her duties;

(c) to take any equipment or materials required for any purpose for which the power of entry is being exercised;

(d) to make such examination and investigation as may in any circumstances be necessary;

(e) to instruct that the premises or any part of them, or anything in them, be left undisturbed. The inspector may require that the premises or the part of the premises under investigation are not disturbed for as long as is reasonably necessary to enable him or her to carry out any examination or investigation;

(f) to take such measurements and photographs and make such recordings as he or she considers necessary;

(g) to take samples, or instruct samples to be taken, of any articles or substances found in or on the premises and also from the air, water or land in, on or in the vicinity of the premises. Specific provisions relate to the possession, safekeeping and use in evidence of such samples;

(h) in the case of any article or substance found in or on premises which appears to him or her to be an article or substance which has caused or is likely to cause pollution of the environment, or harm to human health, to cause it to be dismantled or subjected to any process or test (but not so as to damage or destroy it unless that is necessary);

(i) to require information from any person—the inspector can require any person whom he or she has reasonable cause to believe to be able to give any information relevant to any examination or investigation to answer such questions as the inspector thinks fit to ask. The person answering the questions will be required to sign a declaration of truth to the answers. The interviewee's answers to the questions posed by the EA cannot be used as evidence in any criminal prosecution of the interviewee (because it is contrary to the legal rules concerning self-incrimination) but may be used in evidence against other persons, especially the interviewee's employer;[151]

(j) to inspect any information and to take copies—the inspector can require the production of any information that he or she considers necessary, including information held on computer. He or she also has the right to inspect and take copies of such information or any entry in the records;

(k) to require facilities to afford assistance—here the inspector can require any person to afford him or her such facilities and assistance with respect to any matters or things within that person's control or in relation to which that person has responsibilities. So, for example, the inspector can require an engineer on the premises to show him or her how the monitoring and testing equipment is working (or not working as the case may be);

(l) any other powers conferred by regulation by the Secretary of State.

Certain information can be withheld from the inspector if it is subject to legal professional privilege. This covers correspondence between clients and their solicitors or legal professional advisors. It is an offence to obstruct[152] or fail to comply with the requirements[153] of a duly authorised EA inspector whilst the EA inspector is endeavouring to carry out the tasks assigned to him or her by the EA in accordance with the relevant powers of entry.

---

151 S 108(4) EA 1995.
152 S 110 EA 1995.
153 S 108 EA 1995.

5.15.3 Requests for information (s 71 EA 1995)

Section 71 of EA 1995 empowers the Environment Agency to serve a request for information on any person in order to obtain information relevant to the performance of the Environment Agency's statutory responsibilities. Failure to provide such information or knowingly providing false information is a criminal offence. There is a defence of 'reasonable excuse' but this does not apply to a refusal based on a violation of the rule against self-incrimination.[154] The s 71 power may only be used by the Environment Agency if it already has sufficient information[155] which will form the basis of the s 71 request.[156] The maximum penalty on summary conviction in the magistrates' courts for breach of s 71 is a £5,000 fine. If the matter is committed to the Crown Court, the maximum penalty is an unlimited fine and/or a prison sentence of two years.

5.15.4 Seizure of vehicles (s 6 EPA 1990)

Section 6 of the EPA 1990 empowers the Environment Agency to seize any vehicle which has been used for specified illegal activities. If the Environment Agency has been unable, through its informational powers, to obtain details of the ownership of vehicles suspected of being involved in illegal waste operations, the Environment Agency may make an application to a magistrate for seizure of the relevant vehicle.[157]

5.15.5 Limitations of the EA's investigatory powers

Employees of the EA have no arrest powers, no power to obtain the name and address of any suspect and have limited stop and search powers.

5.16 Clean-up powers (s 59 EPA 1990)

5.16.1 Introduction

Section 59 of the EPA 1990 gives the Environment Agency and the Waste Collection Authorities power to require the removal of controlled (directive) waste (via the service of a Waste Removal Notice (WRN)) where waste has been deposited in contravention of the conditions of a permit or in breach of s 33(1)(c) of the EPA 1990. The relevant authority may serve a notice on the occupier of land, requiring the waste to be removed or specifying the steps to be taken by the recipient of the notice to mitigate the consequences of the deposit. At least 21 days must be allowed to comply with the notice, during which time the recipient has a right to appeal to the magistrates' court. Such an appeal must be allowed if the court is satisfied that the appellant occupier neither deposited nor knowingly caused nor knowingly permitted the deposit, or if there is a material defect in the notice.[158]

The Environment Agency may serve a WRN on a mortgage lender who repossesses property upon which an illegal deposit of waste has taken place.[159]

---

154 See R v Hertfordshire CC ex p Green Environmental Industries Ltd [2000] 2 WLR 373; [2000] 1 All ER 773.
155 E.g. the EA may not use the s 71 power to 'fish around' for any evidence which may incriminate the recipient of the information request.
156 See JB and M Motor Haulage Ltd v London Waste Regulation Authority [1993] Env LR 243.
157 See also regs 20–25 of the Controlled Waste (Registration of Carriers and Seizure of Vehicles) Regulations 1991 (SI 1991/1624).
158 S 59(3).
159 Devonshire WRA v Roberts, Warren and Snow (1995) 7 ELM 105.

If the occupier (who is in receipt of the notice) fails to take necessary action, then the authority can do so and recover its costs from the occupier[160] or, in appropriate cases, from the person who deposited or knowingly caused or knowingly permitted the deposit of waste (provided the person can be traced). In the event of an emergency occurring at a waste management site, the Environment Agency has the power[161] to carry out works and recover its costs from the permit holder. The Environment Agency may, in circumstances in which immediate action is necessary to prevent pollution of the environment or harm to people, remove illegally deposited waste or take other steps if the occupier of the land was not responsible for the deposit, or if the occupier cannot be traced.[162] The Environment Agency may only recover costs which were necessarily incurred from the person or persons who deposited, or knowingly caused, or knowingly permitted, the illegal waste deposit.[163] Where more than one person is responsible for the deposit, as long as the Environment Agency acts reasonably, it does not have to apportion its costs between the unlawful depositors.[164] The s 59 remedial power may be used in conjunction with a s 33 EPA 1990 or reg 38 prosecution or it may be employed independently of any prosecution.

Lodging an appeal will suspend the operation of the WRN until the appeal is determined.[165] Failure to comply with a WRN constitutes a criminal offence, but any prosecution may only be heard in the magistrates' court.[166] The maximum penalty on conviction of the offence is a £5,000 fine. The offence is a 'continuing' offence which attracts a further penalty of a maximum fine of £500 for every day the offence continues after conviction.

5.16.2 Statutory civil liability for the deposit of waste (s 73(b) of the EPA 1990)

In addition to s 59 of the EPA 1990, which empowers the Environment Agency to require the removal of waste deposited in contravention of the conditions of an environmental permit, s 73(6) EPA 1990 imposes civil liability on the person or persons responsible for damage caused by the deposit of controlled (directive) waste in contravention of s 33(1) or s 63(2) of the EPA 1990. Damages may be claimed by any person sustaining property damage or personal injury. Section 73(6) EPA 1990 liability is strict and an action may be commenced by any person. In addition, such persons have the option of commencing a common law tortious action against the person responsible for the damage.[167]

See Chapter ← 11

Section 63(2) of the EPA 1990 provides that it is an offence for any person to deposit or knowingly cause or knowingly permit the deposit of non-controlled waste (that is, waste which is not regulated because, for example, it is exempt) if the relevant waste has hazardous waste characteristics (that is, it is dangerous or difficult to dispose of) and is deposited without a permit, in breach of permit conditions or without some other form of permission.

The circumstances giving rise to an unlawful deposit of waste include:

(a) the deposit of wastes which are not in accordance with the conditions of an environmental permit;

(b) waste deposited in a manner likely to cause pollution of the environment or harm to human health;

(c) the deposit of exempt wastes which constitute an unlawful disposal.

---

160 S 59(6) EPA 1990.
161 S 42(3) EPA 1990.
162 S 59(7) EPA 1990.
163 S 59(8) EPA 1990.
164 *Berridge Incinerators v Nottinghamshire CC* (1987) unreported, 14 April.
165 S 59(4) EPA 1990.
166 S 59(5) EPA 1990.
167 See environmental torts, discussed in Chapter 11.

The person who deposited the waste which caused the damage will be liable, save in those circumstances in which the injured party was totally at fault or chose to run the risk of incurring damage. In those cases, where the defendant was not totally to blame, contributory negligence issues arise.

In addition to the person who deposited the relevant waste, liability may extend to any person or persons who knowingly caused or knowingly permitted the waste deposit (such as the person who arranged with a fly-tipper to dispose of the waste). An illustration of litigation based on an alleged breach of the s 73(6) EPA 1990 statutory (civil law) duty is provided by the case of C v Imperial Design (2001)[168] in which a 13-year-old claimant was badly burnt when he set fire to a drum of solvent belonging to the defendant, lying on land close to the defendant's premises.

5.17 Waste offences

5.17.1 Introduction

The regulation of waste is identical to other Command and Control pollution control regimes in that it is underpinned by a range of criminal offences. The main offences are contained in the EPA 1990 and the Environmental Permitting (England and Wales) Regulations 2010; however, these offences take account of the changes to the definition of waste.[169] Section 33(1) of the EPA 1990 and reg 38 of the Environmental Permitting (England and Wales) Regulations 2010 contain the key waste offences.

5.17.2 Section 33 EPA 1990 offences

Section 33(1) EPA 1990 contains a range of waste offences. These offences exist in parallel to any waste-related offences contained in regulation 38 of the Environmental Permitting (England and Wales) Regulations 2010.

The original wording of s 33(1) EPA 1990 has been amended to reflect the introduction of environmental permitting. The thrust of the three main offences contained in subss (a), (b) and (c) of s 33(1) is maintained. Subsection (a) prohibits the deposit of waste unless an environmental permit is in place and the conditions of that permit are adhered to. Subsection (b) prohibits the treatment (i.e. the submission of directive waste to a 'listed operation') of controlled/directive waste unless an environmental permit is in force and the conditions of the permit are being adhered to. 'Listed operations' include the directive recovery operations listed in the Annexes to Directive 2008/98/EC. Subsection (c) prohibits the treating (e.g. subjecting waste to a recycling process), keeping (storing the waste whether permanently or temporarily) and disposing of waste (e.g. landfilling waste or incinerating waste) in a way which risks causing environmental pollution or harm to human health.

The offences in subss (a) and (b) of s 33(1) may be committed in more than one way. For example an offender may deposit waste or he may knowingly cause or knowingly permit the relevant deposit. In other words the offence may be an offence of strict liability in which the mere deposit of waste constitutes the offence irrespective of the intention of the offender; alternatively the word 'knowingly' requires the offender to have an awareness of what he is doing.

Section 33(1) refers to 'controlled waste'. The original definition of waste in s 75 of the EPA 1990 has been amended to reflect changes to the definition of waste consequent upon the Waste Framework Directive. Waste is defined in s 75(2) EPA 1990:

---

168 C v Imperial Design [2001] Env L R 33 and (2002) JEL 74.
169 See the Waste Framework Directive (91/156/EEC).

'Waste' means anything that is waste within the meaning of Article 3(1) of Directive 2008/98/EC of the European Parliament and the Council on waste.

We set out s 33 of the EPA 1990 in full including amendments to the original wording of subs (1).

33—(1) Subject to subsections (1A), (1B), (2) and (3) a person shall not –

   (a)   deposit controlled waste or extractive waste, or knowingly cause or knowingly permit controlled waste or extractive waste to be deposited in or on any land unless an environmental permit authorising the deposit is in force and the deposit is in accordance with the permit;

   (b)   submit controlled waste, or knowingly cause or knowingly permit controlled waste to be submitted, to any listed operation (other than an operation within subsection (1)(a)) that –

      (i)   is carried out in or on any land, or by means of any mobile plant, and

      (ii)   is not carried out under and in accordance with an environmental permit.

   (c)   treat, keep or dispose of controlled waste or extractive waste in a manner likely to cause pollution of the environment or harm to human health.

(1A) Paragraphs (a) and (b) of subsection 1 above do not apply in relation to a waste operation that is an exempt waste operation.

(1B) Subsection (1) does not apply to the carrying on of any waste operation which is or forms part of an operation which –

   (a)   is the subject of a licence under Part 2 of the Food and Environment Protection Act 1985; or

   (b)   by virtue of an order under section 7 of that Act, does not require such a licence.

(2)   Subject to subsection (2A) below, paragraphs (a) and (b) of subsection 1 do not apply in relation to household waste from a domestic property which is treated, kept or disposed of within the curtilage of the property.

(2A) Subsection (2) above does not apply to the treatment, keeping or disposal of household waste by an establishment or undertaking.

(3)   Subsection (1) (a), (b) or (c) above do not apply in cases prescribed in regulations made by the Secretary of State and the regulations may make different provisions for different areas.

(4)   The Secretary of State, in exercising his power under subsection (3) above shall have regard in particular to the expediency of excluding from the prohibition in subsection (1) –

   (a)   any deposits which are small enough or of such a temporary nature that they may be so excluded;

   (b)   any means of treatment or disposal which are innocuous enough to be excluded;

   (c)   cases for which adequate controls are provided by another enactment than this section.

(5)   Where controlled waste is carried in and deposited from a motor vehicle, the person who controls or is in a position to control the use of the vehicle shall, for the purposes of

subsection (1)(a) above, be treated as knowingly causing the waste to be deposited whether or not he gave any instructions for this to be done.

(6) A person who contravenes subsection (1) above commits an offence.

(7) It shall be a defence for a person charged with an offence under this section:

  (a) that he took all reasonable precautions and exercised all due diligence to avoid the commission of an offence; or

  (b) . . . ; or

  (c) that the acts alleged to constitute the contravention were done in an emergency in order to avoid danger to human health in a case where –

    (i) he took all such steps as were reasonably practicable in the circumstances for minimising pollution of the environment and harm to human health; and

    (ii) particulars of the acts were furnished to the regulation authority as soon as reasonably practicable after they were done.

(8) A person who commits an offence under this section is liable –

  (a) subject to subsection (9) below, on summary conviction to imprisonment for a term not exceeding 12 months or a fine not exceeding £50,000 or both;

  (b) on conviction on indictment, to imprisonment for a term not exceeding five years or a fine or both.

(9) A person (other than an establishment or undertaking) who commits a relevant offence shall be liable –

  (a) on summary conviction, to a fine not exceeding the statutory maximum; and

  (b) on conviction on indictment to a fine.

(10) In this section 'relevant offence' means an offence under this section in respect of a contravention of subsection (1)(c) above consisting of the treatment, keeping or disposal within the cartilage of a domestic property of household waste from that property.

(11) For the purposes of subsection (1)(a) above, the deposit of waste in or on land includes any listed operation involving such a deposit.

(12) For the purposes of subsection (1)(c) above, treating, keeping or disposing of controlled waste includes submitting it to any listed operation.

'Listed operations' are those activities listed in Annex I or II of Directive 2008/98/EC and extractive wastes are mining and quarrying wastes.

5.17.2.1 Elements of the s 33 EPA 1990 offences

5.17.2.1.1 'Knowingly causing' and 'knowingly permitting'

The offences of 'knowingly causing' or 'knowingly permitting' contained in ss 33(1)(a) and 33(1)(b) EPA 1990 are strict even though they require some degree of knowledge on the defendant's part. In *Shanks and McEwan (Teesside) Ltd v Environment Agency* (1997),[170] a waste company was prosecuted by the Environment Agency for knowingly permitting the deposit of controlled waste (directive waste) in contravention of a condition of its waste management licence (permit). The defendant argued, unsuccessfully, that although it knew that a deposit of waste had occurred, it was not aware that the deposit had breached a condition of its operating licence (permit). The court held that the

---

170 *Shanks and McEwan (Teesside) Ltd v Environment Agency* [1997] 2 All ER 332.

defendant's knowledge of the deposit was sufficient to establish liability and it was unnecessary for the prosecution to prove that the defendant knew that the deposit would breach the conditions of its operating licence (permit). Knowledge of a deposit may be inferred from the facts.[171] The very act of operating a landfill site will be interpreted by the courts as constructive knowledge, on the part of the site operator, that deposits are taking place and it is not necessary for the prosecution to demonstrate knowledge of individual breaches of licence (permit) conditions.[172] This interpretation of 'knowingly causing' or 'knowingly permitting' in effect imposes strict liability for breaches of waste management licence (permit) conditions.

The inclusion of 'knowingly causing' appears to have been inserted into ss 33(1)(a) and s 33(1)(b) EPA 1990 to cover the situation where one person orders another to deposit waste (for example, a waste producer contracts a carrier to transport waste to the nearest suitable landfill site, but the carrier fly-tips the waste on waste ground) and the waste consignor is unaware that the consignee deposits the waste illegally.

5.17.2.1.2 'Pollution of the environment' and 'harm to human health'

Section 33(1)(c) EPA 1990 makes it an offence to treat, keep or dispose of controlled (directive) waste in a manner likely to cause pollution of the environment or harm to human health. It makes no reference to knowingly causing or knowingly permitting, nor does it make it a defence to be operating in accordance with a waste management permit. It is possible for a person to be operating in accordance with a waste management permit and yet still be committing an offence under s 33(1)(c) EPA 1990. All that is required is that the treatment, keeping or disposal is likely to cause pollution of the environment or harm to human health. 'Pollution of the environment' refers to harm to flora and fauna, whilst 'harm' refers to both harm to living organisms and ecological systems.

5.17.3 Meaning of 'deposit'

The word 'deposit' has an extended meaning primarily to counter arguments by waste producers and waste handlers that the presence of waste on site does not constitute a 'deposit' because the waste has not reached its final destination. This argument has been raised, unsuccessfully, in order to evade liability for s 33 EPA 1990 offences. In Leigh Land Reclamation Ltd v Walsall MBC (1991),[173] the court held that 'deposit' referred to the tipping and burying of the waste at a landfill site so that the waste became incorporated into the site so that there was 'no realistic prospect of further examination'.

In R v Metropolitan Stipendiary Magistrate ex p London Waste Regulation Authority (1993),[174] the High Court adopted a wider meaning of the term and held that 'deposit' covered both temporary[175] and permanent deposits of waste. Furthermore, 'deposit' includes the continuing activities on a waste management site. In Thames Waste Management Ltd v Surrey CC (1997),[176] the defendant waste management company was convicted of breaching the terms of its waste management licence (permit) and therefore committing an unlawful deposit of waste. One of the licence (permit) conditions required waste, which had been deposited on the site, to be covered over on the day of deposit. The defendant argued, unsuccessfully, that the failure to cover the waste occurred after the waste had already been deposited. The court held that the word 'deposit' could cover continuing activities specified in the

171 See *Kent CC v Beaney* [1993] Env LR 225.
172 *Shanks and McEwan (Teesside) Ltd v Environment Agency* [1997] 2 All ER 332.
173 *Leigh Land Reclamation Ltd v Walsall MBC* (1991) 3 JEL 281.
174 *R v Metropolitan Stipendiary Magistrate ex p London Waste Regulation Authority* [1993] 3 All ER 113.
175 E.g. at waste transfer station.
176 *Thames Waste Management Ltd v Surrey CC* [1997] Env LR 148.

waste management licence (permit). Thus, the 'deposit' continued until it was covered over. Section 33 EPA 1990 offences at a landfill site may not only be committed by the site operator breaching the terms of its licence (permit) but also by waste carriers.[177]

5.17.4 Other EPA 1990 waste offences

In addition to the three offences in s 33(1)(a), (b) and (c) of the EPA 1990, an important 'fly-tipping' offence is created by subs (5) of s 33.

Section 33(5) states:

> 33(5)—where controlled (directive) waste is carried in and deposited from a motor vehicle, the person who controls or is in a position to control the use of the vehicle shall be treated as knowingly causing the waste to be deposited, whether or not he or she gave any instructions for this to be done.

This provision is designed to address the problem of the illegal fly-tipping of waste. Section 33(5) EPA 1990 should be read in the light of the Environment Agency's s 6 EPA 1990 power relating to the seizure of vehicles used for unlawful waste-related activities. If the Environment Agency is unable to obtain information, through its ss 7 and 71 EPA 1990 powers, with regard to any vehicle suspected of being used for fly-tipping, it can apply to a magistrates' court for a warrant to seize the vehicle. After seizure, the Environment Agency may publicise the seizure and, if no one comes forward to claim the vehicle, it may dispose of it.[178] The issue of what constitutes 'control' of a vehicle for the purposes of the s 33(5) EPA 1990 'fly-tipping' offence was considered in *Environment Agency v Melland* (2002).[179] The Environment Agency alleged that Melland had knowingly caused controlled waste to be deposited on land where no waste management licence was in force, contrary to ss 33(1)(a) and 33(6) of the EPA 1990. At the hearing in the magistrates' court, it was established that the registered keeper of the vehicle, at the time of the alleged offence, was a company under which Melland was trading. Prior to the hearing, the Environment Agency had served on Melland a request for information under s 71 of the EPA 1990 in reply to which Melland stated that he had been the owner and registered keeper of the vehicle at the relevant time. Melland argued that there was no case to answer because there was insufficient evidence (that is, the mere fact that his company was the registered keeper) to prove that he was in control of the vehicle at the relevant time the offence was alleged to have been committed. The magistrates dismissed the Environment Agency's case on the basis that the person controlling the vehicle (driving it) was not Melland and therefore control by him had not been established. On appeal, by way of case stated, the Environment Agency argued that the issue of 'control' was one of fact and common sense and vehicle ownership carried with it the ability to control its use. Once ownership had been established, there was evidence to demonstrate control and there followed an irresistible inference of control in the absence of evidence to the contrary. Harrison J held that evidence of vehicle ownership was capable of amounting to prima facie evidence (that is, an initial evidential inference) that the vehicle owner controlled, or was in a position to control, the use of a vehicle. Each case was dependent upon its facts and evidence could be presented (for example, the vehicle had been loaned to someone or stolen) which rebutted the inference the court was entitled to make. In this case, the owner and keeper of the vehicle was Melland, Melland ran a waste (skip hire) business, and waste had been unlawfully deposited from the vehicle. It could therefore be inferred that Melland controlled or was

---

177 With regard to breach of s 33(1)(b) EPA 1990; see *Shanks and McEwan (Teesside) Ltd v Environment Agency* [1997] 2 All ER 332.
178 Reg 23 of the Controlled Waste (Registration of Carriers and Seizure of Vehicles) Regulations 1991.
179 *Environment Agency v Melland* [2002] EWHC 904.

in a position to control the vehicle at the relevant time. This was sufficient evidence to convict Melland in the absence of evidence to the contrary. The Environment Agency was not required to produce evidence linking Melland and the driver of the offending vehicle, although the burden of proof remained with the prosecution. This judgment was consistent with the object of s 33(5) EPA 1990 to make prosecution for fly-tipping easier where some of the relevant circumstances might be obscure.

5.17.5 The household waste exemption

The main exemption from the EPA 1990 waste offences is in relation to household waste. The offences contained in Pt II of the EPA 1990 do not apply in relation to household waste from a domestic property which is treated, kept or disposed of within the curtilage of the dwelling by or with the permission of the occupier of the dwelling.[180] It should be noted that the following will not be treated as household waste for the purpose of this exception: any mineral or synthetic oil or grease; asbestos; or clinical waste.

5.17.6 Defences

5.17.6.1 EPA 1990 defences

It is clear from the wording of ss 33(1)(a) and 33(1)(b) of the EPA 1990 that an offence will not be committed if the deposit, treatment, keeping or disposal of controlled (directive) waste is in accordance with a permit.[181] Therefore, compliance with a permit and all its conditions will provide a defence to these two offences. Compliance with the terms of a permit, however, affords no defence in relation to a s 33(1)(c) EPA 1990 offence.

Section 33(7) also provides a number of additional defences. To succeed in defending a s 33 prosecution, a person charged must prove that:

(a) He or she took all reasonable precautions and exercised all due diligence to avoid the commission of the offence. This defence is often associated with the defendant proving that he or she has set up an adequate system to avoid the commission of an offence. For example, in *Durham CC v Peter Connors Industrial Services Ltd* (1993),[182] a waste carrier who was contracted to make regular visits to a waste producer's premises to collect waste in an awaiting skip was not allowed to take advantage of the s 33(7)(a) defence. The waste carrier had not checked the contents of the skip on every occasion it had collected a skip from the waste producer's premises and the court held that the waste carrier had not done enough to inform itself of the nature of the waste which was being collected. To avail itself of the defence, a specific enquiry had to be made of any person who knew what the waste was and whether a deposit of the waste would be unlawful.[183]

(b) The acts alleged to constitute the contravention were done in an emergency to avoid danger to human health. However, to rely on this defence, it is necessary to fulfil two further criteria, namely that the person seeking to rely on the defence took all such steps as were reasonably practicable in the circumstances for minimising pollution of the environment and harm to health and that, as soon as reasonably practicable after these actions were taken, particulars of

·

---

180 S 33(2) EPA 1990.
181 E.g. it is in accordance with the conditions attached to the licence/permit.
182 *Durham CC v Peter Connors Industrial Services Ltd* [1993] Env LR 197.
183 Note the removal of due diligence defences as a result of the Environmental Permitting (England and Wales) Regulations 2007.

the incident were given to the Environment Agency. Section 33(7)(c) EPA 1990 restricts this defence to circumstances in which emergency action was taken to avoid danger to the public but not danger to the environment. The onus is on the defendant to prove that the circumstances constituted an emergency and the court will employ an objective test (would the reasonable defendant believe that an emergency existed?) in deciding whether the circumstances constituted an emergency.[184]

The courts will determine as a question of fact whether a person can rely on any of these defences.

5.17.6.2 Environmental permitting defences

The Environmental Permitting (England and Wales) Regulations 2010 have made some changes to the defences available in relation to waste offences. Under the new regime there is a single statutory defence regarding breach of permitted activities, the so-called 'emergency defence'—that the action which amounts to a breach of the regulations was taken in an emergency to avoid danger to human health. Particulars of the emergency action must be supplied to the regulator as soon as reasonably practicable.[185] No 'due diligence' defence is available under the 2010 Regulations. Under the previous waste management licensing (permitting) system operators charged with the offence of breaching a condition of a waste management licence (permit) could utilise this due diligence defence. The operator of a waste management facility could not be convicted of breach of licence (permit) conditions if the operator could satisfy the court that it took all reasonable precautions and exercised all due diligence to avoid the commission of the relevant offence (i.e. breach of licence (permit) condition). The withdrawal of the defence signals a more strict liability-based approach to the enforcement of the new permitting regime.

5.17.7 Sanctions

5.17.7.1 EPA 1990 sanctions

Section 33(8) and (9) of the EPA 1990 contain the relevant sanctions relating to breach of s 33(1) EPA 1990. In s 33(8) the penalties are:

(a)   on summary conviction (in a magistrates' court), to imprisonment for a term not exceeding 12 months or a fine not exceeding £50,000 or both; and

(b)   on conviction on indictment (in a Crown Court), to imprisonment for a term not exceeding 5 years or an unlimited fine or both.

5.17.7.2 Sanctions relating to reg 38 of the Environmental Permitting (England and Wales) Regulations 2010

In addition to the waste offences contained in s 33(1) of the EPA 1990 and the sanctions for those offences set out in subss (8) and (9) of s 33 EPA 1990, breach of reg 38 of the Environmental Permitting (England and Wales) Regulations 2010 may occur in regard to a permitted waste facility (e.g. operating a regulated waste facility without a permit or breach of permit conditions). The sanctions for breach of reg 38 are detailed in reg 39.

See Chapter 6 →

---

184 *Waste Incineration Services Ltd v Dudley MBC* [1993] Env LR 29. See reg 40 of the Environmental Permitting (England and Wales) Regulations 2010.

185 Reg 40.

Law in Action

To illustrate typical waste offences which result in EA prosecution and the imposition of penalties upon conviction we set out below three examples of common waste offences:

(i) A Bristol man was given a six-month community service order, a 12-month driving ban and placed under a curfew (i.e. was 'tagged') after admitting to a series of waste offences. The defendant, Christopher Blackwell, appeared before Bristol Magistrates on 23 April 2008 and pleaded guilty to transporting, depositing and disposing of a directive waste without a licence contrary to s 33(1) and (5) of the Environmental Protection Act 1990. The defendant dumped a total of 11 piles of construction waste in a country lane in North Somerset.

(ii) Scrap metal company E J Shanley & Son (Trowbridge) Ltd appeared before Chippenham Magistrates' Court on 25 June 2008 and pleaded guilty in regard to (1) depositing directive waste without the benefit of a waste management licence contrary to s 33(1)(a) EPA 1990 and (2) treating directive waste without the benefit of a waste management licence contrary to s 33(1)(b) EPA 1990. The company was fined £40,000 and £1,813 costs arising out of the operation of a waste transfer station. An Environment Agency officer visited the site in March 2007 and saw that it was being used to store and treat a mixture of household, commercial and industrial wastes, although the site was only licensed to store and recover waste from end-of-life vehicles. The defendant had ignored a warning letter from the Environment Agency to clear the site of unauthorised waste.

(iii) Mark Roberts of Pontardawe in Wales pleaded guilty on 23 September 2008 when he appeared before Neath Magistrates' Court in regard to four charges of unlawfully keeping, depositing and disposing of directive waste contrary to s 33(1)(a) and s 33(1)(b) EPA 1990. The defendant was paid by a householder to take away building waste in November 2007. The EA filmed the defendant tipping waste illegally in a driveway near Alltwen. On investigation the EA found that the garden of the defendant's home was full of household and demolition waste. The defendant's vehicle, which he used to carry out the illegal waste removal, was seized by the police and was subsequently forfeited when the defendant appeared in court. It transpired that the defendant had three earlier waste-related convictions. The defendant was given a four-month prison sentence in regard to his breach of ss 33(1)(a) and 33(6) EPA and 28 days for breach of ss 33(1)(a) and 33(6) EPA.

5.17.8 The personal liability of senior officers of organisations with legal personality

Persons who commit waste offences range from individuals to organisations with legal personality (e.g. a company, a university, and public bodies such as an NHS Trust, a local authority, etc.). Whilst an individual may be fined and sent to gaol, it is not possible to imprison a company, although it is possible to imprison senior company officers. Prison sentences are relatively rare for environmental crimes, but the courts have imposed terms of imprisonment on convicted waste offenders in a number of instances. In most cases, the penalty for a waste offence will be a fine (plus costs, which may be considerably higher than the fine imposed). Although the fine may not always be that great in relation to the company's resources, the poor publicity arising from a prosecution may be more damaging. With regard to senior company officers, the court may order that they be disqualified from holding office (Disqualification of Directors Act 1986).

Senior company (and public authority) officers may be prosecuted and sanctioned for waste-related offences committed by their employing organisation. Where a waste offence has been committed by a company, the senior management may also be personally liable for the offence. However, it has to be proved that the offence was committed with their consent or connivance or was attributable to their neglect.

The relevant legal provision in a waste context was, until the introduction of environmental permitting in 2007, s 157 of the EPA 1990. This section has been repealed and replaced with reg 41 of the Environmental Permitting (England and Wales) Regulations 2010. Regulation 41 is drafted in wider,[186] terms than the provisions, or s 157 EPA 1990, which it replaces.

> 41—(1) If an offence committed under these Regulations by a body corporate is proved –
>
> > (a) to have been committed with the consent or connivance of an officer; or
> > (b) to be attributable to any neglect on the part of an officer,
> > the officer as well as the body corporate is guilty of the offence and is liable to be proceeded against and punished accordingly.
>
> (2) If the affairs of a body corporate are managed by its members, paragraph (1) applies in relation to the acts and defaults of a member in connection with the member's functions of management as if the member were a director of the body.
>
> (3) In this regulation, 'officer', in relation to the body corporate, means a director, member of the committee of management, chief executive, manager, secretary or other similar officer of the body, or a person purporting to act in such a capacity.

Whilst it is clear from company records who the directors are, there has been considerable debate with regard to who is a 'manager' for the purposes of s 157 of the EPA 1990 and similar offences (for example, s 217 of the WRA 1991, s 210 of the WIA 1991 and s 37 of the Health and Safety at Work etc. Act 1974). The courts have developed and applied a 'controlling officer' test to determine who is a 'manager' for the purposes of s 157 of the EPA 1990 and similar offences. In *R v Boal* (1992),[187] the defendant was the assistant general manager of a large bookshop. The defendant took charge of the bookshop whilst the general manager was on holiday. During the time he was in charge, serious breaches of the Fire Precautions Act 1971 came to light. The defendant was prosecuted and acquitted. The court held that, although the defendant was fourth in seniority in the company, he was not a manager within the 1971 Act. In *Woodhouse v Walsall MBC* (1994),[188] the defendant was the general manager of a waste management company. He was prosecuted, under the COPA 1974, for breaches of the company's waste management site licence. The court held that Woodhouse was not a manager for the purposes of the COPA 1974. Although he was a site manager, he was not in a position of real authority regarding the overall running of the company and was not in a position to guide or control company policy. In the Scottish case of *Armour v Skeen* (1976),[189] the Director of Roads of Strathclyde Regional Council was convicted of health and safety offences which led to the death of an employee. In reaching its verdict, the court referred to the fact that the defendant had responsibility for implementing the local authority's health and safety policy and as such was of sufficient seniority to be a 'director, manager, secretary or similar officer'. This case will be of interest to any senior public or private sector manager who has responsibility for devising and implementing an environmental policy.

---

186 The reg 41 offence extends to the chief executive of a corporate body and members of the management committee.
187 *R v Boal* [1992] QB 591.
188 *Woodhouse v Walsall MBC* [1994] Env LR 30.
189 *Armour (John) v Skeen* 1977 SLT 71.

Offences such as those covered in s 157 of the EPA 1990 (and reg 41 of the Environmental Permitting Regulations) are not offences of strict liability and the prosecution must prove that:

(a)   the defendant consented to the commission of the offence; or
(b)   the defendant connived at the commission of the offence; or
(c)   the offence was attributable to the defendant's neglect.

Consent requires some affirmative act or approval (see *Huckerby v Elliott* (1970)[190]). The defendant must be aware that an environmental offence is being committed and acts in a way which indicates that he or she is giving positive approval to the breach (for example, a company's plant malfunctions resulting in a breach of the terms of the company's pollution or operating licences, and a director orders production to continue). Connivance suggests acquiescence in conduct which is likely to lead to the commission of an offence (for example, a director is aware of some illegality and, whilst he or she does not actively encourage the breach, he or she allows it to continue, says nothing about it and chooses not to make any enquiry—i.e. shuts his/her eyes to the problem). Neglect has been defined as 'a failure to perform a duty which the person knows or ought to know' (see *Re Hughes* (1943)[191]). Whether any particular director has been guilty of neglect will depend upon the nature and extent of the director's duties. Managers should therefore be wary of accepting responsibilities relating to the environment and health and safety unless they are provided, by their employing organisation, with sufficient resources to carry out their responsibilities.

5.18 Hazardous waste offences

5.18.1 Introduction

The special waste regulatory regime[192] has been replaced with 'hazardous waste' controls in order to fully implement the Hazardous Waste Directive (91/689). The hazardous waste regime comprises two sets of secondary legislation: (1) the Hazardous Waste (England and Wales) Regulations 2005,[193] and (2) the List of Wastes (England) Regulations 2005.[194] These regulations mirror the definition of hazardous waste to be found in the Hazardous Waste Directive and the EU List of Wastes.

Regulation 47 of the Hazardous Waste Regulations 2005 requires any person who makes a deposit of hazardous waste in or on any land to record the location of the deposit. Records must be kept until the person surrenders his or her waste management licence/environmental permit. The site records will comprise either a site plan marked with a grid or a site plan with overlays on which deposits are shown in relation to the contours of the site. Regulation 19 prohibits any establishment or undertaking which carries out the disposal or recovery of hazardous waste, or which collects hazardous waste, from mixing different categories of hazardous waste, or from mixing hazardous waste with waste which is not hazardous waste.

5.18.2 Offences—reg 65 HWR 2005

Regulation 65 of the Hazardous Waste Regulations 2005 contains a range of offences relating to the failure to comply with obligations set out in the 2005 Regulations. In summary the offences relate

---

190 *Huckerby v Elliot* [1970] 1 All ER 189.
191 *Re Hughes* [1943] 2 All ER 269.
192 See the 4th edition of this text for coverage of the Special Waste Regulations.
193 SI 2005/894.
194 SI 2005/895.

to breach of the following types of obligation: the banning of the mixing hazardous waste, failure to comply with notification requirements, breaches of the hazardous waste consignment process, failure to take appropriate action in an emergency, failure of record keeping/information provision and supplying false or misleading information.

Following a prosecution and conviction for an offence under reg 65 the maximum sanction available to the courts is:

(a)   if the matter is dealt with in a magistrates' court a fine of £50,000 per offence and a maximum term of imprisonment of 12 months;

(b)   if the matter is dealt with in the Crown Court an unlimited fine and/or a sentence of imprisonment of five years (a term of imprisonment is only applicable to humans as opposed to legal persons such as companies or public bodies).

Regulation 70 enables the EA to impose fixed penalty notices[195] regarding breaches of the 2005 Regulations.

The 2005 Regulations provide for limited defences.[196] A defendant may escape conviction if the relevant failure to comply with the 2005 Regulations resulted from an emergency and every reasonable step was taken by the defendant to (1) minimise the danger to the public and/or the environment and (2) rectify the failure as soon as reasonably practicable.

5.19 Waste strategy for England and Wales

5.19.1 National waste policy

Until the dawn of the 1990s, there was no coherent national waste policy in England and Wales. Waste policy was largely a local authority concern due to the ready availability of landfill sites. However, amendments made to the EU Waste Framework Directive (91/156/EC) in 1991 coincided with central government recognition of the need for a more coherent and planned strategy to deal with the ever-increasing quantity of waste produced in England and Wales and the need for better methods of waste management and disposal.

During the period 1990–2000, the government produced several key policy documents: *This Common Inheritance*,[197] DoE Circular 11/94, *Making Waste Work*,[198] *Less Waste: More Value*,[199] *A Way With Waste*[200] and *Waste Strategy for England and Wales*.[201] The latter policy document was updated and reissued in 2007.[202] These policy documents revealed the government's key waste objectives:

(a)   to reduce the amount of waste generated;

(b)   to make the best use of waste;

(c)   to give preference to waste management options which minimise the immediate and future risk of pollution of the environment and harm to human health.

Together, these objectives represent a sustainable waste strategy for the twenty-first century reflecting EU environmental policy objectives. As part of its national strategy, the government set

---

195 Maximum £300 penalty per breach.
196 Reg 66.
197 Cm 1200, 1990.
198 Cm 3040, 1995, DoE.
199 1998, DETR.
200 1999, DETR.
201 Cm 4693, 2000, DETR.
202 Cm 2007 Defra.

national waste reduction, waste recovery and waste recycling targets. The government intended to achieve these targets by a combination of regulatory permit-based controls, eco-taxes, planning controls and information and education initiatives (the first two of these reflecting the EU's 'polluter pays' principle).

Whilst *This Common Inheritance* introduced the concept of the 'waste hierarchy' in 1990, ranking the waste management options in descending order of preference,[203] practical progress, at local level, in achieving the government's waste policy vision has been somewhat steady. The use of s 50 of the EPA 1990 to achieve national coverage of waste management plans, as required by the Waste Framework Directive, was not particularly successful and the WRAs had made rather 'pedestrian' progress in the preparation of waste disposal plans in an attempt to comply with the requirements of the Directive. The attainment of national waste policy objectives (especially waste minimisation) contained in the National Waste Policy (mirroring the objectives of the EU Waste Framework Directive) are likely to depend more upon the use of eco taxes,[204] producer responsibility instruments[205] and target setting[206] than upon the system of permitting and 'policing' waste management disposal and waste management recovery (treatment) sites regulated by the EA under the Environmental Permitting (England and Wales) Regulations 2010.

In 1994, the objectives contained in the Waste Framework Directive, as amended, were transposed into national law by the Waste Management Regulations 1994.[207] Section 50 of the EPA 1990 was repealed and replaced by ss 44A and 44B[208] requiring the Secretary of State to prepare a national waste strategy replacing the previous system of local authority waste disposal plans. The National Waste Strategy requires the Secretary of State to prepare a plan for England and Wales which will contain policies in relation to the recovery and disposal of waste in England and Wales. The strategy details the policies for attaining the objectives set out in Sched 2A to the EPA 1990. Schedule 2A sets out the two key objectives of the strategy:

(1) waste should be recovered or disposed of without endangering human health and without using processes or methods which could harm the environment and in particular without:

    (a) risk to water, air, soil, plants or animals;

    (b) causing nuisances through noise or odours; or

    (c) adversely affecting the countryside or places of special interest, and to secure the implementation of the strategy so as (with regard to waste disposal only) to secure an integrated and adequate network of waste disposal installations taking account of the best available technology; and

(2) ensuring self-sufficiency in waste disposal (having regard to location, need and availability of appropriate facilities), encouraging the prevention or reduction of waste production, and encouraging the recovery of waste by recycling, reuse or reclamation.

The strategy includes provisions relating to each of the following:

(a) the type, quantity and origin of waste to be recovered or disposed of;

(b) general technical requirements; and

(c) any special requirements for particular wastes.

---

203 Minimisation, recycling, recovery and disposal.
204 E.g. the landfill tax.
205 E.g. end of life vehicle recycling.
206 E.g. targets limiting volume of waste going to landfill and the amount of waste to be recycled.
207 Now replaced by the Environmental Permitting (England and Wales) Regulations 2007, as amended.
208 Inserted by the EA 1995.

In preparing the national strategy, the Secretary of State consulted with the Environment Agency, local authorities and industry (and any other bodies or persons that he considered appropriate). The strategy's broad objectives will have major impacts on local authority waste-related responsibilities. The actual preparation of the national waste strategy for England and Wales (and similar plans for Scotland and Northern Ireland) has taken time to come to fruition largely due to informational uncertainties in waste arisings (waste production). The strategy was completed and published in May 2000. 'Waste Strategy 2000 for England and Wales' is[209] the national plan for the purposes of the Waste Framework Directive. The strategy sets the following waste reduction targets, which are to be reviewed at five-yearly intervals:

(a)   to reduce the amount of waste (industrial and commercial) going to landfill by 85 per cent of 1998 levels by 2005;

(b)   to recover value from 40 per cent of municipal waste (EfW incineration generating electricity) and 25 per cent of household waste by 2005;

(c)   to recycle/compost 30 per cent of household waste and 45 per cent of municipal waste by 2010.

Targets in the updated Waste Strategy 2007[210] include:

(a)   the reduction of greenhouse gas emissions from waste management operations by 9.3 million tonnes (mt) of carbon dioxide by 2020 compared to the 2006–07 level;

(b)   the reduction of household waste which is not reused, recycled or composted from 22.2 mt in 2000 to 15.8 mt in 2010 and 12.2 mt in 2010 (a reduction of 45 per cent between 2000–20);

(c)   the reduction of levels of industrial and commercial waste landfilled by 20 per cent compared to the 2004 levels.

The relevant Landfill Directive targets in the 2007 Waste Strategy for biodegradable municipal waste in England are:

(a)   a reduction of 25 per cent by 2010 of the waste that was produced in 1995;

(b)   a reduction of 50 per cent by 2013 of the 1995 level;

(c)   a reduction by 65 per cent by 2020 of the 1995 level.

Since the waste management environmental permitting regime is not the ideal vehicle to address waste minimisation and waste recycling targets, the strategy incorporates the use of eco-taxes[211] and producer responsibility obligations.[212] These non-permit-based regulatory tools are designed to provide the necessary financial incentive to bring about greater waste minimisation and waste recovery efforts. In 2003 the House of Commons Environment, Food and Rural Affairs Select Committee published a report, *The Future of Waste Management*.[213] The report was critical of government waste policy, especially the lack of direction evident in Defra and the underfunding of Environment Agency enforcement. The main criticisms include the following issues: over-reliance on a single eco-tax[214] which could be developed further and other taxes introduced;[215] the adoption, by the

---

209 As amended by an updated waste strategy in 2007.
210 See Ch 8 of the Waste Strategy for England 2007 Cm 7086 Defra.
211 Such as the landfill tax.
212 Such as the Packaging Directive.
213 8th Report, HC 385 I and II (2002–03); summarised in [2003] JPL 1120–24.
214 Landfill tax.
215 For example, a household waste collection charge.

government, of a passive role with regard to the formulation of new waste directives; the failure to provide timely guidance on new directives; poor communication between government and local authorities regarding the role of local authorities with regard to attaining the objectives of the government's waste hierarchy; confusion of waste policy responsibility between Defra, the Office of the Deputy Prime Minister and the Department of Trade and Industry; Environment Agency delays in processing waste management permitting applications; government reticence with regard to waste incineration as a waste management option; and the failure of WDAs and WCAs to work together.

The attainment of the policy objectives (especially waste minimisation) contained in the National Waste Policy (mirroring the objectives of EU Waste Framework Directive) will, it seems, depend more upon the use of eco taxes, producer responsibility instruments[216] and target setting[217] than upon the system of permitting and 'policing' waste management disposal and waste management recovery (treatment) sites.

5.19.2 The significance of EU waste policy

EU waste law and policy has had, and continues to have, a profound impact upon waste management in England and Wales. The EU's waste strategy, set out in the Commission's 'A Community Strategy for Waste Management'[218] and rooted in the waste hierarchy, details the relevant concerns and priorities of the Commission (which largely reflect English and Welsh waste policy). Waste management is also a key 'priority area' of the EU's Sixth Action Programme, Environment 2010; Our Future, Our Choice,[219] the central theme of which is waste prevention and greater efficiency in the use of raw materials (resources) which will minimise waste generation.

The Commission has identified waste policy as one of the seven priority policy thematic strategies in its Sixth Action Programme and in its Communication Towards a Thematic Strategy on the Prevention and Recycling of Waste published in May 2003.[220] The Commission invited discussion from Member States on several issues, including: identifying areas where there is the potential for waste prevention; exchanging best practice; evaluating the relative merits of voluntary and mandatory waste prevention planning; assessing the waste prevention potential of the IPPC Directive; the development of materials-based recycling targets; and placing the onus on producers to recycle waste. Following discussions, the EU Commission produced a Thematic Strategy for the Prevention and Recycling of Waste.[221] The strategy document proposed changes to the Waste Framework Directive including clarification of the definition of waste. In particular the status of recycled materials receives attention, especially in regard to the question of at what point in time do recycled materials cease to be waste? Recycling operations would include 'recovery of waste into products, materials or substances, whether for the original or other purposes'. In addition 'waste recovery' operations, such as 'energy from waste' municipal waste incinerators, which produce energy by burning waste, would be excluded from regulatory control and would cease to be licensed as waste disposal facilities. The Commission desires to impose an obligation on Member States to produce and implement waste prevention programmes. Recycling clearly has an increasingly important role to play in sustainable waste management across Europe.

---

216 E.g. end of life vehicle recycling.
217 E.g. targets limiting volume of waste going to landfill and the amount of waste to be recycled.
218 [1990] OJ L122.
219 COM(2001)31 Final.
220 COM(200)301.
221 COM (2005) 666.

5.19.3 The Waste Framework Directive

The 1975 Waste Framework Directive (75/442/EEC) as amended in 1991 by Directive 91/156/EEC and the current Waste Framework Directive 2008/98/EC has influenced the shape of UK waste law and policy in the following ways:

(a)   the original definition of 'controlled waste' in the EPA 1990 has been amended to reflect the waste definition favoured by the EU—'directive waste';
(b)   EU waste policy created the need for a centralised national waste strategy;[222]
(c)   the EU goal of self-sufficiency in the treatment and disposal of waste[223] has influenced national waste strategy;
(d)   the creation of a 'waste management hierarchy' of waste policy objectives drives EU and Member State national waste policy.[224]

The relevant EU policy objectives are:

(a)   the prevention of and/or reduction of waste;[225]
(b)   the recovery of waste produced;
(c)   the recovery or disposal of waste without endangering human health or the environment.

To a marked degree, the Waste Framework Directive reflects the regulatory structure created by Pt II of the EPA 1990. For example, the Waste Framework Directive:

(a)   imposes a duty of care[226] on all persons in the waste chain;
(b)   obliges all waste disposal and waste recovery operations to be permitted;[227]
(c)   obliges waste producers, handlers, recoverers and disposers to keep proper records.[228]

The Waste Framework Directive objectives were transposed into the law in England and Wales by the Waste Management Regulations 1994.[229] The 1994 regulations do not create legal rights and obligations of benefit to non-decision makers and cannot therefore be relied upon directly by individuals. These objectives are therefore not 'directly effective' in litigation before national courts.[230]

In R v Bolton Metropolitan BC ex p Kirkman (1998),[231] the Court of Appeal held that the Waste Framework Directive expressed objectives rather than legal requirements. The court went on to hold that the effect of transposing the objectives into national law was to create a separate legal duty, applying to regulators, to ensure the attainment of the Sched 4 objectives. There is some debate as to how strict this duty will be in practice. For example, does the duty merely require the regulatory decision maker to have regard to the attainment of the objectives in determining questions which concern the Sched 4 objectives? Are the waste objectives just one of several issues which must be taken into account in regulatory decision making, but leaving the final weighting of the factors to the discretion of the regulator? Alternatively, does the duty oblige the regulatory decision maker to achieve the Sched 4 objectives thereby restricting the extent of the decision maker's discretion and

---

222   Art 6.
223   Art 5.
224   Arts 3 and 4.
225   See Art 174(2) of the EC Treaty.
226   Art 8 and s 34 of the EPA 1990.
227   Arts 9 and 10 and ss 35–42 of the EPA 1990.
228   Art 14 of the EPA 1990 duty of care waste transfer note system and the hazardous waste consignment note system.
229   Now replaced by the Environmental Permitting (England and Wales) Regulations 2010.
230   See Comitato Di Coordinamento per la Difesa Della Cava v Regione Lombardia (Case C-236/92) [1994] ECR I-483.
231   R v Bolton Metropolitan BC ex p Kirkman [1998] Env LR 719.

elevating the Sched 4 objectives above other considerations? In R v Leicestershire CC, Hepworth Building Products and Onyx (UK) Ltd ex p Blackfordby and Boothcorpe Action Group (2001),[232] the judge viewed the Waste Framework Directive objectives as a factor which the decision maker must take into account (the failure of the EA to take the Sched 4 objectives of the Waste Management Regulations 1994[233] into account was held to be unlawful in the case of R v EA ex p Sellars and Petty (1999),[234] but the weight which had to be accorded to the objectives was a matter entirely within the discretion of the decision maker. To hold otherwise would be to give the Sched 4 objectives an 'indeterminate' status—higher than material considerations, but not an absolute obligation. The subsequent decision in R v Daventry DC (2002)[235] seems to accord greater weight to an 'obligatory' objective than other material considerations, without going so far as to establish a hierarchy of relevant considerations, placing the Sched 4 objectives at the top.

In the Daventry DC case, Pill LJ rather helpfully observed that:

> An objective is something different from a material consideration . . . it is . . . a goal. A material consideration is a factor to be taken into account when making a decision, and the objective to be attained will be such a consideration, but it is more than that. An objective which is obligatory must always be kept in mind when making a decision even while the decision maker has regard to other material considerations.

This interpretation of the effect of the waste policy objectives (that they are important but not predominant) appears to be in accordance with the Court of Appeal decision in R (on the application of Blewett) v Derbyshire CC (2005).[236]

This case arose out of a judicial review challenge to a decision to grant planning permission to extend a landfill site. Auld LJ stated that:

> the added focus of waste management calls for particular attention or weight to be given to the objectives of the Waste Framework Directive when considering an application for planning permission for a landfill proposal.

Henceforth decision makers must (1) demonstrate that they understand the objectives contained in the Waste Framework Directive, (2) allocate appropriate weight to those objectives and (3) determine whether other material considerations outweigh the importance attached to attaining those objectives.

5.19.4 The Landfill Directive

In July 1999, the EU issued legislation relating to the harmonisation of landfill standards.[237] The Directive was required to be transposed into national law by July 2001. The Directive's main objective is to bring about a reduction in the amount of methane-producing, biodegradable household and municipal waste which is disposed of in landfill sites. The Directive sets reviewable reduction targets based on 1995 waste arisings.

The deadlines for achievement of these targets could be extended where more than 80 per cent of household and municipal waste was landfilled in 1995. Since waste disposal in England and

---

232 R v Leicestershire CC, Hepworth Building Products and Onyx (UK) Ltd ex p Blackfordby and Boothcorpe Action Group [2001] Env LR 35.
233 Replaced by the Environmental Permitting (England and Wales) Regulations 2010.
234 R v EA ex p Sellars and Petty [1999] Env LR 73.
235 R v Daventry DC [2002] All ER 149.
236 R (on the application of Blewett) v Derbyshire CC [2005] Env LR 25.
237 The Landfill Directive (99/31/EC).

Wales fell into this category, England and Wales were granted an extra four years to achieve each target. The current targets set for England are:[238]

(a)   a 25 per cent reduction by 2010;
(b)   a 50 per cent reduction by 2013;
(c)   a 65 per cent reduction by 2020.

The Landfill Directive is having important impacts upon national landfilling practice. The more important of these impacts are that: disposal of liquid, corrosive, clinical and infectious wastes to landfill is banned, as is the disposal of most types of tyres. The Directive divides landfill sites into three categories: those permitted to accept (a) hazardous wastes, (b) non-hazardous wastes, and (c) inert wastes.

The Directive:

(a)   requires all waste to be pre-treated (for example, sorting and compacting) before disposal;
(b)   bans the co-disposal of wastes (for example, the practice of landfilling hazardous wastes with household wastes);
(c)   requires waste sites to install technology to control landfill gas and leachate (for example, collecting methane and using it to produce electricity);
(d)   requires proper financial provision to deal with site aftercare.

The Landfill (England and Wales) Regulations 2002[239] came into force on 15 June 2002 and implemented the Landfill Directive (99/31/EC). In Pt I of the Regulations, reg 3 details their scope, reg 5 requires planning authorities to have regard to the location requirements of the Regulations when dealing with planning applications for landfills, reg 6 amends the Pollution Prevention and Control Regulations 2000 (PPC Regulations 2000) so that all landfills are Part A(1) installations.[240]

Part II of the 2002 landfill regulations control landfill permit conditions. Of particular note is reg 7, which requires the Environment Agency to classify landfills into sites permitted to accept (a) hazardous waste, (b) non-hazardous waste, and (c) inert waste. Waste acceptance criteria and monitoring procedures are detailed in Sched 1 to the 2002 Regulations. Regulation 16 concerns closure notices.[241] Part III contains relevant offences[242] such as acceptance of waste in contravention of para 3 of Sched 4. Sites which are unable to comply with the Regulations will close.

The Landfill Directive (99/31/EC) regulates the types of waste which are to be accepted at the relevant landfill types (hazardous, non-hazardous and inert). The Commission, in furtherance of the Directive, has published a decision[243] which sets out the rules on waste acceptance procedures for landfills. The Landfill (England and Wales) Regulations 2002 require operators to demonstrate that they have procedures in place which enable them to accept waste in accordance with permit conditions and the waste acceptance procedures.

All landfill sites should have put in place a 'site conditioning' plan. Site operators must monitor their closed landfills for methane emissions and migration of leachate for up to a maximum of 30 years. The Directive requires Member States to improve landfill regulation in the following areas: (a) checking and accepting wastes; (b) monitoring; (c) passing on the full operating costs to

---

238 See Ch 8 of the Waste Strategy for England 2007 Cm 7086 Defra.
239 SI 2002/1559.
240 Regulated by the PPCA 1999 and requiring a permit under the PPC Regulations 2000 but now superseded by the environmental permitting regime contained in the Environmental Permitting (England and Wales) Regulations 2010.
241 For Environment Agency use to accept closure of a landfill.
242 Reg 17.
243 Decision 2003/33/EC.

customers via gate fees (the amount charged by the landfill operator to enable waste to be tipped); and (d) providing adequate aftercare and financial provisions to address post-closure problems.

Following the introduction of the Landfill Regulations 2002, the Environment Agency has consulted, especially with the waste industry, with regard to new best practice guidance on the monitoring of leachate, groundwater and surface water at landfill sites (including closed sites). The resulting guidance[244] takes account of the Environment Agency's draft guidance notes.[245]

Following the implementation of the Environmental Permitting (England and Wales) Regulations in 2007 and amended in 2010 both waste facilities and IPPC facilities are subject to the 2010 Regulations.

The application of the Landfill Regulations 2002 and the Waste Incineration Regulations 2002 are both dependent upon correctly identifying the substances which fall within the definition of 'waste'. Thus, the definition of 'controlled waste'[246] was amended by para 88 of Sched 22 to the EA 1995 to include the list of substances listed in Sched 2B to the EA 1995 (that is, controlled waste includes directive waste).

The case of *Blackland Park Exploration Ltd v Environment Agency* (2003)[247] is an interesting and novel examination of the question of what constitutes a landfill site. A mixture of oil and water was extracted from underground strata at Whisby in Lincolnshire. The oil was separated out and the water was then reinjected into the ground together with imported hazardous liquid wastes. Oil production was IPC-regulated whilst the waste disposal process was covered by a waste management licence (permit). Following the introduction of the Landfill Regulations 2002,[248] the Environment Agency informed the site operator that the disposal of the liquid wastes constituted a landfill operation and that the site would have to be reclassified as a hazardous waste landfill. It followed that, under reg 9 of the Landfill Regulations 2002, liquid wastes could no longer be disposed of to landfill. The site operator disputed the Agency's view and sought a ruling on its legal position. The High Court held that the site was a landfill within reg 3(2) of the Landfill Regulations 2002. Blackbourne J rejected the submission (a) that the word 'deposit' implied placing wastes into a controlled (that is, static) medium (as in the case of normal landfilling operations), and (b) that the reinjection of water and waste constituted a 'discharge' into ground-waters regulated by the Ground Water Regulations 1998.[249] Blackbourne J stated that: 'The site is operated as a waste disposal site. That activity forms a major and distinct part of the claimants' operations at the site. Since the waste is deposited onto or into land it follows that the site is a landfill within the meaning of the Landfill Regulations.'

5.19.5 Other waste directives

5.19.5.1 Introduction

In addition to the general waste controls set out in the Waste Framework Directive, other directives regulate specific waste streams.

5.19.5.2 The Hazardous Waste Directive

The Hazardous Waste Directive (78/319/EEC), as amended by Directives 91/689/EEC and 94/31/EEC, is concerned with the management of wastes which have properties which make the

---

244 To replace the 2001 Environment Agency, *Guidance on Landfill Leachate Monitoring.*
245 *Guidance on Hydrogeological Risk Assessments for Landfills and Derivation of Groundwater Control and Trigger Levels.*
246 See s 75(4) of the EPA 1990.
247 *Blackland Park Exploration Ltd v Environment Agency* [2003] EWHC 691.
248 SI 2002/1559.
249 SI 1998/2746.

relevant wastes dangerous or difficult to handle. These properties are specified in the Annexes to the Directive (for example, toxicity). Much of the Directive has been implemented in England and Wales by the Hazardous Waste Regulations 2005.

The EU is responsible for compiling the list of hazardous substances, based on the capacity of substances to cause harm, which are subjected to tighter control than other directive wastes. The Hazardous Waste Directive requires Member States to prepare and make publicly accessible hazardous waste management plans and to provide the Commission with information relating not only to implementation, but also to the number and type of facilities available in each Member State for the recovery or disposal of hazardous waste. It is the Commission's intention to set up a European network of hazardous waste facilities.

5.19.5.3 Waste shipments

Movements of waste into, within and out of EU Member States is controlled by Directive 84/631/EEC and the directly effective Regulation (EC) 93/259. England and Wales have put in place the Transfrontier Shipment of Waste Regulations 1994.[250] The 1994 Regulations control the shipment of wastes into and out of England and Wales. Any person who wishes to import/export waste into/out of England and Wales must obtain a certificate from the EA authorising the shipment.[251] Breach of the terms of EU Regulation 259/93 is an offence[252] subject to due diligence and emergency defences set out in reg 14 of the 1994 Regulations.

The objective of the EU is to tailor waste movement controls to the health and environmental risks posed by the waste and also the ability of Member States to transport, treat and dispose of it. Regulatory control is based upon a system of prior notification of proposed waste movements. The waste mover/exporter notifies both 'recipient' states and 'transient' states (states through which the waste will be transported). Following receipt of the relevant notice of the proposed consignment, transient and recipient states may: (a) request further information from the exporting state; (b) impose conditions on the waste shipment; or (c) refuse permission. Exporting states must ensure that proper financial provisions regarding shipping, treatment and disposal of the waste are in place before the waste is shipped.

5.19.5.4 Air pollution

Directives 89/369/EEC and 89/429/EEC[253] (on air pollution from industrial plant) regulate the operation of municipal waste incinerators, whilst hazardous waste incineration is dealt with by the Hazardous Waste Incineration Directive (94/67/EC).

5.19.5.5 Waste incineration

The Waste Incineration Directive (2000/76/EC) was passed in order to limit the emission of dioxins from waste incinerators. The Directive has been implemented in England and Wales by the Waste Incineration (England and Wales) Regulations 2002.[254] The regulations came into force on 28 December 2002 and apply (a) to all new plant, and (b) from late December 2005 to existing incinerators, and set a limit of 1 part in 10 billion for dioxin emissions to air from waste incinerators/co-incinerators (co-incineration refers to incinerators which burn waste as a fuel in order to generate energy, e.g. energy (electricity) from waste incinerators). The regulations apply to

---

250 SI 1994/1137.
251 Reg 7.
252 Reg 12.
253 'Daughter' directives of the Air Framework Directive (84/360/EEC).
254 SI 2002/2980.

approximately 950 incinerators/co-incinerators (including the large municipal incinerators, cement kilns and clinical waste incinerators). The aim of the Regulations is to prevent and/or limit, as far as practicable, the negative impacts upon humans and the environment of atmospheric emissions. Operators of incinerators must obtain a permit (licence) authorising their operations.

The Waste Incineration Directive (2000/76/EC) details stringent operating conditions for new incinerators (from the end of December 2002) and for existing incinerators (from the end of December 2005). The Directive consolidates previous EU incinerator directives into one single Directive. The new Directive applies to a much wider range of incinerators (approximately 2,600), including incinerators burning waste oils.

The Waste Incineration Regulations 2002 came into force in late December 2002 implementing Directive 2000/76/EC. Defra concluded a consultation exercise in May 2003 with regard to a guidance note on the new Regulations. The guidance includes commentary upon the definitions of 'waste', 'incineration' and 'co-incineration' (co-incineration is the use of waste fuel to generate energy).[255]

5.19.5.6 Sewage sludge

Directive 86/278/EEC controls the regulation of sewage sludge disposal. Until the mid-1980s, it was common practice to spread sewage sludge on farmland; however, as many sewage treatment plants treat both human and industrial wastes, the processed sludge may contain high levels of heavy metals. The heavy metal content may be so high that the waste will be classified as hazardous waste and must be disposed of appropriately (for example, in a landfill licensed (permitted) to accept sewage sludge). The Directive requires sewage sludge with high levels of heavy metals to be pre-treated before it can be used on farmland. It also sets limits on the number of times annually that sludge may be spread on the same fields.

5.19.5.7 Waste oil

Directive 75/439/EEC regulates the collection and disposal of waste oils. Facilities which collect, keep or dispose of more than 500 litres of waste oils per year are required to keep records of their activities. To avoid harm to human health and the environment, the Directive bans the discharge of: (a) waste oils into watercourses and drains; (b) waste oils on land resulting in damage/harm to soils; and (c) uncontrolled discharges of process residues, and waste oil processing causing atmospheric pollution in excess of the limits detailed in the Directive.

5.19.5.8 Titanium dioxide

The Titanium Dioxide Directive (78/176/EEC) regulates the disposal of waste from the titanium dioxide industry. Titanium dioxide is an important constituent of paints.

5.19.5.9 The Batteries and Accumulators Directive

The Batteries and Accumulators Directive (91/157/EEC) regulates the risks relating to the heavy metal content of waste batteries and accumulators.

5.19.5.10 Directive 76/403/EEC

Directive 76/403/EEC regulates the disposal of waste PCBs and PCTs. Uncontrolled discharges/disposal of these substances are banned. Methods of treatment and disposal must avoid harming human health or the environment.

---

255 See www.defra.gov.uk/environment/ppc.

5.20 Producer responsibility

Section 93 of the EA 1995 enables the Secretary of State to introduce regulations which oblige manufacturers to recycle, recover, or reuse products or materials. The intention is to impose waste reduction targets on business sectors to enable national waste reduction targets to be met and EU legislation to be complied with.

5.20.1 Packaging Directive

The principal example of a producer responsibility initiative is the 1994 Packaging Directive (94/62/EEC), transposed into national legislation by the Producer Responsibility Obligations (Packaging Waste) Regulations 1997 (updated by the Producer Responsibility Obligations (Packaging Waste) Regulations 2007).[256] The function of the Directive is threefold:

(a)   to minimise the environmental impacts of packaging waste;
(b)   to harmonise packaging waste regulation within the EU; and
(c)   to ensure the free movement of packaged goods within the EU.

Article 6 of the Directive set the following reviewable (in 2006) recovery and recycling targets: (a) 50–65 per cent (by weight) of packaging waste to be recovered by mid-2001; and (b) 25–45 per cent of the packaging waste in (a) to be recycled with a minimum of 15 per cent per packaging type.

The waste packaging producer responsibility scheme in England and Wales is subject to a number of restrictions: (a) the burdens imposed by the scheme must be the minimum necessary to achieve the anticipated benefits; (b) the persons subjected to the burdens of the scheme must be those most able to contribute towards the attainment of national waste reduction targets; (c) environmental benefits (such as increased reuse of materials) will result from the scheme's implementation; and (d) the environmental benefits are 'significant' when compared to costs. The scheme adopts a similar definition of 'packaging waste' to that which appears in the Directive and includes all products to contain, handle, protect, deliver and present goods.[257] Packaging may consist of 'primary' packaging,[258] 'secondary' packaging[259] and 'tertiary' packaging.[260]

Member States are required to provide infrastructure for the collection and recovery of packaging waste from the consumer. Member States must also ensure that each type of packaging waste reaches the most appropriate waste facility (for reuse, recovery, treatment or disposal). The 1997 Regulations are based on the concept that the responsibility for meeting the national targets will be shared amongst the producers of packaging materials and the retail users of the producers' products. Businesses (producers) which fall within the ambit of the Packaging Regulations[261] register with the Environment Agency and purchase packaging recovery notes (PRNs) from other businesses which recover and recycle packaging waste. In this way, each business is able to meet the recycling and recovery targets set for it by the Environment Agency. Businesses which engage in the following activities: the manufacture of cardboard, cardboard box manufacturing, the filling or packing of cardboard boxes, and the sale of cardboard packaged goods to retailers, are subject to the producer responsibility obligations provided each business produces, handles, or supplies more

---

256 SI 1997/648.
257 For example, jars, bottles, boxes, shrinkwrap and pallets.
258 The packaging a consumer receives with his goods.
259 The packaging removed by retailers before goods are placed on retailers' shelves.
260 Bulk handling packaging such as shrinkwrap.
261 Regs 3–11.

than 50 tonnes of packaging each year and has an annual turnover of £2 million. Businesses which satisfy these criteria must register with the Environment Agency and supply data upon which the Environment Agency bases its calculation of the volume of waste packaging that must be recycled. Alternatively, any business may join a 'compliance scheme' where several businesses are aggregated together for administrative convenience. Each business certificates its own compliance with the targets set by the Environment Agency.

Recycling includes reprocessing the materials so that they can be used again, either for their original purpose or an alternative purpose. Recovery refers to processes which recover some benefit from the waste, such as burning the waste in an energy from waste incinerator to produce electricity.

The European Commission has proposed a directive to amend the Packaging Waste Directive (94/62/EC) which is intended to clarify the definition of packaging in Art 3(1). Currently 'packaging' is divided into three types of packaging waste (primary, secondary and tertiary); however, the proposal would add a fourth limb to the definition. This draft fourth limb contains a further three criteria and a list of illustrative examples of items which are packaging (or which are not within the definition of packaging). Paper or plastic carrier bags, disposable cups and plates, cling-film, sandwich bags and aluminium foil are packaging waste, whereas flower pots (intended to remain with the plant), tool boxes, tea bags, sausage skins, cheese wax and disposable cutlery are not packaging waste. The proposed directive sets new targets for the recovery of packaging waste. By 2009, 60 per cent (by weight) of packaging waste is to be recovered and 55–80 per cent recycled (including 60 per cent of glass, 60 per cent of paper and board, 50 per cent of metals, 15 per cent of wood and 22.5 per cent of plastics).

The main packaging offences are failing to register with the Environment Agency and failing to take 'reasonable steps to achieve the recycling or recovery target set for the relevant business'. The maximum fine in the magistrates' court on summary conviction is £5,000. Conviction on indictment in the Crown Court is punishable by an unlimited fine.

5.20.2 The End of Life Vehicles Directive

The End of Life Vehicles Directive (2000/53/EC) has been implemented in England and Wales by the End of Life Vehicles Regulations 2003.[262] The directive requires Member States to achieve the following vehicle recycling targets: 85 per cent by weight by 2006 and 95 per cent by weight by 2015. Vehicle manufacturers are, from 2007, responsible for the costs associated with collecting, dismantling and recycling the vehicles which they have manufactured and which now require dismantling (scrapping). Dismantling and recycling are undertaken by authorised treatment facilities, who issue a certificate of destruction, which permits the de-registration of the relevant vehicle.

5.20.3 The Waste Electrical and Electronic Equipment Directive

The Waste Electrical and Electronic Equipment Directive (2002/96/EC) is another producer responsibility scheme which applies to a wide range of (mains and battery) electrical equipment. The scheme requires retailers of electrical equipment to take a product back at the end of its life. Producers of electrical equipment are required to: provide information on the number and type of equipment produced and retailed in the UK or abroad, provide information on recycling and recovery of electrical products, bear the cost of recycling and recovery, label products to facilitate recycling and recovery and design products which facilitate recycling and recovery.

---

262 SI 2003/2635.

5.21 Landfill tax

In 1996, the government introduced a tax on waste going to landfill.[263] The landfill tax reflects the government's principal aim, namely the reduction of waste by taxing waste going to landfill. The regulations classify wastes into three categories: active, inert and exempt.

Landfilled 'active' waste[264] attracts a tax of approximately £48 a tonne, whilst 'inactive' waste[265] is taxed at approximately £2.50 a tonne. Certain wastes are exempt. The tax is paid by landfill companies who pass on the tax, collected via landfill gate fees, charged to waste producers and carriers.

The definition of waste for landfill tax purposes[266] is similar to directive waste but reflects the purposes[267] which underpin the Finance Act 1996 and supplementary regulations. This is illustrated by the case of *Parkwood Landfill v Customs and Excise Commissioners* (2003)[268] in which the Court of Appeal held that directive waste at a landfill site, which had been recycled and used for road construction and landscaping purposes, was not waste within the meaning of s 64 Finance Act 1996.

5.22 International waste law

Whilst the biggest influence on waste management law in England and Wales is the EU, nevertheless some mention should be made of the impact of international law upon waste management because of the UK's signature to and ratification of a number of international treaties and conventions.

The most important international law waste-related activity concerns the regulation of international shipments of waste, especially hazardous waste. The Basel Convention (UN Convention on the Control of Transboundary Movements of Hazardous Waste and their Disposal) was a reactive response to the practice of waste 'dumping'. As the cost of waste disposal in some developed countries rose, it became cheaper to ship hazardous wastes to less developed countries where disposal was much cheaper but, alas, rudimentary. The Basel Convention requires a waste exporter to obtain a consent to the waste shipment from the relevant regulator in the importing country. The consent must include a commitment, by the waste importer, to deal with the imported waste in an environmentally sound fashion. Where a consignment of waste arrives in the importing country and the waste cannot be dealt with in an environmentally sound manner, the exporting state is legally obliged to have the waste returned to it within 90 days. Amendments to the convention ban the export of hazardous waste from OECD countries to non-OECD countries and establish a compensation scheme relating to damage caused by the international shipments of hazardous waste.

International law has also played an important role in restricting or banning the dumping of wastes in international waters.

---

263 See the Finance Act 1996, the Landfill Tax Regulations 1996, the Landfill Tax (Qualifying Materials) Order 1996 and the Landfill Tax (Contaminated Land) Order 1996.

264 E.g., organic methane-producing waste: http://customs.hmrc.gov.uk/channelsPortalWebApp/channels PortalWebApp.portal?_nfpb=true&_pageLabel=pageVAT_ShowContent&propertyType=document& columns=1 &id=HMCE_CL_001206, accessed on 27.2.2010.

265 E.g., construction waste: http://customs.hmrc.gov.uk/channelsPortalWebApp/channelsPortal WebApp.portal?_nfpb=true&_pageLabel=pageVAT_ShowContent&propertyType=document &columns=1&id= HMCE_CL_001206, accessed on 27.2.2010.

266 S 64 Finance Act 1996.

267 E.g. the reduction in the volume of wastes which are landfilled.

268 *Parkwood Landfill v Customs and Excise Commissioners* [2003] Env LR 19.

5.23 Waste planning

5.23.1 Waste prevention programmes

The Waste (England and Wales) Regulations 2011 transpose into law the requirement in the 2008 Waste Framework Directive (Directive 2008/98/EC) to put in place a waste prevention programme which is intended to assist in severing the link between economic growth and the adverse impacts of waste creation. Waste management plans are to give effect and priority to the waste hierarchy in devising waste prevention policy, waste management policy and waste disposal policy. The waste plan is to contain an analysis of the current circumstances (regarding waste creation) in the Member State, general waste policies, policies specific to packaging waste, bio waste and waste separation in addition to arrangements for re-use and recovery of waste (including waste recycling targets).

5.23.2 Development control, Local Development Frameworks and the waste local plan

The town and country planning system controls the geographical siting of all waste management sites. A planning permission must be obtained to authorise the use of land for waste management activities.[269]

Local authorities are responsible for much of the administration of the planning system. The decision (often referred to as 'development control') to grant or refuse planning permission for a waste management site is the responsibility of the County Planning Authority (or metropolitan or unitary authority).[270] Planning permission is required to 'develop' land. 'Development' is defined in s 55(1) of the TCPA 1990 and includes both 'operational' development (for example, building a waste incinerator) and a 'material change of use' of land.[271] Section 55(3)(b) TCPA 1990 provides that 'development' includes the deposit of refuse or waste materials on land.[272]

The decision whether to grant or refuse a planning application for a new waste incinerator, landfill site or waste transfer station will be taken by the County Planning Authority (or metropolitan or unitary authority) on the basis of the policies contained in the relevant Local Development Framework and any material considerations.[273] The content of policies contained in the Local Development Framework will, in the light of s 54A of the TCPA 1990 (replaced by s 38(6) Planning and Compensation Act 1991) have an important effect on the outcome of the application. The Local Development Framework will include policies concerning waste-related developments.

The Town and Country Planning (General Permitted Development) Order (GPDO) 1995 authorises planning permission (without the need for a planning application) for some categories of mining-related waste management activity. For example, Class C, Pt 20 of the GPDO 1995 authorises the construction of waste tips at coal mines. Additional controls apply to such waste tips.[274]

Any conditions attached to a waste-related planning permission should only be imposed for a planning purpose such as access to the site, restoration of the site after closure (especially gas and leachate monitoring), the extent of tipping, the phasing of operations, adverse impacts of the proposed development on adjoining land uses[275] and future land uses in the area ('blight' deterring future development proposals). Conditions should not be imposed which duplicate the operational

---

269 S 55 of the Town and Country Planning Act (TCPA) 1990 and s 36(2) of the EPA 1990.
270 See Sched 1 to the TCPA 1990.
271 For example, using a redundant quarry as a landfill site.
272 See *Roberts v Vale DC* (1997) 78 LGR 368 and *Northavon DC v Secretary of State for the Environment* (1980) 40 P&CR 332.
273 Which include government policy guidance contained in planning policy notes PPS 10 (*Planning and Waste Management*) and PPS 23 (*Planning and Pollution Control*), the national waste strategy, and the Art 4 objectives of the Waste Framework Directive.
274 See the Mines and Quarries (Tips) Act 1969 and the Quarries Regulations 1999.
275 Odour, litter, dust, vermin, birds, visual impact, vehicle movements, hours of operation, contamination of groundwater and gas disposal via flare.

conditions the Environment Agency may choose to impose when determining a waste management permit application for the same site.[276] Typically, such conditions relating to operational matters include the duration of the waste management activities on the site, the types of wastes which are to be tipped and record keeping.

County planning authorities are required by s 38 of the TCPA 1990, as amended, to prepare a waste local plan or, at least, to combine a waste local plan with a minerals local plan. The waste local plan addresses the land use implications of the authority's waste policies. Therefore, it deals with issues such as the need for sites and waste facilities and where these should be located, having regard to geological and hydrological considerations. The waste local plan should not be confused with the now defunct local authority waste disposal plan.

Once granted, planning permission (including conditions) cannot be withdrawn unless compensation is paid to the landowner, and the permission continues to attach to and benefit the land even if ownership changes. In contrast, waste management permits are personal to the permit holder and may only be transferred with the Environment Agency's consent.[277]

5.23.3 Waste recycling policy and waste recycling plans

In 1990, the government set targets for the recycling of household waste[278] to be met by the year 2000. However, according to government statistics, the current average recycling rate for household waste is just under 6 per cent. Although s 49 of the EPA 1990 requires WCAs to prepare recycling plans to ensure that government targets are met, very few local authority recycling targets have been met.

Waste recycling is largely the responsibility of the WCAs, although the WDAs have certain powers and duties in this regard. The main provisions relating to recycling are contained in the following sections of the EPA 1990:

(a) s 49—WCAs are under a duty to investigate what arrangements can practicably be made for recycling household and commercial waste. They must prepare a waste recycling plan and keep it under review;

(b) s 46(2)—WCAs can require household waste to be placed in separate receptacles if certain wastes are going to be recycled (multi-bin schemes and kerbside collection);

(c) s 52—a system of recycling credits to encourage recycling was introduced.

Each WCA is required by s 49 to prepare a waste recycling plan. The WCA in preparing the plan has to consider the effect that recycling proposals will have on the amenities in the locality and also the likely cost or saving (benefit) to the authority. A copy of the plan should be made available for the public to inspect.

5.24 The interface between the waste management regime and other regulatory pollution controls

5.24.1 IPPC

The IPPC Directive introduces integrated controls over waste disposal sites, such as landfill sites.[279] Approximately 900 large landfill sites[280] fall within the IPPC regime. The IPPC regulatory framework

---

276 See PPS 23 replaced by the National Planning Policy Framework.
277 See reg 21 of the Environmental Permitting (England and Wales) Regulations 2010.
278 25% of household waste.
279 See the Environmental Permitting (England and Wales) Regulations 2010.
280 That is, those capable of accepting over 710 tonnes of waste per day and with a total capacity of over 25,000 tonnes.

in England and Wales is contained in the Environmental Permitting (England and Wales) Regulations 2010.

5.24.2 Water pollution

Liquid effluent is not waste which falls to be regulated by the waste management licensing regime in Pt II of the EPA 1990 and the Environmental Permitting (England and Wales) Regulations 2007 as amended. Waste in liquid form is controlled by a combination of the Water Resources Act 1991, the Water Industry Act 1991, the Water Act 2003, the Urban Waste Water Treatment Directive (91/271/EEC) and the Urban Waste Water Treatment (England and Wales) Regulations 1994.

With regard to the threat of groundwater pollution from waste disposed of (but not waste recovery activities) to landfill, the Environmental Permitting (England and Wales) Regulations 2007 as amended provide that a waste management licence/environmental permit will only be granted if the Environment Agency is satisfied that adequate measures exist to prevent pollution of groundwaters by the substances listed in List I and II of the Groundwater Directive (80/68/EEC). In such circumstances, the landfill site will be exempt from the Groundwater Regulations 1998.

5.24.3 Contaminated land

The contaminated land regulatory regime in Part IIA of the EPA 1990 provides regulators (EA and local authorities) with a range of enforcement and clean-up powers. In most circumstances the contaminated land regime controls do not apply to sites covered by waste management licences (now referred to as environmental permits). Any breach of an environmental permit which causes land contamination will be dealt with under the environmental permitting controls. Land contamination caused by an unlawful waste deposit will be dealt with by the EA under its s 59 EPA power and the power to serve a Remediation Notice under the contaminated land controls is removed.[281]

See Chapter 7

5.24.4 Waste policy

The Planning and Compulsory Purchase Act 2004 requires waste planning policy arrangements to be made at the regional level (county, metropolitan or unitary local authorities) via the production of Regional Spatial Strategies which set the policy framework for waste management arrangements at the local level (and which replace Regional Planning Policy Guidance notes). Other waste planning policy guidance (contained in Local Development Frameworks, local waste plans or combined minerals and local waste plans) is now located in the Minerals and Waste Development Framework. Each of these frameworks contains key documents: a Minerals and Waste Development Scheme, a Waste Core Strategy document, an allocation map and supplementary documents.

5.24.5 Town and country planning

Planning permission is required for the development of land or a material change in the use of land. The deposit of waste in or on land will usually be classified as a material change of use and will therefore require planning permission. Section 55(3)(b) TCPA 1990 states: 'the deposit or refuse or waste materials on land involves a material change in its use, notwithstanding that the land is in a site already used for that purpose.'[282]

---

281 See s 78YB(3) EPA 1990.
282 See the Court of Appeal decision in *Bilboe v SoS for the Environment* [1980] P&CR 495 confirming that planning permission is required for a material change of use—in this case tipping unauthorised waste in an inert waste tip.

Before the Environment Agency can issue a waste management environmental permit, it must be satisfied that the waste management operation has planning permission. The applicant will need to demonstrate that either he or she has a full planning permission, certificate of lawful use or development, or an established use certificate.

5.24.6 Statutory nuisance

Statutory nuisances may arise in relation to waste in two instances. The deposit of controlled (directive) waste could amount to an accumulation, prejudicial to health or a nuisance under s 79(1)(e) of the EPA 1990. Alternatively, the resultant smell from the waste could, if prejudicial to health or a nuisance, constitute a statutory nuisance under s 79(1)(d). Radioactive waste[283] is not regulated by Part II of the EPA.[284]

See Chapter 9 →

5.24.7 The Planning (Hazardous Substances) Act 1990

Additional planning controls in regard to hazardous development are available under the Planning (Hazardous Substances) Act 1990. Prior to the introduction of the 1990 Act, the control of developments under the town and country planning regime could exert little control over the use of hazardous substances in developments. It was possible for factories and manufacturers to introduce new hazardous products without requiring the need for further planning consent.

The Planning (Hazardous Substances) Act 1990, which was brought into force on 1 June 1992, requires that the keeping of any hazardous substance on, over or under land, beyond small quantities, will require the consent of the Hazardous Substances Authority (usually the relevant London borough, the district council in a metropolitan county and the district planning authorities elsewhere). Before a 'hazardous substances consent' is granted, the Hazardous Substances Authorities consider whether the proposed storage or use of a hazardous substance is appropriate in a given location.

5.25 The duty of care

5.25.1 Introduction

One of the most significant features of the EPA 1990 was the introduction of a statutory duty of care (on 1 April 1992) in relation to the handling of waste. In its 11th Report, *Managing Waste: The Duty of Care* (1985), the Royal Commission on Environmental Pollution recommended that a duty of care be placed on everybody involved in the waste chain establishing 'cradle to grave' responsibility for waste:

> The producer [of waste] incurs a duty of care which is owed to society, and we would like to see this duty reflected in public attitudes and enshrined in legislation and codes of practice.

The objective of s 34 of the EPA 1990 is to ensure that all persons in the waste chain who produce, handle, treat[285] or dispose of directive waste take reasonable steps to:

(a)   store the waste properly;
(b)   package the waste in adequate packaging or containers;

---

283 As defined in the Radioactive Substances Act 1993.
284 See s 78 EPA 1990.
285 E.g. recycle.

(c)   describe the contents of packaged or containerised waste properly so that the next person in the waste chain can handle it safely;

(d)   hand the waste over only to an authorised person;

(e)   complete a waste transfer note recording details of the consignment of the waste to the next person in the waste chain;

(f)   check that the waste is properly disposed of.

Thus, every person in the waste chain, from waste producer to final waste disposer, is obliged to act responsibly with regard to waste, especially at the point when the waste is handed over (consigned) to the next person in the waste chain. The s 34 EPA duty of care creates statutory 'cradle to grave' responsibility for waste.

Failure to observe the s 34 EPA duty is a criminal offence.[286] This offence is relevant to the issue of an operator's competence to operate a 'regulated facility' such as a waste management facility and hold an environmental permit.

The duty of care is set out in s 34 of the EPA 1990. The duty is supplemented by regulations made under s 34(5) EPA 1990, the Environmental Protection (Duty of Care) Regulations 1991,[287] as amended, and official guidance in the form of a code of practice. The code of practice is intended to assist any person in the waste chain by setting out examples of the appropriate steps which could be taken to fulfil the s 34 duty of care.

The code of practice, initially issued in 1991, was revised in 1996. Any person who fails to comply with the duty imposed by s 34 EPA 1990 or with the Regulations commits a criminal offence.[288] It is not necessary for any environmental damage to have been caused for there to be a breach of s 34 EPA 1990. All that is required is that there has been a breach of the duty. There is no statutory provision allowing for a civil action where damages have been caused as a result of a breach of s 34 EPA 1990. On summary conviction in a magistrates' court, a breach of the duty of care can lead to a maximum fine of £5,000 or, on indictment (in the Crown Court), an unlimited fine.

According to the code of practice, the duty of care is designed 'to be an essentially self-regulating system which is based on good business practice'. For example, the code states that if a waste holder is certain that waste he or she handles is being wrongly managed by another person, then he or she should, at first instance, refuse to deal with that other person (for example, refuse to transfer waste to that person). The code goes on to say that it may not always be possible to take such a course of action, and that, if appropriate, a person should bring the matter to the attention of the Environment Agency.

Section 34 EPA 1990 creates a form of self-regulation underpinned by the criminal law sanction of a s 34(6) prosecution. Any waste producer, broker or waste holder who transfers waste to a 'dodgy' waste carrier who undercuts the going rate charged by legitimate carriers for waste carriage may not only face prosecution for breach of the duty of care,[289] but also prosecution for knowingly causing the deposit of waste[290] if the waste carrier illegally deposits[291] the waste on an unlicensed (non-permitted) site. Furthermore, civil liability may also be incurred with regard to damage caused by the illegal deposit of waste.[292]

---

286   S 34(6) EPA 1990.
287   SI 1991/2839.
288   S 34(6) EPA 1990.
289   S 34(6) EPA 1990.
290   S 33(1)(a) EPA 1990.
291   Fly-tips s 33(5) EPA 1990.
292   S 73(6) EPA 1990.

5.25.2 The duty applies to waste holders

Section 34(1) of the EPA 1990 applies to any person who imports, produces, carries, keeps, treats or disposes of controlled (directive) waste or, as a broker, has control of such waste. Essentially, this means any person in the waste chain from producer to final disposer.[293] Section 34(2) EPA 1990 provides the only exception to the duty: occupiers of domestic premises who produce household waste on their property.

A waste broker is a person who may exercise control over waste, but may not necessarily hold it (such as an environmental consultant). For the purposes of the duty, he or she can be considered as sharing responsibility for any transfer of waste that he or she arranges with the actual parties who effect the transfer.

The Environmental Permitting (England and Wales) Regulations 2010 bring waste brokers and waste dealers within the waste management regulatory regime (i.e. permitting). Waste brokers and waste dealers must register with the Environment Agency and failure to do so constitutes a criminal offence. The Environment Agency has a discretion to refuse registration based on the applicant's previous record of relevant offences. Holders of environmental permits, WCAs, WDAs, registered charitable and voluntary waste carriers are exempt.

5.25.3 What does the duty of care involve?

Any person bound by the duty must take all such measures applicable to him in that capacity as are reasonable in the circumstances:

(a)   to prevent any other person committing the offences in s 33 EPA 1990;
(b)   to prevent the escape of the waste from his control or that of any other person;
(c)   to ensure that if the waste is transferred, it is transferred only to an 'authorised person' or to a person 'for authorised transport purposes'; and
(d)   when waste is transferred, to make sure that it is accompanied by a written description of the waste which will enable other persons to avoid a contravention of s 33 of the Act and to comply with the duty under s 34(1)(b) EPA 1990 to prevent the escape of waste.

The duty applies to all persons in the waste chain[294] from the time the waste is produced to the time it reaches its final destination.[295] Each of these persons must ensure that the waste is dealt with properly and this will, in most cases, require enquiries to be carried out to ascertain that persons further down the waste chain will comply with the s 34 EPA 1990 duty.[296]

5.25.4 Elements of the duty of care

5.25.4.1 To take all such measures applicable to him in that capacity as are reasonable in the circumstances

Section 34(1) EPA 1990 requires any person to whom the duty applies to take 'all such measures as are applicable to him in that capacity as are reasonable in the circumstances' to avoid a breach of the statutory duty. This requirement limits the duty of care in two respects. First, waste holders are only required to take all measures that are applicable to them in their respective capacities. Second, such measures need to be reasonable in the particular circumstances. The responsibility of the individual waste holder is limited and the duty is a subjective one and depends in part upon the holder's relationship to the waste.

---

293 DoE Circular 19/91 uses the shorthand term 'waste holder' to refer to all persons who are subject to the duty.
294 Including a waste producer, waste importer, waste carrier, waste holder, waste disposer, waste broker and waste recycler.
295 E.g. landfill or incinerator.
296 E.g. waste transport company and landfill site operator.

The extent of the waste holder's responsibility under s 34(1) EPA 1990 will vary with the capacity of the waste holder and the extent of control the waste holder has over the waste. The waste holder will therefore be expected to take different measures to comply with the duty of care varying with his capacity as a waste producer, importer, carrier, keeper, treater, disposer, dealer or broker. For example, the waste producer will bear primary responsibility for ensuring that the waste is accurately described (in waste transfer notes and on packaging).

A waste holder is also only expected to take measures that are reasonable in the circumstances. It is here that the code of practice is of importance, since it provides guidance for waste holders on the measures that are reasonable in different circumstances. The circumstances which affect what is reasonable will include:

(a)   what the waste is;
(b)   the dangers it presents in handling and treatment;
(c)   how it is dealt with;
(d)   what the holder might reasonably be expected to know or foresee.

5.25.4.2 To prevent any other person committing offences under s 33 EPA 1990

The first element of s 34 EPA 1990 comprises a duty to prevent any other person committing offences under s 33. A waste holder must not only take steps to ensure that he or she does not breach s 33 EPA 1990, but he or she must take reasonable steps to ensure that any other person who has control of his or her waste does not breach s 33 EPA 1990. For example, a waste producer's s 34 EPA 1990 responsibilities do not end with the transfer of the waste to a waste carrier. Not only must the waste producer check the waste carrier's credentials (carrier's registration certificate), but it is also the waste producer's responsibility to ensure that the waste arrives at the waste management site specified in the transfer documentation.

The code of practice advises waste transferors (consignors) to halt any waste transfer if the waste holder suspects that the waste will not be dealt with properly if handed over to the consignee. Such a situation might arise if a waste carrier arrives at the consignor's premises, very soon after carrying away an initial load of waste, to load up for a second time and arousing the consignor's suspicions that the first consignment of waste has been illegally disposed of (fly-tipped). The waste holder must act responsibly, as judged by an objective (reasonable man) standard, having regard to the waste holder's resources and knowledge. In the circumstances outlined above, the waste holder should first check the position with the waste carrier and, if the explanation given is unsatisfactory, inform the Environment Agency. Higher standards will be expected of the big waste operators in view of their greater resources. Clearly, it is for the waste holder to draw up a contract with a carrier/waste manager which incorporates provisions that enable the waste producer periodically to check the site (for example, a waste transfer station site), check that records and transfer notes are being kept and allow for termination of the contract in the event of the waste manager losing his or her permit. The contract should require the waste disposal contractor to comply with all of the relevant laws and permit conditions and should ideally cover matters of liability, ownership of the waste, insurance and indemnities against liability. In practice, arrangements are made without any written contract or are made by means of a standard contract which does not adequately cover all of the important issues.

The code of practice provides practical advice on complying with this element of the s 34 EPA 1990 duty. However, it should be emphasised that compliance with the code does not ensure that the s 34 EPA 1990 duty of care is being complied with.

5.25.4.3 To prevent the escape of waste from his control or that of any other person

In order to prevent the escape of waste, producers of waste should label it properly and package it in such a way as to prevent escape and leakage whilst on site, in transit or in storage. Consideration should also be given to preventing any escape in subsequent transfer or transfers and up to the final treatment or disposal. Since escape can occur in a variety of circumstances, care will need to be taken to address all possibilities. For example, escape may occur where there is a spillage or where containers have been overfilled; it can occur when adverse weather conditions result in waste being blown away or washed down storm drains. Vandals may cause waste to escape, hence the need for adequate security as well as containerisation. The waste producer, in particular, should take into account the time it will take for the waste to reach its final destination and the mode in which it will be carried or stored at a waste transfer station. Containerisation should be adequate for all of these different situations. For example, black bin bags will almost certainly be inadequate. The suitability of packaging is particularly important where the wastes include flammable or corrosive substances. In *Gateway Professional Services (Management) Ltd v Kingston Upon Hull City Council* (2004)[297] the High Court held that the obligation on legal persons, such as waste holders, to prevent the escape of waste in s 34 EPA 1990 did not apply to the situation where the defendant had itself deposited waste (dumped waste) on land adjacent to one of its retail stores. This was not an 'escape' of waste within the meaning of the section but a deliberate deposit and therefore a s 33 EPA 1990 offence.

5.25.4.4 To transfer the waste only to authorised persons and for authorised transport purposes

To comply with the duty of care, it is also essential to ensure that waste is only transferred to authorised persons or to a person for authorised transport purposes. These are defined respectively in s 34(3) and (4) of the EPA 1990.

Section 34(3) states that the following are authorised persons:

(a)   a WCA;

(b)   a holder of a waste management permit;

(c)   persons exempted by regulations made by the Secretary of State under s 33(3) EPA 1990;

(d)   a registered carrier (registered under s 2 of the Control of Pollution (Amendment) Act 1989);

(e)   any person not required to be registered under the Control of Pollution (Amendment) Act 1989.

Transferors of waste should make sure that they are only transferring their waste to an authorised person. If waste is being transferred to a carrier, then the carrier must be registered under the Control of Pollution (Amendment) Act 1989. Subject to limited exceptions,[298] any person carrying waste in the course of a waste transport business, or in any other way for profit, must be registered with the Environment Agency. It is an offence under s 1(1) of the 1989 Act to carry controlled (directive) waste without registering with the Environment Agency as a waste carrier. The offence may only be dealt with summarily in the magistrates' court. Anyone intending to transfer waste to a carrier should check that the person is registered (or exempt from the need to register) with the Environment Agency. The Environment Agency maintains a register of waste carriers which is open to public inspection. It is necessary for the person handing over the waste to a carrier to check the actual certificate of registration since photocopies are not proof of registration (official duplicates of the original certificate are available from the Environment Agency). Moreover, the transferor should also carry out regular checks to ensure that the registration has not lapsed (for example, due to revocation).

---

297 *Gateway Professional Services (Management) Ltd v Kingston Upon Hull City Council* [2004] Env LR 42.
298 Prescribed in the Controlled Waste (Registration of Carriers and Seizure of Vehicles) Regulations 1991 and 1998 SI 1991/1624 and SI 1998/605.

5.25.4.5 Exemptions

Under reg 2 of the Registration of Carriers (Seizure of Vehicles) Regulations 1991, exemptions are granted to a variety of waste carriers including:

(a) a waste producer who uses its own vehicles to transport waste (except demolition and construction waste);

(b) local authorities, charities and voluntary groups.

The 1989 Control of Pollution (Amendment) Act and 1991 Regulations are targeted at carriers who transport waste as a commercial venture. Therefore, the incidental carriage of waste, on a non-profit basis, by private individuals falls outside the ambit of the legislation.

5.25.4.6 Rejection of registration applications

The Environment Agency may refuse to register any applicant whom it believes not to be a desirable carrier. A carrier will not be desirable if:

(a) the carrier, or a person closely connected with the carrier, has been convicted of a relevant offence;[299] and

(b) the Environment Agency considers it undesirable that the carrier be authorised to carry controlled (directive) waste.[300]

The provisions of the Rehabilitation of Offenders Act 1974 apply to any 'spent' relevant offence.

5.25.4.7 Revocation

The Environment Agency may revoke a carrier's registration certificate where the carrier ceases to be a desirable carrier,[301] for example, a carrier who is convicted of a 'relevant offence', such as illegally fly-tipping waste contrary to s 33(5) of the EPA 1990.

5.25.4.8 Appeals

There is a right of appeal to the Secretary of State against a refusal to grant a carriers' registration certificate (licence) or regarding the Environment Agency's decision to revoke an existing registration certificate.

5.25.4.9 Renewal and surrender

Waste carriers' licences (certificates of registration) are of three years' duration and must be renewed if the carrier wishes to operate lawfully. A carrier may surrender its registration certificate at any time.

5.25.4.10 Stop and search

Section 5(1) COP (A) A 1989 empowers both the Environment Agency and the police to stop and search vehicles which are reasonably believed to be transporting waste but which are not covered by a waste carriers' registration certificate.

5.25.4.11 Authorised transport purposes

Section 34(4) EPA 1990 lists the following as authorised transport purposes:

---

299 Listed in Sched 1 to the 1991 Regulations.
300 Reg 5.
301 Reg 10.

(a)   the transport of controlled (directive) waste within the same premises and between different places in those premises;

(b)   the transport to a place in Great Britain of controlled (directive) waste which has been brought from a country or territory outside Great Britain not having been landed in Great Britain until it arrives at that place;

(c)   the transport by air or sea of controlled (directive) waste from a place inside Great Britain to a place outside Great Britain.

5.25.4.12 The written description

Waste producers are responsible for ensuring that, when they transfer waste, the waste is accompanied by an adequate written description. This description should provide sufficient information to enable all persons who might foreseeably come into contact with the waste to ensure that they can handle the waste safely. The description must be sufficient to ensure that other waste holders in the waste chain can avoid committing offences under s 33 EPA 1990. The level of detail necessary in the transfer note will vary with the properties of the waste.

The Environmental Protection (Duty of Care) Regulations 1991,[302] which came into force on 1 April 1992, established a system of transfer notes and record keeping of waste transfers to help waste holders comply with this element of the duty of care. However, the transfer note does not necessarily provide the full written description. Neither does the transfer note have to accompany the waste, although it is safer if it does so. The Regulations place responsibilities on the transferor and transferee of waste to keep detailed records of all waste transfers. On completion of the transfer of waste, both the transferor and transferee must complete and sign a transfer note. The transfer note provisions contained in these Regulations do not apply, by virtue of reg 2(3), to transfers of hazardous waste where a consignment note system operates.[303] Under the Regulations, a transfer note must include details of the following:

(a)   identification of the waste;

(b)   quantity;

(c)   whether it is loose or in a container at time of transfer;

(d)   place and time of transfer;

(e)   name and address of both the transferor and transferee;

(f)   whether the transferor is the waste producer or importer;

(g)   if the transferee is authorised for transport purposes.

All parties involved in the transfer must keep a copy of the transfer note and the written description for at least two years. The Environment Agency may serve a notice demanding copies of transfer notes and these must be supplied within seven days. While all transfers of waste must be documented, the Regulations do not require each individual transfer to be separately documented. It is possible for a single transfer to cover multiple consignments transferred at the same time or over a period not exceeding a year. However, this can only apply where the description is provided before the first consignment and all the other consignments covered by the note are the same.

---

302 Made under s 34(5).
303 The consignment note system is described in more detail below.

5.25.5 The consignment note system for hazardous waste

The consignment note system relating to hazardous waste, originally established under the Control of Pollution (Special Waste) Regulations 1980 and later amended by the Special Waste Regulations 1996, has now been superseded by the Hazardous Waste Regulations 2005.[304]

The hazardous waste controls, like directive waste controls,[305] create a consignment note system to track the transport of hazardous wastes (see HW Regulations 35–38). A consignment note accompanies each hazardous waste movement and records information which includes: (1) waste description, (2) waste producer, (3) waste carrier and (4) the legal person responsible for final disposal or recovery. The system also applies to movements of hazardous wastes from premises which are not subject to the notification requirements outlined above.

There are record-keeping obligations[306] applying to producers, carriers, holders, disposers and recoverers/recyclers of hazardous waste in much the same way as those which apply to directive waste. Records of hazardous waste consignments must be kept for three years (one year in the case of hazardous waste carriers). Operators of hazardous waste disposal or hazardous waste recovery/recycling plants are required to provide (1) for EA use, every three months, a detailed account of the hazardous wastes which they have received[307] and (2) similar information for use by hazardous waste producers (and hazardous waste holders) who consigned hazardous waste to them.[308]

By virtue of HW regs 47–48, any legal person who (1) deposits hazardous waste in on or under land, or (2) recovers hazardous waste, is required to keep records of the deposit/recovery.

5.25.6 The code of practice

In 1991, the Secretary of State issued a code of practice which provided practical guidance on how to discharge the duty of care.[309] The 1991 code was replaced in 1996. The code recommends a series of steps which would normally be enough to satisfy the requirements of the s 34 EPA 1990 duty. Its importance, however, is reflected in the fact that, by virtue of s 34(10) EPA 1990, the code of practice shall be admissible in evidence and, if any provision of the code appears to the court to be relevant to any question arising in the proceedings, it shall be taken into account in determining that question. It is therefore important that all those who are subject to the duty of care are familiar with the code. The code is not law but ranks as important administrative guidance.

5.25.7 Breach of the duty of care

Any person who fails to comply with the duty of care, or the documentation requirements laid down in the Environment Protection (Duty of Care) Regulations 1991, commits a criminal offence and will be liable, on summary conviction (in a magistrates' court) to a fine not exceeding £5,000. On indictment, the Crown Court can impose an unlimited fine. Once again, directors and senior management may be personally liable for a breach of s 34 EPA 1990. It is therefore in the interests of management to ensure that adequate training programmes and systems are in place to ensure that all relevant staff understand the requirements of the duty of care at all times. Finally, breach of the duty of care is relevant to the issue of operator competence[310] for the purposes of obtaining, maintaining or revoking a waste management licence/environmental permit.

---

304 An explanation of the Special Waste regulations appears in the 4th edition of this text.
305 See 5.21.3.12.
306 HW regs 49–51.
307 HW reg 53.
308 HW reg 54.
309 *Waste Management, The Duty of Care, A Code of Practice.*
310 See page 280.

5.26 Civil liability

5.26.1 Statutory remedy

It has already been noted that s 73(6) EPA 1990 provides a statutory civil remedy for any person who has suffered damages as a consequence of another person's breach of s 33 EPA. However, no such statutory remedy exists in relation to a breach of the duty of care. Damages may be available through common law actions such as nuisance.

5.26.2 EC Directive on Civil Liability for Damage Caused by Waste

The EU Directive on Environmental Damage (2004/35 EC) relating to damage caused by waste on land has been implemented in England and Wales by the Environmental Damage (Prevention and Remediation) Regulations 2009.

5.27 Online resource centre

We recommend that the reader regularly refers to the section of the online resources corresponding to this chapter for information relating to updates, amendments and corrections.

5.28 Summary of key points

Chapter 5 has covered the following topics and issues:

- Waste management (minimisation/treatment/disposal) is a key twenty-first century environmental challenge.
- In recent years there has been a changing emphasis of waste controls, characterised by a move away from an emphasis on waste disposal (e.g. to landfill) to a focus on the management of waste throughout its life cycle (from cradle to grave).
- Developments in policy and law at the European level have been the driving force behind many changes in waste law and policy in England and Wales.
- In an era of sustainable waste management, the EU waste hierarchy is an important factor in encouraging all Member States of the EU to implement measures to minimise waste production and increase the volume of waste which is recycled or reused.
- In a national context, the regulatory framework (of primary and secondary legislation) controls, via a permit-based system, the safe disposal of wastes.
- The importance of the roles, powers and functions of the regulator (Environment Agency).
- The legal controls applying to waste disposal businesses, waste brokers, waste treatment businesses and waste carriers.
- The cradle to grave focus of the waste regulatory regime and how it ensures that control focuses not only on waste disposal and waste treatment, but also on the issue of waste generation/waste minimisation (i.e. upon the whole life cycle of the production process which generates wastes).
- The EU 'waste hierarchy' policy is behind the drive to minimise the amount of waste produced and the obligation imposed upon manufacturers to make the best use of waste actually generated.
- The increased emphasis on recycling, e.g. producer responsibility and obligations such as the End of Vehicle Life Directive, ensures that recycling considerations are taken into account in the design of products such as motor vehicles.

- an increased emphasis on sustainable waste management requiring greater attention to be paid to waste avoidance, minimisation, recycling and recovery.
- The legal definition of 'directive waste' which determines which materials and substances will require to be licensed (permitted) by the regulatory agencies in each Member State (or which escape licensing (permitting) because the activities generating the directive waste are exempt from licensing/permitting control).
- The permit-based (or registration-based) 'Command and Control' regulatory waste regime extends to waste creators, waste disposers, waste treatment/waste recycling businesses, waste brokers and waste carriers/transporters.
- The regulator (the EA) enjoys extensive compliance powers, including a range of notices (e.g. Enforcement Notice) and a range of criminal offences to persuade the polluter to comply with waste law.
- Waste regulation is one area of pollution control in which the use of eco-taxes is evident (e.g. the landfill tax).
- The 'duty of care'[311] obligation applies to all persons who are responsible for waste at some point during its lifetime from the original creation of the waste to the time it is recycled or disposed of and is unique to waste management regulation.
- In regard to waste offences, it is not uncommon for the Environment Agency to commence prosecutions against polluters resulting in convictions and significant penalties.[312]
- Waste regulation is in constant flux: e.g. introduction of the environmental permitting regime.

 ## 5.29 Further reading

Encyclopedias

Bates, J, *UK Waste Law* (2nd edn, Sweet & Maxwell, London 1997).
Garner's Environmental Law (Butterworths, London, updated annually).

Books

Laurence, D, *Waste Regulation Law* (Butterworths, London 2000).

Journal articles and government papers

Abbot, C, 'Waste management licensing: benefit or burden?' (2000) JPL 1003.
Cheyne, I, 'The definition of waste in EC Law' (2002) JEL 61.
Cheyne, I and Purdue, M, 'Fitting definition to purpose: the search for a satisfactory definition of waste' (1995) JEL 149.
Department of the Environment, 'Waste Strategy for England and Wales 2007' (Cm 7086, 2007).
Fluck, J, 'The term "waste" in EU law' (1994) EELR 79.
Krämer, L, 'The distinction between waste and product in Community Law' (2003) 11(1) Env Liability 3.
Lee, M, 'Resources recycling and waste' (2005) Env LR 49.
Pike, J, 'Waste not want not: An even wider definition of waste' (2002) JEL 197.
Purdue, M and van Rossem, A, 'The distinction between using secondary raw materials and the recovery of waste: the directive definition of "waste" ' (1998) JEL 116.

---

311 S 34 EPA 1990.
312 See incidents reported in the ENDS Report.

Royal Commission on Environmental Pollution, 'Incineration of Waste', 17th Report (Cm 2181, 1993).

Royal Commission on Environmental Pollution, 'Managing Waste: The Duty of Care', 11th Report (Cmnd 9675, 1985).

Salter, J, 'The meaning of waste in European Community law' (1997) EELR 14.

Tromans, S, 'Defining recycling' (2004) 16 JEL 80.

Tromans, S, 'EC waste law—a complete mess?' (2001) JEL 133.

Wilkinson, D, 'Time to discard the concept of waste?' (1999) Env LR 172.

Useful websites

Department of Environment Food and Rural Affairs

www.defra.gov.uk/environment/waste/intro.htm

The Environmental Permitting (England and Wales) Regulations 2010

www.opsi.gov.uk/si/si2007/uksi_20073538_en_1

Environmental Services Association – the trade body of the waste industry

www.esauk.org/work/briefings

Information on recycling

www.wastewatch.org.uk

Waste-related producer responsibility compliance scheme

www.valpak.co.uk

Chapter 6

Environmental Permitting

Chapter Contents

> ## Learning Objectives
>
> By the end of this chapter you should have acquired an understanding of:
>
> - how and why the system of environmental permitting developed in England and Wales;
>
> - the system of Integrated Pollution Control (IPC) and its contribution to an holistic system of environmental regulation;
>
> - the impact of the Integrated Pollution Prevention Control Directive (91/156/EC as amended) on the current environmental permitting regime;
>
> - the roles and responsibilities of the regulators and the regulated;
>
> - the scope of the environmental permitting regime and the definition of regulated facilities, including waste operations, which fall within the regime;
>
> - the detailed provisions governing the grant of environmental permits including variation, transfer and surrender of permits and appeals;
>
> - the criminal law offences underpinning the environmental permitting regime;
>
> - the administrative powers of the regulators (often used to persuade regulated activities to comply with pollution control law).

6.1 Introduction

On 6 April 2008 a new system of environmental regulation came into force.[1] The new system, called environmental permitting (EP), was introduced for the specific purpose of simplifying the regulatory burdens placed on business by establishing a common framework for delivering environmental protection objectives in a cost-effective way. The system was developed as part of the government's better regulation agenda, which had the overall aim of cutting the administrative costs of regulation to business.[2] Up until this date the regulatory controls placed upon polluters had developed in an incremental and somewhat piecemeal fashion, resulting in a number of different systems of authorisations and licences despite aiming for the same goal of environmental protection. This incremental development resulted in a regulatory system that was unnecessarily complex. The environmental permitting system aims to remove the unnecessary complexities and provide a single system of environmental permitting that delivers more flexibility for industry, provides a simpler risk-based system of control for regulators whilst at the same time continuing to protect the environment and human health. The Environmental Permitting Regulations 2007 replaced some 41 statutory instruments with a single set of regulations and converted existing Pollution Prevention Control Permits and Waste Management Licences into environmental permits. The 2007 Regulations were revoked and replaced in 2010 by the Environmental Permitting (England and Wales) Regulations 2010.[3] These in turn were amended in 2012 in what was largely a tidying-up exercise.[4] In February 2013

---

1 Environmental Permitting (England and Wales) Regulations 2007 SI 2007/3538. Revoked and replaced by the Environmental Permitting (England and Wales) Regulations 2010 SI 2010/675 as amended by SI 2012/630.
2 Regulation—Less is More, Reducing Burdens, Improving Outcomes (2004), Better Regulation Task Force Report to the Prime Minister.
3 The Environmental Permitting (England and Wales) Regulations 2010 SI 2010/675.
4 The Environmental Permitting (England and Wales) (Amendment) Regulations 2012 SI 2012/630.

Defra commenced consultation on further proposed amendments. This chapter will examine the 2010 Regulations as amended by the 2012 Regulations. For the remainder of this chapter the Environmental Permitting (England and Wales) Regulations 2010 will be referred to as EPR 2010.

Before examining the system of environmental permitting in detail it is necessary to understand the system that was replaced. To this end the chapter will commence with a brief examination of the system of Integrated Pollution Control (IPC), which can be seen as the forerunner of the environmental permitting system. The IPC system, created by Part I of the Environmental Protection Act 1990, regulated some 2,000 seriously polluting processes and introduced the concept of a single IPC 'authorisation' for these processes. By 2007 the IPC system had been replaced with a new system of Integrated Pollution Prevention Control (IPPC) under the auspices of the Pollution Prevention Control Act (PPCA) 1999, which gave effect to Council Directive 96/61/EC.[5] The PPCA 1999 repealed Part I EPA 1990 and replaced the IPC authorisations with PPC permits.[6] Running alongside Part I of the EPA 1990, Part II EPA introduced waste management licences in respect of certain waste management and disposal operations (such as incineration and landfill). The PPCA 1999 brought some of these waste operations within its ambit and as a result some waste operations were regulated by means of a waste management licence under the EPA 1990 and others by means of a permit under the PPCA 1999. There can be little doubt about the veracity of Defra's criticism that the regimes were unnecessarily complex and that there was a compelling need to provide a more streamlined and simplified system. The provisions of the EPA 1990 in relation to IPC authorisations and the provisions of the PPCA 1999 in relation to PPC permits are considered below. The more detailed provisions relating to environmental permits for waste operations are considered in Chapter 5.

See Chapter 5 ◀

6.2 The development of an integrated approach to pollution control

The systems of Integrated Pollution Control (IPC) and Integrated Pollution Prevention and Control (IPPC) were typical Command and Control regulatory regimes in that they used 'licensing' as the primary pollution control mechanism. However, they differed from earlier regulatory regimes in that they were designed to control polluting discharges from a relatively narrow range of highly polluting industries. In contrast to the traditional single environmental medium focus of the water pollution controls contained in the Water Resources Act (WRA) 1991 and the waste management controls contained in Pt II of the Environmental Protection Act (EPA) 1990, the IPC and IPPC regimes were designed to regulate polluting emissions, discharged by industrial processes, into *all three environmental media* (air, water and land). Consequently, industrial sites subject to IPC or IPPC generally required only one authorisation/permit authorising all polluting discharges from that site. IPC and IPPC both aimed to provide a 'one stop shop' approach to environmental regulation and both adopted a *holistic* perspective, paying attention to the polluting impacts of the emissions discharged by industries into the environment as a whole. This holistic, one stop shop approach to environmental regulation remains the backbone of the environmental permitting system, but at the time it was first introduced in 1990 it was quite innovatory.

---

5 Council Directive 96/61/EC of 24 September 1996 concerning integrated pollution prevention and control OJ L 257, 10/10/1996, pp 26–40. This directive was repealed by consolidating Directive 2008/1/EC which has also been repealed with effect from 7 January 2014 by Directive 2010/75/EU.

6 Pollution Prevention and Control (England and Wales) Regulations 2000 SI 2000/1973.

6.2.1 The transferability of pollution and the need for an integrated approach to regulation

The historical development of IPC has its roots in the Industrial Revolution. The creation of the Alkali Inspectorate, by the Alkali Act 1863, was the first attempt to regulate the toxic by-products of the emergent chemical industry. This regime addressed, somewhat ineffectively, only one aspect of the pollution problems associated with industrial production. Meanwhile, smoke and other pollutants were being pumped into the atmosphere at an alarming and unregulated rate.

From the nineteenth century to well into the twentieth century, the standard UK response to pollution problems was to create separate regulatory regimes to deal with problems reactively, as and when they arose. This created a complicated and fragmented jigsaw of overlapping regulatory regimes. Regulated industries experienced difficulties in keeping abreast of the different investigatory and enforcement powers available to the various regulatory authorities. One of the most significant drawbacks of this reactive and piecemeal approach to pollution control was the failure to focus on the environment as a whole. A more sanction-orientated enforcement policy by one regulator might have the undesired effect of encouraging businesses to divert their wastes into less tightly regulated environmental media. This situation was not helped by the absence of environmental quality standards which could provide benchmarks in regard to which the terms of Command and Control licences could be set. Regulatory regimes had an 'end of pipe' focus which took a very narrow view of the impact of environmental pollution on the environment. The 'environment' was essentially the environmental media (air, water and land) into which pollutants were discharged and regulated by the particular regulatory regime. The general public had difficulty identifying the correct regulatory authority to complain to and this reduced the accountability of some regulators.

In 1976, the Royal Commission on Environmental Pollution (RCEP) referred to some of the shortcomings of UK pollution control in its Fifth Report on air pollution.[7] In particular, it recognised the need for a comprehensive regulatory body which could integrate the existing disparate and fragmented legal controls policed by a multitude of regulatory bodies.

The RCEP asserted the need for an integrated approach to pollution control to replace the single environmental medium approach that had developed in the UK. The Report stated that:

> The reduction of emissions to the atmosphere can lead to an increase in wastes to be disposed of on land or discharged to water. If the optimum environmental solutions are to be found, the controlling authority must be able to look comprehensively to all forms of pollution arising from industrial processes where different control problems exist.

In practical terms, this means that where a manufacturer selects a manufacturing process which reduces or eliminates the need to discharge into water, this may have a knock-on effect in terms of the emissions it makes into the atmosphere or the amount of solid waste that needs to be disposed of. The single medium approach, which had developed in a largely piecemeal fashion in this country, could not take account of this interrelationship between different environmental media.

The RCEP Report also referred to the 'transferability of pollution':

> The three principal forms of pollution—of air, water and land—are often very closely linked. In order to reduce atmospheric pollution, gases or dusts may be trapped in a spray of water or washed out of filters. This means polluted water, if not discharged to a sewer or direct to a river or the sea, can be piped into a lagoon to settle and dry out, leaving a solid waste disposal problem. The pollutant may even go full circle by blowing off the lagoon as dust.

---

7 RECEP Fifth Report on *Air Pollution Control: an Integrated Approach* (Cmnd 6731).

The Report identified other examples of the transferability of pollution, such as water seeping through refuse tips and smoke from the incineration of rubbish or sludge. The absence of a co-ordinated view, and the fragmented approach to pollution control that had developed in the UK, meant that this interrelationship was largely ignored. Decisions on water discharges taken by the water authorities were largely taken in isolation of decisions made by the waste disposal authorities, the local authorities exercising their clean air functions or the Alkali Inspectorate. The RCEP could find little evidence of co-ordination between the various agencies. This lack of co-ordination meant that, in practice, industries that had been prevented from releasing hazardous substances into a particular medium could choose another means of disposal—for example, burning or burying— and effectively divert the wastes into another medium where the regulatory regime and rules were less stringent. The RCEP therefore recommended the need for a more co-ordinated approach or a cross-media approach so that pollutants were not simply transferred from one medium to another. There was clear evidence of the need for a new regulatory authority which could control the whole process and achieve the 'best practicable environmental option'. Her Majesty's Inspectorate of Pollution (HMIP) was established in 1987 to provide a more co-ordinated and integrated system of pollution control and was given specific responsibility under Pt I of the EPA 1990 to administer the new system of IPC created under that Act. The functions of HMIP were transferred to the Environment Agency in April 1996 by s 1 of the Environment Act (EA) 1995, demonstrating the continued desire to provide a more co-ordinated system of pollution control.

Part 1 EPA 1990 introduced a new system of regulatory control which aimed to implement the recommendations of the RCEP. The new system became known as Integrated Pollution Control, or IPC, and was initially controlled by HMIP and then by the Environment Agency. To implement the RCEP's recommendations, the system of IPC was established to prevent or minimise pollution of the environment due to the release of substances into any environmental medium (and thus takes a cross-media approach). However, the system of IPC did not cover all industrial processes; instead it concentrated only on the most seriously polluting processes. These seriously polluting processes were regulated by a means of prior approval in which the process operator applied for an IPC authorisation (that is, a form of licence) from the Environment Agency. In deciding whether to grant an IPC authorisation, the Environment Agency was required to consider the impact of the process on all three environmental media and determine the means of operation that would result in the Best Practical Environmental Option (or BPEO).

In its Twelfth Report in 1988, the RCEP dealt with the issue of the 'best practicable environmental option' (BPEO) and defined it in the following way:

> The selection of BPEO requires a systematic approach to decision-taking in which the practicability of all reasonable options is examined and in which environmental impact is a major factor in the final choice.[8]

For a discussion of BPEO in the context of a variation of an IPC authorisation, see *R v The Environment Agency and Redland Aggregates Ltd ex p Gibson* (1999).[9]

6.3 The system of integrated pollution control

The provisions of Part I of the EPA 1990 have been entirely repealed and the system of IPC replaced in its entirety by the system of environmental permitting. However, a brief description of the IPC

---

8 RCEP (1988) Twelfth Report, Best Practicable Environmental Option, Cm 310.
9 *R v Environment Agency and Redland Aggregates Ltd ex p Gibson* [1999] Env LR 73.

regime is necessary because the system of IPC was critical in the evolution of the current system. Essentially Part I EPA 1990 introduced a duel system of environmental regulation:

(a) IPC for the most seriously polluting processes which were regulated by HMIP and then subsequently by the Environment Agency. These were known as Part A processes; and

(b) Local Authority Air Pollution Control (LAAPC) for those processes which were not permitted to operate without an authorisation, but were not so seriously polluting as to fall within the central control of the Environment Agency. Local authorities regulated these less seriously polluting processes with regard solely to their atmospheric emissions.[10]

6.3.1 Prescribed processes

The EPA[11] prohibited the carrying on of certain *prescribed processes* or the release of certain *prescribed substances* into any environmental medium, without prior authorisation from either the Environment Agency or the relevant local authority. In order for an operator to carry on a prescribed process or discharge a prescribed substance he had to apply to the relevant regulatory body for authorisation in order to avoid committing a criminal offence. The Secretary of State issued regulations[12] which prescribed two lists of processes: those in the 'A' list to be controlled by the Environment Agency, and those in the 'B' list to be controlled by the local authority in whose area the process took place. Hence the dual system of control. IPC only related to those processes in the A list. Where a process was prescribed for central control it was regulated by the Environment Agency by means of an IPC authorisation which governed, releases into all environmental media. In essence the Environment Agency had to take into account the process as a whole in terms of the releases into air, water and land. In reaching its conclusions about the levels of discharges and emissions, the Agency was required to have regard to achieving the Best Practicable Environmental Option (BEPO).[13]

On the other hand, where the process was designated for control by a local authority, the local authority could only regulate any emissions that such a process made into air. This did not mean, of course, that processes designated for LAAPC only discharged into air. Where a process was subject 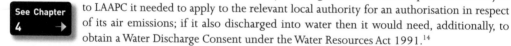 to LAAPC it needed to apply to the relevant local authority for an authorisation in respect of its air emissions; if it also discharged into water then it would need, additionally, to obtain a Water Discharge Consent under the Water Resources Act 1991.[14]

Either the Environment Agency (in respect of IPC) or the local authority (in respect of air pollution) could refuse an application for authorisation or grant it subject to conditions. The Act made it a criminal offence[15] to breach any condition of an authorisation.

The approach adopted under the EPA was to regulate 'processes' and 'substances'. In contrast, as we shall see later, the Environmental Permitting Regulations relate to 'regulated facilities', including regulated waste operations. A process was defined in s 1 EPA 1990 as any activities carried on in Great Britain, whether on premises or by means of mobile plant, which are capable of causing pollution of the environment. 'Activities' were further defined as industrial or commercial activities or activities of any other nature whatsoever.[16] The term 'process' was given a very wide meaning

---

10 Known as Part B processes.
11 S 6 Environmental Protection Act 1990.
12 Environmental Protection (Prescribed Processes and Substances) Regulations 1991 SI 1991/472, as amended.
13 See below at 6.3.2.
14 See Chapter 4 for further discussion of water discharge consents.
15 S 23 EPA 1990.
16 Including, with or without other activities, the keeping of a substance.

and it is clear from the definition that even storage (keeping a substance) could constitute a process if it was capable of causing pollution. The definition of 'process' was considered in HMIP v Safety Kleen UK Ltd (1994).[17] Safety Kleen was prosecuted by HMIP in respect of an incident in which some 13,000 litres of 'cemfuel' (a fuel produced from waste solvents) escaped from a tanker which was parked overnight at the company's premises. Large quantities of the fuel ended up in controlled waters. Safety Kleen had an IPC authorisation in respect of its solvent recovery plant and this expressly excluded the release of substances into controlled waters. At first instance, the defendant company argued that it was not guilty of breaching conditions, since the parked tanker was not a prescribed process and was therefore not subject to any conditions. However, the magistrates' court held that the description of the prescribed process in the authorisation included any other process carried on at the same location by the same person as part of that process. The court accepted therefore that the definition of process included the keeping of a substance in a tanker, and found the defendant guilty. The company was fined £7,500 after it put forward mitigating arguments concerning its speedy response to the incident and the subsequent implementation of measures to avoid future similar incidents.

In practice many companies operated large industrial plants where a number of different industrial processes were carried out at the same location. In these circumstances, the company may have had to apply for one or more IPC authorisations in respect of the different processes.[18]

The 1991 Regulations, as amended, also provided for a number of situations where a process was exempt from the need to obtain an authorisation. Essentially exemptions applied to those processes where the amount of any prescribed substance released was trivial. In Tandridge DC v P&S Civil Engineering Ltd (1995),[19] the Divisional Court held that the burden of proving exceptions was clearly on the defendant.

Part I of the EPA 1990 was brought into force in April 1991. At the time many plants were operating under authorisations from earlier legislation but they were still required to obtain an IPC authorisation from HMIP. However, given the large number of plants concerned and the time it would take to process all of the applications, the government recognised that it needed to include provisions for a phased programme of applications. Consequently, a rolling programme of applications was established, which required applications to be made on a sectoral basis by deadlines specified in Sched 3 to the Environmental Protection (Prescribed Processes and Substances) Regulations 1991. The first sector to be covered under this phased-in programme was the combustion processes. This was necessary in order to meet the deadline of an EC Directive (88/609/EEC) concerned with large combustion plants (that is, power stations). The phased-in programme was completed in 1996. A similar phasing-in process was later utilised in relation to the Pollution Prevention Control Permits (the IPPC regime). However, when the environmental permitting regime came into force an entirely different tactic was adopted; all existing PPC permits and waste management licences automatically became environmental permits on 6 April 2008. As far as new processes were concerned, the phased-in programme was not applicable; an authorisation had to be obtained before operation began. This usually occurred at the same time as planning permission was sought for the development.

6.3.2 IPC authorisations: BATNEEC and BPEO

IPC authorisations could ether be granted subject to conditions or refused. The conditions imposed in an authorisation were the principal mechanism by which the Environment Agency could control

---

17 HMIP v Safety Kleen UK Ltd (1994) ENDS 236.
18 This is something that has been addressed by the Environmental Permitting Regulations 2010, which provide for single and consolidated permits.
19 Tandridge DC v P & S Civil Engineering Ltd [1995] Env LR 67.

or prevent the releases of substances into the environment. This was also the means by which the UK could not only abate pollution, but fulfil its obligations under EU law and other international treaties. In setting conditions the Environment Agency was required by s 7 EPA 1990 to meet the objective laid down in s 7(2). This objective was to ensure that, in carrying on a prescribed process, the best available techniques not entailing excessive cost (BATNEEC) were used for:

(a)   preventing the release of substances prescribed for any environmental medium into that medium or, where that is not practicable, by such means for reducing the release of such substances to a minimum and for rendering harmless any such substances which are so released; and

(b)   rendering harmless any other substances which might cause harm if released into any other environmental medium.

The EPA 1990 introduced the concept of BATNEEC which required that, in setting the specific conditions, the 'best available techniques not entailing excessive cost' were employed to prevent releases or to render them harmless. The BATNEEC requirement applied to the specific conditions laid down by the Environment Agency. However, in addition there was an implied general condition in every authorisation that, in carrying on the process, the person carrying it on must use BATNEEC to achieve the same purposes. The courts demonstrated a marked reluctance to interfere with the discretion of the Agency in determining what conditions to attach to an IPC authorisation. In *Levy v Environment Agency* (2003),[20] the Divisional Court held that the Environment Agency was obliged to consider achieving the statutory objectives, not as a specific requirement that had to be achieved, but as ends to be aimed at. The Agency had to carry out a balancing exercise in deciding what conditions were appropriate. Moreover, the court showed itself unwilling to interfere with a decision which called upon the Agency to exercise sophisticated, specialised scientific knowledge and expertise and which, accordingly, had a wider margin of appreciation than that in the average case. The concept of BATNEEC was reformulated with the Pollution Prevention Control regime and replaced by BAT (Best Available Techniques). The differences between BATNEEC and BAT will be considered later in this chapter.

The important feature of the IPC regime was that it replaced the single medium approach to pollution control with an approach that took into account the environment as a whole. When reaching its conclusions about which conditions to impose the Environment Agency was required to have regard to all of the environmental media involved. Section 7(7) of the EPA 1990 made a specific connection between BATNEEC and BPEO. It specifically required that where a process was subject to IPC and the process involved the release of substances into more than one environmental medium, the BATNEEC conditions should include the objective of ensuring that BATNEEC will be used for minimising the pollution that may be caused to the environment as a whole (the holistic approach), having regard to the best practicable environmental option (BPEO) concerning the substances that may be released. In other words, the aim was clearly to minimise pollution by the application of BATNEEC, having regard to BPEO. Unfortunately, the EPA 1990 did not provide a definition of what was meant by BPEO. It is clear, however, that it involved a balancing exercise, taking into account ways in which, for example, a slight increase in air emissions might radically reduce discharges to water, and weighing up what is 'best' for the environment as a whole.

The statutory duty to ensure that BATNEEC is used, having regard to BPEO, was considered by the Divisional Court in R v Environment Agency and Redland Aggregates Ltd ex p Gibson (1999).[21] The case

---

20 *Levy v Environment Agency* [2002] EWHC 1663 (Admin); [2003] Env LR 11.
21 R v Environment Agency and Redland Aggregates Ltd ex p Gibson [1999] Env LR 73.

concerned three separate applications for judicial review of the Environment Agency's decision to grant variations to existing IPC authorisations so as to allow the burning of substitute liquid fuels (SLF) in three separate manufacturing processes. The applicants claimed that the Agency was obliged to carry out a thorough examination of all of the practicable options and the available techniques relating to the process as a whole and, because the Agency had merely selected the preferred option from a list of two, it had not selected the *best* option. The case very much concerned the fact that what was at issue was the terms of a variation of an IPC authorisation, as opposed to the granting of one. Nevertheless, in the context of the variation, the court held that although the Agency was under a duty to ensure that the terms of a variation to an existing authorisation complied with the statutory objectives of s 7, this did not mean that there was a duty to carry out an exhaustive examination of all practical options and techniques regardless of the circumstances. The extent of this duty to assess BATNEEC and BPEO in an application for a variation was a matter of 'fact and degree' which was dependent upon all the circumstances of the particular case.[22]

6.4 The Integrated Pollution Prevention Control Directive

During the early 1990s the European Commission submitted proposals to develop a system of integrated permitting for industrial processes, along similar lines to the system of Integrated Pollution Control developed in the UK. This eventually resulted, in late 1996, in the enactment of the Integrated Pollution Prevention Control Directive (96/61/EC).[23] The IPPC Directive was based in large part on the IPC experience in the UK but there were a number of differences between the approach adopted in the directive and that in the EPA 1990. Whilst the EPA focused on the control of emissions into air, water and land, the directive was concerned with much wider environmental impacts, including energy efficiency, waste minimisation and noise. The IPPC Directive was enacted at a time when the Commission was also beginning to favour a more flexible approach to environmental regulation with the development of framework directives. To that extent the directive constituted something of a departure from the traditional approach adopted by other EC directives. Earlier directives had also focussed on setting specific emission limits. In contrast, the IPPC Directive did not set any specific environmental limits or targets; it required permits to be set by reference to local conditions and any applicable environmental quality standards. The IPPC Directive obliged Member States to prevent or, where prevention is not possible, reduce pollution *and* environmental impacts from the range of installations listed in Annex 1 of the Directive in order to achieve a high level of protection of the environment as a whole. Annex 1 sets out certain types of installation that are be subject to IPPC by reference to various thresholds. The Annex is broken down into broad industrial sectors and further subdivided to cover detailed specifications within each sector. In addition the Directive laid down the obligations that would apply to the operators of installations and the conditions which should be imposed in permits. The directive introduced the use of Best Available Techniques (BAT); similar, but not identical, to the BATNEEC standard imposed by Part I EPA 1990.

See Chapter 3

Although the IPPC Directive was largely modelled on the IPC regime it did differ in a number of respects. The IPPC regime laid down in the directive was broader in scope than the domestic IPC regime; specifically it aimed to regulate not only environmental emissions discharged to all three environmental media (air, water and land) but also the environmental impacts of the following:

---

22 For further consideration of BPEO in the context of waste management licensing, see R v Bolton MBC ex p Kirkman [1998] Env LR 719; R v Derbyshire CC ex p Murray [2001] Env LR 26; [2001] 2 PLR 1; [2001] JPL 730 (Note).
23 Council Directive 96/61/EC of 24 September 1996 concerning integrated pollution prevention and control OJ L 257, 10/10/1996, pp 26–40.

- energy use and efficiency;
- raw material consumption;
- noise, vibration;
- accident prevention measures;
- heat generation (thermal effects).

The directive also required that regulatory control would extend beyond day-to-day operational controls to include after-care and site remediation. Additionally the IPPC regime also imposed stricter substantive and procedural requirements than those applicable under IPC.[24] As with the IPC regime the IPPC regime did not apply to all polluting activities. It only applied to those *installations* prescribed in Annex 1 of the directive. Since its original enactment the IPPC Directive was subject to a substantial number of amendments. Consequently Directive 96/61/EC was replaced with a codified directive in 2008.[25] The 2008 directive has been amended and will be revoked and replaced with effect from 7 January 2014 by Directive 2010/75/EU.[26] References to the IPPC Directive in this chapter are references to the codified directive 2008.

6.4.1 From EPA 1990 to PPCA 1999; implementation of the IPPC Directive into domestic law

The implementation of the IPPC Directive into domestic law imposed fairly unique problems for the UK in comparison with the other Member States of the EU. The issue for government was how to superimpose a complex system of environmental regulation onto an already established regime. The answer was the repeal of Part I EPA 1990 by the Pollution Prevention Control Act 1999. Like the EPA 1990 before it, the PPCA 1999 was a framework act and was therefore heavily supplemented by detailed subordinate legislation, namely the Pollution Prevention and Control (England and Wales) Regulations 2000[27] (PPC Regulations 2000) as amended. In particular these regulations transposed Annex 1 of the Directive and set down which installations were to fall within the scope of the PPC Act 1999. The regulations also contained further substantial details in relation to the PPC permits that would replace the IPC authorisations.

6.4.2 The differences between the requirements of the IPPC regime and IPC

In order to avoid confusion it should be noted that the Directive uses the phrase Integrated Pollution Prevention Control and required Member States to provide for the regulatory control of those activities listed in Annex 1. The implementing legislation, the Pollution Prevention Control Act 1999, and subordinate legislation dispensed with the term 'integrated' and simply referred to PPC permits. And finally it should also be noted that the PPC Regulations 2000 have now been repealed and replaced by the Environmental Permitting Regulations 2010 which make provisions for environmental permits.[28]

As stated above, the IPPC regime has a wider focus than IPC, regulating environmental impacts rather than environmental emissions. However, its ambit is also significantly wider. The Environment

---

24 See the judgment of Auld LJ in R (on the application of Edwards) v Environment Agency (No 2) [2006] EWCA Civ 877; [2007] Env LR 9; [2007] JPL 82 at para 74.
25 Directive 2008/1/EC of the European Parliament and of the Council of 15 January 2008 concerning integrated pollution prevention and control (Codified version) OJ L 24, 29/1/2008, pp 8–29.
26 Directive 2010/75/EU of the European Parliament and of the Council of 24 November 2010 on industrial emissions (integrated pollution prevention and control) OJ L 334, 17/12/2010, pp 17–19.
27 Pollution Prevention and Control (England and Wales) Regulations 2000 SI 2000/1973.
28 The Environmental Permitting (England and Wales) Regulations 2010 SI 2010/675.

Agency has asserted that whilst the IPPC regime builds upon IPC, it would be 'wrong to view it as IPC with an added "P" '. Like IPC, it covers emissions to air, land and water, but IPPC goes further and covers noise and vibration, energy efficiency, waste minimisation, environmental accidents and site protection. During the currency of PPC permits[29] there were approximately 7,000 listed installations subject to IPPC control as opposed to the 2,000 Part A subject to IPC control. In particular, IPPC extended control to large landfill sites, intensive agricultural production units, and food and drink factories.

IPPC regulates 'installations' rather than 'prescribed processes'. IPPC regulation is therefore a site, or plant-based, method of regulation. This avoided the potential complexity of IPC regulation where several individually licensed processes are all undertaken on the same site.

Unlike IPC, which distinguished between Part A and Part B processes, the PPC Regulations categorised *installations* for control (as required by the directive). The installations were classified as A(1), A(2) and B installations. The Environment Agency regulated the Part 1 installations. In contrast to their previously limited LAAPC responsibilities, local authorities were given a greater regulatory role under IPPC: they were made responsible for regulating Part A(2) installations with regard to *all environmental impacts*, and Part B installations regarding atmospheric emissions only. Thus, for the first time, local authorities extended their remit beyond 'policing' atmospheric emissions from Part B processes.

IPPC controls, like their IPC predecessor, use process standards to determine licence conditions. In particular, 'best available techniques' (BAT) must be employed by installation operators to prevent and/or reduce the environmental impacts of regulated installations.

IPPC's adoption of a BAT standard for all installations contrasts with the BATNEEC condition incorporated in IPC authorisations but, in reality, the two standards are similar since, when determining IPPC permits, the regulator must have regard to the 'proportionality principle' requiring it to take the economic viability of the BAT standard into account.[30]

6.4.3 Pollution prevention control and waste

The IPPC Directive also brought within its scope certain landfill activities above a particular threshold. Prior to the IPPC Directive and the Pollution Prevention Control Act 1999, landfill was entirely regulated by Part II EPA 1990 and landfill sites were required to operate in compliance with a waste management licence granted by the Environment Agency under s 35 EPA 1990. However, the IPPC Directive included a number of waste activities.[31] In consequence these waste activities listed in the IPPC Directive became controlled by the PPCA and PPC permits. Other smaller waste activities remained regulated by Part II EPA 1990. Clearly the presence of two licensing regimes for waste added greatly to the complexity inherent in this system of regulation.

6.4.4 Phasing in PPC permits

Given the differences between IPC and IPPC and also the fact that local authorities now played a new role in regulating A(2) installations the legislation provided for a phased-in application of the PPC regime, added to which certain waste activities (large landfill sites) needed to obtain PPC permits instead of waste management licences. In order to accommodate these significant changes the legislation provided for a transitional period during which existing operators would apply for new PPC permits to replace IPC authorisations and waste management licences. In many respects

---

29 Until 6 April 2008.
30 For a further discussion of BAT see below at 6.12.7.
31 E.g., large landfill.

the period between the enactment of Part 1 EPA 1990 and 2000 can therefore be characterised as a period of almost constant change. There can be little doubt that the whole process was expensive from the point of view of the regulators and the regulated. It also resulted in a complicated system of environmental regulation which was aptly described by the Better Regulation Task Force:[32]

> Many businesses require licences for activities that may pollute the air, water or land. Various licensing requirements are set out in different pieces of legislation and may impose different administrative requirements on industry. The procedures relating to integrated pollution prevention and control (IPPC) for an industrial process that might pollute the air, water or land are different to those required for waste management – yet their objective, to protect the environment, is the same. Many businesses will need to deal with both permitting systems.

6.4.5 The new IPPC Directive

As noted above the first IPPC Directive has been subject to various amendments which were eventually consolidated in 2008 by the current directive (2008/1/EC). However, the 2008 directive has been amended and will be revoked and replaced with full effect from 7 January 2014 by Directive 2010/75/EU on industrial emissions (integrated pollution prevention control) (Recast).[33] The 2010 directive brings together the provisions of seven directives into one piece of legislation. Member States had until 6 January 2013 to transpose its provisions into national law. The directive has various implementation dates; for example it only applies to new installations from 6 January 2013 but does not affect existing installations until 7 January 2014. The new directive will also extend the range of activities subject to IPPC after 7 July 2015 and will apply to existing large combustion plants from 1 January 2016.

6.5 The Better Regulation agenda and the introduction of environmental permitting

As part of the government's Better Regulation agenda Defra was instrumental in putting forward a new system of environmental permitting which would replace PPC permits and waste management licences and simplify environmental regulation. The result was the Environmental Permitting (England and Wales) Regulations 2007 (hereafter EP Regulations 2007), which came into force on 6 April 2008 and which entirely revoked the Pollution Prevention Control Regulations 2000 along with some 40 other statutory instruments relating largely to waste.

When the EP Regulations 2007 came into force they provided[34] that a PPC permit or WML that was in force on 6 April 2008 automatically became an environmental permit and must be treated as if it was granted under the EP 2007 Regulations. In other words, the regulations provided for the immediate conversion of the following into environmental permits:

(a)   Some 20,000 PPC permits governing IPPC installations (including those waste activities regulated by PPC permits).

---

32 Better Regulation Task Force Report to the Prime Minister (March 2005), Regulation – Less is More, Reducing Burdens, Improving Outcomes.
33 Directive 2010/75/EU of the European Parliament and of the Council of 24 November 2010 on industrial emissions (integrated pollution prevention and control) OJ L 334, 17/12/2010, pp 17–19.
34 The Environmental Permitting (England and Wales) Regulations 2007/3538.

(b) Other waste activities previously governed by a waste management licence (and not exempted from the scope of the EP Regulations). The requirement that the environmental permit holder must be the operator is different from the system under waste management licensing. Transitional provisions[35] allowed the holder of a waste management licence (WML) to be treated as the operator for the purposes of the EP Regulations 2007. Any waste activity that had been registered as exempt under the Waste Management Licensing Regulations 1994[36] was deemed to be registered in relation to an exempt waste operation under Sched 2 to the EP Regulations 2007.

(c) Mobile plant carrying out certain waste activities (previously subject to waste management licences under Part II EPA 1990).

The EP Regulations 2007 were made under the auspices of s 2 Pollution Prevention Control Act 1999, which remains in force. The 2007 Regulations were revoked and replaced with the 2010 Environmental Permitting Regulations.[37]

The principal aim of the environmental permitting regime is to provide a simplified stream-lined system of regulatory control in the form of a single permit and common procedures. For example, the new system aims to simplify the process of applying for a permit as well as amending and varying it. In addition the Defra guidance[38] claimed the regime would deliver more flexibility for industry, a simpler risk-based system for regulators whilst continuing to protect the environment and human health. The new regime continues to implement the requirements of the IPPC directive along with a number of other directives relating, inter alia, to waste.[39]

6.5.1 The Environmental Permitting (England and Wales) Regulations 2010: overview

The EPR 2010 as amended set out provisions relating inter alia to the following:

- the regulated facilities that require environmental permits or need to be registered as exempt;
- single Permits, Consolidated Permits and Standard Permits;
- a simple transition to the new regime;
- the process for applying for and determining permit applications (and exemptions);
- provisions for public participation in the permitting process;
- the process for transferring, varying and surrendering environmental permits;
- for the transposition of 18 EU directives which impose obligations required to be delivered through permits or capable of being delivered through permits;
- the functions of the regulatory bodies and the Secretary of State;
- compliance obligations including enforcement powers and criminal offences, the powers and functions of regulators, the Secretary of State and the Welsh Ministers;
- provisions for appeals against permitting decisions.

Each of these will be considered below.

---

35 The Environmental Permitting (England and Wales) Regulations 2010 SI 2010/675 reg 69(2).
36 Waste Management Licensing Regulations 1994 SI 1994/1056, as amended.
37 The Environmental Permitting (England and Wales) Regulations 2010 SI 2010/675.
38 Defra (February 2009) Environmental Permitting, Simplifying Environmental Regulation. Available at http://www.defra.gov.uk/environment/policy/permits/documents/guidance-booklet-090304.pdf.
39 See below at 6.12.3.

6.6 Environmental permitting: regulated facilities

6.6.1 The regulated facilities that require environmental permits or need to be registered as exempt

The purpose of the environmental permitting regime was to bring together facilities previously regulated under the PPC Regulations 2000 and Part II EPA 1990 into a single permitting system. Hence its coverage is wide and so the regulations adopt the generic term 'regulated facility' to describe the activities that fall within its scope. The regulations specify what activities require an environmental permit and also what waste operations are exempt from those requirements.

A 'regulated facility'[40] includes any of the following:

a. an installation that carries out activities listed in Sched 1 to the regulations (these are *Installations* regulated under the IPPC regime). The EP Regulations also includes any activities that are technically linked to the installation;

b. a waste operation not carried out at an installation or by means of a mobile plant;

c. a mobile plant (carrying out either one of the Sched 1 activities or a waste operation);

d. a mining waste operation;

e. a radioactive substances activity;

f. a water discharge activity;

g. a groundwater activity.

Each of these will be considered in turn.

6.6.2 Installations

The term 'installation'[41] refers to any stationary technical unit where one or more activities listed in Part 2 of Sched 1 to the EPR 2010 are carried out. It also includes any other directly associated activities carried out on the same site which have a technical connection with the prescribed activities and which could have an effect on pollution. Rules for determining whether an installation is Part A(1), Part A(2) or Part B are contained in Part 1 of Sched 1 to the Regulations.

Installations that require an environmental permit are listed in Part 2 of Sched 1 to the EPR 2010. The list reflects the requirements of Annex 1 of the IPPC Directive. Certain exclusions from the list and other rules for interpretation are contained in Part 1 of Sched 1.

Schedule 1 to the EPR 2010 classifies 'activities' into six chapters:

(1) energy industries;
(2) production and processing of metals;
(3) minerals industries;
(4) chemical industry;
(5) waste management;
(6) other activities.

Each of the six industry chapters is subdivided into a further set of groupings. Finally, each industry grouping is split into two smaller groups reflecting the regulatory body responsible for 'policing' the relevant installation.

---

40 Environmental Permitting (England and Wales) Regulations 2010 SI 2010/675 reg 8.
41 Environmental Permitting (England and Wales) Regulations 2010 SI 2010/675 reg 2(1).

Part A(1) activities are regulated by the Environment Agency.

Part A(2) and B installations are regulated by local authorities.

Law in Action

Tanning hides and skins at a plant with a treatment capacity of more than 12 tonnes of finished products per day is a Part A1 activity and is therefore regulated by the Environment Agency and is subject to the requirements of the IPPC Directive.

Slaughtering animals at a plant with a carcass production capacity of more than 50 tonnes per day is a Part A1 activity and is therefore regulated by the Environment Agency and is subject to the requirements of the IPPC Directive.

Disposing of or recycling animal carcasses or animal waste by rendering at a plant with a treatment capacity exceeding 10 tonnes per day of animal carcasses or animal waste or both in aggregate is a Part A2 activity. This activity is regulated by the relevant local authority and is also subject to the requirements of the IPPC Directive.

Breeding maggots in any case where 5 kg or more of animal matter, vegetable matter or both in aggregate are introduced into the process in any week is a Part B activity. This activity requires an environmental permit from the relevant local authority. The permit will only regulate the atmospheric emissions. This activity is not subject to the requirements of the IPPC Directive.[42]

A 'mobile plant' is defined as a plant which is designed to move or be moved whether on roads or otherwise and which is used to carry out one or more activities listed in Pt I of Sched 1.

6.6.3 A waste operation not carried out at an installation or by means of a mobile plant

A waste operation is defined in reg 2 as a waste recovery or disposal operation within the meaning of the Waste Framework Directive.[43] Essentially any recovery or disposal of waste is a waste operation and requires an environmental permit (unless it is an excluded waste operation). However, some of the large waste operations will constitute an installation and fall within that classification of regulated facility.

Law in Action

The incineration of hazardous waste in an incineration plant is a Part A1 activity.[44]

The incineration of non-hazardous waste in an incineration plant with a capacity of 1 tonne or more is an A1 activity.

The incineration of non-hazardous waste in an incineration plant with a capacity of less than 1 tonne per hour is an A2 activity.

---

42 Environmental Permitting (England and Wales) Regulations 2010 SI 2010/675 Chap 6, s 6.8, Pt 2, Sched 1.

43 Directive 2008/98/EC of the European Parliament and of the Council of 19 November 2008 on waste and repealing certain directives OJ L312, 22/11/2008, pp 3–30 as amended.

44 Environmental Permitting (England and Wales) Regulations 2010 SI 2010/675 Chap 5, Pt 2, Sched 1.

> The incineration of animal carcasses in a plant, which is not an incineration plant or a co-incineration plant, with a capacity of more than 10 tonnes per day but less than 1 tonne per hour is an A2 activity.
>
> The incineration of non-hazardous waste in a plant which is not an incineration plant or a co-incineration plant, and on premises where there is plant, other than incineration plant or co-incineration plant, which has an aggregate capacity of 50 kg or more per hour but less than 1 tonne per hour is a Part B activity.

6.6.4 Excluded and exempt waste operations

The EPR 2010 draws a distinction between excluded waste operations and exempt waste operations.

Certain waste operations are *excluded* from the permitting regime because they are regulated under other legislation. Excluded waste operations are defined in EPR 2010 reg 2 as any part of a waste operation not carried on at an installation or by means of Part A mobile plant or Part B mobile plant that (a) is the subject of a licence under Part 2 of the Food and Environment Protection Act 1985 (or does not require such a licence by virtue of an order under s 7 of that Act), or relates to waste that is not treated as directive waste by virtue of reg 3(2) of the Controlled Waste (England and Wales) Regulations 2012.[45] Because these operations are regulated under other legislation they are not subject to the additional requirements of the permitting regime.

Other waste operations are exempt from the permitting regime. Article 11 of the Waste Framework Directive permits Member States to exempt certain low-risk waste operations from the permitting regime, but these exemptions only relate to the disposal of waste at its place of production or the recovery of waste. This is transposed by the EPR 2010 in reg 5 which provides for two broad types of exempt waste operations. The first are those that are not carried out at an installation; that is because the waste operation will be covered by the permit for that installation. The second type of exempt waste operation are those that are carried on at an installation but fall within ss 5.3 or 5.4 of Part 2 of Sched 1 (waste recovery or disposal other than by landfill or incineration) and which fall within one of the descriptions of waste activities listed in Part 1 of Sched 3 and also satisfy certain general conditions in Part 1 of Sched 3. The list of activities includes, for example:

● waste storage at the place of production prior to its treatment/disposal elsewhere;
● the deposit of organic waste for fertilising/conditioning land;
● some waste reuse/recovery activities.

Essentially the waste operations listed in Sched 3 are very specific low-risk waste handling operations that do not require a permit. There are no exemptions in regard to facilities handling hazardous waste. Most exemptions need to be registered with the Environment Agency, which is a form of 'light touch' regulation.

---

45   Controlled Waste (England and Wales) Regulations 2012 SI 2012/811.

6.6.5 A mobile plant (carrying out either one of the Sched 1 activities or a waste operation)

A mobile plant is defined as a plant which is designed to move or be moved whether on roads or otherwise. It is only possible for plant undertaking a Part A activity to fall within the definition of 'mobile plant' if it is not an installation. An installation cannot (by definition) be a mobile plant because an installation must be a stationary unit. However, it may be possible for a stationary unit to include plant or equipment which is mobile; if the activity carried out by the mobile plant is directly associated with the stationary unit then it will form part of the installation. If, however, the plant is a separate mobile plant and is not an installation and it carries out one or more activities listed in Pt I of Sched 1 or a waste operation then it too will need an environmental permit.

6.6.6 Mining waste operations

A mining waste operation is the management of extractive waste, whether or not involving a mining waste facility, but excluding activities in Art 2(2)(c) of the Mining Waste Directive.[46]

6.6.7 Radioactive substances activity

Radioactive substances activity was introduced as a regulated facility by the EPR 2010. The principal objective of including radioactive substances within the EPR regime was to enable the Environment Agency to establish and maintain control over the keeping and security of radioactive materials, including sealed radioactive sources and mobile radioactive apparatus; and also to ensure that the accumulation and disposal of radioactive wastes are managed effectively, to limit radiological impact on the general public and the environment. Radioactive substances activities are defined in para 11 of Part 2 of Sched 23. The definition is complex, but essentially a radioactive substances activity is carried on where a person uses premises for the purposes of an undertaking where that person applies, keeps, receives, uses, accumulates or disposes of radioactive material or waste. The provisions do not apply to nuclear sites. Certain low-risk radioactive substances activities are exempt from the need to have a permit. These are set out in Part 7 of Sched 23.

6.6.8 Water discharge activity

Water discharge activities were not regulated under the EPR regime prior to the 2010 regulation. Prior to the EPR 2010, the Water Resources Act 1991 regulated discharges into water and provided for, inter alia, Water Discharge Consents under s 89 of the Act. The EPR 2010 now replaces those parts of the Water Resources Act 1991 that relate to the regulation of discharges to controlled waters. Under the EPR 2010 water discharge activities relate to discharges to surface waters that are controlled waters but do not apply to groundwater. Discharges to groundwater come under ground-water activities.[47] The Defra guidance on water discharge activities states that ' "Water discharge activities" includes both those activities that require a permit, and those activities that are unlawful, for instance causing pollution to surface water, whether deliberate or accidental.'[48] Schedule 21 defines a water discharge activity as meaning:

---

46 Directive 2006/21/EC of the European Parliament and of the Council of 15 March 2006 on the management of waste from extractive industries and amending Directive 2004/35/EC – Statement by the European Parliament, the Council and the Commission OJ L 102, 11/4/2006, pp 15–34.
47 See below at 6.6.9.
48 Defra Environmental Permitting Guidance: Water Discharge Activities For the Environmental Permitting (England and Wales) Regulations 2010, December 2010, Version 2.0.

(a)   the discharge or entry to inland freshwaters, coastal waters or relevant territorial waters of any poisonous, noxious or polluting matter; any waste matter; or any trade effluent or sewage effluent;

(b)   the discharge from land through a pipe into the sea outside the seaward limits of relevant territorial waters of any trade effluent or sewage effluent;

(c)   the removal from any part of the bottom, channel or bed of any inland freshwaters of a deposit accumulated by reason of any dam, weir or sluice holding back the waters, by causing it to be carried away in suspension in the waters, unless the activity is carried on in the exercise of a power conferred by or under any enactment relating to land drainage, flood prevention or navigation;

(d)   the cutting or uprooting of a substantial amount of vegetation in any inland freshwaters or so near to any such waters that it falls into them and failure to take reasonable steps to remove the vegetation from these waters;

(e)   an activity in respect of which the regulator has served a notice requiring a permit (this relates to highway activities or where a person discharges trade effluent or sewage effluent into the waters of any lake or pond which are not inland freshwaters).

A discharge or an activity that might lead to a discharge is not a 'water discharge activity' if the discharge is made, or authorised to be made, by or under any prescribed statutory provision; or the discharge is of trade effluent or sewage effluent from a vessel.

The very broad definition of water discharge activity means that a regulated facility under one of the other limbs discussed above may also include a water discharge activity. For example, an installation may discharge water into a surface drain. However, a single discharge of sewage effluent from a non-regulated facility, for example a hotel, may be a water discharge activity; the guidance refers to these as stand-alone water discharge activities.[49]

See Chapter 4 →

6.6.9 Groundwater activity

Groundwater activities are defined in Sched 22 and include:

●   the discharge of a pollutant that results in or might lead to a direct or indirect input to groundwater;
●   any other discharge that might lead to a direct or indirect input of a pollutant to groundwater;
●   an activity that might lead to a discharge mentioned above where that activity is carried on as part of the operation of a regulated facility of another class;
●   an activity in respect of which a notice under Sched 22 has taken effect.

The regulator has discretion in so far as it may decide that discharge (or an activity that might lead to a discharge) is not a groundwater activity if the input of the pollutant is the consequence of an accident or unforeseen natural event, or is of a quantity so small as to pose no risk to groundwater, or cannot, subject to conditions, be prevented.

As with water discharge activities certain types of groundwater activity are capable of being exempt groundwater activities.

---

49   For further discussion of water discharge activities and the meaning of the terms such as controlled water, entry, polluting matter see Chapter 4 on Water Pollution.

6.7 Environmental permits

EPR 2010 regulation 12 states that no person may operate a regulated facility unless the regulated facility is authorised by an environmental permit. It is a criminal offence to contravene, or knowingly cause or knowingly permit the contravention of, reg 12[50] and it is also a criminal offence to fail to comply with or to contravene an environmental permit condition.[51] Inevitably with such a different range of regulated facilities environmental permits will differ enormously from those regulating complex installations involving hazardous processes and substances to others regulating small-scale activities involving little environmental risk. Unless an operator applies for a standard permit which contains standard conditions the regulator will assess each application on a case-by-case basis having regard to a range of considerations. These are referred to as bespoke permits and they set conditions for those activities where there no standard rules, for example where the necessary controls are too complex or site-specific.

6.7.1 Single permits

It is entirely possible that an operator is carrying out more than one regulated facility at the same site. Regulation 17(a) makes provision for the grant of a single environmental permit provided that the regulator is the same for each facility; the operator is the same for each facility; and all the facilities are on the same site. In determining whether activities are taking place on the same site the regulator is expected to adopt a common-sense approach[52] taking into account the fact that some sites are particularly large. The regulator needs to consider the proximity of the regulated facilities; the coherence of the site and the extent to which the regulated facilities share a common management structure.

The position is slightly more relaxed[53] in relation to mobile plant; providing the regulator and the operator are the same a single environmental permit can be granted to an operator for more than one mobile plant because the mobile plant do not have to be operating on the same site in order to be included in a single permit. Regulation 17(c) provides for the grant of a single environmental permit of more than one standard facility.[54] Standard facilities do not have to be on the same site in order to be included in a single permit. However, standard facilities on different sites cannot be combined in a single permit where the IPPC Directive applies to any of the facilities. A single permit cannot be granted where there are separate regulators. For example if a site includes an A1 installation and an A2 installation they will be regulated by the Environment Agency and the relevant local authority respectively. It is also not possible to combine a permit for a mobile plant with any other regulated facility since mobile plant are not associated with a particular geographical site. The differences in the requirements for mobile plant mean that a single permit cannot cover mobile plant and other facility types.

6.7.2 Consolidated permits

The Regulations[55] also enable the regulator to consolidate environmental permits with a single permit covering the same facilities. This can be done where there is more than one regulated facility with the same operator.

---

50 The Environmental Permitting (England and Wales) Regulations 2010 SI 2010/675 reg 38.
51 For further discussion of offences, see 6.15 below.
52 Defra (March 2012) Environmental Permitting Core guidance, Version 4.0 para 2.31. Available at http://www.defra.gov.uk/environment/policy/permits/guidance.htm.
53 The Environmental Permitting (England and Wales) Regulations 2010 SI 2010/675 reg 17(b).
54 A standard facility is a regulated facility to which the 'standard rules' apply; see below at 6.7.3 and also 6.12.2.
55 The Environmental Permitting (England and Wales) Regulations 2010 SI 2010/675 reg 18.

6.7.3 Standard permits

Regulation 26 allows the Secretary of State and the Environment Agency to prepare standard rules for such regulated facilities as are described in the standard rules. Before issuing standard rules the regulatory body must first consult various persons or bodies that it considers are representative of the communities likely to be affected by the regulated facilities as well as anyone else it considers likely to be affected. In practice this will include industrial associations representing different types of regulated facilities, relevant statutory bodies. The standard rules essentially consist of a set of requirements which are common to the particular class of regulated facility, for example where a number of regulated facilities share similar characteristics. Where standard rules are adopted, the facilities are called standard facilities.[56] The advantage of the standard rules is that they effectively provide an off-the-peg set of permit conditions which can be used instead of site-specific permit conditions. An operator of a standard facility can request[57] that the regulator includes in the environmental permit a term providing that the relevant standard rules are conditions of the permit. This has the effect of reducing the time it takes to determine the application[58] and negates the need for the public consultation requirements.[59] However, once the standard rules become permit conditions the operator has no right of appeal against such conditions.

The regulations require that the standard rules are reviewed as necessary[60] and that they are also made available on the internet.

6.8 The regulatory bodies

The EPR 2010 reg 32 provides for the Environment Agency to act as the regulatory body in relation to the following regulated facilities:

- A1 installations;
- A1 mobile plants;
- waste mobile plant;
- waste operations, including those carried on at a Part B installation or by Part B mobile plant (unless the waste operation is a Part B activity);
- water discharge activities or groundwater activities including those that are carried out at a Part B installation or mobile plant;
- waste operations which are carried out other than at an installation or by a Part A mobile plant or Part B mobile plant;
- mining waste operations, including any carried on at a Part B installation;
- radioactive substances activities.

The local authority in whose area the regulated facility is located is responsible for regulating the following:

- A2 installations or Part A2 mobile plant;
- Part B installations or Part B mobile plant, except any of the following which are carried out at that installation/mobile plant:

---

56 The Environmental Permitting (England and Wales) Regulations 2010 SI 2010/675 reg 2.
57 The Environmental Permitting (England and Wales) Regulations 2010 SI 2010/675 reg 27.
58 To three months.
59 Except where the standard facility is an A installation.
60 For example to incorporate the requirements of any new EU directives.

○ a waste operation (unless it is a Part B activity);
○ a mining waste operation;
○ a water discharge activity;
○ a groundwater activity.

If the principal place of business of the operator of Part A(2) mobile plant or Part B mobile plant is in England and Wales, functions in relation to that regulated facility are exercisable by the local authority in whose area the place of business lies.

Both regulatory bodies are required to work together and the Environment Agency must consult with the relevant local authority in respect of any regulated facility within the local authority's area and vice versa. The Secretary of State for the Environment has power to issue directions transferring regulatory authority to a different regulator either in respect of a class of regulated facility or a specific regulated facility.[61] That said, the Secretary of State cannot direct a local authority to exercise the Environment Agency's functions for a waste operation or a mining waste operation.[62] According to the core guidance these directions are therefore likely to be used mainly where there are regulated facilities on the same site, but with different regulators.[63] The regulators or the operator may make a written request to the Secretary of State to trigger such a direction.

6.9 Applying for an environmental permit

6.9.1 Timing

As was previously noted, existing PPC permits and waste management licences automatically became environmental permits on 6 April 2008.[64] There was no need for any application to be made. However, any new regulated facility will need to apply for an environmental permit before commencing operations in order to avoid criminal liability under reg 38. Therefore an application for an environmental permit for a new regulated facility should normally be made prior to the construction of the facility, preferably alongside the application for planning permission. The regulator will be a statutory consultee in the planning process and therefore submitting the permit application in parallel with the planning application should result in more informed consultation between the relevant authorities. Although there is nothing technically preventing construction prior to a permit application the regulator could impose conditions relating to the design of the infrastructure which could result in considerable cost if the operator has already committed to a different development. Once an operator has an environmental permit he may also apply to vary the permit should there be changes in the operation of the regulated facility. The operator will do this by means of an application to vary a permit.[65]

6.9.2 The applicant must be the operator

An application for an environmental permit must be made by the operator of the regulated facility. The operator is defined as the person who has control over the operation of a regulated facility. If the regulated facility has not yet been put into operation, the operator is the person who will have control over the facility when it is put into operation. Where the regulated facility has ceased to be

---

61 The Environmental Permitting (England and Wales) Regulations 2010 SI 2010/675 reg 33.
62 Unless that waste operation is part of an installation or a mobile plant.
63 See above, in relation to single permits.
64 The Environmental Permitting (England and Wales) Regulations 2010 SI 2010/675 reg 69.
65 This is discussed below at 6.12.

in operation, the operator is the person who holds the environmental permit which authorised the operation of the facility. The regulatory body must refuse the application if it not duly made by the operator.[66]

6.9.3 Operator competence

Underpinning the permitting regime is the notion of operator competence; the operator of a regulated facility must be competent to operate the regulated facility in compliance with the environmental objectives of the regime. The regulator must consider operator competence when considering an application for an EP and also an application for the transfer of an EP (either in whole or in part).

However, the regulator can consider the competency of the operator at any other time that it is exercising its regulatory functions in respect of the regulated facility and has the power to revoke a permit if it considers that the operator is not competent.[67] In making this assessment the regulator may have regard to the operator's management system and level of technical competence as well as his record of regulatory compliance. The financial circumstances of the operator are also relevant considerations in assessing competency. Previously under the WML regime licence holders had to demonstrate that they were 'fit and proper persons' to hold a WML. The operator competency requirements of the environmental permitting regime extend these requirements to all permit holders, although the level of competency required is dependent upon the nature of the regulated facility.

Essentially operator competence has three elements:

(a) Operators must have effective management systems in place in order to achieve a high level of environmental protection; the level will vary depending on the complexity of the regulated facility. Complex regulated facilities should consider the use of formal environmental management systems such as ISO 14001[68] and also registering with the EU's Eco-Management and Audit Scheme (EMAS).

(b) Technical competence: operators must have the required level of technical competence to operate their regulated facility. For waste operations the Certificate of Technical Competence (CoTCs) can be used to demonstrate technical competence as can qualifications from the Chartered Institute of Waste Management (CIWM) and the Waste Management Industry Training Board (WAMITAB).

(c) Financial competence: the operator of any regulated facility must have sufficient financial resources to enable them to comply with the permit conditions.

When the regulator assesses competency it will also need to consider whether the operator or any other 'relevant person' has been convicted of a relevant offence which is an offence relating to the environment or environmental regulation. For these purposes a relevant person includes the operator (which is the legal person and may therefore be a company) but it also extends to a director, manager, secretary or other 'similar officer' of the operator. In respect of a limited liability partnership (LLP) it includes the partners. The regulator should not grant an EP if any such person has been convicted of an environmental offence if it considers that it would be undesirable to let them hold

---

66 Ibid.
67 See below at 6.13.2.
68 International Organisation for Standardisation, ISO 14001 (2004) Environmental Management Systems.

a permit. In other words a previous environmental conviction is not an absolute bar on obtaining an environmental permit but it will make it more difficult. The nature of the offence and the degree of culpability will be relevant considerations.

6.9.4 The application process

The application process is detailed in Sched 5 to the EPR 2010. Although there is no legal requirement operators may engage in pre-application discussions with the regulatory body; this could be particularly useful where the operator is uncertain as to whether a permit is required and also to help the operator understand what is required in the application. An application must be made on the form prescribed by the regulator and include the information specified on the form.[69] The application must also be accompanied by the relevant fee.[70] The core guidance emphasises that the amount of information required in the application process should be proportionate to the environmental risk and must also provide the information required by any relevant EU directives. The process will be determined by the nature of the application; if the operator is proposing a novel or innovative process (for which there may not be published guidance) the regulator is likely to require details of the predicted environmental outcomes of the process. The following information is required as part of the application form:

a. Site condition report (information is required regarding any pollution risks posed by the site). The applicant will need to provide a detailed site plan showing the location of receptors, sources of emissions/releases, monitoring points, site drainage and site surfacing. The applicant may use any environmental impact assessment (EIA), prepared with regard to a linked planning application for the site, to help satisfy this requirement. Details relating to site condition will be used, at the time of site closure, for the purpose of comparing the relative condition of the site before and after the cessation of activities).

b. Details of the operator's competency; in particular the technical competency of the operator and whether he (or any other relevant person – see below) has committed of a relevant offence.

c. Assessment of environmental risks (as relevant) both under normal and abnormal operating conditions including any assumptions that the operator has made in conducting this risk assessment.

d. Details of the operator's finances and management systems.

e. A non-technical summary.

The Environment Agency, in an effort to secure quality applications, has produced guidelines for applicants on how to produce a 'good' application. This information is available on the Environment Agency's website. The core guidance makes it clear that the applicant can draw upon a range of other sources of information in support of their application such as an EIA (mentioned above) or documents relating to an installation's regulation under the Control of Major Accident Hazards (COMAH) Regulations[71] or any site reports prepared for town and country planning purposes. This is consistent with the aim of reducing unnecessary duplication of effort and reducing red tape.

---

69 A copy of the application form is available on the Environment Agency's website.
70 See below at 6.9.6.
71 The Control of Major Accident Hazards Regulations 1999 SI 1999/743.

6.9.5 Requests for further information

The regulator can request further information from the applicant if it considers it necessary in order to enable it to decide whether the proposal meets any requirements of relevant directives[72] and to determine what conditions to impose. In these circumstances the regulator may serve a notice[73] on the applicant requesting the further information within a reasonable period of time; if the applicant fails to supply the required information the regulator can serve a further notice stating that the application is deemed to have been withdrawn. The applicant would forefeit any fee paid if this happened.[74]

6.9.6 Fees

All applications for new permits, and applications to vary, transfer and surrender must be accompanied by the relevant fee. The regulations implement a charging scheme as a practical manifestation of the polluter pays principle and also contribute towards the regulator's costs in exercising their functions under the regulations. In addition the regulator can charge an annual subsistence fee to support the regulator's ongoing costs for monitoring and inspections. Where the Environment Agency is the regulator the provisions governing the charging scheme are in s 41 Environment Act 1995; where the local authority is the regulator, secondary legislation issued under s 65 EPR 2010 makes provision for charging.

Once the application is complete and the fee has been paid, it is regarded as being 'duly made'. Until such time as the application is duly made, the determination period does not start. Therefore if an applicant uses the incorrect form or does not provide sufficient information or the correct fee then the regulator's 'clock' does not start ticking. The core guidance requires regulators to use 'normal standards of reasonableness and common sense'[75] to assess whether applications are duly made.

6.9.7 Determination periods

The regulations prescribe various determination periods depending on the nature of the application. Where public participation is required the determination period is four months for the grant of a new environmental permit except for mobile plant and standard permits. (Although the time period for determining a standard permit for a Part A installation is four months.)

Application	Determination period
Grant of an EP (except mobile plant or standard facility)	4 months
Grant of Standard Permit for standard facility (except Part A installation)	3 months
Grant of EP for Mobile Plant	3 months
Surrender EP	3 months
Variation of EP (other than where public participation is required)	3 months
Variation of EP where public participation is required	4 months
Grant of EP for mining waste operation not involving a mining waste facility	3 months
Application to transfer an EP	2 months

---

72 See below at 6.12.3.
73 Environmental Permitting (England and Wales) Regulations 2010 SI 2010/675, Sched 5, para 4.
74 Environmental Permitting (England and Wales) Regulations 2010 SI 2010/675, Sched 5, para 4.
75 Defra (March 2012) Environmental Permitting Core guidance, Version 4.0, para 6.6.

The determination period may be extended by agreement between the regulator and the applicant/operator. In addition the period may need to be extended where there are questions relating to the inclusion of information on the public register or further information is required.

6.9.8 Notification of determination

The regulator must notify the applicant/operator of its decision and must also give reasons for making its decision.[76] In addition and consistent with the requirements of transparency and openness the decision must be published on the regulator's website. Applicants must be informed of their right of appeal.[77]

6.9.9 Duty to refuse

The regulator is under a duty to refuse a duly made application to grant a permit (or to transfer the whole or part of it) if it considers that the applicant is not the operator and also if it considers that the operator will not operate the facility in accordance with the environmental permit.[78] In addition the regulator reserves the right[79] to refuse an environmental permit application in other circumstances; for example if it believes the operator is not competent to operate the regulated facility in accordance with the permit; or if it considers the environmental risks to be unacceptable. If the regulator considers that the requirements of the relevant EU directives cannot be met, it will refuse the application.

6.9.10 'Call in' power

The Secretary of State has various powers under the EPR 2010. By reg 61 he may issue directions to a regulator either in general or in specific cases. For example he can issue directions about the use of specified powers or in relation to specific applications. The regulator must comply with any directions issued by the Secretary of State. The Secretary of State also has the power to 'call in' an environmental permit application for his own decision.[80] Where an application is called in, the Secretary of State cannot make the decision himself on the application but he directs the regulator as to whether it should grant or refuse the application. In the event that he directs that the application should be granted, he has the power to direct the conditions which are to be included in the permit. Before directing the regulator as to the outcome of the permit application, the Secretary of State will either hold a public inquiry or an informal hearing into the application.

6.10 Public consultation and participation in decision-making

Public consultation is central to the permitting process and the EPR 2010 provide for public participation not only in relation to applications for a permit but also in relation to the variation of an EP

---

76 Environmental Permitting (England and Wales) Regulations 2010 SI 2010/675, Pt1, Sched 5, para 17.
77 See below at 6.14.
78 Environmental Permitting (England and Wales) Regulations 2010 SI 2010/675, Sched 5, Pt 1, para 13.
79 I.e. has discretion.
80 Environmental Permitting (England and Wales) Regulations 2010 SI 2010/675, reg 62.

See Chapter 12 →

in certain circumstances. Environmental permitting is the type of environmental decision that falls within Art 6 of the Aarhus Convention[81] and as such is subject to the specific obligations of that article.[82]

In 2001 the EU adopted Directive 2001/35/EC,[83] which provided for public participation in respect of the drawing up of certain plans and programmes relating to the environment. This amended the IPPC Directive (96/61/EC) in order to bring it in line with Art 6 of the Aarhus Convention. The latter directive now requires Member States to ensure that the public concerned are given early and effective opportunities to participate in the decision-making procedure for granting permits. In addition, a new annex is introduced which sets out detailed provisions on public participation, including a requirement for competent authorities to inform the public of the contents of their decisions (a copy of the permit and any conditions) and of the grounds and considerations on which those decisions are based. The public participation requirements are implemented into the EPR 2010 in Sched 5. In contrast to the earlier PPC regime the EP regulations are far less prescriptive about the precise procedures for public consultation. However, reg 59 requires the Environment Agency to publish a public participation statement of its policies in respect of public participation.[84] This can be accessed via the Agency's website. The consultation process is administered by the regulator responsible for the relevant installation.

6.10.1 Which applications require public consultation?

The public consultation requirements in Sched 5 (Part 1) apply to:

- every application for the grant of an environmental permit;
- applications for standard facilities which are Part A installations;
- mining waste operations that involve a mining waste facility to which Art 7 of the Mining Waste Directive[85] applies.

The public consultation requirements also apply to the variation of an environmental permit if it would entail a substantial change[86] to the permit or if the regulator requires it. An environmental permit can be varied on application by the operator or at the initiative of the regulator (the latter is referred to as regulator-initiated variation).

The public participation requirements therefore do not apply to:

- applications for environmental permits for mobile plant;
- applications for certain radioactive substances activities involving the use of mobile radioactive apparatus for, inter alia, testing purposes;[87]
- applications for standard permits (except in relation to Part A installations);
- mining waste operations not involving a mining waste facility.

---

81 The United Nations Economic Commission for Europe (UNECE) Convention on Access to Information, Public Participation in Decision-Making and Access to Justice in Environmental Matters (1998).
82 See Chapter 12 for further discussion of public participation in environmental decision-making.
83 Directive 2003/35/EC of the European Parliament and the Council of 26 May 2003 providing for public participation in respect of the drawing up of certain plans and programmes relating to the environment and amending with regard to public participation and access to justice Council Directives 85/337/EC and 96/61/EC OJ L 156 25/06/2003, pp 17–25.
84 Environment Agency Environmental Permitting (England and Wales) Regulations 2010-Working Together-Your role in Environmental Permitting. Edition 2, February 2010.
85 Directive 2006/21/EC of the European Parliament and of the Council on the management of waste from extractive industries OJ L 114, 27/4/2006, pp 9–21.
86 Substantial change is defined in Sched 5, para 5 as the change in the operation of an installation which in the regulator's opinion may have significant negative effects on human beings or the environment.
87 Full definition in EPR 2010 Sched 23, Pt 2, para 11(5).

6.10.2 What is required?

If the public consultation requirements in Sched 5 apply, the regulator is under a duty to take the steps it considers appropriate to inform the public about the application (for grant or variation) and where and when they can inspect the public registers. Inspection of the registers is free of charge. The regulator must also invite the public consultees to make their representations and tell them where and by when they should make their representations. The period during which consultation takes place is called the consultation communication period and it commences as soon as the application is duly made to the regulatory body. The period lasts for 30 working days from the date that the application is duly made.[88]

Paragraph 11, Sched 5 provides that the regulator cannot make a determination on an application or a regulator initiated variation unless it has first taken into consideration any representations made by the public consultees or by any person who is required to consent to conditions affecting their land. Therefore the representations become a material consideration in the determination process.

In R (Edwards) v Environment Agency (No 2) (2008)[89] the House of Lords considered the public consultation requirements of the PPC Regulations 2000 and in particular the extent to which the regulations required information to be disclosed to the public. Edwards challenged a decision of the Environment Agency to grant a PPC permit to Rugby Ltd to burn shredded and chipped tyres as a substitute fuel in its cement kilns. The principal ground for challenge was that the Agency had not properly complied with the statutory or common law duties of consultation because it had failed to disclose a report on the potential impact of certain particulates emitted from the proposed installation into air. The report had been compiled by experts within the Agency and in consequence the public had been deprived of an opportunity to comment on this report. Edwards argued that the decision to grant the permit should be nullified because of the alleged procedural irregularity. The Court of Appeal[90] held that the failure to disclose the report was a breach of the common law duty of fairness, but the Court declined to quash the permit on the basis that there would be future opportunities to modify the permit in the light of actual emissions. The Law Lords concluded that the lower courts (and the Agency) had been right to exercise their discretion against quashing the permit on the ground of procedural unfairness. Directive 96/61 specified what information should be made available to the public and the Regulations effected and extended those requirements. However, it was not for the courts to impose a broader duty. On a pragmatic note the Lords held that if the Agency had to disclose its internal working documents for further public consultation, there was no reason why the consultation process should ever come to an end.

6.10.3 Who should be consulted?

Public consultation should be with the public consultees; these are persons who in the regulator's opinion are likely to be affected by, or have an interest in, the application (or variation).[91] The regulator will consult a range of statutory bodies as well as ensuring that the public have the opportunity to submit their representations. The statutory bodies consulted include Natural England, the respective local authorities, the Food Standards Agency, the Health & Safety Executive, Water UK and the Health Protection Agency. In addition to the statutory consultees, the Environment Agency and local authorities consult one another regarding Part A(1) and Part A(2) applications.

---

88 If there has been a determination that information should be withheld from the public register on the grounds of national security or confidentiality then the 30 days runs from the date of the determination—see Public Registers below.
89 R (Edwards) v Environment Agency (No 2) [2008] UKHL 22; [2008] 1 WLR 1587; [2009] 1 All ER 57; [2008] Env LR 34; [2008] JPL 1278.
90 Edwards v Environment Agency (No 2) [2006] EWCA Civ 877; [2007] Env LR 9; [2007] JPL 82 [2007].
91 Environmental Permitting (England and Wales) Regulations 2010 SI 2010/675 Sched 5, para 1.

In some circumstances the regulator may be proposing to include a condition in an environmental permit which requires the operator to carry out works or do things which the permit holder is not entitled to do without the consent of others.[92] For example an environmental permit may require monitoring on land which the operator does not own. Where such a condition is incorporated into the permit the owner or occupier of the land must give consent to the operator to enable him to comply with the condition.[93] The person whose consent is required has a right to be consulted about the proposed condition and accordingly the regulator is required to serve notice on any person who is the owner, lessee or occupier of the land,[94] notifying him of the condition and what works or things are required to be carried out on their land. The person must be given at least 20 days to make any representation in respect of these proposed conditions. If the regulator considers that the application (or regulator-initiated variation) is likely to have significant effects on the environment of another Member State (or if another Member State requests the information), the regulator must enter into bilateral consultations with that Member State. The operator or applicant must be informed where this happens.

6.11 Applications to vary, transfer or surrender an environmental permit

6.11.1 Application to vary an EP

Once an operator has an environmental permit he must ensure that he complies with all of the conditions of the permit. If the operator proposes making any changes to the operation of the regulated facility which would result in a breach of the permit conditions, he will need to apply to the regulator to vary the terms of the permit.[95] Alternatively the regulator may, of its own initiative, vary the permit. Where the proposal involves a 'substantial change' to the permit the public participation requirements discussed above will apply. However, the regulator may decide that public participation is required even if the changes do not amount to a substantial change.[96] A variation application may include an increase to the extent of the site over which the regulated facility operates. However, a variation cannot reduce the extent of the site covered by the environmental permit if the permit requires consideration of the condition of the land. Where the permit relates to or is for stand-alone water discharge activity the regulator cannot vary the terms of the permit that relates to the water discharge for a period of four years after the grant (unless the operator agrees).

6.11.2 Application to transfer an EP

Regulation 21 enables an operator to transfer an existing permit either totally or partially to another operator. A joint application by the existing and proposed operator is necessary specifying the date on which the transfer is required to take effect. The regulator may only reject the application if it considers that the proposed operator would not be able to comply with the permit conditions. If the regulator agrees to the transfer it will issue a new environmental permit.

---

92 Reg 15 makes provision for the imposition of such conditions.
93 And is entitled to compensation under the Environmental Permitting (England and Wales) Regulations 2010 SI 2010/675 Part 2, Sched 5.
94 Ibid Sched 5, para 9.
95 Ibid reg 20.
96 It should be noted that the permit may also be varied at the initiation of the regulator. This is discussed below at 6.13.4.

6.11.3 Application to surrender an EP

The provisions relating to the surrender of an environmental permit are contained in regs 24 and 25 of the EPR 2010 and are very similar to the provisions previously contained in s 39 EPA 1990 in relation to the surrender of waste management licences. The regulator must accept the application to surrender the EP if it is satisfied that the necessary measures have been the taken to avoid a pollution risk resulting from the operation of the regulated facility and to return the site of the regulated facility to a satisfactory state, having regard to the state of the site before the facility was put into operation.[97] Therefore the operator applying for the surrender of an EP will need to supply the regulator with a site report specifying the present condition of the site and any changes which have occurred since the permit was originally granted; and also details of the precautionary steps taken to avoid pollution and any remedial action taken to return the installation to a satisfactory state. The regulator must be satisfied that the installation does not pose any pollution risk before it can accept the surrender. The onus falls squarely on the permit holder to provide the regulator with sufficient information which will convince the regulator that the installation is in a satisfactory condition, poses no risk of pollution and therefore the regulator can safely accept the surrender. The permit holder is presumed to be responsible for any material difference in the condition of the installation as revealed in the pre-permit report and the present condition of the installation.

The requirement to apply for the surrender of an EP is relaxed in relation to the surrender of certain environmental permits whose operation does not affect land. In this respect it is sufficient that the operator 'notifies' the regulator that he is surrendering the permit. This can only apply for a mobile plant, Part B installation (except to the extent that it relates to a waste operation) or certain small non-hazardous waste incineration.[98] The reason why notification is permitted in relation to Part B installations is that they only relate to emissions into the air and there is therefore no requirement to consider the condition of the land prior to the surrender.

In addition to the statutory consultees, the Environment Agency and local authorities consult one another regarding Part A(1) and Part A(2) surrender applications.

6.12 Setting permit conditions and ensuring compliance with the IPPC Directive

6.12.1 Setting permit conditions

The regulator can attach any conditions it sees fit, however, it has an overriding duty to attach certain conditions in order to secure the specific objectives that apply to certain categories of regulated facility. The guidance emphasises that all permit conditions must be both 'necessary' and enforceable. The permit must contain certain information.[99] Conditions must state their objective, standard or desired outcome so that the operator can understand what is required of him. The permit must also identify the operator and the site, by reference to a map or plan. It may be in an electronic form.

6.12.2 Standard permit conditions

The applicant can elect to apply for a standard permit; if the operator does this then they will need to be aware of the standard rules governing the type of facility. The regulator will make the standard rules available and the applicant will need to decide whether their activity falls within the scope of

---

97 The Environmental Permitting (England and Wales) Regulations 2010 SI 2010/675 Pt 1, Sched 5, para 14.
98 Specifically any part of an EP which relates to an activity falling within Pt A(2) of s 5.1 of Pt 2 of Sched 1.
99 The Environmental Permitting (England and Wales) Regulations 2010 SI 2010/675 reg 14.

the standard rules and whether they have suitable control measures to comply with those standard rules. If the regulatory body is satisfied that the applicant can comply with the standard rules it will issue a standard permit which states that the standard rules are the conditions of the permit. Standard permits are not available for any regulated facility that requires a location specific assessment of environmental impact and risk.[100]

6.12.3 Ensuring compliance with EU directives

The decision to grant an application for a permit or refuse it will be taken by the regulator on the basis of the information submitted by the applicant, the representations made by consultees and the public, and the matters specified in the EPR 2010. However, a fundamental consideration for the regulator is that it must ensure that its determination delivers the requirements of the relevant EU directives and provides the required level of protection to the environment. Although the environmental permitting regime establishes a single permitting system this masks the fact that the aim of the regime is to deliver the requirements of a number of key EU directives, which include:

● the IPPC Directive 2008/1/EC (the codified IPPC Directive);[101]
● the Waste Framework Directive 2008/98/EC;[102]
● the Landfill Directive 1999/31/EC;[103]
● the End of Life Vehicles Directive 2000/53/EC;[104]
● the Batteries Directive 2006/66/EC;[105]
● the Mining Waste Directive 2006/21/EC;[106]
● the Waste Incineration Directive 2000/76/EC;[107]
● the Waste Electrical and Electronic Equipment Directive 2012/91/EU;[108]
● the Solvents Emission Directive 1999/13/EC;[109]
● the Large Combustion Plants Directive 2001/80/EC;[110]
● the Groundwater Directive 2006/118/EEC.

The various schedules to the the regulations identify very detailed and precise requirements of how these directives must be delivered through the permitting system. When regulators exercise their functions under the EPR 2010 they are under a duty to achieve the objectives of these directives. This means that if a regulated facility is subject to more than one directive, the permitting system

---

100 Note public consultation is not required for standard permit applications unless they are for a Part A installation.
101 Directive 2008/1/EC of the European Parliament and of the Council of 15 January 2008 concerning integrated pollution prevention and control (Codified version) OJ L 24, 29/1/2008.
102 Directive 2008/98/EC of the European Parliament and of the Council of 19 November 2008 on waste and repealing certain Directives OJ L312, 22/11/2008.
103 Council Directive 1999/31/EC of 26 April 1999 on the landfill of waste, OJ L 182, 16/7/1999, pp 1–19 as amended.
104 Directive 2000/53/EC of the European Parliament and of the Council of 18 September 2000 on end-of-life vehicles OJ L 269, 21/10/2000, pp 34–43 as amended.
105 Directive 2006/66/EC of the European Parliament and of the Council of 6 September 2006 on batteries and accumulators and waste batteries and accumulators and repealing Directive 91/157/EEC OJ L 266, 26/9/2006, pp 1–14 as amended.
106 Repealed from 7 January 2014 by Directive 2010/75/EU.
107 Directive 2010/75/EU of the European Parliament and of the Council of 24 November 2010 on industrial emissions (integrated pollution prevention and control) OJ L 334, 17/12/2010, pp 17–119.
108 Directive 2012/19/EU of the European Parliament and of the Council of 4 July 2012 on waste electrical and electronic equipment (WEEE) OJ L 197, 24/7/2012, pp 38–75.
109 Council Directive 1999/13/EC of 11 March 1999 on the limitation of emissions of volatile organic compounds due to the use of organic solvents in certain activities and installations OJ L 85, 29/3/1999, pp 1–22 as amended. Repealed from 2014 by Directive 2010/75/EU.
110 Directive 2001/80/EC of the European Parliament and of the Council of 23 October 2001 on the limitation of emissions of certain pollutants into the air from large combustion plants OJ L 309, 27/11/2001, pp 1–21. Repealed from 2014 by Directive 2010/75/EU.

requires the objectives of the various directives to be delivered through a single permit. For example, a waste incinerator must meet the requirements of the IPPC, Waste Incineration and Waste Framework Directives. Some Part A installations may, as well as being subject to the IPPC directive, also be subject to the requirements of the Asbestos or Titanium Dioxide directive. Some of the waste directives have been considered in Chapter 5 on waste; it is not the intention of this chapter to re-examine these. Instead the following section will focus specifically on the requirements of the IPPC Directive and the impact this directive has on regulators when they consider applications for regulated facilities falling within the scope of the directive.

6.12.4 Compliance with the IPPC Directive

Schedule 7 requires regulators to exercise their functions to achieve the requirements of the IPPC directive. At a general level this includes achieving the purposes set out in Art 1 of the directive, namely to achieve a high level of protection of the environment taken as a whole by, in particular preventing, or where that is not practicable, reducing emissions into the air, water and land. The provisions of the directive which regulators must secure through the permitting regime include a number of general principles (see immediately below), best available techniques and environmental quality standards and EU emission limit values.

6.12.5 Securing general principles

The general principles of the IPPC directive are listed in Art 3 of the directive. They are:

- All the appropriate preventive measures are taken against pollution, in particular through the application of BAT.
- No significant pollution is caused.
- Waste production is avoided in accordance with the Waste Framework Directive 2008/98/EC.[111]
- Energy is used efficiently.
- The necessary measures are taken to prevent accidents and limit their consequences.
- On cessation of the activities, the necessary measures are taken to restore the site to a satisfactory state and avoid any pollution risk.

These general principals should be reflected in the permit via detailed conditions.

6.12.6 The requirement to use the best available techniques (BAT)

Very specifically the directive requires regulators to ensure that installations are operated in such a way that no significant pollution is caused and also that all appropriate preventive measures are taken against pollution through the application of the best available techniques. This requirement is detailed in Sched 7 of the EPR 2010.

6.12.7 The meaning of BAT

Article 2 of the IPPC Directive defines BAT as 'the most effective and advanced stage in the development of activities and their methods of operation which indicates the practical suitability of

---

111 Directive 2008/98/EC of the European Parliament and of the Council of 19 November 2008 on waste and repealing certain directives OJ L312, 22/11/2008.

particular techniques for providing in principle the basis for Emission Limit Values (ELVs) designed to prevent and, where that is not practicable, generally to reduce emissions and the impact of the environment as a whole'. Schedule 7 of the EPR 2010 imports this definition into the regulations. Essentially, determining what constitutes BAT involves comparing the techniques that prevent or reduce emissions and identifying the best in terms of their impact on the environment. Clearly BAT will differ according to the industry to which it applies; however, each sector will generally be using similar techniques. The European Commission has published guidance on what constitutes BAT for some 30 industrial sectors in the form of BAT Reference Documents (BREFs).[112] These do not constitute absolute and binding standards but the Environment Agency and local authorities should take them into account when framing their BAT conditions in a permit. In addition, the Environment Agency has produced technical guidance for individual sectors (which draw upon the information contained in the BREFs). The guidance that has been issued contains indicative standards for both new and existing installations and they also provide timetables for upgrading existing installations. When an operator submits an application it should consider the relevant guidance note. If the operator wishes to deviate from the industry norm it will have to justify its reasons and explain why alternative standards are BAT-compliant. However, it should be noted that the basic principles for determining BAT should be the same irrespective of whether BAT are indicated in published guidance or are assessed uniquely for a single installation.

Although guidance exists in relation to BAT, regulators will still need to make a site-specific assessment of what constitutes BAT having particular regard to the location in which the regulated facility operates (or proposes to operate). Therefore when assessing BAT the regulator will need to consider local factors such as the proximity to controlled water and the sensitivity of environmental receptors.

6.12.7.1 Best

This term refers to the effectiveness of any technique to be employed by an applicant to achieve a high level of environmental protection. This will require considering the various options available and assessing their relative environmental effects (including direct and indirect effects). In assessing the environmental effects the regulator should have regard to the various factors listed in Annex IV of the IPPC Directive and should then rank techniques according to their overall effects. The factors listed in Annex IV include:

- the use of low waste technology;
- the use of less hazardous substances;
- furthering the recovery and recycling of waste and also substances used in and generated by the process;
- comparable processes, facilities or methods, technological advances and changes in scientific knowledge;
- the nature, effects and volume of emissions;
- the consumption and nature of raw materials used and energy efficiency; and
- the need to prevent accidents.

There may be several techniques which could be employed to achieve the requisite level of environmental protection and in such circumstances they will all satisfy the 'best' criterion. Where there is a choice the technique that is best overall will be BAT unless is not an available technique.

---

112 These are available online from the European IPPC Bureau's website at http://eippcb.jrc.es/reference/.

6.12.7.2 Available

This term refers to the availability of techniques. In order for techniques to be available they do not need to be in general use. Techniques may be available if they have been developed as proven as a pilot provided that the industry could confidently use them. Two issues are material to the question of whether a specific technique is available: (a) what is the balance of costs and advantages, and (b) can the operator obtain the technique. In relation to (a) a technique may be rejected as BAT if its costs would far outweigh its environmental benefits.

6.12.7.3 Techniques

This term is wider than 'technology' and includes considerations such as the design, construction, maintenance and decommissioning of the relevant technique. This is why it is particularly important that where an applicant is seeking approval for a new regulated facility it applies early in the planning stage and before any construction has started.

The use of BAT, combined with a consideration of the installation and its location, provides the basis for setting emission limit values (ELVs) and other permit conditions.

In contrast to BATNEEC in the system of IPC,[113] BAT does not itself include any reference to cost/benefit considerations in determining the techniques which fulfil the BAT test. Nevertheless, cost/benefit considerations are relevant because of the applicability of the EU proportionality principle. Under the BATNEEC test, not only were the costs and benefits of a particular technique taken into account, but also the capacity of each industry sector to buy in the relevant technique. BAT differs from BATNEEC with regard to the materiality of the economic viability of an industry sector as a relevant consideration. Once the various options have been ranked in terms of environmental effectiveness the overall best should be selected unless economic considerations render it unavailable. Therefore cost is a relevant consideration and the cost assessment should include both operating costs as well as capital costs and also any cost savings. For example, using a purer raw material may be more expensive at first but save money overall by improving quality or producing less waste. However, considerations about profitability are irrelevant and should not be taken into account.

6.12.8 Emission limit values (ELVs) and environmental quality standards

The best available techniques are used to achieve a high level of environmental protection and provide the basis for setting ELVs. Article 9(3) of the IPPC Directive requires that the permit must include emission limit values for polluting substances[114] likely to be emitted from the installation in significant quantities. However, this must be read in conjunction with Art 10 of the directive, which states that where an environmental quality standard requires stricter conditions than those achievable by the use of BAT the permit must contain additional measures to comply with the environmental quality standard.

Environmental quality standards are prescribed in EU legislation; an EQS is a numerical standard that specifies maximum concentrations of specific pollutants released into either air or water. In addition there are some national EQS which are sometimes stricter than those prescribed in EU directives.[115] Although these are non-binding in the context of the EP Regulations 2007 they should still be taken into account by the regulator when setting ELVs. The starting point for the regulator when determining permit conditions is to consider

See Chapter 8

---

113 See above at 6.3.2 for discussion of BATNEEC.
114 In particular those listed in Annex 3; Directive 2008/1/EC of the European Parliament and of the Council of 15 January 2008 concerning integrated pollution prevention and control (Codified version) OJ L 24, 29/1/2008.
115 E.g. some air quality standards have been set as part of the national air quality strategy.

whether any EQS may be breached. If the answer is yes, then the regulator will need to specify an ELV to avoid breach of the EQS.

6.13 Enforcement powers

6.13.1 Administrative enforcement powers

The Environment Agency and local authorities have an extensive array of enforcement powers at their disposal to ensure that the permit holder complies with the terms of its permit. These powers enable the regulators to retain tight control over authorised activities without having to resort to prosecution as a control mechanism.

The regulator is required by reg 34 to periodically review environmental permits and also to make 'appropriate periodic inspections' of regulated facilities. The regulations do not stipulate when the reviews should be undertaken. The regulator is required to take any steps which are necessary to ensure that the permit holder complies with the conditions attached to its permit. How the regulator chooses to secure compliance with permit conditions is a matter for regulatory discretion. The following administrative powers are the most significant.

6.13.2 Revocation notice (RN)

The regulator may revoke all or part of the activities authorised by the permit via service of an RN.[116] If it revokes part of the permit it may also vary the remaining part of the permit to the extent that it considers necessary. The effect of an RN is that the permit ceases to have effect from the date specified in the RN. As the service of an RN is a rather heavyweight enforcement option, it is only likely to be used in the face of persistent non-compliance. An appeal against an RN suspends the operation of the notice pending the outcome of the appeal hearing. Where a regulator issues an RN it can still require the operator to take steps to avoid a pollution risk resulting from the operation of the regulated facility and to return the site of the regulated facility to a satisfactory state having regard to the state of the site before the facility was put into operation.[117] If this happens the environmental permit continues to have effect but only to the extent that it requires the steps to be taken.

6.13.3 Enforcement notice (EN)

The regulator may serve an EN on a permit holder if the regulator believes that the permit holder has breached, or is likely to breach, any permit condition.[118] An EN will specify the breach, the remedial action required and the timescale during which the remedial action must be completed. Failure to comply with an EN is a criminal offence.[119]

6.13.4 Suspension notice (SN)

Under the EPRs 2007 the regulator was under a duty to serve an SN if it considered that the operation of an installation involved an imminent risk of serious pollution.[120] The duty was absolute irrespective of whether permit conditions have been observed. However, the corresponding

---

116 Environmental Permitting (England and Wales) Regulations 2010 SI 2010/675, reg 22.
117 Ibid, reg 23.
118 Ibid, reg 36.
119 Ibid, reg 38.
120 Environmental Permitting Regulations, 2007/3538 reg 37.

provisions of the EPR 2010[121] confer discretion on the regulator to serve a suspension notice under the same conditions. The SN must specify what steps must be taken to remove that risk and it may be used to suspend all or part of the permitted activities. In *R (on the application of European Metal Recycling Ltd) v Environment Agency (2012)*[122] the Environment Agency served a suspension notice on the company following complaints from local residents about the noise from the company's metal disposal and reclamation yard. The Agency had concluded that the company's activities involved a serious risk of pollution by noise and the SN required the design and implementation of measures to eliminate the risk by a specified date. In a judicial review action against the Agency's decision to serve the SN the company argued that there was no basis for the Agency to conclude that there was serious risk of pollution by noise; however, the court held that the Agency's decision could only be challenged if it was irrational (and on the facts it was not irrational).

Under reg 37(4) the SN must specify what steps are required to be taken to eliminate the risk. In the *European Metal Recycling* case, referred to above, the company argued the SN was flawed because it did not specify what steps it had to take to eliminate the risk. The court held that as a matter of statutory interpretation the requirement that the regulator states the steps to be required to eliminate the risk could not sensibly be said to be satisfied by a requirement to design and implement measures to eliminate that risk. The SN was quashed. The Agency was not entitled to require the elimination of risk of serious pollution without identifying the steps by which that was to be achieved. Therefore an SN must identify either the outcomes or criteria that are to be achieved by whatever means the recipient chose to adopt or must identify the specific steps that are required. Contrast this requirement with the situation regarding abatement notices under s 80 Environmental Protection Act—see in particular the decision in *R v Falmouth and Truro Port HA ex p South West Water Ltd (2001)*.[123]

See Chapter 9

6.13.5 Variation notice (VN)

It has already been mentioned that an operator may apply to vary the terms of a permit and also that the regulator may vary the permit on its own initiative. Where the regulator decides to do this it will serve a VN and may require the operator to pay a fee. It will consult with the operator. The VN power enables the regulator to tighten permit conditions in response to changes in circumstances, such as changes in industry sector BAT, or the emergence of new environmental risks. The provisions on variation notices are in EPR 2010 reg 20.

6.13.6 Powers to acquire information

Regulation 60(1) gives the regulator the power to serve a notice on any person requiring him or her to provide the information specified within the notice and by the deadline also specified in it. This provision is widely stated, in that the regulator can serve such a notice on 'any person'. The notice may require the person to provide any information on emissions where that requirement is reasonable and this applies even if that information is not in that person's possession and would not normally come into that person's possession. It is a criminal offence not to comply with such a

121 Environmental Permitting Regulations 2010/675 reg 37.
122 *R (on the application of European Metal Recycling Ltd) v Environment Agency* [2012] EWHC 2361 (Admin).
123 *R v Falmouth and Truro Port HA ex p South West Water Ltd* [2001] QB 445.

notice without reasonable excuse. Regulation 60 empowers the Secretary of State to serve a notice on a regulator requiring the regulator to supply him with the information he requires.

6.14 Appeals and public registers

6.14.1 Appeals

Appeals are dealt with in EPR 2010 regs 79 and 82 and further in regs 96–99. In addition Sched 6 lays down the procedures governing appeals. A permit holder has a right of appeal to the Secretary of State against the following:

(a) the service of an RN, VN, EN or SN;
(b) a refusal to grant or a refusal to vary or surrender a permit (refusals include deemed refusals);
(c) the permit conditions;
(d) the regulator's decision that information relating to the permit is not commercially confidential and should be included on the public register.

To exercise the right of appeal the appellant must notify the Secretary of State in writing and must also give notice to the relevant regulator. The Schedule specifies what documents are required in support of the application to appeal. This must include with it a statement indicating whether the appellant wishes the appeal to be in the form of a hearing or dealt with by way of written representations.

Appeals must generally be lodged within six months of the regulatory decision but they do vary and care needs to be taken by operators with regard to this. For example, the time limits vary depending on what is being appealed. Appeals against revocation notices must be made before the revocation takes effect and appeals against enforcement notices and suspension notices must be made within two months. Only in the case of RN appeals is the operation of the notice suspended provided the appeal is lodged in time. Appeals may be heard by way of a full hearing or written representations (that is, a paper-based appeal) and the Secretary of State has the power to order that an appeal proceed by way of a full hearing, in public, irrespective of the wishes of the applicant. On determining an appeal, the Secretary of State may, inter alia, either affirm the decision of the regulator, direct the regulator to grant or vary the conditions or quash all or any of the conditions.

Although appeals are to the Secretary of State he or she may appoint the Planning Inspector to deal with appeals. Appeals may be conducted by written representations, or through a hearing or inquiry under the control of the Secretary of State.

6.14.2 Public registers

Part 5 of the EPR 2010 makes provision for a public register of information in much the same way as previous regimes included public register provisions. The public registers should be viewed in the broader context of the much greater commitment that exists today in relation to access to information. In particular the entry into force of the Freedom of Information Act 2000 and the Environmental Information Regulations (EIR) 2004[124] make it much easier for the public to access information held by public authorities. The regulator is under a duty[125] to maintain a public register containing the information prescribed in Sched 19 of the regulations. However, this is subject to

---

124 Environmental Information Regulations 2004 SI 2004/3391.
125 Environmental Permitting (England and Wales) Regulations 2010 SI 2010/675, reg 46.

various limitations. The register cannot contain anything which relates to criminal proceedings or anything which is the subject matter of pending criminal proceedings. Information may be excluded from the register if it affects national security[126] or on the basis that it is confidential (defined as commercially or industrially confidential).[127]

During the public consultation exercise the regulator is prohibited from telling the public consultees about any information that has been excluded on the grounds of national security unless the Secretary of State requires it to do so. Similarly some of the public consultees must not be told if any information has been withheld on the grounds of confidentiality unless the public consulted is a public authority and requires this information in order to undertake its functions.

6.15 Criminal law enforcement

6.15.1 Offences, personal liability and defences

In common with other Command and Control licence-based regulatory regimes, the environmental permitting regime is underpinned by a number of criminal offences.[128] These offences are not expected to be used frequently given the extensive range of administrative enforcement powers available to regulators.

Amongst the criminal offences listed in reg 38, it is a criminal offence to:

(a)   cause or knowingly cause or knowingly permit the operation of a regulated facility without an environmental permit;

(b)   fail to comply with or breach an environmental permit condition;

(c)   fail to give notice of a change in the operation of that installation;

(c)   fail to comply with an EN or SN;

(d)   fail without reasonable excuse to provide the information required by the register under reg 60(2);

(e)   knowingly or recklessly make a false or misleading statement in purported compliance with the requirement to provide information under the regulations or as part of the process of making an application in respect of an environmental permit;

(f)   intentionally make false entries in a record required to be kept under an environmental permit condition;

(g)   with intent to deceive to forge or use a document issued or authorised to be issued or required for any purpose under an environmental permit condition, or to make or have in his possession a document so closely resembling such a document as to be likely to deceive.

Regulation 38 also lists further offences in respect of exempt waste operations.

If an offence committed by a person under the EPR is due to the act or default of some other person, that other person is also guilty of the offence and liable to be proceeded against and punished accordingly.[129] In addition the regulations also provide for the personal liability of 'officers' of a company. Regulation 41 states that if an offence committed by a body corporate is shown to have been committed with the consent or connivance of an officer, or to be attributable to any neglect on his part, the officer as well as the body corporate is guilty of the offence and liable to be proceeded against and punished accordingly. The term 'officer' in relation to a body corporate

---

126 Ibid, reg 47.
127 Ibid, reg 48.
128 Ibid, reg 38.
129 Ibid, reg 38(3).

is defined as meaning a director, member of the committee of management, chief executive, manager, secretary or other similar officer of the body, or a person purporting to act in any such capacity. The regulations also make provision if the affairs of a body corporate are managed by its members; in which case personal liability (under the same circumstances) can attach to the acts and defaults of a member in connection with his functions of management as if he were a director of the body. This regulation makes it plain that the regulator can proceed against both the company and the individual in such circumstances and both shall be punished accordingly.

The Regulations[130] provide the emergency defence but only in relation to the offences listed in (a) (b) and (c) above. The defence can be used if the person charged can prove that the acts alleged to constitute the contravention were done in an emergency in order to avoid danger to human health in a case and the defendant took all such steps as were reasonably practicable in the circumstances for minimising pollution; and also particulars of the acts were furnished to the regulator as soon as reasonably practicable after they were done.

See Chapter 4 →

6.15.2 Penalties[131]

All offences may be summarily tried in the magistrates' court or on indictment in the Crown Court. The penalties vary depending upon the offence; however, in relation to the offences (a), (b) and (c) listed above, the maximum penalty in the magistrates' court is a fine of up to £50,000 or to imprisonment for up to 12 months or both. The maximum penalty in the Crown Court is an unlimited fine and/or a prison sentence of up to five years. For the offences listed in (d), (e), (f) or (g) above the penalties in the magistrates' court are limited to a fine not exceeding the statutory maximum; or in the Crown Court to an unlimited fine or a prison sentence of up to two years, or both. As the *Hinchliffe* case below demonstrates, the courts are willing to impose custodial sentences where the defendant has shown a flagrant disregard for the regulatory controls. Moreover the courts will take into account a range of factors in deciding what is an appropriate sentence including the financial advantages gained by a defendant by operating in breach of the law.

Law in Action

In April 2009 Envirosol Ltd, a hazardous waste company, was convicted of breaching its environmental permit. The breaches of the EP were identified during inspections by Environment Agency inspectors during late 2007. The breaches were of a significant and potentially dangerous nature, including incorrect storage of incompatible hazardous wastes which could cause fire or explosion and also the release of toxic gases. Further inspection in January 2008 revealed that the company was still not complying with permit conditions. The case is interesting because the Environment Agency served a suspension notice prohibiting receipt of further wastes until the issues were resolved. The company pleaded guilty to three charges in relation to breaches of their environmental permit; they were fined £12,000 for each offence and ordered to pay costs of over £9,000.[132]

---

130 Ibid, reg 40.
131 Ibid, reg 39.
132 Environment Agency, April 2009, 'Company fined for dangerous storage of hazardous waste'. Available at http://www.environment-agency.gov.uk/news/106949.aspx?page=2&month=4&year=2009.

> **Law in Action**
>
> *R v Hinchliffe* (2012)[133]
>
> H was in day-to-day control of a company called Forge Plant Limited that had three waste disposal sites. Only one of the sites had an environmental permit. H's son (N), who was the company director, was mainly located at the site that had the permit. In 2012 H pleaded guilty to three offences under the environmental permitting regime: (1) failure to comply with the conditions of the environmental permit by exceeding the levels of waste stored; (2) knowingly operating a regulated facility allowing controlled waste to be stored, when that facility was not authorised by an environmental permit; and (3) failing to comply with a reg 36 notice requiring him to take steps to reduce the waste on site. The Environment Agency's officers estimated that H and the company had saved about £36,000 by way of avoided permits and associated fees and at £65 per ton it would have cost the business £1,350,000 to dispose of the 20,772 tonnes of waste that were collected but not accounted for in the disposals. The Crown Court in Leeds imposed a custodial sentence of two years' imprisonment concurrent on all four counts. H appealed unsuccessfully against the sentence. The Court of Appeal had no hesitation in concluding that the case called for a sentence of immediate custody. There was a flagrant, deliberate and sustained disregard of the regulations, in spite of the issue of notices and the intervention of the environment officers. This went on for the best part of two years, from about mid-2008 to about mid-2010. H had not made any attempt whatever to comply with the terms of his permit and he continued to store waste unlawfully at the other unlicensed sites in spite of being told that it was not permitted.
>
> The Court of Appeal also drew the 'inescapable inference' that H must have concluded that the risk of the sanctions was outweighed by the financial advantages of continuing to operate in breach of the law. Finally the Court stated that it was not over-impressed by the argument presented in mitigation that H's son had cleaned up the sites at his own expense. In the Court's view it would have been an aggravating feature if this had not been done, and did little to mitigate against the fact that there had been such persistent breaches of the law,

6.15.3 Injunctions

If the regulator considers that proceedings against a person for an offence under reg 38(3) would afford an ineffectual remedy against the person, the regulator may apply to the High Court for an injunction under EPR 2010 reg 42 for the purposes of securing compliance with an EN or SN.

6.15.4 Remedial powers

Both the regulator and the courts have powers in relation to the remediation of environmental damage. Under reg 23 if the regulator has revoked a permit (under reg 22) it can require the operator to take steps to avoid a pollution risk resulting from the operation of the regulated facility; or to return the site of the regulated facility to a satisfactory state, having regard to the state of the site before the facility was put into operation. Under reg 57, if the regulator considers that the operation of a regulated facility under an environmental permit involves a risk of serious pollution, it may arrange for steps to be taken to remove that risk. Similarly the regulator may take steps to

---

133 R v Hinchliffe [2012] EWCA Crim 1691.

remedy the effects of the pollution caused when an operator has operated without an environmental permit, has operated in contravention of the permit conditions or has failed to comply with an EN or SN. Where the regulator does this, it must give the operator five working days' notice of this intention and it may recover the costs of taking those steps from the operator concerned. However, in circumstances where the regulator is of the opinion that the operation of a regulated facility, or the way in which it is being operated, involves an imminent risk of serious pollution, the regulator can arrange for immediate steps to be taken to remove that risk and there is no need for the five-day notification. Again, the regulator can seek to recover its costs except where the operator can prove that there was no imminent risk of serious pollution. In relation to either of these situations, it appears from the wording of the regulation that the operator is not required to pay any costs which have been caused 'unnecessarily' by the regulator.

In circumstances where a person has been convicted for operating without an environmental permit, for contravening the permit conditions or for failure to comply with an EN or SN, then the courts also have the power to make an order requiring that any environmental damage resulting from the offence be remedied by the defendant.[134] The court may do this either as an alternative or in addition to imposing any fine/custodial sentence. This regulation applies where a person is convicted of an offence under reg 38(1)(a), (b) or (c) in respect of a matter which appears to the court to be a matter which it is in his power to remedy.

6.16 The interface of IPPC with other regulatory controls

There are a number of other regulatory regimes whose remits overlap with the environmental permitting regime. The more important of these regulatory controls are referred to below.

6.16.1 Part 2A EPA 1990 (contaminated land)

Site contamination which precedes environmental permit control may be dealt with under the contaminated land regime found in Part 2A EPA 1990. However, s 78YB EPA 1990 states that the provisions of Part 2A cannot be used to remediate contaminated land if the contamination is attributable to the operation of a regulated facility and enforcement action (under regs 36, 37 or 42 EPR 2010) can be taken. The standard of clean-up required under the environmental permitting regime[135] is higher than the standard required under the contaminated land regime. This has ramifications for an applicant who wishes to apply for an environmental permit. An applicant who fails to identify any pre-existing site contamination before commencement of a regulated facility will almost certainly be required to clean up all contamination discovered irrespective of whether the contamination relates to the permit holders' activities or not.

See Chapter 7 →

6.16.2 The Environmental Damage (Prevention and Remediation) Regulations 2009

The Environmental Damage (Prevention and Remediation) Regulations 2009 impose strict liability in respect of environmental damage caused by operators of those activities listed in Annex III of Environmental Liability Directive (ELD) 2004/35/EC[136] (and Sched 2 of the 2009 domestic

---

134 Environmental Permitting (England and Wales) Regulations 2010 SI 2010/675, reg 44.
135 To accord with the condition of the site before commencement of the activities authorised in an environmental permit.
136 Directive 2004/35/EC of the European Parliament and of the Council of 21 April 2004 on environmental liability with regard to the prevention and remedying of environmental damage OJ L 143, 30/4/2004, pp 56–75.

regulations). These are described by reference to various pieces of EU legislation and are referred to in the directive as 'occupational' activities. These include all those activities that require an environmental permit under the Integrated Pollution and Prevention Control Directive[137] including waste management activities. The remedial provisions contained in regs 23, 36, 37 and 57 (see above) enable the Environment Agency and local authorities to take the necessary steps to achieve prevention requirements of the ELD. For example, under reg 23 EPR 2010 the operator may be required to avoid a pollution risk resulting from the operation of the regulated facility and under reg 37 a suspension notice must specify the steps that are required to remove the risk of serious pollution. With regard to remediation if the operation of a regulated facility under an environmental permit involves a risk of serious pollution, the regulator may arrange for steps to be taken to remove that risk (reg 57(1)).

6.16.3 Greenhouse gas emission trading

The EPR 2010 enable the regulators to control emissions of carbon dioxide from any of the activities listed in Sched 1 of the EPR 2010.

6.16.4 The town and country planning system

Planning Policy Statement 23 outlines the government's advice regarding the relationship between the planning and pollution control regimes.[138] It states that the planning and pollution control systems are separate but complementary. Pollution control is concerned with preventing pollution through the use of measures to prohibit or limit the release of substances to the environment from different sources to the lowest practicable level whereas the planning system controls the development and use of land in the public interest. Planning plays an important role in determining the location of development which may give rise to pollution and should focus on whether the development itself is an acceptable use of the land, and the impacts of those uses, rather than the control of processes or emissions themselves.

In practice planning and environmental permitting controls may overlap with regard to the type of conditions which are appropriate to impose in both planning permissions and environmental permits. How far 'land use' considerations extend into and overlap with the environmental permitting (and hence IPPC) regimes will depend upon the circumstances of each case and it is therefore difficult to indicate with any degree of certainty where planning regulation ends and environmental permitting begins. However, it is clear that a decision-maker in the planning system cannot refuse to have regard to the polluting impacts of a proposed development when determining a planning application. The relationship between the town and country planning regime and the Pollution Prevention Control regime was considered in *Harrison v The Secretary of State for Communities and Local Government, Cheshire West and Chester Council (Successor to Vale Royal Borough Council)* (2009)[139] in the context of an appeal against a Planning Inspector's decision not to grant planning permission in respect of a change of use of land from an agricultural site to a mixed use of agricultural and the processing of animal by-products. The facility in question had a PPC permit but the

---

137 Directive 2008/1/EC of the European Parliament and of the Council of 15 January 2008 concerning integrated pollution prevention and control (Codified version) OJ L 24, 29/1/2008, pp 8–29.
138 Albeit it was published in 2004 prior to the introduction of the EP Regulations 2007, but it does consider the relationship between planning and the IPPC regime.
139 *Harrison v The Secretary of State for Communities and Local Government, Cheshire West and Chester Council (Successor to Vale Royal Borough Council)* [2009] EWHC 3382 (Admin); [2009] NPC 146.

planning inspector found that the odours arising from the process caused very significant harm to the amenity of local people. The Inspector doubted that the IPPC regime could be relied upon to prevent this and consequently refused the planning permission. On appeal the Divisional Court held that the purpose of the planning system was to determine whether the development of land was itself an acceptable use of land and also the impact of those uses. In contrast the IPPC regime controlled processes and emissions. However, a planning decision maker[140] was entitled to reach his own conclusions as to the impact of a proposed development on amenity and whether a site under consideration was the appropriate location for a proposed development. It was reasonably open for the Inspector to conclude that, notwithstanding the PPC permit, use of the site for a waste management operation would continue to cause problems to local people. The Court stated that the Inspector had exercised his planning judgment on the broader issue of whether the use of the land for the proposed waste operation by taking into account the level of local complaints and the extent to which the issue of odour emissions was realistically capable of being addressed by the IPPC regime.[141] The relationship between the two regimes was given further consideration in *Ardley Against Incineration v Secretary of State for Communities and Local Government* (2011), albeit the decision was very case-specific.[142]

Law in Action

The applicant, Ardley Against Incineration, as the name suggests was a campaign group which applied to the High Court for an order to quash the Secretary of State's decision to grant planning permission to build an energy for waste facility. The inspector had considered the effects of the facility on air quality and found that they would be insignificant, having noted that the Environment Agency had issued an environmental permit and did not object to the facility on that ground. The Secretary of State accepted the recommendation and granted conditional permission in February 2011. The Court held that the Secretary of State had been entitled to leave matters relating to air quality to the Environment Agency (exercising its powers under the EPR regime).

A further clarification of the relationship between the permitting and planning regimes has usefully been provided by the Waste (England and Wales) Regulations 2011, in that nuisances and hazards arising from traffic beyond the site of a landfill or other waste operation are no longer matters which the regulator is required to consider as part of its permitting functions.[143] These matters now fall solely to the local planning authority to deal with as part of the planning process.

In relation to environmental permits for waste operations, the regulator cannot grant the environmental permit unless the applicant has secured the relevant planning permission for the activity on that site. This requirement dates back to the introduction of waste management licensing in 1994 and reflects the complementary roles of planners and the Environment Agency in delivering

---

140 I.e. planning authority, planning inspector.
141 Assuming that the regime would be properly applied and enforced.
142 *Ardley Against Incineration v Secretary of State for Communities and Local Government* [2011] EWHC 2230 (Admin); [2012] JPL 268.
143 Waste (England and Wales) Regulations 2011 SI 2011/988.

the health and environmental objectives of the Waste Framework Directive. However, in February 2013 Defra put a proposal forward for consultation regarding removing this requirement for certain waste operations. This so called 'planning bar' does not affect the other regulated facilities and therefore its removal would bring waste operations into line with other activities subject to environmental permitting. Having said that it would appear that the main driver behind this proposal is to reduce the administrative burdens placed on businesses and regulators, particularly where planning decisions are delayed by appeals.

6.16.5 Statutory nuisances

Environmental permits will include, if relevant, conditions relating to noise, vibration and similar environmental impacts. Local authorities are barred from using their statutory nuisance powers in Pt III of the EPA 1990 to deal with noise and other problems which the environmental permitting regulator can address, using the relevant environmental permitting enforcement powers. Local authorities may nevertheless use their statutory nuisance powers on a regulated facility in circumstances where the relevant nuisance falls outside the remit of environmental permitting controls. Irrespective of the limitations on local authority power to take statutory nuisance action against an environmental permit holder, an individual may use s 82 of the EPA 1990 to lodge a complaint against an IPPC permit holder in respect of an alleged nuisance.

See Chapter 9

6.17 Online resource centre

We recommend that the reader regularly refers to the section of the online resources corresponding to this chapter for information relating to updates, amendments and corrections.

6.18 Summary of key points

Chapter 6 has covered the following topics and issues:

- the evolution of the permitting regime from its Integrated Pollution Control (IPC) origins under Part I EPA 1990 including discussion of Pollution Prevention Control (PPC) permits and the transitional arrangements as the regimes have evolved;
- the requirements of the IPPC Directive, largely modelled on the IPC regime, and in particular the requirement that operators use the best available techniques to prevent environmental harm;
- the desire on the part of government to secure simpler environmental regulation as part of the Better Regulation agenda;
- the detailed requirements relating to applications for environmental permits, including applications to vary and transfer permits;
- the enforcement powers available to the regulatory bodies (the Environment Agency and local authorities) including the power to prosecute;
- the remedial powers available to the regulatory bodies to secure the prevention and remediation of pollution/environmental damage.

6.19 Further reading

Articles

Henshawe, I, 'The EC Directive on Integrated Pollution Prevention Control: implications for the United Kingdom' [1996] Env Liability 29.

Lea, A, 'BATNEEC, BPEO and the variation of IPC consents—a review of a recent High Court decision concerning the burning of alternative fuels' [1998] JPL 913–18.

Mehta, A, 'The benefits of IPC: views from industry' (1988) 10(4) ELM 190–96.

This article considers the commercial benefits to firms of an IPC regime.

Royal Commission on Environmental Pollution Reports: *Air Pollution Control, An Integrated Approach*, Fifth Report, Cmnd 6371, 1976, HMSO; *Best Practicable Environmental Option*, Twelfth Report, Cmnd 310, 1988, HMSO.

Websites

The Environment Agency

www.environment-agency.gov.uk

The Environment Agency website includes a wide range of official information relating to environmental permitting and IPPC, including Technical Guidance Notes.

Department of Environment, Food and Rural Affairs

www.defra.gov.uk/environment/index.htm

Defra (November 2009) Environmental Permiiting Core guidance, Version 2.0 paragraph 2.31. Available at http://www.defra.gov.uk/environment/policy/permits/guidance.htm

Planning Policy Statement 23: Planning and Pollution Control, available on line at http://www.communities.gov.uk/documents/planningandbuilding/pdf/planningpolicystatement23.pdf (accessed 15 January 2010)

Royal Commission on Environmental Pollution

http://www.rcep.org.uk/

Royal Commission on Environmental Pollution reports are accessible from this site.

Chapter 7

Contaminated Land

Chapter Contents

> ## Learning Objectives
>
> By the end of this chapter you should have acquired an understanding of:
>
> - the problems and risks associated with contaminated land and the government's objectives in bringing contaminated land back into beneficial use;
>
> - the legal definition of contaminated land and the procedures involved in its identification and remediation (clean-up);
>
> - the respective roles of the local authorities and the Environment Agency in securing the remediation of contaminated land;
>
> - the way in which the legislation seeks to determine and apportion liability for the clean-up and the extent to which the legislation applies the polluter-pays principle;
>
> - the relationship between the provisions in Part IIA Environmental Protection Act 1990 (the contaminated land regime) and the planning regime;
>
> - the provisions of the Environmental Damage (Prevention and Remediation) Regulations 2009 as they relate to the remediation of contaminated land.

7.1 Introduction

The UK, as birthplace of the industrial revolution, has been left with a significant legacy of contaminated land. Heavy engineering and manufacturing activity during the twentieth century went largely unregulated before the recognition of the importance of environmental protection began to emerge in the 1970s. However, the problem of Britain's so-called 'Badlands', although recognised for many years, was not addressed until relatively recently, and not specifically until 1 April 2000 when the contaminated land provisions contained in Part IIA of the Environmental Protection Act 1990 came into force. The delay in tackling the contaminated land problem may, in part, be due to the low visibility of the issue since it is not always readily apparent that land may be contaminated. However, the main difficulty faced by government in addressing this issue has been how to bring back land into beneficial use without imposing unnecessary burdens on society, and more specifically in tackling the thorny question of who should pay for past pollution. Not surprisingly it took several years for government, after carrying out numerous consultation exercises, to come forward with a framework for the identification and remediation (clean-up) of contaminated land.

The resulting legislation, Part IIA EPA 1990, is a complex package of legislation and statutory guidance and it remains to be seen whether the regime will, in the long term, achieve the government's stated aspirations of tackling the legacy of contaminated land in the UK. The evidence to date[1] appears to suggest that the majority of contaminated sites are in fact being remediated as a result of redevelopment (via the imposition of planning conditions) or via voluntary remediation. This does not necessarily mean that Part 2A is failing to deliver, but in the government's view such regulatory intervention should be held in reserve for when there is no prospect of a market solution:[2]

---

1 Environment Agency, 'Reporting the Evidence: Dealing with Contaminated Land in England and Wales, A Review of Progress from 2000–2007 of Part 2A Environmental Protection Act 1990' (January 2009). Available at http://publications.environment-agency.gov.uk/pdf/GEHO0109BPHA-e-e.pdf.
2 Defra website www.defra.gov.uk/environment/quality/land accessed on 4 January 2012.

> The contaminated land regime is a valuable tool that helps drive market action to deal with land contamination, and allows regulators to take action to find and deal with significant risks where there is no prospect of a market solution. Since Part 2A was introduced it has played a major role in the very significant progress that has been made in addressing the legacy of land contamination in England and Wales.[3]

This explains the relative paucity of emerging case law which specifically concerns the operation of Part 2A EPA 1990. Therefore in examining the topic of contaminated land this chapter must also consider the operation of the town and country planning regime as it relates to land contamination. In addition the chapter will examine other legislative provisions which may be applied in respect of land that is in a contaminated state.

In contrast to the majority of the 'Command and Control' regulatory controls discussed in this book, the regulation of contaminated land is not licence-based. The damage, in the main, has already been done and the law responds reactively by:

(a) identifying the relevant parcels of land which are 'contaminated';
(b) identifying the person or persons responsible for the contamination; and
(c) allocating the cost of clean-up between the responsible person or persons.

The main function of the contaminated land regime is to address the problem of historic pollution; it does not seek directly to prevent contamination, although whether it could have such deterrent effect in the long term is speculative. Although the government claims that its first priority is to prevent the creation of new contamination[4] it recognises the limitations of this regime in that respect. Instead prevention will be achieved via the traditional Command and Control regimes which are now largely delivered via environmental permitting.

See Chapter 6

7.2 The legacy of contaminated land and the evolution of the statutory regime

Many old industries which existed in the nineteenth and early twentieth centuries have either been swept away or have adapted to modern production methods. Whilst the land upon which these old industries stood has been redeveloped and old buildings replaced with modern ones, it is probable that, in some circumstances, historic contamination of the soil and sub-soil remains as an unwelcome legacy. This is especially true of contaminants which are not biodegradable. The following activities are typically linked to historic land contamination: gas and coking works which produced tars and other residues; closed landfill sites with leachate and methane emission problems; tanning works which used solvents to degrease animal skins; metal works smelting toxic metals such as lead; plating works; heavy engineering works; chemical works using powerful acids and alkalis; petro-chemical works; asbestos production; premises which handled and stored hazardous substances, for example, docks, railways and Ministry of Defence property; and factories which manufactured pesticides.

---

3 Defra Consultation; Changes to the Contaminated Land Regime under Part 2A Environmental Protection Act 1990 at para 55.
4 Statement of Government Policy, Annex 1, Defra Circular 01/2006.

Industry	Contaminated site (England)	Special site (England)	Contaminated site (Wales)	Special site (Wales)
Energy	24%	15%	1%	0%
Metal	13%	3%	0%	0%
Mineral	1%	0%	0%	0%
Chemical	1%	24%	0%	50%
Textiles, printing and coating industries	1%	0%	0%	0%
Waste management	31%	33%	0%	50%
Timber processing	16%	0%	0%	0%
Other	30%	33%	99%	100%
Total number of sites recorded	626	33	120	2

Source: 'Reporting the Evidence', 2008, Table 4[5]

7.2.1 The risks associated with contaminated land

Contaminated land, containing toxic chemicals, poses a threat to the health of humans, plants and animals. Harmful chemicals can enter the food chain via crops grown in contaminated soil. These crops, or the animals which feed upon them, are then eaten by humans and toxic substances are ingested. Alternatively, chemicals, such as solvents or pesticides, may leach out of closed landfills and enter groundwaters. Groundwaters (that is, aquifers) are commonly used to supply water for human consumption. One of the most serious incidences of land contamination occurred in the United States in the 1970s at Love Canal, where an entire community whose homes had been built on a former hazardous waste site had to be evacuated. The Love Canal incident illustrates the extreme risks that humans can face when exposed to serious pollution from land contamination; particularly birth defects, miscarriages and leukaemia. A similar incident occurred in Lekkerkerk in the Netherlands in 1980, drawing further attention to the problems and resulting in the Dutch authorities compiling an inventory of seriously contaminated sites. In the UK, in 1976, a bungalow was destroyed as a result of an explosion caused by the migration of methane gas from a closed landfill at Loscoe in Derbyshire.

The group litigation involving some 18 claimants against Corby District Council has further demonstrated the health risks associated with contaminated land (*Corby Group Litigation v Corby DC* (2009).[6] Although not specifically concerned with Part 2A EPA, the case considered the potential negligence and breach of statutory duty on the part of the District Council in respect of its remediation of a former steel works/industrial site. The claimants alleged a pattern of birth defects (consisting of shortened or missing arms, legs and fingers), which they claimed were caused by their mothers' exposure during pregnancy to airborne contaminants generated by the reclamation works.

---

5 Environment Agency, 'Reporting the Evidence: Dealing with Contaminated Land in England and Wales, A Review of Progress from 2000–2007 of Part 2A Environmental Protection Act 1990' (January 2009), Table 4, p 13.
6 *Corby Group Litigation v Corby DC* [2009] EWHC 1944 (TCC); [2009] NPC 100.

Many chemical substances, which are present in and contaminate land, are either not biodegradable or take many years to break down into less harmful chemicals. The *Cambridge Water* case[7] illustrates the persistence and longevity of solvents and their ability to migrate, through underground strata, over significant distances. Similarly in 2000 the water company, Veolia Water Three Valleys, discovered bromate and bromide in a water borehole, making the water supply unusable. Veolia traced the contaminants back to a housing estate which had been built in the 1980s on land that had been previously used as a chemical works. (See below at 7.6.6 and 7.8.4 for further discussion.)

See Chapter 11

Chemicals which are present in contaminated land may cause damage to crops and livestock. They may even, if they are corrosive, damage building foundations and service pipes and cables. Contaminated land may also result in property blight and property stigma. Residential developments erected on closed landfills may be blighted if methane enters sub-floor areas. If a risk of explosion exists, the property will either become unsaleable, or the price must be reduced to reflect that risk. Property stigma occurs in cases where contamination has been remediated, but the fact that the land on which the property stands was contaminated causes the market price of the property to be depressed. The stigma associated with nuclear waste contamination is apparent in the case of *Blue Circle v Ministry of Defence* (1999).[8]

7.2.2 Growing recognition of the problem of contaminated land and the government's initial response

In comparison to other environmental problems, such as waste and water pollution, the issue of contaminated land is a relative newcomer in terms of the recognition of the problem and the identification of the means to address it. Since the 1970s, various governments sought to examine ways of tackling the problem, but encountered significant difficulties in terms of reaching agreement about how to define contaminated land legally and how to secure the remediation of contaminated sites without resulting in significant property blight. In 1989, the House of Commons Select Committee on the Environment recommended that 'urgent attention [must] be given to the question of creating statutory liability for damage caused by contamination to land'.[9] The Committee also accepted that the establishment of a statutory regime would raise complex questions as to retrospection, insurance cover and limitation periods. As a result of this recommendation, in the following year, the Committee undertook a report on contaminated land (1990). The Committee examined the issue of contamination in detail. Its main recommendations were that records of contamination should be created and open to the public and that a comprehensive framework of regulation should be established. This recommendation led to the inclusion in the Environmental Protection Act (EPA) 1990 of the ill-fated s 143 registers.

7.2.3 The section 143 registers

The EPA 1990, as originally drafted, contained a provision which, if it had ever been brought into force, would have required local authorities to maintain public registers of land in their area 'subject to contamination'. Section 143 EPA 1990 was the first statutory attempt specifically aimed at addressing the issue of contaminated land. The section was a late amendment to the EPA, appearing at the third reading in the House of Lords, and therefore received little Parliamentary debate or scrutiny. It was also highly controversial. One specific problem related to the definition of land

---

7 *Cambridge Water Co v Eastern Counties Leather plc* [1994] 2 AC 264; [1994] 2 WLR 53; [1994] 1 All ER 53.
8 *Blue Circle v Ministry of Defence* [1998] 3 All ER 385; [1999] Env LR 22.
9 Contaminated Land, 1st Report, Session 1989–90, HC170, 1990.

subject to contamination, which the government proposed would be 'land which is being or had been put to a contaminative use', that being 'any use of land which may cause it to be contaminated with noxious substances'. Thus, land would be deemed to be contaminated because of the use to which it had been or was being put, regardless of whether the land was capable of causing harm to humans or property. Under s 143 local authorities would have been required to register sites which were not necessarily contaminated but which had previously been put to a contaminative use. The government carried out extensive consultations with regard to the proposed registers[10] but, in view of the strength of objections, it decided to abandon the s 143 registers. On 24 March 1993, the government announced that the registers would not be introduced, but that a further detailed review of responsibility for contaminated land would be undertaken. Section 143 was repealed by the Environment Act 1995. The principal reasons given by the government for abandoning the s 143 registers were as follows:

(a) the proposed registers were based on the use to which the land had been put regardless of whether or not the use had actually caused the land to be contaminated; this would have led to some sites which were not actually contaminated being included whilst missing other sites which were actually contaminated but by uses not contained on the prescribed list of contaminative uses;

(b) there was no system for removing a site from the register once it had been cleaned up; and

(c) inclusion on the register did not address the potential problem of remediation or the issue of liability for remediation.

7.2.4 Paying for Our Past, and Framework for Contaminated Land

As a result of the abandonment of the registers in 1993, the government formed an inter-departmental group to begin a wide-ranging review of the problems of contamination. The task of the review group was to investigate, inter alia, 'the powers and duties of public authorities which relate to the identification, assessment and appropriate treatment or control of land that could cause pollution of the environment, or harm to human health'.[11] Following this, the then Conservative government published two wide-ranging consultation documents, in March and November 1994.[12] The general tone of *Paying for Our Past* seemed to be one of uncertainty, with questions being posed as to how the regulation of contaminated land might be framed. Nevertheless it did reveal something of the government's basic philosophy in relation to the proposed regime, which placed a particular emphasis on establishing a regime which would remove unacceptable risks of harm and would secure remediation on a suitable for use basis and apply the polluter-pays principle. *Framework for Contaminated Land* represented the definitive statement of government policy. Following this extensive consultation exercise, the government finally enacted the new statutory regime by s 57 of the Environment Act 1995, which inserted a new Part IIA into the Environmental Protection Act 1990. Part IIA includes 26 sections, from s 78A to s 78YC. The provisions of Part IIA came into force on 1 April 2000.

7.2.5 Government objectives and market-based approaches

In the 1994 consultation paper, *Paying for our Past*, the government set out the principles and objectives on which the contaminated land regime was intended to operate:

---

10 Let the buyer be well informed – Recommendations of the Conveyancing Standing Committee of the Law Commission – December 1989.

11 *Hansard*, 24 March 1993, col 634.

12 *Paying for Our Past*, March 1994, and *Framework for Contaminated Land*, November 1994.

(a)   The government recognised that it was necessary to bring large tracts of contaminated land back into beneficial use.

(b)   The standard of clean-up of contaminated land would be based on a 'suitable for use' concept. Clean-up works to remediate the land would only be necessary if the contamination present in the land posed actual or potential risks to man or the environment which were considered to be unacceptable. In assessing what, if any, remediation works were required, it was necessary to have regard to the actual (that is, current) or intended use of the contaminated land. Thus, if planning permission was sought to redevelop a site for housing, the extent of clean-up works would reflect that intended use and its attendant risks, especially to humans. The 'suitable for use' concept is therefore distinguishable from the 'polished earth' approach of the 'Superfund' legislation in the USA (Comprehensive Environmental Response Compensation and Liability Act 1980) or the similar, and now discontinued, 'multifunctional' approach in the Netherlands which required contaminated land to be cleaned up so that it was fit for any use.

(c)   The contaminated land regime would target, prioritise and address the most serious cases of contamination first.

(d)   The financial impact of the contaminated land regime on the economy and specific industries and landowners would be taken into account.

(e)   The creation of a contaminated land regime would clarify responsibility for the clean-up of contaminated land and enable contaminated land to be bought and sold under proper market conditions.

In addition, it was also apparent that the legislation was not intended to provide the only means of addressing contaminated land but rather that it would provide a regulatory regime to address problems of contamination that could not be addressed via other means, most notably via planning conditions and building control. However, since that time the government has made it much clearer that Part 2A should be seen as an 'option of the last resort' only if other market-based approaches fail to deal with the problem.[13] Market-based approaches appear to include voluntary remediation carried out by companies or remediation carried out as part of the redevelopment of land. The latter will usually be subject to specific planning conditions attached to the grant of a planning permission.[14]

7.2.6 The operation of the contaminated land regime to date

In January 2009 the Environment Agency published its second statutory report on the state of contaminated land in England (this report also included, for the first time, statistics relating to Wales).[15] The report provides a valuable and detailed review of the impact of the contaminated land regime and the progress achieved during the seven years following its entry into force in April 2000. In particular, it highlights the fact that, notwithstanding the introduction of this highly complex regime, the majority of contaminated sites in England and Wales are, as the government appears to have intended, currently being dealt with via the town and country planning regime. Local authorities estimate that around only 10 per cent of sites are being dealt with under Part 2A EPA 1990. As noted in the introduction, the above statistic does not necessarily mean that Part 2A is failing to deliver; rather it is claimed that the legislation 'has played a very important role in underpinning the wider (market-based) policy for dealing with land contamination . . . it supports the planning system and acts as a driver to encourage polluters and landowners to clean-up their

---

13 See further at 7.3.2.
14 For further discussion, see 7.11.2.
15 Environment Agency, 'Reporting the Evidence: Dealing with Contaminated Land in England and Wales, A Review of Progress from 2000–2007 of Part 2A Environmental Protection Act 1990' (January 2009).

own land.'[16] The Defra review of 2009 (see later) reports that tens of thousands of hectares of land have been cleaned up as a result of the market-led approach and that probably over 95 per cent of contaminated land work has taken place through redevelopment under the planning system.[17]

7.2.6.1 Impact on residential land

To date the only cases which have specifically addressed the interpretation of Part 2A EPA 1990 have related to residential sites.[18] This highlights the other significant and notable feature of the operation of the regime so far; namely that Part 2A appears to be having the most significant impact on sites which were redeveloped in the past for residential purposes. Over 90 per cent of sites inspected by March 2007 had housing on them when the site was inspected. Clearly this raises some very difficult liability issues where homeowners are largely 'innocent' and have done nothing to cause contamination of the land. Interestingly the report also claims that the legislation has resulted in the development of a new land contamination/brownfield land sector and the emergence of a new range of land contamination professionals and professional qualifications.

7.2.7 Defra review and new statutory guidance

In 2009 Defra conducted a review of the operation of the regime for the first time since 2000. The review concluded that the primary legislation (Part 2A EPA 1990) remained fit for purpose in particular since it had played a major role in driving market action. The review also found a strong case for keeping it on public health and environmental protection grounds. However, the review found flaws in the accompanying statutory guidance which it claimed resulted in unjustified regulatory intervention and inefficient remediation of land. In particular the review concluded that the statutory guidance did not adequately explain key aspects of the Part 2A regime, such as how to decide when land is 'contaminated land', how to ensure that remediation requirements are reasonable and produce value for money, and how to take a precautionary approach without being excessively precautionary. These significant uncertainties had forced developers and other businesses into wastefully expensive remediation, which not only created a burden on the UK economy but also represented poor value for taxpayers. In light of this review a joint public consultation was conducted by Defra and the Welsh Assembly Government between December 2010 and March 2011 on proposals for changes to the statutory guidance. The new statutory guidance was published in April 2012.[19] The intention was that the new guidance would clarify and simplify the regime. Although the guidance is indeed considerably shorter than its predecessors, it doesn't necessarily resolve all of the difficulties identified by the Environment Agency in its 2009 report. It has also been argued that new guidance represents a subtle shift in the underlying philosophy of the regime with a move away from the suitable for use approach that pervaded the previous editions.[20] Two of the notable features of the new guidance are first that it contains an expressly stated presumption that land is not contaminated; 'Under Part 2A the starting point should be that land is not contaminated land unless there is reason to consider otherwise.'[21] Secondly there is a distinct emphasis on the need for the enforcing authorities to show that there is a net benefit in resorting to regulatory action.

---

16 Ibid, para 43.
17 The 'over 95%' figure is a Defra estimate based on experience of the Part 2A and planning regimes and drawing on estimates given e.g. in Environment Agency (2009) 'Dealing with contaminated land in England and Wales: a review of progress with Part 2A of the Environmental Protection Act 2000–2007'. Defra Impact Assessment Simplification of the Contaminated land regime 06/10/2011.
18 The cases are discussed below at 7. 7.
19 Defra, *Environmental Protection Act 1990: Part 2A Contaminated Land Statutory Guidance*, April 2012.
20 See Lees, E 'The contaminated land regime—new guidance and a new philosophy' [2012] Env LR 267.
21 Environment Agency, 'Reporting the Evidence: Dealing with Contaminated Land in England and Wales, A Review of Progress from 2000–2007 of Part 2A Environmental Protection Act 1990' (January 2009), para 1.3.

7.3 The statutory framework of the contaminated land regime

7.3.1 Overview of the legislation

Section 57 of the Environment Act 1995 resulted in the inclusion of a new Part IIA into the Environmental Protection Act, rather gracelessly squeezed between Part II (Waste on Land) and Part III (Statutory Nuisances); hence the somewhat cumbersome section numbering from ss 78A to 78YC. The regime came into force on 1 April 2000. It was subsequently 'extended' with effect from August 2006 as a result of the Radioactive Contaminated Land (Enabling Powers) (England) Regulations 2005,[22] which effectively apply the regime to radioactive contamination of land. The provisions are classically 'framework' in nature with much of the complex, and controversial, detail to be found in the accompanying statutory guidance.[23] By virtue of s 78YA the Secretary of State was empowered to issue statutory guidance, a power exercisable only after consultation with the Environment Agency (or Scottish Environmental Protection Agency) and other such bodies or persons as he considers appropriate. The guidance also had to be laid before Parliament. The first statutory guidance was issued in the form of a DETR Circular (02/2000).[24] This was replaced in October 2006 with Defra Circular 01/2006 *Environmental Protection Act 1990: Part 2A Contaminated Land*.[25] In both these instances the statutory guidance was contained in Annex 3 of the respective Circulars and was accompanied by the following other annexes (Annex 1—A statement of government policy; Annex 2—A description of regime for contaminated land; Annex 3—The Statutory Guidance; Annex 4—A guide to the Contaminated Land (England) Regulations 2006; Annex 5—A guide to other supporting legislation; Annex 6—A glossary of terms).

However, following the review of the contaminated land regime in 2009 and public consultation in 2011 Defra issued revised Statutory Guidance in April 2012.[26] This is in the form of a discreet guidance and is no longer accompanied by the annexes. The objective of the new 2012 guidance is to enable regulators to make quicker decisions about whether or not land is contaminated under Part 2A in order to avoid costly remediation operations being undertaken unnecessarily. The Statutory Guidance is broken down into eight sections as follows: 1—Objectives of regime; 2—Local authority inspection duties; 3—Risk assessment; 4—Definition of Contaminated land; 5—Determination of contaminated land; 6—Remediation of contaminated land; 7—Liability; 8—Recovery of the costs of remediation. The Circular applies only to England and it only applies to non-radioactive sites (radioactive sites are covered by separate guidance).

The Contaminated land (England) Regulations 2006[27] (which replace the earlier 2000 regulations) provide additional detail about Special sites, appeals and the public registers. The 2006 regulations were amended by the Contaminated Land (England) Regulations 2012 SI 2012/263.

7.3.2 The overarching objectives of Part 2A

The overarching objectives of the Part 2A regime are usefully set out in section 1 of the 2012 statutory guidance. Previously these were to be found in the non-binding Annex 1 attached in the 2006 Circular. The inclusion of the objectives in the binding statutory guidance is welcome. Most particularly local authorities are required, at times, to take these broad objectives into account when

---

22 Radioactive Contaminated Land (Enabling Powers) (England) Regulations 2005 SI 2005/3467.

23 Defra, *Environmental Protection Act 1990: Part 2A Contaminated Land Statutory Guidance*, April 2012.

24 Published March 2002.

25 Published September 2006.

26 Defra, *Environmental Protection Act 1990: Part 2A Contaminated Land Statutory Guidance*, April 2012.

27 The Contaminated land (England) Regulations 2006 SI 2006/1380.

making decisions about, inter alia, whether land is contaminated or not. The objectives are also intended to provide an aide to judicial interpretation as and when further questions about the regime are considered by the courts. The aim of Part 2A is to:

1. identify and remove unacceptable risks to human health and the environment;
2. seek to ensure that contaminated land is made suitable for its current use; and
3. ensure that the burdens faced by individuals, companies and society as a whole are proportionate, manageable and compatible with the principles of sustainable development.

There is a very clear mandate in the guidance that local authorities should only seek to use Part 2A where no appropriate alternative mechanisms for clean-up exist. In other words the regime is one of 'last resort' and should only be triggered where other solutions are not available. This means that where, for example, contaminated land is subject to redevelopment, remediation should be secured through the planning regime. It also means that where other statutory provisions exist which can be used to secure the remediation, these should be utilised first.[28]

It is clear from the guidance given in section 1 that the decision to resort to action under Part 2A may be a difficult one. On the one hand local authorities are expected to adopt a precautionary approach to the risks raised by contamination; on the other hand they are also expected to avoid triggering a disproportionate regulatory approach. Overall the aim should be to consider the relative cost and benefits of regulatory action with a view to ensuring that the regime produces net benefits taking into account local circumstances.

7.3.3 Overview of the regime

Local authorities[29] have been allocated the major responsibility for the identification and remediation of contaminated land. The Environment Agency is, however, the enforcing authority in relation to the most severely contaminated sites (known as special sites), the provision of technical guidance, and the preparation (with local authority input) of a periodic report on contaminated land in England and Wales.[30] The contaminated land regime shares some similarities with statutory nuisance controls under Part 3 of the EPA 1990: each regime is largely a reactive form of control; each regulator has a statutory duty to inspect its area; regulation is not licence-based but revolves around the service of a notice specifying the remedial works which are required to be completed within a set timescale; non-compliance with the remedial notice is a criminal offence; the local authority has responsibility for the administration of the regulatory regime (although the Environment Agency regulates the more severely contaminated sites); extensive rights of appeal are available; and details of the remedial notice, and other information, is placed by the regulator on a publicly accessible register of information.

In terms of process the regime can be broken down into the following stages:

1. Local authorities are required to prepare strategies which set out their approach to the identification of contaminated land and they are under a duty to inspect land in their area to determine whether any land is contaminated or a special site. The Environment Agency is responsible for special sites.
2. Local authorities are responsible for making the determination that land is contaminated. They are required to undertake and follow the risk assessment procedures laid down in the

---

28 For the relationship between Part 2A and the environmental permitting and environmental damage (prevention and remediation) regime, see later at 7.9 and 7.11.3.
29 Borough councils, district councils and unitary authorities.
30 S 78U.

statutory guidance and where appropriate produce a written risk summary. Where land is contaminated there must be written determination and various parties must be notified.

3.   The process of notification triggers a minimum three-month consultation period during which the enforcing authority will determine what remediation is required and who will be liable.

4.   The enforcing authority is responsible (subject to certain qualifications) for serving a remediation notice on the appropriate persons who are liable for the remediation.

5.   The remediation must be completed in accordance with the remediation notice. Recipients may appeal a remediation notice.

6.   All of the above documents are available on the publicly accessible register of information.

7.   Failure to comply with a remediation notice without reasonable excuse is a criminal offence.

Each of the above stages is considered below, after an examination of the definition of contaminated land in 7.4.

7.4 The definition of contaminated land

7.4.1 General considerations—presumption against designation and normal levels of contaminants

Of critical significance to the scope of the contaminated land regime is the method by which 'contaminated' land is distinguished from uncontaminated land. The definition is complex and requires local authorities to undertake a detailed risk assessment in accordance with the requirements of the statutory guidance. However, it is important to note that the new statutory guidance makes it very clear that the starting point is that land should not be designated as contaminated unless there is a reason to consider otherwise. This effectively amounts to a presumption that land is not contaminated (within the meaning of the Act) and there must be sufficient evidence to conclude otherwise. In addition the new statutory guidance (unlike its predecessors) addresses the issue of 'normal' levels of contaminants; that is contaminants that are commonplace and widespread throughout England. If land has what is regarded as normal levels of particular contaminants in soil, this should not usually be considered to cause land to be contaminated unless there is a particular reason to think otherwise. Normal level of contaminants in soil may result from the natural presence of contaminants at levels that might reasonably be considered as typical in a given area and have been shown not to pose unacceptable risks and also contaminants caused by low-level diffuse pollution and common human activity, such as pollution caused by the historic use of leaded petrol or the spreading of domestic ash in gardens at reasonably typical levels. However, this latter does not include pollution from specific industrial processes. Essentially here the local authority is required to consider whether the contaminants present in soil are either typical or widespread locally and or regionally/nationally, depending on the circumstances. If the levels are typical, their presence is not likely to result in the land being contaminated, unless there is a specific reason to consider the levels pose an unacceptable risk.

The net effect of the above two provisions is that even fewer sites are likely to be designated, particularly if the sites are 'contaminated' by low-level historic and diffuse pollution. This is perhaps consistent with the regime which emphasises that its aim is to remove 'unacceptable risks'; evidently some contamination is to be regarded as acceptable and insufficient to warrant regulatory action. Hence, Part 2A takes a risk-based approach to defining contaminated land. This requires an assessment of the likelihood that harm will occur as a result of contaminants and the scale and seriousness of such harm if it did occur. Regulatory action will be justified only where the land poses *unacceptable risks*. There were alternative ways of approaching the definition of contaminated land, based on the presence of contaminants in soil at any level or above a given concentration. The government rejected the approach based on the mere presence of contaminants in soil as such an approach would result in large areas of land qualifying in circumstances where there is little or no appreciable risk. The alternative approach, based on contaminants present in soil above specific prescribed concentrations, was also rejected as a poor indicator of risk since it would fail to take into consideration other factors such as the location or use of the land. In order to achieve the aims of Part 2A the thresholds would have to be set at such low levels, resulting again in a great deal of land being caught within the definition unnecessarily.

Clearly the government, when enacting the statute and revising the guidance in 2011, favoured the risk-based approach as providing a more proportionate approach to the problem and one that would focus remediation actions on the reduction of risk, rather than simply the removal of contaminants. Under the approach adopted by the Part 2A regime local authorities have to exercise their judgement in order to strike a balance between dealing with the risks posed by the contaminants in (or on or under) the land and the benefits of remediating the land to reduce those risks and the potential financial impact of taking regulatory action. Although this approach is arguably more proportionate and avoids unsustainable and unnecessary remediation, it inevitably involves difficult questions. Risk assessment is not an exact science and it will often be difficult to make an accurate determination of the risks posed by contaminants in land and will inevitably involve the exercise of discretion in deciding whether the risks are of such significance to qualify the land as legally contaminated. These factors alone pose difficulties not only for local authorities but also for any person wishing to appeal a determination that land is contaminated. In practice, local authorities will often engage the services of specialist environmental consultants to assess the level of contamination and the significance of the risk. The Defra review of 2009 noted that since the contaminated land regime came into force there has been substantial uncertainty over how to decide when land is (and is not) 'contaminated land', and in particular over how to decide when land meets the legal test of 'significant possibility of significant harm to human health'. In some cases, it is inherently difficult to decide when land poses a significant risk because there is often substantial scientific and technical uncertainty over precisely what level of risk is posed at any given site. According to Defra, the technical uncertainty and the broad spectrum of risk has resulted in a substantial potential for 'regulatory creep'. Consequently new statutory guidance was issued in 2012 with the objective of providing a clearer statement about the aims of Part 2A and in particular about the approach to the determination of contaminated land.

7.4.2 The statutory definition of contaminated land

The statutory definition of contaminated land is provided is s 78A(2) of the EPA 1990 (as amended by s 86 Water Act 2003), which defines contaminated land as:

> any land which appears to the local authority in whose area it is situated to be in such a condition, by reason of substances in, on or under land, that:
>
> (a) significant harm is being caused or there is a significant possibility of such harm being caused; or
> (b) significant pollution of controlled waters is being or there is a significant possibility of such pollution being caused
>
> and, in determining whether any land appears to be such land, a local authority shall . . . act in accordance with guidance issued by the Secretary of State . . . with respect to the manner in which that determination is to be made.

The definition was also extended in 2006 to include radioactively contaminated land. However, for the remainder of this chapter the discussion will focus on the position regarding non-radioactive contaminated land. The 2012 statutory guidance does not apply to land contaminated by radioactive substances.

The first thing to note is that the decision as to whether land is contaminated rests with the local authority in whose area it is situated; this is not a determination taken by either central government or the Environment Agency. Essentially there are two distinct requirements for land to be 'contaminated' within the meaning of the legislation:

(1) For land to be contaminated substances (contaminants) must be present, either in, on or under the land. Substances may be naturally occurring, such as methane.

(2) It is not sufficient that substances are present. What is required is that the substances either cause significant harm/pollution, or there is a significant possibility that they will cause such (significant) harm/pollution.

Unfortunately (and not very surprisingly), the Act does not explain what it means by *significant* in the terms *significant harm* and *significant possibility of significant harm*. However, it does require local authorities to act in accordance with the statutory guidance, which in turn attempts to provide guidance on the assessment of significance. According to the statutory guidance it is essential to establish that:

(a) a contaminant linkage is present; and

(b) the contaminant linkage is causing significant harm/significant pollution or there is a significant possibility of it causing significant harm/pollution ('sposh'). In which case, the contaminant linkage becomes a 'significant contaminant linkage'.

The 2000 and 2006 statutory guidance previously referred to this as a pollutant linkage.

7.4.3 The contaminant linkage and significant contaminant linkage

Although the statute makes no reference to a contaminant linkage, it is clear from the guidance that this concept is central to the definition. Unless a contaminant linkage exists, there is no possibility of land being 'legally' contaminated. A contaminant linkage is the link between:

(a) the presence of a substance/contaminant in, on or under the ground;

(b) a 'receptor'; and

(c) a 'pathway' via which the substance/contaminant comes into contact with and harms the receptor.

Terminology

(a) A 'contaminant' is a substance which is in, on or under the land and which has the potential to cause significant harm to a relevant receptor, or to cause significant pollution of controlled waters.

(b) A 'receptor' is something that could be adversely affected by a contaminant, for example a person, an organism, an ecosystem, property, or controlled waters. The various types of receptors that are relevant under the Part 2A regime are explained in later sections.

(c) A 'pathway' is a route by which a receptor is or might be affected by a contaminant.

The term 'contaminant linkage' means the relationship between a contaminant, a pathway three of these. Before a local authority determines that any land appears to be contaminated land, it must as a first step be satisfied that the above three elements have been identified with respect to the land. The absence of either one of the three 'ingredients' will prevent land from falling within the definition. Therefore, theoretically at least, it is possible for land which contains very hazardous substances to fall outside this legal definition because there are no targets/receptors present, or there is no pathway by which the receptors can be exposed to the contaminants. There may be more than one contaminant linkage, depending on the contaminants in the land. A contaminant linkage may arise as a result of substances which are naturally occurring; a contaminant linkage may also arise because substances (such as asbestos) are present in buildings or drains.

7.4.3.1 Normal levels of contaminants

It has already been noted above that the new statutory guidance in 2012 specifically addresses the position of 'normal levels of contaminants'. These are described as contaminants that are commonplace and widespread throughout England. If land has what is regarded as normal levels of particular contaminants in soil this should not usually be considered to cause land to be contaminated unless there is a particular reason to think otherwise.

7.4.3.2 Significant contaminant linkage

The presence of a contaminant linkage does not mean that the land is legally contaminated. For example, all soil will contain substances that could be harmful to either human or environmental receptors, but in the majority of cases the level of risk is likely to be very low. The local authority will need to determine whether the contaminant linkage poses the unacceptable risk needed to trigger the provisions of the act and result in land being classed as contaminated. Essentially the effect of the statutory provisions is to clarify that it is only unacceptable (that is, significantly harmful) risks to man or the environment which convert a contaminant link into a significant contaminant linkage and therefore convert land into contaminated land. This requires the regulator to undertake a risk assessment to determine whether the risks posed by the land are unacceptable. To do this the enforcing authority must 'act in accordance' with the statutory guidance relating to the meaning of 'contaminated land'. The fact that the regulator is obliged to act in accordance with the guidance, to the extent that it addresses the meaning of 'contaminated', will curtail the regulator's discretion as to the identification of which parcels of land fall within the contaminated land control regime.

7.4.4 The process of risk assessment and risk summaries

The statutory guidance requires the risk assessment to determine whether the contaminant linkage results in:

(a)   significant harm being caused;
(b)   a significant possibility of significant harm being caused ('sposh');
(c)   significant pollution of controlled waters being caused;
(d)   significant possibility of significant pollution of controlled waters being caused.

If one of these situations arises, then the 'contaminant linkage' becomes a 'significant contaminant linkage'.

Risk assessment requires an understanding of the risks presented by the land and the associated uncertainties. This may be done in stages starting with a preliminary risk assessment which is informed by a desk-based study (for example searching old maps to discover previous land use) and/or site visit. It may be followed by a generic quantitative risk assessment followed by a more detailed quantitative risk assessment. More detailed site investigation work is likely to be required if is there is evidence that unacceptable risk might reasonably exist. The guidance makes it clear that if a local authority considers there is little reason to consider that land might pose an unacceptable risk, it need not carry out any further investigation. The risk assessment must be relevant to the specific circumstances of the land. For example, in complex cases, there may be a need to consult qualified specialists competent to undertake the work. In undertaking this risk assessment the local authority must only consider the risks in relation to the current use of the land. The current use of the land for these purposes is the use to which the land is currently being put; any reasonably likely future use that would not require planning permission; any temporary use to which the land is put, or is likely to be put, from time to time within the bounds of current planning permission; any likely informal use of the land, for example children playing on the land, whether authorised by the owners or occupiers, or not. The local authority is not required to assess the risks to any receptors which are not likely to be present given the current use of the land or other land which might be affected. The risk assessment must be based on an appropriate, scientific and technical assessment of all the relevant and available evidence and the authority must be satisfied on the balance of probabilities that significant harm is being caused (i.e. that it is more likely than not that such harm is being caused) by a significant contaminant(s).

As mentioned earlier, the government chose not to define contaminated land by quantifiable soil guideline values (SGVs) for particular contaminants. However, the guidance does allow local authorities to use what are referred to as generic assessment criteria (and this includes soil guideline values) subject to certain provisos about the use of such tools. Generic assessment criteria (GACs) are commonly used in contaminated land risk assessment as they provide 'cautious estimates' of levels of contaminants in soil at which there is considered to be no risk to health or at most a minimal risk to health. So for example they may indicate that soil is unlikely to pose the significant risk that triggers the operation of the Part 2A regime. However, the guidance cautions that such GACs should not be used as direct indicators as to whether a significant possibility of significant harm exists. In short they must not be seen as screening levels or thresholds which demarcate whether land is contaminated or not. This is because the level of risk depends on more than just the amount of a particular contaminant in the soil; it will also depend on the extent to which receptors are affected by the contaminants, either by the form the contaminants take or the pathway or the sensitivity of the receptors.

7.4.4.1 Risk summaries

Finally, the guidance requires local authorities to produce a risk summary once it has completed its detailed inspection and risk assessment of the land and has decided that the land may be determined as contaminated. This is a new and welcome innovation. A risk summary must:

- explain the authority's understanding of the risk (and any other factors it considers to be relevant);
- describe the contaminants involved and the identified contaminant linkage (see below);
- describe the potential impacts of the contaminant linkage and the estimated possibility that the impacts may occur and the timescale over which the risk may become manifest;
- describe the risks in context (i.e. by setting them in a local or national context);
- explain/describe the authority's initial views on possible remediation including likely timescales and likely effects of remediation works on local people and businesses and also how much difference the remediation is likely to make to the risks posed by the land;
- include the authority's assessment of whether the remediation will have a net benefit having regard to the broad objectives of the regime;
- if the land is likely to be a special site (see below at 7.5.3) the local authority must consult the Environment Agency and include the Agency's views in the risk summary;

● Be written in a manner that is understandable to the lay person, including the owners of the land. This summary will constitute environmental information and will be accessible to the public under the Environmental Information Regulations 2004.[31]

The risk summary is an essential procedural step which must be taken before an authority makes a formal determination (see below at 7.5.1).

7.4.5 The concept of harm and significant harm-general considerations

Harm is defined in s 78A(4) as 'harm to the health of living organisms or other interference with the ecological systems of which they form a part and, in the case of man, includes harm to his property'. Although this is a very broad definition the Act leaves it to the statutory guidance to deal with the more difficult issue of what harm is to be regarded as significant. The first thing to note is that harm is only relevant if it is harm to either human beings, controlled water or one of the receptors listed in the guidance in Table 1. Harm to any other receptors is not relevant as far as this regime is concerned. The non-human receptors listed in Table 1 are as follows:

● Any ecological system or living organism forming part of such a system within certain locations. These locations are limited and essentially include locations which are already protected under some other environmental or nature conservation legislation. For example, areas protected under the Wildlife and Countryside Act 1981 such as areas of special scientific interest, national nature reserves and special protection areas for birds. Similarly it covers European Sites (under the Natural Habitats Regulations 1994), Special Areas of Conservation and Special Protection Areas.[32]
● Property in the form of crops, produce grown domestically for consumption, livestock and other owned animals (including domestic pets). Wild animals are only regarded as receptors to the extent that they are the subject of shooting or fishing rights.
● Property in the form of buildings.

When deciding whether significant harm has been caused, the local authority must:

(a) carry out an appropriate, scientific and technical assessment of all the relevant and available evidence; and
(b) on the basis of that assessment, the authority is satisfied on the balance of probabilities that significant harm is being caused (i.e. that it is more likely than not that such harm is being caused) by a significant contaminant(s).

However, the 2012 guidance also recognises that there may be considerable uncertainties in the evidence and the facts of particular cases and consequently authorities may be required to take decisions in cases which are not straightforward. This is self-evident, since all risk assessment of contaminated land will involve a degree of uncertainty except in the most extreme of cases; the uncertainty may be about the effects of substances or the assumptions about the future. The guidance seeks to address this by (a) accepting such uncertainties exist, and (b) requiring that local authorities recognise such uncertainties exist. In the face of this authorities should seek to minimise

---

31 Environmental Information Regulations 2004 SI 2004/3391.
32 For full list see Defra, *Environmental Protection Act 1990: Part 2A Contaminated Land Statutory Guidance*, April 2012, Table A, A.26, annex 3.

uncertainty as far as is relevant, reasonable and practical and recognise the remaining uncertainty that exists. It is difficult to predict how this cautionary advice is going to make any difference to local authority decisions. However, it is also unclear quite how this squares with the precautionary approach.

7.4.6 Significant harm to humans and non-human receptors

7.4.6.1 Significant harm to humans

Unlike the 2000 and 2006 statutory guidance, the 2012 guidance distinguishes between human and non-human receptors. This is because the vast majority of determinations to date have been based on land that posed significant risk to human health as opposed to the other non-human receptors. The guidance on significant harm to humans is relatively brief and unequivocal; it states:

- The following should *always* be considered to constitute significant harm to human health: death; life threatening diseases (e.g. cancers); other diseases likely to have serious impacts on health; serious injury; birth defects; and impairment of reproductive functions.
- Local authorities may also consider that other health effects (for example, respiratory tract or cardio vascular effects or physical injury) may constitute significant harm taking into account the seriousness of the harm in question, the impact on the health, and quality of life, of any person suffering the harm; and the scale of the harm. However in relation to these 'other effects' the local authority must consider whether its conclusion would be in accordance with the broad objectives of the regime.
- The harm must be directly attributable to the effects of the contaminants on the body (ies) of the persons concerned.
- The local authority must have carried out an appropriate scientific and technical assessment of all the relevant and available evidence and on the basis of that evidence be satisfied on the balance of probabilities that significant harm is being caused.

Of course it is entirely possible that a local authority will reach the conclusion that harm is being caused but that the harm falls short of significant as described above or harm may be being caused (or is likely to have been caused in the past) and there is a significant possibility that it may happen again. In either of these cases the local authority may consider that such harm is relevant in deciding that the land poses a significant possibility of significant harm.

7.4.6.2 Significant harm to non-human receptors

In determining whether harm to a non-human receptor is significant, the local authority is required to refer to Table 1 which describes what will be significant harm in relation to each receptor. The authority should only regard the forms of harm described in Table 1 as being significant. So, for example, as regards damage to crops and buildings, the guidance requires a substantial reduction in crop value or substantial building damage. With regard to nature conservation sites, the guidance specifies the requirement of irreversible or substantial adverse changes in ecosystem functioning affecting a substantial part of the nature conservation site.

7.4.7 'Sposh' to humans and non-human receptors

In the event that contaminants are not causing significant harm the authority must also consider whether there is a significant possibility that such significant harm will be caused to humans or any of the non-human receptors. In short the authority has to decide whether the possibility of significant harm is sufficiently high so as to justify triggering the regulatory provisions of Part 2A in order to reduce that risk. In taking any decisions under this limb the local authority must take into account the objectives of the regime (as outlined above at 7.3.2). When assessing the risk of 'sposh', the local authority must follow the guidance on risk assessment. The guidance on 'sposh' is quite lengthy and complex; however, fundamentally the local authority is required to:

1. Understand the 'possibility of significant harm' from the relevant contaminant linkage(s). This requires the authority to estimate the likelihood that significant harm might occur to an identified receptor and the estimated impact if the significant harm did occur. For example, it must consider the number of people who might be exposed to the risk and/or who might be harmed. It should also consider the strength of evidence on which the estimate is based and the estimated timescale over which the significant harm might manifest itself.
2. Only when it has done this should it go on to consider and decide whether or not the possibility of significant harm is significant. Essentially this involves the local authority in deciding whether the possibility of significant harm being caused is sufficiently to warrant regulatory action being taken. In deciding this, the local authority must take into account the broad aims of the regime.
3. The local authority will need to compile a risk summary in accordance with the requirements of section 3 of the statutory guidance.

7.4.7.1 'Sposh' to human health

As far as 'sposh' to human health is concerned, the guidance utilises four categories to assist local authorities. First, local authorities should assume that a 'sposh' exists in any case where it considers that the risk to human health is a Category 1 case, which is where there is an unacceptably high probability (supported by robust evidence) that significant harm would occur if no action is taken to stop it. Land is deemed to be Category 1 if:

a. the authority is aware that similar land or situations are known, or are strongly suspected to have caused such harm before in the UK or elsewhere; or
b. similar degrees of exposure to the contaminants in question are known, or strongly suspected (on the basis of robust evidence) to have caused such harm in the UK or elsewhere; or
c. the authority considers that significant harm may already have been caused by contaminants and there is an unacceptable risk that it might continue or occur again if no action is taken.

Local authorities should assume that the land does not pose a 'sposh' in Category 4 cases. Category 4 cases are where no relevant contaminant linkage has been established; normal levels of contaminants are present or do not exceed relevant soil quality values or technical tools or advice; estimated levels of exposure only form a small proportion of what a person may be exposed to through other sources of environmental exposure. Clearly land may fall somewhere between Categories 1 and 4. The guidance details the operation and definitions of Categories 2 and 4 in section 4. Suffice here to note that the local authority will need to decide whether land should be placed into either Category 2 (in which case it would be capable of being determined as contaminated) or Category 3, in which case it would not. Once again in making this assessment the local authority has to take into account the broad objectives of the regime.

7.4.7.2 Significant possibility of significant harm ('sposh') to non-human receptors

In circumstances where the authority has to decide whether a 'significant possibility' of such harm exists to a non-human receptor it is necessary to refer to the third column of Table 1, which was discussed above. So for example, where the receptor is property in the form of crops or livestock, there may be a 'sposh' where significant harm is more likely than not to result from the contaminant linkage taking into account scientific and authoritative information for that type of contaminant linkage particularly in relation to the eco toxicological effects of the contaminants. However, as has been mentioned previously the local authority, when making a decision regarding 'sposh', must only consider determining land as contaminated if it is satisfied that it would be in accordance with the broad aims of the legislation (which include the presumption that land is not contaminated).

7.4.8 Significant pollution of controlled water and 'sposh' of controlled water

Land will be contaminated land if by reason of substances in, on or under land significant pollution of controlled waters is being caused or there is a significant possibility of such pollution being caused. It is important to note that water is treated as a receptor and not as a pathway. Pollution of controlled waters is defined by s 78A(9) as the entry into controlled waters of any poisonous, noxious or polluting matter or any solid waste matter. The definition of controlled waters is the same as in s 104 Water Resources Act 1991, except that 'ground waters' does not include waters contained in underground strata but above the saturation zone. The pollution of controlled water must be 'significant' to result in this designation. If substances cause water to be polluted but the pollution falls short of the significant threshold, then the land will not be contaminated. This is because Part 2A should only be used to deal with pollution that is harmful to human health or the quality of the aquatic ecosystems or terrestrial ecosystems that directly depend on the aquatic ecosystems; or which may result in damage to material property, or impair/interfere with amenities and other legitimate uses of the environment. In relation to this limb of the definition local authorities are also required to strongly regard any technical advice provided by the Environment Agency in support of the guidance and also consult with the Agency before it concludes a determination under this limb.

See Chapter 4

7.4.8.1 Significant pollution

The guidance lists the types of pollution that are to be regarded as being significant, may be considered as significant and should not be regarded as significant. The following are to be regarded as significant:

(a) Pollution equivalent to 'environmental damage' to surface water or groundwater as defined by the Environmental Damage (Prevention and Remediation) Regulations 2009, but which cannot be dealt with under those Regulations.[33]

(b) Inputs resulting in deterioration of the quality of water abstracted, or intended to be used in the future, for human consumption such that additional treatment would be required to enable that use.

(c) A breach of a statutory surface water Environment Quality Standard, either directly or via a groundwater pathway.

(d) Input of a substance into groundwater resulting in a significant and sustained upward trend in concentration of contaminants (as defined in Article 2(3) of the Groundwater Daughter Directive (2006/118/EC)).

The following may be considered as significant providing that the local authority concludes that treating the land as contaminated on this basis would be in accordance with the overriding objectives of the regime:

---

33 See below at 7.9.

(a) significant concentrations of hazardous substances or non-hazardous pollutants in ground-water; or

(b) significant concentrations of priority hazardous substances, priority substances or other specific polluting substances in surface water; at an appropriate, risk-based compliance point.

If pollution of controlled water does not meet the above criteria the land should not be designated as contaminated. Of course any discharge into controlled water that is and in compliance with the conditions of an environmental permit cannot be taken into account. The significant pollution must be 'being caused' and this means that the substances are continuing to enter the controlled water or have entered water and are likely to do so again in such a way that the past and likely future entry are effectively ongoing. On the other hand, land must not be determined as contaminated on this basis if the substances are already present in controlled waters or the entry has ceased and is no further entry is likely.

7.4.8.2 'Sposh' of controlled water

The guidance makes it clear that as regards 'sposh' for controlled water, the test is a positive one; the local authority must reasonably believe there is a significant possibility of significant pollution rather than there is not. As with harm to humans the guidance lays down four categories.

Category	Description	Outcome
1	There is a strong and compelling case for considering 'sposh' exists, in particular where there is robust science-based evidence for considering that high-impact pollution of the type described above would occur (see significant pollution above) if nothing was done to stop it.	Land should be classed as contaminated.
2	Where the evidence to put land into Category 1 does not exist but on the basis of available scientific evidence and expert opinion the authority considers the risks are of sufficient concern that land should be considered to pose a 'sposh' to controlled water on a precautionary basis.	Land should be classed as contaminated.
3	The risks are such that (whilst the authority and others might prefer they did not exist) the tests set out in Categories 1 and 2 above are not met, and therefore regulatory intervention under Part 2A is not warranted. This category should include land where the authority considers that it is very unlikely that serious pollution would occur; or where there is a low likelihood that less serious types of significant pollution might occur.	Land should not be classed as contaminated.
4	Where there is no risk, or the level of risk posed is low. In particular where: (a) no contaminant linkage has been established in which controlled waters are the receptor in the linkage; or (b) the possibility only relates to types of pollution that should not be considered to be significant pollution); or (c) the possibility of water pollution similar to that which might be caused by normal levels of contamination.	Land should not be classed as contaminated.

7.5 The duty to inspect land

Section 78B(1) obliges local authorities to inspect, from time to time, their areas to identify contaminated land. With regard to the more severely contaminated sites,[34] the Environment Agency is the enforcing authority. Each local authority is tasked with the complex job of assessing whether any land in its area satisfies the relevant contaminated land criteria. Local authorities are required to take a strategic approach to the inspection of contaminated land. Authorities are not expected to undertake random inspections; instead they should adopt a rational, ordered and efficient approach, concentrating on those areas where contamination is most likely to be identified, and should seek to ensure that the most pressing and serious problems are located first. The strategy must explain, inter alia, how the authority's approach under the Part 2A regime fits with its broader approach to dealing with land contamination. These strategies are published and are therefore open to public scrutiny. All local authorities in England and Wales have published their strategies and as such, they should provide a useful reference point for lawyers involved in commercial transactions of potentially contaminated land. The strategy should be accessible to the public either as part of a public authority's publication scheme[35] or available on request via the Environmental Information Regulations 2004.[36] The strategies should be kept under review and in any event reviewed at least every five years. The strategy is only the starting point and local authorities are under a statutory duty to inspect land in their area to identify contaminated sites. The Environment Agency's second report on contaminated land notes that whilst 48 per cent of local authorities in England[37] had made 'good' progress in implementing their inspection strategies, 45 per cent of English authorities had made little progress. More significantly the report also reveals that the majority of local authorities had in fact inspected less than 10 per cent of their area since 2000.[38]

In the course of investigating whether land is contaminated, the local authority has identical investigatory powers to those of the Environment Agency contained in s 108 of the Environment Act 1995. The more important of these powers include entry, inspection, experimental boring and sampling. These powers will be available to the regulator if other avenues of information have not been sufficient to establish whether the land is contaminated. It is, however, not always necessary for there to be an intrusive site investigation. However, in the light of what has been said above relating to risk assessment it is difficult to see how the authority can produce a risk summary or make a determination without first obtaining quantitative evidence about the actual presence of contaminants in the soil. However, it should be noted that under the provisions relating to remediation notices, the authority can require the appropriate person(s) to carry out a more detailed and intrusive site investigation as part of a remediation action, as the definition of remediation provided by s 78(7) includes the 'doing of anything for the purposes of assessing the condition of the land in question'.

See Chapter 2

7.5.1 Making the determination that land is not contaminated

The outcome of an assessment of land will be that the land is either contaminated or it is not. Naturally where land is subject to an assessment and/or inspection there will be considerable uncertainty for the landowners which could result in property blight. The guidance recognises this

---

34 Known as 'special sites'.
35 Under s 19 Freedom of Information Act 2000.
36 Environmental Information Regulations 2004 (SI 2004/3391).
37 55% in Wales.
38 Environment Agency, 'Reporting the Evidence: Dealing with Contaminated Land in England and Wales, A Review of Progress from 2000–2007 of Part 2A Environmental Protection Act 1990' (January 2009). Available at http://publications.environment-agency.gov.uk/pdf/GEHO0109BPHA-e-e.pdf.

possibility and requires that assessments should be carried out efficiently and in a timely fashion. Where, at any point, the authority considers that there is insufficient or no evidence that the land is contaminated it is required by the guidance to issue a written statement to that effect. This is far better than leaving the matter inconclusive; however, the written statement can be qualified. For example, the statement may say that the land is considered not to be contaminated given its current use. The written statement must be given to the owners of the land and any other interested parties such as occupiers or neighbouring land owners.

7.5.2 Determining that land is contaminated

Alternatively the local authority may determine that the land is contaminated. It then remains for it to determine the physical extent of the land that is contaminated. This may be difficult where the contamination is not uniformly spread across a piece of land owned by one person. In practice the contamination is likely to affect land owned by various people. The guidance simply offers that the authority should use its judgement on the extent of the land and it may review this decision at a later date if it becomes aware of further relevant information. The land may be subdivided into smaller areas if necessary, for example where the land is in multiple ownership or there are different people responsible for remediation.

7.5.3 Special sites

Having satisfied itself that the land it has investigated is contaminated land, the authority must then decide whether the land qualifies as a special site. The definition of 'special site' is contained in the Contaminated Land (England) Regulations 2006 (as amended),[39] and with regard to which the Environment Agency is the relevant enforcing authority. In general terms, special sites are those: (a) on which the actual or threatened contamination is serious by virtue of the substances used on the land or the harm caused by the land; and (b) which would benefit from the Environment Agency's expertise. The Regulations include the following within the definition of special sites: sites controlled by the Environment Agency under the Environmental Permitting (England and Wales) Regulations 2010,[40] nuclear industry sites, Ministry of Defence sites, and land causing the pollution of controlled waters where the receiving water is intended to be used for the supply of drinking water or breaches of any water quality standards classified under s 82 of the Water Resources Act 1991. The local authority is required to seek the advice of the Environment Agency before desig-nating the site as a special site. If at any time the appropriate Agency considers that any contami-nated land is land which is required to be designated as a special site, that Agency may give notice of that fact to the local authority in whose area the land is situated.

Details of the fact that the site is a special site are entered on the public register. The local authority has a duty[41] to notify the Environment Agency, the owner and/or occupier and any other person who might be responsible for the cost of remediation that the site has been designated as a special site. The Environment Agency retains its[42] investigation powers with regard to special sites.[43] Interestingly, the Environment Agency has the power[44] to de-list special sites, but the site will never-theless remain listed as contaminated land. Where a special site is de-listed, the local authority resumes its role as the enforcing authority.

39 Contaminated Land (England) Regulations 2006 SI 2006/1380.
40 Environmental Permitting (England and Wales) Regulations SI 2010/675 as amended.
41 S 78C EPA 1990.
42 S 108 Environment Act 1995.
43 S 78Q EPA 1990.
44 S 78D EPA 1990.

A total of 781 sites had been determined as contaminated land under Part 2A in England (659) and Wales (122) by the end of March 2007. Of these, 35 were designated special sites (33 for England and two for Wales).[45]

7.5.4 Making the determination

Before it makes its formal determination the statutory guidance requires the authority to inform the landowners/occupiers and any other person who appears to be liable for the remediation. The aim of this pre-determination notification is to allow those persons to make any representations about the determination including proposing a solution (such as voluntary remediation) which might avoid the need for a formal determination. However, thereafter (unless a voluntary solution has been agreed) the local authority is under a duty to make a formal written determination that the land is contaminated (or the Agency that the land is a special site). The determination must be in writing and must include the following information which must be presented in an easily understandable fashion and be available on the authority's public register:

- clearly and accurately identify the location, boundaries and area of the land in question;
- the risk summary;
- an explanation of why the determination has been made including a summary of the relevant assessment methods.

A local authority may:

- postpone determination if somebody undertakes to deal with the problem without determination, and providing the authority is satisfied that the remediation will happen to an appropriate standard and timescale;
- postpone determination of contaminated land if a significant contaminant linkage would only exist if the circumstances of the land were to change in the future within the bounds of the current use of the land or if a more sensitive receptor were to move onto the land or a temporarily interrupted pathway were to be reactivated;
- reconsider any determination made if new information becomes available which significantly alters the basis of its decision or if action has been taken which stops the land being contaminated;
- revoke or vary a determination.

7.5.5 Duty to notify and consult

As soon as the local authority has decided that an area of land/site meets the statutory definition of contaminated land, it is required to follow the procedures laid down in the statute and statutory guidance. The first step involves the formal notification in writing of this determination. Under s 78B the local authority is required to notify the following persons that the land has been formally designated or listed as contaminated land:

(a) the owner;
(b) the occupier;
(c) any other person who appears to the local authority to be liable for all or part of the remediation costs (referred to as the appropriate person(s));

45 Environment Agency, 'Reporting the Evidence: Dealing with Contaminated Land in England and Wales, A Review of Progress from 2000–2007 of Part 2A Environmental Protection Act 1990' (January 2009).

(d)   the Environment Agency. Notification to the Environment Agency triggers consultation on whether the site qualifies as a special site.

The notice must specify to each recipient the capacity in which they are being notified (i.e. as owner or as an appropriate person potentially liable for the clean-up). The local authority may not yet have identified all the persons who are liable for clean-up as this information may only come to light during the consultation. If at a later stage a further person is identified as being an appropriate person then they too should receive formal notification. The issuing of notification triggers the next stage, which is a mandatory process of consultation which must last for a minimum period of three months.[46] The purpose of the consultation is to determine what remediation is required and it involves discussions between the local authority and the person or persons who are thought to be responsible for the cost of the clean-up.[47] During this period the local authority will also be determining the thorny issue of liability and reaching decisions about who is liable for meeting the costs of the remediation and also the extent of their liability.[48] The mandatory three-month consultation is designed to provide the opportunity to reach a negotiated agreement on the extent of and responsibility for remedial works. Even if agreement cannot be reached, it is envisaged that the consultation device will help narrow down areas of dispute between the enforcing authority and the persons responsible for remediation of the contamination. The enforcing authority is prohibited from serving a remediation notice during this mandatory consultation period unless the land is in such a condition that there is imminent danger of serious harm or serious pollution of controlled waters being caused. In this case the enforcing authority can exercise its power under s 78N to undertake the remedial work itself.[49]

7.5.6 Remediation by agreement

The 2012 guidance states that an authority should not serve a remediation notice if it is satisfied that appropriate measures are being taken by way of remediation without the serving of the notice. Specifically the authority should assume that appropriate measures are being taken if (a) it is satisfied that steps are being taken that are likely to achieve an equal or better standard of remediation than would have been specified in the notice, and (b) the timescales of the voluntary remediation are appropriate. To this end the consultation exercise will strive to secure this voluntary agreement. If agreement is reached, the person or persons responsible for remedial works sign an undertaking, referred to as a remediation statement, detailing what remediation works are being or are expected to be done and the time scale for this work to be complete. These details are then entered onto the public register. Provision may be made for the phased completion of these voluntary remedial works. The Environment Agency's 2009 report strongly suggests that the government is relatively successful in achieving voluntary remediation. Between 2000 and March 2007 only 12 formal remediation notices were served; in contrast 277 Remediation Statements were published in the same period.

7.6 The remediation notice

Where the consultation period has elapsed without the successful conclusion of a voluntary agreement and remediation statement, the enforcing authority must, by virtue of s 78E, serve a

---

46 Except in those cases where the contaminated land poses an imminent danger of serious harm or pollution of controlled waters, s 78N(3).
47 S 78H EPA 1990.
48 See below at 7.7.
49 See below at 7.6.3.

remediation notice on the 'appropriate person or persons' who is or are responsible for bearing the cost of clean-up. This will involve the enforcing authority making decisions about the allocation of liability (who is responsible for paying for the clean-up) and the extent of that liability. This involves a highly complex process, which is described more fully below at 7.7. Once the allocation and apportionment processes are concluded, the enforcing authority is subject to a legal duty to serve a remediation notice on the appropriate person or persons.

7.6.1 The form of the notice

The remediation notice is similar in format to a statutory nuisance Abatement Notice. It will specify the works and the relevant timescale to complete them.[50]

Remediation notices must contain sufficient information including:

(a)   a description of the work which is required to be undertaken;
(b)   the identity of the person required to do the work;
(c)   the proportion of the costs each person must bear;
(d)   the timescale within which the work must be completed;
(e)   the identity of each appropriate person;
(f)   the reason(s) for serving the notice; and
(g)   rights of appeal.

A further remediation notice may be served, even if the original notice has been complied with, if it transpires (as a result of the original remediation work) that further works or different works are necessary. Upon successful completion of the remedial works, the enforcing authority is obliged to enter details of the remediation work on the public register. In appropriate circumstances, it may indicate on the register that no further remedial work is anticipated.

7.6.2 Qualifications on service of a remediation notice

There are circumstances in which the enforcing authority is prohibited from serving a remediation notice. As an overriding general prohibition an enforcing authority is not permitted to utilise Part 2A and serve a remediation notice if the land contamination is attributable to the operation of a regulated facility and enforcement action could be taken under the provisions of the Environmental Permitting Regulations 2010 (as amended).[51] Clearly, this aims to eliminate the possible duplication of controls in relation to regulated facilities. Similarly no remediation notice can be served if the land is contaminated by reason of the deposit of controlled waste and either the local authority or the Environment Agency can exercise its clean-up powers under s 59 EPA. No remediation notice can be served during the mandatory three-month consultation period.[52] However, in addition to this temporary restriction s 78H lays down a number of further conditional prohibitions on the service of a remediation notice. These are as follows:

See Chapter 6

See Chapter 5

(a)   where it appears to the enforcing authority that imminent danger of serious harm or water pollution exists and the authority has the power to carry out the remediation under s 78N;
(b)   where remediation may be effected under other regulatory controls;

---

50 S 78E(1) EPA 1990.
51 Environmental Permitting (England and Wales) Regulations SI 2010/675 as amended.
52 Unless the condition of the land poses imminent danger or serious harm or serious pollution of controlled waters.

(c)   where the authority is satisfied that, having had regard to the costs and benefits of remediation, it is not reasonable to serve a remediation notice under s 78E(4) and (5);[53]

(d)   where the remedial works are undertaken voluntarily pursuant to a remedial statement;

(e)   where the person who would be served the notice is the enforcing authority itself;[54]

(f)   where the enforcing authority is satisfied that it has the power to carry out the remediation itself under s 78N;[55]

(g)   where, in the case of pollution of controlled waters, the appropriate persons are owners or occupiers.

Where the enforcing authority is precluded from serving a remediation notice under s 78H(4) or (5) then it is required to publish a remediation declaration which will be accessible via the public register. Basically this must specify the reasons why the enforcing authority would have required the remediation and also the reasons why it has been precluded from serving a remediation notice. This therefore allows the public (and lawyers) to ascertain whether the land is contaminated and the reasons for the authority's lack of intervention under the regime. In the event that the circumstances change, the authority could find it is no longer prevented from serving a remediation notice.

7.6.3 Remediation by the enforcing authority and cost recovery

Despite the fact that the enforcing authority is precluded from serving a remediation notice in the circumstances detailed above, there are situations where the enforcing authority can carry out the remediation works itself. Under s 78H(5) an enforcing authority may not serve a remediation notice where it has the power to carry out the remediation itself under s 78N. Therefore before serving any remediation notice the enforcing authority must first consider whether it is empowered by s 78N to undertake the remediation itself. In some cases this is a relatively simple decision and it should be noted that this does not necessarily mean that the cost will fall to the enforcing authority as s 78N is supported by s 78P, which allows the authority to recover its reasonable costs. First, the enforcing authority has the power to carry out urgent remediation in circumstances where it considers that it is necessary in order to prevent the occurrence of any serious harm, or serious pollution of controlled waters, of which there is imminent danger. The terms 'imminent' and 'serious' are not defined in Part 2A and so the enforcing authority will need to have regard to the statutory guidance, which sets out a number of considerations relating to the seriousness of any harm. In any event the enforcing authority will need to judge each case on the normal meaning of the words and the facts of the case. If the enforcing authority carries out any urgent remediation itself, it needs to prepare and publish a remediation statement. In addition it will also need to consider whether it can recover its reasonable costs from the appropriate person.[56] Additionally the enforcing authority also has the power to undertake the remediation itself:

(a)   on behalf of the appropriate person where the authority and the appropriate person(s) have entered into a written agreement and the appropriate person will meet the costs of the remediation. Thus, the Environment Agency in particular, with its technical expertise can do the remediation on behalf of the appropriate person;

(b)   where the appropriate persons have failed to comply with a remediation notice;

---

53   S 78H(5)(a) EPA 1990.
54   I.e. the enforcing authority is the owner of contaminated land or has caused contamination (s 78H(5)(c) EPA 1990).
55   See below at 7.6.3.
56   See below at 7.6.4.

(c) where, after reasonable enquiry, the authority cannot find either a Class A or a Class B appropriate person; in which case the cost of remediation will fall onto the public purse unless at a later date the enforcing authority is able to identify an appropriate person to recover costs from.

The situations discussed above are relatively clear; however, a more complex situation arises when ss 78H(5) and 78N(3)(e) are read together. Section 78N(3)(e) provides that the enforcing authority has the power to carry out remediation: 'where the enforcing authority considers that, were it to do some particular thing by way of remediation, it would decide, by virtue of s 78P(2) or the statutory guidance not to seek to recover any of the reasonable cost incurred by it in doing that thing; or to seek so to recover only a portion of that cost'. As the guidance notes,[57] this requires the enforcing authority to ask itself a hypothetical question: would it seek to recover all of the reasonable costs it would incur if it carried out the remediation itself?

If the answer is that it would either not seek to recover its costs, or seek to recover only a part of its costs, then the enforcing authority has the power to carry out the remediation itself. What is particularly interesting, though, is that in considering cost recovery the authority is required to consider the issue of hardship (see below). This has the effect of precluding an enforcing authority from serving a remediation notice in circumstances where it would cause hardship on the recipient of the remediation notice.

7.6.4 Cost recovery: section 78P

Section 78P enables the enforcing authority to recover its reasonable costs in circumstances where it has carried out the remediation itself. The guidance recognises that the situations in which cost recovery becomes an issue are going to be varied and accordingly sets out general principles as opposed to detailed criteria; the enforcing authority will need to consider the issue on a case-by-case basis. However, as a general consideration the authority should aim for an overall result which is as fair and equitable as possible to all who may have to meet the costs of remediation, including national and local taxpayers; and it should also be guided by the 'polluter pays' principle. In relation to the latter they should take into account the degree and nature of responsibility of the appropriate person for the creation, or continued existence, of the circumstances which led to the land in question being identified as contaminated land. The authority should also seek to recover all its reasonable costs but should consider waiving or reducing the recovery of costs to the extent that the authority considers is appropriate or reasonable either: to avoid any hardship which the recovery may cause to the appropriate person; or to reflect one or more of the specific considerations set out in the statutory guidance. The new 2012 guidance now includes a new provision which advises authorities that they should bear in mind that cost recovery need not necessarily be an 'all or nothing' matter and it may be reasonable to make an appropriate person pay a contribution to the costs. In the *National Grid Gas* and *Circular Facilities* cases discussed below, it is clear that the Environment Agency and the respective local authority were seeking to avoid the imposition of any cost recovery on the homeowners whose properties were affected by the contamination. The inclusion of this advice in the guidance may encourage authorities to seek to reduce the burden on the public purse by seeking to recover some element of cost from landowners whose land will benefit in value from the remediation undertaken.

The concept of hardship is inevitably going to involve an element of discretion and subjectivity; however, it is limited in application. As far as businesses are concerned the enforcing authority should adopt the same approach to all types of commercial/industrial activities irrespective of whether the business is a public or private company or a sole trader. However, where the appropriate person is a small or medium-sized enterprise or a person who runs such an enterprise, the

---

57 See note 26, para 8.3.

authority needs to consider whether recovery of the full cost would result in the business becoming insolvent, and if it closed, what the cost would be to the local economy of such a closure. If the cost to the local economy appears to be greater than the costs of remediation the authority should consider waiving or reducing the costs it seeks to recover. The guidance also addresses the issue of trustees, charities and social landlords. In relation to Class B homeowners the guidance refers to the knowledge of the homeowner at the time he purchased the property and his income, capital and outgoings. It is evident from both the *Circular Facilities*[58] and *National Grid Gas*[59] cases that the enforcing authorities were of the view that it would cause unreasonable hardship on the homeowners to serve a remediation notice on them.

7.6.5 The standard of remediation

The definition of remediation is provided in s 78A(7) of the EPA 1990 and is much wider than simply 'clean-up'. The remediation notice may require the recipient to undertake remediation in the form of assessing the condition of land; the doing of works, carrying out of operations, taking of steps and also the making of subsequent inspections. Remediation notices (and also statements and declarations) can contain any combination of these actions and will depend on the requirements and stage of the remediation of the site.

Remediation actions: the terminology

Assessment action: an action that assesses the condition of the contaminated land or any water or land affected by it. Assessment actions can be used to gather information to choose or design the most effective remedial treatment action.

Remedial treatment action: an action that will manage the significant harm or pollution of controlled waters caused by the contaminated land. Remedial treatment actions provide the solutions to prevent, minimise, remedy or mitigate the risks from contamination on the land.

Monitoring action: an action where the condition of land or water is monitored. Monitoring actions can be used to provide evidence that a remedial treatment action has been successful or is working.

The previous statutory guidance emphasised that land should be remediated on a suitable for use basis however the new guidance places a greater emphasis on securing a proportionate response to the problem of contaminated land by not demanding remediation beyond that which is necessary. The broad aim of remediation is to remove identified significant contaminant linkages, or permanently to disrupt them to ensure they are no longer significant and that risks are reduced to below an unacceptable level. If harm or pollution has been caused by the contamination them the authority needs to take into account the guidance on what remediation would be reasonable in the given circumstances. It may not always be reasonable to restore land or waters to their former states but it may be possible to achieve some level of clean up albeit of a lesser standard. When deciding what is required by way of remediation, the enforcing authority must take into accounts 78E(4) and (5) of the EPA 1990 which limit what can be required by way of remediation, to those things that the authority considers reasonable, having regard to likely cost and seriousness of harm in question. This section does not prevent an authority from serving a Remediation notice; it simply

---

58 *Circular Facilities (London) Ltd v Sevenoaks DC* [2005] EWHC 865 (Admin), [2005] Env LR 35.
59 *R (on the application of National Grid Gas Plc (formerly Transco Plc)) v Environment Agency* [2007] UKHL 30; [2008] Env LR 4.

limits what the authority might require by way of remediation. The authority must have regard it is always open to the appropriate person to carry out remediation to a higher standard of the guidance in deciding what is reasonable in the circumstances. Of course it is always open to the appropriate person to carry out remediation to a higher standard.

The 2012 Circular provides guidance on the criteria to be considered when assessing whether remediation is reasonable in order to comply with the provisions of s 78E(4) and (5). In some cases though, there may be more than one potential approach to remediation; in which case the authority is expected to select the 'best practicable technique', having regard to the following factors:

(a) the practicability, effectiveness and durability of remediation;
(b) the health and environmental impacts of the chosen remedial options;
(c) the financial costs which are likely to be involved; and
(d) the benefits of the remediation having regard to the seriousness of the harm or pollution in question.

As far as the financial factors are concerned the authority can take into account the direct costs (i.e. feasibility studies, the relevant remedial treatment, management costs) as well as the costs of any tax payable and the cost of managing the land after the remediation has taken place. Additionally the authority can also factor in any depreciation in the value of the land and any estimated increase in the value of the land and whether such increased value would accrue to the appropriate person. But the authority cannot take into account the financial standing of the person who may be made to pay for the remediation. Having said that, the latter may be a consideration when the authority decides whether the costs of such remediation can be imposed on such persons.

7.6.6 Appeals against remediation notices

A right of appeal against the service of a remediation notice is contained in s 78L(1). The appeal must be lodged within 21 days of receipt of the notice and will suspend the operation of the notice. When the provisions first came into force the Act provided a dual system of appeals; appeals against remediation notices served by local authorities were to the magistrates' court whereas appeals against remediation notices served by the Environment Agency, in respect of special sites, were to the Secretary of State. However, this was amended in 2005[60] and since March 2006 appeals against all remediation notices are to the Secretary of State. Prior to this amendment there was only one appeal to the magistrates' court and that was in *Circular Facilities (London) Ltd v Sevenoaks DC*,[61] which resulted in a further case stated appeal to the High Court.

The grounds of appeal as laid down in reg 7 of the Contaminated Land (England) Regulations 2006 are lengthy and complex. Various procedural grounds are listed, particularly the failure to act in accordance with the statutory guidance. In addition the statutory instrument lists a number of more complicated grounds where the appellant will need to prove that the enforcing authority acted unreasonably.[62] This is somewhat unusual since it requires the planning inspector (on behalf of the Secretary of State) to assess the question of reasonableness; this is more suggestive of a judicial review than a standard appeal. With so many grounds on which a person can appeal, this is arguably something of a lawyer's charter. The following list is not exhaustive:

---

60 By s 104 Clean Neighbourhoods and Environment Act 2005.
61 *Circular Facilities (London) Ltd v Sevenoaks DC* [205] EWHC 865 (Admin), [2005] Env LR35. See below at 7.7.5 for further discussion.
62 E.g. it unreasonably determined the appellant to be the appropriate person.

(a) appeals based on submissions that the enforcing authority failed to act in accordance with the statutory guidance;[63]

(b) that the enforcing authority unreasonably determined the appellant to be the appropriate person;

(c) that the enforcing authority unreasonably failed to identify some other person as an appropriate person;

(d) that the enforcing authority failed to apply the exclusion tests and rules on apportionment in accordance with the guidance;

(e) that the enforcing authority was precluded from serving the notice by s 78H or has the power to undertake the remediation itself under s 78N(3);

(f) that the notice is unreasonable.

The Secretary of State can conduct the appeal in the form of a hearing or a local inquiry. It must take the form of a hearing or local inquiry if either the appellant or the enforcing authority requests this and the regulations include provisions about who can be heard. During the appeal process the remediation notice is suspended pending the final outcome even in cases where there is the possibility of imminent danger or serious harm. Costs are generally not available in appeals heard by planning inspectors. Given the complex subject matter of these appeals, it is arguable that the period within which the appeal must be lodged is woefully inadequate.

Law in Action

Two companies (Crest Nicolson and Redlands Minerals) lost their appeal to the Secretary of State for the Environment against a remediation notice requiring them to carry out the remediation of a site in Hertfordshire. The site was designated as contaminated when it became clear that the groundwater supply was contaminated with bromate and bromide. The contamination was traced to a 1980s housing estate built on the site of a former chemical works operated by Steetley Chemical, which made bromide and bromate at the site. Steetley had been taken over by Redland Minerals. Crest bought the site in 1983 and built 66 homes, before selling it to a property management company in 1987. The Environment Agency issued a remediation notice in 2005 but both companies appealed, claiming the other was to blame. The appeals were the first for a special site and the hearing, in early 2007, was the first contaminated land appeal to be held as a public inquiry. The cases have now been considered by the High Court. For further discussion see below at 7.8.4.

7.6.7 Failure to comply with a remediation notice

Non-compliance with a remediation notice without reasonable excuse is an offence.[64] The offence is a summary offence and therefore may only be heard in a magistrates' court. Penalties reflect the distinction between the contamination of industrial and other land. In the case of industrial, trade, or business premises, the maximum financial penalty is £20,000 and there is a further daily penalty of up to £2,000 for every day the remediation notice is not complied with. In the case of other

---

63 E.g. in relation to the determination land is contaminated, the requirements of the remediation notice or the apportionment of costs between appropriate persons.

64 S 78M EPA 1990.

land, the maximum fine and daily penalty are £5,000 and £500 respectively.[65] The enforcing authority has the power to complete the remediation specified in the notice, where the notice has not been complied with,[66] and the authority is entitled to recover reasonable costs,[67] unless this will cause hardship.[68]

The enforcing authority's costs may be secured by means of a legal charge on the legal title of the contaminated land. A person served with a charging order notice has a right to lodge an appeal in the county court within 21 days of receipt of the notice.[69]

Law in Action

According to the ENDS Report,[70] Flintshire County Council was the first council to prosecute a company for failing to comply with a remediation notice. The contaminated site was a residential site; the council had received complaints about heating oil leaking from a tank serving the properties. Friars Management (UK) Ltd, a property management company, was responsible for the underground oil tank and pipe network. The council concluded that a significant pollutant linkage was present because oil was contaminating the gardens of four houses and was rising up the walls of two other houses. In 2004 the Council served a remediation notice on Friars Management, requiring them to undertake the remediation of the properties. Friars Management was taken to court for failing to comply with the notice, contrary to s 78M EPA 1990. In 2005 the company was fined £10,000 with £1,000 costs for failing to comply with the notice. Despite this the company still failed to comply with the notice, and was subject to a further prosecution; the second time the company was fined a further £40,000. The council secured public funding from the Welsh Assembly to carry out the remediation and is reported to be seeking to recover its costs from Friars Management. The costs of the remediation are understood to be about £40,000.

7.7 The appropriate person

The selection of the person or persons responsible for the remediation of contaminated land and the just application of the relevant cost of clean-up between two or more responsible persons is one of the more contentious aspects of the contaminated land regime. The division of liability for remedial costs depends upon the concept of 'the appropriate person'.

7.7.1 The polluter-pays principle

Section 78F(2) defines the appropriate person as 'the person, or any of the persons, who caused or knowingly permitted the substances, or any of the substances, which have been the cause of the

---

65 S 78M(3) and (4)EPA 1990.
66 S 78N EPA 1990.
67 S 78P EPA 1990.
68 See 7.6.4.
69 S 78P(8) EPA 1990.
70 ENDS Report 382, November 2006, p 56.

contamination to be in or under the land'. In essence, this definition seeks to apply the 'polluter-pays' principle by placing primary responsibility on the person(s) who polluted the land. However, it is subject to an important caveat; the liability of such a person is referable only to the particular substances that the person has caused or knowingly permitted to be present.[71] This means that the remedial action to be required is to be taken by the appropriate person only in relation to the substances he or she contributed (s 78F(3)). Consequently the question of liability has to be considered separately for each significant pollutant linkage identified on the land. Section 78K makes it clear that the appropriate person may also be the person from whose land substances have escaped which has caused the contamination of someone else's land.

The enforcing authority is tasked with the job of determining which person or persons caused or knowingly permitted the contaminating substances to be present in/on/under the land. This will not always be easy, given the distinct possibility that a site has been subject, over the years, to a variety of uses and ownership and it will also depend upon the enforcing authority understanding what is meant by 'causing' or 'knowingly permitting'. All that is required under the Act is that the enforcing authority makes reasonable inquiry to find the polluter. The question of what level of inquiry is reasonable remains to be tested by the courts. However, as the case of R (On the application of National Grid Gas Plc) v Environment Agency (2006)[72] demonstrates, the original polluters may no longer exist or they may have been taken over by successive bodies; particularly statutory successors as a result of either nationalisation or privatisation. The National Grid Gas case focussed particularly on the liability of National Grid Gas in 2006 in respect of contamination caused by two private gas companies operating on a site between 1912 and 1948. The case is discussed more fully below.

7.7.2 The transfer of liability to owners/occupiers

The authority is charged with making 'reasonable inquiry'. If, after such reasonable inquiry, no such persons can be found, the liability for the remediation will switch to the 'owner or occupier for the time being of the contaminated land'. Accordingly liability will transfer to the owner/occupier, who will become the appropriate person.[73] This latter step does not apply where the problem caused by the contamination is solely one of water pollution: this reflects the potential liabilities for water pollution as they existed prior to the introduction of Part 2A.

7.7.3 Class A and Class B persons

The guidance seeks to distinguish between these two separate categories of appropriate persons by classifying them as Class A persons (the polluter) and Class B persons (the owner and occupier). In short, primary responsibility rests with the so-called Class A person or persons (referred to as the Class A liability group), but will switch to the Class B persons if the enforcing authority cannot find identify the Class A person or persons. Despite this categorisation it should be noted that in many instances the current owner/occupier of land may in fact be liable as a Class A person if they have caused or knowingly permitted the contaminating substance to be present in the land. It is important to remember that the liability of the Class A person is referable only to the particular substances which the person has caused or knowingly permitted to be present. This means that the remedial

---

71 S 78F (3) EPA 1990.
72 R (On the application of National Grid Gas Plc (formerly Transco Plc)) v Environment Agency [2007] UKHL 30; [2008] Env LR 4.
73 S 78F(4) EPA 1990.

action to be required is to be taken by the appropriate person only in relation to the substances he or she contributed.[74]

7.7.4 Class A persons: causing or knowingly permitting contamination

7.7.4.1 Causing

The terms 'causing' and 'knowingly permitting' have been used as a basis for determining liability in environmental law for over 100 years and have been examined at length elsewhere within this book.[75] It seems likely that 'causing' contamination will be interpreted strictly in much the same way as causing water pollution was under s 85(1) Water Resources Act 1991.[76] The 'appropriate person' in s 78F(2) will be someone who has engaged in, or is engaging in, an active operation which has caused, or is causing, contamination. Maintaining tanks, pipes and cables from which contaminants have escaped will therefore all be active operations attracting liability. More than one person can cause contaminants to be present in or under land.[77]

See Chapters 4–5

Once contaminated land has been identified by an enforcing authority, it is presumed that the owner or occupier of the site, at the date the contamination occurred, caused the contamination. If this presumption does not accord with the facts, the onus is on the owner or occupier to establish that someone else caused the contamination. Significantly, there is no defence to causing contamination based on the use of 'best practice'.[78] However, despite liability for causing being strict, the regime does provide (with regard to the allocation of costs for remediation between the appropriate persons) mechanisms to mitigate the potential impact of liability.[79]

7.7.4.2 Knowingly permitting

The test of 'knowingly permitting' requires both knowledge that the substances in question were in, on or under the land and the possession of the power to prevent such a substance being there.[80] However, it is not necessary to prove that the person knew that the substances could result in the contamination of the land.[81] In the context of the contaminated land regime the question of whether a person knew that substances were present in the land is inevitably made more difficult by the fact that the contamination (and hence knowledge of it) could have happened quite considerably in the past. How does an enforcing authority for example prove that a person knowingly permitted contamination in say the 1960s or 70s? The difficulties in establishing that a person had knowledge are apparent in *Circular Facilities London Ltd v Sevenoaks DC* (2005),[82] a case involving the first appeal against a remediation notice under the Act.

---

74 S 78F(3) EPA 1990.
75 See Chapter 4 in respect of water pollution and Chapter 5 in respect of the waste offences.
76 S 85 WRA 1991 is now repealed.
77 E.g., a contractor who installs an underground storage tank resulting in contamination of the site.
78 Otherwise referred to as a 'state of the art' defence.
79 See 7.8.2 below on exclusion tests.
80 'The test of "knowingly permitting" would require both knowledge that the substances in question were in, on or under the land and the possession of the power to prevent such a substance being there.' (House of Lords Hansard [11 July 1995], col 1497.)
81 See below at 7.7.
82 *Circular Facilities (London) Ltd v Sevenoaks DC* [2005] EWHC 865 (Admin), [2005] Env LR 35.

7.7.5 The *Circular Facilities* case: knowingly permitting

7.7.5.1 The facts

The *Circular Facilities* case involved an appeal by Circular Facilities (CFL) against a remediation notice served by Sevenoaks District Council (SDC). The site in question had formerly been a brickworks on which clay pits had been dug. These were infilled during the 1960s and 70s, initially by the owner (a Mr Kinchen-Goldsmith) and then by the subsequent owner, Mr Scott, who purchased the land in 1978. In December 1979 Mr Scott sold the land to CFL but he continued to develop the site on behalf of CFL. In March 1980 Mr Scott applied for planning permission to construct houses on the site and, as part of the planning process, he submitted a geotechnical report to the council. This report indicated the presence of black organic matter in the trial pits constructed on the site and additionally gases bubbling through water in one of the trial pits. Planning permission was granted and the houses were constructed. The planning permission did not require the removal of the organic matter. Following the entry into force of Part 2A, SDC investigated the site and determined that the land was contaminated and accordingly served a remediation notice on CFL requiring them to take measures to vent the gases and aerate the soil. The council accepted that CFL had not caused the matter to be present on the land but it considered that it had knowingly permitted it to remain there during the construction of the houses. CFL appealed.

7.7.5.2 The issues

In the magistrates' court Judge Kelly found, as a matter of fact, that the geotechnical report must have been available to CFL as it was on the planning register and had been submitted by Mr Scott on its behalf. Additionally Judge Kelly also considered that CFL must have considered the risks of investing in land that had been used as clay pits and therefore in assessing that risk the company must have considered the report. Dismissing the appeal, the magistrates concluded there was evidence of knowledge and the failure to deal with the threats from the gas was sufficient grounds for concluding that CFL had knowingly permitted the contamination. In respect of the other 'players' the court considered that none were liable.

It is not surprising that this first case to come before the magistrates should have resulted in a case stated appeal. The administrative court was asked to consider three questions:

- whether the judge's finding that CFL knew of the presence of buried organic material or gases between 1979 and 1985 was valid;
- whether, assuming that there was knowledge of the contents of the report, such knowledge was sufficient for CFL to be found to have knowingly permitted the substances to be in or on the land;
- whether the judge was right to conclude that the policy of the Act was to make developers liable.

In relation to the first question the High Court concluded that the magistrates' court had not explained on what basis it had concluded that CFL had been aware of the 1978 report, or how that knowledge was imputed to CFL's managing director. The court ordered a retrial. However, before the retrial could take place SDC withdrew its remediation notice and agreed to settle the case with CFL on a confidential basis. On this basis it was not necessary for the court to address the remaining questions. However, Newman J confirmed that knowledge of the presence of the substance alone, which is later found to contaminate, is all that is required to 'knowingly permit'. Despite this being clearly asserted and, in the author's opinion, correct, the statement must be regarded as an obiter statement. Nevertheless, this may offer some comfort to the enforcing authorities in the light of what is otherwise a difficult task of proving liability under this particular limb.

7.7.6 Finding the appropriate person: the *National Grid Gas* case

The *Circular Facilities* case demonstrates the difficulties in establishing that a person or company knew about the presence of contaminating substances in the past. The *National Grid Gas* case also reveals the difficulties faced by the enforcing authorities in finding a Class A person in situations where the contamination was caused by a company that has been taken over by a number of statutory successors.

7.7.6.1 The facts

In 2005 the Environment Agency identified a residential site (with 11 houses on it) as being contaminated by coal tar residues. The Agency carried out the remediation itself (at a cost of approximately £66,000 per residence) but decided (on the basis of the potential hardship it would cause)[83] not to recover its costs from the homeowners. Instead the Agency determined that the appropriate person was Transco Plc.[84] NGG judicially reviewed this decision. The history of the site reveals the difficulties faced by local authorities and the Agency. The site, in Bawtry, Doncaster, had been used by two private companies (for ease of reference, the B&DGC[85] and the SY&DGC[86]) for gas production between 1912 and 1948, when the companies were nationalised by the Gas Act 1948 and taken over by the East Midlands Gas Board (EMGB). Gas production ceased relatively quickly after that and the EMGB sold the land to a company (Kenton Homes Ltd), which in turn sold it on to a developer (Kenneth Jackson Ltd) in 1966. This developer sought planning permission for and built 11 houses on the site. Transco/NGG had never owned or occupied the site; indeed gas production had ceased in the early 1950s well before NGG came into being. However, the Agency contended that NGG was the appropriate person because it was the statutory successor to the EMGB.

Turning to the evolution of the gas industry, the EMGB was established by the Gas Act 1948, which nationalised the industry and provided for the statutory transfer of the assets and liabilities of the privately owned predecessor undertakings to the East Midlands Gas Board. Later in 1972 and 1986 there were further statutory transfers of the assets and liabilities of the EMGB to the British Gas Corporation by the Gas Act 1972 and of the British Gas Corporation to British Gas plc by the Gas Act 1986. Transco and then NGG subsequently acquired the gas transportation and storage undertaking of British Gas plc and the relevant liabilities. In each case the statutory provisions for succession said that the successor company would take over the liabilities of the predecessor company 'immediately before' the transfer date.

The Agency was the enforcing authority for this site and it clearly took steps to identify possible Class A persons. It was clear that if the two private sector gas companies, B&DGC and the SY&DGC, and the EMGB had still existed, they would have been appropriate persons since they caused the contaminating substances to be present. Similarly the Agency considered that both Kenton Homes Ltd and Kenneth Jackson Ltd would have known of the substances and arguably had knowingly permitted their presence. However, both companies had also ceased to exist and could not therefore be 'found'. This left the Agency with the difficult decision to transfer liability to the homeowners, who having bought their houses in good faith could be regarded as 'innocent'. Instead the Agency, having carried out the remediation itself, sought to impose cost recovery liability on Transco/NGG as the appropriate person. In view of the important issue raised by this case and also the potential liability of NGG for numerous other sites, NGG took the decision to seek judicial review of the Agency's decision on the basis that it was not the appropriate person because:

83 See 7.6.3 above.
84 Later to become National Grid Gas (NGG).
85 The Bawtry and District Gas Company.
86 The South Yorkshire and Derbyshire Gas Company.

(a) it had not caused or knowingly permitted the substances to be present;

(b) that at the time of the various transfers of liability through the 'chain' of statutory succession, no relevant liabilities had existed in law, or arisen in fact; and

(c) even if there had been liability under any of the then applicable liability regimes, transfers could only have been effective as to those liabilities and not that under Part 2A which had not been in force at the time of any of the transfers.

Essentially the Agency presented two arguments in favour of its decision that NGG was an appropriate person. First the Environment Agency argued that 'person ... who caused or knowingly permitted' should be construed so as to include every person who became by statute the successor to the liabilities of the actual polluters.[87] The Divisional Court was prepared to accept this argument by adopting a purposive approach to the interpretation. The Divisional Court, referring to Hansard,[88] held that the clear intention of Part 2A was to make the polluter pay, and not innocent homeowners. Although the House of Lords accepted that this was probably true, the fact remained that NGG was not a polluter either. In the opinion of Lord Scott of Foscote, the plain language of the Act did not support such an 'impossible construction' on the term 'person'.

> This is, in my opinion, a quite impossible construction to place on the uncomplicated and easily understandable statutory language. The emphasis in s 78F, both in subs (2) and in subs (3), is on the actual polluter, the person who 'caused or knowingly permitted'.

The critical factor in the Lords' decision was that the statutes which had transferred the rights and liabilities of the various private and public gas undertakers were expressly limited to those existing 'immediately before' the transfer date. The Law Lords were unanimous; since liability under Part 2A had not been created until many years after the transfer dates, that liability had not existed (even as a contingent) 'immediately before' the transfers, and so could not have passed as part of the succession. 'It is true that the legislation was retrospective in the sense that it created a potential present liability for acts done in the past. But that is not the same as creating a deemed past liability for those acts. There is nothing in the Act to create retrospectively in this sense.' The appeal was upheld.

The implications of the decision in *National Grid Gas* remain to be seen. Certainly statutory transfer schemes such as those provided by the Gas Acts occur in relation to those industries which were previously nationalised but are now privatised, such as the coal, electricity and water industries. Local authorities have also been subject to significant statutory reorganisation. The extent to which this decision is 'transferable' to other organisations will depend largely on the precise wording of the statutory transfer schemes. For example, the Water Act 1989 provides for transfers to include future liabilities not existing at the date of the transfer. The decision will no doubt raise concern for property developers and homeowners. In the event that no Class A person can be found, liability may switch to developers who developed on contaminated sites, knowing contaminants were present; or worse, homeowners who bought houses before the issue of land contamination was addressed during the conveyancing transaction.

---

87 I.e. B&DGC, SY&DGC and the EMGB.

88 Relying on the authority in *Pepper v Hart* [1993] 1 All ER 42 that in the event of ambiguity a court could refer to Hansard to ascertain the intention of Parliament.

> **Law in Action**
>
> Gloucester City Council secured £80,000 funding from Defra in order to investigate a site known as Alney Island. The site lies between two branches of the River Severn. The investigation revealed widespread contamination from heavy metals and polycyclic aromatic hydrocarbons in buried ash and clinker. The council considered that a significant pollutant linkage existed, because of the presence of six residential properties and two caravan sites. The land was determined as contaminated land, under Part IIA. After carrying out enquiries the council concluded that no Class A party could be identified, as the polluting activities had occurred over 80 years ago. Liability therefore switched to the Class B landowners. However, the council decided the residents concerned would be put in a position of financial hardship, so it secured financial support from Defra's Capital Support fund to help meet the costs of the remediation.[89]

7.7.7 Liability of site owners and occupiers

As noted above, an owner of land (or occupier) may become liable as a Class A person if they have either caused or knowingly permitted the contaminating substances to be present on land. In which case, their liability arises because they are effectively the 'polluter' and not by virtue of their ownership or occupation of the land. However, an 'innocent' landowner may also become liable in the event that no Class A person can be found.[90] Where land is contaminated with several substances, it will be necessary to establish whether the current owner or occupier is responsible for all or only part of the contamination. If the owner or occupier is only responsible for the presence of some of the substances which are present, the owner or occupier will be liable as a Class A person with regard to the contamination he or she caused. With regard to other contaminating substances on site, the owner or occupier may also be liable as a Class B person if the relevant Class A person or persons cannot be found.

The term 'owner' is defined in s 78A as the person who is entitled to receive the market rent for the property, but mortgagees not in possession and insolvency practitioners are not owners.[91] 'Occupier' is not defined.

7.8 Allocating the cost of remediation, exclusion and apportionment

Having identified the responsible 'appropriate person or persons', the enforcing authority must then determine the extent of each person's liability for clean-up. As with so many other aspects of this regime the task of determining the extent of liability is both complex and governed by the statutory guidance. This makes it clear that the enforcing authority should allocate liability by undertaking the following sequential tasks:

(a) identify the significant pollutant linkages on the land. There may be more than one significant pollutant linkage;

(b) make reasonable inquiry to identify the Class A persons. Liability as a Class A person is referable only to the particular substances which the person has caused or knowingly permitted

---

89 Details available from Gloucester City Council at http://www.gloucester.gov.uk/CouncilServices/EnvironmentalHealth/ PollutionControl/ContaminatedLand-Sitescurrentlybeinginspected-AlneyIsland.aspx.

90 S 78F(4) EPA 1990.

91 S 78X(3) EPA 1990.

to be present. There may be more than one significant pollutant linkage and more than one Class A liability group;

(c) identify, in the absence of Class A persons, the Class B liability group for the relevant significant pollutant linkage;

(d) determine whether any member of a liability groups should be excluded from liability by applying a sequence of exclusion test laid down in the guidance;

(e) apportion the remediation costs between the remaining (non-excluded) liable persons.

In short, the fact that somebody has been identified as an appropriate person does not mean that they will necessarily be liable for meeting the costs of the remediation. This is because the Act requires that where the enforcing authority has identified a liability group, it must go on to consider whether any such member of that liability group should be excluded from liability.

7.8.1 Exclusion of liability

In the government's view there are circumstances where it will not be fair to apportion liability to a person who is 'caught' as either a Class A or Class B person. Hence s 78F(6) requires: 'Where two or more persons would, apart from this subsection, be appropriate persons in relation to any particular thing which is to be done by way of remediation, the enforcing authority shall determine in accordance with guidance issued for the purpose by the Secretary of State whether any, and if so which, of them is to be treated as not being an appropriate person in relation to that thing.' The guidance in turn details the general considerations applying to exclusion and then sets out the detailed exclusion tests for both Class A and Class B persons. As a general consideration the financial circumstances of persons within a liability group are irrelevant at this stage and the exclusion tests cannot result in the exclusion of all of the members of the liability group; at least one member must remain. The guidance states that the intention of the tests is to establish whether, in relation to other members of the liability group, it is fair that he should bear any part of that responsibility. If, after applying the exclusion tests discussed below, a person is excluded from liability he should be treated as not being an appropriate person.

7.8.2 Exclusion of Class A persons

The guidance sets out six tests for determining whether to exclude from liability a person who would otherwise be a Class A person.

The six exclusion tests must be applied sequentially. In applying these tests, the enforcing authority cannot exclude all of the members of the group; in other words, at least one member of the Class A group must remain.

The six tests are summarised as follows:

(1) Test 1: the purpose of this test is to exclude persons who fall within the Class A liability group because of the performance of certain excluded activities. The list of excluded activities is lengthy, but principally includes mortgage lenders and other providers of finance, insurance underwriters and persons who have provided technical, legal or scientific advice.

(2) Test 2: this test excludes persons who have already made payments for the remediation of the land. Such a payment would normally occur when land is transferred (sold) and the vendor either reduces the price to account for the cost of the remediation or makes a payment to the purchaser to cover the costs.

(3) Test 3: the purpose of this test is to exclude from liability those who sold the contaminated land with information regarding the contamination so that it is reasonable to expect the purchaser to bear the costs of the remediation. The test includes an interesting retrospective provision in relation to land transactions where the buyer is a large commercial organisation

or public body. In transactions since the beginning of 1990 where the buyer was a large commercial organisation or public body, permission from the seller for the buyer to carry out his or her own investigations of the land should normally be taken as sufficient indication that the land was sold with information. For further discussion of this test, see the discussion on the *Redland Minerals/Crest Nicholson* litigation below.

(4)   Test 4: this excludes persons from liability in situations where the person has caused substances to be present on the land, but those substances have only formed a significant pollutant linkage because of the unforeseeable introduction of substances by another person at a later date.

(5)   Test 5: this test excludes a person from liability where it can be shown that the land has become contaminated because of the escape of substances from some other (presumably adjoining) land and that another member of the liability group caused that escape.

(6)   Test 6: this test excludes a person from liability where he or she is only liable because of the subsequent introduction by others (such as later developers) who have introduced a relevant pathway or receptors.

The exclusion tests are detailed and complex and, particularly in relation to exclusion tests 2 and 3, there are many conditions to be satisfied before a person can reliably benefit from the test.

In the event that a liability group reaches agreement on the allocation of their respective liabilities and informs the enforcing authority of the voluntary agreement, the terms of the agreement prevail over any other allocation favoured by the enforcing authority except to the extent that the agreement is a sham device intended to avoid liability. This situation could arise if the terms of the agreement purported to transfer liability to a group member who would, in consequence, suffer hardship, thus preventing the enforcing authority serving a remediation notice on that person.

In liability groups whose members include two or more related companies, those companies will be treated as one person for the purpose of applying the exclusion tests.

In the interests of justice, the financial standing of each member of a liability group is irrelevant for the purpose of applying the exclusion tests.

7.8.3 Exclusion of Class B persons

The Class B exclusion tests will only be applied where two or more Class B persons have been identified as appropriate persons. This is most likely to be the case in circumstances where the owner and the occupier are different persons. Class B persons are excluded from liability if they are occupiers or tenants paying a market rent but have no long-term financial interest in the land which would benefit from clean-up works. However, tests should not be applied, and consequently no exclusion should be made, if it would result in the exclusion of all of the members of the liability group. This means that an occupier with no financial interest in the land could be liable, although it is likely in the circumstances that the enforcing authority would consider the potential hardship before serving a remediation notice.

7.8.4 Apportioning costs between appropriate persons

Once the exclusion tests have been applied, the enforcing authority is required to consider the issue of apportionment[92] in accordance with the statutory guidance. In relation to 'polluters' (Class A

---

92 S 78F(7) EPA 1990.

persons remaining after the exclusion tests) the principal determining principle is that liability should be apportioned to reflect the relative responsibility of each of those members for creating or continuing the risk now being caused by the significant pollutant linkage in question. This seems somewhat at odds with the strict liability concept of 'causing', where intention and negligence are irrelevant considerations. This appears to require a subjective assessment which enforcing authorities may feel ill-equipped to make. The enforcing authority will, in arriving at its allocation, have regard to the duration of the period during which each responsible person was in occupation of the land and was using contaminating substances. An accurate assessment will, in most cases, largely depend upon the availability of reliable information. In default of receiving a reasonable amount of information upon which to base an assessment, the enforcing authority may apportion the remediation costs equally between the non-excluded members of the relevant Class A or B.

The applicability of the sold with information exclusion test and the issue of apportionment between two Class A persons were addressed by the High Court in the *Redland Minerals* and *Crest Nicholson* litigation.[93] Redland Minerals (RM) produced chemicals at a site in Hertfordshire between the 1950s and about 1980. Leakages from the works had caused bromide and bromate to be present in the soil. In 1983 RM sold the land to Crest Nicholson (CN), a residential property developer, after CN had conducted some testing of the site. In 1984 CN demolished the chemical works and broke up the hardstanding but left the site exposed to the elements until 1986/87, when it commenced construction of houses. CN had removed a 1-1.5 metre layer of soil from the site with the intention of removing any chemicals; however, due to the exposure to the rain and the removal of the hardstanding, the bromate and bromides had penetrated deeper into the soil than would otherwise have been the case. The contaminants eventually found their way into groundwater. This in turn caused contamination of the water supply. The Environment Agency issues remediation notices to both RM and CN. Both appealed to the Secretary of State, who referred the matter to an inspector and an inquiry was held. In the light of the inspector's report the Secretary of State determined:

- RM were not excluded from liability under the sold with information exclusion test. The exclusion test should apply completely to a contaminant linkage and its partial applicability should only be considered as a factor in the final apportionment. At the time CN purchased the land it knew about the bromide in the upper part of the site but it could not reasonably have been aware of the extent of the bromide contamination likely to have been already present in the aquifer. The High Court agreed that the Secretary of State had the right to reach this conclusion.

- In respect of the bromate, both RM and CN had caused contaminants to be present. Although RM had caused the bromide and bromate to be present CN as a result of action and inaction in the way it dealt with the site caused contaminants that would otherwise have been removed to remain and also caused contaminants to be flushed deeper and faster into the ground. The demolition of the buildings and hard surfaces on the site constituted an active operation which had mobilised the contaminants. Previously the roofs and the hard surfaces had afforded some protection from the rain, but their demolition left the ground open to the leaching effects of infiltration. The Court agreed that both RM and CN had caused the bromate to be present in, on or under land.

---

93 R (on the application of Redland Minerals Ltd) v Secretary of State for Environment, Food and Rural Affairs [2010] EWHC 913 (Admin); [2011] Env LR 2 and R (on the application of Crest Nicholson Residential Ltd) v Secretary of State for Environment, Food and Rural Affairs [2010] EWHC 1561 (Admin); [2011] Env LR 1.

- RM should bear 85% of the costs and CN only 15%. The High Court upheld this too and accepted that the Secretary of State was correct in identifying that there was no simple quantitative causative mechanism in the case. Instead, a broad evaluative judgment on causation had been required. RM had caused all the bromide and bromate to be on the land in the first place and allowed them to filter down to the lower strata during its long period in control of the site. CN had brought no contaminants onto the site but had accelerated the way in which the contaminants already in the land were flushed down to the lower levels.

7.9 The Environmental Damage (Prevention and Remediation) Regulations 2009

7.9.1 Implementing the Environmental Liability Directive

In examining liability for contaminated land it is necessary to reflect on the provisions of the Environmental Damage (Prevention and Remediation) Regulations 2009 as they relate to land.[94] (The provisions of the regulations have a wider scope and include environmental damage to water, protected species and natural habitats, but these are largely outside the subject matter of this chapter.) The 2009 Regulations were brought into force on 1 March 2009, somewhat belatedly since the UK had been required to transpose the requirements of the Environmental Liability Directive (ELD) 2004/35/EC[95] into domestic law by 30 April 2007. Only four Member states met this deadline. By 2010 the Commission had commenced infringement procedures against 23 Member States and subsequently proceeded against a number of states before the Court of Justice, which gave judgment against seven Member States in 2008 and 2009, including the UK.[96] Further details about the implementation and an analysis of the effectiveness of the ELD can be found in the European Commission's report of 2010.[97]

The Environmental Liability Directive 2004 was a long time in the making. The idea of such a directive was first mooted in 1993, when the European Commission published a Green Paper. Seventeen years later, in 2000, the Commission followed this up with a White Paper[98] and the first draft directive was published in 2002. By the time the ELD was finally adopted in 2004 the provisions of Part 2A EPA 1990 had already been brought into force. The ELD 2004 requires Member States to take measures to prevent and remedy certain environmental damage. According to the Europa website it is 'The first EC legislation whose main objectives include the application of the "polluter pays" principle'.[99] However, it is clear that the directive and implementing domestic regulations only cover the most serious cases of environmental damage, and according to Defra the 2009 Regulations are expected to cover fewer than 1 per cent of the total number of cases of damage in England and Wales.[100]

---

94 Environmental Damage (Prevention and Remediation) Regulations 2009 SI 2009/153. Separate regulations were made for Wales. See the Environmental Damage (Prevention and Remediation) (Wales) Regulations 2009 SI 2009/995.
95 Directive 2004/35/EC of the European Parliament and of the Council of 21 April 2004 on environmental liability with regard to the prevention and remedying of environmental damage.
96 Case C-417/08 *Commission v UK* [2009] ECR I-106.
97 Report from the Commission to the Council, the European Parliament, the European Economic and Social Committee and the Committee of the Regions under article 14(2) of Directive 2004/35/CE on the Environmental Liability with regard to Prevention and Remedying of Environmental Damage COM/2010/0581 final.
98 European Commission White Paper on environmental liability COM(2000) 66 final, 9 February 2000.
99 See http://europa.eu/legislation_summaries/enterprise/interaction_with_other_policies/l28120_en.htm, accessed 1 March 2010.
100 Defra, In-depth Guide The Environmental Damage Regulations: Preventing and Remedying Environmental Damage, updated November 2009. See also the corresponding Quick Guide available at: http://www.defra.gov.uk/environment/policy/liability/pdf/quick-guide-regs09.pdf, accessed 1 March 2010.

7.9.2 Prevention and remediation

The ELD/2009 (Part 2) Regulations enable (confer a discretion) on public authorities to require operators to take the necessary preventive steps in situations where there is an imminent threat of environmental damage. Failing that the public authority can take the necessary preventive measures and recover the costs incurred at a later date. However, more specifically within the context of this chapter, where environmental damage has occurred the competent public authority is under a duty (under Part 3 of the regulations) to require remediation where it establishes that there is 'environmental damage' and a liable operator. The Regulations also enable the competent authority to undertake the remediation work and recover its costs at a later date from the operator who caused the damage.

The Directive/Regulations do not create a new common law right of action since the principal concern is to prevent and remedy environmental damage and not to compensate individuals for loss. However, there is provision for natural or legal persons who may be adversely affected by environmental damage and also environment protection organisations[101] to request the competent authorities to act when faced with damage. (This is subject to certain conditions.) Such persons and organisations may then bring judicial review proceedings of the competent body's decisions and actions or its failure to act.

The ELD/2009 Regulations have introduced two types of liability: strict liability and fault-based liability.

7.9.3 Strict liability for damage caused by occupational activities

The regulations impose strict liability in respect of environmental damage caused by operators of those activities listed in Annex III of the Directive (Sched 2 of the 2009 domestic Regulations). These are described by reference to various pieces of EU legislation and are referred to in the directive as 'occupational' activities. These are, inter alia:

- those activities that require an environmental permit under the Integrated Pollution and Prevention Control Directive;
- those waste management activities (including landfill and incineration) that require an environmental permit;
- activities concerning genetically modified organisms and micro-organisms.

In Case C-378/08 *Raffinerie Mediterranee (ERG) SpA and others* the ECJ held, inter alia, that when deciding to impose measures for remedying environmental damage on operators whose activities fall within Annex III to the Directive, the competent authority is not required to establish fault, negligence or intent on the part of operators whose activities are held to be responsible for the environmental damage. However, that authority must first carry out a prior investigation into the origin of the pollution found, and it has a discretion as to the procedures, means to be employed and length of such an investigation. Second, the competent authority is required to establish, in accordance with national rules on evidence, a causal link between the activities of the operators at whom the remedial measures are directed and the pollution.[102]

---

101 E.g. environmental protection pressure groups such as Friends of the Earth.
102 Case C-378/08 *Raffinerie Mediterranee (ERG) SpA v Ministero dello Sviluppo Economico* [2010] 3 CMLR 9; [2010] Env LR 39.

7.9.4 Fault-based liability in respect of damage caused to protected species and natural habitats from all other activities

The regulations also provide for a fault-based liability regime in respect of all occupational activities other than those listed in Annex III/Sched 2 2009 Regulations. However, liability under this limb is confined to damage, or imminent threat of damage, to species or natural habitats protected by EU legislation. Although not directly relevant in this chapter it should be noted that with regard to damage to protected species, natural habitats and water the objective of remediation is to return the environment to the condition it was in before the event giving rise to the damage.

The competent authorities for the purposes of the 2009 Regulations are the Environment Agency and local authorities, depending on which is the regulatory body of the operation (see regs 10 and 11).

7.9.5 Liability for contaminated land

The regulations include environmental damage to land caused by occupational activities listed in Sched 2. Damage to land is defined as 'contamination of land by substances, preparations, organisms or micro-organisms that results in a significant risk of adverse effects on human health'.[103] The definition is similar to the definition of contaminated land under Part 2, but the focus is on adverse effects to human health only (as opposed to other receptors) and does not include 'the significant possibility of harm'.

Also unlike Part 2A EPA 1990, the 2009 Regulations are not retrospective. They only apply to damage that has occurred after the regulations come into force[104] and also to damage that takes place after that date or is threatened after that date but is caused by an incident, event or emission that took place before that date. The regulations will also apply to damage caused by an incident, event or emission that takes place after that date if it derives from an activity that took place and finished before 1 March 2009.[105]

Under reg 17 of the 2009 Regulations the competent authorities can decide whether damage (within the scope of the regulations) has occurred; it is likely that they will be notified of this either by the operator or a third party. If damage has occurred, the regulations provide for procedures to be followed to secure the remediation of the damage. The responsible authority must identify the responsible operator. The operator is defined as the person who operates or controls the activity, including the holder of a permit or authorisation relating to that activity.[106] The operator must then submit proposals for the remediation of the damage (reg 18). The remediation proposals must be consistent with the requirements of Sched 4 of the Regulations which include, inter alia, a description of the environmental damage and the different remediation options as well as the results expected. If the operator fails to make proposals within the time limit specified by the competent enforcement authority or if the operator fails to propose measures, the authority will identify the required remedial measures. The proposals are then subject to a period of consultation (reg 29) after which the authority must serve a remediation notice on the responsible operator (reg 20). On receipt of a remediation notice under the 2009 Regulations the operator is required to undertake the remedial works in accordance with the notice, subject to a right of appeal against the notice. The remediation must ensure, as a minimum, that the relevant contaminants are removed, controlled, contained or diminished so that the land, taking account of its lawful current use or any planning permission in existence at the time of the damage, no longer poses any significant risk of adverse effects on human health.

103 Environmental Damage (Prevention and Remediation) Regulations 2009 SI 2009/153, reg 4(5).
104 In England, 1 March 2009; in Wales, 6 May 2009.
105 Environmental Damage (Prevention and Remediation) Regulations 2009 SI 2009/153, reg 8.
106 Ibid, reg 2.

The regulations create a number of criminal offences; notably failing to comply with a remediation notice (reg 20(3)). On summary conviction, the magistrates' court may impose a fine not exceeding the statutory maximum or a sentence of imprisonment for a term not exceeding three months or both. On conviction on indictment, the Crown Court can impose an unlimited fine, a custodial sentence of up to two years, or both.

7.10 The public register

One of the government's stated aims in relation to the Part IIA regime was to improve transparency. To this end the regime requires that enforcing authorities maintain public registers which detail the actions taken under Part IIA EPA 1990. The contaminated land register, maintained by each enforcing authority, contains details of: remediation notices, remediation statements, declarations, notices, appeals, convictions, remediation work (see s 78R of and Sched 3 to the Contaminated Land (England) Regulations 2000). The information held on the registers will also fall within the definition of environmental information under the Environmental Information Regulations 2004.

See Chapter 12 →

7.11 Interface with other controls

7.11.1 Part 2A as a regime of last resort

The interface between contaminated land controls and other regulatory regimes is particularly important in that the contaminated land regime is designed to 'kick in' only when other statutory controls are unable to tackle contamination effectively. The 2012 statutory guidance clearly states that the enforcing authorities should seek to use Part 2A 'only where no appropriate alternative solution exists'. This is clearly consistent with the government's aim of reducing regulatory intervention. However, it should be remembered that other regimes, such as planning, will only be applicable when land is subject to a redevelopment proposal.

7.11.2 Town and country planning

The contaminated land regime in Part 2A focuses on addressing the risks of contamination on the basis of the current use. The regime was not designed to assess the risks in relation to a future use of the land that would require a specific grant of planning permission. In contrast the planning system aims to control development and land use in the future. Therefore land contamination is a 'material consideration' in individual planning applications and the state of land subject to a development proposal must be taken into account by a planning authority in reaching a planning decision. The local planning authority, if it grants planning permission for development on contaminated land, may impose planning conditions to address risks to man and the environment posed by the presence of contaminants on site—for example, a condition requiring the venting of methane from sub-floor areas if residential development on a closed landfill is contemplated. In setting conditions, the planning authority must ensure that the land would not meet the definition of contaminated land under Part 2A. In these circumstances it is the responsibility of the developer to carry out the remediation and the planning authority to ensure compliance with the planning conditions. In this respect remediation as a condition of planning permission is simple; there is no need for the planning authority to consider who is liable. The evidence to date[107] is that the vast majority of contaminated sites are

---

107 Environment Agency, 'Reporting the Evidence: Dealing with Contaminated Land in England and Wales, A Review of Progress from 2000–2007 of Part 2A Environmental Protection Act 1990' (January 2009).

being dealt with through the planning system. It should be noted that in some cases, the carrying out of remediation activities under Part 2A may itself constitute 'development' and therefore require planning permission.

At a more strategic level contaminated land is also an issue for planning authorities. The content of development plans provides an important mechanism enabling planning authorities (the local authorities) to plan the appropriate redevelopment of 'brownfield' sites which may also be contaminated. The government has set a target of 60 per cent of new housing to be constructed on brownfield sites, and for 100 per cent of contaminated land to be brought back into beneficial use by 2030. Government planning advice relating to contaminated land appears in Planning Policy Statement (PPS) 23.[108]

Law in Action

R (on the application of Gawthorpe) v Sedgemoor DC (2012)[109]

A local resident sought judicial review of Sedgemoor District Council's decision to grant planning permission for the development of 14 houses on a site that was previously used by industrial works. The authority's environmental health officer had advised that the developer should be required to carry out a detailed site investigation in line with PPS 23 in order to determine whether the land was contaminated, and if it was the developer should be required to submit a scheme of remediation before planning permission was granted. PPS 23 advises that where development is proposed on land that is or may be affected by contamination, an assessment of risk should be carried out by the applicant for the local planning authority before the application is determined; and that any existing or new unacceptable risks should be identified and proposals made to deal with them effectively as part of the development process; and that local planning authorities should satisfy themselves that intending developers have addressed effectively the issue of potential contamination in bringing forward their proposal. However, in this case the officer's advice was only attached as a note to the planning permission but was not included as a condition. The court held, having reviewed the guidance in PPS 23, that no reasonable planning authority would have proceeded to grant planning permission without a condition addressing the contaminated land issues in the face of the advice of the Secretary of State and their own Environmental Health Officer, absent a good reason for so doing. The planning permission was unlawful.

7.11.3 Environmental permitting

Regulated facilities that operate within the terms of an environmental permit are excluded from the scope of the contaminated land regime. Section 78YB provides that Part 2A will not apply in relation to any 'significant harm, or pollution of controlled waters, by reason of which land would otherwise fall to be regarded as contaminated, which is attributable to the operation of a regulated facility; and enforcement action may be taken in relation to that harm or

See Chapter 5

---

108 Planning Policy Statement 23: Planning and Pollution Control-Annex 2 Development on Land affected by contamination (November 2004).
109 *R (on the application of Gawthorpe) v Sedgemoor DC* [2012] EWHC 2020 (admin); [2013] Env LR 6.

pollution.' Where a permit holder breaches the terms of his environmental permit (or is likely to breach such terms) the regulatory body may serve an enforcement notice which can include conditions specifying any remedial actions that need to be taken. Similarly Part 2A will not apply in a situation where the land in question is contaminated land, or becomes such land by reason of the

deposit of the controlled waste in question if the Environment Agency can deploy its clean-up powers under s 59 EPA 1990. Inevitably by the very nature of the activity that is regulated there will be land contamination. The issue of remediation is, however, most likely to arise when the operator of the regulated facility seeks to surrender his permit. When this happens the regulatory body (being the relevant local authority or the Environment Agency) must first be satisfied that the necessary measures have been taken to avoid any pollution risk arising from the operation of the facility and second, to return the site of the regulated facility to a satisfactory state, having regard to the state of the site before the facility was put into operation. This may, in practice, be a higher standard of remediation than that required under Part 2A. When applying to surrender a permit applicants are advised to consider whether they might be required to carry out remediation under Part 2A and if so whether it would be more cost-effective to undertake operations for both purposes at the same time.

7.11.4 The Environmental Damage (Prevention and Remediation) Regulations 2009

As stated above, Part 3 of the 2009 Regulations contains a duty for authorities to require remediation where they establish that there is environmental damage and a liable operator. In such cases the regulations would generally take precedence over Part 2A EPA 1990; those responsible for the contamination/environmental damage will not be expected to take preventive or remedial action under both the Regulations and the Act. Part IIA's procedures are primarily designed to deal with complex historical contamination whereas the regulations are designed to provide a quicker response to pollution incidents. Given that the regulations have no retrospective force the date on which the damage has been caused is of course a highly relevant factor. Where the damage has been caused prior to 1 March 2009, Part 2A EPA 1990 will be the applicable regime. Where the cause, date or potential receptors of contamination are uncertain, sites will need to be investigated on the basis that the appropriate regime for fixing liability may be either the Regulations or Part 2A EPA 1990, or if there are proposals for development it may be possible to require action through the planning system. However, the responsible public authorities will need to consider in the particular case whether Part IIA's requirements are more extensive than for the regulations and take a decision on which legislation to apply.

7.11.5 Statutory nuisance

Statutory nuisance abatement controls do not apply where land is in a 'contaminated state'.[110] Statutory nuisance controls do not apply even where the relevant land in a contaminated state does not pose significant harm to man or the environment.[111] Thus, land which is in a contaminated state, but is not posing a risk of significant harm to man or the environment, falls outside the remit of statutory nuisance controls and contaminated land controls. This creates something of a lacuna

in the law. The statutory nuisance regime continues to apply to the effects of deposits of substances on land which give rise to such offence to human senses (such as stenches) as to constitute a nuisance.

---

110 Sched 2, para 89 EA 1995.
111 S 78A(2) EPA 1990.

7.12 Online resource centre

We recommend that the reader regularly refers to the section of the online resources corresponding to this chapter for information relating to updates, amendments and corrections.

7.13 Summary of key points

Chapter 7 has covered the following topics and issues:

- the problems and risks associated with contaminated land and in particular the primary objectives of Part 2 EPA 1990;
- the difficult issues raised in trying to provide a legal definition of contaminated land and the emphasis within the legal definition on the significant risk of harm to humans and the other receptors identified in the statutory guidance;
- the procedures involved in the identification of contaminated land and its remediation;
- the respective roles of the local authorities and the Environment Agency in securing the remediation of contaminated land;
- the way in which the Act seeks to deliver a regime based on the polluter pays principle and the complex and difficult provisions which relate to the exclusion and apportionment of liability;
- the difficulties that the enforcement authorities face in identifying the appropriate person, particularly in circumstances where the contamination was caused some time in the past;
- the emerging case law on the liability of developers and statutory undertakers;
- the relationship between the provisions in Part IIA Environmental Protection Act 1990 and the planning regime and also the Environmental Damage (Prevention and Remediation) Regulations 2009 as they relate to the remediation of contaminated land;
- the actual application of the regime in practice.

7.14 Further reading

Books

Edwards, M, *Contaminated Land: Property Transactions and the New Regime* (CLT Professional, 2000).
Hellawell, T, *Blackstone's Guide to the Contaminated Land Regime* (OUP, 2000).
Tromans, S and Turrall-Clarke, R, *Contaminated Land: The New Regime* (Wildy & Sons, 2007, 2nd edn).

Journal articles and government papers

Carriage, R and Ennis, O, 'Environmental Protection Act 1990 Part 2A: where does the *National Grid Gas* case leave practitioners?' [2007] JPL 1557.
EC law; Environmental damage; Environmental liability; Environmental remediation; Implementation [2009] 7 JPL 849.
Environment Agency, GPLC1 Guiding Principles for Land Contamination (March 2010).
Fogelman, V, '*Circular Facilities (London) Ltd v Sevenoaks District Council*; the first ruling on an appeal against a remediation notice under the contaminated land regime' [2004] JPL 1319.
Langhalm, R, 'Contaminated land—the legal aspect' [1993] JPL 807.

Lee, M, ' "New" environmental liabilities: the purpose and scope of the contaminated land regime and the Environmental Liability Directive' [2009] Env LR.

Planning Policy Statement 23: Planning and Pollution Control — Annex 2 Development on Land affected by contamination (November 2004), available from http://www.communities.gov.uk/corporate/.

Report from the Commission to the Council, the European Parliament, the European Economic and Social Committee and the Committee of the Regions under article 14(2) of Directive 2004/35/CE on Environmental Liability with regard to the Prevention and Remedying of Environmental Damage COM/2010/0581 final.

Thornton, J, 'Contaminated Land: the latest developments' [2009] 1 JPL 8.

Vaughan, S, 'The contaminated land regime: still suitable for use?' [2010] 2 JPL 142.

Winter, G et al, 'Weighing up the EC Environmental Liability Directive' [2008] JEL 20.

Woolley, D, 'Contaminated land—the real world' [2002] JPL 5.

Weblinks

www.environment-agency.gov.uk

An enormous amount of information on the contaminated land regime can be accessed via the Environment Agency's website at the above address. In particular, you can access via this site (by searching for 'contaminated land') a copy of the Agency's first annual report on the contaminated land regime.

The Agency's 2009 report on the state of contaminated land in England gives an overview of progress made in identifying and remediating contaminated land in England since the Pt IIA regime was introduced in April 2000.

http://www.defra.gov.uk/environment/quality/land/contaminated/index.htm

The Defra web page contains a significant amount of information about the contaminated land regime, including a summary of the Act and the statutory guidance. It also includes information about the Environmental Liability Directive 2004.

Chapter 8

Air Pollution

Chapter Contents

Learning Objectives

By the end of this chapter you should have acquired an understanding of:

- the substances discharged into the atmosphere which have adverse impacts upon human health and the environment;

- the nature of air pollution, which poses significant challenges to the use of law to provide an effective set of control mechanisms;

- the dual legal focus on air pollution controls and the maintenance of air quality;

- the global nature of air pollution problems, especially climate change;

- the historical development of air pollution law in England and Wales;

- the impact of the EU upon air pollution law in England and Wales;

- the significance of international environmental law especially in regard to transnational boundary pollution and global climate change;

- the framework of air pollution and air quality controls in place in England and Wales;

- the early air pollution laws regulating visible pollutants, e.g. black smoke and smog;

- the range of regulatory legal tools deployed in England and Wales to tackle the variety of air pollution problems.[1]

8.1 Introduction

Atmospheric (air) pollution in England and Wales is regulated by legislative controls which reflect the historic development of the law as it has moved away from a localised, reactive response to pollution problems to a more integrated and planned response to pan-European and global threats associated with airborne pollutants.[2]

The four main air pollution controls comprise:

(a) the Integrated Pollution and Control (IPPC) permit-based controls, relating to a range of highly polluting industries detailed in Pt I of the Environmental Protection Act 1990 (EPA 1990) and the Pollution Prevention and Control Act 1999 (PPCA 1999) and supplementary secondary legislation, e.g. Environmental Permitting (England and Wales) Regulations 2010;

(b) the criminal law sanction-based controls over the emission of smoke and other particulate matter from chimneys and furnaces detailed in the Clean Air Act 1993 (CAA 1993);

(c) controls relating to vehicle emissions. These controls encompass engine efficiency standards, the chemical composition of fuels, the mandatory use of catalytic converters, the use of traffic management powers, eco-taxes such as price differentials between different types of fuel; and

(d) the establishment and operation of a greenhouse gas emissions trading scheme.

---

1 E.g. static permit-based controls such as IPPC and controls of mobile sources of air pollution such as motor cars.
2 The report of the Intergovernmental Panel on Climate Change in 2007 confirms that the likelihood that increases in global temperature are man-made is over 90%.

These controls are supplemented by the Environment Act 1995 (EA 1995), which has enabled the Secretary of State to create a national air quality strategy and local air quality zones. Due to the inherent mobility of atmospheric pollution and its transboundary impacts, the development of the law is largely driven by a combination of international and European Union (EU) responses to the global threat of climate change.

8.2 Problems caused by air pollution

Atmospheric pollution poses three major threats:

(a)   the *threat to human health*, particularly respiratory illnesses, such as bronchitis and asthma caused by airborne pollutants, skin cancer and eye disorders (e.g. cataracts) linked to ozone layer depletion in the upper atmosphere;

(b)   the *threat to ecosystems*, particularly the damage caused by acid rain (to trees, birds and fish)— acid rain is created by the release of the following gases into the atmosphere: sulphur dioxide, nitric oxide, nitrogen dioxide, ammonia, ozone and hydrocarbons; and

(c)   the *threat of severe climatic disruption* caused by global warming of the atmosphere with excessive levels of greenhouse gases[3]—global warming has not only been linked to the increasing incidence of storms, droughts, desertification, forest fires, floods, and attendant crop and property damage, but there has also been research which suggests that global warming may lead to the disruption of the ocean current systems upon which the world's climatic patterns depend for their stability. It is therefore imperative that effective and timely steps are taken to control the production of greenhouse gases. The problem is compounded by the short-termism of party political systems and the unwillingness of governments to take unpopular decisions (especially those which will financially burden economic activity).

The main human activities which generate air pollutants are summarised below:

(1)   Coal (fossil fuel)-fired power stations and large merchant ships (diesel fuel-powered) produce sulphur dioxide which combines with water vapour to produce acid rain. The burning of fossil fuels is associated with carbon dioxide production.

(2)   Storage and distribution of chemicals, especially fuels and solvents generating volatile organic compounds.

(3)   Depositing or treating wastes.[4] Incineration is associated with emission of dioxins, furans, PAHs, PCBs and metal particulates (e.g. battery disposal).

(4)   Industrial production/manufacturing processes.[5] Industrial processes generate carbon monoxide, carbon dioxide and oxides of nitrogen.

(5)   Oil production, natural gas production and chemical production.

(6)   Use of refrigerants in air conditioning and refrigerators, aerosols, CFCs and solvents.

(7)   Gaseous emissions from motor vehicles.

---

3   E.g. carbon dioxide, methane, CFCs, ozone and oxides of nitrogen.
4   Including agricultural waste, and landfilling of wastes generating methane.
5   I.e. the planned release of chemical substances into the atmosphere.

8.3 Historic controls

The problems associated with air pollution are not new. Legislation aimed at controlling acidic emissions from alkali works dates back to at least 1863.[6] The 1863 Act, like so many that followed it, was reactive; it was introduced following the recommendations of a Royal Commission regarding pollution from alkali works, especially the very damaging emissions of hydrochloric acid gas. The 1863 Alkali Act was extended in scope by the Alkali Act of 1874, and both were consolidated in 1906 in the Alkali Works Regulation Act 1906. The provisions of the 1906 Act were repealed by the EA 1995.

Legislation aimed at controlling smoke and similar atmospheric emissions was later introduced by the Public Health Acts of 1875 and 1936 and the Public Health (Smoke Abatement) Act 1926. These Acts were not successful in dealing with the problems of smoke-related pollution, and it was not until the Clean Air Act (CAA 1956) that there was a comprehensive attempt to control all smoke emissions from domestic fires and commercial and industrial premises.

The CAA 1956, like the earlier legislation, was introduced as a reactive measure to combat an existing air pollution problem. In London in 1952, some 4,000 people lost their lives as a result of the 'great smog'. Smogs, which occur frequently now in places like India, occur when fog combines with smoke particles. The result is that the fog is very dense,[7] visibility is reduced and breathing is impaired. The CAA 1956 was extended in scope by the CAA 1968 and the provisions have now largely been consolidated in the CAA 1993, which is considered in more detail below.

The post-1980 increase in legislation designed to control atmospheric pollution owes much to the UK's membership of the EU and the UK's signature to and ratification of a number of international agreements.

8.4 Government policy

The government's 'early' policy in relation to air pollution was set out in *This Common Inheritance* in 1990. This expression of government policy was, in part, concerned with the protection of public health. In the second year report on the government's programme outlined in the 1990 report, there was a commitment to further action to reduce air pollution. In particular, it was suggested that, in addition to traditional legal controls, the government would also explore the use of economic instruments, for example, measures to ensure that charges incurred by transport users reflect the full costs of their journeys. The landfill tax in relation to waste is a further example of how economic and fiscal measures can be employed to reduce pollution or encourage recycling.

8.4.1 Air quality policy

In March 1994, the Department of the Environment (DoE) published a discussion paper, *Improving Air Quality*, which was followed in January 1995 by *Air Quality: Meeting the Challenge—the Government's Strategic Policies for Air*, which set out the government's policies for air quality management.[8] The 1994 discussion paper recognised that the existing approach to air quality was somewhat fragmented and also that there should be a move to what was described as a more 'effects-based' approach, with revised air quality standards based principally on human health effects. *Meeting the Challenge* put forward the following proposals:

---

6 See the Alkali Act 1863.
7 Smog is a very apt description; it is really a smoke-filled fog.
8 The most recent version of the Strategy is The Air Quality Strategy for England, Scotland, Wales and Northern Ireland 2007.

(a)   A new framework of national air quality standards and targets. Two main levels of air quality were proposed:

   (i)   the first was a long-term target in which nine key pollutants were to be rendered harmless to health and the environment. The following were the pollutants of greatest concern: ozone, benzene, 1.3-butadiene, sulphur dioxide (SO_2), carbon monoxide (CO), nitrogen dioxide (NO_2), particles (especially PM10 emitted from diesel engines), polycyclic aromatic hydrocarbons (PAHs) and lead. This objective was to be achieved through measures such as the introduction of less polluting raw materials, production processes and products;

   (ii)   the second level is essentially a trigger or an alert threshold which indicates when air quality in parts of England and Wales is so poor that an immediate response is justified to prevent serious damage to health, e.g. banning cars from city centres. Local authorities already have legal powers to impose traffic restrictions, but whilst, as yet, they have not used these powers to protect air quality by imposing traffic bans, London has introduced a congestion charging scheme (Transport Act 2000) which has brought about some improvement of air quality in central London.

(b)   The establishment of a framework for local air quality management and, in particular, concentrating action on areas where progress has been slow. Local authorities are responsible for reviewing air quality and they are under a duty to designate Air Quality Management Areas (AQMAs) if they are not attaining the relevant air quality targets. AQMAs are controlled in a similar fashion to smoke control areas[9] and centre upon an Air Quality Plan prepared by the relevant local authority. Local authorities are required to draw up air quality management plans which set out their proposals for meeting air quality targets.

(c)   Vehicle emissions are a major contributor to air pollution and the strategy suggests an action plan to reduce the contribution of road transport to air pollution, particularly in urban areas. In AQMAs, local authorities are required to appraise their development and transport policies against an air quality assessment. Planning Policy Statement 23 on Planning and Pollution Control has been revised to reflect these changes. Planning Policy Guidance Note 13 on Planning and Transport already recognises the relationship between planning, transport and air quality.[10]

8.5 The Environment Act 1995 and air quality in England and Wales

Part IV of the EA 1995 contains provisions to implement the policies set out in *Air Quality: Meeting the Challenge*.[11] Part IV includes provisions designed to secure a national air quality strategy and also provisions concerned with local air quality management. In particular, it provides a framework for ensuring that the UK meets a number of objectives in reducing and controlling the pollutants listed above.[12] The Strategy does not have statutory force and does not impose legal obligations on regulatory bodies, such as the Environment Agency; however, legal obligations may be imposed on regulatory bodies via the power to draft regulations contained in the Environment Act 1995.[13]

---

9 See 8.5.3 for Local Air Quality Management controls.
10 PPS 23 and PPG 13 have been replaced by the National Planning Policy Framework.
11 And subsequent versions of the strategy.
12 See 8.4.1(a).
13 See ss 87 and 91 EA 1995.

8.5.1 National Air Quality Strategy (NAQS)

Section 80 of the EA 1995 imposes a duty on the Secretary of State to prepare and publish a National Air Quality Strategy. The strategy contains policies designed to enable the UK to attain air quality obligations under EU law or international agreements.[14] The Secretary of State is under a duty to review the National Air Quality Strategy[15] from time to time, consulting with the Environment Agency, industry, experts and the public (via a draft strategy).

The NAQS comprises:

(a)   standards relating to air quality;
(b)   objectives for the restriction of levels at which particular substances are present in air;[16] and
(c)   measures which are to be taken by local authorities and other legal persons for the purpose of achieving those objectives.

The current NAQS is detailed in *Air Quality Strategy for England, Wales, Scotland and Northern Ireland*, 2007.[17] The Secretary of State is under a duty to: (a) determine a base (target) air quality standard; and (b) set 'alert thresholds' for particular pollutants[18] which, if exceeded, will result in the adoption of remedial measures (by a local authority) via the designation of an AQMA. The current regulations which implement air pollution policy in England are the Air Quality (England) Regulations 2000[19] as amended. These regulations establish air quality targets for each local authority (for a fixed period and are based upon the effect of each pollutant upon human health and the environment) in regard to pollutants such as carbon monoxide, sulphur dioxide and nitrogen dioxide.

The Environment Agency is required by s 81 of the EA 1995 to have regard to the NAQS when exercising its functions. The NAQS has no legal force, hence ss 87 and 91 of the EA 1995 provide the Secretary of State with the power to make regulations setting standards and objectives.

8.5.2 The Air Quality Limit Values Regulations 2003 (SI 2003/2121)

The 2003 Regulations were passed in order to fully implement the air quality limit values contained in the Framework Directive on Ambient Air Quality (96/62/EC) and the daughter directive, Directive 99/30/EC, setting limit values for sulphur dioxide, nitrogen dioxide, oxides of nitrogen, lead and particulates.

8.5.3 Local Air Quality Management Areas (AQMAs)

Part IV of the EA 1995 places particular responsibilities upon local authorities to achieve, at a local level, the national air quality strategy.

Section 82 of the EA 1995 places each local authority under a duty (the 'appraisal' duty) to carry out a review from time to time of the present and likely future air quality within its area. Where a local authority carries out such a review (an AQR), it must also assess whether air quality standards or objectives are being achieved, or are likely to be achieved within the relevant period. If it appears that any air quality standards or objectives are not being achieved, or are not likely to be achieved, the local authority must identify the parts of its area where this is the case.

---

14 Especially those designed to combat climate change.
15 S 80(4) EA 1995.
16 E.g. benzene, lead, carbon monoxide, nitrogen dioxide, particulates, 1,3 butadiene and ozone.
17 Cm 7169.
18 See n 16.
19 SI 2000/928.

Section 83 EA 1995 makes provision for the establishment of the local air quality management areas. Where it appears that any air quality standards or objectives are not being achieved, or are not likely to be achieved, the local authority must designate, by order, the relevant area as an AQMA.[20] Financial assistance regarding AQMAs is available from Defra and advice from the Environment Agency. Following a subsequent air quality review, the order may be varied or revoked, in the latter case only if it appears that the air quality standards and objectives are being achieved, or are likely to be achieved within the relevant period.

Once an order has been made to designate an area as an AQMA, the local authority (whether district or unitary) is under a duty to exercise its powers in order to reduce the relevant pollutants. Section 84 EA 1995 deals with the duties of local authorities in relation to designated areas. These are as follows:

(a)   to carry out a further detailed investigation and assessment of local air quality;

(b)   to prepare a report regarding the outcome of the detailed assessment referred to above within 12 months of the order becoming operational;

(c)   to prepare a written action plan (air quality plan) which details how and when the local authority intends to exercise its powers to achieve the relevant air quality standards and objectives. If the plan is made by a district council, the relevant county council can make recommendations. These recommendations must be taken into account when finalising the plan.[21] In the event of disagreement, the matter can be referred to the Secretary of State. The Secretary of State enjoys a reserve power to carry out the review and assessment stages, either directly or through a third party (such as the Environment Agency);[22]

(d)   to provide regular information for the public regarding air quality;

(e)   to prepare contingency plans regarding air quality emergencies.

In drawing up its air quality plan, a local authority is obliged to consult government,[23] adjoining local authorities, industry and the general public. The government may provide:

(a)   financial assistance towards the carrying-out of air quality assessments;

(b)   access to government data;

(c)   best practice guidance; and

(d)   research.

The preparation of air quality plans will require local authorities to adopt a more holistic perspective, similar to the wide ambit of Development Plans,[24] and have regard to local pollution control, transport and development policies. The costs falling on the local economy, especially the transport and industry sectors, must be proportionate to plan objectives and be cost-effective. Air Quality Plans may include traffic management controls. Vehicles may be deterred from entering city centres via the use of congestion charging schemes,[25] increasing the number of pedestrianised areas, the provision of park and ride schemes (e.g. York and Cambridge), the introduction of multi-occupancy express vehicle lanes, resident-only parking zones and banning vehicles from city centres at times when air quality is especially poor. Alternative transport measures could include the introduction of cycle lanes, supertrams (light railways, e.g. Sheffield and Manchester) and bus-only lanes.

---

20   Referred to in the 1995 Act as a 'designated area'.
21   S 86 EA 1995.
22   See s 85 EA 1995.
23   E.g. Defra and the Department of Transport.
24   Now contained within Local Development Frameworks.
25   Now operational in London.

Local authority powers to address the deterioration of air quality, especially localised deterioration due to motor vehicles, have benefited from (1) the introduction of Local Transport Plans under the Transport Act 2000 requiring all local authorities to produce a local transport plan (LTP),[26] (2) the road traffic reduction duty imposed on local authorities[27] and the linked national traffic reduction targets created in response to the Road Traffic Reduction (National Targets) Act 1998, and (3) the powers of local authorities to regulate traffic via the use of traffic regulation orders[28] and traffic calming measures.[29]

8.5.4 Powers of the Secretary of State (ss 85, 87 and 88 of the EA 1995)

8.5.4.1 Section 85 EA 1995

The Secretary of State has the power to direct a local authority[30] to take action designed to enable the UK to comply with its EU and international obligations. Local authorities are duty bound to comply with the directions which the Secretary of State gives.[31] The action taken by local authorities designed to respond to air pollution affecting more than one authority will be co-ordinated by government departments via their regional offices.

8.5.4.2 Section 87 EA 1995

In addition to the power to resolve disputes, the Secretary of State is given considerable power under s 87 to make regulations for the following purposes:

(a)   implementing the national air quality strategy;
(b)   implementing EU or international legal obligations;
(c)   prescribing air quality standards;
(d)   prescribing objectives for the restriction of levels at which particular substances are present in air;
(e)   conferring or transferring powers to local authorities;
(f)   controlling the details of reviews; and
(g)   regarding procedural steps.

In regard to the statutory requirements, the Air Quality (England) Regulations 2000[32] specify air quality targets to be attained by local authorities in the period 2003–08. The 2000 Regulations establish quality standards for some pollutants, for example, sulphur dioxide, nitrogen dioxide, carbon monoxide and benzene.[33]

8.5.4.3 Section 88 EA 1995

Before issuing regulations under s 87 EA 1995, the Secretary of State is required to consult with the Environment Agency, local authorities, industry and other appropriate bodies or persons. In addition, s 88 EA 1995 enables the Secretary of State to issue guidance to local authorities which they are obliged to take into account with regard to any relevant matter.

---

26 LTPs are to include policies addressing congestion, parking and public transport.
27 See Road Traffic Reduction Act 1997.
28 See s 1(g) Road Traffic Act 1984.
29 See Highways (Traffic Calming) Regulations 1999 (SI 1999/1026).
30 S 85(5) of the EA 1995.
31 S 85(7) EA 1995.
32 SI 2000/928.
33 Set by reference to the effects of these substances upon human health.

8.6 Other legislative controls

The local authorities,[34] through their environmental health departments and officers, play a key role in controlling air pollution. They are involved in other areas of air pollution control:

(a) providing authorisation (permitting) for some industrial processes governed by the IPPC regulatory controls contained in the PPCA 1999;

(b) enforcing the provisions of the Clean Air Act 1993;

(c) enforcing the provisions of Pt 3 of the EPA 1990 in relation to those statutory nuisances which have an impact on the quality of air;

See Chapter 9

(d) designating AQMAs under Pt IV of the EA 1995.[35]

Emissions into the air are also controlled[36] by the Environment Agency through the system of IPPC permitting.[37]

The town and country planning system regulates the siting of new sources of atmospheric pollution. Policies, including those relating to air quality contained within local authority Local Development Frameworks (LDFs), may guide polluting development to appropriate locations whilst the siting decision itself is based upon a consideration of both LDF policies and 'other material considerations' (a list of factors relevant to planning and relevant to the particular application for development).[38] 'Material considerations' include policy documents which set out national air pollution policy, and the result of consultations with regulators responsible for the day-to-day regulation of activities which discharge pollutants into the atmosphere.[39]

Following the introduction of the NAQS, all local authorities must take account of air quality considerations and standards when updating their Local Development Frameworks.[40] A persistent and knotty problem regarding the grant of planning permission for developments which will discharge pollutants to the atmosphere is the extent to which a decision maker (the planning committee of the local authority or an appeal inspector) may impose conditions[41] on the grant of permission which impinge upon and duplicate the conditions which could be imposed by the regulator responsible for licensing the operational aspects of the development. The leading case here is *Gateshead Metropolitan Borough Council v Secretary of State for the Environment and Northumbrian Water* (1995).[42] The developer applied for planning permission to construct a clinical waste incinerator. The planning committee of the local authority refused to grant permission largely because it believed that the applicant had paid too little attention to the air pollution impacts of the proposal. The planning committee thought that, were it to grant planning permission for the development, HMIP was unlikely to refuse to grant it an IPC licence, and the committee was not convinced that the IPC regime would adequately safeguard the public from environmental damage arising from the operation of the incinerator. In the Court of Appeal, it was accepted that there was an overlap between the planning control and pollution control regimes and that pollution was a material consideration in the planning decision. The court held that the planning committee was entitled to refuse planning permission if, after consulting HMIP,[43] it was clear that an IPC licence (permit)

---

34 The district councils, London borough councils, the metropolitan districts and unitary authorities.

35 As described above in 8.5.3.

36 In addition to local authorities who control the less polluting IPPC processes.

37 The Environment Agency and the local authorities exercise dual regulatory control over IPPC permitted facilities.

38 Note the decision-making legal duties in s 70(2) of the Town and Country Planning Act 1990 and s 38(6) of the Planning and Compulsory Purchase Act 2004.

39 For example, the Environment Agency and local authorities regarding IPPC permitted activities.

40 See the National Planning Policy Framework.

41 See DoE Circular 11/95.

42 *Gateshead MBC v Secretary of State for the Environment and Northumbrian Water Group* [1995] Env LR 37; [1995] JPL 432.

43 Now the Environment Agency.

application would be refused by HMIP. In other cases, pollution control was a matter to be left to HMIP because HMIP could not issue a licence (permit) if the applicant could not satisfy HMIP that the process would comply with the IPC-implied BATNEEC condition and thereby ensure an acceptable degree of environmental protection. Current best practice is to obtain the Environment Agency's views on the acceptability of the proposal at the planning application stage.

In attempting to resolve concerns relating to the harmful atmospheric impacts of development proposals, planning conditions and planning agreements (and unilateral planning obligations) may be employed to address such reservations. By way of example, the applicants' agreement to accept a planning condition providing for a totally enclosed drum-unloading facility, thereby drastically reducing the risk of the escape of malodorous chemical substances, in *Envirocor Waste Holdings Ltd v Secretary of State for the Environment* (1995)[44] was a crucial issue which the planning inspector failed to appreciate fully when he refused permission for a proposed waste transfer station.

Crop residue (stubble) burning is regulated by a combination of s 152 of the EPA 1990 and the Crop Residues (Burning) Regulations 1993.[45] The Regulations prohibit, subject to exemptions and restrictions, the burning of cereal straw (hay), oil seed rape, peas and beans. Breach of the Regulations is an offence punishable by a fine in the magistrates' court. Sections 161 and 161A of the Highways Act 1980 prohibit the lighting of fires on, over or off a highway which injure, interrupt or endanger road users.

Other controls exist under:

(a)   the Health and Safety at Work Act 1974;
(b)   EU legislation;[46]
(c)   international conventions and protocols.[47]

8.7 Local authority air pollution control (LAAPC)

Local authorities are responsible for controlling the atmospheric emissions of certain prescribed industrial processes. Usually, it will be the district council or the London borough council that exercises these powers.

Chapter 6 examines the IPPC regime in regard to which local authorities are responsible for regulating Part A(2) installations with regard to all environmental impacts and Part B installations with regard to atmospheric emissions only.

8.8 The Clean Air Act (CAA 1993)

Whilst the first legislative controls over atmospheric emissions date back to the Alkali Act 1863, nevertheless, this early legislation did not control the emissions of smoke from all industrial processes. The use of coal and the consequent emissions of smoke and grit particles from both houses and factories resulted in serious pollution and health problems. However, it was not until the Clean Air Acts of 1956 and 1968 that there was any comprehensive attempt to control emissions of smoke, dust and grit from industrial and domestic premises.[48] The CAA 1956 was introduced to prohibit the emission of dark smoke from any domestic or industrial chimney. A chimney was

---

44   *Envirocor Waste Holdings Ltd v Secretary of State for the Environment* (1995) EGCS 60.
45   SI 1993/1366.
46   See 8.11.
47   See 8.12.
48   The earlier Public Health (Smoke Abatement) Act 1926 proved to be an ineffective control of domestic smoke.

defined as any structure or opening through which smoke is emitted. Its scope was extended by the CAA 1968 which prohibited emissions of dark smoke from any industrial or trade premises, even though the emission was not made from a chimney. These Acts have now been consolidated into the CAA 1993. Enforcement of the CAA 1993 is the responsibility of the local authorities, which may act both with regard to smoke arising within their areas or affecting their areas. The significance of the CAA 1993 has declined following the increased use of gas-fired boilers.

8.8.1 Definition of 'smoke'

'Smoke' includes soot, ash, grit and gritty particles emitted in smoke, any visible non-carbonaceous vapour (for example, water vapour) and visible fumes (but not invisible gases).[49]

A government report, *Transboundary Air Pollution: Acidification, Eutrophication, and Ground Level Ozone in the UK 1999–2001*, published by Defra, contains data regarding the range of pollution challenges facing the UK.[50] Overall, there appears to be a general decline in levels of atmospheric pollutants, but high levels of NO_x, CO, ozone, volatile organic compounds (benzene) and fine particulates (diesel exhaust emissions) continue to cause concern.

8.8.2 Relationship between the CAA 1993, Part I of the EPA 1990 and the PPCA 1999

Before considering the details of the CAA 1993, it is important to note the relationship between these controls and the controls over atmospheric emissions under Pt I of the EPA 1990[51] and the equivalent IPPC regulatory controls in the PPCA 1999. The provisions of Pts I-III of the CAA 1993 do not apply to any process regulated under Pt I of the EPA 1990. Section 41 of the CAA 1993 excludes IPC and LAAPC processes from the date of authorisation. Similarly, the CAA 1993 does not apply to IPPC- permitted facilities.

8.8.3 Offences under the CAA 1993

The CAA 1993 prohibits emissions of smoke, dust and grit by means of criminal offences. The following are the main offences:

(a)   emission of dark smoke—from a chimney or from industrial premises other than from a chimney;
(b)   emission of dust and grit from non-domestic furnaces;
(c)   emission of smoke from a chimney in a Smoke Control Area;
(d)   various offences relating to the installation of furnaces;
(e)   the burning of insulation cable as part of a metal recovery process unless an LAAPC licence (permit) has been obtained.[52]

Prosecutions under most provisions of the CAA 1993 are dealt with in the magistrates' court.

---

49 For 'dark smoke', see 8.8.4 below and for 'grit, dust and fumes', see 8.8.10.
50 Acid rain, surface ozone and concentrations of the main pollutants.
51 IPC and LAAPC.
52 S 33 of the CAA 1993.

8.8.4 The 'dark smoke' offences (ss 1 and 2 CAA 1993)

The CAA 1993 creates numerous criminal offences, including the so-called 'dark smoke' offences. Sections 1 and 2 of the 1993 Act prohibit the emission of dark smoke from different categories of premises; s 1 requires the relevant emission of dark smoke to be through a chimney whereas s 2 does not. The offences are strict liability offences, although various activities are exempted from the provisions[53] and some statutory defences are available.[54] Section 1 prohibits the emission of 'dark smoke':

(a)   from the chimney of any building;[55] or
(b)   from a chimney which serves the furnace of any fixed boiler or industrial plant.[56]

'Building' includes railway locomotives[57] and vessels in coastal waters.[58]

Section 1 applies to emissions of dark smoke from the chimneys of domestic premises as well as industrial or commercial premises. Where an offence has been committed under s 1(1), liability will rest with the occupier of the building from which the dark smoke is emitted. In the case of dark smoke emissions from a chimney serving a fixed boiler or industrial plant,[59] the person having control or possession of the boiler or plant will be liable if an offence is committed.

A person guilty of an offence under s 1(1) as respects a chimney of a private dwelling is liable to a fine not exceeding level 3 on the standard scale (£1,000), whereas in any other case the fine should not exceed level 5 (£5,000) on the standard scale.

Section 2 prohibits the non-chimney emission of dark smoke from industrial or trade premises. Unlike s 1, the s 2 emission need not be through a chimney. Trade or industrial premises are premises which are used for an industrial or trade purpose or premises on which matter is burnt in connection with any industrial or trade purpose. A s 2 offence may be committed either by the occupier of the premises or any other person causing or permitting the emission. In *Sheffield CC v ADH Demolition Ltd* (1984),[60] it was held that premises could include a demolition site. The burning of rubbish on a demolition site amounted to an industrial or trade process because there was a close relationship between the activity (burning the rubbish) and the trade (demolition) and thus the defendant was properly convicted. Section 2(3) is worded in such a way as to catch offenders who attempt to evade the CAA 1993 by burning substances under cover of night-time. A person guilty of an offence under s 2 is liable on summary conviction to a fine of up to £20,000.

---

53 See 8.8.8 below.
54 See 8.8.9 below.
55 S 1(1).
56 S 1(2).
57 S 43.
58 S 44.
59 S 1(2).
60 *Sheffield City Council v ADH Demolition Ltd* (1984) 82 LGR 177.

Law in Action

To illustrate common pollution incidents giving rise to prosecution by local authorities (and the imposition of sanctions by the courts), we set out below two typical prosecutions:

(i)   In July of 2007 an Environmental Protection Officer (EPO) from North Lincolnshire Council observed smoke being emitted from a bonfire of pallets on Sparkeit's premises in Scunthorpe in an alleged breach of s 2(4) of the 1993 Act. The EPO assessed the shade of the smoke from the bonfire, using a Ringlemann chart, as shade four (smoke in excess of shade two is an offence). Lloyd Dickinson, a director of the defendant company, successfully argued before Scunthorpe Magistrates that the emission of dark smoke was inadvertent and the defendant had taken all practicable steps to prevent the emission of the smoke (i.e. the defendants took advantage of the 'practicable steps' defence). Whilst the court agreed with the prosecution that dark smoke had been emitted, it upheld the defence.

(ii) In contrast, following another incident in Scunthorpe on 7 February 2008 when an EPO from North Lincolnshire Council observed a fire emitting dark smoke burning on a fencing manufacturer's premises (Balmer Lindley (Manufacturing) Ltd), the prosecution was successful in obtaining a conviction relating to the emission of dark smoke contrary to s 2(4) of the Clean Air Act 1993. The defendant was fined £3,000 with £750 costs.

8.8.5 What is dark smoke? (s 3 of the CAA 1993)

'Dark smoke' is defined by reference to a device known as the Ringlemann Chart. Smoke which is determined to be as dark or darker than shade 2 on the Ringlemann Chart is 'dark smoke' for the purposes of the 1993 Act. The Ringlemann Chart indicates differing shades of darkness. The Chart consists of a piece of card with cross-hatching in black on a white background so that a known percentage of white is obscured. The Chart needs to be placed at some distance from the observer who will then be able to see that the lines merge into different greyish/black shades. The different shades are numerically categorised: 0 equals white and 5 equals dense black. Shades 2–4 increase by degrees so that shade 1 indicates a 20 per cent obscuration of the white, shade 2 equals 40 per cent, and so on. In order to compare the shades with the smoke, it is necessary to place the card between the observer and the smoke.[61] The observer usually stands about 50 ft from the Chart in order to match the smoke colour with the Chart. The matching should normally take place in good daylight conditions.

In any legal proceedings for breach of s 1 or s 2, the court must be satisfied that the smoke falls within the statutory definition of dark smoke. However, there is no requirement for an actual comparison of the smoke with the Chart. It is sufficient that the court is certain that the method was properly applied and that the smoke was thereby determined to be dark.

There is no requirement in the CAA 1993 for the defendant to have caused or knowingly permitted the discharge of dark smoke. The offence is one of strict liability. There are, however, a number of defences and exemptions, which are considered below.

---

61 The chart is usually mounted on a wooden or metal frame.

8.8.6 Notification that an offence has been committed

An occupier of premises must be notified of an alleged offence by the local authority environmental officer 'as soon as may be'. This will usually mean that an environmental health officer or officer from the local authority advises the occupier verbally. However, the local authority is required to confirm this notification in writing within a period of four days. Failure to give notice will provide the defendant with a defence to any charges made under ss 1, 2 and 20. Unlike other pollution offences discussed in this book, the offence can only be tried in the magistrates' court.

8.8.7 Strict liability and burden of proof

The CAA 1993 presumes that there will have been an emission of dark smoke from industrial or trade premises in any case where material is burned on those premises and the circumstances are such that the burning would be likely to give rise to the emission of dark smoke. The burden of proof falls squarely on the occupier (or any other person causing or permitting the burning) to show that no dark smoke was actually emitted.

8.8.8 Exemptions

Section 1(3) of the CAA 1993 provides certain exemptions from the above offences. These are contained in the Dark Smoke (Permitted Periods) Regulations 1958,[62] which establish the following exceptions whereby no offence is committed if the emissions of dark smoke are made within certain periods:

(a) the emission of dark smoke is permitted for a defined number of minutes (between 10 and 40) during an eight hour period. The precise number of minutes depends on the number of furnaces which feed into the chimney and whether or not the emission involves the blowing of soot;

(b) in any event, the continuous emission of dark smoke cannot at any time exceed four minutes and the continuous emission of black smoke must not at any time exceed two minutes in any half-hour period.

The Clean Air (Emissions of Dark Smoke) (Exemptions) Regulations 1969[63] also provide exceptions relating to the burning of certain materials in the open. The following are exempt from s 2 of the CAA 1993:

(a) burning timber and other waste material which results either from the demolition of a building or from the clearance of a site upon which there is building operation or engineering construction;

(b) burning explosive which has become waste and any material which has become contaminated by such explosive;

(c) burning tar, pitch or asphalt and other matter in connection with any resurfacing;

(d) burning animal and poultry carcasses where the animals have died or have been slaughtered due to a disease;

(e) burning containers which have been contaminated by any pesticide or toxic substance used for veterinary or agricultural purposes.

---

62 SI 1958/498.
63 SI 1969/1263.

However, for these exceptions to apply, the person seeking to rely on them must satisfy certain conditions. Among other things, there is the requirement that no other reasonably safe and practicable method of disposing of the matter exists. Other conditions relate to the manner in which the burning takes place and that steps are taken to minimise the emission of dark smoke. The burning must be carried out under the supervision of the occupier of the premises.

8.8.9 Defences

Section 1(4) of the CAA 1993 provides that where a breach of the dark smoke provisions occurs, a number of defences may be raised in any proceedings. These defences arise in the following circumstances:

(a) when lighting the furnace from cold; or
(b) when there has been some unforeseeable and unavoidable failure of the furnace or apparatus connected with the furnace; or
(c) when unsuitable fuel has been used when suitable fuel is unobtainable and that the least unsuitable fuel was used.

Garner's Encyclopaedia of Environmental Law[64] suggests that the defence of lighting a furnace from cold might only be available in relation to the initial ignition of the furnace and not each time the furnace is restoked after a period (that is, overnight) of being damped down. These defences are all subject to the important caveat that all practicable steps were taken to prevent or minimise the emission of dark smoke.

As far as the s 2 CAA 1993 offence is concerned, s 2(4) CAA 1993 provides a defence if it can be proved that the emission was inadvertent and that all practicable steps had been taken to prevent or minimise it. It appears from the statute that both these elements will be required before a defendant can rely on the defence. 'Practicable' is defined here in a similar way to practicable in the context of 'best practicable means'. Therefore, regard must be had to factors such as local conditions and circumstances; financial considerations; and the current state of technical knowledge.

Finally, if the person charged with an offence under either of these sections has not been served with a written notification of the offence from the environmental health department of the local authority within the prescribed four-day period, this will provide him with an additional defence.[65]

8.8.10 Grit, dust and fumes

Section 5 CAA 1993 establishes similar offences to the dark smoke offences in relation to grit, dust and fumes emitted from furnaces. Grit is defined by the Clean Air (Emission of Grit and Dust from Furnaces) Regulations 1971,[66] which also prescribe the limits of grit and dust emissions from certain types of furnaces. 'Dust' does not include dust emitted from a chimney as an ingredient of smoke and 'fumes' means any airborne matter smaller than dust.

It is an offence if, on any day, the grit or dust emitted from a chimney serving a specified furnace exceeds the prescribed emission limits laid down in the Regulations. Monitoring equipment is required to measure emissions accurately and the Ringlemann Chart procedure is not applicable. The occupier will be guilty of the offence unless he or she can successfully raise the defence that the best practicable means had been used to minimise or prevent the emission. It should be noted here that

---

64 Garner's Environmental Law eds JF Garner, DJ Harris and H Henderson (London: Butterworths, updated annually).
65 S 51 CAA 1993.
66 SI 1971/162.

the defence requires the best practicable means to be employed rather than any practicable means. However, in circumstances where the Regulations do not specify a prescribed limit (that is, certain furnaces are not covered by the Regulations), an offence will still be committed if the occupier fails to use any practicable means to minimise the emission of grit or dust from the chimney.

8.8.11 Control over the installation of non-domestic furnaces

Section 4 of the CAA 1993 provides that, before installing a furnace over a certain size (basically a non-domestic boiler), the person seeking to make the installation must obtain the approval of the local authority. The section also stipulates that all new non-domestic boilers should, so far as practicable, be smokeless. Anyone who installs a furnace in contravention of this requirement is committing an offence, but if the local authority has approved the installation, it is deemed to comply with the requirements of the section.

Additionally, all non-domestic furnaces over a certain energy value must comply with the provisions contained in ss 6–8 CAA 1993. Furnaces falling under these sections must be fitted with local authority-approved grit and dust arrestment equipment. The arrestors must be properly maintained, if used for the following purposes:

(a)   to burn pulverised fuel; or
(b)   to burn, at a rate of 45.4 kg or more an hour, any other solid matter (waste); or
(c)   to burn, at a rate equivalent to 366.4 kilowatts or more, any liquid or gaseous matter.

There are certain exemptions from these provisions specified in s 7 CAA 1993. In particular, the Secretary of State has used his powers under s 7 CAA 1993 to prescribe by regulation that furnaces of a certain class (for example, mobile furnaces) may be exempted.[67] Alternatively, it is possible to apply to the local authority for an exemption under s 7 CAA 1993. The local authority can only grant an exemption if it is satisfied that the emissions of grit or dust will not amount to a statutory nuisance. The local authority may also require the occupier of these furnaces to comply with certain monitoring requirements in relation to the measurement of grit, dust and fumes. In turn, the occupier has the right to request that the local authority make and record such measurements and the local authority will be required to do so from time to time. A right of appeal to the Secretary of State is available if the local authority refuses to approve the proposed equipment.

8.8.12 Control over chimney height

Section 14 CAA 1993 applies to furnaces connected to a chimney and empowers local authorities to control the height of chimneys for the purposes of regulating air pollution. These controls are based on the principle of dilute and disperse. Tall chimney stacks are supposed to enable the more effective dispersion of pollution in order to dilute it to harmless levels. The control under s 14 CAA 1993 exists in addition to the normal planning controls which the planning authority can exert.

If any person is intending to:

(a)   erect a new chimney to serve a furnace;
(b)   enlarge an existing chimney to serve a furnace; or
(c)   replace a chimney with an increased combustion space,

---

67 See the Clean Air (Arrestment Plant) (Exemption) Regulations 1969 SI 1969/1262.

then he or she must make an application to the local authority for chimney height approval. The local authority will determine the application by reference to the 1981 *Third Memorandum on Chimney Heights*,[68] which assists with the calculation on chimney heights. The local authority must take into account various factors[69] and, in particular, must not grant approval for a chimney unless it is satisfied that its height will be sufficient to prevent, as far as practicable, the chimney emissions becoming prejudicial to health or a nuisance.

The local authority can approve the chimney height either with or without conditions. Once again, there is a right of appeal against the decision of the local authority to the Secretary of State.

8.8.13 Smoke Control Areas

The ability to establish Smoke Control Areas is one of the principal features of the CAA 1993 and provides an important means by which local authorities can control smoke from domestic properties. A local authority has the power[70] to declare all or part of its area as a Smoke Control Area and does so by designating a Smoke Control Order. The relevant steps to create a Smoke Control Area are set out in Sched 1 to the CAA 1993. In addition, the Secretary of State has the power, by virtue of s 19 CAA 1993, to order a local authority to designate a Smoke Control Area. Two or more local authorities may combine to declare a larger Smoke Control Area.[71] Smoke Control Orders may be varied or revoked at any time. The Smoke Control Order may designate certain classes of building; it may exempt specific buildings or classes of buildings or fireplaces. It has been suggested that the widespread adoption of Smoke Control Areas has been an important factor in achieving compliance with the Sulphur Dioxide Directive (80/779/EEC).

Once an area has been designated as a Smoke Control Area, then an occupier of a building in the area is guilty of an offence if smoke (note that this includes any shade of smoke) is emitted from a chimney of that building. However, defences are available if:

(a) the emission resulted from the use of an authorised fuel; or

(b) the emission resulted from the use of a fireplace exempted by regulations.

Authorised fuels are defined by the Smoke Control Areas (Authorised Fuel) Regulations 1991.[72] Various regulations exempt certain classes of fireplace (the Smoke Control (Exempted Fireplaces) Orders). It is also an offence to buy solid non-authorised fuel for use in a Smoke Control Area (unless of course it is for an exempt fireplace) and it is also an offence to retail unauthorised fuel for unauthorised use in a Smoke Control Area.

8.8.14 Air pollution research and data collection responsibilities of local authorities

Local authorities are empowered[73] to undertake or make financial contributions towards the cost of research into air pollution and publication of research results.[74] In furtherance of the s 34 CAA 1993 power, authorities may serve notices[75] on the occupiers of non-domestic premises requiring

---

68 DoE Circular 25/81.
69 Proximity of neighbouring property, topography and current levels of atmospheric pollution.
70 See s 18 of the CAA 1993.
71 See s 61(3) CAA 1993.
72 SI 1991/1282.
73 S 34 of the CAA 1993.
74 S 38 of the CAA 1993 and the 1997 Regulations SI 1997/19.
75 S 36.

the provision of air pollution emissions data. A right of appeal to the Secretary of State exists with regard to service of such a notice.[76] In the event that the data requested is not forthcoming, local authorities have a power of entry, subject to giving the occupier a minimum of 21 days' notice, to take the necessary measurements.[77] Air pollution emissions data may be recorded by the occupier and supplied to the local authority under the terms of an agreement.[78]

Of considerable importance is the Secretary of State's power[79] to direct, subject to prior consultation, a local authority to acquire and operate air pollution monitoring and recording equipment and to forward the data collected to him. The resultant network of air pollution monitoring stations forms a key component of the government's pollution reduction strategy. The data collected enables the Secretary of State to comply with his duty to provide the public with ozone information.

8.8.15 Measuring and monitoring atmospheric pollution

The National Air Quality Strategy is largely dependent upon the technical capacity of the systems in place to measure and monitor atmospheric pollution. Local authorities in England and Wales utilise a large number of air monitoring stations to sample, record and transmit data on air pollution levels. This locally generated information is supplemented by (1) the National Atmospheric Emissions Inventory,[80] which is organised on an industry sector basis, (2) a range of air quality inventories located in densely urbanised areas,[81] and (3) ozone data compiled under the Ozone Monitoring and Information Regulations 1994[82] which implement the Air Pollution by Ozone Directive (92/72/EC). The 1994 Regulations require the relevant regulatory authorities to put in place a system to warn the public of excessive ozone levels and provide guidance on what action to take.

8.9 Statutory nuisances relating to air quality

Statutory nuisance is considered in Chapter 9. However, in the context of controls over air pollution, it should be noted that the following matters may constitute a statutory nuisance if they are either prejudicial to health or a nuisance:

(a) any premises in such a state so as to be prejudicial to health or a nuisance (this could cover odour emissions from such premises, even though smell is specifically mentioned in (c) below);

(b) smoke, fumes or gas emitted from premises so as to be prejudicial to health or a nuisance;

(c) any dust, steam, smell or other effluvia arising on industrial, trade or business premises.

However, it should be noted that, in relation to (b) above, where the emission of smoke can be controlled under the CAA 1993, the statutory nuisance provisions do not apply. Therefore, this statutory nuisance is largely concerned with smoke which is less than 'dark' from non-domestic premises.

Civil actions, based on the tort of private nuisance, may arise out of activities on the defendant's land which result in air pollution and either consequent physical damage to the claimant's

---

76 S 37.
77 S 35(1)(b).
78 S 36(6) of the CAA 1993 and the 1997 Regulations SI 1997/18.
79 Under s 39 of the CAA 1993.
80 www.naei.org.uk.
81 E.g. London, West Yorkshire, West Midlands and Greater Manchester.
82 SI 1994/440.

land[83] or an unreasonable interference with the use or enjoyment of the claimant's property. Nuisance actions relating to odour, smoke, dust and airborne litter occur from time to time,[84] in which smells emanating from a poorly managed landfill site gave rise to a successful action. Public nuisance actions are less frequent than private nuisance actions[85]—e.g. acidic deposits damaging a car parked on the public highway.

8.10 Pollution from motor vehicles

There is no doubt that emissions from motor vehicles are a major source of atmospheric pollution.[86] Approximately 98 per cent of the UK's benzene emissions arise from vehicle emissions; 89 per cent of the UK's carbon monoxide emissions, 10 per cent of CO_2, 51 per cent of NO_X, 70 per cent of lead and 36 per cent of hydrocarbons come from petrol and diesel engine vehicles. Linked to these statistics is the fact that vehicle emissions have increased by approximately 50 per cent since 1970, although there is some evidence of a temporary downward trend since the introduction of cars fitted with catalytic converters. Pollution emission 'gains' linked to improvements in motor vehicle engine efficiency and the development of less polluting fuels have been offset by increases in the number of motor vehicle journeys made and the number of vehicles in circulation.[87] Vehicles are also relatively cheaper now than at any time before. Vehicle emissions are also largely responsible for emissions of other pollutants such as 1.3-butadiene, which has been shown to be linked to increased risks of lymphoma or leukaemia.

Vehicle emission limits relating to NO_X, CO_2 and hydrocarbons are set by the EU according to the age of motor vehicles, with tighter limits being progressively imposed on vehicle manufacturers. The relevant EU Directives[88] are implemented in the UK via the Road Traffic Acts[89] and the Road Vehicles (Construction and Use) Regulations 2003.[90] Breach of the Regulations is an offence.[91] New motor cars and commercial motor vehicles arriving in the UK must comply with the Motor Vehicle (Type Approval)(Great Britain) Regulations 1984.[92] Annual Ministry of Transport Tests (MOTs) set limits for carbon monoxide and smoke emissions from vehicle exhaust systems.

The problem of vehicle emissions was one of the main themes in *Air Quality: Meeting the Challenge*,[93] which put forward five proposals. These were:

(a) new technological standards for fuels, vehicle engine efficiency (economy), vehicle exhaust systems (especially particulate filters), catalytic converters and air pollution monitoring, recording and data transmission equipment;

(b) planning policies and local transport strategies aimed at reducing the need to travel and encouraging more environmentally friendly modes of transport;

(c) new environmental partnerships with public service and fleet operators, involving improved consultation with bus service operators, road haulage companies and taxi firms regarding their respective contributions to achieving NAQS and AQMA pollution reduction targets;

---

83 For example, airborne acidic deposits or fumes. See *St Helens Smelting Co v Tipping* (1865) 11 HL Cas 642; (1865) 11 ER 1483.
84 See *Blackburn v ARC Ltd* [1998] Env LR 469.
85 *Halsey v Esso Petroleum Co Ltd* [1961] 1 WLR 683; [1961] 2 All ER 145.
86 Especially NO_X, CO_2 and hydrocarbons.
87 Currently 24 million, estimated to rise to over 50 million by 2025. Seee the RCEP's 18th report: *Transport and the Environment* (1994) Cm2674, which drew attention to the estimated 140% growth in road traffic in the period 1988–2025.
88 78/665/EEC, 83/351/EEC, 88/76/EEC, 89/458/EEC, 91/441/EEC, 91/542/EEC, 93/59/EEC and 94/12/EC.
89 Especially the Road Traffic Act (RTA) 1988.
90 SI 2003/2695.
91 S 42 of the Road Traffic Act 1988.
92 SI 1984/981.
93 See 8.5 above.

(d)   stricter enforcement of emissions regulations and, in particular, targeting those vehicles doing the most damage to the environment;

(e)   voluntary action and guidance, especially best practice guidance for industry, commerce and the public.

The composition of fuels is an important factor in reducing traffic-related air pollution. Section 30 of the CAA 1993 empowers the Secretary of State to make regulations relating to fuel content. The Secretary of State may prevent or restrict the production, treatment, importation, distribution, use or sale of fuels. Section 30 CAA 1993 imposes an obligation on the Secretary of State to consult the key stakeholders[94] before introducing new regulations. The current regulations implementing Directives (98/70/EC (petrol)) and (93/12/EEC (diesel)) are the Motor Fuel (Composition and Content) Regulations 1999.[95] Local authorities have responsibility for enforcing the regulations.[96] Similar regulations to the 1999 Regulations apply to fuels with high sulphur content (for example, gas oil) used in non-motor vehicle engines and furnaces. The use of kerosene in aircraft and ships is exempt.

It is clear that for many local authorities with heavy traffic flows and congestion problems, vehicle emissions are going to pose the biggest single problem in terms of meeting air quality standards and objectives. Better traffic management and local transport strategies are seen as important in reducing the use of vehicles. In areas which designate AQMAs, the action plan may need to embrace traffic management issues; for example, restricting access to a particular area or roads, regulating traffic flows and speed, and encouraging other transport modes, such as park and ride. Local authorities have the power, under the Road Traffic Regulation Act 1984 (RTRA 1984), in the interest of preserving local amenity to prohibit, restrict or regulate vehicles, or particular types of vehicles.

The objectives of the NAQS are incorporated into the RTRA 1984 by Sched 22 to the EA 1995. Sections 1, 6 and 122 RTRA 1984, as amended, enable local authorities[97] to make orders with a view to achieving the national strategy objectives. The Road Traffic (Vehicle Emissions) (Fixed Penalty) Regulations 1997[98] enable local authorities to issue fixed penalty notices to road vehicle users who fail to comply with the emission limits set out in regs 61 and 98. Only the police have powers to stop and check vehicles regarding their emissions.

An emergency traffic re-routing power is included in the RTRA 1984, enabling local authorities to divert traffic away from heavily polluted city centres and urban areas when threshold pollution limits have been exceeded.

8.11 EU legislation

The EU had a relatively slow start in terms of its programme of legislation designed to control air pollution. The first directive establishing air quality standards was not adopted until 1980 (Directive 80/779/EEC). Since then, the EU has adopted a variety of measures to tackle air pollution including: (1) permit-based regulatory control of polluting processes,[99] (2) product standards which apply to polluting products (i.e. controls on production and consumption),[100] (3) the use of prohibitions,[101]

---

94 Motor vehicle manufacturers, vehicle buyers and users, fuel companies and air pollution regulators.
95 SI 1999/3107.
96 S 201 of the Local Government Act 1972.
97 Shire counties, metropolitan district authorities, metropolitan borough councils, London borough councils and unitary authorities.
98 SI 1997/3058.
99 E.g. the industries falling within IPPC control.
100 E.g. composition of motor vehicle fuels and manufacture and installation of catalytic converters in motor vehicles.
101 E.g. bans on the use of CFCs and HFCs.

(4) the use of strict emission limits in regard to products[102] and processes,[103] (5) the deployment of air quality standards to measure and limit the presence of substances in the air, (6) economic instruments,[104] (7) voluntary agreements[105] and (8) the collection of reliable data.

Generally speaking, EU air pollution measures can be categorised into the following broad types:

(a) *Emissions from large industrial plants* Of particular importance is the Large Combustion Plant Directive (88/609/ EEC (power stations)). This was implemented in the UK via the IPC regulatory regime (now replaced by IPPC regulatory control). In addition, Directive 84/360/ EEC required that new industrial plants use the best available techniques not entailing excessive cost (BATNEEC). Directive 89/369/EEC deals with emissions from municipal waste incineration plants. In 1996, the EU introduced an Integrated Pollution Prevention and Control Directive (96/61/EC) which has been implemented into national law by the PPCA 1999. The IPPC Directive is, in effect, an extension to the existing IPC and LAAPC licence-based controls over a number of highly polluting industries. The IPPC Directive requires licensed/permitted process operators to use the Best Available Techniques (BAT) to prevent (if possible) or minimise polluting emissions to air. Directive 2001/80/EC, applying to large power stations producing energy only,[106] replaces Directive 88/609/EC and sets new emission limits for sulphur dioxide, oxides of nitrogen and dust.

Process standards to limit air pollution also apply to storage facilities. The Volatile Organic Compounds Directive (1994/63/EC) controls the emission or evaporation of petrol vapours from both storage tanks (tank farms, such as the one at Buncefield in Hertfordshire) and petrol service stations. Similarly the Volatile Organic Compounds Directive (1999/13/EC) regulates the storage, use and evaporation of organic solvents.

(b) *Air pollution affecting the ozone layer* EU Regulations 3322/88 and 549/91 have now banned the use of CFCs (chlorofluorocarbons) and HFCs (hydrofluorocarbons).[107]

(c) *Air quality standards* The EU passed the Air Quality Framework Directive (96/62/EC) in 1996. This is a framework directive whose function is to protect both the general public and the environment from the damaging atmospheric effects of a range of polluting substances. This Directive is intended to be supplemented by a number of daughter directives to control 12 pollutants. The first of the daughter directives (99/30/EC) specifies binding limits for lead, sulphur dioxide, nitrogen dioxide, and small particulate matter.[108] The remaining pollutants are ozone, carbon monoxide, benzene, polyaromatic hydrocarbons (PAH) and the toxic metals—arsenic, mercury, cadmium, and nickel.

Directive 2001/18/EC, which sets national emission ceiling limits for sulphur dioxide, oxides of nitrogen, ammonia and volatile organic compounds in Member States, has been implemented in the UK by the National Ceilings Regulations 2002.[109] The Secretary of State must, as of 2010, ensure that emissions of the gases listed above do not exceed the ceiling limits specified in the Schedule to the Directive. In addition, the Secretary of State must prepare plans for the progressive reduction of the relevant gases, require local authorities to take the reduction programme provisions into account when exercising their functions, and

---

102 E.g. from motor vehicles.
103 E.g. emissions from industrial plants.
104 E.g. eco taxes on motor vehicle fuels, waste going to landfill and emission trading schemes.
105 E.g. with motor vehicle manufacturers.
106 Power plants, of all fuel types, with a thermal input of at least 50 megawatts.
107 See SI 1994/199 and SI 1996/506.
108 PM 10.
109 SI 2002/3118.

prepare annual inventories of the relevant polluting emissions. The Air Quality Standards Regulations 2010 (SI 2010/1001) implement Directive 2008/50/EC on ambient air quality and Directive 2004/107/EC relating to arsenic, cadmium, mercury, nickel and polycyclic aromatic hydrocarbons in ambient air.

(d) *Vehicle emission standards*[110] The EU has enacted various directives which aim to control vehicle emissions. Initially, the directives in this area were intended to harmonise standards in order to promote the free movement of goods (namely vehicles). In 1991, the EU adopted Directive 91/441/EC which imposed strict standards on emissions from passenger cars and a similar Directive 93/59/EC, was adopted in relation to light commercial vehicles. However, since then, emission limits have been tightened via further directives relating to passenger cars (94/12/EEC). Currently the Cars and Light Vans Directive (2001/100/EC) specifies the emission limits (carbon monoxide, nitrogen dioxide, hydrocarbons and particulates) applicable to cars and vans whilst emissions from heavy goods vehicles and large commercial vehicles are controlled by the Vans and Heavy Duty Vehicles Directive (1988/77/EC) as amended. In addition to setting emission limits, the EU has also sought to control the content and composition of fuels in order to reduce emissions of lead and sulphur. These are dealt with below. It is worth noting that the Commission recognises that the problem of vehicle emissions cannot simply be addressed by legislative measures. The Commission has also proposed a variety of other measures concerned with traffic management. The Commission's Green Paper on the impact of transport on the environment[111] considers the impact that vehicle emissions will have on the environment by the year 2010 and suggests actions which are required to be taken.

(e) *Product quality standards* A variety of directives have been concerned with improving product quality standards particularly in relation to fuel products. Examples include Directive 76/716/EEC and Directive 99/32/EC on the sulphur content of liquid fuels and Directive 98/70/EC on the chemical composition of fuels.

(f) *Atmospheric pollution and waste reduction* The Landfill Directive (99/31/EC) came into force in July 1999 and has now been transposed into UK law. One important aspect of the Directive is that it will drastically reduce the amount of municipal waste currently being landfilled: a 65-per-cent reduction of 1995 levels by 2016. This will result in an increase in the amount of municipal waste that is recycled and/or incinerated. Whilst the Directive will deliver an important reduction in methane emissions (a significant contributor to global warming and climate change) from landfill sites, it will increase atmospheric emissions from incinerators.[112] The Incineration of Waste Directive (2000/76/EC) imposes emission limits on polluting substances[113] discharged to air.

(g) *The EU Emissions Trading Scheme* The EU ETS forms a central pillar of the EU's European Climate Change Programme. The relevant European legislative enactment is contained in Directive 2003/87/EC. The EU ETS applies to the industries listed in Annex I[114] in respect of one or more of the greenhouse gases listed in Annex II. The EU ETS is designed to have a phased application (linked to the five-yearly Kyoto Protocol emission reduction targets). Member States are required to produce a national allocation plan (produced in consultation with each of the relevant industries and forwarded to the Commission for approval) setting emission allowances for all industrial installations to which the EU ETS applies (and setting greenhouse

---

110 See 8.10 above.
111 COM(92)46 Final (1992).
112 See Directives 89/369/EEC and 89/429/EEC relating to municipal waste incinerators.
113 Sulphur dioxide, oxides of nitrogen and dust.
114 E.g. oil refineries, steelmaking, papermaking, cement-making, brickmaking and glass.

gas emission allowances for individual installations). The emissions trading scheme has been implemented in England and Wales by secondary legislation: the Greenhouse Gas Emissions Trading Scheme Regulations 2005.[115]

(h) *Voluntary agreements* In the last decade the EU has demonstrated an increased interest in the use of voluntary agreements (voluntary instruments). Whilst these are legally binding agreements entered into voluntarily by polluting industries, they are not laws. Probably the best example of the use of such agreements is to be found in the motor manufacturing industry. In 1996 the Council of Ministers proposed a strategy to reduce the level of carbon monoxide emitted by motor cars. Subsequently the Commission entered into voluntary agreements with the car industry associations in Europe, Japan and Korea to reduce carbon dioxide emissions in new cars, sold to European citizens, to 140g per kilometre by 2008–09.[116]

(i) *Data* In recognition of and response to the need for (1) accurate data relating to air pollution and (2) the dissemination of that data to users, via publicly accessible registers, the EU has established a European Pollutant Emissions Register.[117] The Register enables the EU Commission, European Environment Agency, European Parliament, Member States, NGOs and citizens to search for air pollution data across all Member States. Searches may be made by reference to a range of criteria including specific pollutants and activities generating emissions.[118] The register is maintained jointly by the European Environment Agency and the Commission. Member States are obliged to report, initially, on a tri-annual basis on a range of 50 pollutants (mostly air pollutants) listed in Annex 1 of Decision 2000/479. The Register is to be replaced by the more comprehensive Pollutant Release and Transfer Register established by the Aarhus Convention.

8.12 Acid rain, ozone, global warming and the international dimension

Air pollution is a global environmental issue and attracts international attention. The study of international environmental law falls outside the scope of this book, but the transboundary nature of atmospheric pollution and the global problem of greenhouse gas emissions and climate change[119] make it necessary to include some commentary.

The UK (and the EU) are signatories to a number of international conventions which require the government to take steps to reduce the emission of certain pollutants.

The EU is a party to both the UN Framework Convention on Climate Change and the Kyoto Protocol. It has established a European Climate Change Programme which has led to a range of initiatives designed to reduce greenhouse gas emissions including the establishment of an emissions trading scheme, the promotion of cogeneration of heat and electricity, the promotion of renewable energy, promotion of biofuels, energy performance and energy efficiency.

(a) *The 1979 Convention on Long Range Transboundary Air Pollution* Agreed in Geneva in 1979 became effective in 1983. The Convention signatories (including the EU, the UK and USA) have agreed to endeavour to limit and, as far as possible, reduce and prevent air pollution

---

115 The 2005 Regulations have been updated by the Greenhouse Gas Emissions Trading Scheme Regulations 2012.
116 See a consideration of the utility of these agreements: G.Volpi and S. Singer, 'Will voluntary agreements at EU level deliver on environmental objectives? Lessons from the agreement with the automotive industry', WWF Discussion Paper (2000).
117 See Decision 2000/479/EC.
118 I.e. by industry.
119 Of particular interest are the 2006 Stern Report, *The Econmics of Climate Change* (HM Treasury, London) and the Intergovernmental Panel on Climate Change (www.ipcc.ch).

(especially pollutants associated with the production of acid rain) using best available technology subject to economic feasibility. This flexible framework Convention does not contain provisions to sanction non-compliant signatory states but has resulted in several protocols which set specific pollution-reduction targets including: (1) the reduction of sulphur dioxide (SO2) emissions, (2) the reduction of oxides of nitrogen (NO_x) emissions, and (3) the reduction of emissions of volatile organic compounds (VOCs) and heavy metals.

The UK ratified the first Protocol to the Convention (the Oslo Protocol) in 1994. This committed the UK to achieving a 20 per cent reduction of sulphur dioxide by 2010.[120] Upon signing the Second Protocol to the Convention (the Sofia Protocol) the UK committed itself to limiting nitrogen oxide emissions levels by 1987.[121] The UK's compliance with the Oslo Protocol has been largely due to the construction of gas-fired power stations, which has reduced reliance upon coal-fired power stations and their associated polluting emissions, for example, SO_2 and CO_2.

(b)   *The 1985 Vienna Convention and the 1987 Montreal Protocol relating to the Protection of the Ozone Layer* The Vienna Convention contains provisions requiring signatory states to assess the causes and effects of ozone loss and requires co-operation in information exchange and relevant abatement technology transfer. Signatory states are required to take appropriate measures to prevent 'adverse effects' to the ozone layer.[122] Parties to the Vienna Convention, including the UK (and EU) which ratified it in 1987, have signed up to the Montreal Protocol on Substances that Deplete the Ozone Layer. The Montreal Protocol, as amended in 1991 and 1992, sets binding targets requiring the signatory states to freeze, reduce and phase out the production of various CFCs, HCFCs, methyl bromide and halons. The Protocol also included provisions relating to: (1) the creation of a fund to speed up the adoption of alternative substances to CFCs; (2) derogation provisions especially for the benefit of developing states which were unable to meet the Protocol deadlines for phasing out CFC use. In contrast to the Geneva Convention, the Montreal Protocol to the Vienna Convention includes formal procedures to deal with non-compliant states, and a range of financial sanctions such as the withdrawal of funding from bodies such as the World Bank; and (3) signatory states are banned from trading with non-signatory states which continue to produce CFCs.

(c)   *The 1992 UN Framework Convention on Climate Change* This Convention, ratified by 50 parties who attended the United Nations Earth Summit in Rio de Janeiro,[123] is designed to reduce current emissions of greenhouse gases to a level which will restrict the adverse impacts of greenhouse gas emissions upon the global climate, enabling ecosystems to adapt to change whilst maintaining sustainable economic activity and food production.[124] The Convention incorporates the concept of 'common but differentiated responsibility' to reflect the different obligations placed upon developed and developing states. In regard to the attainment of the Art 2 objectives, the Convention incorporates a range of principles, including (i) common but differentiated responsibility, (ii) a right to sustainable development, (iii) the precautionary principle, and (iv) co-operation within an international economic system. Article 4 details the commitments applicable to developed and developing signatory states.

The 1997 Kyoto Protocol to the Convention establishes binding emission targets for each developed signatory state[125] in regard to the following six greenhouse gases: carbon dioxide, oxides of

---

120 Based on the 1980 level of SO2 production.
121 Based on the 1984 level of production of these emissions.
122 I.e. a precautionary approach to the emission of substances which were likely to cause ozone depletion.
123 In force from 1994.
124 The Art 2 objectives.
125 See Annex 1.

nitrogen, methane, HFCs (hydrofluorocarbons), PFCs (perfluorocarbons) and ozone in the lower atmosphere. The combined target for the six gases represents a very modest 5 per cent reduction of 1990 emission levels for these gases. Targets are to be achieved by 2012. Developing countries, in contrast to developed countries, are not bound by the reduction targets.

The common but differentiated responsibility principle, underpinning the Convention and Protocol, requires some states to reduce their emissions, some states to increase emissions and other states to maintain their level of emissions of the relevant gases.

The Rio Convention and Kyoto Protocol have generated debate with regard to the factors which may be taken into account when assessing whether a state has attained its Protocol targets. For example, provisions contained within the Protocol enable developed (Annex 1) states to use the presence of existing forests, the planting of new forests and forest management activities as 'carbon sinks'[126] to offset part of their greenhouse gas reduction target obligations contained in the Protocol.

Article 4 of the Protocol enables two or more Annex 1 parties to aggregate their emissions provided the total emissions of the two parties does not exceed the combined emission total of the two parties.[127] Thus, regional groupings of states, such as the EU, obtain a degree of flexibility in meeting the aggregated protocol targets for the relevant individual states. Article 6 provides for joint implementation of the Protocol's provisions. Thus an Annex 1 state can receive allowances for the transfer of clean technology to a developing state. Articles 4 and 7 enable emissions trading systems to be established. Article 12 provides for a 'clean development mechanism' whereby Annex 1 states are allowed to assist developing states with projects which will result in greenhouse gas emission reductions.[128] The Convention obliges signatory states to produce annual reports of greenhouse gas emissions. A Compliance Committee relating to the Protocol assists parties with compliance and also acts as an enforcement body.

States which fail to comply with the Protocol may be required to submit action plans detailing the reasons for non-compliance and proposed remedial action. In addition non-compliant states could be disallowed the use of the clean development mechanism (and/or the emissions trading scheme and/or the joint implementation mechanism) to help meet the Protocol targets.

8.13 Climate change and England and Wales

The recognition of the probable implications of climate change has forced the UK government to consider the utility of a range of legal and policy tools to address the global issue of the adverse effects of greenhouse gas emissions. The government's Climate Change Programme, designed to reduce greenhouse gas emissions, is based upon the following measures: (1) licence-based regulatory controls, especially the PPCA 1999 and supplementary secondary legislation, to meet the requirements of a range of EU Directives including the Large Combustion Plants Directive (2001/80/EC) and the National Ceilings Emissions Directive (2001/81/EC), (2) an increased reliance on renewable energy. Section 62 of the Utilities Act 2000 set a binding target of 10 per cent of the national energy supply to be derived from renewable sources of supply by 2010, (3) improved energy efficiency standards in building construction,[129] (4) the provision of a greater range of powers to reduce traffic congestion, and (5) a range of economic instruments including the climate change levy, the national emissions trading scheme, motor vehicle fuel pricing, road tax and company car tax.

---

126 'Carbon sink' refers to carbon dioxide locked up in trees.
127 An example of a joint implementation mechanism which underpins the Convention and Protocol.
128 E.g., the construction of less polluting power stations.
129 See Building Act 1984 and Sustainable and Secure Buildings Act 2004.

The government's programme to tackle climate change exempts aviation and atmospheric marine emissions and emissions from agriculture.[130]

8.13.1 The Climate Change Levy

The combined effect of s 30 and Sched 6 of the Finance Act 2000 is to introduce a tax upon energy consumption—the Climate Change Levy. The tax apples to all industrial users and public bodies, but (1) excludes small businesses, (2) excludes domestic consumers and (3) does not apply to energy consumers whose energy comes from renewable sources and combined heat and power plants. By reducing energy consumption, the government intends to lower the production of greenhouse gases in the UK and thereby meet its Convention/Protocol commitments.

The levy is payable by energy suppliers of both primary fuels and secondary fuels used for lighting, heating, powering appliances and machinery. Energy suppliers will recover the levy from their customers. There are some important exemptions, including domestic use of fuel and power, vehicle fuel, fuel products which are not energy-related (for example, raw material usage and lubricants), renewable energy production and energy from combined heat and power plants. The levy is based on the energy content of the relevant fuel rather than its carbon content. There are reductions in the levy for energy-intensive industries such as steel, glass, paper, aluminium, metal foundries, food and drink production, and cement,[131] which may claim an 80 per cent discount from the levy provided the relevant energy consumer has entered a climate change agreement obliging the energy user to introduce energy efficiency measures in order to reduce its 'carbon footprint'.[132]

8.13.2 Emissions trading

In 2002 the government seized the initiative to introduce a national emissions trading scheme, but this was followed in 2003 by the introduction of an EU scheme which came into effect in 2005.[133]

The primary objective of emission trading schemes is to reduce greenhouse gas emissions by establishing a market, regulated by an Emissions Trading Authority, in which scheme participants buy and sell greenhouse gas 'allowances'.[134] An assessment of the emissions trading scheme has been prepared by the Public Accounts Committee of the House of Commons: *The UK Emissions Trading Scheme: A New Way to Tackle Climate Change* (2003–04 session).

Scheme participants enter into an agreement which specifies a greenhouse gas reduction target which the participant must attain. The allowances which the participant receives are based on the agreed reduction target. Scheme participants may meet their reduction target by: (1) achieving the reduction target, (2) exceeding the reduction target and banking or selling the unused allowances to other scheme participants or (3) purchasing allowances from other participants.

There are four types of scheme participant: Direct Participants, Agreement Participants and two other classes. Direct Participants bid, in an auction, for a share of emission allowances and enter into a binding agreement to meet their greenhouse gas reduction target. Section 39 of the Waste and Emissions Trading Act 2003 specifies the financial penalty payable by any Direct Participant who fails to purchase enough allowances to meet its reduction target. In contrast to Direct

---

130 Save for large production units regulated under the IPPC regime—large pig units, battery hen units and dairy herds.
131 Listed in Part 1 of Sched 1 to the Pollution Prevention and Control (England and Wales) Regulations 2000 SI 2000/1973.
132 ENDS Report 339 at p 23.
133 The Greenhouse Gas Emissions Trading Scheme Directive (2003/87/EC) was implemented in England and Wales by the Greenhouse Gas Emissions Trading Scheme Regulations 2005 which have been updated by the Greenhouse Gas Emissions Trading Scheme Regulations 2012.
134 I.e. an allocation of the right to produce a set amount of greenhouse gas emissions.

Participants, Agreement Participants belong to an industry sector whose reduction targets are set in a Climate Change Agreement.[135] The remaining two classes of scheme participant do not require greenhouse gas reduction targets because they simply trade in the emissions trading scheme.

There has been some criticism of the emissions trading scheme,[136] especially concerning (1) the overlap with permit-based regulatory regimes[137] in regard to which some scheme participants were already obliged by permit conditions to achieve emission reductions despite the fact that the permit holder was bidding for trading emission allowances based on the reductions it was required to achieve via permit conditions, (2) scheme participants who met their reduction target through a planned cut-back in production and (3) scheme participants who cut back on production and bank trading allowances in anticipation of using them when economic conditions improved and production increased.

The Greenhouse Gas Emissions Trading Scheme Directive (2003/87/EC) became operational in the UK in 2005. It is comparable, but not identical, to the UK Emissions Trading Scheme. The key differences of the EU scheme are (1) the EU scheme is permit-based and is run by the Environment Agency, (2) the EU scheme is limited to a range of industries and (3) the EU scheme currently only apples to carbon dioxide emissions. The EU scheme was implemented in England and Wales by the Greenhouse Gas Emissions Trading Scheme Regulations 2005, which were updated by the Greenhouse Gas Emissions Trading Scheme Regulations 2012.[138]

8.13.3 The Climate Change and Sustainable Energy Act 2006

This Act plays a subsidiary role to the Climate Change Act 2008 and the EU Emissions Trading Scheme. It is designed to (1) encourage the production and use of small-scale electricity-generating equipment, (2) encourage the installation of energy efficiency measures, and (3) address the issue of fuel poverty. The Act requires the government to report to Parliament on an annual basis regarding greenhouse gas emissions and measures to reduce those emissions.[139] Electricity-generating companies benefit from a 'carbon emissions reduction obligation' enabling them to buy electricity generated from small-scale (microgeneration, e.g. small-scale wind turbines and solar panels) systems to offset against their own greenhouse gas emissions.

8.13.4 The Climate Change Act 2008

In passing the Climate Change Act 2008 the UK was the first country in the world to introduce legally binding targets relating to the reduction of carbon dioxide, a key greenhouse gas. Carbon dioxide currently accounts for approximately 85 per cent of the UK's total emissions of greenhouse gases. The government has agreed to reduce these by 20 per cent by 2010 and by 60 per cent by 2050.[140] The Act provides an incentive for organisations (to which the Act applies) to achieve greater efficiency in energy usage.

The Act requires the government to publish five-yearly carbon budgets. The Secretary of State is legally obliged to ensure that the net UK carbon account does not exceed budget limits. Carbon budget periods are to last five years; the first budget covers the period 2008–12. The Act creates an independent advisory body called the Committee on Climate Change, whose function it is to advise government on carbon budgets and options to meet greenhouse gas reduction targets. The

---

135 See 18.3.1 above.
136 See ENDS Report 326 at p 25.
137 E.g. IPPC.
138 SI 2003/3311.
139 In a similar vein to the Climate Change Act 2008.
140 Based on 1990 levels of greenhouse gas emissions.

Committee reports to Parliament every five years regarding (1) the current impacts and predicted impacts of climate change and (2) how best to adapt to those impacts.

The 2008 Act also implements the Carbon Reduction Commitment.[141] The organisations to which the scheme applies consume a minimum of 6,000 megawatt hours per year.[142] The Carbon Reduction Commitment scheme operates on a 'Cap and Trade' basis. The government sells carbon allowances to participating organisations at an initial price of £12 per tonne of carbon dioxide. Each participating organisation is required to demonstrate, via a self-certification process, that it has sufficient allowances which correspond to the amount of its carbon dioxide emissions. Any participating organisation which emits more than its allowance must buy additional allowances from other participants in the trading scheme.

8.14 Online resource centre

We recommend that the reader regularly refers to the section of the online resources corresponding to this chapter for information relating to updates, amendments and corrections.

8.15 Summary of key points

Chapter 8 has covered the following topics and issues:

- Climate change is a complex problem requiring a range of regulatory responses at national, regional (e.g. EU) and international levels.
- Air pollution regulation dating back to at least the nineteenth century with a focus upon visible air pollutants, has evolved from a localised issue to a national regional (e.g. EU) and global challenge.
- International law has responded to climate change issues by agreeing a series of framework Conventions supplemented by more detailed Protocols mirroring the pattern of EU and Member State air pollution regulation.
- The UK and the EU have adopted new policy instruments to address greenhouse gas emissions (e.g. the UK Climate Change Levy and the EU Emissions Trading Scheme).
- In regard to emissions from transport the EU uses a product-standard regulatory approach e.g. standards relating to the composition of motor vehicle fuels.
- The EU is the most important regulatory body involved in the setting of air quality standards which apply in England and Wales. The EU's framework strategy on air quality and daughter directives specify quality limits for particular substances.
- Permit-based regulatory controls relate to emissions from industry and power stations.
- The EU has adopted innovative policy instruments to tackle air pollution (e.g. voluntary agreements with the motor vehicle industry and a European-wide emissions trading scheme).
- In view of the fact that EU directives are addressed to the governments of Member States, the Secretary of State has national responsibility for compliance with European law relating to air pollution, but at local level it is the Environment Agency and the local authorities who have practical responsibility for air pollution regulation.

---

141 An emissions trading scheme for large non-energy-intensive organisations e.g. (1) public-sector bodies such as local authorities, water companies and rail operators and (2) businesses such as supermarkets.
142 Energy-intensive industries e.g. steel production are subject to the EU Emissions Trading Scheme and the Act does not apply to other significant sources of carbon dioxide emissions e.g. marine vessels and aircraft.

- Air-quality law in England and Wales is tied to the national air quality strategy. Compliance with the strategy is achieved via a system of local air quality management.
- Local authorities regulate emissions of dark smoke and fumes under the clean air legislation.

 ## 8.16 Further reading

Books

Environmental Protection UK, *Pollution Control Handbook 2008* (Environmental Protection UK, Brighton 2008).
Harvey, L, *Global Warming: The Hard Science* (Prentice Hall, New Jersey 2000).
Helm, D, *Climate Change Policy* (OUP, Oxford 2006).
Hughes, D, Parpworth, N and Upson, J, *Air Pollution Law and Regulation* (Jordans, Bristol 1998).
National Society for Clean Air, *Pollution Handbook* (updated annually).

Journal articles and government papers

Bongaerts, J, 'Carbon dioxide emissions and cars: an environmental agreement at EU level' (1999) EELR 101.
Commission of the European Communities, Green Paper on Greenhouse Gas Emission, COM(2000)87.
Defra, 'Air Quality Strategy for England, Wales, Scotland and Northern Ireland' (Cm 7169, 2007).
Department of the Environment, 'Air Quality Strategy for England, Scotland, Wales and Northern Ireland' (Cm 4548, 2000).
Department of the Environment, 'Ozone', DoE Expert Panel on Air Quality Standards (DoE, 1994).
DETR Circular 15/97, 'The UK National Air Quality Standards: Guidance for Local Authorities' (DETR, 1997).
DETR Guidance G3 (97), 'Air Quality and Traffic Management' (DETR, 1997).
House of Commons Environment Committee, 'UK Climate Change Programme', 5th Report (1999–2000).
HM Treasury and Cabinet Office, 'The Stern Review: The Economics of Climate Change' (2006) .
Monbiot, G, 'Climate Change: A Crisis of Collective Denial' (2005) ELM 57.
Royal Commission on Environmental Pollution, 'Air Pollution Control: An Integrated Approach', 5th Report (Cmnd 6371, 1975).
Royal Commission on Environmental Pollution, 'Energy—The Changing Climate' (Cm 4749, 2000).
Royal Commission on Environmental Pollution, 'Transport and the Environment' (Cm 2674, 1994).
Stradling, D, 'The smoke of great cities: British and American efforts to control pollution 1860–1914' (1999) Environmental History 6.
United Nations, 'Strategies and Policies for Air Pollution Abatement' (United Nations Economic Commission for Europe, ECE/E13.AIR/65, 1999).
Warren, L, 'Global climate change: a stern response?' (2007) Env L Rev 77.

Useful websites

The Inter-governmental Panel on Climate Change
www.ipcc.ch

The Royal Commission on Environmental Pollution
www.rcep.org.uk

The National Air Quality Archive
www.airquality.co.uk

The National Atmospheric Emissions Inventory
www.naei.org.uk

The National Society for Clean Air
http://www.environmental-protection.org.uk/

United Nations (climate change)
www.unfccc.int

Chapter 9

Statutory Nuisance

> ## Learning Objectives
>
> By the end of this chapter you should have acquired an understanding of:
>
> - the provisions of Part III Environmental Protection Act 1990 in relation to statutory nuisance and the associated case law;
>
> - the various statutory nuisances and the test for determining whether something constitutes a statutory nuisance;
>
> - the procedure involved in determining and abating statutory nuisances including the rights of appeal against abatement notices and the criminal liability arising when an abatement notice is breached;
>
> - the developing case law in relation to the requirements of abatement notices;
>
> - the role of the statutory nuisance provisions in combating localised environmental problems and an understanding of the relationship between Part III EPA 1990 and other regulatory controls discussed in this book.

There is a further discussion of the statutory nuisance regime with specific reference to noise nuisances in Chapter 10, while Chapter 11 considers the various ways in which the common law might be used in environmental litigation and examines some of the inherent difficulties faced when bringing common law actions.

9.1 Introduction

In the main, tortious actions are brought because the claimant is seeking an injunction to prevent something occurring and/or some form of compensation for damages as a result of a nuisance or negligent act. Inevitably these types of actions involve expensive protracted litigation and there is no guarantee that any action will be successful because of the difficulty in fulfilling the requirements under each cause of action. Common law actions, especially tort actions, are however supplemented by the provisions of Part III of the Environmental Protection Act (EPA) 1990, which provides that certain states of affairs may constitute 'statutory nuisances'. The control of statutory nuisances rests largely with the environmental health departments of local authorities, which are empowered by Part III EPA to take steps to bring statutory nuisance to an end (or to use the language of the statute, to abate the nuisance). Any person who is affected by a statutory nuisance may complain to the local authority of the area in which the nuisance arises. The local authority is under a duty to take reasonable steps to investigate. If a local authority is satisfied that something constitutes a statutory nuisance, it is under a duty to serve an abatement notice on the perpetrator of the nuisance in order to bring the statutory nuisance to an end. Failure to comply with an abatement notice constitutes a criminal offence. This procedure effectively means that the local authority is responsible for dealing with the problem rather than the individual having to bring a civil claim against the person responsible for the nuisance. However, it should be noted that, although a local authority may use the provisions to prevent the occurrence of a statutory nuisance, the Act is largely used as a reactive tool, enabling local authorities to deal with problems once they have arisen. Finally it is also possible for a 'person aggrieved' by a statutory nuisance to commence proceedings[1]

---

1 Under s 82 EPA 1990.

in the magistrates' court[1] in order to secure the abatement of the nuisance (effectively bypassing the local authority statutory provisions).

9.1.1 Background

The statutory nuisance provisions were not originally introduced as an environmental protection measure. The provisions of Part III EPA can be traced back to the very first 'statutory nuisances', which were created by temporary legislation in 1846.[2] This early legislation provided for 'the more speedy removal of certain nuisances'; prosecution could follow in respect of 'the accumulation of any offensive or noxious matter, refuse, dung, or offal, or of the existence of any foul or offensive drain, privy, or cesspool'. This legislation ultimately led to the Public Health Act (PHA) 1875 and the PHA 1936. These early statutes placed certain nuisances on a statutory footing, in recognition of the growing health problems associated with industrial development and some of the limitations of the common law in addressing these problems. The statutory nuisance provisions contained in the PHA 1936 have been repealed and re-enacted verbatim by the EPA 1990. However, one of the problems with this straightforward re-enactment relates to the fact that the legislation serves different purposes and this raises questions about the extent to which the purpose should be taken into account, by the courts, when approaching the question of interpretation. The Public Health Act 1936 was, as its title makes clear, enacted to protect public health, particularly given the insanitary conditions of the times. Although the provisions were indirectly capable of dealing with pollution, the primary objective of the legislation was clear; the protection of public health (see in particular *Coventry City Council v Cartwright* (1975)[3] and also *Oakley v Birmingham City Council* (2000)).[4] The objective of the EPA 1990 was to restate the law defining statutory nuisances and improve the summary procedures for dealing with them. The extent to which the overall purpose of the provisions has altered remains questionable (and will be considered below). Many of the cases cited in this chapter relate to statutory nuisances under the provisions of the PHA 1936. However, they are still relevant in the context of the EPA 1990 and it is clear that the courts, when approaching the interpretation of the relevant provisions in the EPA 1990, have close regard to the statutory origins of the provisions (see discussion below on nuisances prejudicial to health). (However, see *Hounslow LBC v Thames Water Utilities Ltd* (2003)[5] for a contrasting position.)

The reason for putting certain nuisances on a statutory footing was to provide a quicker, cheaper and more effective means of dealing with nuisances than by means of a common law action. Nevertheless, the provisions do provide a means of indirect environmental protection, in that they can be used to deal with a range of local environmental problems. The list of matters that may potentially constitute statutory nuisances is wide and covers many different situations, ranging from noise as a result of a party, to the accumulation of waste materials on land, and more recently to artificial light emanating from premises. The common feature of these statutory nuisances is that they relate, in practice, to very localised incidents or situations that cause aggravation and annoyance to local people. In this respect the statutory nuisances differ from many of the other 'controls' discussed in this book. However, the fact that 'environmental' problems are localised does not mean that they are less important to the people affected by them. A vacant site used for dumping rubbish may not have serious or global environmental consequences, but can cause considerable problems for people living and working near the site. It may attract vermin, it may give rise to noxious or offensive smells, and it may result in a loss of local amenity. In that sense, the vacant site affects the environment of those affected by it and as such is no less of an environmental problem to the people concerned. Similarly, noise may

---

2 The Wreck and Salvage Act 1846, 9 and 10 Vict. c 96.
3 *Coventry City Council v Cartwright* [1975] 1 WLR 845; [1975] 2 All ER 99.
4 *Oakley v Birmingham City Council* [2001] 1 AC 617; [2000] 3 WLR 1936; [2001] 1 All ER 385; [2001] Env LR 37.
5 *Hounslow LBC v Thames Water Utilities Ltd* [2003] EWHC 1197 Admin; [2004] Env LR 4.

only affect people in a relatively small geographical area, but exposure to unwanted noise can cause recipients to experience a level of discomfort which warrants a legal resolution.

The current statutory nuisance provisions can be found in Pt III of the EPA 1990 (ss 79–82), as amended. The noise nuisance in s 79(g) was drawn from the Control of Pollution Act (COPA) 1974 and s 79(ga) (noise emitted from or caused by a vehicle, machinery or equipment) was inserted by the Noise and Statutory Nuisance Act (NSNA) 1993. In April 2006 two 'new' statutory nuisances came into effect by virtue of ss 101 and 102 of the Clean Neighbourhoods and Environment Act (CNEA) 2005, which inserted new subss 78(fa) and (fb) respectively.

9.2 What are the statutory nuisances?

The matters or activities that constitute statutory nuisances are listed in s 79 as follows:

(a)   any premises in such a state as to be prejudicial to health or a nuisance;

(b)   smoke emitted from premises so as to be prejudicial to health or a nuisance;

(c)   fumes or gases emitted from premises so as to be prejudicial to health or a nuisance;

(d)   any dust, steam, smell or other effluvia arising on industrial, trade or business premises and being prejudicial to health or a nuisance;

(e)   any accumulation or deposit which is prejudicial to health or a nuisance;

(f)   any animal kept in such a place or manner as to be prejudicial to health or a nuisance;

(fa) any insects emanating from relevant industrial, trade or business premises and being prejudicial to health or a nuisance;

(fb) artificial light emitted from premises so as to be prejudicial to health or a nuisance;

(g)   noise emitted from premises so as to be prejudicial to health or a nuisance;

(ga) noise that is prejudicial to health or a nuisance and is emitted from or caused by a vehicle, machinery or equipment in a street;

(h)   any other matter declared by any enactment to be a statutory nuisance.

 See Chapter 10 →   Noise nuisances are considered in greater detail in Chapter 10.

9.2.1 The contaminated land exception

It should be noted that Part III EPA specifically excludes contaminated land from the statutory nuisance regime. Section 79(1)(a) states that 'no matter shall constitute a statutory nuisance to the extent that it consists of, or is caused by, any land being in a contaminated state'. However, the definition of land being in a contaminated state is not the same as the definition of contaminated land in Part IIA EPA 1990, causing something of a lacuna in the statutory provisions. This will be discussed more fully at 9.11.1 below.

9.3 Prejudicial to health or a nuisance

The matters listed in s 79 EPA 1990 are not automatically statutory nuisances. They only become so if they are either prejudicial to health or a nuisance. This phrase includes two separate and alternative limbs, and it is not necessary to show that a matter is both a nuisance and prejudicial to health. This was affirmed in *Betts v Penge UDC* (1942).[6] In practice it is likely to be easier to establish that

---

6 *Betts v Penge UDC* [1942] 2 All ER 61.

something is a nuisance than prejudicial to health (see Oakley[7]). In *Vella v Lambeth LBC* (2005),[8] Poole J accepted the reasoning of Lambeth Council that it was difficult to see how noise could fail to give rise to a nuisance at common law yet at the same time be prejudicial to health. This did not assume a 'link' between the concepts of nuisance and prejudicial to health, but rather reflected the fact that if the 'lower level of the test for common law nuisance failed to be satisfied it was difficult to foresee how the higher hurdle of prejudice to health could be cleared'.[9]

9.3.1 Prejudicial to health

Section 79(7) defines 'prejudicial to health' as meaning 'injurious, or likely to cause injury'. This definition includes two limbs: 'injurious to health', that is, actual harm, and 'likely to cause injury', that is, anticipated harm. The definition is the same as that given in the predecessor provisions of the PHA 1936, a fact that has remained important in the interpretation of the existing provisions in the EPA (see R v Bristol City Council, ex p Everett (1999)[10] and below).

The meaning of prejudicial to health was considered by the Divisional Court in the case of *Cartwright*,[11] which concerned a vacant site owned by the city council. The council took no steps to prevent people from depositing household refuse and building materials, such as brick, tarmacadam, earth, scrap iron and broken glass, on the site. A local resident complained that the deposits constituted a statutory nuisance, in that there was an accumulation or deposit which was prejudicial to health and a nuisance. The argument that it was a nuisance was based on the loss of amenity, an argument soundly rejected by the Court. However, the case is important because of its consideration of the meaning of the phrase 'prejudicial to health'. Initially, the magistrates' court found that the building materials on the site were prejudicial to health on the basis that anyone entering the site might injure himself or herself on the rubble, and they consequently made an abatement order. However, on appeal, that decision was overturned by the Divisional Court, which concerned itself with the question of whether or not the inert materials on the site could be prejudicial to health. The Court came to the conclusion that they could only be prejudice to health if the deposit was likely to cause a threat of disease, or attract vermin. In his judgment, Widgery CJ stated that, in relation to the words prejudicial to health: 'the underlying conception of the section [s 92(1)(c) of the PHA 1936] is that that which is struck at is an accumulation of something which produces a threat to health in the sense of a threat of disease, vermin or the like.' The concept of prejudice to health did not extend to physical injury.

This reference to the statutory origins of the provisions in the EPA was examined in some depth in R v Bristol City Council ex p Everett (1999),[12] a case concerning s 79(1)(a)—'premises in such a state as to be prejudicial to health'. Although the Court of Appeal accepted that in their *ordinary meaning* the words 'injurious, or likely to cause injury, to health' are capable of including accidental physical injury caused by the state of premises, the court felt it necessary to interpret the provisions of the EPA by reference to its predecessor, the PHA 1936: 'The limitation of the reach of this Statute to disease and ill-health is too long standing and deep rooted to be susceptible now to any different interpretation.' Accordingly the Court of Appeal held that the risk of physical injury from a steep internal staircase did not fall within the definition of prejudicial to health. The House of Lords in Oakley[13] reached the same conclusion in a case concerning the physical layout of premises. Oakley confirmed that the language of s 79(1)(a) must be construed in the light of its legislative history

---

7 Oakley v Birmingham City Council [2001] 1 AC 617.
8 Vella v Lambeth LBC [2005] EWHC 2473 (Admin); [2006] Env LR 33.
9 Ibid, para 41.
10 R v Bristol City Council ex p Everett [1999] Env LR 587.
11 Coventry City Council v Cartwright [1975] 1 WLR 845; [1975] 2 All ER 99.
12 Ibid.
13 Oakley v Birmingham City Council [2001] 1 AC 617.

of the provision and that prejudicial to health denoted some form of 'possible infection or disease or illness'. *Cunningham v Birmingham City Council* (1998)[14] confirms that the test for whether something, such as the state of premises, is 'prejudicial to health' is an objective test.

See also *R (On the application of Anne) v Test Valley BC* (2001),[15] which confirmed the objective test approach. The authority must determine whether the health of the average person would be prejudiced. In *O'Toole v Knowsley MBC* (1999)[16] the Divisional Court held that, when determining whether the state of premises was prejudicial to the health of the tenant, it was sufficient to rely on expert evidence as to the condition of the premises, where there was no evidence of the medical condition of the tenant.

9.3.2 What is meant by nuisance?

The courts have equated nuisance in this context with common law nuisance, especially private nuisance involving interference with enjoyment of property. In *National Coal Board v Neath BC* (1976),[17] it was held that the word 'nuisance' meant either a public or a private nuisance at common law. It therefore involved an act or omission materially affecting the comfort and quality of life of a class of the public or an interference for a substantial period with the use and enjoyment of neighbouring property. In *National Coal Board v Thorne* (1976)[18] the Divisional Court held that 'nuisance' in the context of statutory nuisance had the same meaning as public or private nuisance at common law and did not arise if the acts complained of affected only the persons occupying the premises where the nuisance allegedly took place. This requirement appeared to have been relaxed in later cases, such as *Carr v Hackney LBC* (1995),[19] where the nuisance consisted of condensation, dampness and mould caused by the state of the premises, as opposed to an interference from neighbouring property. Similarly in *Network Housing Association Ltd v Westminster City Council* (1995)[20] the nuisance arose from the lack of soundproofing between flats, as opposed to interference from neighbouring tenants. However, the issue was considered in *Vella v Lambeth LBC* (2005)[21] (judicial review proceedings against the council's decision not to serve an abatement notice), where (citing Lord Hoffman's judgment in *LB Southwark v Mills* (2000)[22]) the claimant conceded that a nuisance must be caused to neighbouring property. This is an important consideration in respect of complaints by tenants in respect of any 'nuisance' that they suffer as a result of defective premises. In *Vella* it was noted that as a result of this requirement, many actions against landlords in respect of the state of residential property have been under the prejudicial to health limb and not the nuisance limb.

The problem with using the common law concept of private nuisance is that there is no clearly applicable standard or threshold against which one can say absolutely that a statutory nuisance exists. The question of whether a nuisance exists will depend (subjectively) on the particular circumstances of the case. As will be illustrated in Chapter 11 (and Chapter 10 in relation to noise), one of the features of the common law of nuisance is the achievement of a balance between competing rights, with each case turning on its facts. Deciding whether a nuisance exists using the common law will require an assessment of all of the relevant factors, including whether the activity complained of has the benefit of planning permission. (This issue will be considered further in relation to noisy activities in Chapter 10.) This 'balancing' of competing

See Chapters 10–11 →

---

14 *Cunningham v Birmingham City Council* [1998] Env LR 1.
15 *R (On the application of Anne) v Test Valley BC* [2001] EWHC Admin 1019; [2002] Env LR 22; [2002] 1 PLR 29.
16 *O'Toole v Knowsley MBC* [1999] Env LR 86.
17 *National Coal Board v Neath BC* [1976] 2 All ER 478.
18 *National Coal Board v Thorne* [1976] 1 WLR 543.
19 *Carr v Hackney LBC* [1995] Env LR 372.
20 *Network Housing Association Ltd v Westminster City Council* [1995] 27 HLR 189.
21 *Vella v Lambeth LBC* [2005] EWHC 2473 (Admin); [2006] Env LR 33.
22 *LB Southwark v Mills* [2001] 1 AC 1; [1999] 3 WLR 939; [1999] 4 All ER 449; [2000] Env LR 112.

factors is amply demonstrated in R (London Borough of Hackney) v Moshe Rottenberg (2007),[23] a case concerning noise emitted from premises. The Divisional Court confirmed that there is no prescribed standard of what is and is not a permissible level of noise from neighbouring property. On the contrary:

> When considering whether noise amounts to a nuisance, it is necessary to have regard to a number of factors, which include the nature and context of the neighbourhood; the competing and conflicting interests of adjoining owners and occupants and other people affected; and the fact of any activities in the premises, and whether those are activities permitted by planning permission and the like.[24]

In its guidance on the 'new' statutory nuisances (insects and artificial lights) Defra states that the factors to be taken into consideration by local authorities and the courts include: duration, frequency, impact (i.e. material interference with use of property or personal well-being) the state of the local environment, the motive of the creator of the nuisance and also the sensitivity of the complainant.[25]

Where there is no actual physical damage to person or property, but only a reduction in the enjoyment of a property (for instance, as a consequence of loud noise or offensive smells), the courts have also indicated that much will depend upon the location where the nuisance is complained of. In the often-quoted case of Sturges v Bridgman (1879),[26] Thesiger LJ stated that 'what would be a nuisance in Belgrave Square would not necessarily be so in Bermondsey'.[27] This narrow approach is problematic in the context of environmental protection. Environmental problems often transcend spatially defined areas, and should not be seen in such narrow terms. Moreover, it is precisely in the industrial, urban and run-down areas where there are more likely to be statutory nuisances occurring. There can be no justifiable reason why in these more vulnerable areas the protection of the law should be less than in those areas where the chances of statutory nuisances occurring are more remote.

9.3.3 Interference with personal comfort

The common law test for private nuisance is that there is an interference to property or the enjoyment of property. However in Wivenhoe Port v Colchester BC (1985),[28] the Court of Appeal stated that, in the context of statutory nuisance, nuisance did not have its wide common law meaning but should be confined to personal discomfort. In the judgment, Butler J made the following statement:

> To be within the spirit of the Act [PHA 1936] a nuisance, to be a statutory nuisance, had to be one interfering materially with the personal comfort of the residents, in the sense that it materially affected their well-being although it might not be prejudicial to their health. Thus, dust falling on motor cars might cause inconvenience to their owners; it might even diminish the value of their motor car; but this would not be a statutory nuisance. In the same way, dust falling on gardens or trees, or on stock held in a shop would not be a statutory nuisance. But dust in eyes or hair, even if not shown to be prejudicial to health, would be so as an interference with personal comfort.[29]

---

23 R (London Borough of Hackney) v Moshe Rottenberg [2007] EWHC 166 (Admin).
24 Ibid, at 11.
25 Defra, 'Statutory Nuisance from Insects and Artificial Light'.
26 Sturges v Bridgman [1879] 11 Ch D 852.
27 Ibid, at 865.
28 Wivenhoe Port v Colchester BC [1985] JPL 396 affirming; [1985] JPL 175.
29 Ibid.

Butler J's reference to the 'spirit of the Act' demonstrates a purposive approach to statutory interpretation and he was undoubtedly correct that the principal purpose of the PHA 1936 was to protect public health. However, as noted earlier, the statutory nuisances are now contained in the EPA 1990, which has as its raison d'être the wider aim of protection of the environment. It is questionable whether this restrictive approach is compatible with the aims of the EPA 1990; indeed, dust falling on grass and trees seems to be precisely the type of activity that causes environmental problems. However, the approach adopted in *Wivenhoe* appears to have been relaxed in more recent cases considering the EPA 1990 provisions. In *Godfrey v Conwy County BC* (2000)[30] the Divisional Court held, in relation to a noise nuisance, that it is sufficient that the noise merely interferes with another's quiet enjoyment of their property.

9.4 The specific statutory nuisances and corresponding exemptions

The following section includes a brief examination of each of the different statutory nuisances. In addition it should be noted that s 79(2)–(6) of the EPA 1990 provides a number of specific exemptions from the list of statutory nuisances. These are dealt with below under each limb.

9.4.1 Premises in such a state

> 79—(1)(a)—Any premises in such a state as to be prejudicial to health or a nuisance.

Premises does not simply mean buildings, but is defined in s 79(7) as including land and any vessel other than one powered by steam reciprocating machinery; the definition encompasses the garden of a dwelling house (see *Stevenage BC v Wilson* (1993)[31]). In *East Riding of Yorkshire Council v Yorkshire Water Services Ltd* (2000),[32] it was held that sewers are not 'premises' within the meaning of this limb of statutory nuisance. The Divisional Court rejected submissions based upon the potentially wider remit of statutory nuisance contained within the EPA 1990 (as opposed to a public health statute).

Council house tenants seeking to force their landlords (the council) to deal with defective premises have used this particular head of statutory nuisance on many occasions—see, for example, *Carr v Hackney LBC* (1995).[33] The premises may be in such a state as to be prejudicial to the health of the occupants, in which case a statutory nuisance may arise where there is no interference from a neighbouring property. In *Birmingham City Council v Oakley*[34] Lord Slynn held that the provision was directed at the presence of some feature which in itself is prejudicial to health, in that it is a source of possible infection or disease or illness such as dampness, mould or dirt or evil-smelling accumulations or the presence of rats. Accordingly, in R v Bristol City Council ex p Everett (1999),[35] it was held that a steep internal staircase which could potentially cover physical injury (but not ill health) was outside the remit of the section. In *Oakley*[36] the House of Lords held that the layout of premises

---

30 *Godfrey v Conwy County BC* [2000] All ER (D) 1809 G; [2001] Env LR 38.
31 *Stevenage BC v Wilson* [1993] Env LR 121.
32 *East Riding of Yorkshire Council v Yorkshire Water Services Ltd* [2001] Env LR 7; [2000] COD 446.
33 *Carr v Hackney LBC* [1995] Env LR 372.
34 *Oakley v Birmingham City Council* [2001] 1 AC 617.
35 *R v Bristol City Council ex p Everett* [1999] Env LR 587.
36 *Oakley v Birmingham City Council* [2001] 1 AC 617.

would not be sufficient to render the premises to be in such a state so as to be prejudicial to health. Once again the House of Lords referred to the statutory origins of the provision in concluding that the PHA 1936 were concerned only with the *state* of the premises, not with their layout or any facilities which ought to be installed.

This particular category of statutory nuisance has been considered in a number of cases concerning sound insulation and the extent to which inadequate sound insulation may render premises to be prejudicial to health. For example, where the noise levels from neighbouring premises are reasonable and therefore not a nuisance but it is still argued that the poor sound insulation renders the noise to be prejudicial to health. This head of statutory nuisance was used successfully in (*Southwark London BC v Ince* (1989)[37]) where premises were held to be prejudicial to health by virtue of inadequate sound insulation. However, in *Vella v Lambeth LBC*[38] Poole J concluded that the argument that inadequate sound insulation can cause premises to be in such a state so as to be prejudicial to health is no longer sustainable following *Everett* and *Oakley*: 'The words in s 79(1)(a) can be given no wider meaning than that which has attached since the enactment of the "sanitary statutes" of the mid-nineteenth century.'

See Chapter ◀ 10

The nuisance or prejudice to health need not arise on the premises, but may be caused by some external interference. However, disturbance due to external, traffic-generated noise is excluded from the ambit of statutory nuisance (see *London Borough of Haringey v Jowett* (1999)[39]).

9.4.2 Smoke emitted from premises

79(1)(b)—Smoke emitted from premises so as to be prejudicial to health or a nuisance.

This particular statutory nuisance was not included in the Public Health Acts, but replaces provisions from the Clean Air Act (CAA) 1956. In *Griffiths v Pembrokeshire CC* (2000),[40] a case stated appeal, the Divisional Court held that for the purposes of s 79(1)(b), smoke could include the smell of smoke. The applicant had argued that the smoke, which passed over a neighbour's property, was at too high a level to cause a nuisance. However, although the smoke was not visible to the naked eye, it did leave a detectable smell.

Premises occupied by the armed forces are exempt from this section. So are certain activities listed in s 79(3), such as smoke emitted from a chimney of a private dwelling within a smoke control area, and dark smoke emitted from a chimney of a building serving a boiler or furnace. These latter exempt activities will not constitute a statutory nuisance under Pt III of the EPA 1990 but are controlled under the provisions of the Clean Air Act (CAA) 1993.

9.4.3 Fumes or gases emitted from premises

79(1)(c)—Fumes or gas emitted from premises so as to be prejudicial to health or a nuisance.

Section 79(1)(c) only applies to domestic premises. Fumes are defined as any airborne solid smaller than dust, and gas is defined as vapour and moisture precipitated from vapour.

---

37 *Southwark LBC v Ince* [1989] COD 549.
38 *Vella v Lambeth LBC* [2005] EWHC 2473 (Admin); [2006] Env LR 33.
39 *London Borough of Haringey v Jowett* [1999] NPC 52; [2000] Env LR D6.
40 *Griffiths v Pembrokeshire CC* [2000] Env LR 622; [2000] EHLR 359.

9.4.4 Dust, steam, smell or other effluvia arising on industrial, trade or business premises

79(1)(d)—Any dust, steam, smell or other effluvia arising on industrial, trade or business premises so as to be prejudicial to health or a nuisance.

Steam emitted from a railway locomotive engine is exempted. The term 'effluvia' refers to the flow of harmful or unpleasant substances, such as vapours or gases, onto the complainant's property (see *Malton Borough Health Board v Malton Farmers Manure* (1879)[41]). The terms 'industrial, trade or business premises' are defined widely in s 79(7). The definition includes premises used for manufacturing, treatment or processing purposes. However, until recently, the definition of premises excluded public sewers and sewage works. In *R v Parlby & Ors* (1889)[42] it was held that sewage works were excluded from the definition of 'premises in such a state' under s 91 of the PHA 1875 (the predecessor of s 79(1)(a)). This decision was upheld and applied in *East Riding of Yorkshire Council v Yorkshire Water* (2000),[43] where the Divisional Court held that it was beyond dispute that a public sewer could not be 'premises' in the sense used by the 1875 Act, and that there was a presumption that the judicial interpretation of wording in an Act would be carried forward to the same wording used in a subsequent Act. However, in *Hounslow LBC v Thames Water Utilities Ltd* (2003)[44] the nuisance concerned the smell from the sewage works (a section 79(1)(d) statutory nuisance rather than a s 79(1)(a) nuisance). The Divisional Court distinguished *Parlby*, holding that the ratio in *Parlby* related to 'premises in such a state so as to be a nuisance', and could not be transplanted to the word 'premises' in s 79(1) (d). The Court concluded that the plain meaning of s 79(1)(d) was that it covered the emission of odours from sewage treatment works. The case is interesting and important on several fronts:

(a) From a statutory interpretation perspective the Divisional Court made it clear that the definition of statutory nuisance was completely recast by the 1990 EPA, confirmed by the preamble to the 1990 Act, which expressed Parliament's intention to restate the law in the area of environmental protection.

(b) Section 79(1) was drafted in an inclusive way, with specific exclusions and was not intended to exclude any particular premises, unless by necessary implication or express exclusion.

(c) Policy considerations applicable in 1893 were no longer relevant. Today local authorities are able to take action against large undertakings to regulate nuisance.

(d) Sewage treatment works often create very unpleasant smells. This decision will enable local authorities to respond to the increasing number of complaints against sewerage undertakers.

9.4.5 Any accumulation or deposit

79(1)(e)—Any accumulation or deposit which is prejudicial to health or a nuisance.

This has been held to mean 'an accumulation of something which produces a threat to health in the sense of a threat of disease, vermin or the like' (*Coventry City Council v Cartwright* (1975)[45]). In this particular case, the accumulation of building materials, scrap iron and broken glass was not an

---

41 *Malton Borough Health Board v Malton Farmers Manure* [1879] (1878–79) LR 4 Ex D 302.
42 *R v Parlby & Ors* [1889] 22 QB 520.
43 *East Riding of Yorkshire Council v Yorkshire Water Services Ltd* [2001] Env LR 7; [2000] COD 446.
44 *Vella v Lambeth LBC* [2005] EWHC 2473 (Admin); [2006] Env LR 33.
45 *Coventry City Council v Cartwright* [1975] 1 WLR 845; [1975] 2 All ER 99.

accumulation that was prejudicial to health, so as to be within the intent (or purpose) of the legislation. The fact that the materials could cause injury when walked on was not relevant (see earlier discussion of prejudicial to health). In R v Carrick DC ex p Shelley (1996),[46] it was held that pollution from sewage outfalls, such as sanitary towels and condoms washed up on a beach, constituted a statutory nuisance under s 79(1)(e). However, a mere accumulation that does not create any physical interference with the legitimate activities of anyone else is not likely to be a statutory nuisance. The relevant deposit need not result from human action (see Margate Pier v Town Council of Margate (1869),[47] a case involving the natural accumulation of seaweed).

9.4.6 Any animal kept in such a place or manner

> 79(1)(f)—Any animal kept in such a place or such a manner as to be prejudicial to health or a nuisance.

Both smells and noise from animals may constitute statutory nuisances although, in Morrisey v Galer (1955),[48] it was held that on its true construction this particular category of statutory nuisance dealt with nuisances arising from premises in which animals were kept, i.e., insanitary or defective premises, and not with noisy animals. Nevertheless, noise from animals is covered under s 79(1)(g) below. It should also be noted that wild animals in their natural state are not 'kept' within the meaning of the Act.

9.4.7 Any insects emanating from relevant industrial, trade or business premises

> 79(1)(fa)—Any insects emanating from relevant industrial, trade or business premises and being prejudicial to health or a nuisance.

This new category of statutory nuisance was inserted into the EPA by s 102 Clean Neighbourhoods and Environment Act (CNEA) 2005. Section 79(5A) EPA 1990 states that this head of statutory nuisance does not apply to insects that are wild animals that are protected (listed in Sched 5 to the Wildlife and Countryside Act 1981). This particular head of statutory nuisance only applies in relation to relevant industrial, trade or business premises. These are defined in s 79(7)(c) as industrial, trade or business premises, but this excludes land used as or for arable, grazing, meadow, pasture, osier land, reed beds or woodland. In addition land used for market gardens, nursery grounds or orchards are excluded, as is land used for agricultural purposes or land included in a site which is a site of special scientific interest.

9.4.8 Artificial light emitted from premises

> 79(1)(fb)—Artificial light emitted from premises so as to be prejudicial to health or a nuisance.

This new category of statutory nuisance was inserted into the EPA by s 102 CNEA 2005. Premises occupied by the armed forces are exempt from this section, as are certain other public and transport

46 R v Carrick DC ex p Shelley [1996] Env LR 273 [1996] JPL 857.
47 Margate Pier v Town Council of Margate (1869) 33 JP 437, 20 LT 564.
48 Morrisey v Galer [1955] 1 WLR 110; [1955] 1 All ER 380.

premises such as airports, harbours, bus stations, railway premises and prisons. A rather obvious, but nevertheless reassuring, exemption operates in favour of lighthouses. It remains to be seen what types of premises will be caught by this statutory nuisance, but clearly it has the potential to be used in cases of houses decked with flashing Christmas lights, and also possibly sports stadiums with floodlights. Where the light is emitted from trade, industrial or business premises, the defence of best practicable means (BPM) (see later in this chapter) is available. The BPM defence is also available where the artificial light is emitted by lights used for the purposes only of illuminating an outdoor relevant sports facility.

The Defra guidance[49] on this new limb of statutory nuisance indicates that Defra anticipates that much artificial light nuisance will be caused by excessive levels of illumination and glare, which is inappropriate to its need and which has been poorly designed, directed, operated and maintained. It is also anticipated that simple remedies, such as re-aiming or screening, should be sufficient in many cases. This point is illustrated in the case below.

Law in Action

The case of *R (on the application of Broxbourne BC) v North and East Hertfordshire Magistrates' Court* [2009][50] doesn't add a great deal to our understanding of this particular limb of statutory nuisance but it does make fascinating (if not illuminating (pun intended)) reading. A resident complained to the local authority about light from a neighbouring veterinary practice which was lit up at night time (allegedly to allow safe access for clients and to protect against burglary). The vet appealed the abatement notice and the magistrates allowed the appeal. The judicial review was brought by the council on the grounds that the chairman of the bench had acted improperly when he had gone to see the light himself and had told the other magistrates of his views. The Divisional Court quashed the decision of the magistrates and remitted the appeal to a differently constituted bench for reconsideration. Much of this is outside the scope of this chapter; however the case is interesting in that it appears that the whole thing could have been avoided at minimal cost. The EHO had recommended to the vet alternative lighting which would have resolved the problem for less than £100.

9.4.9 Noise emitted from premises

79(1)(g)—Noise emitted from premises so as to be prejudicial to health or a nuisance.

Noise nuisance was previously contained in ss 58 and 59 of the COPA 1974. 'Noise' is defined as including vibration. Aircraft noise (other than noise from a model aircraft) is exempt from this provision but controlled under other specific legislation. Premises occupied by the armed forces are exempt from this particular section.

See Chapter 10 →

---

49 Defra, 'Statutory Nuisance from Insects and Artificial Light'.
50 *R (on the application of Broxbourne BC) v North and East Hertfordshire Magistrates' Court* [2009] EWHC 695 (Admin); [2009] NPC 60.

9.4.10 Noise emitted from or caused by a vehicle, machinery or equipment in a street

79(1)(ga)—Noise that is prejudicial to health or a nuisance and is emitted from or caused by a vehicle, machinery or equipment in a street.

This statutory nuisance will be considered in full in Chapter 10.

9.4.11 Any other matter declared by any enactment

79(1)(h)—Any other matter declared by any enactment to be a statutory nuisance.

This catch-all provision enables other statutory nuisances created by any other Act to be dealt with under the statutory nuisance procedures of the EPA 1990, for example, nuisances caused by mines and quarries (see the Mines and Quarries Act 1954).

9.5 Responsibility of the local authorities

9.5.1 Duty to inspect and respond to complaints

Section 79(1) of the EPA 1990 places all district councils and London borough councils under a duty to inspect their area from time to time to detect any statutory nuisance actually occurring or likely to occur, which ought to be dealt with under ss 80 and 80A of the Act. They are also under a duty to take such steps as are reasonably practicable to investigate complaints made by people living in the area about statutory nuisances. The duty is therefore twofold. On the one hand the local authority has to carry out its own checks to detect any statutory nuisances. In addition it has a duty to respond to the complaints that it receives. In practice, local authority environmental health departments and officers are responsible for enforcing this legislation and they carry out the inspections and deal with the complaints. In some areas, particularly the large cities, some local authorities have night patrols that are concerned primarily with noise control. The duty to inspect and detect statutory nuisances is tempered by the requirement that these inspections only have to be carried out from time to time. One of the problems here is that the expression 'from time to time' is not defined by the EPA 1990, thus making the obligation very imprecise.

The duty to respond to complaints was established by the EPA 1990. Prior to its introduction, local authorities were not actually required to respond to complaints, although, in practice, complainants provided useful information about the occurrences of statutory nuisances within the local authority area. The duty to respond to complaints made by people living in the area is qualified by the fact that the authority only has to take such steps as are reasonably practicable to investigate the complaint. This expression is not defined and could potentially cause problems.

Law in Action

In R (On the application of Anne) v Test Valley BC (2000)[51] A commenced judicial review proceedings in respect of the alleged failure of the council to act in relation to their complaints about

51 R (On the application of Anne) v Test Valley BC [2001] EWHC Admin 1019; [2002] Env LR 22.

a lime tree in their neighbour's garden. A claimed that the tree harboured aphids that excreted honeydew, and which fell on his property. A also complained that the tree was a source of mould and mould spores which accelerated the decay of his thatch roof and which had a seriously adverse effect on his health. In response to these complaints the council visited the property on a number of occasions and engaged a consultant to carry out a number of tests, including taking various samples of the tree and the mould on the roof. The court held that the steps carried out by the council were reasonably practicable in the circumstances; they were properly conducted and in accordance with the requirements of the Act. Moreover, the court held that the conclusion drawn by the authority that there was no statutory nuisance was adequately reasoned.

However, if the complainant presents credible evidence of the existence of a nuisance to the local authority and the local authority declines to fulfil its statutory duty by inspecting the alleged nuisance, the complainant could judicially review the local authority's adopted course of action. (Albeit that this would of course be a very costly exercise and the cost alone might deter most complainants from pursuing this course of action.)

Local authorities are increasingly finding that they are facing severe financial problems. Whether the authority can take into account its own financial situation in determining what is reasonably practicable is not clear. However, if the Secretary of State finds that a local authority is in default of these duties, he can, by virtue of Sched 3 to the EPA 1990, transfer the function to himself.

9.5.2 Local authorities' investigative powers

In order to carry out their functions of inspection and investigation, local authority environmental health officers (EHOs) can enter any land with the people and equipment that they consider necessary. The officers can also carry out any inspections, measurements and tests, and can also take away samples and articles. These powers are provided by Sched 3 to the EPA 1990. The purpose of the inspection and investigation is to establish whether or not there is a statutory nuisance (or whether one is likely to occur) and to gather any evidence which may be needed in subsequent court proceedings. The powers of entry are exercisable in respect of any premises. This means that the EHO can investigate not only the premises from which the alleged nuisance emanates, but also neighbouring premises in order to further the investigation. The EHO can exercise powers of entry at any reasonable time. However, where the premises are private dwellings, the EHO will need to obtain the occupiers' consent and also give 24 hours' notice. The EHO is not required to have a warrant, but one will be required where entry is refused or a refusal is apprehended, where the premises are permanently or temporarily unoccupied or where, in an emergency, the EHO believes there to be a danger to life or health. Where the EHO believes that a request for admission would defeat the purposes of entry (for example, where he or she anticipates that evidence may be concealed), then he or she should also secure a warrant. Sometimes, the EHO may be accompanied by a police officer. It is a criminal offence under Sched 3 EPA 1990 to obstruct an EHO exercising his or her powers of entry.

9.5.3 Making the determination

In practice, the local authority environmental health officer will make an initial determination whether the matter complained of constitutes a statutory nuisance on the basis of it being prejudicial to health or a nuisance. The officer will therefore be required to take into account the nature of the neighbourhood and also whether the matter complained of amounts to a nuisance in common law or is just (as sometimes happens) a vexatious complaint. The environmental health officer will pay particular attention to the following considerations: the nature of the activity alleged to constitute a nuisance; the locality; the relevant time; the duration of the alleged nuisance; and the utility of the activity creating the alleged nuisance. The EHO will only need to satisfy himself or herself on the balance of probabilities that a nuisance has occurred or is likely to occur before he or she is obliged to take abatement action. The local authority has no authority to act unless it is satisfied that a statutory nuisance exists or is likely to occur or recur (s 80(1) of the EPA 1990).

9.6 Abatement notices

9.6.1 Duty to serve an abatement notice
Section 80 of the EPA 1990 provides that an authority shall serve an abatement notice when it is satisfied that a statutory nuisance:

(a) exists;
(b) is likely to occur; or
(c) is likely to recur in its area.

This demonstrates that not only can the authority use its powers to bring a statutory nuisance to an end, it can also use an abatement notice in order to take preventive action to stop a statutory nuisance happening or reoccurring. The section does not say anything about the need for the likely occurrence to be imminent. It is enough that it is likely to occur. Also, when one considers that the concept of 'prejudicial to health' also extends to 'likely to cause injury', the local authority must serve an Abatement notice if it believes that circumstances exist which make injury likely.

If a local authority is satisfied that the statutory nuisance exists or is likely to occur or recur, s 80 EPA 1990 provides that the authority *shall* serve an abatement notice. The statute confers no discretion in this matter; a point confirmed by the High Court in R v Carrick DC ex p Shelley (1996).[52] In this case the district council received a complaint relating to the presence of sewage debris (from a sewage outfall pipe) washed up on a beach in its area. The authority refused to utilise its statutory nuisance powers, pending the outcome of other proceedings, which were not directly related to its statutory nuisance functions. The complainant successfully challenged, by means of judicial review, the authority's decision to do nothing. The court held that once it was clear that a statutory nuisance existed, the authority was obliged by law to serve an abatement notice, in this case on the water and sewerage company responsible for the statutory nuisance. (See also R v Falmouth and Truro Port Health Authority ex p South West Water Ltd (2000).[53])

Since the Shelley case, s 80 has been amended by the CNEA 2005, which modifies the duty in relation to statutory nuisances under s 79(g) (noise emitted from premises). Where a local authority is satisfied that a statutory nuisance falls within this limb it has a choice of how to respond. It can, as an alternative to serving an abatement notice, take such steps as it considers appropriate for the purpose of persuading the appropriate person to abate the nuisance (or stop it occurring or recurring) (s 80(2A)). The introduction of this provision enables local authorities to try to resolve noise issues in a more flexible and immediate way without having to resort to serving an abatement notice. In such circumstances the local authority can seek to persuade the person causing the

52 R v Carrick DC ex p Shelley [1996] Env LR 273.
53 R v Falmouth and Truro Port Health Authority ex p South West Water Ltd [2001] QB 445, [2000] 3 All ER 306, [2000] 3 WLR 1464.

nuisance to bring it to an end within a period of up to seven days. If, however, the authority is satisfied that at any time during this period its attempts to persuade the person to bring the nuisance to an end will fail, it is bound to serve an abatement notice. The authority must also serve an abatement notice if after the relevant period the nuisance still exists (or is likely to occur or recur).

9.6.2 The form of the notice

Section 80(1) provides that:

> Where a local authority is satisfied that a statutory nuisance exists, or is likely to occur or recur, in the area of the authority, the local authority shall serve a notice ('an abatement notice') imposing all or any of the following requirements –
>
> (a) the abatement of the nuisance or prohibiting or restricting its occurrence or recurrence;
> (b) the execution of such works, and the taking of such other steps, as may be necessary for any of these purposes.

Although there is no prescribed form for an abatement notice, it must nevertheless state the following in a manner that is clear and understandable to the recipient:

(a)   the nature of the statutory nuisance and whether it exists or is likely to occur or recur;
(b)   time limits for compliance;
(c)   the right of appeal to the magistrates' court.

What appears to have been less clear is whether a local authority is required to spell out exactly what a recipient of a notice is required to do to abate the nuisance. Section 80(1) states that the notice must contain 'all or any' of the requirements listed in s 80(1)(a) and (b). This has given rise to a considerable and growing body of case law centring on whether local authorities should be required to specify the steps required to bring the nuisance to an end or whether they have discretion simply to require abatement of the nuisance.

9.6.3 Specifying the nature of the nuisance

The abatement notice must inform the recipient about the nature of the statutory nuisance that the notice seeks to address. In most cases this will be obvious but in a number of cases recipients have sought to challenge abatement notices on the ground that the notice does not provide sufficient clarity about the nature of the nuisance. For example, in *Budd v Colchester BC* (1999) B challenged an abatement notice that referred to 'dog barking'.[54] Schiemann LJ and Smedley J held that the Crown Court had been correct in holding that there was no necessity for the notice to set out the levels or times of barking which were alleged to constitute the nuisance. In *Godfrey v Conwy CBC* the Divisional Court upheld a notice which referred to nuisance arising from 'drumming and amplified music'.[55] The challenge to the notice, which was rejected by the Court, was in essence that the notice did not specify objective criteria by which compliance could be determined. In *R (on the application of Elvington Park Ltd) v York Crown Court* (2012)[56] EPL was served an abatement notice that included the following:

---

54 *Budd v Colchester BC* [1999] Env LR 739; [1999] EHLR 347.
55 *Godfrey v Conwy County BC* [2000] All ER (D) 1809 G; [2001] Env LR 38.
56 *R (On the application of Elvington Park Ltd) v York Crown Court* [2011] EWHC 2213 (Admin); [2012] Env LR 10.

> Nuisance arises as a result of excessive emissions of noise from Elvington Airfield, Elvington Lane, Elvington, York, affecting occupation of nearby residential properties. The emissions of noise arise from motor vehicle activities, motor sport events and activities associated with them including the use of public address systems.

The company (E) argued that the abatement notice was defective because it only referred in general terms to excessive emissions of noise and failed to inform it what it was the council was complaining of, and therefore it couldn't know what it had to do to abate the nuisance, short of closing down the motor racing circuit. E argued that in order for the abatement notice to be valid it should, as a minimum, have either identified the particular activities which are said to constitute the nuisance or specified the noise level above which any activities would amount to a nuisance. The Crown Court disagreed and upheld that abatement notice. E appealed against the Crown Court's decision by way of case stated appeal. The High Court held, having regard to the wording of s 80(1) EPA 1990 and the two cases mentioned above, that:

> One can accept without hesitation that a notice which referred to a nuisance simpliciter, without stating in general terms what kind of nuisance it was (noise, smoke, fumes, etc.) would be invalid. But, beyond that, the courts have set the required threshold of description at a low level.

9.6.4 Should a local authority be required to specify what steps need to be taken?

This question was considered by the Divisional Court in *Sterling Homes v Birmingham City Council* (1996).[57] An abatement notice was served on Sterling Homes which required the recipients 'to carry out such works as may be necessary to ensure that the noise and vibration does not cause prejudice to health or a nuisance, and take any other steps as may be necessary for that purpose'. Sterling Homes failed to comply with the notice and were prosecuted; they appealed on a point of law to the Divisional Court arguing that the notice was a nullity because it failed to specify what it was they were supposed to do. The Divisional Court, following a review of previous authorities held that:

> As the law stands, local authorities are not, in any event, obliged to require works to be done or other steps to be taken: they can ... simply require the nuisance to be abated; the obligation to specify the 'works' and the 'steps' only arises if they choose to include in their notices a requirement for work to be done or steps to be taken.[58]

In reaching this conclusion the Divisional Court considered some pragmatic reasons why it might be fairer if the recipient of the notice is given the option of deciding what is required rather than being told what to do by the officials of the local authority. The recipient of the notice is more familiar with the problem and may be able to abate the nuisance by doing works less expensive than those required by the local authority. Additionally there would be less drain on the authority's resources if it were not required to spend time and money telling those responsible for nuisances how to abate them. McCullough J thought that there could be circumstances where it would be 'helpful' if local authorities specified what should be done but despite this he felt that the Act did not impose any such requirement.

---

57 *Sterling Homes (Midlands Ltd) v Birmingham City Council* [1996] Env LR 121.
58 Ibid, p 133.

Two years later, in *Kirklees MBC v Field and Others* (1998),[59] a specially constituted three-judge Court of Appeal cast doubt on this. The Court of Appeal held that in circumstances where the authority requires the recipient to take positive steps (as opposed to refraining from doing something), it 'could be necessary to specify those steps to avoid doubt'. In this case, the statutory nuisance constituted a rock face in serious danger of collapse. The Court of Appeal held that the abatement notice was invalid because it did not specify the works that were necessary to abate the nuisance. Rather confusingly, though, the Court of Appeal approved the earlier decision in *Sterling Homes*, in that it approved the idea that a notice may simply require the abatement of the nuisance.

The decision in *Kirklees* was eventually overruled by the subsequent decision of the Court of Appeal in *R v Falmouth and Truro Port Health Authority ex p South West Water Ltd* (2000).[60] The Court of Appeal held that, in all cases, the authority could if it wished leave the choice of means of abatement to the perpetrator of the nuisance and should not be obliged to specify what works were necessary, since this could interfere with the ability of the recipient of the notice to choose the works that would enable it to comply with the abatement notice. Consequently a local authority may simply require that the recipient of the notice abate the nuisance, leaving it entirely for the recipient to decide how best to do this.

9.6.5 Are there circumstances where it might be wholly unreasonable for a local authority to simply require the abatement of a nuisance?

In *Sevenoaks DC v Brands Hatch Leisure Group Ltd* (2001)[61] Laws LJ recognised that 'Conceptually, every abatement of a nuisance must require some steps to be taken if only because, by definition, the status quo is being changed; so the taking of some steps is inherent in the requirement of a notice which is strictly expressed only in terms of section 80(1)(a).'[62] Bearing this in mind, some recipients have argued that although the local authority has complete discretion whether to require abatement or to specify steps/undertaking of works, there may be circumstances where it is wholly unreasonable for a local authority to simply require the nuisance be abated. In *Budd v Colchester BC* (1999)[63] Swinton Thomas LJ accepted (on an obiter basis) that he could envisage facts where it would be wholly unreasonable for a local authority to serve a notice merely requiring the recipient to abate the nuisance without stating the works or steps which the Local Authority required to be taken for that purpose. Similarly in another obiter statement in the *Brands Hatch* case Laws LJ considered the utility in recognising a class of cases where it may be '*Wednesbury*[64] irrational' for the local authority not to specify works.

The irrationality argument was put forward to the Divisional Court in *Elvington Park Ltd & Another v City of York Council* (2009).[65] In this case York City Council served a notice on Elvington Park Ltd in respect of a noise nuisance caused by motor racing. The notice required the abatement of the noise nuisance and required the recipient to 'take the steps necessary to prevent noise from motor vehicles and associated activities causing a statutory nuisance'. The notice was appealed but both the magistrates' court and the Crown Court dismissed the appeal. In a case stated appeal the Divisional Court was asked whether the notice was invalid because it failed to specify what steps were required (the invalidity question), and secondly whether in the circumstances it was irrational of the respondents not to set out those steps (the irrationality question). On the first question the Divisional Court held that, on the facts, the notice was invalid, therefore negating the need to consider the second 'irrationality' question. Nevertheless the

---

59 *Kirklees MBC v Field and Others* [1998] Env LR 337.
60 *R v Falmouth and Truro Port Health Authority ex p South West Water Ltd* [2001] QB 445, [2000] 3 All ER 306, [2000] 3 WLR 1464.
61 *Sevenoaks DC v Brands Hatch Leisure Group Ltd* [2001] Env LR 5; [2001] EHLR.
62 Ibid, at para 19.
63 *Budd v Colchester BC* [1999] Env LR 739; [1999] EHLR 347.
64 *Associated Provincial Picture Houses Ltd v Wednesbury Corp* [1948] 1 KB 223; [1947] 2 All ER 680.
65 *Elvington Park Ltd & Another v City of York Council* [2009] EWHC 1805 (Admin); [2010] Env LR 10.

Court rejected the argument that a notice could be nullified on this ground. First, the Court found it difficult to see how a valid notice, which did not require any steps to be taken, could be irrational if it did not particularise the steps. Second the Court upheld the right of a local authority to refrain from specifying what steps are to be taken acknowledging the difficulties faced by local authorities in specifying the steps needed. In support of this Silber J recognised how difficult it had been for the experts (for the appellant and respondent) to agree what steps were to be taken, given the particular complexities of dealing with this type of noise nuisance. Hence it could not be irrational if the council failed to specify these steps. Whilst this case must be considered in the light of the particular facts and difficulties associated with abatement of this type of noise nuisance the ruling does appear to have rendered the irrationality argument of little value to appellants.

9.6.6 Specifying the steps to be taken

Notwithstanding the discussions above, if a local authority decides to require steps to be taken or work to be undertaken, it must specify what these steps/works are with sufficient clarity and particularity for the recipient to be clear what is required.

In *Network Housing Association Ltd v Westminster CC* (1995),[66] the city council served an abatement notice on the housing association requiring it to carry out alterations in order to reduce the noise between flats to a specific decibel level. Since the abatement notice 'fell short of the minimum legal requirement to convey to its recipient clearly what it had to do', it was quashed.[67] In *London Borough of Camden v London Underground Ltd* (2000)[68] the Divisional Court considered the validity of an abatement notice which required the recipient to 'pay special attention to' a particular element of the noise nuisance (the low frequency noise) and which also concluded with the sentence 'if you fail to execute all or any of the works in accordance with this notice the council may execute the works'. The Court considered that the requirement to pay special attention to a particular element of the noise nuisance necessarily required the taking of appropriate remedial steps, i.e. the words require work to be carried out and this view was supported by the last sentence. In the light of this construction the Divisional Court held that the local authority was required to detail what work was required, and since it had failed to do this the notice was invalid.

This point was emphasised once again by the Divisional Court in *Elvington Park Ltd & Another*[69] In this case the abatement notice was drafted as follows:

HEREBY REQUIRE YOU as the person responsible for the said nuisance within 3 months from the service of this notice, to abate the same and also

HEREBY PROHIBIT the recurrence of the same and for that purpose require you to:

take the steps necessary to prevent noise from motor vehicles and associated activities causing a statutory nuisance at other premises.

The Council may also take proceedings in the High Court for securing the abatement, prohibition or restriction of the nuisance. Further if you fail to execute all or any of the works in accordance with this notice, the Council may execute the works and recover from you the necessary expenditure incurred.

---

66 *Network Housing Association Ltd v Westminster City Council* [1995] 27 HLR 189.
67 Ibid (per Buckley J), at p 183.
68 *London Borough of Camden v London Underground Ltd* [2000] Env LR 369.
69 *Elvington Park Ltd & Another v City of York Council* [2009] EWHC 1805 (Admin); [2010] Env LR 10.

The Divisional Court held that the authorities clearly show that if an abatement notice requires not merely abatement of noise but also steps to be taken, they should be specified. If they failed to specify what was required the notice would be invalid because 'the recipients of these notices would not know what they had to do to avoid criminal proceedings being brought against them'.[70] Interestingly, in the *Elvington Park* case the local authority issued two further abatement notices which made no reference to any steps and this time simply required the abatement of the nuisance and prohibited any further recurrence. These two abatement notices became the subject of further litigation.[71] The degree of specification will no doubt vary on a case-by-case basis, and in some circumstances may be elaborated in a covering schedule, annex or letter. In the *Camden LBC*[72] case discussed above it was held that the notice served on London Underground, which was expressed to be an abatement notice, was to be construed in the light of the letter that accompanied it. Where the authority does prescribe steps to be taken, the recipient may choose to challenge these steps by way of appeal (see below). In view of this, it would appear that the simplest option for a local authority is simply to require the abatement of the nuisance, thus passing the burden to the recipient to determine how best to do this and reducing the likelihood of appeal.

9.6.7 Is there a duty to consult?

In *R v Falmouth and Truro Port Health Authority ex p South West Water Ltd* (2000)[73] it was found that the local authority is not under a duty to consult the alleged perpetrator of a statutory nuisance before serving an abatement notice. Thus, for example, where a local authority elects to specify what steps are required to abate a nuisance, the authority is not required to conduct any prior consultation with the recipient of the notice. Notwithstanding the fact that there is no duty to consult, the Court of Appeal did suggest that consultation may often be appropriate and that there may in some circumstances be a duty to consult where the recipient has a legitimate expectation of being consulted. On the facts in this case, the Court of Appeal held that the recipient did not have a legitimate expectation of being consulted, but also added that there was a strong case for consultation. In practice, many EHOs will actually embark on some form of dialogue with the parties involved before serving an abatement notice.

9.6.8 On whom must the notice be served?

The provisions regarding the serving of abatement notices are contained in s 80 of the EPA 1990. Normally, the local authority is required to serve the notice on the person responsible for the nuisance. There are two exceptions to this in ss 80(2)(b) and (c). These are considered below.

The person responsible for the nuisance is defined in s 79(7) as the person to whose:

(a)   act;
(b)   default; or
(c)   sufferance,

the nuisance is attributable.

This is a wide definition and could include not only the person who created the nuisance, but also a third person/party who failed to take any appropriate preventive or corrective action where

---

70   Ibid, at para 36.
71   *R (On the application of Elvington Park Ltd) v York Crown Court* [2011] EWHC 2213 (Admin); [2012] Env LR 10.
72   *London Borough of Camden v London Underground Ltd* [2000] Env LR 369.
73   *R v Falmouth and Truro Port Health Authority ex p South West Water Ltd* [2001] QB 445, [2000] 3 All ER 306, [2000] 3 WLR 1464.

he or she had some legal requirement to do so. It can also include third persons who, on becoming aware of the problem, took no steps to remedy the situation. This was confirmed in *Clayton v Sale UDC* (1926),[74] where an owner was held liable for a statutory nuisance on his land consequent upon the activities or defaults of another. In *Carr v Hackney LBC* (1995),[75] the Divisional Court held that where a tenant had refused to allow his landlord to enter in order to do works to abate the nuisance, the landlord could not be a person whose act or default or sufferance caused the nuisance to arise. It would also appear that a local authority can serve a notice on a previous owner of land, rather than the current owner, if it decides that the previous owner was the person who caused the nuisance rather than the present owner.

Section 80(2)(b) provides that where the nuisance arises from any defect in the structural character of a building, then the notice should be served on the owner of the premises. Section 80(2)(c) states that in circumstances where the person responsible for the nuisance cannot be found, or the nuisance has not yet occurred, then the notice must be served on the owner or occupier of the premises. The terms 'owner' and 'occupier' are not defined in this particular part of the statute. In the case of *London Borough of Camden v Gunby* (1999)[76] an abatement notice was served on a property managing agent (G) in respect of a structural defect in the property which constituted a s 79(1)(a) statutory nuisance. G appealed the notice arguing that it should have been served on the freehold owner as per s 80(2)(b). The Crown Court allowed the appeal and the council appealed by way of case stated, contending that the managing agent was to be regarded as the owner. The Divisional Court considered the definition of the term 'owner' in s 81A(9) but noted that the definition here applied to 'this section'. The court held that in view of this an ambiguity was posed as to the meaning of the word where it appeared undefined in s 80(2) and that the ambiguity was to be resolved by recourse to the legislative history of the provision. This showed that a series of statutes regulating statutory nuisance had defined 'owner' as the person for the time being receiving the rack rent of the premises in connection with which the word was used, whether on his own account or as agent or trustee for any other person; that the word in s 80(2) should be given the same well-established meaning and was therefore apt to include a managing agent who received rack rent as an agent or trustee.

Where the statutory nuisance relates to a vehicle the person responsible is the person in whose name the vehicle is registered and any other person who is driving the vehicle and in relation to machinery or equipment the person responsible can also include any person who is for the time being the operator of the machinery or equipment (s 79(7)).

Law in Action

R (on the application of Khan) v Isleworth Crown Court (2011)[77]
Mr Khan had been served an abatement notice which required him to prevent the repetitive and uncontrolled barking of a dog at his home. The notice was delivered to his home and addressed to 'the occupier'. However, K had moved out of that property before the notice was delivered. K was not aware of the notice and so he did not appeal it. In fact, K's brother lived at the address and was in fact the owner of the dog. A month later the local sent a summons to the address alleging that K was in breach of the notice without reasonable excuse. He was

---

74 *Clayton v Sale UDC* [1926] 1 KB 415.
75 *Carr v Hackney London BC* [1995] Env LR 372.
76 *London Borough of Camden v Gunby* [2000] WLR 465.
77 *R (on the application of Khan) v Isleworth Crown Court* [2011] EWHC 3164 (Admin); [2012] Env LR 12.

subsequently convicted in his absence and when he became aware of the problem he appealed to the Crown Court. However, the Crown Court found that despite K not owning the dog and not being present at the property at the relevant times he had been responsible for the nuisance and had no reasonable excuse for not knowing about the statutory nuisance and so being unable to appeal the notice. The Crown Court considered that K should have made arrangements to collect his post and so upheld the conviction. The case was referred to the High Court, which quashed the conviction. The High Court held it was entirely obvious that K was not the person responsible for the nuisance. That person had manifestly been his brother whose dog it was and who had plainly been in control (or not) at the relevant times. For further discussion of this case in respect of the reasonable excuse defence see later at 9.9.1.

9.6.9 What if more than one person is involved?

Section 81(1) deals with the situation where more than one person is responsible for the statutory nuisance. In these circumstances, s 80 still applies to each of the persons, irrespective of whether or not that which any one of them is responsible for would, by itself, amount to a statutory nuisance. Therefore, if two persons are involved in an action which jointly amounts to a statutory nuisance, they will both be responsible for the statutory nuisance even if their individual actions do not by themselves amount to such a nuisance. Although the abatement notice should be served in the first instance on the person responsible for the nuisance, this should be read as meaning that the authority is obliged to serve separate notices on all the parties that may have contributed to the statutory nuisance.

9.7 Appeals against an abatement notice

By virtue of s 80(3) of the EPA 1990, a person upon whom an abatement notice is served is entitled to appeal against it by making a complaint to the magistrates' court. He or she must be informed of this right in the abatement notice. Where a person decides to lodge an appeal, he or she must do so within 21 days from the day on which the abatement notice was served.

9.7.1 Grounds for appeal

The grounds of appeal and powers of the magistrates' courts are laid down in the Statutory Nuisance (Appeals) Regulations 1995[78] as amended. The grounds are as follows:

(a) the abatement notice is not justified by s 80 of the EPA 1990—here the appellant would be arguing that the matter did not constitute a statutory nuisance;
(b) the abatement notice has some informality, or is defective or contains an error;
(c) the authority has refused unreasonably to accept compliance with alternative requirements, or the requirements laid down in the abatement notice are unreasonable or unnecessary;
(d) the period(s) for compliance in the notice is (are) not reasonably sufficient for the purpose;
(e) there has been an error in the service of the notice—for example, the notice has been served on the wrong person. An appeal may also be made if the appellant argues that it is 'equitable' for the notice to be served on some other person, either *instead of* the appellant or as well as him. Whether the wrong person has been served will be determined by reference to s 80(2);

---

78 Statutory Nuisance (Appeals) Regulations 1995 SI 1995/2644.

(f) the best practicable means were used to prevent or counteract the effect of a nuisance from trade or business premises or, for a noise nuisance under s 79(1)(ga), that the best practicable means were used to prevent or counteract the noise from or caused by a vehicle, machinery or equipment being used for industrial or trade purposes;

(g) in relation to a nuisance under s 79(1)(g) or (ga), the requirements imposed by the abatement notice are more onerous than the requirements which may have been determined by means of other noise controls under the COPA 1974;

(h) in relation to a nuisance under s 89(1)(ga) (noise emitted from or caused by vehicles, machinery or equipment), the requirements imposed by the abatement notice are more onerous than the requirements of any condition of a consent given under the NSNA 1993 (provisions relating to loudspeakers in streets or on roads).

The ground specified in (f) above, that the best practicable means were used to prevent or counteract the effect of a nuisance from trade or business premises, is considered below in relation to defences since best practicable means (BPM) also constitutes a defence against non-compliance with an abatement notice.

9.7.2 Magistrates' powers in respect of appeals

The magistrates' court has wide powers when dealing with appeals against abatement notices. It can:

(a) quash the abatement notice;
(b) vary the abatement notice in favour of the appellant;
(c) dismiss the appeal.

If a person has appealed on the grounds of some defect or error in the abatement notice, the court must dismiss the appeal if it is satisfied that the defect or error is not a material one. Therefore, there seems little value in appealing against 'minor' defects or informalities.

In addition to this, the court can also make an order as it thinks fit regarding:

(a) any works which need to be carried out and the contribution to be made by any person to the cost of the work; or
(b) the proportion of expenses that a local authority may recover from the appellant and from any other person.

Law in Action

In *Brighton & Hove Council v Ocean Coachworks (Brighton) Ltd* (2001)[79] an abatement notice was served on OCB in relation to noise from tools and machinery used for vehicle repairs. The notice required abatement 'forthwith' by keeping the workshop doors closed except where there was a genuine business reason for opening the doors. The notice also included a reference to the expenditure required in carrying out works in compliance with the notice not being disproportionate (in order to prevent the suspension of the notice pending an appeal—see

---

79 Brighton & Hove Council v Ocean Coachworks (Brighton) Ltd [2001] Env LR 4.

below). OCB appealed a the notice arguing that the term 'forthwith' did not comply with the statutory requirements of s 80(b) as to specification of time for compliance. The magistrates concluded that the notice had breached natural justice by requiring unspecified works and by the failure to set a clear deadline. In a case stated appeal the Divisional Court was asked four questions:

(a) whether the notice was invalid for failing to adequately specify the steps required;

(b) whether the notice was invalid for failing to provide a 'window of time' in which to comply;

(c) whether the notice was invalid for making the time for compliance 'forthwith'; and

(d) whether in all the circumstances the notice was a nullity.

The Divisional Court concluded that the notice left OCB in no doubt as to what was required despite the erroneous and superfluous reference to 'carrying out works'. Since the notice was clear and unambiguous in its requirements it was not a realistic consideration to include a window of time within which to comply and so the notice was not invalid for making the time for compliance forthwith.

9.7.3 Effect of an appeal upon an abatement notice

In general, and provided the abatement notice is appropriately worded by the relevant local authority, the lodging of an appeal will not suspend it and the person served with the notice will still be required to comply with its conditions. This is particularly so where the nuisance to which the abatement notice relates is either injurious to health or likely to be of such a limited duration that suspension of the notice would render it of no practical effect. The fact that the notice will not be suspended pending the appeal should be clearly stated in the notice. However, this general provision does not apply in the following alternative situations when the abatement notice will be suspended pending the appeal:

(a) where compliance with the abatement notice would involve any person in expenditure or the carrying out of works before the hearing of the appeal and the works or cost would be out of proportion in relation to the expected public benefit;

(b) in the case of a nuisance under s 79(1)(g) or (ga) of the EPA 1990, the noise to which the abatement notice relates is noise necessarily caused in the course of the performance of some duty imposed by law on the appellant.

These provisions are to be found in reg 3 of the Statutory Nuisance (Appeals) Regulations 1995.[80]

9.7.4 Duration of an abatement notice

Unless it is otherwise stated, an abatement notice is of unlimited duration. In *Wellingborough DC v Gordon* (1991),[81] the defendant, Mr Gordon, was served an abatement notice in 1985 in respect of a noise nuisance. Three years later in 1988 he held a birthday party at which the police intervened in the early hours of the morning, requesting that the volume of the music be turned down. The district council prosecuted Mr Gordon for breach of the abatement notice served in 1985. The magistrates found the defendant not guilty but, on appeal, the High Court held that the abatement

---

80 Statutory Nuisance (Appeals) Regulations 1995 SI 1995/2644.
81 *Wellingborough DC v Gordon* [1990] 155 JP 494; [1991] JPL 874.

notice was still valid. Interestingly, in this case, there had been no complaints about the noise levels in 1988, and the High Court acknowledged that this was an isolated incident. In the Court's view, however, these factors did not constitute a reasonable excuse for breaching the original notice.

9.8 Non-compliance with an abatement notice

Section 80(4) of the EPA 1990 establishes that it is a criminal offence for a person to contravene or fail to comply with any requirement or prohibition imposed by an abatement notice, without reasonable excuse. If an abatement notice is not complied with, the authority that has issued the notice has three options:

(a) abate the nuisance and do whatever may be necessary in execution of the notice;
(b) institute summary proceedings;
(c) take proceedings for an injunction in the High Court.

9.8.1 The authority can abate the nuisance

The authority can abate the nuisance and do whatever may be necessary in execution of the notice (s 81(3)). In relation to noise from premises under s 79(g) this power includes the power to remove any equipment which is being used or has been used in the emission of the noise (s 80(3A)). The authority can take this course of action irrespective of whether it takes proceedings for non-compliance under s 80(4) (see below). In the event that the authority does take action either to abate the nuisance or prevent it happening it can, by virtue of s 81(4), recover any expenses reasonably incurred. This would normally be from the person whose acts or omissions caused the nuisance. If that person is the owner of the premises, the expenses can be recovered from any person who is for the time being the owner of them. This would cover situations where, for instance, a previous owner caused a nuisance, but the present owner could be made responsible for the reasonable expenses incurred by the authority. Should the matter of cost recovery go before the court, the court has the power to apportion the expenses between persons whose acts (or omissions) caused the nuisance, in a manner that the court considers fair and reasonable.

The NSNA 1993 inserted s 81A into the EPA 1990, providing additional assistance to local authorities by enabling them to recover costs by making a charge on the premises owned by the person in default.

9.8.2 The authority can institute summary proceedings

If a person fails to comply with an abatement notice without reasonable excuse they commit an offence under s 80(4) and the authority can only institute proceedings in the magistrates' court. Clearly the potential of incurring criminal liability for non-compliance with an abatement notice provides an effective deterrent against non-compliance. In this regard the statutory nuisance provisions contrast starkly with the civil tort of nuisance. However, as noted earlier, it also means that the criminal standard of proof applies in summary proceedings.

Prior to the decision in R (on the application of Ethos Recycling Ltd) v Barking and Dagenham Magistrates' Court [2009][82] it was not entirely clear whether a local authority had to obtain the Secretary of State's consent to commencing criminal proceedings before the magistrates, or whether it also meant that

---

82 R (on the application of Ethos Recycling Ltd) v Barking and Dagenham Magistrates' Court [2009] EWHC 2885 (Admin); [2010] Env LR 25.

consent must be sought before issuing an abatement notice. The EPA fails to define the term 'summary proceedings' and hence the lack of clarity about its precise meaning. In this case Ethos Recycling Ltd (E) held an environmental permit which included a condition requiring the installation of a dust suppression system at the company's waste recycling plant. The Environment Agency had issued a warning regarding the levels of dust from the site. However, the local authority, having received complaints about the dust, served an abatement notice on the company. E appealed the notice, arguing that it was a nullity because the local authority had served it without first obtaining the consent of the Secretary of State. This argument was rejected by the district judge on the basis that if Parliament had intended that a local authority could not serve an abatement notice without the consent of the Secretary of State, then s 80 would have made this clear. Instead the district judge considered that the local authority could serve an abatement notice but could not commence court proceedings without consent: 'By using the words "institute summary proceedings" they have in my view prevented double jeopardy in the criminal sense by leaving the final decision of enforcement to the Environment Agency without preventing the local authority from taking the preparatory steps necessary to allow them to institute summary proceedings if necessary.'[83] In a judicial review of this decision the Divisional Court upheld the decision of the district judge stating that his interpretation was correct, and on its true constriction s 79(10) did not include service of an abatement notice. Moreover the Court considered that it was the local authority rather than the Environment Agency that was the natural recipient of complaints and as such has a statutory duty to investigate and serve a notice to prevent the continuation or recurrence of the nuisance where it was satisfied that such a nuisance existed. On a practical note the Court also held that it would be wholly artificial to require the local authority first to obtain the consent of the Secretary of State. 'Such a step would inevitably take time and frequently time was of the essence where neighbours were complaining and expected prompt action from the local authority.'

Section 79(10) limits the capacity of a local authority to commence summary proceedings in respect of a nuisance falling within s 79(1)(b), (d), (e) or (fb). If, in any of these cases, proceedings might be instituted under s 2 Pollution Prevention Control Act 1999 the local authority must first obtain the consent of the Secretary of State before commencing statutory nuisance proceedings.

9.8.2.1 Penalties

The penalty for breaching an abatement notice (see s 80(5) and (6)) depends on whether the nuisance has occurred on industrial, trade or business premises. For nuisances arising on non-industrial, trade or business premises, the maximum penalty is £5,000 plus a further £500 for each day that the offence continues after the conviction. However, where the nuisance occurs on industrial, trade or business premises, the maximum fine is £20,000 (but no additional daily fines can be made).

Law in Action

The exercise of discretion in determining the level of fines was considered by the Divisional Court in *R (on the application of Islington LBC) v Inner London Crown Court* (2003).[84] The council sought judicial review of the decision of the Inner London Crown Court to impose a fine of £4,000 on the council for a statutory nuisance involving a flat for which the council was the

---

83 Ibid at para 22.
84 *R (on the application of Islington LBC) v Inner London Crown Court* [2003] EWHC 2500 (Admin); [2004] Env LR 20.

landlord. The council had been found guilty of offences under s 82 EPA (see below) following its failure to comply with a magistrates' notice to abate the nuisance. The council pleaded guilty and was fined £4,000 together with compensation orders of £2,500 to each of the two tenants. The magistrates had set the fine of £4,000 in view of the degree of the statutory nuisance and the state of the premises in question (which suffered from damp and mould); a decision that was upheld by the Crown Court (although the Crown Court reduced the compensation orders to £1,000). The Divisional Court held that whilst the offence in question had been serious, there was a wide range of nuisances that were required to be censured by the imposition of a fine up to a maximum of £5,000, and there were offences which could be much worse. In these circumstances, and given the mitigating circumstances (the council had pleaded guilty and had substantially carried out the works required) a fine of £4,000 had clearly been outside the broad area of the Crown Court's sentencing discretion. Thus it seems clear that when a court is imposing a fine in respect of non-compliance with an abatement notice it should have regard to the nature and gravity of the statutory nuisance and the attitude of the defendant.

9.8.2.2 Anti-Social Behaviour Orders (ASBO)

Given that many of the statutory nuisances that occur do so in the context of neighbour disputes it is no surprise that a court may consider imposing an ASBO on the person responsible for the statutory nuisance. Section 1C Crime and Disorder Act 1998 provides that where an offender is convicted of an offence, it is possible for an Anti-Social Behaviour Order (ASBO) to be imposed where the court considers the offender has caused, or is likely to cause, harassment, alarm or distress to others and the ASBO is necessary to protect them from antisocial behaviour. In R (on the application of Joseph McGarrett) v Kingston Crown Court[85] the claimant sought judicial review of the Crown Court's decision to impose an indefinite ASBO on him, in addition to fining him for breach of an abatement notice. (The fine was £75 and in addition there was a victim surcharge of £15 and the defendant was ordered to pay costs of £290.) The Divisional Court, however, disagreed and quashed the ASBO; the purpose of an ASBO was not to punish and the terms of the order had to be proportionate to the risk to be guarded against. On the facts, the Divisional Court considered that although there was no objection to the Crown Court taking the initiative in considering whether to impose an ASBO, in the instant case there had been no findings of fact by the court on which to base the ASBO. The breach of the abatement notice was a single offence and no other relevant offending had occurred.

9.8.3 The authority can take proceedings in the High Court

The third option available to the authority against a person who fails to comply with or contravenes an abatement notice is to take proceedings in the High Court (s 81(5) of the EPA 1990). This option is available if the authority is of the view that proceedings in the magistrates' court (under s 80(4)) would afford an inadequate remedy. The aim would be to obtain an injunction to secure the abatement, prohibition or restriction of the statutory nuisance. The authority can take this course of action at any time after service of an abatement notice, even if summary proceedings have not been concluded (see Hammersmith London BC v Magnum Automated Forecourts Ltd (1978)[86]). In East Dorset DC v Eaglebeam Ltd & Others (2006)[87] an injunction was granted restraining a company from running motocross activities

---

85 R (on the application of Joseph McGarrett) v Kingston Crown Court [2009] EWHC 1776 (Admin).
86 Hammersmith LBC v Magnum Automated Forecourts Ltd [1978] 1 WLR 50.
87 East Dorset DC v Eaglebeam Ltd & Others [2006] EWHC 2378 (QB) LTL 2/10/2006.

on its land. The company, E, had been served an abatement notice in respect of the noise from the site.

E had taken some steps to reduce the noise following receipt of the notice but it had also been aware that the motocross was sufficiently noisy to be both a statutory nuisance and also a public nuisance. The injunction was granted because, even in the light of these facts, E had deliberately continued to carry on with the motocross activities.

Failure to comply with an injunction may result in a prison sentence. In *Bristol City Council v Huggins* (1995[88]), Mr Huggins was jailed for three months for breaching an injunction which was obtained by Bristol City Council after two prosecutions under the EPA 1990 failed. The circumstances surrounding the application for an injunction must be sufficiently serious otherwise there is little prospect of the High Court exercising its discretion to grant the remedy. See also *Lloyd v Symonds and Others* (1998).[89]

9.9 Defences against non-compliance with an abatement notice

Any person who contravenes or fails to comply with the terms of an abatement notice, without reasonable excuse, is guilty of an offence (s 80(4) of the EPA 1990). However, s 80(7) provides a defence of best practicable means. Subject to certain exceptions, it will be a defence to prove that the best practicable means were used to prevent or counteract the effects of the nuisance. Section 80(4) provides that it will only be an offence to contravene or to fail to comply with the requirements of an abatement notice provided the defendant does not have a reasonable excuse.

9.9.1 What is meant by 'reasonable excuse'?

The EPA 1990 does not define 'reasonable excuse'. The test laid down by the courts appears to be an objective one; that is, whether a reasonable person would consider the excuse consistent with a reasonable standard of conduct. Therefore, what constitutes 'reasonable excuse' will be a matter of fact. In *Saddleworth UDC v Aggregate and Sand* (1970),[90] the Divisional Court held that the difficulty in obtaining credit and the lack of finance could not constitute a reasonable excuse for non-compliance with an abatement notice. The alleged reasonable excuse must relate specifically to a problem encountered in attempting to comply with the abatement notice. In *Wellingborough BC v Gordon* (1993),[91] the court rejected a submission that there was a 'reasonable excuse' based on the length of time (three years) between service of the notice and its breach. Neither is there a 'reasonable excuse' based on the argument that a common law action on identical facts would fail. If the defendant produces evidence to support its submission that the defendant had a reasonable excuse for carrying on the activity alleged to constitute a statutory nuisance, the local authority must prove, beyond reasonable doubt, that the activity was not reasonable (see *Polychronakis v Richards and Jerrom Ltd* (1998)[92] and *Hope Butuyuyu v London Borough of Hammersmith & Fulham* (1997)[93]).

The 'reasonable excuse' element of the offence under s 80(4) of the EPA 1990 should not be used as the means to challenge the grounds upon which the abatement notice was served. In *Lambert Flat Management Ltd v Lomas* (1981)[94] the Divisional Court considered the meaning of 'reasonable

88 *Bristol City Council v Huggins* (1995, unreported).
89 *Lloyd v Symonds and Others* Lawtel, 20 March 1998.
90 *Saddleworth UDC v Aggregate and Sand* [1970] 69 LGR 103, 114 Sol Jo 931.
91 *Wellingborough DC v Gordon* [1990] 155 JP 494; [1991] JPL 874.
92 *Polychronakis v Richards and Jerrom Ltd* [1998] JPL 588; [1998] Env LR 347.
93 *Hope Butuyuyu v London Borough of Hammersmith & Fulham* [1997] Env LR D 13.
94 *Lambert Flat Management Ltd v Lomas* [1981] 1 WLR 898.

excuse' under equivalent provisions to the 1990 Act found in the Control of Pollution Act 1976 and held 'an excuse cannot be "reasonable" . . . if it involves matters which could have been raised on appeal . . . unless such matters arose after the appeal was heard or, if there was no appeal, after the time for appeal had expired'. Ackner LJ agreed that a 'reasonable excuse' could not be provided by a matter which could have been raised on appeal, on the assumption 'that there was no special reason such as illness, non-receipt of the notice, or other potential excuse for not entering an appeal'. This obiter statement suggests that where a person has a special reason for not entering an appeal they may be able to raise one of the grounds for appeal as a reasonable excuse. This was examined further in Butuyuyu v Hammersmith & Fulham LBC (1997).[95] The borough council successfully prosecuted B for failing to comply with an abatement notice without reasonable excuse. B had not appealed the notice, but challenged the conviction by way of case stated, arguing that she had a reasonable excuse for not appealing the notice, namely that she was diagnosed as HIV positive and her eldest child who had cancer died two days after she was served the notice. The Divisional Court allowed the appeal and held that it was not possible to provide a comprehensive definition of what matters could amount to a reasonable excuse for failure to appeal an abatement notice, as the circumstances of each case will vary considerably. The examples given in Lambert Flat Management provided a guide but no more than that; the magistrates' view that the defence of 'reasonable excuse' was only available in circumstances where the defendant had not received the abatement notice was too restrictive. In Khan v Isleworth Crown Court (2011)[96] (the facts were discussed above at 9.6.8) K had not appealed the notice because he was not aware of it. In a case stated appeal against his conviction in the Crown Court, the Divisional Court held that the rule in Lambert Flat Management Ltd (1981) did not apply if there were special reasons for that non-compliance, but an attempt to evade the notice would not amount to a reasonable excuse. On the facts of this case the Court said there was no suggestion that K had sought to evade the notice and K's failure to respond (if it could even be classed as a failure) could not deprive him of the opportunity to raise a cast iron point in appealing against his conviction. K's conviction was quashed.

Notwithstanding these cases, which are very fact-specific, the recipient of an abatement notice would be well advised that challenges to abatement notices are best addressed through the appeal process (see further AMEC Building Ltd v London Borough of Camden (1997)[97]). It should be noted that in raising the reasonable excuse defence the magistrates' court or Crown Court may legitimately consider whether the nuisance existed in the first place or was sufficient to constitute a breach of the abatement notice.

Law in Action

In R (London Borough of Hackney) v Moshe Rottenberg (2007)[98] Rabbi Rottenberg was served an abatement notice in respect of noise generated from a dwelling house that was used as a school and synagogue. The investigating environmental health officers concluded that the noise levels amounted to a nuisance. The Rabbi failed to comply with the abatement notice and the council commenced summary proceedings. Following his conviction by the magistrates the Rabbi appealed to the Crown Court on the grounds of reasonable excuse. Following a rehearing the Crown Court considered that there was insufficient evidence of the nuisance

---

95 Butuyuyu v Hammersmith & Fulham LBC (1997) 29 HLR 584; [1997] Env LR D13.
96 R (on the application of Khan) v Isleworth Crown Court [2011] EWHC 3164 (Admin); [2012] Env LR 12.
97 AMEC Building Ltd v London Borough of Camden [1997] Env LR 330.
98 R (London Borough of Hackney) v Moshe Rottenberg [2007] EWHC 166 (Admin).

itself (they were not satisfied so that they could be sure to a criminal standard that the noise intrusion was sufficient to cause a nuisance rather than an irritation). The council appealed by way of case stated to the Divisional Court, which confirmed 'It is to be noticed that the offence of breach of an abatement order is committed when a nuisance is created "without reasonable excuse". The Crown Court did not decide the appeal on this ground. Having found that the incidents complained of did not amount to a nuisance, it did not need to form a conclusion.' In reaching this conclusion the Divisional Court accepted that the issue of reasonable excuse may be closely related to the question whether there was a nuisance at all.

9.9.2 The 'best practicable means' defence

Section 80(7) provides the defence that the best practicable means were used to prevent or counteract the nuisance. The defendant must be able to establish the defence on the balance of probabilities (that is, more likely than not) rather than beyond reasonable doubt.

The defence is, however, only available where the nuisance arises on industrial trade or business premises. Section 80(8) lists its availability as follows:

(a)   in the case of nuisances (a), (d), (e), (f), (fa) or (g) of s 79(1), the defence is only available if the nuisance occurs on industrial, trade or business premises;

(b)   if the nuisance falls within s 79(fb) the defence is only available if the artificial light is emitted from industrial, trade or business premises or from lights used for the sole purpose of illuminating an outdoor relevant sports facility;

(c)   if the nuisance falls under category (ga) of s 79(1), the defence is generally not available unless the noise is emitted from or caused by a vehicle, machinery or equipment being used for industrial, trade or business purposes;

(d)   in the case of smoke emitted from premises (s 79(1)(b)), the defence of best practicable means is not available except where the smoke is emitted from a chimney;

(e)   the defence of best practicable means is not available at all in relation to the nuisances under s 79(1)(c) and (h).

Examples of cases where BPM was used as a defence are *Tewkesbury BC v Deacon & anor* (2003)[99] and *Chapman v Gosberton Farm Produce Co Ltd* (1993).[100]

9.9.3 BPM as a ground for appeal

It should also be recalled that one of the grounds for appeal in relation to an abatement notice is that the best practicable means were used to:

(a)   prevent or counteract the effect of a nuisance from trade or business premises or, for a noise nuisance under s 79(1)(ga); or

(b)   prevent or counteract the noise from or caused by a vehicle, machinery or equipment being used for industrial or trade purposes.

Examples of cases where BPM has been used as a ground for appeal include *East Devon DC v Farr* (2002).[101]

---

99 *Tewkesbury BC v Deacon & anor* [2003] EWHC 2544 (Admin) [2004] Env LR 22.
100 *Chapman v Gosberton Farm Produce Co Ltd* [1993] Env LR 191.
101 *East Devon DC v Farr* [2002] Env LR 31.

9.9.4 The definition of 'best practical means'

The definition provided in s 79(9) of the EPA 1990 states that best practicable means is to be interpreted by reference to the following provisions:

(a) 'practicable' means reasonably practicable having regard among other things to:

    (i) local conditions and circumstances;

    (ii) the current state of technical knowledge; and

    (iii) the financial implications;

(b) the means to be employed include:

    (i) the design, installation, maintenance and manner and periods of operation of plant and machinery; and

    (ii) the design, construction and maintenance of buildings and structures;

(c) the test is to apply only so far as compatible with any:

    (i) duty imposed by law;

    (ii) safety and safe working conditions; and

    (iii) exigencies of any emergency or unforeseeable circumstances.

In circumstances where a code of practice under s 71 of the COPA 1974 (noise minimisation) is applicable, regard must be given to the guidance given in the code. It has been argued that the defence is in reality a 'reasonably practicable means' defence[102] in which the defendant/appellant has to prove that he has satisfied the test by taking reasonably practicable steps to prevent or minimise pollution.

The BPM defence/ground for appeal raises a number of points:

1. The onus is on the defendant/appellant seeking to rely on the defence/ground for appeal to prove that the best practicable means were employed.

2. The expression best practicable means must be construed having regard to the factors set out in s 79(1) but requires ultimately that a decision be reached that the person relying on the defence/ground for appeal has established that he has used the best practicable means on the balance of probabilities.

3. The defendant/appellant must establish why all other obvious or practicable means are not the best practicable means (St Albans City and District Council v Patel (2008)[103]). However, note that when assessing whether BPM have been used, a failure to refer to the specific statutory provisions in s 79(9) does not necessarily invalidate the determination (East Devon DC v Farr (2002)[104]).

4. If the means undertaken are not established to be the best then the defence/ground for appeal has not been made (St Albans City and District Council v Patel (2008)[105]).

5. The court is entitled to reach a decision on the evidence before it but it is under an obligation to assess whether the defendant/appellant has examined all the possible options (Farr). It is open to the local authority to put forward arguments about the availability of other options or means of abating the nuisance.

102 Stookes, P 'Current concerns in environmental decision making' (2007) JPL 536.
103 St Albans City and DC v Patel [2008] EWHC 2767 (Admin); [2009] Env LR 22.
104 East Devon DC v Farr [2002] Env LR 31.
105 St Albans City and DC v Patel [2008] EWHC 2767 (Admin); [2009] Env LR 22.

6. The assessment of BPM relates to the specific premises from which the nuisance exists. In *Manley v New Forest DC* (1999),[106] it was established that the defendant dog breeder was already using best practicable means to minimise noise at the time an abatement notice was served on him. The High Court reversed the decision of the Crown Court that best practicable means could be established by the defendant agreeing to relocate his business to a non-residential area. The Court held that relocation in such circumstances was going beyond the purpose of the statutory nuisance controls contained in Pt III of the EPA 1990. See also *Chapman v Gosberton Farm Produce* (1993).[107]

The definition of BPM includes reference to the financial implications, and it is of little surprise that this argument has been advanced in a number of cases. In *Wivenhoe Port v Colchester BC* (1985)[108] the port authority argued that it had used the best practicable means to abate a dust nuisance but it was not able to use certain dust arrestment equipment because of the cost and impact on profitability. The High Court accepted that the profitability of the defendant was a relevant factor to be taken into account, but went on to say that the company needed to show, on the balance of probabilities, that the operation would go from profit to loss, or become so uneconomical that the company could not profitably continue if the dust machinery was used. In *East Devon DC v Farr* (2002),[109] in the context of an appeal against an abatement notice, the Divisional Court upheld the magistrates' decision to quash the notice where the recipient had done all that he could be expected to do in the circumstances to abate a noise nuisance. Following complaints about the noise from his small industrial unit, the abatement notice required that the doors on the industrial unit be kept closed when the machinery was in operation. Farr appealed the notice on the grounds that, inter alia, he had investigated the possibility of installing air conditioning and dust extraction equipment so as to avoid having to open the doors, but had concluded that this would have been ineffective, noisier and expensive.

Law in Action

The noise from pubs and bars continues to present problems for residents, local authorities and landlords. The case of *St Albans City and DC v Patel*[110] illustrates some of the difficulties in dealing with pub noise and involved a consideration of the defence of best practical means. P was the landlord of a bar which included a small garden in which customers could drink in the summer. P was served an abatement notice relating to noise from the garden, and the question before the magistrates' court was whether P was using the best practicable means to abate the nuisance. P had taken steps to reduce the number of people who could be in the garden and only using part of the garden. He had also explored reducing the amount of time customers could stay in the garden, but the impact of this was that patrons went elsewhere and he consequently lost money. The courts will examine the accounts in support of arguments about the financial implications of different options. In this case the magistrates considered that P had adequately made out the defence. The council appealed by way of case stated, arguing that the magistrates had failed to apply the proper test of best practicable

106 *Manley v New Forest DC* [1999] EWCH Admin 752.
107 *Chapman v Gosberton Farm Produce Co Ltd* [1993] Env LR 191.
108 *Wivenhoe Port v Colchester BC* [1985] JPL 175.
109 *East Devon DC v Farr* [2002] Env LR 31.
110 *St Albans City and DC v Patel* [2008] EWHC 2767 (Admin); [2009] Env LR 22.

means since they had only considered the practicability of one option (closing the garden altogether) and had not considered lesser measures such as further reducing the area of the garden used or restricting the hours of use. The council's appeal was dismissed. The Divisional Court considered that the magistrates had been well aware of these lesser measures and when the case stated was read as a whole, it was plain that the magistrates agreed with P's evidence that financial effects prevented him from employing those lesser measures. On the balance of probabilities, the lesser measures were not practicable. The case demonstrates the difficulties in deciding the issue of best practicable means. See further *R (on the application of South Kesteven DC) v Grantham Magistrates' Court* (2010) in which the Divisional Court applies the approach in *Patel*.[111]

9.9.5 Special defences

Special defences exist regarding noise and other nuisances in relation to construction sites, and noise abatement zones.

See Chapter
◄ 10

9.10 Action by citizens

Section 82 EPA 1990 provides that any person aggrieved by a statutory nuisance has the right to complain to the magistrates' court in order to obtain a court order to bring the nuisance to an end. Failure to comply with a court order under this section is an offence. Section 82 enables any person to bypass the local authority statutory nuisance process. The provision enables any person who is aggrieved by the nuisance to commence proceedings which are likely to be cheaper and quicker than a common law private nuisance action. There is no requirement that the complainant is an occupier of premises or a neighbour of adjoining premises.

The phrase 'person aggrieved' has appeared in various other statutes and has been widely interpreted by the courts. In *AG (Gambia) v N'Jie* (1961),[112] Lord Denning asserted (albeit in a case not related to statutory nuisances) that the words 'person aggrieved' should not be subjected to a restrictive interpretation. However, he went on to say that the words:

> do not include, of course, a mere busybody who is interfering in things which do not concern him; but they do include a person who has a genuine grievance because an order has been made which prejudicially affects his interests.

It seems, therefore, that a person must at least be in some way prejudicially affected by the alleged nuisance. In *Sandwell MBC v Bujok* (1990),[113] a council tenant alleged that the defective state of her council house gave rise to a statutory nuisance under the PHA 1936. Mrs Bujok was entitled to bring proceedings against the council as a person whose health, and that of her family, was prejudicially affected by the premises. Section 82 is of particular value when the person concerned is complaining about a statutory nuisance created by a local authority and has been useful in enabling people to bring actions against the local authority in respect of council houses and premises which are prejudicial to health or a nuisance. The number of these cases has been increasing in recent years. The fact that the local authorities act as the statutory bodies responsible for controlling

111 *South Kesteven DC v Grantham Magistrates' Court* [2010] EWHC 1419 (Admin); [2011] Env LR 3.
112 *AG (Gambia) v N'Jie* [1961] [1961] AC 617; [1961] 2 WLR 845; [1961] 2 All ER 504.
113 *Sandwell MBC v Bujok* [1990] 1 WLR 1350.

statutory nuisances does not provide them with any immunity against actions against them, as can be seen in the *Sandwell* case.

Aggrieved persons can only commence proceedings to secure the abatement of an existing nuisance or its recurrence. They cannot, under these provisions, bring an action to prevent a statutory nuisance, such as a potentially noisy party, since the magistrates' court, unlike the local authority, does not have anticipatory powers.

9.10.1 Section 82 proceedings

When a person complains to the magistrates' court, there is a requirement that the defendant is informed, in writing, of the matter complained of and that such action is going to be taken. For noise nuisances, the complainant must give three days' notice, but the period of notice is 21 days in respect of the other nuisances. Before taking action in proceedings brought under s 82, the magistrates must be satisfied of one of the following conditions:

(a)   the alleged nuisance exists; or
(b)   an abated nuisance is likely to recur on the same premises, or in the same street.

The court can make the following orders:

(a)   requiring the defendant to abate the nuisance within a specified time and to carry out any works necessary for that purpose;
(b)   prohibiting a recurrence of the nuisance and requiring the defendant to carry out any necessary works to prevent the recurrence. A time period for carrying out such works will be specified in the order;
(c)   imposition of a fine of up to £5,000;
(d)   requiring the relevant local authority to do anything which the convicted person was required to do by the court order, after it has given the authority the opportunity to be heard.

Where the nuisance is such as to render premises unfit for human habitation, the court can prohibit the use of the premises for human habitation until the court is satisfied that the premises have been made fit for such a purpose.

Failure to comply with a nuisance order from the magistrates is an offence and can result in a fine of up to £5,000 (plus £500 for each day that the offence continues). In *R (on the application of London Borough of Islington) v Inner London Crown Court and another* (2003)[114] the Divisional Court considered the sentencing powers of a court under s 82. In this case the borough council sought judicial review of the Crown Court's decision to uphold a fine of £4,000 in respect of a s 82 action brought by two council house tenants. The tenants commenced s 82 proceedings because the council had failed to respond to their complaints dating back to 1999. Although the council had pleaded guilty, the Crown Court considered the fine was appropriate, having regard to the seriousness of the offence. Judicial review should not be used to offer a backdoor appeal against a sentence; however, the Divisional Court will review a sentence if it clearly falls outside the broad area of the lower court's sentencing discretion. In this case the Divisional Court considered the factors that should be taken into account including the very wide range of statutory nuisances that may be embraced by the fine of £5,000, some of which can be very serious. Accordingly it was held that the maximum penalty should be reserved for the worst possible type of case under s 82 and where the council has contested the proceedings.

---

114 *R (on the application of London Borough of Islington) v Inner London Crown Court and another* [2003] EWHC 2500 (Admin).

In addition s 82(12) provides that the court may also order the payment of compensation in addition to a fine. In *R v Crown Court at Liverpool and another, ex p Cooke* (1996)[115] Leggatt LJ held that the legislation 'provides for both alternatives, I see nothing contrary to principle about ordering compensation "instead of" rather than "in addition to" a fine. If a compensation order is itself large enough to be punitive, as the magistrate's order was here, there is no occasion to impose a fine as well. If, on the other hand, the compensation order is relatively small, as the Crown Court decided it should be, it is necessary to add a fine for punitive effect.' Additionally, the Court added that when assessing compensation the court should only take into account the injury, loss or damage caused by the continuation of the nuisance from the date when the period stated in the complainant's s 82 notice expired to the date of the hearing.

For a further discussion of a protracted case involving s 82, see *Roper v Tussauds Theme Parks Ltd* (2007)[116] in Chapter 10.

See Chapter 10

From the point of view of a person subjected to a situation which constitutes a statutory nuisance, the provisions of Pt III of the EPA 1990 provide a relatively simple mechanism for addressing problems without recourse to expensive and lengthy litigation. In contrast to civil proceedings, which are expensive and usually very fraught, the statutory nuisance provisions enable the local authority to 'step in' to deal with problems before litigation becomes necessary. The statistics produced annually by the Chartered Institute for Environmental Health Officers demonstrate that the vast majority of substantiated complaints that are dealt with can be resolved informally without legal action. The 'burden' of dealing with statutory nuisances rests with the local authority and the mechanisms, backed up by the possibility of criminal sanctions, can afford a very effective means of dealing with problems. Since proceedings under Pt III of the EPA 1990 are heard before the magistrates' court, the speed of dealing with cases is likely to be much faster than private actions before the county court and High Court. Moreover, from the point of view of the 'complainant', the legal costs are borne by the local authority.

9.11 Relationship with other legislative controls

9.11.1 Contaminated land

Until the implementation of Part IIA EPA 1990 which established a statutory regime for dealing with contaminated land, it was possible for local councils to utilise their powers under Part III EPA to secure the clean-up of sites that were contaminated (although the author has no particular evidence about the use of this power in this context). However, with the enactment of Part IIA,[117] s 79(1)(a) was inserted into Pt III of the EPA. This section states clearly that no matter shall constitute a statutory nuisance to the extent that it consists of, or is caused by, any land being in a contaminated state. Although the intention of the government was to avoid an overlap of the provisions, it has in fact created something of a lacuna in the law. The reason for this is that the definition of land that 'is in a contaminated state' provided by s 79(1)(b) is not the same as land that is contaminated under Part IIA. Land that is in a contaminated state includes any land on which contaminants are present and on which harm is being caused or there is a possibility of harm being caused or pollution of controlled waters is being, or is likely to be, may cause harm. This is a much broader definition than the definition of contaminated land in s 82A EPA 1990, which requires the presence of contaminating substances which cause *significant* harm or have a *significant possibility* of causing *significant harm*. Consequently, any land which is in a

See Chapter 7

---

115 *R v Crown Court at Liverpool and another, ex p Cooke* [1996] 4 All ER 589.
116 *Roper v Tussauds Theme Parks Ltd* [2007] EWHC 624 (Admin); [2007] Env LR 31.
117 Inserted into the EPA 1990 by s 57 Environment Act 1995.

contaminated state, but is not 'contaminated land' because the risks it poses are not significant, will effectively fall between the two regimes and a local authority will have no power to deal with it. However, the statutory nuisance regime continues to apply to the effects of deposits of substances on land which give rise to such offence to human senses (such as stenches) as to constitute a nuisance.

9.11.2 Relationship with the environmental permitting regime

The relationship between the enforcement role of the Environment Agency and local authority responsibilities under Part III has already been considered above at 9.8.2 in R (*on the application of Ethos Recycling Ltd*) *v Barking and Dagenham Magistrates' Court* (2009).[118] In that case the Divisional Court considered the provision of s 79(10) EPA 1990, which prevents a local authority from commencing summary proceedings in respect of statutory nuisances falling within s 79 (1)(b), (d), (e) or (fb). If in any of these cases proceedings might be instituted under s 2 Pollution Prevention Control Act 1999, then the local authority must first obtain the consent of the Secretary of State before commencing statutory nuisance proceedings. According to the district judge in this case the purpose of this provision is to avoid double jeopardy in the criminal sense. The upshot of the case was that it is now clear that in respect of these categories of statutory nuisance which involve regulated facilities a local authority still has the right to serve an abatement notice on the operator of the regulated facility; however, they must seek consent if they wish to secure compliance by means of summary proceedings. The court stated that this accorded with the practicalities of local authorities meeting their responsibilities for dealing with statutory nuisances in the context of their relationship with the Environment Agency.

9.11.3 Relationship with planning law

Many of the activities that are alleged to constitute a statutory nuisance will have been specifically authorised by the grant of planning permission. This raises the question about the extent to which the grant of planning permission for the intensification of an existing use or a new use changes the locality of the area.

See Chapter 10 →

9.12 Online resource centre

We recommend that the reader regularly refers to the section of the online resources corresponding to this chapter for information relating to updates, amendments and corrections.

9.13 Summary of key points

Chapter 9 has covered the following topics and issues:

- the statutory background of Part III EPA 1990 including a reflection on the impact that the 'public health' origins of the legislation has had an impact on the approach taken by the courts to the interpretation of the current legislation, particularly in relation to the interpretation of 'prejudicial to health';
- an examination of each of the statutory nuisances including relevant case law;

---

118 R (*on the application of Ethos Recycling Ltd*) *v Barking and Dagenham Magistrates' Court* [2009] EWHC 2885 (Admin); [2010] Env LR 25.

- the procedures that are to be followed once a local authority is satisfied that a statutory nuisance exists or is likely to recur or occur;
- the provisions and case law relating to abatement notices and in particular whether local authorities can simply require the abatement of a nuisance without having to prescribe the steps to be taken;
- statistics which demonstrate that the majority of statutory nuisance complaints are resolved informally without recourse to the provisions of the Act.

This chapter, read in conjunction with Chapter 11, should enable the reader to evaluate the relative merits of the statutory nuisance provisions in securing a relatively quick and cheap resolution to the resolution of localised nuisances.

 ## 9.14 Further reading

Articles

Lewis, R, 'Dealing with nuisance: all about abatement' (2000) 3(6) Journal of Local Government Law 117.
This article considers whether abatement notices must spell out the necessary abatement requirements or whether the steps needed to abate the nuisance may be left to be determined by the perpetrator of the nuisance.
Lewis, R, 'Statutory nuisance abatement notices—a response' [2000] JPEL 1011.
This article examines a number of statutory nuisance cases and the possible implications of the implementation of the Human Rights Act 1998.
Loveland, I, 'And now wash your hands—statutory nuisance under the Environmental Protection Act 1990 section 79(1)' [2001] JPEL 1144.
This reviews the decision of the House of Lords in *Birmingham City Council v John Oakley* (2000) concerning statutory nuisance in a council house.
Malcolm, R, 'Statutory nuisance: the validity of abatement notices' [2000] JPEL 894.
Malcolm, R and Ponting, J, 'Statutory nuisance, The Sanitary Paradigm and Judicial Conservatism' [2006] 18(1) JEL 37.
McCracken, R, Jones, G and Pereira, J: a series of six articles on various aspects of the statutory nuisance regime published in the Solicitors Journal ((2001) 145(42) SJ 1028–29 to (2001) 145(47) SJ 1152–53).
The articles cover the following topics: scope of the regime, responsibilities of the local authorities, abatement notices, appeals and s 82 provisions.
Parpworth, N, 'Statutory nuisance abatement notices under s 80 of the Environmental Protection Act 1990' (2003) 167(12) Justice of the Peace and Local Government Law 204.
Taylor, M and Hughes, D, 'Exterior Lighting as a statutory nuisance' [2005] JPL 1131.

Weblinks

www.cieh.org
The official website of the Chartered Institute of Environmental Health. Documents available on the site include Policy Unit responses to Noise Act Review, annual statistics relating to noise complaints and statutory nuisance procedures.

Chapter 10

Noise Pollution

Chapter Contents

Learning Objectives

By the end of this chapter you should have acquired an understanding of:

- why noise is a problem and how noise can adversely affect health and the enjoyment of land;

- some of the difficulties in using legal mechanisms to control unwanted noise, in particular having regard to the transient and subjective nature of noise;

- how the law has adopted a variety of approaches to dealing with noise, both preventive and reactive in nature;

- the government's Noise Policy statement (2010);

- how noise law has developed in a piecemeal fashion and includes a very diverse range of mechanisms, yet there appears to be some impetus (albeit delayed) towards the development of a national noise strategy;

- how noise law is developing as a distinct branch of environmental law, as evidenced by the increasing regulation of noise through environmental permitting, the introduction of an EU-wide Environmental Noise Directive and the amendments to the Noise Act 1996;

- the difficulties in securing the resolution of noise problems using the common law tort of nuisance;

- the statutory provisions which seek to provide remedies for noise problems, including the statutory nuisance provisions in Part III EPA 1990 and the Noise Act 1996.

10.1 Introduction: the problem of noise and the legal regulation of noise

This chapter will start with some general observations about noise: the extent to which it is an environmental problem; the adverse effects of noise; different types of noise; the way noise is measured; and the different approaches to the legal regulation of noise. That will be followed by a discussion of European Union and domestic noise policy, including an examination of the EU Directive on Environmental Noise and the national noise strategy. The chapter will then examine the different approaches to noise regulation; in the first instance focusing on preventive measures and then examining the legal provisions which enable persons aggrieved by noise nuisances to seek redress before the courts. The chapter does not purport to be exhaustive. It does not include any examination of the law relating to occupational noise (noise in the work place), nor does it consider any property law issues relating for example to covenants for the quiet enjoyment of land. Some areas are only dealt with in the minimum of detail; for example, the use of planning laws to prevent noise is only addressed in general terms.

Noise is a natural consequence of everything that we do. It forms part of our everyday background, and for the most part we just accept it, or at least tolerate it. Nevertheless, noise has the capacity to cause conflict between those who are generating it and those who hear it but do not wish to. Indeed, the Wilson Committee[1] recognised the subjective and conflictual nature of the

---

1 Committee on the Problem of Noise (1963) Noise: Final Report, Cmnd 2056. London: HMSO.

problem when it defined noise as 'sound which is undesired by the recipient'. A 2010 Health Protection Agency Report stated that noise needs to be distinguished from sound, which is a term used to describe wave-like variations in air pressure that occur at frequencies that can stimulate receptors in the inner ear. In contrast, 'Noise implies the presence of sound but also implies a response to sound: noise is often defined as an unwanted source.'[2]

In comparison with waste and water, the issue of noise appears at first instance to be a relatively minor problem; after all, it does not cause damage to the ozone layer, contribute to climate change, or pose the type of health risks one would associate with contaminated land or fly tipping. However, in July 2009 the ENDS Report claimed: 'Noise comes of age as an environmental issue.'[3] The article asserted that although noise has been a relatively neglected environmental issue, it is growing in importance following confirmation of its quantifiable adverse health effects, including high blood pressure, increased stress and poor mental health. Certainly it is clear, when one looks at statistics concerning the number of complaints about neighbourhood noise, that noise can cause a variety of problems and considerable distress to members of the public who are exposed to levels of noise that they consider are unacceptable.

10.1.1 The adverse effects of noise; damage to health

Although unwanted noise or excessively loud noise may be annoying to those who do not wish to hear it, does it have any harmful effect? Unlike other types of pollution, noise is transient, it exists at the time that it is generated and cannot be said to have a permanent harmful effect on the environment in the same way that toxic wastes can contaminate land. Nevertheless, it can have a long-term or even permanent detrimental effect on hearing, health and mental wellbeing. CS Kerse in his book The Law Relating to Noise[4] notes that exposure to excessive noise can result in a range of physiological effects. Quoting Dr Samuel Rosen, he states that: 'At an unexpected or unwanted noise, the pupils dilate, skin pales, mucous membranes dry; there are intestinal spasms and the adrenals explode secretions. The biological organism, in a word, is disturbed.' More recently, reports confirm the health risks associated with noise. In 2010 the Health Protection Agency (HPA) published a government-sponsored study of environmental noise.[5] The report, prepared by a committee of experts, reviews current research into the health and social impacts of environmental noise, including annoyance, sleep disturbance and physiological effects. It notes that whilst it has been recognised for a long time that exposure to loud noise in the workplace (occupational exposure) is capable of causing health problems such as circulatory problems, it is only relatively recently that research has shown environmental noise to have similar effects. According to the HPA review a 2008 EU report concluded that exposure to night-time aircraft noise and daytime road traffic noise was associated with increased blood pressure, and that the risk of heart attack and heart disease was increased by a factor of 1.09 from exposure to road traffic noise and by a factor of 1.26 from aircraft noise. One of the key recommendations of the HPA is the establishment of an independent expert committee (similar to the Committee on the Medical Effects of Air Pollution) to address the effect of environmental noise on health and monitor developments in knowledge in this area.

Noise can cause both temporary and permanent hearing loss. Temporary loss of hearing is typified either by sounds being perceived as muffled, or by a ringing in the ears. Once the exposure to the noise has ended, hearing should return to normal after about 45 minutes. Repeated exposure to noise might prevent the ear from recovering so readily, and may cause permanent hearing loss.

---

2   Health Protection Agency (2010) *Environmental Noise and Health in the UK: A Report by the Ad Hoc Expert Group on Noise on Health.*
3   ENDS Report 414, July 2009, p 18.
4   Kerse, CS, *The Law Relating to Noise* (Oyez Publishing, 1975).
5   Health Protection Agency (2010) *Environmental Noise and Health in the UK: A Report by the Ad Hoc Expert Group on Noise on Health.*

Excessive levels of noise continued over a sustained period can cause serious damage to hearing and may even cause hearing loss (noise-induced hearing loss). There are many occupations that expose workers to enough loud noise to cause this type of hearing loss. Equally, deafness may occur as a result of a very sudden and loud noise. The most likely and immediate health problems that can occur in relation to noise are that the recipient has a headache and associated discomfort, or that the noise is causing them to lose sleep. Loss of sleep and health problems arising from loss of sleep are a common complaint. Aeroplane noise in particular has a much more significant impact on sleep loss than do other noises. Residents living close to major airports, notably Heathrow, will testify to this particular problem. Loss of sleep can result in a person becoming irritable; he or she may find it difficult to concentrate, and it may in turn result in a diminution of physical wellbeing and health. It has been estimated that around 20 per cent of the EU's population[6] suffer from noise levels that scientists and health experts consider to be unacceptable, where most people become annoyed, where sleep is disturbed and where adverse health effects are to be feared. An additional 170 million citizens are living in so-called 'grey areas' where the noise levels are such as to cause serious annoyance during the daytime.[7]

Unwanted noise can cause negative attitudes such as irritation and annoyance, and these can be manifested in a number of ways. For some people annoyance can result in a heightened emotional state which can lead to increased risk-taking and possibly even anger or violence. Alternatively it can lead to a sense of frustration or powerlessness on the part of the recipient. In *Dennis & Dennis v Ministry of Defence* (2003),[8] the claimants described the noise caused by RAF Harrier jets taking off from a nearby RAF base as not only deafening and highly intrusive, but also 'frightening'. Similarly, in *Middlesbrough CC v Stevens* (1993),[9] the constant and repetitive playing of Whitney Houston's song 'I Will Always Love You' was said to have caused 'psychological torture' for a neighbour.[10]

10.1.2 The difficulties in regulating noise

Noise regulation poses its own distinctive problems:

(a)   Noise is localised, and mostly it is a source of temporary irritation.

(b)   Noise is not inherently dangerous. It does not accumulate in our bodies or the wider environment. It is not toxic to man and the environment as many chemical substances are.

(c)   The impact of noise on humans is highly subjective. Although it is possible to measure the level at which noise begins to damage hearing, the impact of less damaging sound is problematic. The differential impact of noise upon humans varies with the time of day and the susceptibility of the individual. Unwanted noise at night which disturbs sleep is a serious issue.

(d)   Can exposure to noise breach any of the fundamental human rights guaranteed by the ECHR?

(e)   It may be difficult to disentangle offending noises from background noises or the general noise level in the area.

---

6 About 80 million people.
7 Source http://ec.europa.eu/environment/noise/greenpap.htm#situ.
8 *Dennis & Dennis v Ministry of Defence* [2003] EWHC 793.
9 *Middlesbrough CC v Stevens* (1993) The Times, 7 September.
10 For further examination of the impact of environmental noise on health, see Health Protection Agency (2010) *Environmental Noise and Health in the UK: A Report by the Ad Hoc Expert Group on Noise on Health.*

(f)   How should regulatory controls tackle the problem? Should controls 'bite' at: (i) the immediate point of noise production;[11] (ii) some point between the noise producer and the noise recipient,[12] or (iii) the point at which the noise reaches the recipient's property;[13]

(g)   What type of regulatory controls should be employed? For example: (i) product standards;[14] (ii) licence based controls;[15] (iii) reactive controls;[16] (iv) public order controls and anti-social behaviour orders and (v) separation controls.[17]

(h)   Noise is regulated by a patchwork of fragmented controls.

In most circumstances, unwanted noises will not cause people to complain, but there are clearly circumstances where the volume, duration or repetition (or all three) will cause sufficient aggravation to cause the recipient of the unwanted noise intrusion to take legal action, or in some instances resort to more dramatic measures. Most people are familiar with complaints between neighbours concerning excessive noise from music systems, dogs barking or the constant drone of lawnmowers, but these complaints rarely lead to legal proceedings. However, people are increasingly concerned about noise levels and neighbourhood noise in particular. They are also more aware of the effects that noise can have upon them and are consequently more likely to complain. This is clearly borne out by statistics, some of which are shown later.

Modern industrial society generates an enormous quantity of noise and this is bound to increase as more and more aeroplanes arrive and depart at airports and as more and more cars take to the roads. There are also more opportunities for creating noise in a society which relies heavily upon domestic appliances (the noisy washing machine and lawnmower). Stereo and audio equipment have become more sophisticated, more powerful, more affordable and more commonplace, and people are able to play music at high volumes.

Whilst excessive or continued levels of noise may be unacceptable, certain levels of noise must be accepted in order that modern society can function. Construction sites, for instance, generate a significant amount of noise from mobile plant, pneumatic drills, etc and cause many local residents to complain. Yet we nevertheless expect and, in most instances, welcome new developments, which can create jobs and which can enhance towns and cities. All activities and processes generate noise and we all expect to be able to continue those activities without interference from others. This raises certain problems regarding the legal regulation of noise, in that there will necessarily be a need to achieve a balance between the rights of individuals, groups or companies to make noise and the rights of others not to suffer at their expense. This weighing of considerations is familiar in the common law of nuisance where the courts have to consider whether what is complained of is unreasonable.

Law in Action

The case of *Southwark LBC v Mills* and *Baxter v Camden LBC (No 2)*[18] illustrates the difficulties the courts face in reconciling domestic noise disputes. Camden LBC was the owner and landlord of a Victorian house that it converted into three flats. B moved into one of the flats in 1992;

---

11 E.g., motor vehicle exhaust systems and construction site noise.
12 E.g., construction of a noise barrier, either internally via sound insulation, or externally via a 'bund' to deflect noise away from the recipient.
13 E.g., installation of double glazing.
14 Noise emission limits applying to tyres, lawnmowers, car exhaust systems, etc.
15 E.g. environmental permitting and Health and Safety at Work controls in factories.
16 E.g., statutory nuisance.
17 E.g., planning controls providing geographical separation between incompatible land uses.
18 *Southwark LBC v Mills & Baxter v Camden LBC (No 2)* [2001] 1 AC 1; [1999] 4 All ER 449; [1999] 3 WLR 939.

the other two were occupied at the time. B brought proceedings in nuisance (and also for breach of the covenant of quiet enjoyment) against the CLBC, claiming that she could hear the normal domestic activities of the other two adjoining flats. There was nothing unreasonable about the noise; but the flats had no sound insulation and she was disturbed by the noise of her neighbour's television, baby crying and routine sounds of cooking and cleaning. It was accepted that this caused distress and tension. Initially the county court held that the noise from the ordinary domestic use of the flats constituted an unreasonable interference with B's enjoyment of her flat, but CLBC was not liable in nuisance because a tenant who took premises in a defective condition had no right to complain of their conditions (unless one arose under the terms of the tenancy or statute). On appeal the House of Lords held that the ordinary use of residential premises was incapable of constituting a nuisance. Where a tenant complained of noise nuisance from a neighbouring tenant's premises, their common landlord could not be liable in nuisance for having authorised the commission of an actionable nuisance if the noise arose from the ordinary and reasonable use for which the neighbouring tenant could not be liable. See also *Faidi v Elliott Group* (2012).[19]

This balancing of competing considerations is also particularly evident in some of the cases relating to noise from aircraft. The demand for more flights and the proposals to build new runways at various airports throughout the country has given rise to enormous controversy and raised issues of human rights and public interest. For example, see *Hatton v United Kingdom* (2003)[20] in which H, who lived near Heathrow Airport, complained that the airport's policy on night-time flights (and the subsequent noise that she had to suffer) constituted a breach of her rights under Arts 8 and 13 of the European Convention on Human Rights (ECHR).[21] For an examination of these issues in the context of military aircraft, see *Dennis & Dennis v Ministry of Defence* (2003),[22] in which the Divisional Court held that the noise from RAF Harrier jets could not be classed as 'ordinary' and that, whilst a public interest argument might excuse what would otherwise be an actionable nuisance, the claimants in question should not bear the cost of that public benefit.

The other problematic feature of controlling noise is that it is a particularly subjective issue. What amounts to intolerable noise for one person may be disregarded or even considered desirable by others. Pop concerts, raves and parties are typical examples. Some people will be able to accept certain levels of noise, whereas others may suffer in terms of their mental or physical health as a consequence of that same noise. The sensitivity of hearing varies from person to person, and other factors such as age can play a large part in determining responses. Noise may be problematic not only in relation to its volume, but also with regard to its capacity to irritate the recipient. Intermittent, disturbing and repetitive noises, whilst not inherently dangerous, may cause significant annoyance and emotional disturbance.

10.1.3 The nature of legal controls: prevention, sanctions and cure

Traditionally, noise problems have been addressed through the common law, principally by means of private nuisance actions and also via the statutory nuisance provisions contained in Part III of the Environmental Protection Act (EPA) 1990. In relation to the latter, noise can be controlled where it constitutes a statutory nuisance. Local authorities have various powers which enable them to abate

---

19 *Faidi v Elliott Group* [2012] EWCA Civ 287; [2012] HLR 27 (CA Div)).
20 *Hatton v United Kingdom* (2003) 37 EHRR 28.
21 This case is discussed further below at 10.10.4.
22 *Dennis & Dennis v Ministry of Defence* [2003] EWHC 793.

noise nuisances and bring criminal proceedings if the person responsible for the noise nuisance fails to comply with an abatement notice. In general terms, both the common law and the statutory nuisance provisions have been utilised to bring noise nuisances to an end either by abatement or injunction. A successful action in nuisance may also result in a claimant being awarded damages as compensation for the nuisance suffered. Although the common law and the statutory nuisance provisions are used to provide a resolution to noise problems they do not provide a direct means of preventing noise nuisances occurring in the first place.

Part III EPA 1990 and the Noise Act 1996 impose sanctions for noise nuisances. For example, the Noise Act (NA) 1996 provides for immediate sanctions in the form of on-the-spot fines, designed to bring night-time noise nuisances to an immediate end. The Anti-Social Behaviour Act (ASBA) 2003 also contains provisions which enable local authorities to deal with noisy premises, and the Criminal Justice Act 1994 contains provisions relating to raves.[23]

Noise problems may be anticipated and controls put in place that seek to prevent noise nuisances from occurring. To this end the EU has introduced a raft of legislation which seeks to lay down precise noise emission levels for particular classes of machinery and vehicles. In addition there are a number of codes of practice which set out recommended noise levels for the likes of intruder alarms and ice cream van chimes. Predicted noise from construction works can be regulated in advance by means of a noise consent issued by a local authority.[24]

In addition to these legal measures, the levels of noise can to some extent be controlled (and therefore prevented) through good planning which takes account of the potential noise generation of developments at the planning stage. Planning authorities are required to consider the problems of noise when taking planning decisions in order to avoid noise nuisances occurring. Planning Policy Guidance Note 24[25] gives guidance to local authorities on the use of their planning powers to minimise the adverse impact of noise. Noise may be an issue that needs to be addressed during the Environmental Impact Assessment process for a project or indeed as part of a Strategic Environmental Impact Assessment. Noise and planning will be considered later in this chapter.

10.1.4 Measuring noise

Despite the fact that responses to different noises vary widely, it is possible to measure sound objectively. Sound can be measured either in hertz (Hz), which measures the frequency of sound (the number of pressure variations per second), or in decibels.

The decibel (dB(A)) measure is more widely used because it provides a better measure of the response of the human ear to loudness as the ear responds to changes in the noise level. The decibel is effectively a logarithmic scale with 0 dB corresponding to the quietest audible sound (the threshold of hearing). 20 dB(A) is said to be equivalent to a gentle breeze or a soft whisper, whereas 120 dB(A) is equivalent to a military aircraft taking off.[26] 140 dB represents a sound at which pain would probably occur. As stated above, the usual form of measurement is dB(A), where the 'A' refers to the frequency weighting used in sound meters, enabling them effectively to mimic human hearing.

The Control of Noise (Measurements and Registers) Regulations 1976[27] prescribes the decibel as the method for measuring noise in relation to the legal controls discussed in this chapter. In

---

23 Ss 63–67 Criminal Justice Act 1994.
24 Under the provisions of the Control of Pollution Act (COPA) 1974; see below, on specific noise controls.
25 Planning Policy Guidance 24: Planning and Noise (1994).
26 www.transportandenvironment.org.
27 The Control of Noise (Measurements and Registers) Regulations 1976 SI 1976/37.

addition, they also provide some guidance on how noise levels can be calculated when it is not possible to make a precise measurement.

The courts are familiar with the use of decibels as measurements of noise although they will often seek a further description of the noise from the complainant. In *Halsey v Esso Petroleum Co Ltd* (1961),[28] the use of decibels was affirmed by the court, and an indication was given as to the effect of different levels of noise:

> Between 40 and 60 decibels the noise is moderate, and between 60 and 80 it is loud. Between 80 and 100 it is very loud and from 100 to 120 it is deafening.

The issue of noise has in recent years started to receive more attention from government and the European Union.

10.2 Noise policy and the EU Environmental Noise Directive

10.2.1 The development of an EU noise policy

At the European level, noise has traditionally received less priority than other environmental problems such as water pollution and waste. Although the EU has enacted various directives addressing noise emissions from specific products (by fixing maximum permissible levels of noise emissions), the principal aim of this legislation has been to harmonise standards to achieve a single market in goods. However, amidst increasing recognition of noise as an environmental problem in its own right, in 1996 the EU published a Green Paper on Future Noise Policy (COM(96) 540). This recognised, inter alia, the paucity of information about levels of noise exposure as well as particular issues relating to noise generated by traffic. The Green Paper also recognised the local nature of noise as a problem and the fact that many Member States had already developed national noise abatement laws, particularly in relation to new developments in sensitive areas. However, the Commission considered that, notwithstanding the local nature of noise, it was appropriate for the EU to develop its own noise policy.

10.2.2 The Environmental Noise Directive

In pursuance of this policy the EU enacted Directive 2002/49/EC[29] (commonly known as the Environmental Noise Directive, or END) which aims to 'define a common approach intended to avoid, prevent or reduce on a prioritised basis the harmful effects, including annoyance, due to exposure to environmental noise'.[30] The Environmental Noise Directive requires the development of a long-term EU noise strategy. In common with the approach adopted in other environment policy directives, the directive has four key strands:

● Member States are required to draw up 'strategic noise maps' for major transport infrastructure (major roads, railways, airports and agglomerations of over 100,000 people). The directive employs harmonised noise indicators L_{den} (day-evening-night equivalent level) and L_{night} (night equivalent level). The information compiled on the maps will enable authorities to assess

---

28 *Halsey v Esso Petroleum Co Ltd* [1961] 1 WLR 683.
29 Directive 2002/49/EC of the European Parliament and of the Council of 25 June 2002 relating to the assessment and management of environmental noise – Declaration by the Commission in the Conciliation Committee on the directive relating to the assessment and management of environmental noise OJ L 189, 18/7/2002, pp 12–25.
30 Directive 2002/49/EC, Art 1.

the number of people within the EU who are annoyed and have their sleep disturbed by noise.

- Information on environmental noise and its effects is to be made available to the public. This limb of the directive complies with the requirements of the Aarhus Convention[31] on access to information and public participation in environmental decision-making.
- Competent authorities in the Member States are required to address local noise issues, prepare action plans to reduce noise where necessary and to maintain environmental noise quality where it is good. The directive is not prescriptive; it does not set any limit value, nor does it prescribe the measures to be used in the action plans. However, it did require publication of these action plans by June 2008.
- As part of the action plans, Member States were required to introduce specific measures and draw up action plans to protect quiet areas in agglomerations against an increase in noise.

In June 2011 the European Commission published a report on the implementation of the directive to date.[32] Twelve Member States failed to communicate their implementing measures to the Commission by the required date, including the UK. By October 27 all Member states had introduced implanting legislation and the report notes that the overall quality of transposition was 'satisfactory'. However, the report identifies a number of problems in implementation. In particular, many aspects of the directive were not prescribed in detail, or left considerable discretion to Member States which have resulted in different interpretations and approaches.

Although Art 5 of the directive introduced noise indicators for reporting, it did not fix any legally binding EU-wide noise limit values or targets. Member States were required to report their national limit values, and almost inevitably the Member States have taken different approaches. Whilst the majority set legally binding noise limit values, others (including the UK) have established guideline values. Very few Member States based their limit, trigger or guideline values on WHO health-based assessments. The difficulty with such varied approaches is that the Commission has been unable to summarise or compare the different levels in the Member States.

Using the information from the first round of noise mapping the Commission report states that around 40 million people across the EU are exposed to noise above 50 dB from roads within agglomerations during the night. 25 million people are exposed to noise at the same level from major roads outside agglomerations. These numbers are expected to be revised upwards as more noise maps are received and/or assessed. Despite the improvements of comparability of strategic noise mapping, the Commission reports that it remains difficult to present comparable figures on the number of people being exposed to excessive noise levels. The difficulties are caused by the differing approaches to data collection, quality and availability and assessment methods used in the Member States. Consequently the Commission has started work on developing a harmonised method for assessing noise exposure.

Despite its delayed communication of implementing measures, the UK was one of only five Member States to submit its action plan by the deadline of 18 January 2009. As far as the designation of quiet areas was concerned, the directive gave the Member States discretion on the delimitation of such areas. This has resulted in very divergent approaches and although most Member States have designated quiet areas in agglomerations, very few have designated any in the open country.

Overall the report identifies that the directive has resulted in some benefits, but a significant number of implementation problems and shortcomings have also been highlighted. In the main, these are linked to the divergent approaches adopted by the Member States. On the plus side of the

31 UNECE Convention on Access to Information, Public Participation in Decision-making and Access to Justice in Environmental Matters (1998).
32 COM (2011) 321 Final Report from the Commission to the European Parliament and the Council on the Implementation of the Environmental Noise Directive in accordance with Article 11 of Directive 2002/49/EC.

equation the report concludes that the mapping exercise has given the EU its first overview on the extent of noise pollution problems, and a comprehensive set of noise data at EU level, which did not exist before. The noise action plans have helped to identify noise 'hot spots' where further action is required. In addition implementation of the directive has enabled the Commission to identify gaps in the legislation on sources of noise (such as vehicles, railways and aircraft).

10.2.3 The Environmental Noise Regulations—domestic implementation of the directive

The directive, which had to be transposed into national law by July 2004, was implemented into English law by the Environmental Noise (England) Regulations 2006.[33] The Regulations have been amended on a number of occasions, particularly in 2009 when amendments were made[34] to seemingly reduce some of the obligations imposed in the 2006 regulations whilst maintaining the 'minimum' degree of protection afforded by the directive. In keeping with the directive the regulations apply to environmental noise to which humans are exposed in particular in built-up areas, in public parks or other quiet areas in an agglomeration, near schools, hospitals and other noise-sensitive buildings and areas. The Regulations, however, do not apply to noise that is caused by the exposed person himself, noise from domestic activities, noise created by neighbours, noise at work places or noise inside means of transport or due to military activities in military areas.

10.2.4 Strategic noise mapping

The directive provides for two stages in the noise mapping exercise. Member States were required to complete the noise mapping exercise by June 2007 for major roads with more than 6 million vehicle passages annually; major railways with more than 60,000 train passages annually; major airports;[35] and urban agglomerations with populations greater than 250,000 people. The Environmental Noise (Identification of Noise Sources) (England) Regulations 2007[36] identify the first-round agglomerations, which include 22 places including London, Tyneside, Manchester and Blackpool[37] and the first-round major roads, railways and airports. The noise maps for these were published (in England) by Defra and the relevant airport operators. Defra published in May 2008,[38] almost 12 months after the deadline. The next round of noise mapping should have been complete by 30 June 2012 for all agglomerations[39] and for all major roads[40] and major railways.[41] However, at the time of writing (March 2013) the second-round mapping exercise had not been completed and no second-round maps published.

A strategic noise map is defined in the directive as a map designed for the global assessment of noise exposure in a given area due to different noise sources or for overall predictions for such an area. The Defra website[42] provides a slightly more user-friendly explanation: 'A noise map is rather

---

33 Environmental Noise (England) Regulations 2006 SI 2006/2238 as amended by SI 2008/375. The Regulations came into force on 1 October 2006.
34 Environmental Noise (England) Regulations 2009 SI 2009/1610.
35 Airports with more than 50,000 aircraft movements annually except for training on light aircraft.
36 Environmental Noise (Identification of Noise Sources) (England) Regulations 2007 SI 2007/415 (as amended by SI 2007/2458).
37 Blackpool, Bournemouth, Brighton, Bristol, Coventry, Hull, Leicester, Liverpool-Birkenhead, London, Manchester, Nottingham, Portsmouth, Preston, Reading, Sheffield, Southampton, Southend, Teesside, the Potteries, Tyneside, West Midlands, West Yorkshire.
38 They cover 22 large urban areas. For current noise maps see the Defra website at: http://services.defra.gov.uk/wps/portal/noise.
39 Whose population exceeds 100,000.
40 Includes regional and national roads which have more than three million vehicle passages a year.
41 One which has more than 30,000 train passages per year. At the time of writing, the Welsh Assembly Government has completed strategic noise maps for major roads, railways and Cardiff and Vale and Swansea/Neath Port Talbot.
42 http://www.defra.gov.uk/.

like a weather map for noise but it shows areas which are relatively louder or quieter. Just as a weather map might have isobars joining points of equal air pressure, a noise map can have contours joining points having the same noise level.' The Defra website also provides interactive access to the published noise maps and also population exposure charts which show the number of people exposed to the different noise levels from each source within each agglomeration. These can be searched by postcode. However, the principal aim of the noise maps is to provide information for the development of noise action plans to manage and reduce noise as appropriate. The directive requires that noise maps must be reviewed every five years.

10.2.5 Noise action plans

Member States were required to draw up noise action plans by July 2008. The directive defines action plans as plans designed to manage noise issues and effects, including noise reduction if necessary. The action plans are based on the results of the noise mapping and are intended to apply in particular to the most 'important areas' identified by the noise maps. Implementation of this aspect of the directive was also delayed; Defra did not publish its first round of draft actions plans until July 2009, some 12 months after the deadline. However, the first Noise Action Plans for the 23 agglomerations (large urban areas), major roads, and major railways in England were formally adopted by the Secretary of State on 15 March 2010 and are available on the Defra website. Operators of major airports were also required to produce noise action plans for the period 2010–2015. These are accessible via the individual airport websites.

Noise action plans must contain a description of the agglomeration, the major roads, the major railways or major airports and other noise sources being taken into account in the plan and a summary of the results of the noise mapping. The plan must evaluate the estimated number of people exposed to noise and identify any problems that need to be improved and any noise reduction measures already in force and in the course of preparation. Plans must also include a long-term strategy which includes information about any actions to be taken in the next five years. In preparing and revising action plans the Secretary of State and the relevant airport operator must comply with the public participation requirements laid down in reg 20 Environmental Noise Regulations 2006. This requires that the public is consulted about proposals for action plans; and that the public is given early and effective opportunities to participate in the preparation and review of the action plans. The results of that public participation must be taken into account and when the action plans are adopted the public must be informed of the decisions taken. At all stages reasonable time must be allowed to ensure proper public participation.

10.2.6 Quiet areas

The aim of the action plan is to prevent and reduce environmental noise where necessary and particularly where exposure levels can induce harmful effects on human health and to preserve environmental noise quality where it is good. The directive requires action plans to contain details on measures taken by the Secretary of State (or airport operators) to preserve quiet areas inside and outside agglomerations. Initially the 2006 Environmental Noise Regulations required the Secretary of State to publish (by means of regulations) a list of designated quiet areas by September 2007. However, the 2009 amendment relaxed this requirement and all that is now required is that the Secretary of State publishes the list in whatever form he considers appropriate. The change was made in order to facilitate liaison with local authorities on what might be appropriate areas to identify, and also to enable the quiet areas to be published through the action planning process rather than in regulations. Interestingly the regulations do not ascribe any role to local authorities although of course it is anticipated that there will be the aforementioned liaison. Quiet areas in the second round of agglomerations were supposed to have been identified by September 2012 but at the time of writing this does not appear to have happened. There appear to be no plans in the regulations to recognise quiet areas outside agglomerations.

Plans should also address any priorities which must be identified, having regard to the relevant criteria laid down by the Secretary of State. (Regulation 14[A] requires the Secretary of State to set out limit values or other criteria for the identification of priorities for action plans.) Essentially, the noise maps have enabled Defra to identify so-called 'important areas' which are the noisiest areas, which exceed limit values set by Defra. As part of the action plan consultation exercise, Defra identified a group of 'first priority areas', where particular attention may be needed to reduce noise levels or exposure to noise through mitigation measures. The thresholds that have been used define first priority areas as those containing about 60,000 dwellings, or 122,000 people. This constitutes some 1 per cent of the population exposed to the 'highest noise levels'—defined as above 50 decibels, expressed as the maximum weighted daytime and evening noise levels (LA10, 18hr). However, Defra also state that all areas where noise exposure exceeds higher thresholds (76 dB LA10, 18hr for road or 73 dB LAeq from rail) will be investigated as priority areas.

10.2.7 Noise management measures

Implementation of the noise action plans will rest with the various 'noise making authorities', who will need to investigate first priority areas and consider what further noise management measures, if any, might be implemented. The noise making authorities for roads are the Highways Agency and local highway authorities; for railways, the Department for Transport and the Office of Rail Regulation. For airports, the noise making authority is the airport operator. Before taking any noise management measures there must be public consultation.

Regulation 21 states that where an action plan (or a revision to an action plan) had been properly adopted and it also identified a public authority as being responsible for a particular action then that public authority must treat the action plan as its policy in relation to that action. The types of action that can be taken appear to be very wide from simple solutions such as sound insulation to properties, the erection of noise barriers, the use of traffic management systems and low-noise road surfaces. All proposed measures must be subject to a cost-benefit analysis (which for roads includes the impact on transport disruption).

10.3 National noise strategy and noise policy statement

The government's Rural White Paper in 2000 promised a national strategy to tackle ambient noise from transport and industry, and this was followed in 2001 by a Defra consultation paper, 'Towards a National Ambient Noise Strategy'. The consultation document was written prior to the adoption of, but in anticipation of, the EU Environmental Noise Directive (see above), which had been in the pipeline since 1996. Towards a National Ambient Noise Strategy proposed a three-phase approach and timetable. It was anticipated that the first phase would be used to collect information on noise levels across England and to develop methods to assess the impact of noise. Central to this phase was the preparation of noise maps covering major town and transport routes. The initial consultation suggested that this would be complete by 2005; however, clearly the EU Directive, with its requirement for noise maps for agglomerations and major road, rail and airports, has had an impact on this schedule. The deadline for the first round of noise maps in the directive was June 2007 (albeit that implementation of this was delayed in England by almost 12 months). The second phase, which was due to run between 2004 and 2006, aimed to evaluate the techniques for assessing and mitigating noise pollution identified in phase one and the final third phase was to be the preparation of a national noise strategy by 2007. During the consultation exercise a large number of respondents indicated that they supported more action to tackle neighbourhood noise. Consequently in 2006 Defra announced that it aimed to publish a national strategy that would include ambient and neighbourhood noise in 2008. However, this has never happened, mainly for resource reasons, and the strategy was abandoned in favour of a new Noise Policy Statement for England.

10.3.1 The Noise Policy Statement for England

In 2010 Defra published its first Noise Policy Statement for England (NPSE).[43] Although the Policy approach is radically different to the Strategy discussed above, it does appear to pick up some of the threads from the aborted strategy, particularly in that the NPSE deals with neighbourhood noise. The NPSE applies to the following types of noise:

● environmental-defined as including noise from transportation sources;
● neighbour noise, which includes noise from inside and outside people's homes;
● neighbourhood noise, which includes noise arising from within the community, such as industrial and entertainment premises (such as pubs), trade and business premises, construction sites and noise in the street.[44]

In contrast to the aborted national strategy, which ran to some 192 pages, the NPSE is very short in length and very short in detail. The NPSE seeks to set out the long-term vision of government noise policy and to provide clarity about the underlying principles and aims in the legislation that relates to noise. The vision is backed by six brief paragraphs, a statement of three aims and five guiding principles for sustainable development, which set the statement in its broader context. In addition, the policy is accompanied by four pages of explanatory notes. Consistent with the risk-based approach adopted elsewhere,[45] the NPSE aims to:

1. Avoid significant adverse impacts on health and quality of life within the context of government policy on sustainable development.
2. Mitigate and minimise adverse impacts on health and quality of life from within the context of government policy on sustainable development. This second principle refers to situations where the impact lies between LOAEL and SOAEL and requires that reasonable steps should be taken to mitigate and minimise adverse effects on health and quality of life while also taking into account the guiding principle of sustainable development.
3. Where possible, contribute to the improvement of health and quality of life through the effective management and control of environmental, neighbour and neighbourhood noise within the government policy on sustainable development.

By describing clear policy vision and aims, the NPSE aims to provide clarity and direction to enable decisions to be made regarding what is an acceptable noise burden to place on society. The aspiration of the policy is that noise should not be considered as an isolated issue, or when it is too late to find an appropriate solution. Rather, the noise implications of a particular policy or activity should be considered at an appropriate stage and alongside other relevant issues. It recognises that over time other government departments and agencies will be expected to review existing policies against the statement.

Although the principles are couched in very general terms, the policy draws a distinction between three different categories of noise exposure, as follows:

---

43 Defra Noise Policy Statement for England, March 2010.
44 The NPSE does not cover occupational noise (noise in the work place).
45 See e.g. the 2012 Statutory Guidance on Contaminated Land, in Chapter 7.

- NOEL (No Observed Effect Level). This is the level below which no effect can be detected. In simple terms, below this level, there is no detectable effect on health and quality of life due to the noise.
- LOAEL (Lowest Observed Adverse Effect Level). This is the level above which adverse effects on health and quality of life can be detected.
- SOAEL (Significant Observed Adverse Effect Level). This is the level above which significant adverse effects on health and quality of life occur. The NPSE recognises that it isn't possible to have an objective noise-based measure that defines SOAEL because this will depend on the source of the noise, and will affect people in different ways and at different times. Further research is required to increase understanding of what may constitute a significant adverse impact on health.

Although the NPSE is not particularly prescriptive, it is intended to provide guidance to a range of decision-makers across central and local government, and in this respect is to be welcomed, but it remains to be seen what impact it will have in practice.

10.4 Noise prevention; emission standards

The following part of this chapter will examine various statutory controls (both EU and domestic) which seek to reduce noise either from specific sources (such as motor vehicles and aircraft) or from particular activities, such as construction sites and loudspeakers. This section is not exhaustive; instead it attempts to cover some of the main sources of noise and key statutory provisions, which the reader will note are varied.

One way of reducing noise generated by certain types of transport, machines or activities is to set source emission standards. This is the approach that has been taken in a number of EU directives. As noted earlier, the European Union has relatively recently began to develop a noise policy. However, its initial forays into noise control were largely concerned with prescribing maximum acceptable levels of noise for certain types of machinery and products such as lawnmowers, motor cycles and aircraft.

10.4.1 Noise from motor vehicles and traffic

Traffic-related noise nuisance arises from a combination of engine noise, road noise[46] and the volume of traffic using a particular stretch of road. The EU has been influential in developing product-based controls, such as exhaust silencers and tyre standards, which help to combat these problems. The first EU-harmonised noise requirements were introduced in the 1970s by EC Directive 70/157/EEC, as amended.[47] The directive limits the maximum acceptable noise levels from different types of vehicle which must conform to these type approvals. The original directive has been amended several times to make the noise emission limits more stringent. For example, the current position is that maximum noise levels from a vehicle intended for the carriage of passengers and comprising not more than nine seats (including the driver's seat) is 74 decibels (dB(A)). The provisions of this directive and subsequent amendments have been transposed into national law by various statutory instruments including the Motor Vehicles (Type Approval) (Great Britain) Regulations 1984[48] and the Motor Vehicles (Type Approval of Reduced Pollution Adaptions)

---

46 Caused by the composition of the road surface: tarmac or concrete.
47 Council Directive 70/157/EEC of 6 February 1970 on the approximation of the laws of the Member States relating to the permissible sound levels and the exhaust system of motor vehicles OJ L 42, 23/2/1970.
48 Motor Vehicles (Type Approval) (Great Britain) Regulations 1984 SI 1984/981.

Regulations 1998,[49] as amended. The EU has also adopted similar type approval legislation for motorcycles, such as Directive 97/24/EC,[50] which sets maximum permissible sound levels from two- and three-wheel vehicles and their exhaust systems.

The noise of tyres rolling across road surfaces has also been identified as a particular problem aggravated by the sheer volume of traffic on the roads. Therefore in 2001 the EU adopted Directive 2001/43/EC,[51] which seeks to complement the legislation discussed above by providing for the testing and limiting of tyre rolling noise levels and for their phased reduction. The directive sets different limits for different types of vehicles and tyre width. The directive requires tyre noise rolling tests as part of a certificated type approval process which must be met by any new tyres being placed on the European market.

10.4.2 Aircraft noise

Aircraft noise is now largely regulated by the European Aviation Safety Agency (EASA), which seeks to promote a uniform level of environmental protection throughout the EU. From an environmental protection perspective EASA is concerned with regulating atmospheric emissions (such as carbon dioxide) and noise from aircraft. The Civil Aviation Authority, along with other European national authorities, has largely ceded its responsibilities for aviation environmental protection to EASA. All aircraft are governed by EU Regulation 216/2008,[52] known as the Basic Regulation. This EU regulation adopts the standards of the International Civil Aviation Organisation which are contained on Annex 16 of the 1944 Chicago Convention on Civil Aviation (which has been updated on several occasions). The Chicago Convention is in its ninth edition (dated November 2007). Certain aircraft which are not regulated by the basic EASA regulation are required to comply with the Air Navigation (Environmental Standards for Non-EASA Aircraft) Order 2008.[53]

10.4.3 Plant and machinery

The Secretary of State has the power under s 68 of the Control of Pollution Act (COPA) 1974 to make regulations which reduce or limit the noise caused by plant or machinery both inside and outside factories and construction sites. However, this power has not been exercised, and the Secretary of State has preferred the use of codes of practice rather than legally binding standards. Section 71 of the COPA 1974 enabled the Secretary of State to prepare and approve codes of practice for the purpose of giving guidance on the appropriate methods of minimising noise in relation to specified types of plant and machinery. A number of s 71 codes were introduced, for example, the Control of Noise (Codes of Practice for Construction and Open Sites) Orders 1984 and 1987. These were revoked in 2002 by SI 2002/461, which basically approves the British Standards Institution (BSI) Codes of Practice as being suitable for giving guidance on appropriate methods for minimising noise. Codes of Practice exist for audible intruder alarms,[54] ice cream van chimes[55] and model aircraft.[56] Although codes of practice are not legally binding, they may be taken into account in legal proceedings, for example, in determining whether best practical means (BPM) have been employed.

---

49 Motor Vehicles (Type Approval of Reduced Pollution Adaptions) Regulations 1998 SI 1998/3093 as amended.
50 Directive 97/24/EC of the European Parliament and of the Council of 17 June 1997 on certain components and characteristics of two- or three-wheel motor vehicles OJ L 226, 18/8/1997.
51 Directive 2001/43/EC of the European Parliament and of the Council of 27 June 2001 amending Council Directive 92/23/EEC relating to tyres for motor vehicles and their trailers OJ L 211, 4/8/2001.
52 Regulation (EC) No 216/2008 of the European Parliament and of the Council of 20 February 2008 on common rules in the field of civil aviation and establishing a European Aviation Safety Agency OJ L 79, 19/3/2008, pp 1–49.
53 Air Navigation (Environmental Standards for Non-EASA Aircraft) Order 2008 SI 2008/3133.
54 Control of Noise (Code of Practice on Noise from Audible Intruder Alarms) Order 1981 SI 1981/1829.
55 Control of Noise (Code of Practice on Noise from Ice-Cream Van Chimes) Order 1981 SI 1981/1828.
56 Control of Noise (Code of Practice on Noise from Model Aircraft) Order 1981 SI 1981/1830.

10.5 Controlling noise from construction sites

The COPA 1974 includes a number of provisions which enable local authorities to control various aspects of noise. In particular, ss 60 and 61 introduced the first legislative controls over noise from construction sites. These sections enable local authorities to exercise control over the level of noise in their areas arising from construction works. The definition of 'construction' extends to the erection, construction, alteration, repair or maintenance of buildings, structures or roads. It also includes demolition and dredging works. Where it appears to a local authority that any of these activities are being, or are going to be, carried out on any premises, the authority can serve a notice imposing requirements as to the way in which the work is to be carried out.[57] It is not necessary that a nuisance exists or could occur for the authority to resort to these powers. Sometimes, local authorities will publish details of the notice in the local press.

The notice can specify the following:

(a) plant and machinery which must or must not be used;
(b) permitted hours of operation;
(c) noise levels by reference to the time of the day or to a part of the site;
(d) the time within which the notice is to be complied with;
(e) the execution of works necessary for the purpose of the notice.

When the local authority issues a notice under s 60 COPA 1974, it must take into account the matters specified in s 60(4), which are:

(a) relevant codes of practice issued under s 71 of the COPA 1974;
(b) the need to ensure that the best practicable means (BPM) are employed to minimise noise;
(c) the need to protect people in the locality from the effects of noise.

It should be noted that the definition of BPM under s 72 of the COPA 1974 is very similar to the definition provided under the EPA 1990 (s 79(9)). The local authority is required to serve the s 60 notice on the person who appears (to the local authority) to be either carrying out or going to carry out the works. In addition, a notice can also be served on the person(s) who is (are) responsible for or controlling the carrying out of the works. In *City of London Corp v Bovis Construction Ltd* (1992),[58] it was held that it was sufficient that the notice was served upon the person having control of the site even if the contractor actually doing the work is not served.

It is an offence not to comply with a s 60 notice without reasonable excuse. The magistrates can impose a fine of up to £5,000, with a daily fine of £50 for continuing offences. However, it is possible to raise the defence of reasonable excuse. The phrase reasonable excuse is not defined in the Act, but was considered in the case of *City of London Corp v Bovis*, where Lord Bingham stated that:

> Nothing much short of an emergency, unless an event beyond a party's control, could in my view provide a reasonable excuse for contravention in a case such as this.[59]

Where a party fails to comply with the s 60 notice, the local authority also has the option to apply for an injunction. The court may grant an injunction where it appears that the criminal proceedings

---

57 s 60(2) COPA 1974.
58 City of London Corp v Bovis Construction Ltd [1992] 3 All ER 697.
59 See also *Wiltshire Construction (London) Ltd v Westminster City Council* CO/1374/96 and *Walter Lilly & Co Ltd v Westminster City Council* (1994) 158 JP 805.

will not provide an adequate remedy to ensure compliance with the notice and to protect the inhabitants from noise.

A right of appeal exists against a s 60 notice, providing the appeal is made within 21 days of service. The grounds for appeal are set out in the Control of Noise (Appeals) Regulations 1975[60] as amended. An appeal can suspend the notice unless the notice expressly states otherwise.

10.5.1 Prior consents

Given that local authorities have powers to restrict construction noise under s 60 of the COPA 1974, contractors have the right to reach some agreement with the local authority, in advance of the works taking place, about the levels and timing of noise that will take place. Section 61(3) provides that contractors can apply for consent prior to the construction work taking place. To do so, the applicant must provide details of the work that is to be carried out, and also the method by which it is to be carried out. In addition, details must be given regarding the measures that will be taken to minimise the noise resulting from the works. If the authority considers that the application contains sufficient information that no s 60 notice would be served if the steps proposed are observed, then it must grant a consent. The authority, however, has the right to attach conditions to the consent. In setting the conditions, it must take into account the relevant codes of practice, BPM and the need to protect persons in the locality from noise.

The authority must respond to the application for prior consent within 28 days of receipt of the application. The authority can either refuse or approve the application, or alternatively it may approve the application subject to conditions. An applicant can appeal if the authority refuses to give its consent, fails to deal with the application within the 28 days, or attaches conditions to which the applicant objects. An appeal is made to the magistrates' court and must be lodged within 21 days after the expiry of the 28 days.

It is an offence to carry on the works other than in compliance with the terms of the consent. Obtaining the prior consent from the local authority can prove to be valuable since the existence of a consent can protect the contractor from any statutory nuisance proceedings brought by a local authority. However, the consent does not provide the same protection in relation to actions brought by private individuals.[61] The existence and compliance with a prior consent will not provide a defence in such actions. A citizen can also seek an injunction in respect of a noise nuisance irrespective of whether there is a s 61 prior consent. Although prior consent would appear to be a sensible step for any contractor, in practice relatively few have applied under these provisions. One of the suggested reasons for this is the view that contractors have thought that the local authorities would be too restrictive in setting conditions. Contractors have preferred to run the risk of proceedings under s 60.

10.6 Noise from loudspeakers and intruder alarms

10.6.1 Noise from loudspeakers

Noise from loudspeakers is controlled by s 62 COPA 1974, which provides that loudspeakers are not to be operated in streets at all for advertising any entertainment, trade or business. There is a blanket ban as far as advertising is concerned. In *Westminster City Council v French Connection Retail Ltd* (2005),[62] French Connection used audio pucks or suckers connected to the window panes of its

---

60 Control of Noise (Appeals) Regulations 1975 (SI 1975/2116).
61 Under s 82 of the EPA 1990.
62 *Westminster City Council v French Connection Retail Ltd* [2005] EWHC 933 (Admin); [2005] LLR 533.

shop in Regent Street London to broadcast pop music and advertising. Westminster City Council prosecuted French Connection under s 62 COPA but the magistrates dismissed the case because they considered that the loudspeakers were not in the street. The Divisional Court, in a case stated appeal, took a more common-sense approach; once it was established that the window pane itself was functioning as a loudspeaker, its outer face was clearly in the street even if its inner face was in the shop. The case was remitted back to the magistrates with a direction to convict.

Loudspeakers may be used for non-advertising purposes, but they may not be operated in any event between 11 pm and 8 am the following morning. Section 62(2) of the COPA 1974 provides exceptions for the use of loudspeakers:

(a)   at any time in the street for, inter alia, various public service reasons, such as the police, the ambulance or fire service or the Environment Agency;

(b)   in an emergency;

(c)   inside vehicles for the entertainment of passengers;

(d)   by ice cream vans (or vans selling perishable foods). These may play their music between noon and 7 pm;

(e)   at pleasure fairs.

In relation to the last three of these exceptions, there is a caveat that the noise must not give reasonable cause for annoyance to persons in the vicinity.

Section 8 of and Sched 2 to the Noise and Statutory Nuisance Act (NSNA) 1993 amended s 62 of the COPA 1974 in order to allow local authorities to permit the use of loudspeakers in certain circumstances where it would otherwise be a breach of s 62. The maximum penalty for the illegal use of a loudspeaker in a street is £5,000.

10.6.2 Noise from burglar alarms

There cannot be many people who have not been annoyed by the sound of burglar alarms going off for what sometimes seems like for ever in the middle of the night. Burglar alarms are designed to be noisy and to arouse attention, but all too often they go off for no other reason than the operator has misused the system or a 'door has blown open'. Provisions regulating audible intruder alarms were first introduced by s 9 of the NSNA 1993, which enabled local authorities to adopt a regime to deal with the problem of burglar alarms. Local authorities were given the power to impose obligations on installers of audible intruder alarms requiring the alarms to conform with requirements laid down in secondary legislation (enacted by the Secretary of State). The provisions contained in s 9 NSNA 1993 were repealed and replaced with largely similar provisions in the Clean Neighbourhoods and Environment Act (CNEA) 2005. The current provisions relating to intruder alarms are now to be found in Part 7 CNEA 2005. Section 69 CNEA enables local authorities to designate all or part of its area as an alarm notification area. There is no obligation on local authorities to do this; the provision is discretionary. However, if a local authority proposes to designate an alarm notification area it must comply with the publicity requirements contained within s 69 and consider any representations made regarding the proposed designation. Following designation of an area, the local authority must publish a notice in a local newspaper and must also send a copy of the notice to the address of all premises within the area. Once an area has been designated, then s 70 provides that where an intruder alarm has been installed on premises within the area, the occupier (or if there is no occupier, the owner) must (a) nominate a key holder and (b) notify the local authority (in writing and within the required period) of the name and address and telephone number of the nominated key holder. A person can only be nominated as a key holder if he holds the keys which enable him to gain access to the part of the premises where the control panel for the alarm is installed. He must also normally reside within the vicinity of the premises, be able to silence the alarm and agree to act in this capacity. The nominated key holder may be a key holding company. A person commits an offence if he fails to comply with the requirement to nominate a key holder and notify the local authority.[63] The local authority may commence criminal proceedings before the magistrates' court that may impose a fine of up to level three on the standard scale. However, s 73 CNEA 2005 provides for the use of fixed penalty notices. Where a local authority authorised officer considers that an offence has been committed under s 71(4) he can, as an alternative to prosecution, serve a fixed penalty notice which enables the recipient to discharge any liability to conviction by the payment of the fixed penalty. The local authority must give the person 14 days to pay, during which no criminal proceedings can be commenced. A person may not be convicted if he pays the fixed penalty within 14 days of the notice. Local authorities can specify the amount of the fixed penalty, or if no amount is specified the amount is £75.[64] The local authority may, if it wishes, set a lower penalty for early payment.

In the event that an intruder alarm does go off, s 77 provides the local authority with the power to enter premises. To trigger the powers of entry the alarm must have been sounding continuously for more than 20 minutes or intermittently for more than one hour and the sound must be likely to cause annoyance to people living or working within the vicinity of the premises. However, if the alarm goes off in an alarm notification area, before exercising this power of entry the local authority must first take reasonable steps to get the nominated key holder to switch the alarm off. The local authority should not use force to enter premises unless a magistrate has issued a warrant[65] authorising the officer to use reasonable force if necessary.

10.7 Control of industrial noise: environmental permitting

Prior to the Integrated Pollution Prevention Directive (96/61/EC)[66] the Environment Agency did not exercise any control over the noise emissions from industrial plant subject to the system of Integrated Pollution control (IPC) under Part I EPA 1990. Part I EPA 1990 was concerned with the regulation of emissions into air, water and land. However, the IPPC Directive required a much more holistic approach and included within its scope vibration and noise. The requirements of the IPPC Directive were initially implemented into domestic law by the Pollution Prevention Control Act 1999 and the Pollution Prevention and Control (England and Wales) Regulations 2000.[67] However, the current regulation is via the Environmental Permitting (England and Wales) Regulations 2010.[68] Any industrial activity that falls within the scope of the IPPC Directive[69] is classed as an A1 or A2 installation for the purposes of the environmental permitting regime. The Environment Agency regulates AI installations and the relevant local authority regulates A2 installations. The purpose of the IPPC regime is to prevent and reduce and reduce pollution and environmental impacts from installations. IPPC requires installations to be operated in such a way that all appropriate preventative measures are taken against pollution, in particular through the application of Best Available Techniques (BAT). BAT includes both the technology used and the way in which the installation is designed, built and operated. In deciding what level of control constitutes BAT for a given installation, a number of factors need to be considered

See Chapter 6

---

63 S 71 (4) CNEA 2005.
64 S 74 CNEA 2005.
65 Ibid.
66 Council Directive 96/61/EC of 24 September 1996 concerning integrated pollution prevention and control OJ L 257, 10/10/1996. Now repealed and replaced by Directive 2008/1/EC of the European Parliament and of the Council of 15 January 2008 concerning integrated pollution prevention and control.
67 Pollution Prevention and Control (England and Wales) Regulations 2000 SI 2000/1973.
68 Environmental Permitting (England and Wales) Regulations 2010 SI 2010/675, as amended.
69 Listed in Annex 1 of the directive.

and balanced. The impacts that must be addressed by BAT conditions include discharges to air, water and land and also energy use and efficiency; raw material consumption; noise, vibration, accident prevention measures; heat generation (thermal effects).

To assist the Agency and the local authorities in relation to noise controls and the assessment of the Best Available Techniques (BAT) in relation to noise the Agency has produced a horizontal, cross-sectoral guide.[70] This requires applicants to conduct a risk assessment in relation to noise, having regard to the potential for the noise to cause annoyance and complaint and also having regard to any particularly sensitive receptors.[71] A permit holder will usually be required to monitor sound emissions and will be required as appropriate to install the necessary sound insulation to meet specified sound emission limits. Conditions can be imposed which require noise levels to be minimised at source, and to ensure adequate distance between the source and receiver and the use of barriers between the source and receiver. It is a criminal offence under reg 38 of the Environmental Permitting Regulations 2010 to breach any condition of an environmental permit.

Local authorities are barred from using their statutory nuisance powers in Pt III of the EPA 1990 to deal with noise and other problems which the environmental permitting regulator can address, using the relevant environmental permitting enforcement powers. Local authorities may nevertheless use their statutory nuisance powers on a regulated facility in circumstances where the relevant nuisance falls outside the remit of environmental permitting controls. Irrespective of the limitations on local authority power to take statutory nuisance action against an environmental permit holder, an individual may use s 82 of the EPA 1990 to lodge a complaint against an IPPC permit holder in respect of an alleged nuisance.

See Chapter ◄ 9

10.8 Prevention of noise through the planning system

10.8.1 Noise abatement zones

In addition to the specific powers in ss 60–61 of the COPA 1974 (described above), local authorities can also take preventive action to control noise by designating noise abatement zones. The provisions relating to noise abatement zones are found in ss 63–67 of the COPA 1974. Section 63 of the COPA 1974 makes provision for local authorities to designate all or any part of their area as a noise abatement zone. The purpose of noise abatement zones is to 'prevent deterioration in environmental noise levels and achieve reductions in noise levels wherever practicable'.[72] Originally, such an order had to be confirmed by the Secretary of State, but this requirement was removed by the Local Government and Planning Act 1980.

Where a local authority designates an area as a noise abatement zone, it must measure the level of noise emanating from those classes of premises specified by the order. It is also under a duty to maintain a noise level register of all measurements taken. In a noise abatement zone, it is an offence to exceed the level of noise recorded in the noise level register without the written consent of the local authority. The local authority can consent to a noise level being exceeded by virtue of s 65 and any consent may be subject to conditions. Where such consent is denied by a local authority, an applicant can appeal to the Secretary of State. Where the local authority consents to the registered level being exceeded, this is also recorded in the register.

---

70 Horizontal Guidance Note: IPPC H3, Integrated Pollution Prevention and Control (IPPC) Horizontal Guidance for Noise Part 2 – Noise Assessment and Control.
71 E.g. residential properties close to the installation.
72 Sched 1 to the COPA 1974 defines the procedures for establishing noise abatement zones.

If the local authority records a measurement in the register, it is obliged to serve a copy of that record on the owner or occupier of the premises from which the measurement was taken. Any person who is served with a copy of a record has the right to appeal against the record to the Secretary of State within 28 days by virtue of s 64. The Control of Noise (Appeals) Regulations 1975[73] provide for the appeals procedure. The precise methods of measurement are determined by the Control of Noise (Measurement and Registers) Regulations 1976.[74]

In addition, the local authority can require the reduction of noise emanating from premises covered by the noise abatement order. The local authority will issue a noise reduction notice, which will state:

(a)   that the level of noise must be reduced to the stated levels;
(b)   the noise level allowable at different times of the day and on different days;
(c)   what steps are to be taken to achieve the noise reduction; and
(d)   the deadline for achieving the noise reduction.

The noise reduction stated in the notice must be practicable and achievable at a reasonable cost. It must also generate some public benefit. Parties served with a noise reduction notice have the right to appeal to the magistrates' court against the notice (the appeal must be made within three months of service of the notice). Failure to comply with the terms of a notice without reasonable excuse constitutes an offence. By virtue of s 74 of the COPA 1974, the fines may not exceed level 5 on the standard scale (£5,000) and there is provision for a daily penalty of £50. As in statutory nuisance, the local authority may execute works itself and recover reasonable costs.[75]

Noise abatement zones have not found widespread support. In 2006 Defra reported that only about 100 Noise Abatement Zones had been created.[76] This is probably because of the time it takes to establish a NAZ and the resources that are needed to implement the provisions. Local authorities have largely relied on their powers under the statutory nuisance provisions in the EPA 1990 to control noise. In December 2012 Defra opened a two-month consultation on proposals to abolish Noise Abatement Zones and at that time Defra noted that only two NAZs were in active use.[77]

10.8.2 Planning and noise control

The town and country planning regime can play a large part in causing, exacerbating or reducing noise problems. Bad planning can result in noisy developments being built alongside more noise-sensitive activities. For this reason, planning authorities are required to consider the potential for noise problems in the exercise of their planning functions. In 1994, a new Planning Policy Guidance Note[78] was introduced on planning and noise to replace the advice previously given in DoE Circular 10/73. It also takes into account the recommendations of the Noise Review Working Party, which reported in October 1990.

PPG 24 provides advice to local authorities on how to use their planning powers to minimise the adverse impact of noise. In particular, it outlines the considerations that should be taken into account when the authority is considering planning applications for activities which will generate

---

73 Control of Noise (Appeals) Regulations 1975 SI 1975/2116.
74 Control of Noise (Measurement and Registers) Regulations 1976 SI 1976/37.
75 s 69 of the COPA 1974.
76 Defra, Neighbourhood Noise Policies and Practice for Local Authorities – a Management Guide, September 2006.
77 Defra Consultation on Repeal of ss 63 to 67 of the Control of Pollution Act 1974 Abolishing Noise Abatement Zones December 2012.
78 Planning Policy Guidance 24: Planning and Noise (1994).

noise and also for proposals in noise sensitive areas. The PPG highlights the measures that may be taken to control noise.

These include:

(a) ensuring that there is adequate distance between the source of noise and noise-sensitive areas;
(b) engineering solutions to reduce noise at the point of generation;
(c) controlling the times when noise-generating activities can take place.

10.8.2.1 Noise exposure categories

In addition, PPG 24 introduces the concept of 'noise exposure' categories (NECs) for residential developments. When determining an application for a residential development near a source of noise, such as a motorway, planning authorities must first determine into which of the four noise exposure categories the proposed site falls, taking account of noise levels during the day and night. The four NECs are rated A to D. An A category means that noise need not be considered as a determining factor in granting planning permission, whereas a D category means that planning permission should normally be refused. Annex 2 of the PPG sets out detailed 'noise exposure' categories:

A—noise need not be considered as a determining factor in granting planning permission.
B—noise should be taken into account.
C—planning permission should normally be granted, but where it is granted appropriate conditions should be applied.
D—planning permission should normally be refused.

10.8.2.2 Environmental Impact Assessment (EIA) and noise

Where a proposed development is subject to the requirements of the Environmental Impact Assessment Directive[79] and the corresponding domestic legislation,[80] an environmental impact assessment must be conducted before planning consent can be granted. The purpose of the EIA process is to enable decision makers to gather information about the environmental effects of a proposed development and to take this into account in the decision-making process. Only certain projects are subject to the requirements of the directive and these are listed in Annexes 1 and 2 of the directive.[81] If a project is of the type listed in Sched 1, then an EIA is mandatory. If a project is of a type listed in Sched 2 the planning authority is required to consider whether the project is likely to have significant effects on the environment having regard, inter alia, to its nature, size and location. If the project is likely to have significant environmental effects, then an EIA is required. A considerable body of case law has emerged in relation to the degree of discretion involved in making this decision, but that falls outside the scope of this chapter. Where an EIA is required, the developer will be required to produce an environmental statement which will identify any adverse environmental effects that the development is likely to have together with proposed mitigation measures. The Environmental Statement must be made available to the public so that they can make their representations known to the planning authority. In essence, the EIA process is procedural, the aim being to inform the decision-making process.[82]

---

79 Council Directive 85/337/EEC on the assessment of the effects of certain private and public projects on the environment OJ L 175, 5/7/1985, pp 40–48 (as amended).
80 Principally the Town and Country Planning (Environmental Impact Assessment) (England and Wales) Regulations 1999.
81 And correspondingly Scheds 1 and 2 of the the Town and Country Planning (Environmental Impact Assessment) (England and Wales) Regulations 1999.
82 And hopefully make for better decisions in respect of the environment.

The developer can seek a scoping opinion from the relevant planning authority which essentially enables the developer and authority to agree the scope of the Environmental Statement. In most instances noise will be a relevant consideration and the developer will be required to consider the likely noise levels from the proposed development. As part of this process the developer will also be expected to consider what steps can be taken to reduce noise levels and noise exposure. The planning authority may then impose a range of conditions which seek to minimise the noise impact of the development.

10.8.2.3 Planning conditions

Local planning authorities can grant planning permission for development subject to conditions which are aimed at minimising noise levels. PPG 24 is useful once again in that it describes the sorts of conditions that might be used to achieve this objective. For example, the planning authority can lay down conditions which determine that construction work cannot begin until a scheme for protecting a noise-sensitive development has been approved by the authority. Other relevant conditions include:

(a)   layout conditions;
(b)   engineering conditions;
(c)   administration conditions (such as operating times).

A planning authority may impose conditions relating to the hours of operation for the purposes of controlling noise. In *Penwith DC v Secretary of State for the Environment* (1977),[83] the local planning authority, in relation to an application for the extension to a factory, granted permission subject to a condition that no machinery be operated in the extension or the existing factory between the hours of 6 pm and 6 am on weekdays or between 1 pm on Saturday and 8 am on Monday, or on statutory holidays. The court held that the planning authority could lawfully impose such conditions.[84] However, when a planning authority grants planning permission it may, but is not required to, prescribe particular noise standards for the development to meet nor does it have to fix noise limits.[85]

A planning authority can refuse to grant planning permission on the ground that the development would cause noise disturbance to the neighbourhood. In *Barnet LBC v Alder* (2009)[86] retrospective planning permission was sought for the change of use from a semi-detached house to a school. The Council refused planning permission, because of the increased activity from the premises and the noise disturbance which caused significant harm to neighbouring premises. The refusal was upheld on appeal by the planning inspector and eventually the Divisional Court granted the Council an injunction because the school continued to operate without planning permission.

10.8.3 Building regulations

There can be no doubt that poor sound insulation, particularly in flats, is a contributory factor to neighbour noise problems. However, new buildings must comply with building regulations which can to some extent prevent noise problems occurring. Building regulations are enacted under the enabling powers contained in s 1 of the Building Act 1984.[87] The Building Regulations 2010[88]

---

83 *Penwith DC v Secretary of State for the Environment* (1977) 34 P & CR 269; [1977] JPL 371.
84 See also the Planning Inspector's decision in *Blanchard Wells Ltd v Winchester City Council* [2011] PAD 57.
85 *R (On the application of TWS) v Manchester City Council* [2013] EWHC 55 (Admin).
86 *Barnet LBC v Alder* [2009] EWHC 2012 (QB).
87 As amended by the Sustainable and Secure Buildings Act 2004.
88 Building Regulations 2010 SI 2010/2214.

prescribe various technical requirements relating to building structures including noise insulation. The technical details relating to sound insulation are contained in the Approved Document Resistance to the Passage of Sound, which was last updated in 2013 and is available on the UK planning portal.[89] It is a criminal offence to carry out building works in contravention of the Building Regulations, subject to a fine of up to £5,000 and up to £50 for each day the contravention continues. In *Baxter v Camden LBC* (2001)[90] in a case concerning a nuisance claim, the Court of Appeal held that the ordinary use of residential premises was incapable of constituting a nuisance, unless the use was unusual or unreasonable in terms of the purpose for which the premises were constructed. However, on the facts, the Court had regard to the fact that when the property had been converted by the landlord, the sound insulation between the floors was done in accordance with the building standards prevailing at the time. Consequently this did not change the purpose for which the premises were constructed and accordingly nothing unusual or unreasonable was done at that time so as to render ordinary use of the house a nuisance.

10.9 Neighbourhood noise

In this section we shall consider the specific problem of neighbourhood noise, which poses its own set of difficult problems and which is also a major cause for complaint amongst the public. Neighbourhood noise, defined for the purposes of this text as the noise inside and outside homes, has been a growing area of concern for the last decade. The National Noise Incidence Study 2000/2001[91] concluded that some 55 per cent of the population of England and Wales live in dwellings exposed to daytime noise levels above the World Health Organisation (WHO) recommended daytime level of 55 dB (decibels). In addition, the study found that 68 per cent of the population of England and Wales live in dwellings exposed to night-time noise levels above the WHO recommended level of 45 decibels. Among the findings of the study which included a survey of more than 5,000 people, were the following:

- 21 per cent of respondents reported that noise spoilt their home life to some extent, with 8 per cent of respondents reporting that their home life was spoilt either 'quite a lot' or 'totally';
- 84 per cent of respondents heard road traffic noise and 40 per cent were bothered, annoyed or disturbed to some extent;
- 28 per cent of respondents reported that road traffic noise at their homes had got worse in the last five years;
- 81 per cent of respondents heard noise from neighbours and/or other people nearby and 37 per cent were bothered, annoyed or disturbed to some extent;
- the proportion of respondents who reported being adversely affected by noise from neighbours has increased from 21 per cent to 26 per cent over the last 10 years whilst, for all other categories of environmental noise, the proportion adversely affected remained unchanged;
- only a small proportion of respondents who were bothered by noise from neighbours complained to the environmental health department of their local authority, which means that noise complaint statistics may greatly underestimate the extent of community dissatisfaction.

---

89 Available at: http://www.planningportal.gov.uk/uploads/br/BR_PDF_ADE_2003.pdf (accessed 26 January 2010).
90 *Southwark LBC v Mills & Baxter v Camden LBC (No 2)* [2001] 1 AC 1; [1999] 4 All ER 449; [1999] 3 WLR 939.
91 National Noise Incidence Survey (England and Wales) 2000 (Defra).

There is also an environmental justice aspect to the problem of neighbourhood noise. As with so many other environmental problems, it is likely to be the poorest members of the community who are at most risk of exposure to neighbourhood noise. Neighbourhood noise is more likely to be a problem in areas of high-density housing, such as flats and social housing and deprived areas. 'In contrast, the profile of those not concerned by neighbour noise is consistent with circumstances which would be expected to limit exposure, for example detached housing, high home ownership, and residence in rural/suburban locations in some of the least deprived areas nationally.'[92]

The Chartered Institute of Environmental Health (CIEH) publishes annual statistics which provide a detailed breakdown of the number of complaints received by local authorities in England and Wales.

In 2010/2011 152 local authorities[93] were recorded as receiving 137,977 noise complaints, of which 92,245 were about domestic noise, representing the largest source of noise complaints by a significant margin.[94] Interestingly, of these 92,245 domestic noise complaints received, only 18,654 were confirmed to be statutory nuisances by the local authorities.[95] These noise statistics also need to be put into context; the figures have been provided by only 44 per cent of local authorities suggesting that the number of actual noise complaints will be much higher. Also it should be borne in mind that, according to MORI,[96] 'The majority of people who have complained about noise do so in person to the noise maker, with around one in four complaining to the police and one in five to the council.' In short, the official statistics do not reveal the full picture. However, they do demonstrate that the public perception of noise as a problem is high.

The principal mechanism available for local authorities in dealing with domestic noise complaints is the statutory nuisance provisions contained in Pt III of the EPA 1990.[97] The 2010/2011 CIEH statistics reveal that the vast majority of substantiated complaints were in fact resolved without any recourse to the formal proceedings under the Act:

CIEH Noise Nuisance 2010/2011 summary data for all respondents (England, Wales)[98]

Complaints received re domestic noise	92,245
Complaints per million population	4,206
Sources confirmed as a statutory nuisance	18,654
Nuisances resolved informally without notices being served	6,268
Abatement notices served	1,682
Noise Act warning notices	87

However, before examining the statutory nuisance provisions relating to noise it is worth first reconsidering the use of the common law as a means of addressing noise disputes. The following section focuses on noise cases; for a fuller discussion of all of the common low torts, see Chapter 11.

See Chapter 11 →

---

92 MORI Social Research Institute (October 2003), Neighbour Noise: Public Opinion Research to Assess its Nature, Extent and Significance Research Study Conducted for Department for Environment, Food and Rural Affairs (Defra).

93 Some 44% of all local authorities.

94 The next highest figure being 17,110 in respect of noise from commercial and leisure activities.

95 See below and also Chapter 9.

96 MORI Social Research Institute (October 2003), Neighbour Noise: Public Opinion Research to Assess its Nature, Extent and Significance Research Study Conducted for Department for Environment, Food and Rural Affairs (Defra).

97 See below and also Chapter 9 for a fuller discussion of these provisions.

98 CIEH Annual Survey of Noise Enforcement–Results for 2011/201. Available from http://www.cieh.org/policy/noise-statistics-research.html?terms=noise+complaints (accessed March 2013).

10.10 The common law as a tool for the resolution of noise disputes

10.10.1 Nuisance

It is well established that noise can constitute an actionable nuisance at common law. Noise may give rise to either a public nuisance or a private nuisance. In some circumstances it may be both. In *Halsey v Esso Petroleum Co Ltd* (1961),[99] it was held that noise from tanker lorries at night on the public highway was both a public and a private nuisance. However, private nuisance actions are the most common because the impact of a public nuisance must be widely felt if it is to form the basis of a common law action.

10.10.2 Private nuisance: unreasonable interference

A private nuisance is one which unlawfully interferes with a person's use or enjoyment of land or some right connected with it. The nature of the interference will be a significant factor in determining whether an action succeeds. A minor interference may still amount to a nuisance where there is physical damage, either to property or person, whereas in other cases the interference must be substantial. In *Walter v Selfe* (1851),[100] the test was said to be whether there was 'an inconvenience materially interfering with the ordinary comfort physically of human existence, not merely according to plain and sober and simple notions amongst the English people'. As far as noise nuisances are concerned it is far more likely that a noise nuisance will interfere with a person's enjoyment of property, as opposed to causing actual physical damage (although of course noise vibration may cause physical damage). In 1931 the Divisional Court held in relation to a noise nuisance claim that that noise will create an actionable nuisance only if it materially interferes with the ordinary comfort of life.[101] In *Halsey*[102] the noise from boilers at night was held to be a nuisance for which the defendants were liable, since night was the time when the ordinary man took his rest and the noise was an inconvenience materially interfering with the ordinary comfort physically of human existence. In *Godfrey v Conwy CBC* (2000)[103] the Divisional Court affirmed the test, adding that that noise that is obtrusive and out of character with the area in which it occurs is capable of amounting to a nuisance.

In each case the question of whether something materially interferes with the enjoyment of property will be judged by 'ordinary plain and simple notions, and having regard to the locality; the question being one of degree in each case.'[104] In a nuisance action, the courts are required to balance the rights of the owner of land to do what he or she wants against the rights of the owners of neighbouring land to be free from unreasonable interference. This necessarily involves the court dealing with each case on its merits, taking into account all the relevant circumstances. The courts have developed a number of general principles and will take into account a number of factors.

10.10.3 Temporary interferences

The duration of an alleged nuisance is a factor which any court must take into account. It is here that noise can pose particular problems, because noise is often a temporary occurrence. As a general rule, the courts have found that a temporary interference is less likely to constitute a nuisance than

---

99 *Halsey v Esso Petroleum Co Ltd* [1961] 1 WLR 683.
100 *Walter v Selfe* (1851) 64 ER 849; (1851) 4 De G & Sm 315.
101 *Vanderpant v Mayfair Hotel Co Ltd* (1930)) [1930] 1 Ch 138.
102 *Halsey v Esso Petroleum Co Ltd* [1961] 1 WLR 683.
103 *Godfrey v Conwy CBC* [2000] All ER (D) 1809 G; [2001] Env LR 38.
104 Ibid.

one which is permanent or occurs regularly. A classic example of this reasoning can be found in the case of *Leeman v Montagu* (1936).[105] Here it was held that the noise from cockerels sounding their dawn chorus was not an actionable nuisance whereas, if the noise from the cockerels had taken place in a residential area for weeks, damages and an injunction might have been granted. Notwithstanding that it has been held that noise which results in loss of a single night's sleep can amount to a nuisance (*Andreae v Selfridge & Co Ltd* (1938)[106]). In a more recent case brought under the statutory nuisance provisions of the EPA 1990, *East Northamptonshire DC v Fossett* (1994),[107] the defendant F argued that 'nuisance' under the EPA 1990 has its common law meaning and therefore a single isolated instance of noise was not enough since there must be a 'course of action'. This argument was rejected by the Divisional Court, which stated that no case had held that excessive noise continuing all night could not amount to a nuisance to neighbouring residences.

The time of day, however, may be a factor for consideration. Noise disturbances during the night are more likely to constitute a nuisance than a noise made during the day.

10.10.4 Locality

It is well known that the courts will take into account the character of an area when determining whether an action is unreasonable and constitutes a nuisance.[108] The logical conclusion of this in relation to noise is that in peaceful suburban areas, the courts are more likely to regard noise as a nuisance than in built-up industrial areas. However, this does not exclude the possibility of bringing an action in private nuisance in industrial areas, nor does the fact that an area is already noisy remove the possibility of success. In *Roskell v Whitworth* (1871),[109] a congregation at a Roman Catholic Church succeeded in obtaining an injunction to restrain the use of a steam hammer in an iron and steel works because it interfered with their prayers and the comfortable enjoyment of the rectory house.[110]

Since it is a well-established principle in the law of nuisance that locality will have a bearing on whether a nuisance action will succeed, to what extent will the grant of planning permission alter the characteristics of a neighbourhood and provide a defence against a nuisance action? In *Gillingham BC v Medway (Chatham) Dock Co* (1992),[111] planning permission had been granted to the Medway Port Authority for the construction of a port facility on the site of the former Chatham Royal Naval Dockyard. The Royal Naval Dockyard when it was operational had not generated much traffic, unlike the new port facility. Local residents complained to the local authority about the noise and other pollution from the round-the-clock heavy goods vehicle traffic to and from the port. In proceedings against the port authority, the council sought to restrain the passage of the heavy goods vehicles through the neighbourhood at night on the grounds that it constituted a public nuisance.

The court held that the grant of planning permission could alter the character of the area and may have the effect of rendering 'innocent activities which prior to the change would have been an actionable nuisance'. In other words, the question of whether the noise constituted a nuisance had to be considered in the light of the situation *after* planning permission had been granted, a planning permission which in itself changed the character of the area. Central to the court's reasoning was the fact that during the planning permission process the local planning authority was required to

---

105 *Leeman v Montagu* [1936] 2 All ER 1677.
106 *Andreae v Selfridge & Co Ltd* [1938] Ch 1.
107 *East Northamptonshire DC v Fossett* [1994] Env LR 388.
108 *Sturges v Bridgman* (1879) 11 Ch D 852.
109 *Roskell v Whitworth* (1871) 19 WR 804.
110 See also *Rushmer v Polsue and Alfieri Ltd* [1906] Ch 234; [1907] AC 121.
111 *Gillingham BC v Medway (Chatham) Dock Co* [1993] QB 343 [1992] 3 WLR 449 [1993] Env LR 98.

balance the interests of the community against those of individuals and that it would have taken into account concerns relating to noise. On this basis it was held that the noise from the traffic was not an actionable nuisance.

The Gillingham ruling was considered by the Court of Appeal in Wheeler v JJ Saunders Ltd (1995).[112] Here, planning permission was granted for two pig-weaning houses. An action in private nuisance was brought because of the smell generated by the pigs. The defendants in the action sought to rely on the Gillingham case by arguing that the grant of planning permission for the pig houses meant there could not be an actionable nuisance. This argument was rejected by the Court of Appeal, which held that it is wrong to state that any planning decision authorised any nuisance which must inevitably flow from the grant of that permission. As Staughton LJ made clear:

> the court should be slow to acquiesce in the extinction of private rights without compensation as a result of administrative decisions which could not be appealed and were difficult to challenge.

The Court distinguished the Gillingham decision, saying that it could only be applied to a major development which altered the character of the neighbourhood or with wide consequential effects such as required balancing of competing public and private interest before planning permission was granted. In the Wheeler case there had not been a change in the character of the neighbourhood, nor did it appear that the local planning authority had balanced the relevant competing interests. The Wheeler decision was applied in Watson v Croft Promo-Sport Ltd,[113] which concerned an action in nuisance against the operators of the Croft motor racing circuit in County Durham. Planning permission for the circuit had been granted in 1963 and further in 1998, and included a set of monitored noise restrictions for the benefit of those affected by the circuit's use. The claimants were local residents and sought a restraining order to stop the motor racing and also compensation for the past nuisance. The Divisional Court had held that a planning authority had no jurisdiction to authorise a nuisance via the grant of planning permission. On appeal the Court of Appeal affirmed this point, stating that it was well established that the grant of planning permission as such does not affect the private law rights of third parties. The Court of Appeal also confirmed a second well-established principle: that planning permission may alter the nature and character of the locality as to shift the standard of reasonable user which governs the question of nuisance. The issue of whether a planning permission had changed the character of a neighbourhood so as to defeat what would otherwise constitute a claim in nuisance was a question of fact and of degree. On the facts, the Court of Appeal accepted the Divisional Court's conclusion that the essential character of the area had not changed despite the gradual development of the circuit. However, the Court of Appeal also considered that the lower court was wrong not to have granted an injunction restricting the use of the circuit to the level which was the threshold of the nuisance.

Not surprisingly noise from motor racing circuits continues to generate litigation. In 2012 the Court of Appeal was forced once again to consider the relationship between noise and planning permission in Coventry (t/a RDC Promotions) v Lawrence (2012).[114] Coventry (C) operated a stadium and track in Suffolk for various forms of motor sport racing. There was a long planning history for the track and stadium, including a 1975 planning permission for the stadium, various temporary permissions and a certificate of lawful use and finally permanent planning permission for the track in 2002. The track was used for speedway and stock car racing. During the period 1992–2002

112 Wheeler v JJ Saunders Ltd [1996] Ch 19 [1995] 3 WLR 466 [1995] Env LR 286.
113 Watson v Croft Promo-Sport Ltd [2009] EWCA Civ 15; [2009] 3 All ER 249; [2009] 18 EG 86; [2009] JPL 1178.
114 Coventry (t/a RDC Promotions) v Lawrence [2012] EWCA Civ 26; [2012] Env LR 28.

reports from the planning authority showed that the local planning authority had given careful consideration to the differing interests of those who lived in the locality, including the need to protect residents from undue disturbance and also the valuable social function of the facility. In 2006 Lawrence (L) bought a bungalow which was only 560 metres from the stadium; it isn't clear whether he was aware of the motor racing activities. L complained to the district council about the noise from the stadium and track and the council served an abatement notice on C, which C complied with to the satisfaction of the district council. Consequently L bought a private nuisance action seeking damages and an injunction. The High Court granted an injunction limiting the noise that could be generated and awarded damages to L. C appealed on the ground that the judge had failed to take into account that the implementation of the various planning permissions had changed the character of the locality. In addition C also argued that if the noise did constitute a nuisance, L could not pursue their claim as they had moved into an area where nuisance had been present for many years and/or C had had acquired a right by prescription to cause such nuisance. The Court of Appeal followed the decisions discussed above and held that the law could be summarised in four propositions:

(i)   a planning authority by the grant of planning permission could not authorise the commission of a nuisance;

(ii)   nevertheless the grant of planning permission followed by the implementation of such permission might change the character of a locality;

(iii)   it was a question of fact in every case whether the grant of planning permission followed by steps to implement such permission did have the effect of changing the character of the locality; and

(iv)   if the character of a locality was changed as a consequence of planning permission having been granted and implemented, then:

    (a)   the question whether particular activities in that locality constituted a nuisance had to be decided against the background of its changed character; and

    (b)   one consequence might be that otherwise offensive activities in that locality ceased to constitute a nuisance.

On the facts the Court of Appeal held that when L had bought the bungalow, the noise of motor sports emanating from the track and the stadium were an established part of the character of the locality. They could not be left out of account when considering whether the matters complained of constituted a nuisance. Had C conducted their business at noise levels above those permitted by the planning permissions, L might have been able to make out a case in nuisance. However, on the facts this was not the case. The judge's finding of private nuisance had been based upon an error of law and could not stand.

10.10.5 Nature of the noise-generating activity

The nature of the activity that gives rise to the alleged nuisance is a factor which a court should take into account in determining whether the user of land is reasonable. This is clearly demonstrated in *Dennis & Dennis v Ministry for Defence* (2003),[115] in which the Divisional Court examined the public interest argument in the context of a claim against the Ministry of Defence in respect of the excessive noise caused by RAF Harrier jets. D, a husband and wife, owned and lived at an estate adjacent to an RAF air base where Harrier squadrons trained; the jets flew directly (and at very low altitude)

---

115 *Dennis & Dennis v Ministry for Defence* [2003] EWHC 793 (QB); [2003] Env LR 34.

over D's property. The claimants sought a declaration that the noise of the jets constituted a nuisance (it being deafening) and they also sought damages. In addition D also claimed that the noise infringed their human rights under the Human Rights Act 1998.[116] The issue here was the extent to which a court should consider the public utility of the activity that is causing the nuisance. The MOD argued that the flying activity was necessary in the interests of national security. The Divisional Court had no difficulty finding that the noise constituted a nuisance; the Harriers were not an ordinary use of land and the noise levels were extreme. However, the court also recognised that the public interest demanded that the flying activity should continue in order to protect national security. Therefore the rights of the individual had to be subjugated to the greater public interest in this case. However, the court went on to say that although the public interest had to be considered it was not the case that selected individuals (such as D&D) had to bear the cost of the public benefit. It was not proportionate to give effect to the public interest without compensating D.

In respect of noise nuisances the courts have demonstrated some reluctance to interfere with noise arising from construction sites. This reflects the principle that the courts must have regard to the nature and desirability of the operation that is causing the alleged nuisance. In *Andreae v Selfridge & Co Ltd* (1938),[117] the defendant company was developing a site close to the plaintiff's hotel. It was held that if operations of this particular nature are reasonably carried out, and all proper steps are taken to ensure that no undue inconvenience is caused to neighbours, then the neighbours must put up with the noise. However, in *De Keyser's Hotel Ltd v Spicer Bros Ltd and Minter* (1914),[118] it was held that the defendant's building operations constituted a nuisance because they were not carried out in a reasonable and proper manner. The case was brought by the hotel on the grounds that the noise from the construction was so loud that the guests at the hotel and after-dinner speakers were unable to make themselves heard.

It appears that the courts have recognised that building operations cannot happen without generating noise, and that they are usually only short-lived operations where the benefits outweigh the temporary discomforts. Legislation now exists to control the noise from construction sites,[119] although it is still possible to bring a private action in nuisance.

10.10.6 Sensitivity of the claimant

It is well established that for an interference to be actionable, it must be one which affects an ordinary person, and not one who is abnormally sensitive. In *Robinson v Kilvert* (1889),[120] where the plaintiff claimed that heat from the defendant's property which was situated in the basement was having an adverse effect on the brown paper stored in his premises, it was held that there was no actionable nuisance because:

> a man who carries on an exceptionally delicate trade cannot complain because it is injured by his neighbour doing something lawful on his property, if it is something which would not injure anything but an exceptionally delicate trade.

The rationale behind this principle is consistent with the law of nuisance. An example of abnormal sensitivity was given in *Heath v The Brighton Corp* (1908).[121] In this case the vicar of a church sought an injunction to restrain the noise from the defendant's power station. The vicar failed because the

---

116 For a further discussion of noise and human rights see below at 10.10.3.
117 *Andreae v Selfridge & Co Ltd* [1938] Ch 1.
118 *De Keyser's Hotel Ltd v Spicer Bros Ltd and Minter* (1914) 30 TLR 257.
119 Ss 60 and 61 of the COPA 1974.
120 *Robinson v Kilvert* (1884) 41 Ch D 88.
121 *Heath v The Brighton Corp* (1908) 72 JP 225, 98 LT 718.

noise was neither interrupting services nor had it affected attendance at church; it merely irritated the vicar. Therefore, it appears to follow that there can be no regard to a claimant who has, for example, an acute sense of hearing or who suffers from tinnitus.

10.10.7 Intention of the parties

In relation to noise nuisances, the courts have been willing to take into account the malicious intent of the parties. In *Hollywood Silver Fox Farm Ltd v Emmett* (1936),[122] the court granted an injunction to the plaintiff which restrained his neighbour from firing his guns during breeding time. The guns were fired by the defendant in spite, following an argument between the defendant and the plaintiff. Therefore, if the defendant's noise is made with the intention of causing annoyance to his neighbour, he may be liable even if the interference would not amount to a nuisance if done in the ordinary and reasonable use of property. A good example of this occurred in *Christie v Davey* (1893).[123] The defendant's intentional banging of trays on a party wall in retaliation for the noise caused by the neighbour's musical sessions was held to constitute a nuisance.

10.10.8 Nuisance: the relationship with recommended World Health Organisation guidelines

In assessing whether a noise constitutes an actionable nuisance is it appropriate to take into account any recommended noise guidelines? Does noise which exceeds, for example, guidelines suggested by the World Health Organization (WHO) automatically become a nuisance, and vice versa? Clearly, as the discussion above demonstrates, the courts will assess the question of nuisance by considering a range of factors to determine whether the user of land was reasonable or whether it constitutes an unreasonable interference with the enjoyment of land. To what extent can a court take into recommended noise levels in answering these questions?

In *Murdoch and Murdoch v Glacier Metal Co Ltd* (1998)[124] the Court of Appeal considered whether something could constitute an actionable noise nuisance where the noise complained of had reached a level just above that at which, according to a WHO report, the value of sleep could be affected. The Court held that although the noise exceeded the maximum level recommended by the WHO it did not constitute an actionable nuisance per se. It was not necessarily the case that there was a common law nuisance if sleep was disturbed by noise. Although the question of sleep disturbance was an important matter to take into account, it was necessary to consider the overall situation; this includes taking into account the standards of the average person and the character of the neighbourhood when deciding whether the noise was sufficiently serious to amount to a nuisance.

10.10.9 Impact of the Human Rights Act 1998

In any consideration of the law of tort it is now necessary to reflect on the impact of the Human Rights Act (HRA) 1998. As McManus (2005) notes,

> Given the pronounced limitations of the law of nuisance to deal effectively with all forms of noise pollution it is likely that we will witness the provisions of Art 8 of the European Convention on Human Rights (ECHR) and Art 1 of Protocol No 1 to the ECHR (which guarantee respect for

---

122 *Hollywood Silver Fox Farm Ltd v Emmett* [1936] 2 KB 468.
123 *Christie v Davey* [1893] 1 Ch 316.
124 *Murdoch and Murdoch v Glacier Metal Company Limited* [1998] Env LR 732.

family life and home as well as the right to peaceful enjoyment of property and possessions) being more frequently enlisted in relation to various forms of noise pollution as practitioners become more aware of human rights law.[125]

The European Convention on Human Rights does not grant an explicit right to a quiet environment (or a clean one). However it is clear that litigants in noise cases have sought to argue that other rights, notably Art 8.1, have been infringed. Article 8.1 protects the individual's right to respect for his or her private and family life, home and correspondence. However, this right is not absolute; an interference with Art 8 rights can be justified in the in the interests of national security, public safety or the economic well-being of the country, for the prevention of disorder or crime, for the protection of health or morals, or for the protection of the rights and freedoms of others (Art 8.2 ECHR). Herein lies much of the difficulty. In the cases discussed below it becomes clear that the noise generated by aircraft (both civil and military) can cause a very significant deterioration of an individual's rights under Art 8.1, but the courts have accepted that the right, being qualified, must be balanced against the wider public interest in maintaining a viable international airport (see Hatton[126] below) and military capability in the air (see Dennis[127] below).

Since courts are public bodies under the Human Rights Act (HRA) 1998,[128] they are required to act in a way that is compatible with the rights enshrined in the European Convention of Human Rights (ECHR). As a result it is evident that the common law, which is organic and evolving, has felt the impact of this duty. In McKenna v British Aluminium Ltd (2002)[129] a number of claimants brought a claim in nuisance against British Aluminium for noise, emissions and invasions of the privacy of their homes caused by the operation of one of their plants. The difficult issue in this case was that the claimants were children and therefore lacked the property interest required to bring an action in nuisance (see Hunter v Canary Wharf Ltd (1997)[130]). BA argued that accordingly the case should be struck out. However, Neuberger J refused to strike out the action; he held that the application should proceed on the basis that the court should develop the common law so as to be Convention-compliant: 'There is a real possibility of the court concluding that in light of the different landscape, namely Article 8.1 now being effectively part of our law, it is necessary to extend or change the law, even though, in circumstances where the Convention was no part of English Law.'[131]

There have been a number of cases involving noise in which the claimants have raised arguments about infringements of their rights under Art 8.1 of the ECHR. In Powell and Rayner v United Kingdom (1990)[132] the applicants lived in very close proximity to one of the Heathrow Airport's runways. The applicants maintained that, as a result of excessive noise generated by air traffic in and out of Heathrow Airport, they had each been victim of an unjustified interference by the United Kingdom with the right guaranteed to them under Art 8. The applicants argued that the noise levels permitted by air traffic regulations were unacceptable and also that they had no legal redress through the courts because of s 76 of the Civil Aviation Act 1982 which effectively limited the liability of airlines in nuisance if they complied with air traffic regulations. In short the applicants argued that this meant they had no legal redress to deal with the noise nuisance. The European Court of Human Rights (ECtHR) seemed to recognise the adverse effect of the noise on one of the applicants; however the court considered that the Art 8 rights had not been infringed because any

---

125 McManus, F, (2005) 'Noise Pollution and Human Rights' [2005] EHRLR 6, 575–587.
126 Hatton v United Kingdom (2003) 37 EHRR 28.
127 Dennis & Dennis v Ministry of Defence [2003] EWHC 793.
128 S 6 HRA 1998.
129 McKenna v British Aluminium Ltd [2002] Env LR.
130 Hunter v Canary Wharf Ltd [1997] 2 WLR 684; (1995) 139 SJ LB 214.
131 Ibid.
132 Powell and Rayner v United Kingdom (1990) 12 EHRR 355.

potential interference was justified by the state's need to operate an international airport in the wider interest of the community. The issue of noise from Heathrow Airport was raised once again in the case of *Hatton v United Kingdom*.[133] In this case the Grand Chamber of the ECtHR was faced with the question of whether the UK government's policy on night-time flights from Heathrow infringed the applicant's rights under Arts 8 and 13 of the ECHR. The applicants lived near Heathrow Airport. The ECtHR considered that the policy was capable of adversely affecting the quality of the applicants' private life and the scope for their enjoying the amenities of their respective homes, and thus their rights protected by Art 8. The noise disturbances were not caused by the state but were caused by the private flight operators. However, a breach of an individual's ECHR rights may arise from the failure of the state to regulate private industry in a manner securing proper respect for the rights enshrined in Art 8. On the facts, though, the ECtHR concluded that when the government adopted its policy it struck a fair balance between the competing interests of the individuals affected by the night noise and the wider interests of the community. It was in the national economic interest for a state to maintain an international airport. The state enjoyed a wide margin of appreciation in these cases.

The case of *Dennis & Dennis v Ministry of Defence* (2003)[134] has already been referred to earlier. Here the claimants, D & D, were faced with a serious noise problem generated by RAF Harrier jets taking off from a nearby RAF base close to their home/business. The couple alleged that the noise constituted a nuisance (it being deafening and extremely intrusive), infringing their rights under Art 8, and also that it had resulted in a significant diminution in the value of their property. The Divisional Court accepted that the noise was capable of breaching the Art 8 rights of persons living nearby and also constituted a nuisance. However, turning to Art 8.2 the Court also accepted that there was a significant wider public interest that demanded the aircraft should continue to fly. The defence of the realm and the cost and inconvenience of uprooting the military airbase meant that D's private rights were subjugated to the public interest. However, the Court also went on to say that whilst the public interest demanded the continuation of the flying, selected individuals were not to bear the cost of the public benefit. It was not proportionate that a small number of individuals had to tolerate the nuisance in the wider public interest. Therefore the claimants were entitled, exceptionally, to damages of £950,000 to cover capital loss, loss of amenity and loss of commercial opportunities caused by the nuisance.

See also *Andrews v Reading BC*,[135] in which the he Divisional Court, following *Hatton*[136] and *Dennis*,[137] concluded that Art 8 could be invoked in noise cases but the question of whether it did so was a question of fact. (The case concerned noise from traffic.) The Court stated that it was up to the claimant to prove that the noise interfered with his Art 8 rights and for the defendant to prove the justification under Art 8.2.

10.10.10 Remedies

The main remedies available in private nuisance actions are:

(a) abatement;
(b) injunction;
(c) damages.

---

133 *Hatton v United Kingdom* (2003) 37 EHRR 28.
134 *Dennis & Dennis v Ministry of Defence* [2003] EWHC 793.
135 *Andrews v Reading BC* [2005] EWHC 256 (QB); [2006] RVR 56.
136 *Hatton v United Kingdom* (2003) 37 EHRR 28.
137 *Dennis & Dennis v Ministry of Defence* [2003] EWHC 793.

The advantage of common law actions, despite the problems noted, is that they enable claimants to seek damages. If the intention of the claimant is to bring an end to the noise problem, a swifter and cheaper remedy is to ask a local authority to commence proceedings under the statutory nuisance provisions of the EPA 1990.[138]

See Chapters
◀ 9 and 11

10.10.11 Limits of nuisance: the requirement to have a legal interest in land

There are several problems in bringing an action in private nuisance and traditionally it has been necessary to demonstrate that the claimant has an interest in land. The House of Lords reaffirmed that a complainant must have an interest in land in *Hunter v Canary Wharf Ltd* (1997).[139]

The creator of the relevant nuisance is the person who is liable and, unlike the claimant, does not need to have a proprietary interest in land where the nuisance arises. The occupier of the property from which the nuisance emanates will normally also be liable, although usually the creator of the nuisance and the occupier will be the same person.[140] A landlord will only be liable for any nuisance which emanates from premises where such a state of affairs is the ordinary and necessary consequences of granting the lease.[141]

10.10.12 Public nuisance

A public nuisance is defined as an unlawful act or omission which materially affects the reasonable comfort and convenience of a class of Her Majesty's subjects who come within the sphere or neighbourhood of its operation. Unlike private nuisance, there is no need to prove any interest in land. In *AG v PYA Quarries Ltd* (1957),[142] it was held that it is a question of fact whether a large enough group of people have been affected for the nuisance to be called public.

A public nuisance is both a tort and a criminal offence and the case is brought by the Attorney General (or an individual with the consent of the Attorney General and in his name), who may also seek an injunction to prevent a public nuisance.

Law in Action

In *R v Conrad Ryder-Large & John Castrillion* (2008)[143] both defendants were charged with causing public nuisance by organising a 'rave' (a large outdoor party, with about 200 people and live music playing from a music system powered by a generator). The music could be heard up to four miles away and the police had received about 39 complaints from the public. At 4.00 am the police asked the defendants to turn the music down but they refused. The police eventually switched the generator off at 5.00 am (which was later hotwired and repowered). Both defendants were arrested for causing a public nuisance.

Both initially argued before the Crown Court that it was an abuse of process to charge them with the common law offence of public nuisance, that they should have been charged

---

138 For further discussion of the statutory nuisance regime see Chapter 9; for further discussion of the common law remedies see Chapter 11.
139 *Hunter v Canary Wharf Ltd* [1997] 2 WLR 684; (1995) 139 SJ LB 214.
140 See *Sedleigh-Denfield v O'Callaghan* [1940] AC 880; [1940] 3 All ER 349.
141 See *Tetley v Chitty* [1986] 1 All ER 663; (1985) 135 NLJ 1009.
142 *AG v PYA Quarries Ltd* [1957] 2 QB 169; [1957] 1 All ER 894; [1957] 2 WLR 770.
143 *R v Conrad Ryder-Large and John Castrillion* [2008] EWCA Crim 2966.

with offences under statute, but the court rejected this argument and convicted. On appeal, however, the first defendant (R-L) did not challenge this point, because he accepted that there was no statutory offence for which they could be charged. He could not be charged under Part III EPA 1990 because it was first necessary to serve an abatement notice before criminal proceedings could be brought. He could not be charged under s 63 Criminal Justice Act 1994 because he was an occupier of the land. The second defendant (C) argued this point before the Court of Appeal; however, the Court concluded that s 63 provides a power to the police that is additional to common law offences of causing a nuisance.

The defendants, however, did appeal their convictions and sentences. The first defendant was given a three-month sentence suspended for two years and made the subject of a prohibited activity requirement for two years. The second defendant was fined £2,000 with 28 days' imprisonment in default of payment. The Court of Appeal upheld both conviction and sentence; the suspended custodial sentence for RL was appropriate given his attitude and his lack of recognition of the disturbance he had caused.

For a private claimant to seek damages in a case of public nuisance, he or she must prove that he or she has suffered some special damage over and above that suffered by the general public. It is not necessary for the claimant to have an interest in land. Damages may be available to compensate for personal injury and for economic loss from the responsible party. As in private nuisance, an action may be brought against the creator of the nuisance, the occupier of premises and/or the landlord. In relation to noise problems, public nuisance actions are relatively rare.

10.11 Noise as a statutory nuisance

See Chapter 9 →

The provisions in the EPA 1990 relating to noise nuisances were amended by the Noise and Statutory Nuisance Act (NSNA) 1993 and also the Clean Neighbourhoods and Environment Act (CNEA) 2005. The majority of the new provisions came into force in January 1994. In particular, the NSNA 1993 incorporated a new noise statutory nuisance into the EPA 1990 at s 79(1)(ga). The following section focuses exclusively on the two noise statutory nuisances contained in s 79(1)(g) and (ga).

10.11.1 Section 79(1)(g) and (ga) of the EPA 1990

Sections 79(1)(g) and (ga) of the EPA 1990 provide that noise can be a statutory nuisance in the following circumstances:

(a) Section 79(1)(g): 'noise emitted from premises so as to be prejudicial to health or a nuisance'; and

(b) Section 79(1)(ga): 'noise that is prejudicial to health or a nuisance and is emitted from or caused by a vehicle, machinery or equipment in a street'.

The EPA 1990 does not provide any particular definition of noise other than to say in s 79 that it includes 'vibration'. Although the two statutory nuisances noted above refer specifically to noise, the more general statutory nuisance listed in s 79(1)(a)—'Any premises in such a state as to be prejudicial to health or a nuisance'—has also been utilised in some noise cases. This particular limb of statutory nuisance will therefore be considered briefly below.

10.11.2 Prejudicial to health or a nuisance?

Before considering the noise statutory nuisances in any detail, it is necessary to consider the general provisions relating to statutory nuisance. Although s 79 of the EPA 1990 lists certain states of affairs that may constitute statutory nuisances, they will only be statutory nuisances if they are either prejudicial to health or a nuisance. The definition includes two separate and alternative limbs and it is not necessary to show that a matter is both a nuisance and prejudicial to health. This was affirmed in *Betts v Penge UDC* (1942).[144]

10.11.2.1 Prejudicial to health

Section 79(7) of the EPA 1990 defines 'prejudicial to health' as meaning 'injurious, or likely to cause injury'. This definition includes two limbs, 'injurious to health', that is, actual harm, or 'likely to cause injury', that is, anticipated harm. The definition is the same as that given in the Public Health Act 1936. However, in the context of noise nuisance it was held in *Southwark LBC v Ince* (1989)[145] that a house which was inadequately insulated against noise, so that noise from a nearby railway adversely affected the occupants, was prejudicial to health.[146]

See Chapter 9

10.11.2.2 What is meant by nuisance?

The courts have equated nuisance in this context with common law nuisance, private or public, with the focus primarily on private nuisance, therefore involving interference with enjoyment of property. In *National Coal Board v Neath BC* (1976),[147] it was held that the word 'nuisance' meant either a public or a private nuisance at common law. It should also be noted that, like the common law nuisance, the interference must be with *neighbouring* property.[148]

In *Godfrey v Conwy County BC* (2000),[149] in a case stated appeal, the Divisional Court held that noise can constitute a statutory nuisance even if it does not exceed background noise in the locality if it is of a character which makes it intrusive and irritating. It is not necessary for the noise to be prejudicial to health; it is sufficient that it merely interferes with another's quiet enjoyment of his or her property. In this case, G had converted a barn in a quiet rural area for use as a music studio where rock bands practised. On investigation, the Environmental Health Officer was clearly able to hear the noise and accepted the complaints made, but she was unable to take a recording of the noise satisfactorily because of the interference of background noise caused by haymaking in the adjacent field. G argued that the noise from his recording studio was no higher than the background noise and that, in the absence of a decibel reading, the noise could not be prejudicial to health.

10.11.3 Premises in such a state as to be prejudicial to health or a nuisance

At first glance this particular limb of statutory nuisance may not appear to be of any assistance in the context of a noise complaint and indeed that now appears to be the case following the decision of the Divisional Court in *Vella v Lambeth LBC*.[150] However, it was used successfully in *Southwark London BC v Ince* (1989).[151] Here, council house tenants had successfully complained to the

---

144 *Betts v Penge UDC* [1942] 2 All ER 61.
145 *Southwark LBC v Ince* (1989) 21 HLR 504.
146 See also *R (on the application of Wakie) v Haringey Magistrates' Court* [2003] EWHC 2217 (Admin).
147 *National Coal Board v Neath BC* [1976] 2 All ER 478.
148 *National Coal Board v Thorne* [1976] 1 WLR 543.
149 *Godfrey v Conwy CBC* [2000] All ER (D) 1809 G; [2001] Env LR 38.
150 *Vella v Lambeth LBC* [2005] EWHC 2473 (Admin); [2006] Env LR 33.
151 *Southwark LBC v Ince* [1989] COD 549.

magistrates for an order against the council; their complaint was that the noise and vibration from the road and rail traffic running near the building in which they lived was so bad that it was prejudicial to their health. The magistrates found that when the flats had been converted, no adequate sound insulation measures had been taken by the local authority, as a result of which the flats suffered from severe noise penetration which was capable of causing and had in fact caused injury to the health of the tenants. They made an order requiring the authority to sound-insulate the building and the council appealed. The Divisional Court held that the question was not whether the noise was itself a statutory nuisance but whether the premises were in such a state as to be prejudicial to health, and that the magistrates were justified in deciding that a house which was inadequately insulated against external noise was prejudicial to the health of the occupants.

However, in *Vella v Lambeth LBC*[152] the Divisional Court held that the argument that a lack of adequate sound insulation can cause premises to be in such a state as to be prejudicial to health for the purposes of s 79(1)(a) is no longer sustainable following the decisions of the Court of Appeal in *Everett*[153] and the House of Lords in *Oakley*.[154] Both these cases concerned this limb of statutory nuisance but they were not cases about noise. In interpreting this limb of statutory nuisance, Lord Hoffman in *Oakley*, recalling the public health origins of the provision, emphasised that the section contemplates a case in which the premises as they stand present a threat to the health of the occupiers or neighbours which requires summary removal. Therefore the Divisional Court in *Vella* concluded that 'If the words used in s 79(1)(a) can be given no wider meaning than that which has attached to the same words since the enactment of the "sanitary statutes" of the mid-nineteenth century, there can be no room for holding that a lack of sound insulation sufficient to comply with current standards renders premises in such a state as to be prejudicial to health.'[155]

The case is also interesting because Poole J considered that it was not appropriate to use this section of the EPA 1990 to deal with noise cases when Parliament had provided for a separate statutory code under which local authorities have express powers under s 79(g) to deal with noise nuisances. Additionally he considered that 'The immense financial burden that would be imposed on social and private landlords if the court were, by the statutory nuisance route, to require the immediate upgrading of properties generally to a standard of sound insulation not required when they were constructed or adapted, is also very real' and that this is a matter of housing management, not environmental health.

10.11.4 Noise from premises—s 79(1)(g)

Like all of the statutory nuisances in s 79 of the EPA 1990, noise from premises may only constitute a statutory nuisance if it is either:

(a)   noise emitted from premises so as to be *prejudicial to health*; or
(b)   noise emitted from premises so as to be a *nuisance*.

This particular statutory nuisance was not included in the Public Health Act 1936 but was drawn from ss 57–59 of the COPA 1974. The term 'premises' was not defined in the COPA 1974. In *Tower Hamlets LBC v Manzoni and Walder* (1984),[156] brought under s 58 COPA, the court held that the term 'premises' did not include a street and therefore noise from a street could not be controlled under

---

152   *Vella v Lambeth LBC* [2005] EWHC 2473 (Admin); [2006] Env LR 33.
153   *R v Bristol City Council ex p Everett* [1999] 1 WLR 1170; [1999] Env LR 587.
154   *Oakley v Birmingham City Council* [2001] 1 AC 617 [2000] 3 WLR 1936 [2001] Env LR 37.
155   *Vella v Lambeth LBC* [2005] EWHC 2473 (Admin); [2006] Env LR 33, Poole, J at para 69.
156   *Tower Hamlets LBC v Manzoni and Walder* [1984] JPL 436.

the statutory nuisance provisions of the COPA 1974.[157] However, the EPA has rectified this by providing a definition of 'premises' as including land. It remains unclear whether this definition encompasses a street.

When called to investigate a complaint concerning noise from premises the Environmental Health Officer (EHO) will need to assess whether the noise is either prejudicial to health or a nuisance; it need not be both. As the Court noted in *Vella*,[158] if the 'lower level of the test for common law nuisance failed to be satisfied it was difficult to foresee how the higher hurdle of prejudice to health could be cleared'.[159] Therefore in practice, and unless there is clear prejudice to health, an EHO will be best advised to consider first whether the noise constitutes a nuisance at common law. Therefore, he should consider the following factors:

(a) the duration and time of the noise;
(b) the nature of the activity giving rise to the noise;
(c) the harm suffered by the person affected;
(d) the neighbourhood where the noise took place.

As the statistics discussed above (at 10.9) show, the vast majority of complaints do not result in the use of formal statutory nuisance proceedings, let alone litigation. However, the following cases provide some examples of statutory nuisance under the s 79(1)(g) limb of the EPA 1990.

Law in Action

In *R (London Borough of Hackney) v Moshe Rottenberg* (2007)[160] Rabbi Rottenberg was served with an abatement notice in respect of noise generated from a dwelling house that was used as a school and synagogue. The investigating environmental health officers concluded that the noise levels amounted to a nuisance. The noise consisted of shouting, chanting, jumping on internal floors and clapping. On appeal against the abatement notice the Rabbi argued, inter alia, that the noise did not amount to a nuisance. The local authority argued that their EHOs are professional, experienced and independent people, that they had heard the noise themselves on the occasions of their visits, and that the court must accept their evidence or give sufficient reason for rejecting it. The Divisional Court, however, held that the court was entitled to reject the opinion of the officers; on the facts the court considered that there was insufficient evidence that the noise intrusion was sufficient to cause a nuisance rather than an irritation.

It also means that, in practice, the EHO who is usually responsible for exercising the local authority's statutory nuisance functions will need to make a similar determination.

10.11.5 Noise in a street which is emitted from a vehicle, machinery or equipment—s 79(1)(ga)

This particular statutory nuisance was incorporated into s 79 EPA 1990 by the NSNA 1993. The amendment was made largely because the EPA 1990 did not provide sufficient protection from

---

157 The case concerned noise made by animal rights protesters using megaphones in the street.
158 *Vella v Lambeth LBC* [2005] EWHC 2473 (Admin); [2006] Env LR 33.
159 Ibid at para 41.
160 *R (London Borough of Hackney) v Moshe Rottenberg* [2007] EWHC 166 (Admin); [2007] Env LR 24; [2008] JPL 177.

noise in the streets. A street is defined as a 'highway and any other road, footway, square or court that is for the time being open to the public'. It is clear that a great deal of noise is generated in streets not only from vehicles but from ice cream vans, people playing loud music and of course the interminable sounds of car alarms going off. Not all street noises are covered. Certain exceptions are provided: it does not apply to noise created by traffic, the armed forces or by political demonstrations (or demonstrations supporting or opposing a campaign or cause). Traffic is understood to mean vehicles in motion.

In *Haringey LBC v Jowett* (2000),[161] in a case concerning a complaint by a council house tenant about the noise from traffic caused by poor sound insulation of his property, the court found that although the lack of sound insulation meant that the premises were a potential source of injury to Jowett's health, the authority was not responsible for the statutory nuisance in respect of the traffic noises, the reasoning being that the restriction on traffic under s 79(1)(ga) was limited by s 79(6A) of the 1990 Act,[162] thereby precluding traffic noise.

Section 79(1)(ga) only refers to street noises emitted from vehicles, machinery or equipment. The question remains about the position of noise which emanates from the street but is not emitted from any of these particular sources.

10.11.6 Responsibility of the local authorities

Section 79(1) of the EPA 1990 places all district councils and London borough councils under a duty to inspect their area from time to time to detect any statutory nuisance which ought to be dealt with under ss 80 and 80A of the EPA 1990. They are also under a duty to take such steps as are reasonably practicable to investigate complaints about statutory nuisances made by people living in the area. The duty is therefore twofold. The local authority has to carry out its own checks and has to respond to complaints. In practice, it is usually the environmental health departments and officers that are responsible for enforcing this legislation and they will carry out the inspections and deal with the complaints. In some areas, particularly the large cities, some local authorities have night patrols which are concerned primarily with noise control. This means that the degree of attention that a council pays to a complaint may vary depending on locality and the level of resources that the local authority makes available for this service.

Some local authorities may operate their own internal policies; for example they may have discretion not to respond to certain noise complaints unless they receive more than one complaint. Some local authorities operate a policy of first sending a warning letter to the person they have received the complaint against:

(a) *Duty to inspect*. The duty to inspect and detect statutory nuisances is tempered by the requirement that these inspections only have to be carried out from time to time. One of the problems here is that the expression 'from time to time' is not defined by the EPA 1990, thus making the obligation very imprecise.

(b) *Duty to respond to complaints*. This duty to respond to complaints was established by the EPA 1990. Prior to its introduction, local authorities were not actually required to respond to complaints made although, in practice, complainants provided useful information about the occurrences of statutory nuisances within the local authority area. The duty to respond to complaints made by people living in the area is qualified by the fact that the authority only has to take such steps as are reasonably practicable to investigate the complaint. Again, this expression is

---

161 *Haringey LBC v Jowett* (2000) 32 HLR 308 (1999) 78 P & CR D24.
162 As amended by s 2 of the NSNA 1993.

not defined and could potentially cause problems. Local authorities are increasingly finding that they are facing severe financial problems. Whether the authority can take into account its own financial situation in determining what is reasonably practicable is not clear. However, if the Secretary of State finds that a local authority is in default of these duties, he can, by virtue of Sched 3 EPA 1990, transfer the function to himself.

(c) *Local authorities' investigative powers.* In order to carry out their functions of inspection and investigation, local authority environmental officers can enter any land with the people and equipment that they consider necessary. The officers can also carry out any inspections, measurements and tests and can also take away samples and articles. These powers are provided by Sched 3 to the EPA 1990. The purpose of the inspection and investigation is to establish whether or not there is a statutory nuisance (or whether one is likely to occur) and to gather any evidence which may be needed in subsequent court proceedings. The general position is that once a local authority environmental officer is satisfied that a statutory nuisance is occurring or is likely to occur, an abatement notice must be served on the person responsible for the nuisance.[163] However, in relation to the noise nuisances the position is different in that it is possible for the local authority to take alternative steps to try to bring the nuisance to an end (see 10.11.7).

(d) *Determining whether a statutory nuisance exists.* In practice, the local authority environmental health officer will make an initial determination whether the matter complained of constitutes a statutory nuisance on the basis of it being prejudicial to health or a nuisance. He or she will therefore be required to take into account the nature of the neighbourhood and also whether the matter complained of amounts to a nuisance in common law or is just (as sometimes happens) a vexatious complaint. As with the common law, this makes it very difficult to predict whether or not a noise will amount to an actionable statutory nuisance. An EHO may have to make a number of visits to determine whether a nuisance exists, particularly in relation to noise nuisances which by their very nature are often sporadic. Complainants are well advised to keep a written record of the times and frequency that noise disturbances take place and also, where possible, to get third parties to witness the disturbances for evidential purposes. In relation specifically to noise complaints, the EHO may take noise measurements where this is possible; however, there is absolutely no requirement to do this under Part III EPA 1990.

10.11.7 The duty to serve an abatement notice or to take steps to persuade

Once it has been determined that a statutory nuisance exists or is likely to occur, an abatement notice must be served on the person responsible. Section 80 of the EPA 1990 provides that an authority must serve an abatement notice when it is satisfied that, in its area, a statutory nuisance:

(a) exists;
(b) is likely to occur; or
(c) is likely to recur.

However, this provision was amended by the Clean Neighbourhoods and Environment Act 2005 specifically in relation to noise nuisances falling under s 79(g). Section 80(2A) states that where a local authority is satisfied that a statutory nuisance falling within s 79(1)(g) exists, or is likely to

---

163 See *Carrick DC ex p Shelley* [1996] Env LR 273; [1996] JPL 857.

occur or recur, the authority has a choice. It must either serve an abatement notice or it can 'take such other steps as it thinks appropriate for the purpose of persuading the appropriate person to abate the nuisance or prohibit or restrict its occurrence or recurrence'. This is an interesting innovation and reflects a willingness to allow local authorities to exercise a more pragmatic and flexible response to noise nuisances. For example, if an EHO receives a complaint from a resident about noise from his neighbour's house and the EHO is satisfied it constitutes a statutory nuisance, it will invariably be enough for the EHO to speak to the neighbour, explain the situation and ask them to reduce the noise; all without resort to an abatement notice, which is formal and takes time to draft. However, if an EHO does prefer this informal means of resolution he will still be required to serve an abatement notice if:

(a)   the authority is satisfied that it will not be able to persuade the appropriate person to abate the nuisance within seven days;[164] or

(b)   the authority is satisfied that at the end of the seven days the nuisance continues to exist, or continues to be likely to occur or recur.

The appropriate person is either the person who is responsible for the nuisance (for example, the person playing the drums or controlling the audio equipment), or, where the person responsible cannot be found, or the nuisance hasn't yet occurred, the owner or occupier. In practice the person responsible is highly likely to be the owner or occupier.

It should be apparent from the discussion immediately above that the authority can take preventive action in order to stop a statutory nuisance from occurring. The requirement to serve the abatement notice (or taking persuasive steps) is mandatory. However, s 80 does not say anything about the need for the likely occurrence to be imminent. It is enough that it is likely to occur. Also, when one considers that the concept of 'prejudicial to health' also extends to 'likely to cause injury', the local authority must serve an abatement notice, if it believes that circumstances exist which make injury likely.

10.11.8 Abatement notices in respect of noise in the street

With regard to statutory nuisances falling within s 79(10)(g)(a), the relevant provisions relating to abatement notices are contained in s 80A, which modifies the procedures relating to the service of abatement notices. In circumstances where the noise is caused by or emitted from an unattended vehicle or unattended machinery or equipment the abatement notice must be served on:

(a)   the person responsible for the vehicle, machinery or equipment;[165] or

(b)   if that person cannot be found then the authority can fix the notice to the vehicle, machine or equipment. However, if the person can be found within one hour of this, the notice must also be served on the person. Any person who removes or interferes with a notice fixed to a vehicle, machine or equipment commits a criminal offence.[166]

This also applies in circumstances where the statutory nuisance has not yet occurred (but the authority must be satisfied that it is likely to occur).

---

164 From the day on which the authority was satisfied that there was a statutory nuisance.
165 Where they can be found; this is likely to be the driver or the machine operator.
166 Unless he is the person responsible or he has been authorised by the person responsible

10.11.9 The form of the notice

Although there is no prescribed form for an abatement notice, it must nevertheless state the following in a manner which is clear and understandable to the recipient:

(a)   the nature of the statutory nuisance;
(b)   the action or works required to abate it;
(c)   time limits for compliance;
(d)   the rights of appeal to the magistrates' court.

The abatement notice can impose a variety of conditions, including:

(a)   conditions requiring the abatement of the nuisance or prohibiting or restricting its occurrence or recurrence;[167]
(b)   conditions requiring the execution of such works, and the taking of such other steps, as may be necessary for any of these purposes.[168]

10.11.9.1 How prescriptive must the notice be?

There has been a significant amount of litigation relating to the abatement notices; particularly on the extent to which a local authority should be required to specify what works or steps are required. Suffice to say that local authorities have considerable discretion in framing abatement notices; they can simply require the abatement of the nuisance. However, the authority can, if it wishes, decide to specify the steps or works that need to be undertaken by the recipient of the notice. If the authority elects to do this, the notice must be sufficiently certain.

See Chapter ◀ **9**

   The following section will look almost exclusively at cases which concern noise nuisances under s 79(1)(g) and (ga).

   In R v Fenny Stratford JJ ex p Watney Mann (1976),[169] three residents were disturbed by the noise from a jukebox in a local public house. Proceedings were brought under s 99 of the Public Health Act 1936 against the company that owned the pub and the local magistrates' court issued a nuisance order which stated that the 'nuisance should be abated' and 'the level of noise in the premises should not exceed 70 decibels'. Watney Mann applied for judicial review, arguing that the terms of the notice were not clear. The Divisional Court quashed the notice on the grounds that it was void for reasons of uncertainty, in that:

(a)   it did not state where the noise meter should be positioned; and
(b)   the magistrates had failed to consider the likelihood and relevance of other sources of noise such as general conversation.

However, in two later cases, the courts appeared to take a more lenient attitude towards this issue. In East Northamptonshire DC v Fossett (1994),[170] F was served with an abatement notice which required F to control all activities, including musical ones, so as not to cause a nuisance. The district council had served the notice because it was aware that an all-night rave was to take place at F's club. The rave took place and the noise could be heard within one mile of the club. F was prosecuted for breach of the notice. The magistrates held that the noise levels amounted to a nuisance, but stated that the abatement notice was void on the grounds of imprecision and uncertainty. The district

167 S 80(1)(a) EPA 1990.
168 S 80(1)(b) EPA 1990.
169 R v Fenny Stratford JJ ex p Watney Mann [1976] 1 WLR 1101; [1976] 2 All ER 888.
170 East Northamptonshire DC v Fossett [1994] Env LR 388.

council appealed by way of case stated. In response F argued, following *Watney Mann*,[171] that a decibel level should have been set by the notice. The Divisional Court distinguished that case as one on a recurrence of a nuisance. In *Fossett*, the Divisional Court held that since the notice was served to prevent a likely nuisance, the district council would have had to speculate unnecessarily if they had tried to set a decibel level and, on the facts, the district council had been forced to act quickly. F further argued that the notice was uncertain and he could not possibly know what an acceptable level of sound should be since the notice had failed to set one down. The Divisional Court rejected these arguments.

In a further case, *Myatt v Teignbridge DC* (1994),[172] M kept 17 dogs. The district council served an abatement notice on her which required her to 'cease the keeping of dogs'. A further notice was served which stated that she had to 'reduce the number of dogs kept at the premises to no more than two and to take such steps as are necessary in the housing, welfare and management of the dogs to ensure they do not cause a nuisance'. M failed to comply with either notice and was prosecuted by the district council. She appealed by way of case stated. The Divisional Court held that the issue was whether or not the recipient of the notice knows what is wrong from the notice. On the facts, the court held that M must have known what the cause of complaint was and, although the notice could have been drawn up more carefully, it was sufficient to make clear to the recipient what was wrong. However, a court will quash a notice if it considers that it is too vague and uncertain as it did in *Lambie v Thanet DC* (2001).[173] Here the Divisional Court held that a requirement in an abatement notice that 'amplified music and raised voices were not intrusive in nearby or adjoining properties' was too vague and too uncertain. However, in this same case the abatement notice required L to allow the authority to set up a sound-restricting device on his premises. The Divisional Court held that the local authority's power under s 80(1)(b) was a wide one and could legitimately include a requirement to allow an officer to enter premises so as to install such a device.

Law in Action

In *Sevenoaks DC v Brands Hatch Leisure Group Ltd* (2001)[174] BH was served an abatement notice which required them to abate the nuisance (the noise from squealing tyres at the motor racing circuit) and 'to take steps necessary for the purposes of prohibiting the recurrence of the said nuisance as are specified in the schedule attached hereto'. This schedule specified maximum decibel levels but it did not specify how BH was to achieve these levels and BH appealed on the grounds that the notice was invalid because it failed to adequately specify the steps or works that were required. The Divisional Court held that it was inherent in every abatement notice that some action would be required, and the local authority was only required to specify works or steps where the method for achieving abatement was specified. The court went on to say that in a noise case it might be important for the authority to spell out what level of noise it would find acceptable and how sound measurements should be taken (as it had done here). Although the words 'steps' had been used in the notice, such steps were not set out and particular steps were not expressly or impliedly identified. The court upheld the validity of the notice.

171 *R v Fenny Stratford JJ ex p Watney Mann* [1976] 1 WLR 1101; [1976] 2 All ER 888.
172 *Myatt v Teignbridge DC* [1994] Env LR D 18.
173 *Lambie v Thanet DC* [2001] Env LR 21; [2001] EHLR 3.
174 *Sevenoaks DC v Brands Hatch Leisure Group Ltd* [2001] [2001] Env LR 5; [2001] EHLR 7.

See further the discussion of R (*On the application of Elvington Park Ltd*) *v York Crown Court* (2011)[175] in Chapter 9.

See Chapter 9

There is no need to specify a time limit when prohibiting the recurrence of a nuisance. In R v *Birmingham City Justices ex p Guppy* (1988),[176] the city council served an abatement notice on G, who was having a noisy party. The notice imposed the three following requirements:

(a)   to prohibit the noise amounting to a nuisance;
(b)   immediately to cease permitting the use of the sound equipment to produce a noise so as to be a nuisance; and
(c)   to take all other steps as may be necessary for that purpose.

Two months later, the noise nuisance recurred on three successive nights and G was convicted of three offences of non-compliance with the notice. G sought judicial review of the convictions specifically on the grounds that the prohibition of recurrence in the notice was invalid since no time limit for compliance was specified. The Divisional Court held that it is necessary for a notice to include a time limit for compliance where it requires the abatement of a nuisance or the execution of works, but not where it prohibits the recurrence of a nuisance. The decision in *Guppy* was applied in R v *Tunbridge Wells Justices ex p Tunbridge Wells BC* (1996).[177]

10.11.10 On whom must the notice be served?

The provisions regarding the serving of abatement notices are contained in s 80 of the EPA 1990. Normally the local authority is required to serve the notice on the person responsible for the nuisance.[178] Where the nuisance arises from any defect in the structural character of a building, the abatement notice should be served on the owner of the premises. In circumstances where the person responsible for the nuisance cannot be found, or the nuisance has not yet occurred, the notice must be served on the owner or occupier of the premises.

In relation to vehicles, machinery or equipment, the person responsible will be the driver or operator. In circumstances where the noise nuisance has not occurred or arises from an unattended vehicle, machinery or equipment, the abatement notice should be served on the person responsible for the vehicle. If that person cannot be found, the abatement notice can be affixed to the vehicle following a determination of the authority to that effect. This particular provision was introduced by the NSNA 1993 and is now contained in s 80(A) of the EPA 1990.

The abatement notice must specify the time for compliance. With noise nuisances, that may be immediately. Non-compliance with an abatement notice without reasonable excuse is a criminal offence.

The person responsible for the nuisance is defined in s 79(7) of the EPA 1990 as the person to whose:

(a)   act;
(b)   default; or
(c)   sufferance,

the nuisance is attributable.

This is a wide definition and could include not only the person who created the noise nuisance,

---

175 R (*On the application of Elvington Park Ltd*) *v York Crown Court* [2011] EWHC 2213 (Admin); [2012] Env LR 10.
176 R v *Birmingham City Justices ex p Guppy* (1988) 152 JP 159.
177 R v *Tunbridge Wells Justices ex p Tunbridge Wells BC* [1996] Env LR 88.
178 See the discussion in Chapter 9 of R (*on the application of Khan*) *v Isleworth Crown Court* [2011] EWHC 3164 (Admin); [2012] Env LR 12.

but also a third person/party who failed to take any appropriate preventive or corrective action where they had some legal requirement to do so. It can also include third persons who on becoming aware of the problem took no steps to remedy the situation. This was confirmed in the case of *Clayton v Sale UDC* (1926),[179] where an owner was held liable for a statutory nuisance on his land consequent upon the activities or defaults of another.

In *Network Housing Association Ltd v Westminster CC* (1995),[180] an abatement notice was served on a housing association landlord in respect of noise under s 79(1)(e) of the EPA 1990 (noise emitted from premises) following a complaint from a tenant to the city council. The complainant claimed he was being disturbed by the ordinary residential use of the flat above. The notice required the housing association to carry out alterations to the flat to reduce the noise levels to a prescribed decibel level. The court found that the noise in question was the noise of everyday living and it was the lack of sound insulation between his and a neighbour's flat that constituted it a nuisance. The housing association argued that there was no act on its part, nor indeed any default or sufferance, since it had no knowledge of the nuisance when it acquired the premises. However, the court rejected these arguments and held that the landlord was the person responsible. The housing association had allowed the nuisance to continue after it had come to its attention in 1991. However, on appeal to the Divisional Court, it was held that the abatement notice did not specify the type of works to be carried out and was void because of lack of certainty.

10.11.11 Appeals against an abatement notice

A person who is served an abatement notice is entitled to appeal against it by making a complaint to the magistrates' court.[181] He or she must be informed of this right in the abatement notice. Where a person decides to lodge an appeal, they must do so within 21 days from the day when the abatement notice was served. The grounds for appeal are not laid down in the EPA 1990, but are provided in the Statutory Nuisance (Appeals) Regulations 1995.[182]

The grounds are as follows:

(a)　the abatement notice is not justified by s 80 of the EPA 1990. In other words, the appellant argues that the matter did not constitute a statutory nuisance;

(b)　the abatement notice contains some informality, is defective or contains an error;

(c)　the authority has unreasonably refused to accept compliance with alternative requirements, or the requirements laid down in the abatement notice are unreasonable or unnecessary;

(d)　the period for compliance in the notice is not reasonably sufficient;

(e)　there has been an error in the service of the notice; for example the notice has been served on the wrong person. An appeal may also be made if the appellant argues that it is 'equitable' for the notice to be served on some other person either instead of the appellant or in addition to the appellant. Whether the wrong person has been served will be determined by reference to s 80(2). In relation to noise nuisances, an appeal may be brought on the grounds that the notice should have been served on the person responsible for the vehicle, machinery or equipment instead of the appellant;

(f)　the best practicable means (BPM) were used to counteract the effect of a nuisance from trade or business premises.

---

179 *Clayton v Sale UDC* [1926] 1 KB 415.
180 *Network Housing Association Ltd v Westminster CC* [1995] Env LR 176.
181 S 80(3) EPA 1990.
182 Statutory Nuisance (Appeals) Regulations 1995 SI 1995/2644.

As far as the noise nuisance contained in ss 79(1)(g) and (ga) of the EPA 1990 is concerned, there is an additional ground of appeal, namely that the requirements imposed by the abatement notice are more onerous than the requirements which may have been determined by means of other noise controls under the COPA 1974 or the NSNA 1993 (such as consents relating to construction sites and loudspeakers).

The magistrates' courts have wide powers when dealing with appeals against abatement notices. They can:

(a)   correct any procedural defect in the notice, quash the notice or vary the notice;

(b)   dismiss the appeal;

(c)   make such order as they think fit regarding:

  (i)   any works which need to be carried out and the contribution to be made by any person to the cost of the work; or

  (ii)   the proportion of expenses that a local authority may recover from the appellant and from any other person.

10.11.11.1 Effect of an appeal upon an abatement notice

In general, the lodging of an appeal will not suspend the operation of an abatement notice and therefore the person served with a notice will still be required to comply with the conditions of the notice. However, this general provision does not apply in circumstances where:

(a)   the abatement notice requires expenditure on works and the expenditure required would be out of proportion to the expected public benefit; or

(b)   in the case of a nuisance under s 79(1)(g) or (ga), the noise to which the abatement notice relates is noise necessarily caused in the course of the performance of some duty imposed by law on the appellant.

10.12 Failure to comply with an abatement notice

Section 80(4) of the EPA 1990 establishes that it is an offence for a person served with an abatement notice either to contravene or fail to comply with any requirement or prohibition imposed by the notice, without reasonable excuse. (Note, creating a statutory nuisance is not a criminal offence; the offence only occurs because of the failure to comply with the abatement notice without reasonable excuse.)

If an abatement notice is not complied with, the authority that has issued the notice has three options available to it, as follows.

10.12.1 The authority can abate the nuisance and recover its cost

The authority can abate the nuisance and do whatever may be necessary in execution of the notice (s 81(3) EPA 1990). A typical example of this is where audio equipment is removed to abate a noise nuisance. Police support may often be required when environmental health officers try to seize equipment. Prior to 1996 there had been some uncertainty about the use of s 81(3) to temporarily confiscate noise-making equipment, as there was no specific provision for the return of seized equipment to owners. Local authorities often used s 43 of the Powers of Criminal Courts Act 1973 to obtain a court order to confiscate permanently equipment used to commit or facilitate the commission of an offence. The provisions relating to seizure of equipment were amended by the NA 1996 and are covered more fully at 10.12.5 below. If the noise is from a car alarm, the officer has the power to open the vehicle, if necessary by force, and immobilise the alarm.

An authority can abate a nuisance irrespective of whether it takes proceedings for non-compliance.[183] In the event that the authority does take action either to abate the nuisance or prevent it happening, then it can, by virtue of s 81(4) EPA 1990, recover any expenses reasonably incurred. This would normally be from the person whose acts or omissions caused the nuisance. If that person is the owner of the premises, the expenses can be recovered from any person who is for the time being the owner of them. This would cover situations where, for instance, a previous owner caused a nuisance, but the present owner could be made responsible for the reasonable expenses incurred by the authority. Should the matter of cost recovery go before the court, the court has the power to apportion the expenses between persons whose acts (or omissions) caused the nuisance, in a manner that the court considers fair and reasonable.

The NSNA provides additional assistance to the local authorities in the form of a newly inserted s 81A EPA 1990, which enables the local authority serving a notice to recover costs to make a charge on the premises owned by the person in default. If the noise is from a car alarm, the officer has the power to open the vehicle, if necessary by force, and immobilise the alarm. The expenses incurred by a local authority in abating a nuisance can be recovered with interest.[184] The local authority can also place a charge[185] on the premises. This new provision was inserted into the EPA 1990 by s 10 of the NSNA 1993.

10.12.2 The authority can institute summary proceedings

If a person commits an offence under s 80(4) EPA 1990, the authority can institute proceedings in the magistrates' court. The offence is failing to comply with an abatement notice without reasonable excuse.

In *Lewisham LBC v Hall* (2003),[186] the council appealed against a decision by the magistrates' court to acquit Hall on charges of contravening a noise abatement notice. Hall had failed to comply with the notice and the council had commenced summary proceedings, but was unable to produce any acoustic measurement evidence, relying on the experience of the environmental health officer. The Divisional Court held that the production of acoustic measurement evidence (such as a decibel recording device used under the NA 1996) was not a precondition for conviction. It was open to magistrates to convict on the basis of the evidence of an environmental health officer or any other lay witness.

The penalty for failure to comply with an abatement notice, without reasonable excuse, depends on whether the nuisance has occurred on industrial, trade or business premises or not. For nuisances arising on non-industrial, trade or business premises, the maximum penalty is £5,000 plus a further £500 for each day that the offence continues after the conviction. However, where the nuisance occurs on industrial, trade or business premises, the maximum fine is £20,000 (but

no additional daily fines can be made). Interestingly the fine in Scotland was increased to £40,000 in 2004 but remains £20,000 in England and Wales. See also *R (on the application of McGarrett) v Kingston Crown Court* (2009).[187] In this case the Crown Court imposed an Anti-Social Behaviour Order for one offence of failing to comply with an abatement notice (that related to noise). The Divisional Court held that the ASBO was so far outside the reasonable area of the court's discretion that it constituted a manifest error of law.

---

183 See below.
184 S 81A EPA 1990.
185 That is, a debt secured on property and recouped when the property is sold.
186 *Lewisham London BC v Hall* [2003] Env LR 4.
187 *R (on the application of McGarrett) v Kingston Crown Court* [2009] EWHC 1776 (Admin); [2010] Env LR 21.

10.12.3 The authority can seek an injunction

The third option available to the authority against a person who fails to comply with or contravenes an abatement notice is to take proceedings in the High Court (s 81(5) of the EPA 1990). This option is available if the authority is of the view that proceedings in the magistrates' court (under s 80(4)) would afford an inadequate remedy. The authority can take this course of action even if summary proceedings have not been exhausted and equally there is no requirement that the authority has suffered damage from the nuisance.

Law in Action

Hammersmith LBC v Magnum Automated Forecourts Ltd (1978)[188]

Following a number of complaints about noise coming from a 24-hour taxi company, HLBC served an abatement notice on MAF Ltd requiring them to cease their taxi operations between 11 pm and 7 am. The company lodged an appeal to the magistrates' court. Although the pending appeal did not suspend the abatement notice, the company continued to operate throughout the night. The local authority decided not to bring a prosecution for failure to comply with the notice, but instead decided to apply to the High Court for an injunction to prevent activities at the taxi centre between 11 pm and 7 am. The Divisional Court held that as the company had made no effort to comply with the notice, the local authority was fully justified in seeking an injunction rather than in bringing a prosecution for an offence, and the court awarded an injunction pending the outcome of the appeal against the notice.

In *East Dorset DC v Eaglebeam Ltd & Others* (2006)[189] an injunction was granted restraining a company from running motocross activities on its land. The company, E, had been served with an abatement notice in respect of noise from the site. E had taken some steps to reduce the noise following receipt of the notice but had also been aware that the motocross was sufficiently noisy to be both a statutory nuisance and also a public nuisance. The injunction was granted because E had deliberately continued to carry on with the motocross activities. Failure to comply with an injunction may result in a prison sentence. In *Bristol CC v Huggins* (1994),[190] Mr Huggins was jailed for three months for breaching an injunction which was obtained by Bristol City Council after two prosecutions under the EPA 1990 had failed. This enables the local authority to obtain an interlocutory injunction to stop a nuisance, despite the availability of appeal proceedings in the magistrates' court.

10.12.4 Defences

The following defences are available in relation to charges for failing to comply with an abatement notice:

(a)   *Reasonable excuse.* It will be a defence if the defendant can prove that there was a reasonable excuse for not complying with the abatement notice. Unfortunately, the EPA 1990 does not define 'reasonable excuse'. The test is whether it is an excuse that a reasonable man would

---

188   *Hammersmith LBC v Magnum Automated Forecourts Ltd* [1978] 1 WLR 50.
189   *East Dorset DC v Eaglebeam Ltd & Others* [2006] EWHC 2378 (QB); LTL 2/10/2006.
190   *Bristol CC v Huggins* (1994, unreported).

consider consistent with a reasonable standard of conduct. What constitutes a reasonable excuse will therefore be a matter of fact. Reasonable excuses have included non-receipt of the abatement notice.[191] A birthday celebration or party will not constitute a reasonable excuse. However, in *Butuyuyu v Hammersmith & Fulham LBC* (1997)[192] the Divisional Court said it was not possible to provide a comprehensive definition of what matters could amount to a reasonable excuse for failure to appeal an abatement notice, as the circumstances of each case will vary considerably. Although the examples given in *Lambert Flat Management* provided a guide, they did no more than that. On the facts of this case the court accepted that the defendant had a reasonable excuse; she was diagnosed as HIV positive and her eldest child, who had cancer, died two days after she was served the notice.

See Chapter 9 →

(b) *The best practicable means (BPM) defence.* Where a person has been served with an abatement notice in respect of statutory nuisance under s 79(1)(g) or (ga), the best practical means defence is available provided that the nuisance arises on industrial, trade or business premises, or the noise is emitted from or caused by a vehicle, machinery or equipment being used for industrial, trade or business purposes. Essentially the BPM defence requires the defendant to prove that the best practicable means (BPM) were used to prevent or counteract the nuisance. The defence was considered in *Chapman v Gosberton Farm Produce Co Ltd* (1993),[193] where a company in Boston, Lincolnshire received prepared packed horticultural produce from heavy goods vehicles during the night. Complaints were made to the district council about the noise from the lorries and also about the noise from the refrigeration equipment. In proceedings before the magistrates' court, the company argued that the BPM had been used to counteract the effect of the noise. The company maintained that it had sought planning permission to erect a soil bank and screening (to provide a sound screen) as part of a wider application to extend its business and this fulfilled the BPM. The magistrates accepted this defence, but their decision was overruled by the Divisional Court. The upper court held that the burden of proof in establishing the BPM lies on the defendant[194] on a balance of probability, and it could not be said that a simple planning application was enough to discharge the burden of proof since the application for planning permission had not been determined.

In *East Devon DC v Farr* (2002)[195] the Divisional Court upheld the magistrates' decision to quash an abatement notice where the recipient had done all that he could be expected to do in the circumstances to abate a noise nuisance. The abatement notice required that the doors on his industrial unit be kept closed when the machinery was in operation in order to reduce the noise emissions. Farr appealed on the grounds that, inter alia, he had investigated the possibility of installing air conditioning and dust extraction equipment so as to avoid having to open the doors, but had concluded that this would have been ineffective, noisier and expensive. See also *Manley v New Forest DC* (1999),[196] where the Divisional Court held that that best practicable means could be not be established by the defendant agreeing to relocate his business to a non-residential area. The court held that relocation in such circumstances was going beyond the purpose of the statutory nuisance controls contained in Pt III of the EPA 1990. In *Manley v New Forest DC* (2007)[197] the Divisional Court made it clear that if M was to advance the defence of BPM, he had to demonstrate that he was doing something and that this constituted the BPM. If he had done nothing then the argument could only succeed if he

---

191 *A Lambert Flat Management Ltd v Lomas* [1981] 1 WLR 898; [1981] 2 All ER 280.
192 *Butuyuyu v Hammersmith & Fulham LBC* (1997) 29 HLR 584; [1997] Env LR D13.
193 *Chapman v Gosberton Farm Produce Co Ltd* [1993] Env LR 191.
194 S 101 of the Magistrates' Court Act 1980.
195 *East Devon DC v Farr* [2002] EWHC 115 (Admin); [2002] Env LR 31.
196 *Manley v New Forest DC* [1999] [2000] EHLR 113; [2000] Env LR D11.
197 *Manley v New Forest District Council* [2007] EWHC 3188 (Admin); [2008] Env LR 26.

could prove that nothing could be done. In the context of dogs and noise, that would be an almost impossible task.

In considering what constitutes BPM in this context, s 79 adds an additional factor not relevant in other statutory nuisances. In circumstances where a code of practice[198] is applicable, then regard must be had for the guidance given in the code.

(c) *Codes of practice.* Section 71 of the COPA 1974 enables the Secretary of State to prepare and approve codes of practice for the purpose of giving guidance on the appropriate methods of minimising noise in relation to specified types of plant and machinery. Codes of practice issued under s 71 include construction and open sites, audible intruder alarms, ice cream van chimes and model aircraft.

(d) *Additional defences.* In addition, s 80(9) of the EPA 1990 contains a defence specific to a failure to abate a noise nuisance or act in accordance with a prohibition or restriction in a noise abatement notice. The basis of this defence is essentially that the local authority has given its consent to a particular level of noise under the provisions of ss 60–67 of the COPA 1974 and that the abatement notice attempts to impose a higher standard.

10.12.5 The aggrieved citizen's action—s 82 of the EPA 1990

The right exists in relation to all of the statutory nuisances contained in the EPA 1990 for an aggrieved person to make a complaint in the magistrates' court.[199] Before a person can do this, he or she must give notice. In relation to noise nuisances under s 79(1)(g) and (ga), only three days' notice is required, rather than the standard 21 days' notice. One of the main limitations with the so-called aggrieved citizen's action is that the magistrates' court cannot make an order unless a statutory nuisance has occurred. In other words, preventive action cannot be taken by an individual.

Before taking action in proceedings brought under s 82, the magistrates must be satisfied that one of the following conditions exists:

(a) the alleged nuisance exists;
(b) an abated nuisance is likely to recur on the same premises, or in the same street.

The court can make the following orders:

(a) requiring the defendant to abate the nuisance within a specified time and to carry out any works necessary for that purpose;
(b) prohibiting a recurrence of the nuisance and requiring the defendant to carry out any necessary works to prevent the recurrence. A time period for carrying out such works will be specified in the order;
(c) the imposition of a fine of up to £5,000, with a further fine of up to £500 for each day that the offence continues after conviction;
(d) order the relevant local authority to do anything which the convicted person was required to do by the court order, after it has given the authority the opportunity to be heard. This is only likely to happen where the court makes a second nuisance order because the first has not been complied with.

Where the nuisance is such as to render premises unfit for human habitation, the court can prohibit the use of the premises for human habitation until the court is satisfied that the premises have been made fit for such a purpose.

---

198 Issued under s 71 of the COPA 1974.
199 s 82 of the EPA 1990.

Failure to comply with a nuisance order from the magistrates is an offence and can result in a fine of up to £5,000.[200] The magistrates' court can make a compensation order in favour of persons aggrieved by the nuisance.[201]

One of the most interesting noise cases for some time, *Roper v Tussauds Theme Parks Ltd* (2007),[202] concerned a s 82 citizen's action brought by a person living close to the Alton Towers theme park, particularly since it illustrates some of the real difficulties faced by litigants and the courts in dealing with noise problems. In consequence of the s 82 action brought by Roper (R) the magistrates' court made an abatement order against the theme park and also convicted the site operator and fined them £5,000. T appealed the conviction, fine and order, but the Crown Court upheld the conviction, reduced the fine to £3,500 and amended the terms of the abatement order. R then appealed by way of case stated on a number of grounds (not all of which are considered here). First, R argued that the terms of the new abatement were irreconcilable with the facts. The noise that constituted the statutory nuisance had been measured at 43 dBA and therefore it was argued that it was irrational to suppose that the statutory nuisance could be abated by permitting a noise level of up to 40 dBA; and that this would be likely to result in complaints. The Divisional Court, however, upheld the dBA level that was set, stating that even such a marginal difference 'could prove the difference between what was acceptable and what was not acceptable'. In reaching this decision the Crown Court had also, correctly, considered that the noise levels were well below the WHO guidelines that indicated that few people would be moderately annoyed, and in addition the Crown Court had been right to remind itself of the character of the area (in which local residents inevitably must expect some inconvenience from noise from Alton Towers.).

R also argued that the court's order was illegitimately influenced by commercial considerations (and that such commercial considerations could only be relevant in the context of a person advancing the defence of BPM for breach of an abatement notice). Again the Divisional Court rejected this argument and held that far from being precluded from having regard to commercial considerations, the court was

> obliged to have regard to all relevant circumstances in ensuring that the discharge by them of their obligation to make an abatement order, having potential penal consequences, was proportionate and no more than was reasonably necessary in order to achieve the statutory requirement. In fact, in connection with that part of the order, the court rightly found that the evidence of any adverse commercial impact was exiguous and indirect and that the respondent would have no difficulty in complying with its terms.[203]

10.13 The Noise Act 1996

The NA 1996 received Royal Assent on 18 July 1996. The provisions of the Act do not create a new noise nuisance, but provide for a special summary procedure in relation to night-time noise. The 1996 Act introduced for the first time a night noise offence relating to domestic premises and a procedure for the seizure and forfeiture of noise-making equipment.

When the NA first came into force the provisions were adoptive, that is to say local authorities were not obliged to comply with the provisions of the Act. If a local authority determined it wanted

---

200 Plus £500 for each day that the offence continues.
201 S 82 (12) EPA. Also, see *R v Crown Court at Liverpool and another, ex parte Cooke* [1996] 4 All ER 589.
202 *Roper v Tussauds Theme Parks Ltd* [2007] EWHC 624 (Admin); [2007] Env LR 31.
203 Ibid at para 15.

to apply the Act it was required to adopt a formal council resolution to adopt its provisions. This adoptive element was criticised at the time with the suggestion that very few authorities would seek to adopt a statute which imposed significant resource implications and this turned out to be the case. By 2000 only 14 authorities had adopted the Act. The low take-up was attributed by many to the obligation, having once adopted the 1996 Act, that local authorities maintain an out-of-hours noise response service that might not be justified by local circumstances and their own best value reviews.

In compliance with the requirements of the Act, Defra embarked on a review and consultation exercise in 2000 to evaluate its effectiveness. The outcome of this and a subsequent public consultation, concluded in March 2001, was the amendment of the 1996 Act so that it now provides local authorities with a further tool to use without the need for formal adoption as had been required originally. Although very few authorities had adopted the NA 1996, the conclusion of the consultation exercise was that the Act had acted as a form of catalyst in encouraging local authorities to operate some form of out of hours complaints service. In 1994, only 52 per cent of authorities (responding to the consultation exercise) operated some form of out of hours service, whereas the percentage had significantly increased to 90 per cent in 2000. More particularly, the review indicated that one of the key successes of the NA 1996 was the clarification of the powers of seizure and the clear incorporation of these powers into the EPA 1990.

However, the Act was not without its critics, one of the principal criticisms being that the act only really offered one advantage over the provisions of Part III EPA 1990, namely the possibility of serving a fixed penalty notice without having to go through the protracted procedures of serving an abatement notice. The requirement that noise exceed a fixed threshold was also criticised because of the need to invest in specific recording devices, and the difficulties in taking recordings.

See Chapter 9

Following the review of the NA 1996, the government announced that it would seek to make amendments to it in order to make the night noise offence more accessible to local councils. Consequently the Noise Act 1996 was amended by the Anti-Social Behaviour Act 2003 so that the night-time noise offence may be used by any local authority in England and Wales without the need to formally adopt the Act. The amendments to the 1996 Act made by the Anti-Social Behaviour Act 2003 came into force in England and Wales on 31 March 2004. The Act applies to every local authority in England and Wales.[204]

Before embarking on an explanation of the provisions of the Noise Act 1996 the reader should note that this Act does not replace the statutory nuisance provisions in Part III EPA 1990. The Noise Act is intended to complement Part III EPA 1990 by providing another tool to local authorities to enable them to deal swiftly and specifically with night-time noise from residential premises.

10.13.1 Night-time noise complaints

By s 2(1) NA 1996, if a local authority receives a complaint of the type described below, it may arrange for an officer of the authority to take reasonable steps to investigate the complaint. This contrasts with the original version of s 1 NA 1996[205] when the local authority was under a duty to investigate. The mandatory nature of the original section explains why so many local authorities took the decision not to adopt the Act. It also contrasts with s 79 EPA 1990, where the authority is under a duty to take reasonable steps to investigate complaints of statutory nuisance. Section 1 NA enables the local authority to exercise discretion in deciding whether to investigate night-time noise complaints within the scope of this Act.

---

204 S 1 NA 1996.
205 Prior to amendment by the Anti-Social Behaviour Act 2003.

The type of complaint that is covered by the NA 1996 is a complaint made by any individual present in a dwelling (the complainant's dwelling) during night hours[206] that excessive noise is being emitted from either:

(a) another dwelling (the offending dwelling); or

(b) any premises which have a premises licence or a temporary event notice[207] (referred to as the offending premises).

10.13.2 Investigation; noise in excess of permitted levels

If, after carrying out an investigation, the local authority officer (usually the EHO) is satisfied that:

(a) the noise is being emitted from the offending dwelling or premises during night hours; and

(b) the noise, if it were measured from within the complainant's dwelling, would or might exceed the permitted level, the officer may serve a notice about the noise.

The officer may serve a notice.

In contrast to the EPA 1990, which requires an EHO to make an assessment as to whether noise is either prejudicial to health or a nuisance, the NA 1996 utilises objective noise thresholds. Noise that exceeds the permitted levels can be dealt with by the Act.[208]

The permitted levels are laid down by the Secretary of State in directions.[209] The permitted levels are 34 dB (if the underlying noise level does not exceed 24 dB) or 10 dB above the relevant background noise (if the underlying noise level is 24 dB or more)—an increase of 10 dB over a background level of 25 dB will double the loudness of the noise).

It is clear that it is the local authority officer who is responsible for making the decision as to whether the noise does or is likely to exceed the permitted level. He needs to be satisfied that the noise is being emitted from the offending dwelling or premises and that if it were measured from within the complainant's dwelling it would or might exceed the permitted levels.

The officer needs to decide whether it is necessary to assess the noise levels either within or outside the complainant's dwelling and also it appears to be a matter of discretion whether or not the noise level needs to be measured using any noise-measuring device.[210] There is no requirement to measure the noise at this stage.

It should be noted that an officer may reach the conclusion (either by judgement or by taking a measurement) that the noise complained of does not exceed the permitted level. However, if they are satisfied that the noise constitutes a statutory nuisance the officer will be under a duty under s 80 EPA 1990 to serve an abatement notice. If the investigating officer is satisfied that a statutory nuisance is being caused as well as the permitted noise level being exceeded, the mandatory duty to serve an abatement notice also applies.

10.13.3 The warning notice[211]

If the officer is satisfied that the noise does or might exceed the permitted levels (recalling that he can make this judgement without actually measuring the noise), the officer has discretion in

---

206 Defined as being between 11 pm and 7 am.
207 Both defined in the Licensing Act 2003.
208 Although this does not necessarily mean that that same noise would constitute a statutory nuisance, and vice versa.
209 S 5 NA 1996.
210 S 2(5)(b) NA 1996.
211 S 3 NA 1996.

relation to whether or not to serve a warning notice. The purpose of the notice is to effectively warn any person who is responsible for noise which is emitted from the offending dwelling or premises and which exceeds the permitted levels that they may be guilty of an offence. The warning notice may start as little as 10 minutes after the service of the notice and must end at 7 am. Clearly the idea is that on receipt of such a warning the person responsible will reduce the volume of the noise to avoid any criminal liability. To that extent the provision seeks to provide a speedy (almost immediate) reduction in noise. In respect of noise from a dwelling the officer must serve the notice on any person present at or near the offending dwelling who appears to be the person responsible for the noise. In circumstances where it is not reasonably practicable to identify this person the officer is permitted to leave the notice at the offending dwelling (for example by posting it through a letterbox). Where the noise is being emitted from offending premises the officer should serve the notice on the person he believes to be the responsible person in relation to the premises.

The person responsible is defined as the person to whose act, default or sufferance, the emission of the noise is wholly or partly attributable. This test is the same as that used under the statutory nuisance provisions discussed earlier.

10.13.4 Offences, evidence and defences

Criminal liability arises if, after receiving a warning notice, the noise that is emitted from the offending dwelling or premises exceeds the permitted levels (as measured from within the complainant's dwelling) during the period of the notice. So, for example, if the warning notice comes into effect 10 minutes after service, the recipient must reduce the noise to the permitted levels within 10 minutes in order to avoid the commission of an offence. Section 4 establishes the offence in relation to offending residential dwellings and s 4A for offending premises. In relation to s 4 (noise from offending dwellings) the person charged with the offence has only one defence available: namely that there was a reasonable excuse for not complying with the warning notice. The maximum penalty is set at is level three on the standard scale. However, turning to the offence under s 4A, 'noise from offending premises', the NA does not provide any defence; liability appears to be absolute and the penalty for this offence is greater and is set at a maximum of level five on the standard scale (currently £5,000).

Section 7 of the NA 1996 lays down the evidence that may be admitted to a court in summary proceedings for an offence under s 4 or s 4A. It includes:

(a) documentary evidence of an offence without the attendance in court of the local authority officer;[212] and

(b) evidence from noise-measuring devices. This may include the record of the measurement produced automatically by a noise-measuring device.

10.13.5 Powers of entry and seizure and disposal of equipment

Section 10 of the NA 1996 provides a power of entry by force under a magistrate's warrant. The NA 1996 makes specific provision for the seizure and disposal of equipment, such as audio and stereo equipment. The relevant provisions are s 10 of and Sched 1 to the Act. The provisions of the NA 1996 in this regard also extend to the statutory nuisance provisions under Part III EPA 1990 and make it clear that the power of a local authority to abate a nuisance under s 81(3) of the EPA 1990 includes the power to seize and remove equipment which it appears to the local authority is being or has been used in the emission of a noise nuisance under s 79(1)(g) of the Act.

---

212 Unless by virtue of s 7(6) attendance is required by the defendant.

10.13.6 Fixed penalty notices

The NA 1996 was introduced to provide a speedy resolution of noise problems. Where a local authority officer has reason to believe that a person is committing or has just committed an offence under ss 4 or 4A, the officer may issue a fixed penalty notice. This essentially gives the person in receipt of the penalty notice the opportunity of discharging any liability under the Act upon payment of a fixed penalty.

The fixed penalty notice can be served by delivering the notice to the responsible person. If it is not reasonably practicable to deliver it, the officer can leave the notice, addressed to the responsible person, at the offending dwelling or premises. Once a person has been served a fixed penalty notice the authority cannot commence any further criminal proceedings until a period of 14 days (following the service of the notice) has elapsed. If the person pays the fixed penalty within the 14 days he discharges his liability under the Act and no further proceedings can be taken. Criminal proceedings may be taken if the payment is not made.

Local authorities can set a fixed penalty; otherwise, the penalty is £100[213] for s 4 offences. However, where the offence is committed from offending premises,[214] s 8A sets the fixed penalty at £500, again reflecting the harsher nature of the provisions in relation to noise emitted from non-residential dwellings.

10.14 Other statutory provisions

In addition to all of the measures discussed above, there are a number of further statutory provisions which can be used to deal with noise problems. The following list does not purport to be exhaustive.

10.14.1 By-laws

The first legislation in the UK expressly dealing with noise was in the form of by-laws. Section 235(1) of the Local Government Act 1972 allows district councils to make by-laws for the 'good rule and government of the whole or any part of the district or borough, as the case may be, and for the prevention and suppression of nuisances therein'. The breach of a by-law is a criminal offence.

10.14.2 Anti-social behaviour orders

Anti-social, threatening and disruptive behaviour which causes, or is likely to cause, alarm, harassment and distress may be dealt with by means of an anti-social behaviour order under the Anti-Social Behaviour Act 2003. The Act deals with a range of anti-social behaviour, but Part 6 specifically addresses anti-social behaviour in an environmental context. As far as noise is concerned, s 40 allows the chief executive of a local authority to order the closure, for up to 24 hours, of certain licensed premises (or premises where a temporary events licence has effect). He can make this order if he reasonably believes that a public nuisance is being caused by noise coming from the premises, and the closure of the premises is necessary to prevent that nuisance. It is a criminal offence to breach such a closure order and a person guilty of an offence may be given a custodial sentence of up to 51 weeks and/or a fine of up to £20,000.

---

213 S 8 NA 1996.
214 Under s 4A.

10.14.3 'Rave' parties

The Criminal Justice and Public Order Act 1994 is relevant to the control of 'rave' parties. A 'rave' is defined as 'a gathering of 20 or more people on land in the open air that includes the playing of amplified music during the night and as such, by reason of its loudness and duration and the time at which it is played, is likely to cause serious distress to the inhabitants of the locality'. Section 63 empowers the police to stop a rave in circumstances where the music is likely to cause serious distress to local residents. If a police officer (of at least the rank of superintendent) reasonably believes that two or more persons are making preparations to hold the 'rave' and more than 10 people are attending or waiting for it to begin, the police officer has the power to instruct those persons to leave the land and also to remove any vehicle that they have with them on the land. This does not apply to the occupier of the land, who is exempt. The Divisional Court held that s 63 provides a power to the police that is additional to common law offences of causing a nuisance).[215]

10.15 Alternative dispute resolution and mediation

Noise disputes are often part of a much wider neighbour dispute. Unwelcome noise is often a symptom of the disagreement between neighbours, rather than the original cause. In this case, the noise laws discussed above may be of limited use in controlling the noise, and other alternative methods of resolution may be required, either in other branches of law or possibly through mediation. Equally, genuine noise disputes may be dealt with outside the framework of legal control discussed so far. The following section is intended to consider the possibilities of alternative forms of dispute resolution which may lend themselves to the resolution of noise disputes.

It will often be the case that a dispute between neighbours over noise can be resolved informally. Often an environmental health officer can facilitate this informal resolution by helping the neighbours to reach some sort of compromise solution.

Defra has shown itself keen to encourage informal resolution of problems and has published a guide to assist people who are facing noise problems (*Bothered by Noise?*, 1994).[216] However, it is recognised that not all problems can be dealt with so easily. Nevertheless, Defra has also sought to promote the use of more formal means of alternative dispute resolution and has issued a guidance note on the mechanics and benefits of alternative dispute resolution, in particular, the use of mediation.

The advantages of mediation are clear. Mediation is normally quicker and almost certainly less expensive than legal action because its use only requires one mediator. The costs of mediation are split between the parties involved. Mediation was argued for most strenuously during the passage of the Noise Bill before Parliament. According to the MP for Lewisham and Deptford, Joan Ruddock, 'about 60 per cent of all mediated neighbour disputes involve noise, and estimates of their success range from 40 per cent to 77 per cent. Mediation is cost-effective and usually costs between £200 and £300 per hour'.[217]

---

215 See above at 10.10.6 for further discussion of *R v Conrad Ryder-Large and John Castrillion* [2008] EWCA Crim 2966.
216 Available from the Defra website at: http://www.defra.gov.uk/environment/quality/noise/neighbour/suffer/suffer2.htm.
217 Hansard, 16 February 1996—during the Second Reading of the Noise Bill.

Law in Action

The case for mediation—*Faidi v Elliott Group* (2012)[218]

The Faidi family owned a flat in Sloane Square, London. The lease of the flat contained two covenants that prohibited tenants from 'doing, permitting or suffering, in or upon the demised premises, any act or thing which may be or become a nuisance or annoyance to the lessors or the tenants of the lessors or the occupiers of any part of the building or of any adjoining or neighbouring premises'. The second covenant required tenants to keep all the floors (except the bathroom and kitchen) covered with carpet and underlay. In 2006 the former tenants of Flat 8 (the flat above the Faidi's flat) obtained the landlord's permission to take up the existing carpets and underlay in each of the habitable rooms and lay a new solid timber floor. The consent was granted subject to a proviso that there was adequate sound proofing in accordance with building regulations. The work was completed with sound insulation that exceeded the minimum required and the evidence of the architect was that the sound insulation was now better than it had been when carpets were laid directly onto the old concrete floor. The problems started when new tenants moved into Flat 8. The Faidis complained that they were disturbed by the noise of heels clicking on the new timber floor above them. The Faidis failed in their action for breach of the covenants because the landlord had consented to the leaseholder installing wooden floors and had waived the covenant which required the floor to be covered with carpet and underlay, as enforcing that clause would have frustrated the purpose of the works carried out. As far as the nuisance was concerned, the Court of Appeal restated the decision of *Southwark LBC v Mills*[219] that a person who uses his premises in a normal way cannot be guilty of a noise nuisance. The Faidis legal costs of litigating as far as the Court of Appeal were £140,000. Each of the appeal judges commented that this was a classic neighbour dispute over noise which should never have reached the courts. In particular Jackson LJ stated:

> This case concerns a dispute between neighbours, which should have been capable of sensible resolution without recourse to the courts. During the course of his submissions in the Court of Appeal Mr Pearce for the claimants observed that this may not be an 'all or nothing' case. A moderate degree of carpeting in flat 8 might (a) reduce the noise penetrating into flat 6 and (b) still enable the occupants of flat 8 to enjoy their new wooden floor. This is precisely the sort of outcome which a skilled mediator could achieve, but which the court will not impose.

10.16 Online resource centre

We recommend that the reader regularly refers to the section of the online resources corresponding to this chapter for information relating to updates, amendments and corrections.

10.17 Summary of key points

Chapter 10 has covered the following topics and issues:

---

218 Faidi v Elliott Group [2012] EWCA Civ 287; [2012] HLR 27 (CA Div).
219 *Southwark LBC v Mills & Baxter v Camden LBC (No 2)* [2001] 1 AC 1; [1999] 4 All ER 449; [1999] 3 WLR 939.

- the nature of noise, which unlike many of the environmental problems addressed in this book, does not damage the environment per se in the sense of causing lasting pollution. Noise problems are generally localised and temporary; however, that does not mean that noise does not cause harm. There is growing evidence about the adverse effects of noise on human health and the statistics strongly suggest that the public consider noise, particularly neighbourhood noise, to be a particular problem;
- the difficulties in regulating in relation to noise. The control of noise poses a range of difficulties not least because all activities generate noise and such activities are unavoidable or desirable (take air travel and the noise from planes as an example). Noise is transient and the assessment of it can be subjective. Noise occurs in such a widely diverse range of circumstances (construction noise, transport noise, domestic household noise for example) and it is therefore extremely difficult to regulate by a single piece of legislation which can accommodate all of the different issues;
- the lack of a coherent set of rules that deal with noise as an environmental problem; instead the legal mechanisms that have developed have done so in a piecemeal fashion;
- the laws that have developed seek to either prevent noise at source by setting specific noise limits for different types of products and vehicles or avoiding the creation of noise nuisance by means of the imposition of planning conditions which minimise the impact of noise;
- public authorities (mainly local authorities) can control and regulate certain types of noise such as noise from construction sites and loudspeakers. The environmental permitting regime which delivers the requirements of the Integrated Pollution Prevention Control Directive enables the regulatory bodies to impose noise controls over regulated facilities and therefore industrial activities are now required to utilise the best available techniques to minimise noise;
- the law also seeks to provide a form of resolution when noise causes disagreement or constitutes a nuisance. Traditionally, noise problems have been resolved through the courts by means of common law actions in private nuisance. However, Parliament has provided additional statutory mechanisms which enable local authorities to deal with noise problems. Specifically, Part III EPA 1990 (the statutory nuisance regime) and the amended Noise Act 1996 enable local authorities to respond to complaints about noise in order to secure the abatement of noise within relatively quick timescales;
- the EU has taken the lead in legislating noise emission limits for a variety of products (vehicles, white goods, tyres etc) and this legislation aims to control the emission of noise at source. However, the EU has relatively recently recognised the impact of noise on citizens and in consequence has begun to adopt a more strategic approach to noise control, principally by means of the adoption of the EU Environmental Noise Directive. Implementation of this has been delayed but is in progress. The adoption of a national noise strategy, however, has not yet transpired, despite government assertions.

10.18 Further reading

Books

A useful, but now somewhat out-of-date examination of noise law can be found in Adams, M and McManus, F, *Noise and Noise Law* (Wiley Chancery, 1994).

Journal articles and government papers

Dymond, A, 'Noise and the Limits of the Law' (2000) 3(1) *Journal of Local Government Law* 11.
Joseph, M and Bradburn, P, 'Ambient noise strategy: A solution for noise control?' Noise Health (serial online) 2003 [cited 2010 Jan 28; 5:39–41]. Available from http://www.noiseandhealth.org/text.asp?2003/5/18/39/31819.

Lee, M, 'Nuisance and regulation in the Court of Appeal' [2013] 3 JPL 277.
McManus, F, 'Noise law in the United Kingdom—a very British solution?' (2000) 20(2) LS 264.
McManus, F, 'Noise Pollution and Human Rights' [2005] 6 EHRLR 575.
'Noise comes of age as an environmental issue', ENDS 2009, 414, 18.
'Nuisance: penalties for excessive noise', Env LM 2009, September 6–8.

Websites

www.environment-agency.gov.uk
The official website of the Environment Agency.

www.cieh.org
The official website of the Chartered Institute of Environmental Health. Documents available include Policy Unit Response to the Review of the Noise Act and annual statistics relating to noise complaints and statutory nuisance procedures.

http://noise.eionet.europa.eu/
NOISE is the Noise Observation and Information Service for Europe maintained by the European Environment Agency (EEA). It contains data related to strategic noise maps delivered in accordance with European Directive 2002/49/EC relating to the assessment and management of environmental noise.

http://www.noiseabatementsociety.com/
The Noise Abatement Society. The objective of the Noise Abatement Society is to raise awareness of, and find solutions to, noise pollution.

Chapter 11

Environmental Torts

Chapter Contents

Learning Objectives

By the end of this chapter you should have acquired an understanding of:

- the largely compensatory role of civil law actions (environmental torts) in the protection of the interests of private legal persons arising out of pollution-related damage;

- the main grounds upon which a civil environmental action may be commenced—the torts (civil wrongs) of private nuisance, public nuisance, trespass, the rule in *Rylands v Fletcher* and negligence;

- tortious remedies (damages and injunctions);

- defences to civil actions/environmental torts;

- the advantages and disadvantages of torts-based litigation as an environmental protection mechanism;

- the role of statutory civil actions;

- the EU and civil liability issues in an environmental context;

- environmental civil actions based on allegations of breach of human rights.

11.1 Introduction

Most of this book is devoted to a study of the public regulation of private pollution. Command and Control regulatory regimes are employed by the government to regulate the polluting emissions of private industry. Such legislative controls task public bodies, such as the Environment Agency and the local authorities, with regulating polluting emissions from a wide range of industries.

Command and Control legislation such as the Environmental Protection Act 1990 (EPA) and the Water Resources Act 1991 (WRA) are examples of public law. These laws differ from criminal laws or civil laws in that each piece of legislation comprises an administrative framework designed to regulate a particular type of polluting activity, often through the use of permit-based controls. In contrast to the regulation of pollution by public regulators 'policing' compliance with the law as detailed in legislation and permits, this chapter considers the role of the common law as a component of the patchwork of controls which currently comprise the environmental law of England and Wales. The common law, in contrast to the law in legislation, comprises various legal principles which have been developed by the judiciary in decided cases over many years. This is 'judge made' law rather than statute law (Acts of Parliament). Common law actions consist of 'one on one' disputes involving an action commenced by an injured claimant in the civil courts against the person (defendant) who allegedly caused the injury. Thus, the common law is a mechanism to regulate the legal relations between private persons, whether individuals or companies. In the context of this book, the relevant legal relations upon which we shall focus concern the resolution of disputes relating to pollution damage to property, property-related interests, or personal injury. Most of these disputes require the courts to resolve competing land uses.

The most important set of common laws which have application to environmental problems in general, and pollution in particular, is the law of torts (a tort is a wrong). The primary function of the law of torts is to provide a range of remedies for any person who suffers a wrong consisting of damage to property or person (personal injury) caused by the activities of another person. As we shall see, these environmental torts have a role to play in compensating pollution victims for damage caused by polluters (and in limited circumstances restricting or prohibiting the defendant's activities).

11.2 Common law actions (environmental torts)

Where a legal person, such as an individual or a company,[1] has suffered environmental harm which takes the form of damage to person or property, an action in tort is usually the most appropriate response. The common law of torts is used to provide redress, usually in the form of compensation, for a victim of pollution-related damage.

Although common law actions have been criticised for 'being too expensive, too long-winded and too uncertain',[2] nevertheless, they have, in recent years, proved to be a fertile ground for environmental litigation, although the judiciary have demonstrated a rather lukewarm response to attempts to use torts as a mechanism to control the adverse impacts of pollution on people, property and the wider environment. The courts have shown a preference for specific pollution legislation, such as the EPA 1990, and have shown minimal support for attempts to develop the common law as a means of resolving modern-day environmental problems.

Before we consider each environmental tort in detail, a few general points will be made:

(a) common law actions are largely concerned with the protection of *private rights*. These rights, such as property rights, are 'private' in the sense that they relate to legal persons (individual humans, companies and similar legal persons). Currently, no corresponding legal rights exist to bring an action on behalf of the environment or flora and fauna.[3] It is humans (and also other legal persons such as companies) who resort to the common law to engage in civil litigation in order to protect their own interests from actual or threatened damage arising out of the use of a neighbouring landowner's property;

(b) in contrast to the Command and Control regulatory frameworks in the EPA 1990 and the WRA 1991, with their permit-based pollution controls linked to precise and monitorable permit conditions, the common law has traditionally been associated with imprecise standards. The common law attempts to balance competing private interests and looks to the reasonableness of the activities of competing landowners. It does not lay down strict numerical limits for substances contained in emissions from one person's property discharged into the environment and affecting a neighbouring property;

(c) proving that the defendant's activities caused the damage sustained (the process of causation) may be a difficult and expensive task, bearing in mind the degree of scientific uncertainty which may exist.[4] Damage caused by airborne pollutants may pose a significant evidential problem for the claimant, especially if the claimant's and defendant's properties are some distance from one another and there are other properties in the area which are generating identical or similar polluting emissions;

(d) the right to take action in most cases is strictly limited to those persons whose property or property-related interests have been harmed;[5]

(e) in a common law action, the court makes a largely subjective decision as to whether the defendant's activities are unreasonable, taking into account the degree of tolerance which would be expected of a reasonable neighbour;

(f) the grant of, and compliance with, a pollution permit issued by a regulator under Command and Control legislation, such as the WRA 1991, does not prevent the defendant being liable in an action based on tort (except negligence);

---

1 Or similar legal persons such as an NHS Trust or a local authority.
2 S Bell, *Environmental Law: The Law and Policy Relating to the Protection of the Environment* (4th edn, Blackstone, Oxford 1997).
3 CD Stone, 'Should Trees Have Standing? Towards Legal Rights for Natural Objects' (1972) *Southern California Law Review* 45, 540–541.
4 See *Graham and Graham v Rechem International Ltd* [1996] Env LR 158.
5 See *Hunter v Canary Wharf Ltd* [1997] 2 WLR 684; (1995) 139 SJ LB 214 and *Blackburn v ARC Ltd* [1998] Env LR 469.

(g) the common law is mainly a reactive and compensatory mechanism. Only rarely[6] will the courts, in such an action, grant an injunction to prevent anticipated future damage or interference;

(h) the usual remedy, in the event that an action is successful, is an award of damages to the claimant to put him or her back in the same position that he or she would have been in had the tort not been committed. Except in the case of negligence actions, the claimant may seek an injunction to restrain the defendant's behaviour which is causing injury to the claimant's interests. The award of an injunction will almost certainly be more important to both parties than damages. Injunctions are generally only awarded to stop or restrict continuing activities;

(i) a successful claimant is not obliged to spend any damages received on restoring the environment, even if this was the basis of the complaint;

(j) injury or damage relating to some aspect of the environment valued by the public or harm to people is often a powerful factor which motivates the claimant to pursue a case in order to make a defendant accountable for the alleged wrong;[7]

(k) the legal standard of proof in civil cases requires the claimant to prove his or her case 'on the balance of probabilities'. In other words, it is more likely than not that the defendant's actions caused the relevant injury to the claimant or his or her interests.

11.3 Remedies

The common law offers various remedies which will be sought by the claimant depending upon the particular circumstances of each case. Each remedy is discussed below.

11.3.1 Damages

The object of damages in the law of torts is to put the claimant into the position he or she would have been in had the harm or damage not occurred. This is particularly difficult to calculate in relation to environmental damage, because it is often the case that the cost of environmental damage can never be calculated for many years, as clean-up may take several years, or the damage can never be fully rectified.

The most common form of damages to be awarded by the courts are compensatory damages, where the claimant is compensated for any loss that has been suffered.

There are several other forms of damages which may be awarded, for example:

(a) *aggravated damages*—awarded where the court wishes to express disapproval of the defendant's conduct and compensate the claimant who has suffered more than would normally be expected;

(b) *punitive/exemplary damages*—awarded where it is the court's intention to punish the tortfeasor (defendant) by adding an additional award onto the compensatory damages awarded, which may also have the effect of deterring others from acting in a similar fashion. The award of exemplary damages is largely governed by the rules established in *Rookes v Barnard* (1964),[8] in which it was stated that damages of this type could be awarded in three classes of case:

---

6 In *Blackburn v ARC Ltd* [1998] Env LR 469 the applicants were refused an injunctive remedy to close down a landfill which was breaching its permit conditions and was causing a nuisance.
7 C Pugh and M Day, *Pollution and Personal Injury: Toxic Torts II* (Cameron May, London 1995).
8 *Rookes v Barnard* [1964] 2 WLR 269.

(i)   where servants of the government act in an oppressive, arbitrary or unconstitutional way. In a claim in private nuisance it was held that this could not apply to private individuals or corporations;[9]

(ii)   where the defendant's conduct was calculated to profit from the tort. This is particularly appropriate in environmental cases, because industrial operators may feel that it would be more profitable to continue with the polluting activity and to face the consequences when paying damages, rather than to cease production or to operate with less polluting techniques;

(iii)   where a statute forming the basis of the tortious action expressly permits the payment of exemplary damages.

11.3.2 Injunction

In addition, or as an alternative to damages, the claimant may seek an injunction.

Injunctions essentially allow the courts to require that the defendant discontinues the offending operation and/or takes action to prevent or remedy the damage or pollution that has been caused. Injunctions can be classified as:

(a)   mandatory injunctions, in which case the court will order the defendant to undo or remedy the damage, or prevent further damage from occurring;

(b)   prohibitory injunctions, which order the defendant not to continue with the wrongful act. The duration of a prohibitory injunction is determined by the court with regard to the offending activity and the nature of its effects.

Injunctions provide the potential for a powerful common law weapon against polluters and their activities because they allow the courts to tailor the exact remedy to the nature of the damage being caused. For example, it may be possible for the court to order a mandatory clean-up of a gradual chemical spillage, or prohibit the operation of a polluting activity.

The effect of injunctions can be particularly damaging for those upon whom they are imposed; for example, in the Irish case of *Bellew v Cement Ltd* (1948),[10] an injunction closed the defendant's cement factory for three months. The financial and commercial implications of injunctions are potentially very damaging, but common law injunctions are awarded in few cases. Interlocutory injunctions (temporary injunctions) allow the courts to compel the defendant to take action to cease operating or remedy the damage caused pending a full hearing. Injunctions are restricted in that they may only be granted by the court when the activity complained of is substantial, and when it would be reasonable. In order to determine this, it is necessary to balance the interests of not only the claimant and defendant but also the polluting activity and the significance of its impact on the environment.

To illustrate the current approach of the courts to the imposition of injunctive relief we set out the following two decisions.

---

9   *Gibbons and Others v South West Water Services* [1992] 2 WLR 507; [1993] Env LR 244.
10 *Bellew v Cement Ltd* [1948] Ir R 61.

> **Law in Action**
>
> (1) In a 2006 Court of Appeal case (*Regan v Paul Properties Ltd and Others* (2006) EWCA Civ 1319) involving an interference with the claimant's right to light amounting to a nuisance, the Court held that a claimant is prima facie entitled to an injunction to protect his legal rights against a person who has committed a wrongful act such as a continuing nuisance. The case involved a five-storey development in Brighton located opposite the claimant's home. The claimant warned the developers that the development would substantially interfere with natural light entering the claimant's sitting room. The claimant commenced legal proceedings and sought an injunction to force the developer to redesign the building to prevent the light interference. The Court of Appeal held that the obstruction of light was a substantial interference. In granting an injunction the Court was disinclined to force the claimant to accept compensation from the defendants, even though the loss resulting from modifying the development was assessed at £175,000.
>
> (2) Residents commenced a private nuisance claim against a recycling and composting company (*Morgan and Baker v Hinton Organics (Wessex) Ltd* (High Court QBD, 21.12.2007)) in regard to the unpleasant smell produced by a composting process. The claimants commenced legal proceedings and obtained an interim injunction, effectively putting a stop to the odour problem; however, the injunction was subsequently discharged by the High Court, primarily because of difficulties relating to the wording of the injunction, which made the Environment Agency or local authority the adjudicator of whether there had been an infringement of the terms of the injunction. In contrast, readers should note the successful private nuisance action relating to unpleasant odours from a landfill site in *Blackburn v ARC Ltd* (1998) Env LR 469.

11.3.3 Abatement

The remedy of abatement dates back many years, although it is rarely used today and its use is not encouraged by the courts. It is an important remedy in statutory nuisance actions. Under the common law, abatement is known as the 'self-help' remedy because an occupier of land affected may take action to abate the damage.

The definition of abatement appears in *Blackstone's Commentaries on the Laws of England Book III*:

> And the reason why the law allows this private and summary method of doing one's self justice, is because injuries of this kind, which obstruct or annoy or such things as are of daily convenience and use, require an immediate remedy; and cannot wait for the slow progress of the ordinary forms of law.

This point was discussed in *Burton v Winters* (1993),[11] in which it was stated that abatement was a summary remedy which was only justified in clear and simple cases where the nuisance or trespass would not justify the expense of legal proceedings, or in an emergency where an urgent remedy is required. A simple example of abatement was given in *Smith v Giddy* (1904),[12] in which it was held that the plaintiff was entitled to cut back the overhanging branches of his neighbour's ash and elm trees which were damaging the growth of his fruit trees.

---

11 *Burton v Winters* [1993] 1 WLR 1077.
12 *Smith v Giddy* [1904] 2 KB 448.

11.4 General defences to intentional torts

An action in tort may fail if the defendant is able to rely on one of the general defences discussed below. There are also defences which are specific to particular torts, which will be discussed in relation to each tort.

11.4.1 Statutory authority

If the tort has been authorised by a statute, this will provide a complete defence, and will not allow the injured party to recover damages. The exact application of the defence of statutory authority will depend on the statute in question. The defendant must prove that the conduct complained of has arisen as an inevitable result of the activity authorised by the statute and that the defendant has exercised reasonable care in carrying out that activity. The authority to carry out the activity must be expressly or impliedly authorised by the statute. An example of implied authority was given in *Allen v Gulf Oil Refining Ltd* (1979).[13] The Gulf Oil Refining Act 1965 authorised the compulsory purchase of land, by the defendants, for the construction of a refinery. It did not explicitly authorise the operation of the refinery. The plaintiff claimed that the operation of the refinery caused a nuisance. The House of Lords held that the defence must apply because the operation of the refinery was implied by the statute and was therefore authorised. However, this defence may not succeed where the Act specifically envisages that an action in nuisance may be brought.[14]

In the case of *Budden v BP Oil Ltd and Shell Oil Ltd* (1980),[15] the Court of Appeal accepted an argument put forward by the defendants that they had complied with the relevant statutory provision, s 75(1) of the Control of Pollution Act 1974 (COPA), and accepted that the statutory standard establishes the common law standard.

In *Barr v Biffa Waste Services Ltd* (2012)[16] the Court of Appeal rejected the defendant's argument, in an odour-related private nuisance action, that its environmental permit to operate a landfill site gave it statutory authority to emit odours.

11.4.2 *Volenti non fit injuria* (consent)

Meaning literally 'no injury is done to a person who consents', the defence of *volenti non fit injuria* can be pleaded by the defendant. In order for this defence to succeed, the claimant must voluntarily assume the risk. In order to do this, the claimant must be in position to make a choice as to whether or not to assume the risk and he or she must also know of the nature and extent of the risk.

11.4.3 Necessity

The defence of necessity is used where the defendant must choose between causing damage to the claimant's property and preventing some greater damage to the public or to a third party. This defence is effective in limited circumstances. Where the defence is raised, it can only succeed if the necessity did not arise from the defendant's negligence. It must also be proved that the defendant has acted in the public benefit, or for the protection of his own property. When determining the applicability of the defence, it is necessary for the courts to judge which of the possible outcomes

---

13 *Allen v Gulf Oil Refining Ltd* [1981] AC 1001; [1981] 2 WLR 188; [1981] All ER 353. See also 11.7.7.1.
14 See *Lloyds Bank v Guardian Assurance, Trollope and Colls Ltd* (1987) 35 Build LR 34.
15 *Budden and Albery v BP Oil Ltd and Shell Oil Ltd* [1980] JPL 586.
16 *Barr v Biffa Waste Services Ltd* [2012] EWCA Civ 312, [2012] 3 All ER 380.

would be preferred. The limitation attached to the defence of necessity is that the defendant must have acted as a reasonable man in order to avoid a greater danger.

11.4.4 Contributory negligence

Section 1 of the Law Reform (Contributory Negligence) Act 1945 provides:

> Where any person suffers damage as the result partly of his own fault and partly of the fault of any other person or persons, a claim in respect of that damage shall not be defeated by reason of the fault of the person suffering the damage, but the damages recoverable in respect thereof shall be reduced to such extent as the court thinks just and equitable having regard to the claimant's share in the responsibility for the damage.

The burden of proof is placed on the defendant to establish that the claimant contributed to the damage resulting in his injuries. This defence allows the amount of damages to be reduced in line with the claimant's contribution to his or her own loss or injury. Damages are often reduced by anything from 10 per cent to 75 per cent.

11.5 Torts and environmental damage

The common law actions which are of most relevance to the private regulation of environmental pollution are the torts of nuisance, trespass, negligence and the rule in *Rylands v Fletcher* (1868).[17] Of all the four torts, it is nuisance which appears to be the most popular ground of action. In an environmental context we refer to these civil actions as *environmental torts*. We consider below the elements of each tort, relevant defences and available remedies.

11.6 Nuisance

Actions in nuisance may be divided into private nuisance, public nuisance and also statutory nuisance as contained in ss 79–82 of the EPA 1990, and supplemented by the Noise and Statutory Nuisance Act 1993. Statutory nuisance was dealt with in Chapter 9. A distinction must be made between the three types of nuisance because they are each significantly different from each other. The tort of private nuisance attempts to reconcile the competing interests of landowners; public nuisance is both a civil wrong and a crime which protects public rights, although an individual may bring an action where he or she has suffered damage over and above that suffered by the public generally; a statutory nuisance is one which is largely controlled by local authorities exercising their statutory powers. Today, the tort of nuisance is recognised as the area of common law which has contributed most significantly to environmental protection, although, in most cases, the claimant is only interested in pursuing his own interests, rather than seeking to confer a benefit upon the public and/or the environment.

11.7 Private nuisance

Private nuisance attempts to achieve a balance of competing rights of neighbours to use their property as they wish. It must be stressed that not every interference with another's use or enjoyment of

---

17 *Rylands v Fletcher* (1868) LR 3HL 330.

land can constitute a private nuisance. In order to be actionable, the conduct complained of must constitute an unreasonable interference with an occupier's interest in the beneficial use of his or her land. Most nuisance actions relate to continuing unreasonable land uses.

11.7.1 Definition

Private nuisance was defined in *Read v Lyons & Co Ltd* (1947)[18] as an 'unlawful interference with a person's use or enjoyment of land or some right over, or in connection with it'.

11.7.2 The two categories of private nuisance

Traditionally, private nuisance has been subdivided into two categories:

(a) actions involving physical damage to the claimant's land; and
(b) actions involving interference with the claimant's use or enjoyment of land (often referred to as the 'sensibility' or 'amenity' cases).

Typically, private nuisance actions, in an environmental context, relate to physical damage to property and chattels caused by the defendant's polluting emissions which come into contact with and damage the claimant's property. For example, pollutants may be blown by the wind onto the claimant's land. This is the most common type of nuisance action and it is generally the easiest to prove. Successful actions in private nuisance have been taken against defendants engaged in running various types of activities, reported in the law reports, including: an oil depot, a metal foundry, a brickworks, a cokeworks, a landfill site and a coal distribution depot. The phrase 'physical damage' includes damage to premises, land, vegetation, chattels and livestock.

Private nuisance actions also relate to cases in which there is no physical damage to property, but injury is caused to the claimant's use or enjoyment of his or her land; for example, cases concerning interference with property stemming from unreasonable amounts of noise, unpleasant smells, dust, vibration and infestations emanating from the defendant's land. In order to succeed, the claimant must prove that he or she has suffered 'inconvenience materially interfering with the ordinary physical comfort of human existence, not merely according to elegant or dainty modes and habits of living, but according to plain and sober and simple notions and habits obtaining among the English People'.[19] The focus in these cases is on what the ordinary claimant would find intolerable and not what an especially sensitive (that is, hypersensitive) person would find unreasonable and/or intolerable. The essence of damage in these cases is unlawful interference with the use and enjoyment of the claimant's property.

11.7.3 The characteristic features of private nuisance

The tort of private nuisance is characterised by the following features:

(a) the nuisance must arise from a continuous state of affairs and not a one-off, isolated event; however, a sufficiently continuous state of affairs arose out of a single firework display in *Crown River Cruises Ltd v Kimbolton Fireworks Ltd* (1996);[20]

---

18 *Read v Lyons & Co Ltd* [1947] AC 156; [1946] 2 All ER 471.
19 See *Walter v Selfe* (1851) 4 De G & S 315.
20 *Crown River Cruises Ltd v Kimbolton Fireworks Ltd* [1996] 2 Lloyd's Rep 533.

(b) the defendant's actions do not have to have been the original cause of the problem. An action may be brought even though the nuisance arises as a result of pre-existing conditions on the defendant's land, for example, historic contamination. The nuisance must emanate from the defendant's land;

(c) the nuisance must affect land belonging to the claimant or in which the claimant has a proprietary interest. In *Hunter and Others v Canary Wharf Ltd* (1997),[21] the House of Lords rejected the proposition that occupiers of property, other than owners and tenants, could sue in private nuisance. This decision has been followed in *Blackburn v ARC Ltd* (1998),[22] in which the plaintiff's common law wife, who had no proprietary interest in the plaintiff's house, had her claim in nuisance rejected;

(d) the claimant must prove that the damage sustained, whether in the form of physical damage to person, premises, or chattels or personal discomfort, has been caused by the alleged nuisance. In many environmental pollution cases, it may be difficult to prove a causal link between the nuisance and the damage sustained by the claimant;

(e) the type of damage sustained by the claimant must have been reasonably foreseeable at the time when the actions which caused the damage occurred.[23] The plaintiff water company in *Cambridge Water Co Ltd v Eastern Counties Leather plc* (1994)[24] failed in its nuisance action because, at the time polluting chemicals escaped from the defendant's tannery, it was not reasonably foreseeable that solvents could migrate through sub-strata over several years and travel significant distances before contaminating the aquifer from which the claimant water company abstracted drinking water;

(f) where the nuisance causes personal discomfort, as opposed to physical damage, the characteristics of the neighbourhood where the alleged nuisance occurs is taken into account.[25] Residents living in an established industrial area[26] will be expected to be more tolerant of such interference than people living in a purely residential area;

(g) nuisance does not enable a hypersensitive (especially sensitive) claimant to obtain redress in circumstances in which the ordinary reasonable person would not find the defendant's activities to be a nuisance;

(h) the grant of planning permission will not confer immunity upon the defendant for liability in nuisance[27] except to the extent that planning permission for a major development, when implemented, changes the character of the area.[28] Similarly the grant of, and compliance with, a permit to pollute issued by the Environment Agency will not provide the defendant with immunity from a common law action in nuisance;

(i) where a nuisance is found to exist, the claimant will generally be awarded damages to place him or her in the position he or she would have been in had the nuisance not occurred. However, where the defendant is liable for a nuisance which he or she did not originally cause, he or she will only be expected to have taken reasonable steps to remedy the situation in the light of his or her means. No remedy is available in private nuisance for personal injury: private nuisance is a land/property-based tort;

(j) in appropriate circumstances the court may grant an injunction.[29]

---

21 *Hunter and Others v Canary Wharf Ltd* [1997] AC 156.
22 *Blackburn v ARC Ltd* [1998] Env LR 469.
23 See *Cambridge Water Co v Eastern Counties Leather plc* [1994] 2 AC 264; [1994] 2 WLR 53; [1994] 1 All ER 53.
24 Ibid.
25 *St Helens Smelting Co v Tipping* (1865) 11 HL Cas 642; (1865) 11 ER 1483.
26 E.g. polluted.
27 *Wheeler v J J Saunders Ltd* [1996] Ch 19; [1995] 3 WLR 466; [1995] 2 All ER 697.
28 See *Gillingham BC v Medway (Chatham) Dock* [1993] QB 343; [1992] 3 WLR 449; [1992] 3 All ER 923; [1992] Env LR 98 and contrast *Wheeler v J J Saunders Ltd* [1996] Ch 19; [1995] 3 WLR 466; [1995] 2 All ER 697.
29 See *Wheeler v J J Saunders Ltd* [1996] Ch 19; [1995] 3 WLR 466; [1995] 2 All ER 697.

11.7.4 Reasonableness

The key issue in an action based on nuisance is that the court must judge whether the defendant is using his or her property reasonably. In *Saunders-Clark v Grosvenor Mansions and D'Allesandri* (1900),[30] Buckley J stated:

> the court must consider whether the defendant is using his property reasonably or not. If he is using it reasonably, there is nothing which at law can be considered a nuisance: but if he is not using it reasonably . . . then the plaintiff is entitled to relief.

Whilst giving consideration to the question of whether the defendant is using his or her property reasonably, the court attempts to balance the competing interests of the claimant and the defendant. On the one hand, the defendant has a right to conduct activities on his or her land as he or she pleases, and on the other hand the claimant has a right to use and enjoy his or her property without an unreasonable amount of interference. The court must therefore determine whether, on the facts, the defendant is using his or her property unreasonably. The ordinary day-to-day use of domestic premises, such as an apartment in a block of flats (constructed with poor noise insulation), will cause some disturbance to occupiers of neighbouring premises but because such user is, in the circumstances, reasonable, the disturbance will not be actionable in private nuisance.[31]

In balancing the competing interests of the claimant and the defendant, the courts apply a 'give and take' test and pay particular attention to the following factors:

(a)   locality;
(b)   duration;
(c)   sensitivity of the claimant;
(d)   intention of the defendant;
(e)   the defendant's use of best practicable means (BPM) to minimise the nuisance;
(f)   the foreseeability of the type of harm or damage complained of;
(g)   the utility of the defendant's conduct.

Each of these is discussed below.

11.7.4.1 Severity

A significant number of private nuisance actions stem from the impact of odour or noise. The following case, involving landfill-related odour complaints, illustrates the application of the tort of private nuisance in a twenty-first-century context.

The private nuisance action in *Barr v Biffa Waste Services Ltd* (2012)[32] arose out of complaints, relating to odour, made by residents of houses located close to a waste landfill site operated by Biffa Waste Services Ltd in Ware (Hertfordshire). The waste which was being disposed of had been 'pre-treated' in the sense that recyclable materials, such as plastics, had been removed from the material before it was tipped. The pre-treatment of the waste caused the waste to have a higher odour level, when compared to untreated waste, because (1) the waste was not tipped and covered over as quickly as untreated waste, and (2) the waste contained a higher proportion of organic matter than untreated waste. Coulson J, the trial judge, rejected the claimants' nuisance action. The judge decided that the claimants could not demonstrate that the defendant had used its land unreasonably and unlawfully because the claimants had not alleged that the defendant had breached the conditions attached to its landfill environmental permit. In addition the judge held that the defendant's

---

30 *Saunders-Clark v Grosvenor Mansions and D'Allesandri* [1900] 2 Ch 373.
31 See *Baxter v Camden (No 2)* (2000) Env LR 112.
32 *Barr v Biffa Waste Services Ltd* [2012] EWCA Civ 312, [2012] 3 All ER 380.

environmental permit had the effect of changing the character of the area (i.e. there had been a change in locality), and, as such, tipping waste in accordance with the conditions of an environmental permit amounted to a reasonable use of land. Coulson J went on to hold that even if his interpretation of these legal issues was wrong, the vast majority of claimants could not establish that they had suffered an unreasonable level of interference with the use and enjoyment of their homes. Coulson J attempted to identify a threshold (based on a yearly average of 'one odour complaint day each week') above which the claimant's nuisance action would succeed.

The complainant's appeal to the Court of Appeal was successful. The Court found that:

(1)   Compliance with the conditions of an environmental permit is not the correct test to determine whether the impact of the defendant's use of its land upon the claimant is reasonable or not. The correct approach is to ask whether a normal person would find the interference unreasonable.

(2)   The grant of an environmental permit does not transform the nature of the locality in a private nuisance action.

(3)   The trial judge was wrong to hold that a private nuisance claim would succeed only if the threshold he had set was exceeded.

(4)   The defendant's cross-appeal, based on the argument that it had statutory authority to emit odour, was rejected.

11.7.4.2 Locality

The character of the local environment is a key factor which the courts have regard to in the 'sensibility' nuisance cases (otherwise referred to as amenity damage, intangible damage or personal discomfort). These are nuisance actions which do not involve physical damage but the claimant alleges that the defendant's actions have caused injury to the use or enjoyment of the claimant's property. As a general rule, a claimant who lives in a highly industrialised or urbanised neighbourhood must accept higher levels of noise and air pollution than might exist in a rural area. The classic statement of the 'locality doctrine' appears in the case of *Sturges v Bridgman* (1879):[33] 'What would be a nuisance in Belgrave Square would not necessarily be so in Bermondsey.'

The locality doctrine does have limits. For example, in *Rushmer v Polsue and Alfieri Ltd* (1906),[34] the House of Lords upheld the grant of an injunction to the plaintiff to stop the operation of the defendant's noisy printing press during the night. The injunction was granted despite the existence of many other printing presses in the area also operating at night. The court expressed the limits of the locality doctrine as follows:

> It does not follow that because I live, say, in the manufacturing part of Sheffield I cannot complain if a steam-hammer is introduced next door, and so worked as to render sleep at night almost impossible, although previously to its introduction my house was a reasonably comfortable abode, having regard to the local standard; and it would be no answer to say that the steam-hammer is of the most modern approved pattern and is reasonably worked. In short, if a substantial addition is found as fact in any particular case, it is no answer to say that the neighbourhood is noisy, and that the defendant's machinery is of first class character.

The reasoning of the Court in regard to the issue of 'locality' in the case of *Rushmer v Polsue and Alfieri Ltd* was referred to with approval by the trial judge in the recent case of *Dennis v MOD* (2003).[35] In

---

33 *Sturges v Bridgman* (1879) 11 Ch D 852.
34 *Rushmer v Polsue and Alfieri Ltd* [1906] Ch 234; [1907] AC 121.
35 *Dennis & Dennis v Ministry of Defence* [2003] EWHC 793; see 11.7.4.10 for the facts of the case.

that case the trial judge observed that if, at some stage in the future, the next generation of noisier fighter planes were to operate from RAF Wittering, a new nuisance tortious claim would arise.

Also of relevance to the locality doctrine is the decision in *Gillingham BC v Medway (Chatham) Dock Co Ltd* (1993).[36] This case concerned the grant of planning permission to transform a former naval dockyard into a commercial port. The development generated high levels of heavy goods vehicle traffic throughout day and night which disturbed residents living adjacent to the roads giving access to the port. The local residents persuaded their local authority to take an action in public nuisance. The court held that the grant of planning permission had changed the character of the neighbourhood and therefore any allegation of nuisance was to be judged by reference to what was acceptable in a commercial, rather than a residential, area. The decision in the *Gillingham* case was subsequently clarified by the Court of Appeal in *Wheeler v JJ Saunders Ltd* (1996).[37] Planning permission had been granted for development consisting of pig-rearing units.[38] A private nuisance action was commenced with regard to smells emanating from the pig unit. The court rejected the proposition that the grant of planning permission automatically operates to create a defence to a nuisance action based on the grant of planning permission changing the character of the area. The plaintiff was awarded an injunction. The court sought to limit the application of the *Gillingham* case to developments which concerned 'strategic' planning developments (major developments). In the context of a planning decision relating to a commercial port, interference with private rights had been weighed against the public interest, and the level of interference was found to be acceptable. The decision clarified that it is the implementation of planning permission, rather than the grant of permission, which changes the character of the area.

11.7.4.3 Sensitivity of the claimant

Where the claimant is deemed to be abnormally sensitive to the defendant's activities, there can be no actionable nuisance. In *Robinson v Kilvert* (1889),[39] the claimant argued that heat from the defendant's property, which was situated below the plaintiff's premises in the basement, was having an adverse effect on the brown paper stored in the plaintiff's premises. It was held that there was no actionable nuisance because:

> a man who carries on an exceptionally delicate trade cannot complain because it is injured by his neighbour doing something lawful on his property, if it is something which would not injure anything but an exceptionally delicate trade.

The rationale behind this principle is consistent with the law of nuisance, namely that each owner of property should have a right to reasonable use and enjoyment of his land.

See Chapter 10

A further example of abnormal sensitivity was given in the case of *Heath v Brighton* (1908).[40] In this case, the vicar of a church sought an injunction to restrain the noise from the defendant's power station. The vicar failed because the noise had neither interrupted services nor had it affected attendance at church; it merely irritated the vicar.

11.7.4.4 Duration of the nuisance

The ability to obtain redress in a private nuisance action depends, in part, upon the claimant being able to prove that the activity alleged to constitute a nuisance is a continuing problem. In *Bolton v*

---

36 *Gillingham BC v Medway (Chatham) Dock* [1993] QB 343.
37 *Wheeler v J J Saunders Ltd* [1996] Ch 19.
38 An extension to an existing pig farm.
39 *Robinson v Kilvert* (1884) 41 Ch D 88.
40 *Heath v Brighton Corp* (1908) 98 LT 718.

Stone (1951),[41] the Court of Appeal rejected a nuisance action relating to the activities of the defendant cricket club because the plaintiff could only establish that cricket balls had been hit out of the ground six times in 30 years. However, an unreasonable level of interference arising from a temporary activity may amount to a nuisance, as the following case illustrates.

In *De Keyser's Royal Hotel Ltd v Spicer Bros Ltd* (1914)[42] the defendant's building operations were so loud that guests at the claimant's hotel were unable to sleep and after-dinner speakers were unable to make themselves heard. The court held that the defendants were not carrying out the operations in a reasonable and proper manner.

Interferences do not have to be continuous to be a nuisance. Isolated incidents which occur on a regular basis may amount to an actionable nuisance.

Single incidents may give rise to a nuisance action. In *British Celanese v AH Hunt (Capacitors) Ltd* (1969),[43] the defendant stored bails of metal foil on its property. Foil was blown onto neighbouring property causing damage to an electricity substation. The court held that an isolated incident could create an actionable nuisance,[44] because the storage method constituted a state of affairs (i.e. there was a continuing threat of damage).

11.7.4.5 Intention of the defendant

The defendant's motives may also be a factor in determining the reasonable use of property. In *Hollywood Silver Fox Farm v Emmett* (1936),[45] the defendant's malicious intent to disrupt the claimant's fox farm by discharging a shotgun during the silver fox mating season was held to be an actionable nuisance. The defendant was aware that female silver foxes may kill and eat their cubs if disturbed. Environmental malice includes the deliberate making of noise to antagonise neighbours in neighbour disputes.[46]

11.7.4.6 Utility of the defendant's conduct

If the defendant is carrying out operations which provide a general benefit to the whole community, then the nuisance will be more reasonable or justifiable than if his or her motive is purely selfish or malicious. There is clearly a link between the defendant's motives and the utility of his or her conduct (e.g. where the defendant operates a sewage treatment facility or a landfill). Whilst the courts do take account of the social utility of the defendant's activities, it appears that this factor is not a key consideration.[47]

11.7.4.7 The defendant's use of best practicable means to minimise the nuisance

The defendant's use of best available abatement technology (best practicable means) to minimise the impact of the alleged nuisance upon the claimant will be taken into account by the court and will be given appropriate weight. Utilisation of the best practicable means (including 'best available techniques' in an IPPC regulated facility) by the defendant does not provide an automatic defence. The courts will have regard to the severity of the impact of the defendant's activities upon the claimant and whether any further preventive action could have been taken by the defendant. Thus, a defendant who is complying with the terms of a permit to pollute may not necessarily be able to

---

41 Bolton v Stone [1951] AC 850.
42 De Keyser's Royal Hotel Ltd v Spicer Bros Ltd (1914) 30 TLR 257.
43 British Celanese Ltd v AH Hunt (Capacitors) Ltd [1969] 1 WLR 959; [1969] 2 All ER 1252.
44 See also Crown River Cruises Ltd v Kimbolton Fireworks Ltd [1996] 2 Lloyd's Rep 533, in which debris from a fireworks display fell to earth over a period of some 20 minutes, and set light to the defendant's barges.
45 Hollywood Silver Fox Farm Ltd v Emmett [1936] 2 KB 468; [1936] 1 All ER 825.
46 E.g. banging a tin tray on a shared wall to disrupt music lessons. See Christie v Dovey (1893) 1 ch 316.
47 Kennaway v Thompson [1980] 3 WLR 361; [1980] 3 All ER 329; Blackburn v ARC Ltd [1998] Env LR 469; see also the discussion of public benefit in 11.7.4.10 below.

defeat a nuisance action. In *Read v J Lyons and Co Ltd* (1947),[48] the House of Lords, in a nuisance action in respect of an explosion at a munitions factory, held that if a man commits a nuisance, it is no answer to his neighbour's complaint that he took the utmost care not to commit the nuisance. Even if a factory has been operated with reasonable care, it is still open to the court to find that the defendant's activities constitute a nuisance.

11.7.4.8 The foreseeability of the type of harm or damage complained of

It is necessary for the claimant to prove that the type of damage caused to his or her use or enjoyment of land was *foreseeable at the time the relevant damage occurred*. The leading case on this issue is *Cambridge Water Co Ltd v Eastern Counties Leather plc* (1994).[49] The House of Lords, in rejecting the claimant's private nuisance action, held that liability depended upon the foreseeability of the relevant type of damage occurring. The damage in this particular case consisted of the presence of polluting solvents in an aquifer from which the claimant abstracted drinking water. Although it was proved that the solvents had emanated from the defendant's property, the court held that at the time the spillages of solvents had occurred, it was not reasonably foreseeable that the escape of those solvents would result in damage to the aquifer.

The 'hypersensitive' claimant cases operate to filter out nuisance actions which have little prospect of success, but the mere fact that a claimant engages in a hypersensitive trade will not automatically debar a nuisance action. If a defendant's activities would have caused a nuisance for a normal (i.e. non-hypersensitive) neighbour, a claimant engaging in a hypersensitive trade may still succeed in a nuisance action.[50]

Some academic commentators have suggested that recent case law[51] is indicative of a trend by the courts to treat hypersensitivity as one aspect of the wider question of whether the defendant ought to have realised that his activities, which were causing the claimant a degree of interference, would result in the claimant sustaining reasonably foreseeable damage.

11.7.4.9 Human rights

Is the existence of such rights a relevant factor in a private nuisance action, or is the action based on the ground of breach of an article of the European Convention on Human Rights (incorporated into English law by the HRA 1998)? In *Marcic v Thames Water Utilities Ltd* (2002),[52] the claimant brought a successful action against his sewerage services provider based on a breach of Art 8 of the ECHR (right to respect for a person's home and private life).

11.7.4.10 Public interest

The tort of nuisance continues to be a fertile basis of civil actions. In *Dennis v Ministry of Defence* (2003),[53] the claimants owned an historic mansion located close to an RAF base at Wittering in Lincolnshire. The base was used for jump jet pilot training and the noise of aircraft was very loud.[54] The claimants sued the Ministry of Defence (MOD) in nuisance and Buckley J found that the operation of the jets constituted a very serious interference with the enjoyment of the claimant's property. The MOD put forward the following arguments (unsuccessfully) to justify its activities: (a) training pilots for the defence of the realm was one of the ordinary usages land for the benefit of humankind—the court held that the generation of such extreme noise was not an ordinary use

---

48 *Read v Lyons & Co Ltd* [1947] AC 156.
49 *Cambridge Water Co v Eastern Counties Leather plc* [1994] 2 AC 264; [1994] 2 WLR 53; [1994] 1 All ER 53.
50 See *McKinnon Industries Ltd v Walker* (1951) 3 DLR 577.
51 E.g. *Network Rail Infrastructure Ltd v C J Morris (trading as Soundstar Studios)* (2004) Env LR 41.
52 *Marcic v Thames Water Utilities Ltd* [2001] 3 All ER 698; [2002] 2 All ER 55.
53 *Dennis & Dennis v Ministry of Defence* [2003] EWHC 793.
54 An average of 77–113 db(A).

of land; (b) defence of the realm was a public interest of a different and greater order than commercial interests (that is, the public interest 'trumped' the private commercial interests of the claimants). Buckley J declined to attempt a general answer to the question of the effect of public interest in a nuisance action; however, if the public interest were automatically to prevail (when balancing the competing interests of the parties) over private interests, then the claimants would have no remedy at all and would suffer unjust damage for the benefit of all (i.e. for the public benefit). Buckley J was clearly of the opinion that public interest considerations were relevant to the question of the appropriate remedy (rather than whether the activities complained of constituted a nuisance). Thus, whilst the public interest might dictate that jump jet training continue, it was just that the claimants receive compensation; (c) the MOD submitted that the character of the neighbourhood was to be assessed in the context of the airbase as an established feature of the locality. This was rejected by the court as otherwise the defendant could change the character of the neighbourhood over time (i.e. by intensifying use) and create a nuisance with impunity; and (d) the MOD's argument that it had acquired a prescriptive right was also rejected because such a right was too uncertain. The court also upheld the claimant's claim based on breach of their human rights.[55] The court awarded £950,000 damages based on property 'blight', loss of potential revenue from the commercial exploitation of the property, and loss of amenity.

11.7.5 Who can bring an action in private nuisance?

It is a long-established principle that, in order to sue in nuisance, the claimant must have an interest in the land affected.[56] This will include the occupier of the land, a tenant in possession, and it can extend to those with a variety of other legal interests in land (such as a squatter with possessory title). A person merely occupying property[57] does not have a property interest on which to base a nuisance action but such a person may be able to base a civil action on breach of Art 8 of the European Convention on Human Rights.[58]

11.7.6 Against whom can a nuisance action be brought?

A civil action can be brought against a variety of parties, not only the 'polluter', but also those who allowed or authorised the pollution or environmental damage.

A nuisance action can be brought against the following:

(a) the creator of the nuisance: the party who creates the nuisance may always be sued. This is the case whether or not the creator of the nuisance is the occupier of the land at the time;[59]

(b) the occupier of premises: the occupier will be liable in three situations:

(i) if he or she creates the nuisance; or
(ii) if the nuisance is caused by his or her servant or agent; or
(iii) if he or she continues (adopts) a pre-existing nuisance created by a previous occupier.

In *Leakey v National Trust* (1980),[60] it was stated that if the nuisance was not created by the occupier, he or she is only expected to do what is reasonable in the circumstances to prevent or minimise a known risk to his or her neighbour;

---

55 Art 8—right to home and family life, and Art 1, Protocol 1—peaceful enjoyment of possessions.
56 See *Hunter and Others v Canary Wharf Ltd* [1997] AC 156.
57 E.g. as a married spouse or relation of the property owner or tenant.
58 See *Khatun v UK* see page 584 and *McKenna v British Aluminium* [2002] Env LR 30.
59 See *Thompson v Gibson* (1841) 7 M & W 456.
60 *Leakey v National Trust* [1980] 2 WLR 65; [1980] 1 All ER 17.

(c)   the landlord: there is a generally recognised rule that a landlord will generally not be liable because he or she is not in occupation of the property and has no knowledge of the nuisance, unless he or she has authorised the nuisance, as in *Tetley v Chitty* (1986).[61] In that case, the local authority, as landlord, was held liable for the noise caused by go-karting activities because the authority knew (by granting a lease it knew what its land would be used for), or should have known, of the nuisance before the property was let;

(d)   any person who is creating a nuisance by making a 'material contribution' to the damage (from several sources) suffered by the claimant.[62]

11.7.7 Defences

11.7.7.1 Statutory authority

This defence is only available to legal persons exercising statutory powers whose activities are alleged to be causing a nuisance. To be able to take advantage of this defence, the defendant must be able to show that it did not cause any unnecessary inconvenience in the way in which it carried out the activities authorised by the relevant legislation. The court will take into account the methods and equipment used by the defendant to complete the works. It will also have regard to the scale of the development, its social utility and the timescale within which it took the defendant to complete the development. In *Allen v Gulf Oil Refining Ltd* (1981),[63] a private Act of Parliament provided the defendant oil company with statutory authority to acquire land in Milford Haven for the purpose of building an oil refinery. Once the refinery was constructed and was operational, local residents brought a nuisance action in regard to the smells, noise and vibration generated by the defendant's activities. The plaintiffs argued that the defence of statutory authority did not apply in this case because the relevant Act did not specifically refer to, and therefore authorise, the operation of the plant in a manner which created a nuisance. The House of Lords rejected this submission and held that the Act conferred an immunity for all acts inevitably flowing from the authority to build the refinery. The plaintiffs could only succeed if they could establish that the nuisance complained of was much greater than was necessary or where the defendant had carried out its activities negligently. In short, redress is only possible if it can be proved that the defendant failed to exercise reasonable care to minimise the nuisance. An example of a case in which the defendant failed to exercise reasonable care is *Tate & Lyle Industries Ltd v GLC* (1983).[64] The defendant local authority constructed a ferry terminal with the benefit of statutory authority, but the development caused the silting-up of the River Thames around the plaintiff sugar refiners' river jetties. The plaintiff sued in nuisance to recover the £50,000 it had incurred in dredging the river in order to maintain access to its jetties. The court found in favour of the plaintiff but awarded only 75 per cent of its claim on the ground that even if the defendant had exercised reasonable care in the construction of the terminal, some dredging would still have been necessary.

Whilst it is clear that Acts of Parliament will entitle a defendant to claim the defence of statutory authority, it seems that other legislative provisions, such as the grant of a pollution permit by the Environment Agency, will not, in most cases, entitle the defendant to the defence of statutory authority. In *Wheeler v JJ Saunders Ltd* (1995),[65] Gibson LJ stated that 'the court should be slow to acquiesce in the extinction of private rights without compensation as a result of administrative decisions which could not be appealed and were difficult to challenge'. Gibson LJ went on to concede,

---

61   *Tetley v Chitty* [1986] 1 All ER 663.
62   See 11.7.7.4.
63   *Allen v Gulf Oil Refining Ltd* [1981] AC 1001; [1981] 2 WLR 188; [1981] All ER 353.
64   *Tate & Lyle Industries Ltd v GLC* [1983] AC 509.
65   *Wheeler v JJ Saunders Ltd* [1996] Ch 19.

however, that there might be instances where a regulatory body may legitimately override private rights.

One case which considers private nuisance in an environmental context is *Blackburn v ARC Ltd* (1998).[66] The case concerned a landfill site which was alleged to be causing a nuisance due to (a) litter escaping from the site, (b) odour problems relating to the failure of the defendant properly to cover over the waste and also from landfill gases, and (c) noise from lorry traffic, site machinery and gas flare. The High Court held that the defence of statutory authority only applied if the statutory authority changed the character of the area or there was direct statutory authorisation for the development. In this case, there was no change in character because the relevant planning permission and landfill permit were of a temporary nature (i.e. the interference would end when the landfill site was full). The plaintiff's claim would fail if the nuisance would have inevitably resulted from the authorised activities. However, in this case, the nuisance was not inevitable and could have been avoided if the defendant had operated its site properly. The Court went on to hold that where the defendant's activities did inevitably lead to the release of odours and gas in circumstances where the release could not have been avoided, in order to establish nuisance, the plaintiff must prove that the defendant's use of land was not a reasonable use. It was clear that the use of land as a waste tip which generated odours and gases was not a reasonable use of land. If the odours and gas were more than must be tolerated in modern living conditions, the defendant will be liable. Additionally, the court held that the principle of 'give and take', applying to the activities of neighbouring landowners (and referred to by Lord Goff in *CambridgeWater*),[67] depended upon the defendant's use of land being a reasonable use, but, in this case, the defendant's activities 'fell well outside any latitude which the law may have allowed'.

11.7.7.2 The defendant takes reasonable precautions to minimise the nuisance

The courts make a distinction between those cases in which the defendant is the original cause of the nuisance and those cases in which the defendant acquires land and continues a pre-existing nuisance. In the former case, the fact that the defendant took all reasonable care to minimise the nuisance will not provide a defence because liability is strict. In *Read v Lyons* (1947),[68] Lord Symons stated: 'If a man commits a legal nuisance, it is no answer to his injured neighbour that he took the utmost care not to commit it. There the liability is strict.' In the latter case, in which the defendant subsequently becomes aware that a nuisance is being caused and takes all reasonable precautions to minimise the nuisance, then the defendant will have a defence.[69]

11.7.7.3 The claimant came to the nuisance

It is not a defence for a defendant to allege that the claimant exposed himself to a nuisance by moving to it (i.e. moving into an area with the result that the claimant is exposed to the defendant's activities). This is relevant to the owners of factories which, at some point after construction, became surrounded by residential development. The law does not prevent residential property owners from taking action with regard to nuisance caused by the operation of factories. The leading case on this issue is *Bliss v Hall* (1838),[70] in which the defendant established and operated a business as a tallow chandler. Three years later, the plaintiff moved into the neighbouring property and commenced a nuisance action against the defendant with regard to the fumes produced by the tallow works. Tindall CJ stated: 'The plaintiff came to the house he occupies with all the rights

---

66 *Blackburn v ARC Ltd* [1998] Env LR 469.
67 *CambridgeWater Co v Eastern Counties Leather plc* [1994] 2 AC 264; [1994] 2 WLR 53; [1994] 1 All ER 53.
68 *Read v Lyons & Co Ltd* [1947] AC 156.
69 See *Leakey v National Trust* [1980] 2 WLR 65; [1980] 1 All ER 17.
70 *Bliss v Hall* (1838) 4 Bing NC 183.

which the common law affords, and one of them is the right to wholesome air. Unless the defendant shows a prescriptive right to carry on his business in the particular the plaintiff is entitled to judgment.' Awareness of the possibility that conflicts might arise between competing property owners will not be allowed to interfere with the operation of the town and country planning system. The High Court held in *R v Exeter County Council ex p JL Thomas and Co Ltd* (1991)[71] that a planning authority may grant planning permission for development which may, when implemented, give rise to complaints and legal action against the owners of existing development by owners of new developments.

11.7.7.4 One of many polluters

It is no defence to a nuisance action for the defendant to argue that the defendant's contribution to the nuisance suffered by the claimant is so insignificant that it is not actionable. The authority for this principle is *Blair v Deakin* (1887),[72] a case in which effluent from several upstream defendants created a nuisance for a downstream factory owner. This principle should be viewed with some caution since the means to detect, measure and identify pollutants is now very much more advanced than when this case was decided.[73]

11.7.7.5 Prescription

The likelihood of this defence succeeding in most circumstances is remote. Whilst, in theory, it is possible to acquire an easement to pollute, in practice this defence is very difficult to establish. To succeed, the right to pollute which is claimed must be lawful (that is, not a discharge in breach of the conditions of a pollution permit), which is openly exercised, which is continuously exercised for a period of at least 20 years, and which is exercised without the permission of the person against whom the right is being acquired. In *Sturges v Bridgman* (1879),[74] the defendant had operated noisy machinery on his land for over 20 years. An adjoining landowner, a doctor, extended his premises by constructing a consulting room close to the boundary with the defendant's property. The doctor then commenced, and succeeded in, an action in nuisance against the defendant due to the unreasonable level of noise and vibration generated by the defendant's machines. The court rejected the defendant's argument that he had acquired an easement authorising the nuisance. The time from which the prescriptive right in this case was calculated was the time, or point, at which the nuisance began, and the time ran from the date of construction of the consulting rooms.

11.7.8 Remedies

11.7.8.1 Injunctions

To succeed in obtaining an injunction, the claimant must have a strong case. The courts are reluctant to grant injunctions unless there is good evidence that the defendant's activities are having a significant and adverse impact upon the claimant which justifies restricting, totally or partially, the defendant's activities which are causing the nuisance. The following cases illustrate the circumstances in which a claim for an injunction may succeed or fail. In *Halsey v Esso Petroleum Co Ltd* (1961),[75] the plaintiff successfully obtained an injunction relating to the noise from the defendant's boilers and vehicle movements to and from the plant. In *Allison v Merton, Sutton and Wandsworth AHA* (1975),[76]

---

71 *R v Exeter CC ex p JL Thomas and Co Ltd* [1991] 1 QB 471.
72 *Blair v Deakin* (1887) 57 LT 522.
73 See also 11.2.c and especially the case of *Graham and Graham v Rechem International Ltd* [1996] Env LR 158.
74 *Sturges v Bridgman* (1879) 11 Ch D 852.
75 *Halsey v Esso Petroleum Co Ltd* [1961] 1 WLR 683; [1961] 2 All ER 145.
76 *Allison v Merton, Sutton and Wandsworth AHA* [1975] CLY 2450.

the plaintiff was granted an injunction to restrain the noise from the defendant's hospital boilers which interfered with the plaintiff's sleep and caused feelings of depression falling short of a clinical depressive illness. In *AG v Gastonia Coaches Ltd* (1977),[77] the plaintiff successfully obtained an injunction against the defendant coach company to restrain a nuisance consisting of diesel odours and noise disturbance caused by the defendant 'revving' coach engines in a residential street. In *Blackburn v ARC Ltd* (1998),[78] the plaintiff applied for an injunction to close down the defendant's landfill site which was alleged to be causing a nuisance due to litter, odour and vehicle movements. The landfill site only had a further three years of 'life' left and the court declined to grant an injunction closing the site down. Whilst the court accepted that the primary remedy for continuing nuisances was an injunction, it was a discretionary remedy and in the circumstances of this case damages provided adequate compensation for the diminution in value of the plaintiff's property. The court stated that it would be open to the plaintiff to seek a further injunction at any time in the future if a repetition of the serious failures of the past were to recur.

11.7.8.2 Compensation

Compensation may be awarded to the claimant with regard to damage to property and chattels. The position regarding the recovery of compensation for personal injury caused by nuisance is unclear and therefore the claimant ought to include a negligence claim to cover any personal injury.

11.7.8.3 Sensibility claims

An award of damages is the norm in such cases and the sum awarded will reflect the severity and persistence of the nuisance.[79]

11.7.8.4 Loss of profits

In contrast to negligence actions, in which pure economic loss (i.e. cases in which the claimant suffers financial loss but no personal injury or property damage) is not recoverable, once damage has been proved in a nuisance action, liability is strict. In appropriate cases, loss of profits are recoverable. In *Blackburn v ARC Ltd* (1998),[80] the plaintiff included a claim for loss of profits relating to renovation works carried out at the plaintiff's home. The court rejected the claim on the basis that such losses were not a foreseeable consequence of the particular nuisance. Although the loss of profits claim failed, the plaintiff did recover £25,000 in respect of the diminution of the value of his home.

11.7.8.5 Exemplary damages

The circumstances in which exemplary damages may be claimed are very limited. The claimant will succeed if the defendant has deliberately interfered with the claimant's property rights and has cynically calculated that his or her interference will produce a financial gain greater than the cost of the damage to the claimant.[81]

11.8 Human rights

With the advent of the Human Rights Act 1998, lawyers acting on behalf of claimants whose interests have been injured by the polluting activities of defendants began to consider basing a claim for

---

77 *AG v Gastonia Coaches Ltd* (1977) RTR 219.
78 *Blackburn v ARC Ltd* [1998] Env LR 469.
79 Eg *Allison v Merton, Sutton and Wandsworth AHA* [1975] CLY 2450.
80 *Blackburn v ARC Ltd* [1998] Env LR 469.
81 See *AB v South West Water Services Ltd* [1993] 1 All ER 609.

redress on the breach of the claimant's human rights in addition to one or more of the environmental torts. In recent years a number of cases have been argued on the basis of both torts and breach of human rights.[82] Of particular relevance are the cases of *Marcic v Thames Water Utilities Ltd*—a case involving sewage pollution,[83] *Dennis v MOD*—a case involving noise interference[84] and *Hatton v UK*—a noise nuisance case arising out of the operation of Heathrow Airport.[85]

See Chapter ◄ 12.11

11.9 Public nuisance

The tort of public nuisance shares many of the elements of private nuisance, although there are several distinguishing factors. It is also possible for an alleged nuisance to be actionable as both a public and private nuisance.[86]

11.9.1 Definition

Public nuisance was defined in the case of *AG v PYA Quarries* (1957):[87]

> A public nuisance is one which materially affects the reasonable comfort and convenience of life of a class of Her Majesty's subjects who come within the sphere or neighbourhood of its operation; the question whether the number of persons affected is sufficient to constitute a class is one of fact in every case and it is sufficient to show that a representative cross-section of that class has been so affected for an injunction to issue.

11.9.2 The characteristic features of public nuisance

Actions in public nuisance have the advantage that no interest in land is required by a claimant in order to commence an action. The House of Lords decision in *Hunter and Others v Canary Wharf Ltd* (1997),[88] with its rejection of private nuisance actions by occupiers of property who have no legal rights as owners or tenants of property, is likely to increase interest in the use of public nuisance by licensees (e.g. persons with a mere contractual right to occupy property) who cannot otherwise sue in private nuisance.

Public nuisance must affect a class or section of the public. In contrast to private nuisance, public nuisance is a crime and this enables the Attorney General or a local authority to prosecute the defendant. An action in public nuisance may be brought by an individual or a group of citizens provided that he, she or they can establish that he, she or they have suffered special damage (damage over and above that which is suffered by the general public which is calculable in financial terms). Typically, public nuisance actions involving infringement of public rights might relate to:

(a)   repeated exposure to offensive smells generated by landfill sites or waste incinerators;

(b)   intolerable noise created by a factory which is operating 24 hours a day and disturbs many

---

82   Especially breach of Art 8—the right to home and family life and Art 1 of Protocol 1—the peaceful enjoyment of possessions.
83   E.g. *Marcic v Thames Water Utilities Ltd* [2001] 3 All ER 698; [2002] 2 All ER 55.
84   *Dennis & Dennis v Ministry of Defence* [2003] EWHC 793.
85   *Hatton v UK* (2001) The Times, 8 October.
86   *Allen v Gulf Oil Refining Ltd* [1981] AC 1001; [1981] 2 WLR 188; [1981] All ER 353.
87   *AG v PYA Quarries* (1957) 2 WLR 770.
88   *Hunter and Others v Canary Wharf Ltd* [1997] AC 156.

people;

(c) widespread contamination of water supplies posing a threat to the health of a large number of people; or

(d) interference with public rights of way (on land and on navigable waters).

Public nuisance is founded on the commission of an actionable wrong which has a material effect on a 'large' number of people. Some guidance on the numbers of people who must be affected to justify an action in public nuisance is provided by the Docklands case, *Hunter v Canary Wharf* (1997).[89] In that action, approximately 600 people constituted a sufficiently wide class of the public to mount an action relating to disturbance caused by construction dust and interference with TV reception. In contrast, in *R v Johnson* (1996),[90] the Court of Appeal held that 13 women who had received harassing telephone calls were a 'class' upon which a public nuisance action could be founded.

The case of *R v South West Water Authority* (1991)[91] was brought following the water pollution incident at Camelford, Cornwall, which attracted a considerable amount of press coverage at the time. In July 1988, 20 tonnes of aluminium sulphate was pumped into the wrong tank at a water treatment works. Although the alarm was raised almost immediately, remedial action was not taken for several hours, during which time there were reports from water consumers that the water smelt and tasted foul, that it was black, it burnt mouths and hair and stuck fingers together. It was later reported that the water had caused considerable personal injury in the form of hair loss, nail deformities, rheumatism, diarrhoea and memory loss. The action was brought as criminal proceedings against South West Water Authority. The authority was found guilty of committing a public nuisance by supplying water contaminated with aluminium sulphate which endangered the health or comfort of the public. The authority was fined £10,000 and ordered to pay costs of £25,000.

11.9.3 Who can bring an action in public nuisance?

Public nuisance actions may be commenced by members of the public, a local authority, or the Attorney General. Public nuisance actions will, as a general rule, only be commenced where the relevant local authority is unwilling to take action (using its statutory nuisance powers). If a member of the public commences an action, he or she must have suffered substantial damage (that is greater than that suffered by the public in general). The damage must also be of a type which was reasonably foreseeable. In *Halsey v Esso Petroleum Co Ltd* (1961),[92] a public nuisance action was possible because oily smuts had damaged vehicles parked on the public highway, as opposed to being parked on private property. In addition, the noise of heavy vehicles travelling to and from the refinery on the public highway also justified an action in public nuisance. The special damage sustained by Halsey was damage to the paintwork of his motor car.

A public nuisance action may be commenced by a claimant where interference with a public right also violates the claimant's private rights. In *Tate & Lyle Industries Ltd v GLC* (1983),[93] an action in public nuisance was possible because not only did the defendant's construction work interfere with public navigation rights, but it also interfered with the plaintiff's right of access to its river jetties.

Section 222 of the Local Government Act 1972 provides local authorities with a discretionary power to commence public nuisance actions. This power is used infrequently due to the preference of local authorities to use their statutory nuisance powers

---

89 Ibid.
90 *R v Johnson* [1996] 2 Cr App R 434.
91 *R v South West Water Authority* (1991) 3 LMELR 65.
92 *Halsey v Esso Petroleum Co Ltd* (1961) 1 WLR 683.
93 *Tate & Lyle Industries Ltd v GLC* (1983) AC 509.

instead. In contrast to private nuisance, the use of best practicable means to abate a public nuisance is a complete defence to a statutory nuisance action. This may be a factor in the decision by a member of the public to commence a public nuisance action rather than relying upon the local authority. Also, if a local authority does commence a public nuisance action, aggrieved citizens will not be able to claim compensation for the damage they have suffered. Worse still, if a local authority fails to establish that a public nuisance exists, it will not be able to claim injunctive relief and aggrieved citizens may be left without a remedy.

The Attorney General is entitled to take action to redress public wrongs. In the event that an individual who wishes to commence an action in public nuisance cannot prove that he or she has suffered special damage, he or she may request either the Attorney General or the local authority to take action.

11.9.4 Against whom can the action in public nuisance be brought?

As in private nuisance, an action may be brought against the following:

(a)   the creator of the nuisance;
(b)   the occupier of the relevant premises;
(c)   the landlord.

11.9.5 Can a claim for personal injury be based upon public nuisance?

The Court of Appeal[94] has held that damages for personal injury are potentially recoverable in the tort of public nuisance. The relevant litigation related to a public nuisance claim brought by 18 claimants who had been born with upper limb deformities. The claimants claimed damages in the tort of public nuisance, asserting that their deformities had arisen from their mothers' exposure to toxic materials during the course of their pregnancies. The claimants alleged that their mothers' exposure to toxic materials was caused by the defendant's programme of reclamation and decontamination relating to land in Corby. The defendants applied to strike out the claimants' claim, based upon the defendant's submission that even if, historically, a claim to damages for personal injury had lain in public nuisance, such a claim no longer existed. Dyson LJ rejected that contention and held that the claimants' civil action could not be found to have no reasonable prospect of success.

11.10 Defences in public nuisance and private nuisance actions

The following are defences in public and private nuisance actions:

(a)   statutory authority;
(b)   contributory negligence;
(c)   prescription (only available in private nuisance)—the law will not allow an action in nuisance to succeed if the state of affairs which constitutes the actionable nuisance has continued for more than 20 years. For this defence to succeed, the claimant must show that the actionable

---

94   *Corby Group Litigation v Corby Borough Council* (2008) EWCA Civ 463. See also http://www.lawreports.co.uk/WLRD/2008/CACiv/
      may0.8.htm, accessed on 28.2.2010.
95   *Sturges v Bridgman* (1879) 11 Ch D 852.

nuisance has run from the beginning of this 20-year period (*Sturges v Bridgman* (1879));[95]

(d)   consent of the claimant—in circumstances in which the claimant has consented, either expressly or impliedly, to the nuisance, the defendant cannot be liable, unless there is some negligence on his or her part;[96]

(e)   ignorance—ignorance of the nuisance can only be classed as a defence if it is not a result of the defendant's failure to act with reasonable skill and care in order to discover the nuisance;

(f)   other defences—many other defences have been raised, although few have been successful; for example, it would be no defence for the defendant to argue that the claimant had 'come to the nuisance', nor could the defendant argue that the activity is of some use to the public in general, although it may be an issue which is considered in determining whether the defendant's use of the land is reasonable.

11.11 Remedies in nuisance actions

Remedies[97] in nuisance actions are:

(a)   abatement;
(b)   injunction;
(c)   damages.

Damages are available for (i) physical damage to the claimant's property, and (ii) personal injury to the claimant in the torts of negligence and public nuisance.

11.12 Negligence

The largest number of civil compensation claims are based upon the tort of negligence, but this tort has limited utility in an environmental context. Negligence actions have advantages and disadvantages. The claimant does not require an interest in land in order to sue and damages are available to compensate personal injuries. Conversely, injunctions are not available, pure economic loss and exemplary damages are not recoverable, the negligent actions of the defendant's independent contractors may shield the defendant from liability, and in contrast to other torts, fault must be proved. A negligence claim may be the only option for some claimants who suffer damage but have no interest in the property which would enable them to commence actions in nuisance, trespass or the rule in *Rylands v Fletcher* (for example, a guest in a hotel who is poisoned by fumes emanating from a factory located adjacent to the hotel).[98]

11.12.1 Definition

Negligence is the omission to do something which a reasonable man, guided upon those considerations which ordinarily regulate the conduct of human affairs, would do, or doing something which a prudent and reasonable man would not do.[99]

In order to establish negligence, the claimant must prove the following:

---

96 *Kiddle v City Business Properties Ltd* [1942] 1 KB 269.
97 See generally 11.3.
98 *Rylands v Fletcher* (1868) LR 3HL 330.
99 *Blythe v Birmingham Waterworks Co* (1856) 11 Exch 781.

(a)   the defendant owes the claimant a duty of care;
(b)   the defendant breaches that duty; and
(c)   the breach causes damage to the claimant.

11.12.2 Duty of care

A general guide to the circumstances in which it would be appropriate to impose a duty of care upon a defendant in the tort of negligence was established in *Donoghue v Stevenson* (1932).[100] The general guiding principle behind the duty of care is the 'neighbour principle'—meaning that 'you must take reasonable care to avoid acts or omissions which you can reasonably foresee would be likely to injure your neighbour'. Neighbours are defined as 'persons who are so closely and directly affected by my act that I ought reasonably to have them in contemplation as being so affected when I am directing my mind to the acts or omissions which are being called into question'. The judges use the duty of care concept (and the other key negligence criteria: breach of duty and damage) as control devices to regulate the number of negligence actions which are litigated before the civil courts.

The neighbour principle has, in recent times, been given a restrictive judicial interpretation. The judiciary generally favour an incremental approach to the development of the law of negligence. In novel factual situations, the courts apply the approach set out in the case of *Caparo Industries v Dickman* (1990)[101] in order to determine whether a duty of care is owed by the defendant to the claimant.

Three criteria must be established:

(a)   the harm must be reasonably foreseeable (that is, an objective test of what the reasonable man would foresee and not what the defendant might foresee);
(b)   the claimant and defendant must have a sufficiently proximate relationship; and
(c)   it must be just, fair and reasonable to impose a duty of care.

The courts currently appear to be reluctant to take a principled, as opposed to an incremental approach (i.e. the judges look back to similar factual situations in which previous courts imposed or refused to impose a duty of care), to the development of the law by upholding claims which support the imposition of a duty of care in novel environmental contexts. This is especially true where a claimant seeks to make a regulatory agency liable for loss caused by a failure (omission) to warn the claimant of danger.[102]

11.12.3 Breach of duty of care

Once a duty of care has been established, it is necessary to go on to establish that the defendant was in breach of his duty of care and, further, that his or her breach resulted in damage to the claimant. In order to determine whether there has been a breach of the duty of care, it is necessary to look at the conduct of the defendant and ask whether he or she has achieved the standard of care that is necessary if he or she is not to be liable. The standard used is that of the 'reasonable man'. This is an objective standard and as such no concessions are made for individual weaknesses. The courts will consider the following factors in order to determine whether the defendant has acted as a reasonable man:

---

100 *Donoghue v Stevenson* [1932] AC 562.
101 *Caparo Industries v Dickman* [1990] 2 AC 605.
102 See *Dear v Thames Water Ltd* (1992) WLAW 116, but contrast the decisions in *Barnes v Irwell Valley Water Board* [1939] 1 KB 21 and *Scott-Whitehead v National Coal Board* [1987] 2 EGLR 227; (1987) 53 P & CR 263.

(a)   the likelihood of harm;
(b)   the seriousness of the risk;
(c)   the end to be achieved;
(d)   the cost and practicability of avoiding the risk.

Where the duty of care relates to a specialised area (e.g. a profession), the duty of care expected is one which would be expected from someone with those skills in the same profession.[103] Where industrial practices are concerned, one must look to standards which are deemed reasonable (especially as described in industry and regulatory guidance documents) by the industry concerned.

11.12.4 Foreseeable damage arising from the breach of the duty of care

An action in negligence can only be brought where the negligence has caused, or contributed to, personal injury or damage to property. The courts normally use the 'but for' test to determine whether the defendant's breach of duty was the cause of the damage (that is, would the claimant's loss or injury have occurred in any event and irrespective of the defendant's negligence?). The classic illustration of the 'but for' test is *Barnett v Chelsea and Kensington Hospital Management Committee* (1969),[104] in which a person suffering from arsenic poisoning attended hospital but would have died even if the hospital had not been negligent in its failure to properly diagnose the patient's condition. The 'but for' test and its limitations are examined below (see also the tort texts listed in the further reading section at the end of the chapter).

Damage must also be reasonably foreseeable, as the defendant will not be liable for the unforeseen consequences of his or her negligent act.[105]

Following the House of Lords' decision in *Cambridge Water Co Ltd v Eastern Counties Leather plc* (1994),[106] foreseeability of the relevant *type of harm* or damage is a necessary prerequisite of liability in negligence, nuisance and the rule in *Rylands v Fletcher*.[107] The test of foreseeability in the *Cambridge Water* case was based on what the reasonable supervisor, who was overseeing the operation of the defendant's tannery, would have foreseen as the consequence of repeated spillages of solvents over a prolonged period of time. The court held that, at the material time, the supervisor might reasonably have foreseen that repeated spillages of solvents, in relatively small quantities, might result in solvent fumes affecting the breathing of the defendant's employees, but not contamination of groundwaters. Little was known about the migration of chemicals in subsurface strata (underground bands of rock) at the relevant time the spillages were occurring and the supervisor could not reasonably have foreseen the relevant type of harm which actually occurred.

It should be noted that in recent years, greater emphasis has been placed on the prudence of businesses employing risk assessments to identify pollution risks associated with their activities. The harmful practices which formed the basis of the *Cambridge Water* litigation occurred in the late 1970s at a time when industrial practice regarding the identification of pollution risks tended to be reactive. It was not uncommon to find that industry would do little to address pollution risks until the regulator produced guidance on specific environmental risks which it had identified. This is no longer an acceptable practice as employers and others have an obligation to keep up to date with best practice.[108]

---

103 See *Bolam v Friern Hospital Management Committee* [1957] 1 WLR 582.
104 *Barnett v Chelsea and Kensington Hospital Management Committee* [1969] 1 QB 428.
105 See, further, *Overseas Tankship (UK) Ltd v Morts Dock & Engineering Co Ltd (The Wagon Mound)* [1961] AC 388; [1961] 2 WLR 126.
106 *Cambridge Water Co v Eastern Counties Leather plc* [1994] 2 AC 264; [1994] 2 WLR 53; [1994] 1 All ER 53.
107 *Rylands v Fletcher* (1868) LR 3 HL 330.
108 See *Thompson v Smiths Shiprepairers (North Shields) Ltd* [1984] 1 All ER 881.

11.12.5 What counts as 'damage' in a negligence action?

Environmental compensation claims often stem from actions based on the tort of private nuisance; however, one significant property-related negligence action arose in *Blue Circle Industries plc v Ministry of Defence* (1998).[109] This case concerned a claim for compensation arising out of a delayed sale of the claimant's property; the original purchaser dropped out when the prospective purchaser realised that the property was contaminated, caused by flood waters negligently emanating from MOD property carrying with them radioactive substances. Those substances became mixed with (and therefore formed part of) the defendant's soil.[110] Although the level of radioactive contamination posed no threat to human health, the level present in the defendant's land exceeded the level permitted by the Nuclear Installations Act (NIA) 1965. This aspect of the case is similar to that of *Cambridge Water v Eastern Counties Leather*,[111] in which the House of Lords accepted that the presence of solvents in controlled waters in concentrations exceeding those permitted by the EC Drinking Water Directive could constitute actionable damage (see Carnwath LJ's judgment in *Blue Circle*).

In allowing the claimant's action for damages under the NIA 1965, the court drew attention to the physical damage to Blue Circle's land which constituted an adverse change in the property's usefulness and value.[112]

In the comparable case of *Merlin v British Nuclear Fuels plc* (1990),[113] the claimant was a homeowner living close to the Sellafield civil nuclear power plant in Cumbria. The claim for damages related to the presence of radioactive dust in the claimant's property which the claimant alleged had adversely affected (blighted) the value of his home. In rejecting the claim, the High Court held that the radioactive dust from Sellafield which was present in Merlin's home had not caused any damage to the property (that is, the presence of the dust did not constitute damage to property). Only the airspace within Merlin's home had changed and since the airspace was not capable of being owned by Merlin, there could be no damage to his property, in spite of the fact that the presence of dust adversely affected the market value of the property. The *Merlin* case may be contrasted with *Hunter and Others v Canary Wharf Ltd* (1997),[114] a nuisance case in which the presence of excessive levels of dust in Hunter's property was accepted (see the judgment of Pill LJ) as constituting property damage, provided cleaning costs (for example, in regard to internal fabrics) were reasonably incurred.

11.12.6 Damage is a prerequisite of liability

A claimant will fail in a negligence action unless damage is proved. Damage may comprise personal injury (including psychiatric injury), property damage, consequential losses (i.e. financial loss consequent upon damage to property or personal injury), but not pure economic loss.[115] Damage to the unowned environment is not a recoverable head of damages in England and Wales. In some circumstances, there might be difficulty in determining the precise date when the relevant damage occurred. For example, in the *Cambridge Water* case,[116] the damage to the plaintiff's proprietary right to abstract wholesome water from its borehole only occurred when the water became unwholesome and unsaleable. This occurred when tests, carried out by the claimant, revealed that the water breached water quality standards contained in a European Community Drinking Water Directive

---

109 *Blue Circle v Ministry of Defence* [1998] 3 All ER 385; [1999] Env LR 22.
110 See the judgment of Aldous LJ.
111 *Cambridge Water Co v Eastern Counties Leather plc* [1994] 2 AC 264; [1994] 2 WLR 53; [1994] 1 All ER 53.
112 M Lee, 'Civil liability in the nuclear industry' [2000] JEL 317.
113 *Merlin v British Nuclear Fules plc* [1990] 2 QB 557.
114 *Hunter and Others v Canary Wharf Ltd* [1997] AC 156.
115 'Economic loss' is a term which refers to damage that is purely financial. It is damage which is not consequent upon physical damage or personal injury.
116 See 11.15.

(80/778/EC) which set maximum permissible levels for certain chemicals, including solvents. The presence of solvents in the water exceeded the limits contained in the Directive and the water could therefore no longer be supplied for human consumption.

In the absence of statutory standards, the damage occasioned to the claimant must be 'substantial' if the negligence action is to be actionable. The courts employ a 'fact and degree' test to determine when damage is substantial. In the Docklands case,[117] the court referred to substantial damage as 'injury impairing value or usefulness'. In determining whether substantial damage has occurred, the courts do not take into account the impact of continuing damage. This may cause problems for the claimant in deciding when to commence an action. If the action is commenced too early, there may be difficulties in establishing that damage has actually occurred, but if the claimant leaves it too long to commence an action, he or she may have his or her claim statute barred.[118] The court has the power to strike out an action if it is of the opinion that the damage occurred at a much earlier time than the date on which the claimant commenced the claim.[119]

11.12.7 Proof

The doctrine of *res ipsa loquitur* (the thing speaks for itself)[120] may be invoked by a claimant to reduce the burden of proof in those cases where the claimant is alleging that the injury or damage was caused by negligence, such as the poor design or faulty operation of industrial plant. Any conviction for a criminal offence which the defendant has and which is material to the claimant's claim, for example, a public nuisance conviction, may be used in evidence to support the claimant's claim. Depending upon the degree of relevance to the claim, this may be conclusive in establishing the civil liability of the defendant.

11.12.8 Causation

The general rule is that the claimant must prove his or her case on the balance of probabilities (that is, it is more likely than not that the defendant's breach of duty caused the claimant's loss). Where there are conflicting explanations of the loss or injury sustained by the claimant, it is not the defendant's job to prove which of the competing explanations is the correct one.

Causation problems may arise in circumstances in which the defendant's negligent acts or omissions compete with an 'innocent' (that is, non-negligent) cause of the loss. The problem often relates to the fact that medical science cannot prove (with the necessary degree of certainty) that the defendant's act or omission caused the claimant's loss because the relevant biological processes are not fully understood.[121] This problem is illustrated by the case of *McGhee v National Coal Board* (1973),[122] in which the claimant, an employee of the defendant, contracted dermatitis due to exposure to brick dust whilst working in a brick kiln. Exposure to some brick dust during the working day was inevitable and lawful. The claimant's allegation of negligence related to the fact that the defendant had not provided shower facilities at work and the extra time the claimant was exposed to the dust, before he could shower at home, was the cause of the disease. The defendant admitted that it had been negligent in not providing showers, but argued that its negligence was not the cause of the disease. Whilst the medical evidence confirmed that exposure to brick dust caused dermatitis, nevertheless, medical experts could not agree that, on the balance

---

117 *Hunter and Others v Canary Wharf Ltd* [1997] AC 156.
118 Because the claim was not commenced within the relevant limitation period; see section 11.16.1.4.
119 S 14 of the Limitation Act 1980.
120 See *Scott v London & St Katherine's Docks Co* (1865) 3 H & C 596.
121 See J Adams, Risk (UCL Press, London 1995).
122 *McGhee v National Coal Board* [1973] 1 WLR 1.

of probabilities, the *additional* exposure to dust had caused the disease. The disease might have been caused by the 'innocent' lawful dust to which the claimant was exposed during working hours.

The House of Lords held the defendant liable because its failure to provide showers had *materially increased the risk* that the claimant would contract dermatitis. In circumstances in which the defendant may escape liability due to evidential difficulties, the courts may relax the 'but for' test in the interests of justice. Not to relax the burden of proof would be unfair to the claimant, since the claimant had sustained exactly the sort of damage which the defendant had a duty to protect the claimant against.

The decision in *McGhee* should be compared with *Hotson v East Berkshire AHA* (1987)[123] (a 'lost chance' case) in which the delay in the treatment of the plaintiff's hip injury resulted in the plaintiff losing a 25 per cent chance of making a full recovery from the injury. The House of Lords rejected the claim because the plaintiff had failed to prove his case on the balance of probabilities. There was a 75 per cent chance that the disabling condition stemming from the injury would have occurred irrespective of the defendant's negligence. In *Hotson*, the court could, on the evidence before it, draw an inference that the plaintiff's injury had not been caused by the defendant's negligence, whereas in *McGhee*, the court based its decision on the evidence that the plaintiff's negligent additional exposure to brick dust was an operative cause of the plaintiff's disease materially contributing to its onset. Thus, the exposure to the 'guilty' dust need not be the main cause of the plaintiff's disease. A majority of the House of Lords treated a material increase in risk as equivalent to a material contribution to the disease.

McGhee and similar cases are important to environmental litigants because actions in negligence are a common basis of action in claims for personal injury concerning exposure to polluting substances (for example, dioxins from waste incinerator chimneys). Occasionally, litigation may be prompted by so-called 'cancer cluster' cases in which emissions from a factory are alleged to have caused illness in the population living in the vicinity of the factory. Whilst expert evidence may be able to demonstrate that statistically there will be a 25 per cent increase in cancer-related mortality in the area surrounding the factory in the next five years, it will be rare for the courts to allow claimants to succeed in such circumstances unless there are good reasons for relaxing the burden of proof.

In *Wilsher v Essex AHA* (1986),[124] the House of Lords stated that *McGhee* supported the basic rule that the claimant must prove that the defendant caused the claimant's loss but, although the burden of proof remains with the claimant, the claimant may establish that the defendant's breach of duty was a material contributory cause of the loss. This interpretation of *McGhee* has not found support in the recent House of Lords' decision in *Fairchild and Others v Glenhaven Funeral Services Ltd* (2002).[125] In this case, negligent exposure of employees to asbestos fibres resulted in the claimant contracting mesothelioma, an invariably fatal type of cancer with a long latency ('gestation') period. Unfortunately, medical science does not fully understand the disease and this resulted in further causation problems. The claimant had worked for a number of employers who had all negligently exposed him to asbestos fibres. Mesothelioma is not, unlike pneumoconiosis, a cumulative illness (that is, the greater the exposure, the worse the disease). There is a minimum exposure (dose) level which has no adverse impact upon humans (each human is unique in their toleration of asbestos fibres) but, once that level is exceeded, it takes only one fibre to trigger the disease. Whilst the risk of contracting the disease increases with greater exposure to asbestos fibres, once the disease has been triggered, the severity of the disease does not increase with further exposure. The claimant could not prove which of his former employers had exposed him to the 'fatal fibre' which had

123 *Hotson v East Berkshire AHA* [1987] AC 750.
124 *Wilsher v Essex AHA* [1986] 3 All ER 801.
125 *Fairchild and Others v Glenhaven Funeral Services Ltd* [2002] 3 All ER 305.

triggered the disease and, on the basis of the normal causation rules, his action was bound to fail. The House of Lords held that in the special circumstances of this type of case (fatal disease and breach of duty to protect the claimant from exposure to asbestos), the 'but for' test ought to be relaxed. Lord Bingham expressed the court's reasoning in the following terms:

> there is a strong policy argument in favour of compensating those who have suffered grave harm, at the expense of their employers who owed them a duty to protect them against that very harm and failed to do so, when the harm can only have been caused by the breach of that duty and science does not permit the victim accurately to attribute, as between several employers, the precise responsibility for the harm he has suffered.[126]

Proving, to the satisfaction of the court, that the defendant's activities caused injury to the claimant is commonly an area where many negligence claims founder. For example, in *Graham and Graham v Rechem International Ltd* (1996),[127] the court rejected an allegation of damage caused to the claimant's cattle due to alleged dioxin poisoning from the defendant's chemical waste incinerator. In this action, the defendant supported its case by referring to the absence of regulatory enforcement action to indicate that its emission of dioxins was not causing harm.

11.12.9 Who can bring an action in negligence?
There is no need to prove an interest in the land which is affected, as there is in an action based on private nuisance. It is not necessary to demonstrate loss by other members of the public, which is necessary in cases brought on the grounds of public nuisance.

11.12.10 Against whom can an action in negligence be brought?
An action can be brought against any legal person where it can be proved that he, she or it owes a duty of care to the claimant, that there was a breach of this duty and that this resulted in reasonably foreseeable damage or injury to the claimant. There are, however, policy factors which will limit actions against certain defendants, for example, regulatory agencies.

11.12.11 Defences

11.12.11.1 Compliance with regulations
It has been suggested that the possession of a permit (for example, a planning permission or permit granted by the Environment Agency) may act as a defence to a negligence action. There is, however, no applicable blanket defence which applies automatically in such circumstances. In *Budden and Alberry v BP Oil Ltd and Shell Oil Ltd*[128] it was alleged that the defendant petrol companies had been negligent in not eliminating or reducing the lead content of their petrols by July 1978 and that this had caused personal injury to the plaintiffs. The defendants applied to have the action struck out on the basis that compliance with the relevant regulations made under s 75(1) of the COPA 1974 provided them with either a complete statutory defence or a complete answer to the allegation that the defendants had been at fault. The court accepted the second submission but not the first.

---

126 In regard to 'fatal fibre' asbestos cases, readers should note the case of *Barker v Corus* [2006] 2 WLR 1027 and the Compensation Act 2006.
127 *Graham and Graham v Rechem International Ltd* (1996) Env LR 158.
128 *Budden and Alberry v BP Oil Ltd and Shell Oil Ltd* (1980) JPL 586.

In *Blackburn v ARC Ltd* (1998),[129] a case involving a claim (in nuisance) for an injunction and/or damages relating to odour and litter emanating from a poorly run landfill, the defendant argued unsuccessfully that possession of planning permission and a waste management permit provided it with a defence to the action. The court held that those permits would only provide the defendant with a defence if the relevant permit conditions were being observed so that any resulting nuisance would be an inevitable consequence of the defendant's permitted operations. This approach seems to accord with earlier authority regarding the application of the defence of statutory authority.[130]

11.12.11.2 Fault

In order to avoid liability in negligence, industrial defendants must be able to establish that they were, at the material time, operating in accordance with the objectively determined standards of knowledge and best practice applicable in the relevant industry.[131] In assessing whether a defendant has attained the standard required by the duty of care in the particular set of circumstances, the court will take a number of factors into account, including:

(a)   the object to be attained;
(b)   the practicability of taking precautions;
(c)   the existence of approved or general practice;
(d)   the defendant's compliance with approved or general practice; and
(e)   the risks created by the defendant's activities.

In assessing whether the defendant kept reasonably abreast of emerging risks in the relevant industry, the court is likely to apply *Stokes v GKN* (1968),[132] a case concerning awareness of developing knowledge of occupational health risks.

11.12.12 Remedies

11.12.12.1 Damages

It is a general principle of the tort of negligence that it is possible to claim damages for physical damage to the person or to property and for loss consequent upon such damage. It is not possible to claim for pure economic loss.[133] Following this, it would be possible to claim damages for injuries caused by a chemical spillage which caused damage to people and property; it would be possible to claim for the clean-up costs, but it would not be possible to claim money for lost profits for the time the site was shut.

11.12.12.2 Injunction

In *Miller v Jackson* (1977),[134] it was held that an injunction is not an available remedy in an action based upon the tort of negligence.

11.13 Trespass

The tort of trespass to land has many functions. Its application for environmental purposes is a more recent development, although its use for such purposes appears to be limited as the trespass must

---

129 *Blackburn v ARC Ltd* [1998] Env LR 469.
130 *Allen v Gulf Oil Refining Ltd* [1981] AC 1001; [1981] 2 WLR 188; [1981] All ER 353.
131 E.g., that they were operating in accordance with an industry code of practice.
132 *Stokes v GKN* [1968] 1 WLR 1776.
133 See, further, *Murphy v Brentwood DC* [1990] 3 WLR 414; [1990] 2 All ER 908.
134 *Miller v Jackson* [1977] 3 WLR 20; [1977] All ER 338.

constitute a direct interference with the claimant's property without lawful excuse. There is some overlap between trespass to land and private nuisance, although it may be easier to bring an action on the basis of trespass because there is no requirement to prove damage as there is with nuisance. This is an obvious advantage and it may make an action in trespass in respect of fly-tipped waste, for example, more likely to succeed than an action in private nuisance. The utility of a trespass action is illustrated by the case of *League Against Cruel Sports v Scott* (1985)[135] in which the claimant used its ownership of land on Exmoor to impede the defendant's deer hunting. The mere presence of the hunt, without permission on the claimant's land, and without causing any damage, would clearly have constituted a trespass and this enabled the court to grant the claimant an injunction preventing the entry of the hunt onto the claimant's land.

11.13.1 Definition

Trespass to land is the unjustifiable physical interference with land, arising from intentional or negligent entry onto the land. A continuing trespass may be caused by continuing entry onto the land or by allowing physical matter to remain on the land.

In addition to trespass to land, an action may be brought with regard to trespass to the person. Whilst it is possible to envisage a situation in which pollution generated by the defendant's activities might give rise to a claim for trespass to the person, in practice the requirement that the interference to the claimant's property or person must be direct has restricted the development of this tort.

The defendant's activities in *McDonald v Associated Fuels Ltd* (1954)[136] illustrate the significance of the intentional nature of the defendant's activities which it is necessary to prove if the claimant is to succeed. The defendant delivered sawdust to the plaintiff's home by blowing it from the defendant's lorry into a storage bin at the plaintiff's home. Exhaust gases from the defendant's lorry were blown into the plaintiff's home along with the sawdust. In consequence, the plaintiff was overcome by fumes, collapsed and suffered injury. The plaintiff's claim based on the negligent actions of the defendant was successful and the court went on to confirm that an action in trespass would also have been successful on the facts. Whilst the defendant did not intend to blow exhaust fumes into the plaintiff's home, it intended to do the act which directly caused the injury.

11.13.2 The characteristics of trespass

The following factors which must be present in order for an action for trespass to land or the person to be brought are:

(a)   that the trespass was direct;
(b)   that the act was intentional or negligent;
(c)   a causal link must be proved between the directness of the act and the inevitability of its consequences.

11.13.3 Direct

The interference must be direct rather than consequential. For example, fly-tipping tyres onto someone's property would constitute trespass, whereas migration of methane from a landfill would

---

135 *League Against Cruel Sports v Scott* (1985) 2 All ER 489.
136 *McDonald v Associated Fuels Ltd* (1954) DLR 775.

not. The dumping of rubbish on land is a common form of trespass, even if it causes very little damage, as in *Gregory v Piper* (1820),[137] in which the defendant disposed of his rubbish in such a way as to block a right of way. Some of the rubbish rolled against the plaintiff's wall and it was held that the defendant was liable in trespass. In this case, it was stated that, in order to be direct, the injury must result from an act of the defendant. An example of this may be found in *Jones v Llanrwst UDC* (1911),[138] in which it was held that sewage, which the defendant had released into a river and which had passed downstream and settled on the plaintiff's land, was direct and amounted to trespass. If the trespass is indirect,[139] then any action should be brought in nuisance.

11.13.4 Intentional or negligent acts

In order for a trespass to be actionable, it is necessary to prove that the defendant acted intentionally or negligently. The intent requirement essentially means that the defendant, or someone under his or her control, must voluntarily enter the claimant's land. Involuntary entry onto, or into, the claimant's land is not sufficient to constitute trespass.

11.13.5 Causal link between the directness of the act and its effects

It is also imperative to establish a causal link between the directness of the act and the inevitability of its consequences. If the effects of the act are indirect, there can be no trespass, although there may be a remedy in nuisance or negligence. Establishing a causal link between the defendant's act and both the directness and inevitability of the resultant damage are important restrictions on trespass actions. In *Jones v Llanrwst UDC*,[140] sewage flowing from the defendant's drains into a river polluted a section of riverbank belonging to the plaintiff (when the sewage was carried in a defined river channel and was deposited on the claimant's riverbank). Whilst the defendant local authority had not intended to deposit sewage onto the plaintiff's land, the court held the defendant liable because it had intended the sewage to pass from its drains into the river. The court held that the trespass was sufficiently direct despite the plaintiff's property being some way downstream of the defendant's drain. By contrast, in *Esso Petroleum Co Ltd v Southport Corp*,[141] the defendant's tanker ran aground in the Ribble Estuary. To refloat the tanker, oil was emptied into the estuary where it was carried by the wind and the tide onto the plaintiff's beach. The House of Lords distinguished this case from *Jones v Llanrwst* on the ground that, unlike the inevitability of a river flowing downstream, it was not inevitable that the oil would wash up on Southport beach. The outcome of this case means that it is virtually impossible to bring a trespass action with regard to an air pollution incident due to the unpredictability of air currents, which negates the necessary degree of directness. In contrast, rivers flow in defined channels.

11.13.6 Who can bring an action in trespass?

Any person who is in exclusive possession of the land can bring an action in trespass. Exclusive possession refers to the occupation or physical control of the land.

As trespass is actionable per se (i.e. without proof of damage), the party bringing the action does not have to prove that the trespass has caused actual damage.

---

137 *Gregory v Piper* (1829) 9 B & C 591.
138 *Jones v Llanrwst UDC* [1911] 1 Ch 393; [1908] All ER 922; see 11.13.5.
139 See *Esso Petroleum Co Ltd v Southport Corp* [1956] AC 218; see 11.13.5.
140 *Jones v Llanrwst UDC* [1911] 1 Ch 393; [1908] All ER 922.
141 *Esso Petroleum Co Ltd v Southport Corp* [1956] AC 218.

11.13.7 Against whom can a trespass action be brought?

The action can be brought against a defendant (the wrongdoer) who has interfered with the possession of the claimant's land. An example of this would be where someone has exceeded permission to remain on the land.

11.13.8 Defences

Defences are:

(a)   necessity;
(b)   compliance with the conditions attached to a licence or permit. A licence gives the express or implied authority which will prevent the trespass from being actionable.

11.13.9 Remedies

Remedies are:

(a)   *damages*—the amount of damages awarded in actions of trespass will usually depend upon the act complained of, particularly as trespass is actionable without any evidence of damage being caused. If the trespass is deemed to be trivial, the damages awarded will usually be nominal. Substantial damage will, however, result in an appropriate award of compensation. Yet, where the trespass has physically damaged the land, the level of damages awarded will reflect the reduction in the value of the land rather than the costs of remediation;[142]
(b)   *injunction*—it will generally be easier to obtain an injunction in an action for trespass than under any other tort because there is no need to prove any damage.

The claimant may require an injunction to prevent a continuing trespass, for example, to prevent the recurrence of tipping.

11.14 The rule in *Rylands v Fletcher*

11.14.1 Definition

The classic definition of this tort is found in the judgment of Blackburn J in *Rylands v Fletcher* (1868),[143] that is, 'the person who for his own purposes brings on his land and collects and keeps there anything likely to do mischief if it escapes, must keep it in at his peril, and, if he does not do so, is prima facie answerable for all the damage which is the natural consequence of its escape'.

The case involved the construction of a reservoir on the defendant's land by independent contractors. The contractors failed to block off a number of mine shafts under the defendant's land which connected to the plaintiff's mine. When the reservoir was filled with water, the plaintiff's mine became flooded. The defendant, although personally not at fault, was held strictly liable for the damage. He had brought onto his land and collected there something which was likely to do damage if it escaped. The defendant failed in his duty to prevent the escape and was therefore liable for all the damage which was the natural consequence of the escape.

The *Rylands v Fletcher* principle imposes strict, but not absolute, liability for damage caused by the escape of dangerous things. The principle has been applied to a wide range of escapes of substances

---

142   *Lodge Holes Colliery Co Ltd v Wednesbury Corp* [1908] AC 323.
143   *Rylands v Fletcher* (1868) LR 3HL 330.

or objects including: water, fire, gases and fumes, electricity, oil, chemicals, colliery waste, poisonous vegetation, acid smuts, explosives, vibrations, trees and animals. Because the rule imposes strict liability, the claimant does not need to prove that the defendant was negligent. The claimant will succeed if he or she establishes a causal connection between the escape and the damage sustained.

An extra facet to the rule was added by Lord Cairns when the case reached the House of Lords. The rule was restricted to circumstances where the defendant had made a 'non-natural' use of his land. The rule applies to things not naturally (ordinarily) present on the defendant's land. The defendant incurs liability by bringing these things onto his or her land which subsequently escape and cause damage. This has, until the decision in *Cambridge Water v Eastern Counties Leather plc* (1994),[144] played an important part in restricting the application of the rule. This restriction came to be associated with the idea that, to fall within the rule, the defendant's use of his land had to pose an increased risk of injury to others. This idea of 'non-natural' use was referred to in *Rickards v Lothian* (1913)[145] as 'some special use bringing with it increased danger to others and must not merely be the ordinary use of the land or such a use as is proper for the general benefit of the community'. To be able to commence an action, the claimant was required to establish that the defendant's use of his or her land was an abnormal use involving an especially hazardous activity. Subsequent cases do not support this interpretation of the *Rylands v Fletcher* principle.[145a]

11.14.2 Which factors must be established for the rule to apply?

In *Read v Lyons* (1947),[146] the key criteria to establish liability under the rule in *Rylands v Fletcher* were stated to be:

(a)   dangerous thing likely to do mischief;
(b)   brought on to land;
(c)   escape;
(d)   non-natural user of the land.[147]

11.14.3 Dangerous thing likely to do mischief

The first essential factor in the application of the rule in *Rylands v Fletcher* is that it applies to 'anything likely to do mischief if it escapes'. There are numerous examples of 'dangerous things' which have escaped and caused damage, including oil,[148] noxious fumes,[149] and explosives.[150]

In determining the presence of a 'dangerous thing', the courts will use a factual test 'whether the thing is likely to do mischief if it escapes'. Following the decision in *Cambridge Water*,[151] it would appear that there is a requirement that the type of damage which occurs is reasonably foreseen as a result of the escape, and possibly that the escape itself (the relevant pollution pathway) is foreseeable.[152] A seemingly innocuous substance, such as water, may be a 'thing likely to do mischief if it escapes' (note the circumstances of *Rylands v Fletcher* (1868)).

---

144 *Cambridge Water Co v Eastern Counties Leather plc* [1994] 2 AC 264; [1994] 2 WLR 53; [1994] 1 All ER 53.
145 *Rickards v Lothian* [1913] AC 263; [1911–13] All ER 71.
145a See *Transco v Stockport MBC* (2004) 2 AC 1.
146 *Read v Lyons & Co Ltd* [1947] AC 156.
147 Note that the additional criterion that the type of damage sustained must be foreseeable was added by the House of Lords decision in *Cambridge Water Co v Eastern Counties Leather plc* [1994] 2 AC 264.
148 *Smith v Great Western Railway* (1926) 135 LT 112.
149 *West v Bristol Tramway Co* [1908] 2 KB 14; [1908–10] All ER 215.
150 *Miles v Forest Rock and Granite Co (Leicestershire) Ltd* (1918) 34 TLR 500; storage of explosives.
151 *Cambridge Water Co v Eastern Counties Leather plc* [1994] 2 AC 264; [1994] 2 WLR 53; [1994] 1 All ER 53.
152 See 11.14.5 below.

11.14.4 Brought on to land

It is not enough for the dangerous thing to be naturally present on the land; it must have been brought onto the land. In *Giles v Walker* (1890),[153] there was no liability for self-sown thistledown which blew from the defendant's land onto the plaintiff's land. There may, however, be liability in nuisance or negligence in such circumstances.[154]

11.14.5 Escape

There must also be an escape of the 'dangerous thing' from the defendant's land before there can be any liability under the rule in *Rylands v Fletcher*. It is not sufficient that there was merely the potential for escape. This is clear from the case of *Read v Lyons* (1947),[155] in which it was held that escape meant an escape from a place where the defendant has occupation or control over land to a place which is outside his or her occupation or control.[156] The case of *Rainham Chemical Works Ltd v Belvedere Fish Guano Co* (1921)[157] confirms that liability may arise under the rule in *Rylands v Fletcher* where the relevant 'escape' from the defendant's land is not simply an escape of the substance collected on the defendant's land. In the *Rainham* case an explosion in a munitions factory propelled pieces of the defendant's factory (rather than the dangerous raw materials stored on the defendant's land) onto the claimant's premises.

11.14.6 Non-natural user of the land

It is a fundamental principle of the rule that the defendant should have brought onto his or her land something which was not naturally there. The term 'natural' was interpreted in *Rylands v Fletcher* to mean 'that which exists in or by nature and is not artificial', although more recent cases have centred on the wider definition which covers the concept that a non-natural use is one that brings with it 'increased danger to others and must not merely be the ordinary use of land or such a use as is proper for the general benefit of the community'.[158] The *Rickards v Lothian* decision was followed in *Read v Lyons* by what was essentially a policy decision, that uses which provide some public benefit would be classed as 'natural'. This point was illustrated in *British Celanese Ltd v AH Hunt (Capacitors) Ltd* (1969):[159]

> The manufacturing of electrical and electronic components . . . cannot be adjudged to be a special use . . . The metal foil was there for use in the manufacture of goods of a common type which at all material times were needed for the general benefit of the community.

The decision of the House of Lords in *Cambridge Water Co v Eastern Counties Leather plc* (1994)[160] has altered the 'non-natural user' requirement. In determining what was a non-natural use, the House of Lords took a fairly broad approach, in line with the original concept of non-natural use, and held that there should be a distinction between something naturally occurring, for example a flood, and an artificial creation such as a reservoir.[161]

---

153 *Giles v Walker* (1890) 24 QBD 656.
154 See 11.12 above.
155 *Read v Lyons & Co Ltd* [1947] AC 156.
156 In which an explosion occurred in a munitions factory but no liability under the rule in *Rylands v Fletcher* arose because there was no escape of anything onto the neighbouring premises belonging to the claimant.
157 *Rainham Chemical Works Ltd v Belvedere Fish Guano Co.* (1921) 2 AC 465.
158 *Rickards v Lothian* [1913] AC 263; [1911–13] All ER 71.
159 *British Celanese Ltd v AH Hunt (Capacitors) Ltd* [1969] 1 WLR 959; [1969] 2 All ER 1252.
160 *Cambridge Water Co v Eastern Counties Leather plc* [1994] 2 AC 264; [1994] 2 WLR 53; [1994] 1 All ER 53.
161 See 11.15.6 below.

There is clearly less need to rely on the non-natural user restriction because the House of Lords has limited future claims by holding that foreseeability is now an essential requirement of the tort.

The House of Lords decisions in *Cambridge Water*[162] and the case of *Transco v Stockport MBC* (2004)[163] indicate that the courts are minded not to develop the rule in *Rylands v Fletcher* into a tort of strict liability regarding ultra-hazardous substances brought onto the defendant's land and which subsequently escape.

In *Transco* the defendant local authority owned a block of flats. Drinking water was supplied, by a water company, to the block of flats via a pipe. The water supply pipe developed a leak and a large quantity of water collected on the defendant's land (under the block of flats) from where it migrated causing (a) a railway embankment to collapse and (b) exposing a gas pipe belonging to the defendant gas transmission company. The claimant gas company commenced an action against the local authority under the rule in *Rylands v Fletcher* to recover the costs associated with rectifying the unsupported gas supply pipe. The House of Lords rejected the claim on the ground that, by bringing water onto its land via a piped supply, the defendant local authority was not using its land in an extraordinarily risky fashion. The water had not been deliberately accumulated but had been piped under normal water main pressure. The *Transco* decision suggests that in order to succeed under the rule in *Rylands v Fletcher*, the claimant must prove that the defendant's use of its land was an extraordinary use giving rise to an extraordinary level of risk.

11.14.7 Foreseeability of the type of damage (remoteness)

In *Cambridge Water*,[164] the House of Lords stated that the rule in *Rylands v Fletcher* should be considered as an extension of the law of nuisance relating to isolated incidents rather than continuing problems:

> it would moreover lead to a more coherent body of common law principles if the rule was to be regarded as essentially an extension of the law of nuisance to isolated escapes from land.

As a result of making this connection, it was stated that the damage must be foreseeable:

> The historical connection with the law of nuisance must now be regarded as pointing towards the conclusion that foreseeability of damage is a prerequisite of the recovery of damages under the rule.

11.14.8 Who can bring an action under *Rylands v Fletcher?*

It is not clear whether it is necessary for a claimant to have an interest in land in order to bring an action under the rule in *Rylands v Fletcher* (there are several cases where the claimant has not had an interest, although it was suggested in *Read v Lyons* that some interest in land will be necessary). The House of Lords decisions in *Cambridge Water* and *Transco v Stockport MBC* suggest that the rule in *Rylands v Fletcher* is merely an extension of the law of nuisance and, if this is so, the ordinary principles of nuisance will apply, namely that the claimant must have an interest in land.

---

162 *Cambridge Water Co v Eastern Counties Leather plc* [1994] 2 AC 264; [1994] 2 WLR 53; [1994] 1 All ER 53; see 11.15.
163 *Transco v Stockport MBC* [2004] 2 AC 1.
164 *Cambridge Water Co v Eastern Counties Leather plc* [1994] 2 AC 264; [1994] 2 WLR 53; [1994] 1 All ER 53.

11.14.9 Against whom can an action in *Rylands v Fletcher* be brought?

It would appear that the defendant does not need to have any proprietary interest in the land; it is enough that he merely controls the 'dangerous thing', as was stated in *Rainham Chemical Works v Belvedere Fish Guano* (1921).[165] This suggestion is consistent with the law of nuisance and reflects the close link between nuisance and *Rylands v Fletcher*.

11.14.10 Defences

Although it is widely acknowledged that the rule in *Rylands v Fletcher* created a regime of strict liability, liability is not absolute and the courts have developed a number of defences:

(a) statutory authority;

(b) necessity;

(c) act of God. The act of God defence is very limited and applies to 'forces of nature which no human foresight can provide against, and of which human prudence is not bound to recognise the possibility';[166]

(d) common benefit. Where the 'dangerous thing' is for the benefit of both the defendant and the claimant, the defendant will not be liable for its escape. This defence is very close to the defence of consent;[167]

(e) independent act of a third party. The unforeseeable act of an independent third party is a defence where the defendant has no control over the actions of the third party. The burden of proving this defence lies with the defendant. Where the third party's act could have been foreseen or action could have been taken to prevent the consequences, the defendant will still be liable;[168]

(f) default on the part of the claimant. Where the claimant suffers as a result of his or her own act or default, the defendant cannot be liable. Where there is contributory negligence on the part of the claimant, the provisions of the Law Reform (Contributory Negligence) Act 1945 apply.

11.14.11 Remedies

Because the rule in *Rylands v Fletcher* has its origins in nuisance, the remedies available appear to be the same as nuisance, namely:

(a) damages—in *Read v Lyons*[169] it was decided that damages would not be available for personal injury;

(b) injunction—although there is little judicial guidance on this point.

11.15 *Cambridge Water Co v Eastern Counties Leather plc*

The House of Lords decision in the case of *Cambridge Water Co v Eastern Counties Leather plc* (1994)[170] has made a considerable impact on the interpretation and application of the common law to environmental problems.

---

165 *Rainham Chemical Works Ltd v Belvedere Fish Guano Co.* (1921) 2 AC 465.
166 *Tennent v Earl of Glasgow* (1864) 2 Macph (Ct of Sess) (HL) 22.
167 See the decisions in *Dunne v North Western Gas Board* (1963) 3 All ER 916 and *Transco v Stockport MBC* [2004] 2 AC 1; especially Lord Bingham's judgment upon the validity of this defence.
168 *Northwestern Utilities v London Guarantee and Accident Co Ltd* [1936] AC 108.
169 *Read v Lyons & Co Ltd* [1947] AC 156.
170 *Cambridge Water Co v Eastern Counties Leather plc* [1994] 2 AC 264; [1994] 2 WLR 53; [1994] 1 All ER 53.

11.15.1 The facts of the case

In September 1976, Cambridge Water Company bought a piece of land which was formerly used as a paper mill at Sawston, Cambridgeshire, attached to which was a permit to abstract water from a borehole (linked to an underground aquifer) on the site. Cambridge Water Company began to abstract water from the aquifer for public consumption in June 1979. Unknown to the water company, the water was contaminated by solvents (PCE and TCE) which had leached into the aquifer from a tannery operated by Eastern Counties Leather. The spillages of the relevant solvent occurred regularly between 1950 and 1976, after which the tannery began to operate more efficiently. This contamination was not considered an issue (it did not make the water unwholesome and unusable) until, in 1976, the EC issued Directive 80/778/EC. This Directive set standards for drinking water used for human consumption and contained a limit relating to the maximum level of perchloroethylene solvent which could be present in the water. The water abstracted from the borehole was found to exceed these limits and use of the borehole was discontinued. It was originally thought that the litigation related to this case would be commenced under the WRA 1991; however, this proved to be impossible as the pollution pre-dated its enactment (the solvent took several years to migrate to and pollute the aquifer). Cambridge Water Company began civil proceedings against Eastern Counties Leather on the grounds of nuisance, negligence and the rule in *Rylands v Fletcher*.

11.15.2 The High Court decision

The action was dismissed in nuisance and negligence because it was held that the defendants, Eastern Counties Leather, could not at the relevant time that spillages of solvent were occurring have foreseen the damage caused to the aquifer.

Kennedy J also considered the application of the rule in *Rylands v Fletcher* and decided that the defendant's activities on its site, including the use of solvents, was a 'natural use' of land.

11.15.3 The Court of Appeal decision

The High Court decision was reversed by the Court of Appeal and Cambridge Water Company was awarded £1 million in damages plus costs. The decision of the Court of Appeal was based on the tort of nuisance and the decision in the case of *Ballard v Tomlinson* (1885).[171] The Court of Appeal held that the pollution of the aquifer by Eastern Counties Leather plc constituted an interference with Cambridge Water Company's 'natural rights' to abstract naturally occurring water which arrived beneath Cambridge Water's land by percolation through undefined underground channels. It was held that interference with this natural right to abstract uncontaminated groundwater constituted an actionable nuisance. The Court of Appeal did not comment on the rule in *Rylands v Fletcher*.

The Court of Appeal's reversal of the High Court's decision alarmed industry, which feared that it could be liable for so-called historic contamination. Appeal to the House of Lords was inevitable.

11.15.4 The House of Lords' decision

The decision of the House of Lords was awaited with a great deal of interest as it was widely anticipated that the outcome would considerably affect the future application and development of the common law and that it would clarify the principles of the common law relating to environmental damage. The judgment contained important pronouncements on the relationship between nuisance and the rule in *Rylands v Fletcher*.

---

171 *Ballard v Tomlinson* (1885) 29 Ch D 115.

11.15.5 Foreseeability

The House of Lords considered the issue of foreseeability in great detail. The following passage indicates the tone of the judgment:

> it by no means follows that the defendant should be held liable for damage of a type which he could not reasonably foresee; and the development of the law of negligence in the past 60 years points strongly towards a requirement that such foreseeability should be a prerequisite of liability in damages for nuisance, as it is of liability in negligence.

Lord Goff went on to state that foreseeability of harm 'is a prerequisite of recovery of damages in private nuisance, as in the case of public nuisance'. Therefore, there could only be liability where the interference was of a type which could be reasonably foreseen by a person in the defendant's position at the relevant time the solvents escaped from the defendant's control. The House of Lords therefore held that the damage caused to the aquifer by the solvents was not reasonably foreseeable at the time the pollution occurred.

11.15.6 Non-natural user

The House of Lords observed that 'the storage of substantial quantities of chemicals on industrial premises should be regarded as an almost classic case of non-natural use' and in so doing freed up the non-natural user restriction on liability under the *Rylands v Fletcher* tort.

11.15.7 The courts and environmental protection

Also contained in the judgment was a statement referring to the development of the common law as a means of environmental protection. It was implied that it was the function of Parliament, rather than the courts, to create a statutory regime of liability for environmental damage:

> But it does not follow from these developments that a common law principle, such as the rule in *Rylands v Fletcher*, should be developed or rendered more strict to provide for liability in respect of such pollution. On the contrary, given that so much well informed and carefully structured legislation is now being put in place for this purpose, there is less need for the courts to develop a common law principle to achieve the same end, and indeed it may well be undesirable that they should do so.

11.15.8 The implications of the judgment

The judgment has been viewed by many environmentalists as being restrictive because of the introduction of the requirement of foreseeability of the type of damage as a component of the rule in *Rylands v Fletcher*. Critics of the judgment say that only very rarely will it impose liability for pollution cases such as this one (i.e. a historic pollution case). However, many commentators feel that the judgment was the only reasonable and practicable step to be taken in the circumstances, because it is unfair to penalise anyone and impose retrospective liability for operations which were considered perfectly normal and effective at the relevant time. Neither is the judgment as restrictive as some originally interpreted, as it can provide the basis for liability where industry's poor environmental practices, after 1994, result in the escape of substances which contaminate neighbouring property.[172]

---

172 We refer the reader, at the end of this chapter, to several articles which analyse the implications of *Cambridge Water Co v Eastern Counties Leather plc* [1994] 2 AC 264; [1994] 2 WLR 53; [1994] 1 All ER 53.

11.16 An evaluation of the environmental torts as a means of environmental protection

Whilst it is clear that the environmental torts do have a valid role to play in the protection of the environment, they do have a number of both limitations and advantages.

11.16.1 Disadvantages

The first fundamental problem associated with the use of the environmental tort to secure environmental protection is that it cannot prevent damage (it is reactive) to the environment (although the use of an injunction can halt threatened damage or continuing damage); its purpose instead is to compensate the owner of the land affected. The award of compensation to remediate environmental damage may not necessarily be used by the claimant for that purpose.

Because the development of common law controls has taken place over many years and at a time when the environment was not considered important, common law does not meet the specific needs of environmental protection for a number of reasons:

(a)   it operates on the basis of reactive 'cure' rather than prevention;
(b)   the common law creates an uncertain level of liability (it does not set clear permit-based conditions which determine an acceptable level of pollution);
(c)   it permits individuals to be guardians of the environment only on an ad hoc basis, given the uncertainty of establishing that the behaviour complained of was unreasonable and the evidential difficulties associated with this.

Modern (Command and Control) environmental laws which have been developed in response to specific environmental problems are better placed to address the needs of environmental protection because they contain express standards and provisions which relate directly to many industrial operations (they have industry-wide application).

Current environmental regulation is also better suited to the needs of industry as it provides clear standards of acceptable environmental behaviour via permit-based regulatory controls. Through these legislative frameworks, industry can also seek advice and guidance as to acceptable levels and types of pollution from the relevant regulator.

In the late nineteenth century, it was established that the courts could not assume the place of the legislature in such cases. This was affirmed in *Cambridge Water Co v Eastern Counties Leather plc*,[173] in which the House of Lords confirmed that it would not be appropriate for the courts to develop the common law principles further.

11.16.1.1 Evidence

It may often be difficult to (a) prove the source of the pollution causing damage, and (b) establish a causal link between the pollution and the damage caused. Experts may need to be employed to help prove the claimant's case and this often causes considerable delay and expense when bringing an action under the common law.[174]

---

173   *Cambridge Water Co v Eastern Counties Leather plc* [1994] 2 AC 264; [1994] 2 WLR 53; [1994] 1 All ER 53.
174   In regard to this issue see the High Court decision in *Corby Litigation Group v Corby BC* (2008) EWCA Civ 463 that remediation works relating to contaminated land had the ability to cause birth defects.

11.16.1.2 Costs

The cost of financing a common law action is often extremely prohibitive, especially as the availability of legal aid in such cases is very restricted. An example of a legally aided action is the Docklands litigation.[175] Where legal aid is not available, it is usually only the wealthy who can take action, an example of this being the rock star Roger Daltry, who brought an action in respect of agricultural pollution which damaged his fish farm in *Beju-Bop Ltd v Home Farm (Iwerne Minster) Ltd* (1990).[176]

The financial problems are exacerbated by the fact that an unsuccessful claimant may have to bear the defendant's legal costs as well as his or her own.

An action in tort brought following environmental damage is often one that is hard fought by the defendant, who may be a large multinational company anxious to avoid defeat because this may damage the image of the company, with the potential to affect trade adversely. In order to avoid defeat, the defendant will spend a considerable amount of money on legal advice, representation and presentation of alternative scientific evidence (often far more than the claimant can afford to pay his or her own legal and scientific experts). An example of such a case is that of *Hanrahan v Merck, Sharp and Dohme* (1988),[177] an Irish case which, had it not been for the sheer determination of the plaintiff, and the hardship suffered by him and his family to raise the finances necessary to appeal, the case would not have reached the Supreme Court, where the earlier decision in favour of Merck, Sharp and Dohme was reversed.

The introduction of contingency fees by the Law Society could potentially have a significant impact on environmental litigation. The proliferation of claims-handling companies and 'no win, no fee' deals may stimulate an increase in environment-related claims.

11.16.1.3 Remoteness

The House of Lords' decision in *Cambridge Water Co v Eastern Counties Leather plc*[178] introduced the element of foreseeability as a prerequisite to the rule in *Rylands v Fletcher*. The introduction of the foreseeability element will have the effect of limiting claims for historic pollution. However, as foreseeability is to be determined from the state of knowledge at the time the pollution takes place, it is unlikely that a great deal of the pollution which is currently taking place will be unforeseeable.

11.16.1.4 The Limitation Act 1980

A further limitation as to the effectiveness of the common law in the protection of the environment is that the Limitation Act 1980 applies. Section 2 of the Limitation Act 1980 provides:

(a) an action founded on tort shall not be brought after the expiration of six years from the date on which the cause of action actually accrued;

(b) where the action is brought in respect of personal injury, the basic limitation period is reduced to three years under s 11(4) of the Act, although the court has discretion to override this limitation period if it would be equitable to do so;

(c) the limitation period is calculated 'from the date on which the cause of action occurred'. The reason for the existence of the limitation period is that it would be unfair on the defendant if an action could be brought against him or her for an indefinite period of time.

---

175 *Hunter and Others v Canary Wharf Ltd* [1997] AC 156.
176 *Beju-Bop Ltd v Home Farm (Iwerne Minister) Ltd* [1990] WLAW 90.
177 *Hanrahan v Merck, Sharp and Dohme* [1988] 1 LRM 629.
178 *Cambridge Water Co v Eastern Counties Leather plc* [1994] 2 AC 264; [1994] 2 WLR 53; [1994] 1 All ER 53.

11.16.2 Advantages

The strengthening of the statutory framework for the control of environmental pollution and environmental damage may have lessened the significance of the common law. However, it still remains an important basis of action in several circumstances and it has the capacity to react quickly and flexibly to emerging issues:

(a) for environmental pressure groups (for example, anglers' associations, Friends of the Earth and Greenpeace);

(b) for individuals who are affected by environmental damage and for whom there is no relief under statutory provisions;

(c) for enforcement agencies, such as the Environment Agency, where a prosecution under a statutory provision is not possible (although this is likely to be a rare occurrence);

(d) where the pollution has taken place before the relevant legislation providing a remedy has come into force. This was the case in *Cambridge Water*, where the pollution pre-dated the WRA 1991.

11.16.2.1 Environmental torts may supplement statutory provisions

An environmental tort action may also supplement statutory provisions. For example, in the case of *National Rivers Authority (NRA) and Anglers Co-operative Association v Clarke* (1994),[179] the NRA attempted to prosecute a pig farmer, Mr Clarke, who was responsible for the release of three million gallons of slurry into the river Sapiston in Suffolk, affecting a 75 km stretch of the river Sapiston and the Little Ouse and destroying a fishery. The action against Mr Clarke was brought under ss 31(1)(a) and 32(1)(a) of the COPA 1974 and s 4(1) of the Salmon and Freshwater Fisheries Act 1975. The Court of Appeal decided that the pig farmer could not be liable because his knowledge of the discharge could not be proven.[180] Following the failure of the action under the statute, the NRA, along with the Anglers Co-operative Association who were representing the interests of the local angling club, then proceeded with a civil action against Mr Clarke. This time the action succeeded and the NRA was awarded £90,000 to cover its legal costs, to investigate the extent of the damage to the fishery and to pay for restocking.

The Anglers Co-operative Association was awarded £8,400 for legal expenses, and the local angling club was awarded £8,450 in damages.

11.16.2.2 Remedies

The chief remedy sought in environmental tort actions is compensatory damages. A significant advantage of an action under common law over statutory provisions is that the claimant may (depending upon the tort) recover damage for property damage or personal injury. This is only rarely possible under statute. One example, however, is s 73(6) of the EPA 1990.

The remedies available in cases based on the common law are not specifically intended to meet modern environmental challenges; rather, their aim is to address affected property rights. Injunctions can be granted in a variety of situations. They may be prohibitive, in which case they will simply require that the defendant should cease operations to prevent further damage from occurring; they may be mandatory, in which case the defendant will be required to take some positive action, such as the clean-up of a contaminated site. Both types of injunction may be granted on a *quia timet* basis, which would prevent damage being done where there was a threat of it occurring.

---

179 *National Rivers Authority (NRA) and Anglers Co-operative Association v Clarke* (1994) 232 ENDS 45.
180 Had the NRA based the action on 'causing' pollution, it might have succeeded.

11.16.2.3 Actions need not be restrictive

A major advantage associated with a tort action is that it need not be limited to a single tort. It is not uncommon for the torts of nuisance, negligence, trespass and the rule in *Rylands v Fletcher* to be tested in one case.

11.17 Statutory civil actions

11.17.1 Introduction

In addition to the civil law torts, legislation can also provide a means by which individuals can pursue civil claims for breach of environmental law.

Civil liability actions arising from statutes are available as follows:

(a) express statutory rights to be compensated for certain types of damage;
(b) breach of statutory duty;
(c) certain statutory provisions which extend, or sometimes restrict (e.g. s 100(b) WRA 1991) rights under the common law.

Each of these will be considered in turn. It may also be possible for an individual privately to prosecute a polluter for an offence under the statute, providing such action is not prohibited by the statute.[181] Where a statute provides for enforcement of the statute via the criminal law (i.e. a range of criminal offences built into the relevant statute) this is thought to rule out the possibility of lodging a civil claim for damage caused by breach of statutory duty.

11.17.2 Express statutory rights to damages

An example of such an express provision is s 73(6) of the EPA 1990, which provides that where damage is caused by waste deposited in or on land, the person who deposited it, or knowingly caused or knowingly permitted it to be deposited, commits an offence under ss 33(1) or 63(2) EPA 1990 and is liable in damages for the cost of remediation. Section 73(6) provides that where the damage was wholly the fault of the person who suffered it, or the person who suffered voluntarily accepted the risk of the damage, the defences of contributory negligence and *volenti non fit injuria* are applicable. It is not necessary for a prosecution to be brought in order to commence a statutory civil action; it is enough that the offence has been committed.

11.17.3 Breach of statutory duty

The general rule defining breach of statutory duty was established in *Bishop of Rochester v Bridges* (1831):[182]

> where an Act creates an obligation and enforces performance in a specified manner . . . that performance cannot be enforced in any other manner.

A breach of statutory duty is only actionable where it can be shown that Parliament intends that the statute should grant a civil remedy. Many environmental statutes which prohibit an activity or make such activity a criminal offence also provide for some degree of civil liability. The question of civil liability for breach of statutory duty is addressed in both the EPA 1990 and the WRA 1991.

---

181 See 11.3.
182 *Bishop of Rochester v Bridges* (1831) 1 B & Ad 847.

In order to bring an action for breach of statutory duty, the claimant must prove the following:

(a)   that the statute creates an obligation;
(b)   that the statute allows a civil action/remedy;
(c)   that the harm suffered by the claimant is within the general class of risks at which the statute is directed;
(d)   that the claimant is a member of the class of persons protected by the statute;
(e)   that the defendant has breached the statute; and
(f)   that this breach has caused the damage complained of.

If the relevant statute does not specifically refer to the right of an aggrieved person to commence an action for breach of statutory duty, the courts may infer such a right but the wider the discretion granted by the statute to the relevant public authority, the less likely it will be that an individual will have a successful cause of action.[183]

Legislation (such as pollution control) which empowers a public body, such as the Environment Agency, to protect environmental interests rather than the interests of individuals will constitute an unlikely basis for a civil action for breach of statutory duty.

11.17.3.1 Defences
There are two defences available for breach of statutory duty:

(a)   *volenti non fit injuria*—the defence of *volenti non fit injuria* (that is, the claimant's voluntary assumption of risk, sometimes referred to as consent) applies to cases of breach of statutory duty. In ICI v Shatwell (1965),[184] the House of Lords held that the defence applied in cases of breach of statutory duty except where there is a statutory provision to the contrary. This defence is not available where a worker sues his or her employer for breach of the employer's statutory duty;
(b)   contributory negligence.

11.17.3.2 Examples of civil actions for breach of statutory duty
Gibbons and Others v South West Water Services (1992)[185] was an action brought on behalf of 80 plaintiffs in respect of damage suffered by them when their drinking water supplies were contaminated with aluminium sulphate. The plaintiffs claimed damages on the grounds of breach of statutory duty, public nuisance and breach of contract. The defendants, South West Water Services, in an out-of-court settlement, admitted liability for breach of statutory duty and the plaintiffs were awarded compensatory damages. See also the High Court decision in *Bowden v South West Water Services Ltd* (1998)[186] concerning the rejection of the claimant's claim for damages on the ground that the obligations contained in three EU water directives were insufficiently specific to entitle shell fishermen[187] to mount a successful civil action for breach of statutory duty.

11.18 Statutory provisions which alter rights under common law

A range of statutory provisions provide a variety of civil law-based mechanisms to remediate environmental damage and enable injured persons to recover compensatory damages from the person

---

183 See X (Minors) v Bedfordshire County Council (1995) 2 AC 633.
184 ICI v Shatwell (1965) AC 656.
185 Gibbons and Others v South West Water Services (1992) 2 WLR 507.
186 Bowden v South West Water Services Ltd (1998) Env LR 445.
187 E.g. a class of persons.

See Chapters

4.14 →

5.16.2 →

7 →

responsible for the relevant injury. These civil law provisions include: (1) the water pollution clean-up powers contained in s 161 WRA 1991, (2) the clean-up power relating to illegal waste disposal contained in s 73(6) EPA 1990, (3) the contaminated land remediation regime contained in Part IIA EPA 1990, (4) the marine oil spill remediation and compensation regime contained in the Merchant Shipping Act 1995 (sections 153 and 154 impose strict liability on ship owners regarding property damage and personal injury caused by oil pollution incidents) and (5) the compensation and remediation regime contained in the Nuclear Installations Act 1965 relating to damage and personal injury caused by the operation of nuclear power plants. The 1965 Act imposes absolute civil liability for damage caused by the type of incidents detailed in ss 7–10 of the Act.[188]

Statutory nuisance provisions in the EPA 1990 allow an individual to bring action in a magistrates' court against a person who has created the nuisance.[189] This section is used where the local

See Chapter

9 →

authority has not acted to prevent or abate the statutory nuisance. An individual aggrieved by a statutory nuisance may bring an action under s 82 of the EPA 1990.[190] These proceedings will be brought against the person responsible for the nuisance. If the responsible party cannot be found, the owner of the premises may be liable or, where more than one person is responsible for the nuisance, each party may be liable under s 82 'whether or not what any one of them is responsible for would by itself amount to a nuisance'. This action can only be brought in a magistrates' court and there is no power enabling an individual to serve an Abatement Notice. Notice of the individual's intention to bring proceedings must be given to the responsible parties. In the case of a noise nuisance, three days' notice must be given and, in all other cases, 21 days' notice must be given.

11.19 Civil liability and the EU

The EU has introduced an environmental liability regime. The Environmental Liability Directive (2004/35/EC) came into force in 2007 in order to provide a degree of protection for the unowned environment. The types of 'environmental damage' covered by the Directive are: (1) damage to habitats and species specified in EU nature conservation legislative provisions (e.g. the Wild Birds Directive (79/409/EEC) and the Habitats Directive (92/43/EC)), (2) damage to the types of waters specified in the Water Framework Directive (2000/60/EC), (3) contamination of soils and (4) subject to the consent of Member States, damage to habitats and species protected under the national nature conservation laws of the relevant Member States.

A key restrictive feature of the Environmental Liability Directive is that it excludes damage to property, personal injury and financial loss (pure economic loss). Neither does the Directive apply to environmental liabilities arising out of the operation of the nuclear industry or in regard to marine oil pollution incidents.

Any award of damages made under the terms of the Directive must be used to restore the relevant environmental damage except where restoration is not possible. Whilst regulatory authorities in Member States retain the primary enforcement role in regard to the Directive's provisions, individuals whose interests are adversely affected by the damaging activities specified in the Directive and non-governmental organisations (NGOs) may request that the relevant regulatory authority in a Member State take appropriate action (but individuals and NGOs cannot compel regulatory authorities to take action). The regulator is required to give reasons for its enforcement

---

188 See discussion of the nuclear contamination cases of *Merlin* and *Blue Circle* in 11.12.5.
189 S 82 EPA 1990.
190 Which re-enacts s 99 of the Public Health Act 1936.

decision (to take or refuse to take action) and NGOs may challenge the regulator's decision before the Member State courts or other competent adjudicatory body. The rights granted to individuals and NGOs are not as extensive as those granted in some US states to pursue so-called 'citizen suits'.

Partial defences are available where (1) the relevant environmental damage has been authorised, via permit, in regard to an activity which is subject to EU regulation (e.g. IPPC permit) or (2) the defendant was, at the time the environmental damage occurred, carrying on his or her activities in accordance with 'state of the art' scientific or technical knowledge which did not require action to be taken regarding the environmental damage which ultimately occurred.

The Environmental Damage (Prevention and Remediation) Regulations 2009 are now in force. These regulations impose liability on operators of commercial activities that cause or may cause significant environmental damage.[191]

11.20 Online resource centre

We recommend that the reader regularly refers to the section of the online resources corresponding to this chapter for information relating to updates, amendments and corrections.

11.21 Summary of key points

Chapter 11 has covered the following topics and issues:

- Victims of environmental pollution-related damage to land, land-related interests or personal injury may seek redress (primarily in the form of compensatory damages) from the polluter using civil law actions (environmental torts).
- The key torts are: private nuisance, public nuisance, trespass, the rule in *Rylands v Fletcher* and negligence. Save for negligence and possibly public nuisance, these torts have evolved to protect property and property-related interests.
- The most important environmental tort is private nuisance. The courts balance the competing land-related interests of the claimant and defendant in order to determine whether the defendant is using his/her land unreasonably and is therefore infringing the claimant's interests.
- In contrast to public law environmental controls (e.g. WRA 1991 and EPA 1990) the development of the law of torts has been ad hoc and largely dependent upon the claimant having an interest in land to protect and the financial resources to engage in litigation to protect those interests.
- The utility of trespass as an environmental tort is limited by the requirement that the relevant injury or damage must constitute a direct interference with the claimant's property.
- The rule in *Rylands v Fletcher* is concerned with liability for damage caused by 'one-off' (isolated) escapes of substances from the defendant's property. The rule has been subject to important House of Lords decisions in the last two decades (e.g. *Cambridge Water v Eastern Counties Leather plc* and *Transco v Stockport Metropolitan Borough Council*).
- The victims of pollution-related damage will normally obtain redress in the form of damages (monetary compensation) but may, in an appropriate but rare case, obtain an injunction to prohibit or restrict the defendant's activities.

---

191 Occurring after 1.3.2009.

- The judiciary have in the last two to three decades demonstrated a lack of enthusiasm to develop the law of torts as a means to control environmental pollution. The courts prefer to leave Parliament to pass legislation (often in response to an EU Directive) designed to regulate polluting emissions from particular industries or types of polluting activity.
- Breach of human rights as a basis for the redress of damage caused by polluting activities has emerged as an additional liability mechanism (in addition to torts).
- A limited number of statutory provisions exist which enable a claimant to seek redress for environmental damage.

11.22 Further reading

Books

Buckley, R, *The Law of Nuisance* (Butterworths, London 1981).
Conaghan, J and Mansell, W, *The Wrongs of Tort*, (2nd edn, Pluto, London 1998).
Lowry, J and Edmunds, R (eds), *Environmental Protection and the Common Law* (Hart, Oxford 2000).
O'Neill, O, *Justice, Property and the Environment* (Ashgate, Farnham 1997).
Pugh, C and Day, M, *Pollution and Personal Injury: Toxic Torts II* (Cameron May, London 1995).
Rogers, WVH, *Winfield and Jolowicz on Tort* (17th edn, Sweet & Maxwell, London 2011).
Wetterstein, P, *Harm to the Environment: the Right to Compensation and the Assessment of Damages* (Clarendon, Oxford 1997).

Journal articles and government papers

Bowman, M, 'Nuisance, strict liability and environmental hazards' (1995) Env Liability 105.
Brenner, JF, 'Nuisance law and the Industrial Revolution' (1974) J Legal Studies 403.
Campbell, D, 'Of Coase and corn: a (sort of) defence of private nuisance' (2000) MLR 197.
Cane, P, 'Are environmental harms special?' [2001] JEL 3.
Cross, D, 'Does the careless polluter pay?' (1995) 111 LQR 445.
Gearty, C, 'The place of nuisance in the modern law of torts' (1989) CLJ 214.
Greve, M, 'The private enforcement of environmental law' (1999) 65 Tulane L Rev 339.
Hilson, C, '*Cambridge Water* revisited' [1996] WLAW 126.
Holder, J, 'The Sellafield litigation and questions of causation in environmental law' (1994) CLP 287.
Lee, M, 'Civil liability in the nuclear industry' [2000] JEL 317.
McLaren, J, 'Nuisance law and the Industrial Revolution: some lessons from social history' (1983) OJLS 155.
Newark, F, 'Non-natural user and *Rylands v Fletcher*' (1961) MLR 557.
O'Sullivan, J, 'Nuisance, local authorities and neighbours from hell' (2000) CLJ 11.
Ogus, A and Richardson, G, 'Economics and the environment: a study of private nuisance' (1977) CLJ 284.
Penner, J, 'Nuisance and the character of the neighbourhood' [1993] JEL 1.
Pontin, B, 'Tort interacting with regulatory law' (2001) NILQ 597.
Rabin, R, 'Environmental liability and the tort system' (1987) Houston Law Review 27.
Spencer, J, 'Public nuisance: a critical examination' (1989) CLJ 55.
Steele, J, 'Private Law and the environment: nuisance in context' (1995) 15 LS 236.
Steele, J, 'Remedies and remediation: foundational issues in environmental liability' (1995) MLR 615.
Steele, J and Jewell, T, 'Nuisance and planning' (1993) MLR 568.
Steele, J and Wikeley, N, 'Dust on the streets and liability for environmental concerns' (1997) MLR 265.

Stone, C, 'Should trees have standing?: Towards legal rights for natural objects' (1972) Southern
    California L Rev 450.
Stone, C, 'Should trees have standing revisited. How far will law and morals reach—a pluralist
    perspective' (1985) 59(1) Southern California L Rev 1.
Tromans, S, 'Nuisance—prevention or payment?' (1982) CLJ 87.
Wightman, J, 'Nuisance—the environmental tort?: *Hunter v Canary Wharf* in the House of Lords'
    (1998) MLR 870.
Wilde, M, 'The EC Commission's White Paper on environmental liability: issues and implications'
    [2001] JEL 21.

Chapter 12

The Private Regulation of Environmental Pollution

Public Concern, Private Prosecution, Judicial Review, Access to Information and Human Rights

Chapter Contents

Learning Objectives

By the end of this chapter you should have acquired an understanding of:

- the importance of public participation in environmental decision-making and how access to environmental information facilitates this participation;

- the causes of public concern and why it is important that the public plays a role in ensuring that public authorities and private companies adhere to the legal rules relating to the protection of the environment;

- the requirements of the Aarhus Convention 1998 and in particular the inextricable link between access to environmental information, public participation and access to justice in environmental matters;

- the provisions of the Environmental Information Regulations 2004;

- the role of judicial review and private prosecutions in the enforcement of environmental law;

- the access to justice requirements of the Aarhus Convention and an appreciation of the extent to which the UK complies with its Convention obligations in this respect;

- the emerging role of the Human Rights Act 1998 in the armoury of litigants seeking to enforce environmental laws.

12.1 Introduction

In Chapter 11, we noted that legal persons, such as individuals and companies, are able to use the law of torts to obtain redress for damage to property and person caused by the polluting activities of other persons. The role of private individuals, companies and other organisations or groups is not, however, confined to litigation in the civil courts. Legal persons also have an important role to play in ensuring that the Command and Control regimes examined in Chapters 4–10 are properly regulated and the relevant regulators are made accountable for their decisions. Private individuals (and this includes legal and natural persons) have two courses of action open to them if they are unhappy with any regulatory action (or inaction) or decision. First, in the event that a regulator exercises its discretion not to prosecute a person who has breached environmental law, any person who disagrees with this decision may exercise the right (provided the right is not excluded by the relevant statute) to mount a private prosecution to bring the alleged offender to account before the criminal courts.[1] Secondly, any person may challenge a wide range of regulatory decisions[2] by means of an application to the courts to have the relevant decision judicially reviewed. These two mechanisms enable the private person to 'police' the activities of public regulators. In order for private persons effectively to police a regulatory body's decision it is essential that they have access to regulatory records, especially those relating to pollution licences/permits.[3]

The importance of the participation of private citizens in the protection of the environment is widely recognised, particularly by the United Nations and the European Union. In June 1998 the

---

1 Including the right to prosecute the regulator where the regulator has committed an offence.
2 Including a decision not to prosecute.
3 That is, applications for licences/permits, the conditions attached to them, the monitoring of polluting emissions to confirm that licences/permits are complied with, etc.

UNECE Convention on Access to Information, Public Participation in Decision-making and Access to Justice in Environmental Matters[4] was adopted in Aarhus, Denmark. The UK ratified the Convention on 23 February 2005. The Convention, known as the Aarhus Convention, is based on the premise that sustainable development can only be achieved through the involvement of all stakeholders and that every person has a duty, both individually and in association with others, to protect and improve the environment for the benefit of present and future generations.[5] In particular the Convention requires signatory states to take the necessary measures to ensure that the public has access to information about the environment, can participate in environmental decision-making and has access to justice in the event that these 'rights' are denied. The EU, as a signatory of the Convention, has translated these rights into a number of EU directives which are in turn binding on the Member States of the EU. In addition the Human Rights Act 1998 continues to prove fertile ground for some interesting environmental claims.

12.2 Public concern

12.2.1 What is public concern and why is it important?

Public concern, in an environmental pollution context, is the fear of actual or threatened adverse impacts of emissions from industrial, commercial and agricultural activity upon an individual's core interests. Public concern may extend to fears about developments such as nuclear power or wind farms or airport extensions. In short, anything which threatens the security of an individual, especially with regard to health, family, property, money or employment will trigger a strong defensive reaction. Quite simply, the public will vehemently oppose those pollution-related risks which it considers to be unacceptable. Furedi (1997)[6] captured the essence of such concerns when he observed:

> Safety has become the fundamental value of the 1990s. Passions that were once devoted to a struggle to save the world (or keep it the same) are now invested in trying to ensure that we are safe.

In order to appreciate fully the significance of public concern and its potential impact on government, regulatory agencies, and regulated businesses, we must take note of the role of the media. The media reports on what it believes to be the chief concerns of its principal client, the public. The media, through their editorial control of the items they deem newsworthy, sensitise the public to selected risks. Pollution-related concerns are high on the media's agenda and, over time, pollution-related issues have become a pressing concern for most people. This shift in the public perception is borne out by one leading law firm specialising in pollution-related claims which has noted the 'enormous increase in public concern regarding environmental pollution'.[7]

The public is assailed on all sides by both local and global threats including climate change, acid rain, destruction of habitat, resource depletion, industrial pollution and nuclear waste disposal. At the same time, public confidence in science and scientific experts has been severely dented by a string of environmental controversies which have been linked with adverse health impacts: genetically modified crops, ozone depletion and traffic-related asthma. The controversy surrounding the credibility of

4   United Nations Economic Commission for Europe Convention on Access to Information, Public Participation in Decision-making and Access to Justice in Environmental Matters (1998).
5   Ibid, Recital 7 of the Convention referred to in n4.
6   Furedi, F, *Culture of Fear* (Cassell, 1997).
7   Pugh, C and Day, M, *Pollution and Personal Injury: Toxic Torts II* (Cameron and May, 1995).

scientific evidence about climate change reached new heights with the 'theft' in 2009 of documents and emails from the Climatic Studies Unit at the University of East Anglia. The whole saga reheated the debate about the scientific basis for man-made global warming and there can be little doubt the story left members of the public at best confused, and at worst cynical about climate change science.

What the public values and what the public fears are two related issues which are capable of forming important inputs into environmental policy and environmental decision-making. The public values a healthy environment and any development, such as the construction of a waste incinerator, which appears to threaten such deeply held values, beliefs or convictions, is likely to generate controversy. Currently, the planning system seems to be the main forum in which development decisions, relating to permission to build 'risky' developments, come head to head with public concerns relating to health, safety and environmental issues. Almost without exception, any development proposal which is believed to impact adversely upon humans will stimulate vociferous opposition. Controversies over the siting of waste incinerators, landfill sites, electricity power lines, low-level nuclear waste storage facilities and similar unwanted developments are reported daily in the media. However, even developments which are more environmentally friendly, such as wind farms, may encounter very vocal opposition.

The issues which concern the public undoubtedly have an influence upon what the media deem newsworthy. The more the media report on an issue of public concern, such as climate change, the more the public are sensitised to that issue and its attendant risks. In turn, public concern impacts upon government pre-occupations and may generate policy proposals, at both central and local levels. In some instances, public concern may force the government to propose new legislation, as in the case of dangerous dogs or firearms.[8] Public concerns permeate society and impact upon the activities of the regulators[9] and the regulated.[10]

Public concern is not only instrumental in influencing government policy and proposals for new legislation, but it can also have a powerful localised impact on regulators and regulated businesses. Media coverage of pollution incidents may alert the public to the pollution risks associated with the operation of specific company plants.[11] In turn, this may result in public pressure on the regulator to prosecute the offending polluter. Regulators such as the Environment Agency operate in a political environment and are acutely aware that they need to be seen to be doing their job as this is understood by the public. In such circumstances, the regulator may exercise its discretion to prosecute to placate the public rather than employing its administrative enforcement powers. Regulated businesses are also increasingly aware of the power of public concern and opposition. Unpopular development proposals, such as the proposed construction of a new factory or extension to an existing facility, or a new wind farm development may be blocked by widespread opposition to the relevant proposal. Usually, public concern is expressed at the planning stage, but increasingly the public will seek participation in the decision-making of environmental regulators, especially with regard to the issue and variation of licences.

12.2.2 Public concern and the legitimacy of environmental decision-making

Tapping into public concerns and values is problematic for both central and local government. It is not easy to discern, or measure, the extent of public concern with regard to a specific risk. The

---

8 Following the Dunblane massacre in 1996.
9 As can be seen in the Environment Agency's enforcement and prosecution policy, and in its agreement to trial an extended public consultation process with regard to licensing applications which generate high levels of public concern.
10 As was evident in the decision of Shell to reverse its plan to decommission the Brent Spar oil rig at sea.
11 E.g. the BP Deepwater Horizon oil spill in the Gulf of Mexico in 2010.

public is not a homogeneous group whose opinions are easily sounded out. Experience at local government level in the drafting and consultation upon development plans[12] is illustrative of the problem. Only major landholders and businesses tend to make inputs into the development plan process. They do so primarily to protect their own interests. In contrast, few individuals bother to master the background detail to the consultation process (which requires a major investment of time and effort) prior to making any input into the process. In an effort to address this problem, both central and local government have experimented with focus groups, citizen juries and citizen advisory forums, in an effort to ascertain reliable indications of public values and concerns. These initiatives recognise, to a greater or lesser extent, the need to bring the public 'up to speed' before reliable information on public concerns and values may be elicited. Obtaining accurate information is vital because only then will the government be reasonably certain that its policies will be perceived as legitimate by the public. Values and concerns thus form an essential element of policy-making. Policies which do not reflect the true concerns and values of the public will be unreliable guides for decision-makers. Failing to consult properly can wrongfoot the government and lead to a public outcry which may force the government to rethink its proposals. An example of the consequences of failing to obtain reliable information on public concerns can be seen in the public outcry and subsequent rejection, by Hampshire County Council, of a proposal to build a large waste incinerator on the outskirts of Portsmouth.[13]

Often the environmental protection non-governmental organisations (NGOs) are very well placed to play an active and informed role in policy formulation. They also have the financial resources (albeit these need to be prioritised) and expertise to mount judicial review actions when they consider the public consultation is flawed.

Law in Action

R (on the application of Greenpeace Ltd) v Secretary of State for Trade and Industry (2007)[14]

In February 2003 the government issued a White Paper on the future of energy production in the UK. The White Paper stated that the main thrust of energy policy should be on energy efficiency and renewable energy; it did not support new nuclear build. However, the government promised 'the fullest public consultation' before it reached any decision to change its policy. In January 2006 the Secretary of State issued a consultation document which it claimed was part of that public consultation process; this also claimed that the government was not, at this stage, bringing forward policy proposals. The public was given 12 weeks to submit their views. By July 2006 the government had issued an Energy Review which included the conclusion that new nuclear power stations would make a significant contribution to meeting the government's energy policy goals. This decision to support new nuclear build was challenged by Greenpeace, who argued they had a legitimate expectation of being consulted, and the 2006 exercise did not constitute a consultation of this new policy; it was more in the form of a consultation about issues that need to be considered in a consultation exercise. The Divisional Court found in favour of Greenpeace and held that that the consultation was very seriously flawed, procedurally unfair and a breach of Greenpeace's legitimate expectation that there would be the fullest consultation. The decision was therefore unlawful.

---

12 Which comprise a collection of policies guiding development control decisions in the planning process.
13 Stanley, N., 'Contentious planning disputes; an insoluble problem?' [2000] JPL 1226.
14 R (on the application of Greenpeace Ltd) v Secretary of State for Trade and Industry [2007] EWHC 311 (Admin); [2007] Env LR 29; [2007] JPL 1314; [2007] NPC 21.

Until the late 1990s, the principal Command and Control decision-making process in which the public vented its concerns about the tolerability of risks created by development proposals was the town and country planning system. There are signs that the demand for public participation in the licensing/permitting decisions of the Environment Agency and the local authorities is growing. The Environment Agency follows the government's Consultation Principles (2010),[15] which replace the government's Code of Practice on Consultation (2008).[16] The Consultation Principles are not legally binding and are subject to any legal or mandatory consultation requirements. In general terms they require government departments and public bodies to give more thought on how to engage with and consult those who are affected by proposed policies. Consultation should be proportionate and may range from two weeks to 12 weeks, depending on the circumstances and also whether there has been earlier consultation. Taking into account the availability of the internet and email, the guidance is that consultation should be 'digital by default'. However, other forms should be used where they are needed to reach groups affected by a policy. In addition the Environment Agency has also published a public participation statement, under the heading of 'Working together' for the purposes of explaining how the public can get involved in the permitting decisions taken by the Agency. In 2012 the Agency used YouTube to make the public aware of other consultation exercises, for instance in relation to its river basin management plans in England and Wales.[17]

In the past, the government has responded to important shifts in public concern by adopting reactive, legislative 'fixes', as demonstrated by the passage of the Deposit of Poisonous Wastes Act 1972 and the Clean Air Acts of the 1950s. These laws were passed in response to environmental problems (fly-tipping dangerous waste, and the health effects of smogs) which captured the attention of the public and media and led to demands for decisive action. Legislation which goes with the grain of society's perceptions of acceptable environmental behaviour will have widespread support because it is perceived as necessary. The government must learn the lesson that it cannot afford to wait until a situation becomes intolerable before it acts. There are encouraging signs that the government is beginning to adopt a less reactive approach to environmental pollution problems, as demonstrated by its proactive policy development of the national air, waste and water strategies.[18]

12.2.3 The causes of high levels of public concern

Since public concern often arises from actual or threatened exposure to levels of pollution which the public perceives as too risky and therefore unacceptable, we need to consider the following linked issues: what is risk, and what factors help to generate public perception of unacceptable risk exposure?

12.2.3.1 What is risk?

Every one of us, of necessity, is a risk-taker. In the act of a crossing a public highway, overtaking another vehicle in our own motor car, or smoking cigarettes, we are all involved in a continual process of risk-taking. Our own experiences of risk-taking, be they rewards or losses, influence our own risk-taking behaviour and the opinion each of us holds of what constitutes a 'risky' activity. Why then are some risks surrounded by controversy and considered to be less acceptable than other

---

15 Consultation Principles Guidance 2010, available at https://www.gov.uk/government/publications/consultation-principles-guidance accessed March 2013.
16 Her Majesty's Government Code of Practice on Consultation 2008.
17 http://www.youtube.com/watch?v=kh_UhCquA_U&feature=youtube_gdata_player.
18 Although it could be argued that the government is only responding to EU pressure for change.

activities which also involve the taking of risks? Why is environmental pollution, such as the airborne emissions from waste incinerators, associated with unacceptable risk-taking and the creation of high levels of public concern?

These questions can only be effectively answered if we develop a better understanding of the concept of risk.[19] John Adams, a leading author on risk, has divided risk into three categories in an effort to explain why the public is more fearful of some risks than others.[20] Risks may be directly perceptible to each of us through our own, unaided senses; risks may be perceptible with the aid of science and technology; or risks may be 'virtual risks'. In crossing a busy road, we are using our own unaided senses to perceive the direct risk that oncoming vehicles may injure us. We do not need to carry out a formal risk assessment to convince us that we should exercise a high degree of care in such circumstances. Similarly, the risks and rewards of driving fast are directly apparent to us. Each individual has an in-built 'risk thermostat' which guides his or her risk-taking behaviour. Some people are risk-seeking, whilst others are risk averse, and the setting of each individual's risk thermostat will vary with that person's life experiences. Occasionally, an individual's risk thermostat will conflict with attempts by regulators and safety experts to manage risks for him or her. We may choose to ignore speed limit warning signs in the pursuit of speed. Despite the efforts of government, many of us will continue to insist on taking more risks than the safety authorities believe we should take.

Risks perceived through science require us to use scientific apparatus to perceive the relevant risk. We cannot see a virus with the naked eye but we can observe it under the microscope. However, without training, we cannot understand what we are seeing or form any impression with regard to the risk of infection. Science helps us to assess risk in those cases in which the mechanism between exposure to infection and the onset of the disease is well known. It also helps us assess the relevant risk and its acceptability or tolerability. In those cases where the science is uncertain, we may resort to the use of objective risk assessments to provide us with statistical information to guide our risk-taking behaviour. In the world of risk assessments, activities which have less than a 'one in a million' risk of resulting in death are generally considered to be safe. Risk assessments are frequently used in assessing the risk of workplace accidents and they have also been used to demonstrate the relatively remote risk of chemical spillages occurring at a waste transfer station. See, for example, *Envirocor Waste Holdings Ltd v Secretary of State for the Environment* (1996).[21] Whilst these assessments are helpful aids in environmental decision-making, they nevertheless represent an expert's best 'guesstimate' of the likelihood of an adverse outcome actually materialising. Whilst risk experts may be familiar with the statistical risk ratings of various activities, the ordinary individual may have rather more difficulty in coming to a satisfactory conclusion on whether a one in a million risk of dying of cancer caused by polluting emissions from a new factory is an acceptable risk.

Virtual risks are those risks, such as the risk to health associated with the consumption of meat potentially infected with BSE,[22] which are surrounded by great uncertainty and with regard to which scientists themselves cannot agree whether the relevant activity is safe. An environmental pollution example is the public concern generated by the emission of carcinogenic dioxins from waste incinerators. When faced with scientists who profoundly disagree with one another, the public is forced to impose meaning on uncertainty. In such circumstances, the public makes an assessment of the relevant risk based upon the subjective criteria discussed below.

Public concern is increasingly relevant to environmental decision-making. Public concern is now a consideration which, when relevant, must be taken into account by local planning

---

19 The Royal Society, *Risk: Analysis, Perception, and Management*, 1992.
20 Adams, J, *Risk* (UCL Press, 1995).
21 *Envirocor Waste Holdings Ltd v Secretary of State for the Environment* [1996] Env LR 49; [1996] JPL 489.
22 Bovine spongiform encephalopathy.

decision-makers when determining the outcome of planning applications. The pollution risks asso-ciated with granting environmental permits to industry to discharge substances into the environ-ment may generate public concern. Increasingly, affected members of the public wish to participate in regulatory decisions which affect their wellbeing. Public concern is also instrumental in the commencement of some common law actions in which residents living in the vicinity of polluting industry choose to take on big business or public authorities in the courts because of the fear of the ill-effects of pollution in their neighbourhood.[23]

12.2.3.2 The factors generating public perception of unacceptable risk exposure
Research has demonstrated that the public uses 'rules of thumb' to reduce the burden involved in processing the mass of information available to it with regard to the assessment of risks. The public largely relies upon what it is able to recall about a particular risk when calculating the likelihood of an event occurring or recurring. This may lead to significant differences of opinion between what activities the risk experts tell us are safe and what the public perceives as safe. For example, the public tends to overestimate the risk of death and injury from infrequent causes, such as hurricanes, but underestimates the loss of life from asthma.

The nature and extent of media coverage of a risk is a key factor influencing public perception and public concern. A specialist law firm, which has considerable experience of environmental pollution claims, believes that media interest in environmental pollution will ensure that health problems associated with these activities are well reported. The same firm reported that it had received a total of 1,500 telephone calls from potential plaintiffs, concerned about the risks of breast implants, following two television appearances by a representative of the firm on the ITN news.[24]

The types of events which the media deem newsworthy, the graphic imagery employed and the timescale within which an issue remains newsworthy, all influence public recollection. The media report on what they believe to be of most concern to most of the public for most of the time. Reporting is biased in favour of stories relating to health, money, crime, education and the environ-ment. Media reporting of industrial accidents causing death, injury and environmental damage create a climate in which the public will voice its objections to both existing and proposed develop-ments which threaten the fundamental concerns of the public: the ability to live in a healthy, pollution-free and safe local environment. It is not surprising to discover that the public is concerned with threats to its health. Where industrial activities threaten these fundamental concerns, the following expressions of concern are to be expected: is this waste incinerator poisoning the neighbourhood with toxic atmospheric emissions? Will the construction of this chemical plant close to residential properties blight property values? These are typical and rational reactions to what the public perceives as threats to its core concerns.

The degree of public trust in the organisation which will be managing a risk influences the opinion of the public as to the acceptability of the activity creating the risk. If the organisation which will be managing the risk has a poor track record in risk management, it can expect public opposition. For example, would the public in the immediate years after the Bhopal disaster have been behaving irrationally if it steadfastly resisted a proposal by Union Carbide to build a chemical plant in the heart of the British countryside, even though the chemical company could demonstrate, using objectively calculated risk assessments, that the proposed plant would be safe?

If a hazard is perceived by the public as being imposed on it, the risks created by the relevant activity will be less acceptable than if the risks were assumed voluntarily.

---

23 E.g., see *Corby Group Litigation v Corby DC* [2009] EWHC 1944 (TCC); [2009] NPC 100.
24 Pugh, C and Day, M, *Pollution and Personal Injury: Toxic Torts II* (Cameron and May, 1995).

R v Secretary of State for Trade and Industry ex p Duddridge (1996)[25] illustrates the heightened public opposition to risky development which the public perceives as being unjustly imposed upon it against its will. If the public believes that it has no personal control over a risk, the level of public concern experienced will be higher than in those circumstances in which the public retains some degree of control over risk exposure. For example, public concern relating to polluting emissions from a new factory may be defused if the site operator provides equipment and training to enable the public to monitor plant emissions independently of data collected by the factory itself.

The number of people potentially at risk from, for example, the risk of explosion at a petrochemical plant is a further factor which the public takes into account when assessing the tolerability of a hazard. Also of significance is the way in which the hazard manifests itself. Contrast the graphic media depiction of how the victims of the Piper Alpha oilrig inferno met their deaths with the minimal media interest in the plight of shipworkers whose hearing has been severely damaged by constant exposure to loud noises. In the former incident, the injuries caused were immediate, graphic and horrific, whilst in the case of widespread deafness in shipyards, the injuries were neither observable nor immediately apparent.

New risks are problematic because the public is unfamiliar with the extent and nature of the risks generated by the relevant activity. Genetic engineering, biotechnology and the risks of exposure to electro-magnetic field radiation are three examples of the uncertainty created by newly emergent risks which are not yet fully understood by experts and the public. Any accident involving new technologies, such as biotechnology, may be perceived by the public as confirmation that the activity is inherently dangerous, and therefore any risks associated with such risky technology are not acceptable.

Man-made risks, such as those associated with the nuclear power industry, cause the public to fear far more than hazards which are 'natural', such as the risk of property damage caused by living on a flood plain.

The perception that risks are inequitably distributed in society also affects their acceptability. The waste industry is currently grappling with this issue with regard to finding sites to 'host' new landfills or waste incinerators. The perception of the local community that it is to be the dumping ground for waste generated by the entire county often galvanises affected members of the public to take action to resist the proposal.

Research has demonstrated that a combination of the factors outlined above may combine to evoke a powerful negative public reaction. Hazards may cause 'dread' or 'unknown' risk reactions amongst the public. Dread risks are those which are characterised by a lack of personal control, the inequitable distribution of risks and benefits, the existence of a threat to future generations, the fact that the risk increases over time, and the fact that the risk has catastrophic potential to injure people or the environment. The issues raised by objectors to the construction of a waste incinerator in Gateshead illustrate the dread risk caused by public concern over exposure to dioxins emitted from the incinerator.[26] 'Unknown' reactions relate to hazards which are unobservable, which are not fully understood by science, and whose impacts on people and the environment are difficult to assess. Hazards generated by nuclear power plants may prompt this type of extreme reaction. Occasionally, the combination of public concern criteria produces a public outcry compelling the government and the regulators to take swift and decisive action to address such concerns. The post-Dunblane disaster 'Snowdrop' campaign subjected the then government to intense and sustained pressure to ban certain types of firearms.

One final, yet significant issue is the failure of stakeholders in risk decision processes to hear and understand one another's points of view. The supporters of an objective perspective on risk and

---

25 *R v Secretary of State for Trade and Industry ex p Duddridge* [1996] 2 CMLR 361; [1996] Env LR 325.
26 See *Gateshead MBC v Secretary of State for the Environment, Gateshead MBC v Northumbrian Water Group Plc* [1995] Env LR 37.

hazards favour the use of statistics to calculate the probability and severity of a range of adverse incidents. They may fail to appreciate the wide range of factors which the public employs to 'calculate' risk and its tolerability. This problem is neatly encapsulated in Sandman's equation: 'Risk = Hazard + Outrage', where hazard is 'objective' risk and outrage is public, 'subjective' risk.

Public concern continues to raise its head in planning disputes. In *Trevett v Secretary of State for Transport, Local Government and the Regions and Others* (2002),[27] the applicant challenged the grant, on appeal, of planning permission for the erection of three police radio masts on the ground that the inspector who heard the planning appeal had regarded the public perception of health risks as irrelevant. The High Court rejected this submission and held that the inspector had considered the perceived health risks from the radio masts, but had concluded, on the facts, that the perceived risks did not justify refusing planning permission.[28]

12.3 Recognition of the need for public participation

It is not possible within the constraints of this chapter to provide a detailed examination of the various policy statements or legal instruments that provide for some form of public participation in environmental decision-making. Instead the principal focus of the examination will be on the provisions of the Aarhus Convention on Access to Information, Public Participation in Decision-making and Access to Justice in Environmental Matters 1998.[29] This is proving to be an extremely important legal instrument that has resulted not only in a number of EU directives and corresponding national legislation, but also a potent source of rights for the public. Before embarking on a discussion of the Aarhus Convention it is worth noting that as far as international law is concerned non-governmental organisations (NGOs) have increasingly played an important role in the formulation of international environmental law. This was particularly the case at the UN Conference on Environment and Development held in Rio de Janeiro in 1992. Informally known as the Earth Summit, the Rio Conference involved some 172 governments and about 2,400 representatives from NGOs throughout the world.[30] Not only were NGOs accredited at the conference, many of them played a significant part in the parallel negotiations leading up to the Bio-Diversity Convention (1992) and the Convention on Climate Change (1992). The role played by NGOs was well recognised and in fact a whole Chapter of Agenda 21 was devoted to their activities. One of the significant outcomes of the Rio Conference was the Rio Declaration which, although not legally binding, lists 27 principles. In this context, Principle 10 of the Rio Declaration is particularly important:

Principle 10

Environmental issues are best handled with the participation of all concerned citizens, at the relevant level. At the national level, each individual shall have appropriate access to information concerning the environment that is held by public authorities, including information on hazardous materials and activities in their communities, and the opportunity to participate in decision-making processes. States shall facilitate and encourage public awareness and participation by making information widely available. Effective access to judicial and administrative proceedings, including redress and remedy, shall be provided.

---

27 *Trevett v Secretary of State for Transport, Local Government and the Regions and Others* [2002] EWHC 2696 (Admin); [2003] Env LR D10.
28 See the article by Ray Kemp in [2003] JPL 13 with regard to public concern and telecommunication masts.
29 United Nations Economic Commission for Europe Convention on Access to Information, Public Participation in Decision-making and Access to Justice in Environmental Matters (1998).
30 Two further Earth Summits were held, in Johannesburg 2002 (Rio +10) and Rio in 2012 (Rio +20) and both involved significant numbers of NGO participants.

Unlike the Rio Declaration, the Aarhus Convention is legally binding upon its parties. It contains specific provisions which enshrine the three rights embedded in Principle 10, namely access to information, public participation and access to justice. To this end the Convention has been described as 'the most impressive elaboration of Principle 10 of the Rio Declaration, which stresses the need for citizens' participation in environmental issues and for access to information on the environment held by public authorities.'[31] The UNECE website declares that the Convention goes to '[the] heart of the relationship between people and governments. The Convention is not only an environmental agreement; it is also a Convention about government accountability, transparency and responsiveness'.[32] The basic philosophy underpinning the Convention is that in the field of the environment improved access to information and public participation in environmental decision-making will enhance the quality and implementation of decisions; giving the public the right to express their concerns will enable public authorities to take due account of such concerns. This in turn will further the accountability and transparency in decision-making. The Convention also recognises that the public has a role to play in ensuring that public bodies comply with environmental law and should have access to administrative and judicial procedures that enable them to assert these rights and exercise their duties.

The EU has also recognised the important role that citizens can play in, inter alia, ensuring that environmental legislation is enforced. For example, the EU's Fifth Environmental Action Programme (1993–2000)[33] stated that:

> Individuals and public interest groups should have practicable access to the courts in order to ensure that their legitimate interests are protected and that prescribed environmental measures are effectively enforced and illegal practices stopped.

The EU was central in the negotiations leading up to the adoption of the Aarhus Convention, and indeed much of the Convention is based upon the experience of the EU's earlier directives on access to environmental information and environmental impact assessment. As a party to the Convention the EU has adopted a number of new and amending directives to incorporate the obligations of the Convention into EU law and has also adopted the Aarhus Regulation[34] in order to ensure that the institutions of the EU also comply with the Convention.

At the national level Defra, as lead department on environmental policy, asserted that the commitment to environmental democracy is demonstrated by the UK's ratification of the Aarhus Convention.

> The government believes that improved access to information and wider participation of the public in decision-making processes are essential for building trust within communities, increasing public authority accountability and making better environmental policy. Backed by access to justice, this will create greater transparency and openness in environmental matters, and will contribute towards society's goals of more sustainable and environmentally sound development.[35]

---

31 Kofi A Annan, former Secretary-General of the United Nations (1997–2006).
32 http://www.unece.org/env/pp/, accessed 18 March 2013.
33 See Chapter 3 for further discussion of the Fifth Environmental Action Programme.
34 Regulation (EC) No 1367/2006 of the European Parliament and of the Council of 6 September 2006 on the application of the provisions of the Aarhus Convention on Access to Information, Public Participation in Decision-making and Access to Justice in Environmental Matters to Community institutions and bodies, OJ L 264, 25/09/2006 pp 13–19.
35 http://www.defra.gov.uk/environment/policy/international/aarhus/index.htm. Accessed 13 March 2010.

12.4 The Aarhus Convention

12.4.1 Overview and ratification

The Aarhus Convention[36] was agreed in the Danish city of Aarhus in June 1998 and entered into force on 30 October 2001. The Convention was signed in by the European Union in its capacity as a regional economic integration organisation.[37] The EU has legal capacity to conclude international agreements with states that are not members of the EU and international organisations, within the areas provided for by the Treaties.[38] In terms of the conclusion of the Aarhus Convention the legal basis was to be found in the Environment title of the EC Treaty, specifically in what was Art 174 EC Treaty.[39] In addition all of the 27 Member States are signatories and parties to the Convention since in matters relating to environmental protection policy the EU shares competence with the Member States.[40] In this respect the Aarhus Convention is typical of so many international agreements which are concluded jointly by the EU and its member states. Such treaties are generally referred to as mixity and are said to be the 'hallmark' of the EU's external relations.[41] In essence, therefore, the Convention binds both the Member States in their own right as sovereign signatory states and, as a matter of EU law, through their membership of the EU and the legal instruments adopted by the EU in fulfilment of its Convention obligations.

See Chapter 3

As at September 2012 there were 46 parties to the Convention, including all the EU states, the EU, and other countries such as Bosnia and Herzegovina, Albania and Armenia, Tajikistan, the former Yugoslav Republic of Macedonia, Ukraine and Turkmenistan. The parties to the Convention are required to take the necessary legislative, regulatory and other measures to ensure compliance with the provisions of the Convention and also to ensure proper enforcement measures are put in place. The Convention is said to be based on three pillars:

1.   access to environmental information;
2.   public participation in environmental decision-making;
3.   access to justice in environmental matters.

The Convention seeks to provide minimum guarantees and accordingly its provisions do not affect the right of a party to maintain or introduce measures providing for broader access to information, more extensive public participation in decision-making and wider access to justice in environmental matters than required by the Convention.

12.4.2 The Compliance Committee

Article 15 of the Convention required the parties to establish arrangements for reviewing compliance with the Convention. Consequently in 2002 the parties adopted a decision and elected the first Compliance Committee. The Compliance Committee can examine complaints submitted by the parties or the Convention Secretariat. However, uniquely in international environmental law, the Compliance Committee can also examine complaints made directly from members of the public.

---

36   United Nations Economic Commission for Europe Convention on Access to Information, Public Participation in Decision-making and Access to Justice in Environmental Matters (1998).
37   Ibid, Art 17. The Convention was open for signature by, inter alia, regional economic integration organisations constituted by sovereign Member States of the Economic Commission for Europe to which Member States have transferred competence over matters governed by the Convention. The EU is the only regional economic integration organisation currently party to the Convention.
38   Art 216 TEU.
39   Now Art 191 TFEU.
40   Art 4 TFEU.
41   See Eeckhout, P, EU External Relations (Oxford EU Law Library, 2011, 2nd edn).

The process of examining complaints is very transparent, with all correspondence being published on the UNECE website making it possible for the public to track the progress of a complaint. First the Committee will determine whether a complaint is admissible. If the complaint is admissible it is referred to the respective party which has the opportunity to submit its observations. Following this the Committee will consider information supplied by both the complainant (referred to as the communicant) and the party and it will prepare draft recommendations and findings which are again subject to further discussion. Finally the Compliance Committee will report its recommendations and findings to the meeting of the parties.

The meeting of the parties may, upon consideration of any recommendations of the Committee, decide upon appropriate measures to bring about full compliance. For example, it could request that the party submit a strategy and schedule for ensuring compliance. Although the meeting of the parties cannot issue binding decisions, it can issue declarations of non-compliance and issue cautions.

Since its establishment the Committee has reached a number of findings with regard to compliance by the parties. For example on 28 September 2010 the Committee published its findings in relation to the UK in case ACCC/C/2010/53. This followed a complaint lodged by a subcommittee which represented the interests of a group of residents in Moray Feu, Edinburgh and which alleged that Edinburgh City Council had acted in breach of the Convention in relation to the rerouting of traffic to facilitate the development of a tram system. Specifically it was alleged that the council had failed to collect relevant environmental information and to provide it on request; had denied meaningful public participation regarding traffic rerouting; and by using a private Act of Parliament to approve the tram system had removed the requirement to hold a public hearing, which resulted in the residents being denied access to justice. In relation to the public participation and access to justice complaints, the Committee considered the communicants' allegations were not sufficiently substantiated, which shows that communicants must be able to adduce evidence in support of their complaints. However the Committee found that by not providing the requested raw data to the public the UK had failed to comply with the access to information provisions of the Convention. This is just one example. In fact the UK has been held to be in breach of the Convention in other cases, most notably ACCC/C/2008/33 in which the Committee found the UK to be in breach of its obligations under Art 9(4) of the Convention. This case is discussed further below.

12.5 Access to environmental information

12.5.1 The Aarhus Convention

The Aarhus Convention recognises that public authorities hold a great deal of environmental information in the public interest. Much of this information is either about the state of the environment or the measures that are being taken to protect it. It is therefore not 'private' information because it concerns our environment. The preamble to the Convention states that:

> in the field of the environment, improved access to information and public participation in decision-making enhance the quality and the implementation of decisions, contribute to public awareness of environmental issues, give the public the opportunity to express its concerns and enable public authorities to take due account of such concerns.

The public should also have access to information to enable them to obtain evidence of any unlawful activity and to ensure that both private and public organisations comply with environmental law. The public needs to be able to access reliable information in order to ascertain whether and how polluting activities are authorised and what steps the regulatory bodies are taking (or not taking) to enforce environmental laws. The public also needs to access information from public authorities in order to hold them to account, possibly through the courts by means of judicial review. Environmental information may also be used for less litigious purposes, for instance, by consumers and customers to identify the environmental track record of companies and factor such information into their respective decision-making processes. In order to be able to participate in environmental decision-making and hold public authorities to account the public should have the fullest access to this information. The access to environmental information pillar is contained in Arts 4 and 5, supplemented by Art 9(1) which deals with the procedures for redress and remedies where environmental information is wrongly withheld. Article 9(1) will be considered in detail below at 12.8.3.

Article 4 requires public authorities to provide environmental information to the public on request. The terms 'environmental information' and 'public authorities' are both broadly defined in the Convention. In addition Art 4 lays down certain procedural requirements for handling requests, including the time allowed for handling requests and when a charge may or may not be levied. Importantly, Art 4 confers a right on any member of the public to ask for environmental information without having to state a reason. Like all access to information provisions Art 4 lists a number of grounds upon which a public authority may refuse to disclose environmental information. These are called exceptions and they are all subject to a public interest test. Significantly, the Convention includes an expressly worded mandate that the exceptions to disclosure must be interpreted in a restrictive way, taking into account the public interest served by disclosure and taking into account whether the information requested relates to emissions into the environment. The Convention implicitly recognises that improving public awareness about the environment requires more than simply giving the public the right to request information. Therefore in addition to being required to provide environmental information on request the Convention includes provisions requiring the more active dissemination of environmental information, particularly by electronic means.

Article 5 requires that public authorities possess and update environmental information which is relevant to their functions and make it available in a manner that is transparent and effectively accessible. Public authorities can do this by establishing and maintaining publicly accessible lists, registers or files of information and taking other practical steps which make the public aware about how and where they can access environmental information. Of course the advent of the internet has made this much easier. Each party is required to ensure that the environmental information that it holds is progressively made available in electronic databases and as a minimum the accessible information must include the following:

(a)   Reports on the state of the environment.
(b)   Texts of legislation relating to the environment.
(c)   As appropriate, policies, plans and programmes on or relating to the environment, and environmental agreements.
(d)   Other information, where the availability of such information would facilitate the application of national law implementing this Convention.

Interestingly Art 5 also encourages each party to urge operators whose activities have a significant impact on the environment to inform the public regularly of the environmental impact of their activities and products, where appropriate within the framework of voluntary eco-labelling or eco-auditing schemes or by other means.

12.5.2 EU legislation

Prior to signing the Convention in 1998 the EU had already adopted the Environmental Information Directive in 1990 (Directive 90/313/EEC),[42] which required Member States to

---

42   Directive 90/313/EEC of 7 June 1990 on the freedom of access to information on the environment OJ L 158, 23.6.1990, pp.. 56–58.

disclose environmental information on request. The weaknesses inherent in the 1990 Directive informed much of the discussion in the Aarhus negotiations. Certainly the Convention sought to address and overcome these weaknesses by widening the definition of public authorities and environmental information and reducing the number of exceptions and making them all subject to a public interest test. The conclusion of the Convention meant that it was necessary for EU law to align itself with the provisions of the Convention and for the EU to ensure compliance on the part of the Member States and the EU institutions. As far as the Member States were concerned, the solution was the repeal of the 1990 Directive and the adoption of Directive 2003/4/EC on public access to environmental information. [43] In addition the EU also adopted the so-called Aarhus Regulation,[44] which included provisions relating to access to environmental information held by the EU's institutions and bodies.

12.5.3 Access to information in the UK: from secrecy to openness

Historically, the UK has been characterised by limited public access to environmental information. Hughes (2002) asserts: 'Environmental regulation has traditionally been shrouded in secrecy, due to both legally enforceable obligations of confidentiality and voluntary practices of secrecy by the regulatory authorities.'[45] The policy of secrecy was given a formal basis when, in 1974, the Health and Safety at Work Act specifically prohibited the Health & Safety Inspectorate from publicising any details of any recordings or measurements taken during the exercise of its duties under the Act. Early environmental legislation made it very difficult for the public to obtain information about polluting activities. Various later statutes also incorporated specific provisions that forbade the disclosure of information relating to polluting activities. For example, the Rivers (Prevention of Pollution) Act 1961 only permitted the disclosure of information about water discharge consents if the company making the discharge expressly permitted the disclosure. The dearth of information available has, arguably, increased the public's concerns regarding the adverse health impacts of exposure to polluting emissions and undermined the public's trust of regulators and government.

The Royal Commission on Environmental Pollution can take much of the credit for ensuring the introduction of the statutory provisions which established publicly accessible pollution control registers. In its 2nd Report in 1972,[46] the RCEP suggested that the arguments in favour of restricting the accessibility of commercial environmental information were not well founded:

> We doubt some of the reasons for this confidentiality and our doubts are shared by many of the witnesses from industry with whom we have spoken. It is a practice which on occasion hinders the flow of information and it leads to risks of misunderstanding on the part of the public which may be harmful to industry and government alike.

Later in 1984 in its 10th Report,[47] the Royal Commission recommended that the public should be entitled to the fullest possible information with regard to all forms of environmental pollution, and that the onus should be placed on the polluter to substantiate a claim for exceptional treatment

---

43 Directive 2003/4/EC of the European Parliament and of the Council of 28 January 2003 on public access to environmental information and repealing Council Directive 90/313/EEC OJ L 41, 14/2/2003, pp 26–32.

44 Regulation (EC) No 1367/2006 of the European Parliament and of the Council of 6 September 2006 on the application of the provisions of the Aarhus Convention on Access to Information, Public Participation in Decision-making and Access to Justice in Environmental Matters to Community institutions and bodies, OJ L 264, 25/09/2006 pp 13–19.

45 Hughes, D, *Environmental Law* (Oxford University Press, 4th edn).

46 RCEP 2nd Report (1972) *Three Issues in Industrial Pollution.*

47 RCEP 10th Report (1984) *Tackling Pollution – Experience and Prospects.*

(that is, exclusion of information). It accordingly recommended that a guiding principle behind all legislative and administrative controls relating to environmental pollution information should be a presumption in favour of unrestricted access for the public to information which the pollution control authorities receive by virtue of their statutory powers, with protection for secrecy only in those circumstances where a genuine case can be substantiated. It was also suggested that cases where genuine secrets are involved are, in fact, comparatively rare. The basic premise of the Royal Commission's arguments was that the public has a right to know, that there is a need to restore public confidence in the enforcement system and, importantly, that the public has a beneficial interest in the environment.

The EPA 1990 introduced important new provisions requiring that certain information held by the regulatory bodies empowered by the Act be available for inspection by the public. The stated aim was that information must be freely available. Unnecessary secrecy undermines public confidence that pollution has been properly controlled. The intention was that the new system of public registers which the EPA 1990 introduced would increase confidence in pollution control. According to the Royal Commission this would facilitate public participation in helping to protect the environment and would allow every individual to become an environmental watchdog in his or her own right.

12.5.4 Access to information: the public registers

The most important source of environmental information prior to the entry into force of the Environmental Information Regulations 2004 (EIR 2004) was the public registers established under various pieces of planning and environmental legislation. For example, the Town and Country Planning Act 1947 established the first public register which contained details of planning applications. Now under s 69 Town and Country Planning Act 1990 every local planning authority is under a duty to maintain a public register of information. The exact information content is prescribed under Part 7 (art 36) of the Town and Country Planning (Development Management Procedure) (England) Order 2010 SI 2010/2184. Other public registers were established under the Water Resources and Water Industries Acts 1991. Today the principal register of importance is the register of activities regulated under the environmental permitting regime, but other registers continue to be of importance such as the register of contaminated land under Part 2A EPA 1990. It is not the intention of this book to list all the public registers.[48] The purpose of the public register legislation is to ensure that public authorities with responsibilities for regulating polluting activities are required to disclose information to the public. Each individual piece of legislation prescribes the precise content of the register. The use of the term 'register' can be a little misleading because the information may be held in a traditional filing cabinet, but more likely now in a series of electronic files. It is quite rare for the legislation to prescribe how the information should be stored or made accessible, but in general terms the registers are required to be available for inspection at all reasonable times, and copies of entries can be obtained at a reasonable charge. However, a public authority is not permitted to impose any charges for in situ inspection of the public registers, as this would breach the provisions of the EIR 2004.

---

48 For a more detailed discussion of the contemporary public registers see Wolf, S, *Environmental Information Regulations; A Practical Guide* (Law Society Publishing, 2011).

Law in Action

The Environment Agency's website enables members of the public to do an online search of information held on the Agency's public registers. The online registers provide summary data backed up by the facility to request further details and copy documents.

The environmental permitting register is a particularly important source of information about those activities that are subject to the permitting regime. The detailed provisions governing the duty to maintain the registers are to be found in the Environmental Permitting Regulations 2010, Part 5, regs 45–56 and Sched 24. Both the relevant local authority and the Environment Agency are obliged to maintain the registers about the activities they regulate.

The registers also contain information about any administrative notices served by the Environment Agency/local authority,[49] appeals, applications to remove information from the register,[50] monitoring data,[51] details of breaches of permit conditions[52] and enforcement action.[53] The registers do not contain information relating to breaches of the law by non-licence holders. Although the registers provide a great deal of information about permitted activities they are limited to just that and do not extend to more general information, such as policy documents or information about the state of the environment. However, this information is now accessible via the EIR 2004. Finally it should be noted that certain information may be withheld from the public registers.

In general terms the various statutory provisions have tended to allow or require the regulator to withhold information on the grounds of national security and commercial confidentiality. However, these provisions must now be read in conjunction with the EIR 2004. Although the EIR do not expressly or impliedly repeal any legislation which excludes information from the public registers, it is necessary to take into account EIR reg 5.6. This states that any enactment or rule of law that would prevent the disclosure of environmental information in accordance with the EIR shall not apply. This means that a public authority maintaining a register would need to 'dissapply' any statutory provision excluding environmental information from a register and re-examine whether information should be disclosed/withheld by reference exclusively to the EIR 2004.

12.6 Environmental Information Regulations 2004

The Environmental Information Regulations 2004 give effect to the Access to Environmental Information Directive (Directive 2003/4/EC),[54] which, as was noted earlier, was adopted by the EU in fulfilment of its obligations under the first pillar of the Aarhus Convention. The EIR 2004 repealed and replaced the Environmental Information Regulations 1992,[55] which had enacted the earlier 1990 Directive. It is interesting to note that the EIR 1992 had entered into force some 12 years before the Freedom of Information Act (FOIA) 2000, which came fully into force on

---

49 E.g., enforcement notices.
50 National security or commercial confidentiality reasons.
51 Including sampling data.
52 E.g., the number of breaches.
53 Including the outcome of prosecutions.
54 Directive 2003/4/EC of the European Parliament and of the Council of 28 January 2003 on public access to environmental information and repealing Council Directive 90/313/EEC OJ L 41, 14/2/2003, pp 26–32.
55 Environmental Information Regulations 1992 SI 1992/3240.

1 April 2004. It therefore should have represented a significant landmark on the general 'information rights' landscape. Certainly the EIR 1992 provided a more generous right to information than that provided for by the public registers. However, the reality is that the EIR 1992 were rarely utilised, other than by some NGOs or commercial companies seeking to obtain information about competitors. The definition of public authorities caught within the scope of the 1992 Regulations was vague and the privatised water companies argued that they were not bound by the Regulations. The grounds for withholding information (the exceptions) were widely drafted, and fundamentally there was no statutory right of appeal in relation to a refusal to disclose information. The only mechanism for challenging a decision under the EIR 1992 was by way of judicial review, which explains why the cases are few and far between.

The Environmental Information Directive 2003 has largely addressed these defects in so far as there is now a much wider definition of environmental information and public authorities; the exceptions are more narrowly drafted and the EIR 2004 provide for a free independent review by the Information Commissioner (see below at 12.6.8). However, the issue of whether the privatised water companies are subject to the EIR 2004 remains a contentious issue and will be discussed below.

12.6.1 What is environmental information?

In its Review of Directive 90/313/EEC[56] the Commission noted that one of the main problems highlighted by complainants about the application of the Directive throughout the Member States related to the definition of information relating to the environment:

> In some Member States a strict interpretation [of information relating to the environment] had led to refusals to provide information not considered to fall within the scope of the definition. Examples of such information included information on the public health effects of the state of the environment, on radiation or nuclear energy and on the financial or needs analyses in support of projects likely to affect the environment.[57]

The Aarhus Convention sought to eliminate these problems by providing a wide, non-exhaustive definition of environmental information. In fact:

> What constitutes environmental information is explained rather indirectly in terms of what environmental information can be about. The subjects of environmental information are broken into three categories and within each category illustrative lists are set forth. These are non-exhaustive lists.[58]

The definition of environmental information in Art 2 of the Convention is repeated practically verbatim in Art 2 of the 2003 Directive and reg 2(1) of EIR 2004. In fact the EIR expressly states that the definition has the same meaning as the Directive. The definition of environmental information is lengthy, broad and non-exhaustive. Environmental information can take many forms, including information in written, visual, aural, electronic or any other material form. It includes, for example, information contained in all types of documents such as decision letters, applications,

56 Report from the Commission to the Council and the European Parliament on the experience gained in the application of Council Directive 90/313/EEC of 7 June 1990 on freedom of access to information on the environment COM (2000) 400 final.
57 Ibid, fn 46.
58 Stec, S and Casey-Lefkowitz, S et al, UN/ECE Convention on Access to Information, Public Participation in Decision-making and Access to Justice in Environmental Matters, The Aarhus Convention: An Implementation Guide (2000). Available at http://www.unece.org/env/pp/acig.pdf.

inspection reports, concession agreements, contracts, tables, databases, spreadsheets, emails, photographs, sketches and handwritten notes or drawings and covers opinions and advice as well as facts. Information in raw and unprocessed form is capable of being environmental information as well as documents, so, for example, it has been possible for applicants to obtain copies of plans,[59] maps, graphs and satellite images.

However, the information must be on one of the six limbs of the definition. The first limb of the definition is central and it refers to the so-called 'elements' of the environment. Rather than producing a finite and exhaustive list of these elements, the EIR provides a widely drafted illustrative list which contains the traditional media of air, water and land, but also includes landscape, natural sites and biological diversity. Environmental information is defined in the first instance as any information on the *state* of the elements of the environment; a request concerning air quality clearly falls within this but so would a question to a highways authority about the state of the highway or footpaths.

The second limb includes any information on the factors affecting or likely to affect the elements of the environment. Interestingly this is not limited to traditional emissions or discharges or waste but includes energy, noise and radiation. Although factors are defined widely the limb is qualified in so far as the factors must affect or be likely to affect the elements of the environment. However, the ICO Guidance on this states that it is hard to imagine a factor that is not likely to have an effect on one of the elements and that there is no possible de minimis limitation. Additionally the Information Rights Tribunal has shown a marked reluctance to engage in any detailed scientific analysis of effect, preferring to give the words of the definition their plain and ordinary meaning.[60] Moving on, the third limb refers to any information on measures (including administrative measures), such as policies, legislation, plans, programmes, environmental agreements, and activities affecting or likely to affect the elements and factors referred to above. The Information Commissioner and Tribunal have found that legal advice given to a public authority in respect of planning issues constitutes a measure likely to affect one of the elements of the environment.[61] Similarly, advice given to Ministers by civil servants during policy formulation or decision-making falls within this limb, as does information supplied by the public in questionnaire form during a process of public consultation.[62]

The fourth and fifth limbs of the definition include reports on the implementation of environmental legislation and cost-benefit and other economic analyses and assumptions used within the framework of the measures and activities referred to above. The final limb includes any information on the state of human health and safety, including the contamination of the food chain, where relevant, conditions of human life, cultural sites and built structures inasmuch as they are or may be affected by the state of the elements of the environment or through those elements by any of the factors or measures referred to.

There is a degree of cross-reference between the limbs so that, for example, the inclusion of material in a body of information on the factors covered by subpara (b) will only bring that information within the definition if the factors affect or are likely to affect the elements of the environment listed in subpara (a).

The Defra guidance[63] cautions public authorities to ensure that the information that is made available to a requestor is 'up to date, accurate and comparable, so far as the public authority reasonably believes'. Information can include opinions and if this is the case the applicant should be made aware of this. Moreover the guidance suggests that since information may come from third

---

59 See ICO Decision, *Chesterfield Borough Council* FS502060693.
60 See *Office of Communications (Ofcom) v Information Commissioner*, Information Tribunal Appeal 04/09/07 EA/2006/0078.
61 See *Kirkaldie v Information Commissioner and Thanet District Council*, Information Tribunal Appeal, 04/07/06 EA/2006/001.
62 See ICO Decision FS50079628, 29/11/06 Transport for London.
63 See Defra Guidance Chapter 3, 'What is covered by the Regulations?'

parties it could be unreliable. Public authorities have been advised that where this is the case they should issue a disclaimer addressing issues to be taken into account by the public, for example in relation to the reliability, source and accuracy of the information.

A number of public authorities have failed to identify requests as being for environmental information, treating them as general requests for information under the FOIA 2004. Defra has published guidance[64] to authorities on the boundaries between environmental information and there are an increasing number of ICO and Information Rights Tribunal decisions to assist public authorities in making this determination.

12.6.2 Public authorities falling within the scope of the regulations

The definition of public authority is important in defining the scope of the regulations; if a body is not a public authority it is not obliged to disclose information under the EIR 2004. The Aarhus Implementation Guide[65] makes it clear that the Convention aims to provide as broad a coverage as possible and it is intended that 'privatised solutions[66] cannot take public services or activities out of the realm of the public environmental information regime. However, the litigation relating to the private water companies (discussed below) demonstrates that the private water companies are resistant to attempts to make them disclose information; the issue remains unresolved at the time of writing.

The definition of public authorities is contained in reg 2(2) EIR 2004, but reg 3 specifically excludes any public authority to the extent that it is acting in a judicial or legislative capacity and either House of Parliament to the extent required for the purpose of avoiding an infringement of the privileges of either House. Significantly the definition is wider than the definition of bodies subject to the FOIA 2000. Consequently some bodies will escape obligation under the FOIA 2000 but are still under a duty to disclose any environmental information that they hold. For example, the Port of London Authority, which is not subject to the FOIA 2000, was required to disclose environmental information that it held about the construction of Temple Pier at Victoria Embankment in London.[67]

The term 'public authority' is initially defined by giving it the same meaning that it has under s 3(1) FOIA. It includes government departments and any other public authority as defined under the Act. However, the EIR 2004 also include[68] the special forces and any unit or part of a unit which is for the time being required by the Secretary of State to assist the Government Communications Headquarters in the exercise of its functions. In contrast those bodies which are subject to FOIA but only in relation to the information specified in Sched 1[69] are excluded from this part of the definition.[70] Similarly any person designated by Order under s 5 FOIA is also excluded from the definition of public authorities in reg 2(2)(b).

To provide the broad coverage required by the Convention and Directive, the EIR includes two further categories of bodies that fall within the definition of public authorities. The first is any other body or other person that carries out functions of public administration.[71] These functions need not relate to the environment; however, they must be *administrative* functions.[72] A private body may carry

64 Ibid.
65 Stec, S and Casey-Lefkowitz, S et al, UN/ECE Convention on Access to Information, Public Participation in Decision-making and Access to Justice in Environmental Matters, The Aarhus Convention: An Implementation Guide (2000). Available at http://www.unece.org/env/pp/acig.pdf.
66 E.g. the privatisation of governmental activities.
67 Port of London v Information Commissioner EA/2006/0083.
68 By disregarding the exception granted in para 6 of Sched 1 FOIA.
69 Such as the Bank of England, or the BBC.
70 Although arguably they may fall within other parts of the EIR definition.
71 Reg 2(2)(c).
72 See Network Rail v Information Commissioner, Information Tribunal Appeal, 17/07/07, EA/2006/0061, EA/2006/0062.

out functions of public administration, for example a private company that is contracted to perform a function normally performed by governmental authorities.

The final, and perhaps most difficult, part of the definition, in reg 2(2)(d), covers any other body or other person that is under the control of a person falling within subparas 2(2) (a)–(c) and:

(i)   has public responsibilities relating to the environment;
(ii)   exercises functions of a public nature relating to the environment; or
(iii)   provides public services relating to the environment.

Essentially this involves a two-stage test. First, does the person/body fall under the control of a public authority, and second, does the body demonstrate at least one of the responsibilities relating to the environment, functions of a public nature relating to the environment, or provide public services relating to the environment. The Information Rights Tribunal and Commissioner found no difficulty in holding that private sector waste companies that are carrying out statutory duties on behalf of a public authority fall under this limb. So, for example, South Downs Waste Services Ltd, a private waste company, was held to be a public authority by virtue of the integrated waste management contract it had entered into with two councils.[73] This clearly has important implications for private sector providers who enter into contracts to carry out the statutory responsibilities of public authorities and authorities who put such contracts out to tender should make companies aware of this possibility under the EIR 2004.

Law in Action

Environmental Resources Management Ltd, a private environmental consultancy firm, carried out a strategic environmental assessment and produced a report on behalf of the Regional Assembly for North East England (RANE). RANE was under a statutory duty to carry out the environmental assessment. The Information Commissioner decided that ERM Ltd was a public authority for the purposes of the Regulations. Because ERM carried out the assessment and prepared the report, reg 2(2)(d)(ii) of the EIR applied to it. Furthermore, ERM was under the control of RANE, a body to which reg 2(2)(c) applied. This control was both contractual and statutory. [ICO Decision FER0090259, 07/06/2006]

12.6.3 Are the privatised water companies public authorities for the purposes of the EIR?

This vexed question has resulted in a request for a preliminary ruling to the ECJ and a complaint to the Aarhus Compliance Committee. The question was considered at some length by the Upper Tribunal in *Smartsource Drainage and Water Searches Ltd v The Information Commissioner* (2010).[74] The focus of the Tribunal's examination was on the extent to which the water companies could be said to be under the 'control' of a public authority. The Upper Tribunal considered the way in which 'control' had been interpreted by the courts in other contexts. Although these were of limited assistance in interpreting the EIR the Tribunal felt the ruling of McKenna J in *Ready Mixed Concrete v Ministry of Pensions* (1968)[75] gave a taste of what control means:

---

73 ICO Decision FS50114241, 18/03/08.
74 *Smartsource Drainage and Water Searches Ltd v The Information Commissioner* (2010) (GIA/2458/2010); [2010] UKUT 415 (AAC).
75 *Ready Mixed Concrete v Ministry of Pensions and National Insurance* [1968] 1 All ER 433 at 440C.

> Control includes the power of deciding the thing to be done, the way in which it should be done, the means to be employed in doing it, the time when, and the place where it shall be done.

Having regard to this, but more specifically the aims of the Convention, the Upper Tribunal concluded that the aim of the legislation was to capture governmental and executive functions in the various guises. In the Tribunal's view it was necessary to draw a distinction between control and regulation; private companies may be subject to extensive regulation but still remain at arm's length from the machinery of the state. Applying this reasoning the Tribunal concluded that the water companies are not public authorities for the purposes of the EIR. However, in 2012, faced with a similar case (*Fish Legal v Information Commissioner*—see below) the Upper Tribunal decided that it was necessary to seek a preliminary ruling from the Court of Justice on the interpretation of the definition of public authority under the directive.[76]

Law in Action

In 2009, Fish Legal, a non-profit-making organisation set up to use the law to fight against pollution, submitted requests for environmental information from several water and sewerage companies, including United Utilities and Yorkshire Water. The requests related to information on the performance of their combined sewage overflows, which allow sewage including faeces, urine and washing detergents to pass untreated into rivers, lakes and coastal waters when wastewater treatment works are overwhelmed by rain. United Utilities and Yorkshire Water argued that they were not subject to the EIR 2004, and therefore not obliged to release the information. The Information Commissioner agreed with the water companies and so Fish Legal appealed to the First Tier Information Rights Tribunal. The case was stayed pending the outcome of *Smartsource*. Following the *Smartsource* decision, the First-tier Tribunal dismissed the appeals, but gave permission to appeal to the Upper Tribunal. On appeal, the Upper Tribunal decided that it was necessary to refer five questions to the ECJ regarding the interpretation of public authorities.

At the time of writing the request for a preliminary ruling was still pending before the Court of Justice.[77] In addition Fish Legal had submitted a complaint to the Aarhus Compliance Committee.

12.6.4 The duty to make information available on request

Regulation 5 EIR specifies that (subject to certain conditions) a public authority that holds environmental information shall make the information available on request. The unique feature about the EIR 2004 is that it includes a requirement to respond to oral requests for information. The regime is also said to be applicant blind, meaning that the public authority cannot respond to a request on the basis of the applicant's identity or motive (for example, even if the applicant is going to use the information to embarrass an authority). The word 'available' is emphasised here because of the interpretation placed upon it by the Information Rights Tribunal in the *Rhondda Cynon Taff* decision.[78]

---

76 *Fish Legal v Information Commissioner* (GIA/0979 & 0980/2011); [2012] UKUT 177 AAC.
77 Case C-279/12 *Fish Legal v Information Commissioner* (decision pending).
78 *Rhondda Cynon Taff County BC v Information Commissioner*, Information Tribunal Appeal, 05/12/07, EA/2006/0065.

In this case the Tribunal adopted a particularly literal approach to the interpretation of the EIR 2004 by contrasting and distinguishing the wording of reg 5(1) EIR with s 1(1) FOIA. Under the EIR a public authority is only required to make the information *available* on request. In contrast, s 1(1) FOIA provides that an applicant is entitled to have that information *communicated to him*. According to the Tribunal this distinction is important. Whereas under FOIA an applicant has a right to receive the information, under the EIR the obligation is to provide access to the information and this 'may not mean physically providing an applicant with a copy of the information i.e. there is no obligation to communicate it to the applicant'. It is arguable that the Tribunal, in this instance, failed to adopt the wider purposive approach to interpretation generally regarded as essential when approaching the interpretation of national legislation that gives effect to EU law. However, it should be stated that the Tribunal's decisions do not set any precedents and it remains to be seen whether this limited view would be supported by the courts. What is clear is that when the courts have been called upon to interpret the EIR 2004 they caution against using the FOIA as an aid to interpretation:

> Both measures promote increased openness in the public sector; but as it seems to me one would have to be very cautious in using either as a guide to the interpretation of the other since the EIR are, and are only, a measure to implement European legislation. If their interpretation is to be coloured by anything, it must be by the Directive.[79]

An applicant has the right to ask for information to be supplied in a particular form or format, and where this happens, the public authority is required[80] to comply with the applicant's request. However, this is qualified in so far as the authority can decline if it is either reasonable for the authority to make the information available in another form or format, or the information is already publicly available and easily accessible in another form or format. In either case, the public authority must provide the applicant with a written explanation of this as soon as possible or within 20 working days of the request.

Public authorities can make reasonable charges for making the information available but if the applicant is invited and willing to examine the information at the offices of the public authority then no charge may be made. Authorities cannot charge for the time taken to retrieve the information; they can only charge for actual costs incurred[81] and these must be reasonable.[82]

The EIR only confers a right of access to environmental information that is held by a public authority. For the purposes of the Regulations, environmental information is held by a public authority if the information:

a.   is in the authority's possession and has been produced or received by the authority; or
b.   is held by another person on behalf of the authority.

The noteworthy aspect of this is that it includes information in the authority's possession[83] which has been received from a third party. This means that where a public authority receives information from a third party (such as a company or individual) and then stores it within the authority's building or elsewhere on its behalf, the information is 'held' for the purposes of the request. So, for example, if a local authority receives information from waste companies as part of a waste contract tendering exercise this information is 'held' by the local authority for the purposes of the EIR 2004. It is, therefore, subject to the application of any appropriate exception, potentially disclosable.

---

79 *R (on the application of the Office of Communications v Information Commissioner* [2008] EWHC 1445 (Admin).
80 By reg 6 EIR 2004.
81 I.e. paper, printing, photocopying and postage costs.
82 See *Markinson v Information Commissioner*, Information Tribunal Appeal, 28/03/2006 EA/2005/0014.
83 Or held by another person on behalf of the authority.

Unless the public authority intends to withhold the information requested in reliance of one of the exceptions contained in reg 12, it is required by reg 5 to make the information available as soon as possible and in any event within 20 working days after the date of the receipt of the request.[84] The 20 working day period starts the day after receipt of the information request. The information that is made available must be up to date, accurate and comparable so far as the public authority reasonably believes. The time period may be extended to 40 working days if the authority reasonably believes that the complexity and volume of the information requested means that it is impracticable either to comply with the request within 20 working days or to make a decision to refuse to do so.

Applicants and prospective applicants have the right to receive reasonable advice and assistance in the formulation of a request.[85] Where the public authority takes the view that the request has been formulated in too general a manner, it must then ask the applicant[86] to provide more particulars in relation to the request and should also assist the applicant in providing these particulars. This provision can be particularly important for individuals and ad hoc pressure groups trying to find out about environmental issues where they lack the specific knowledge or expertise to identify exactly what information they require. The Defra Code of Practice[87] suggests that public authorities publish details of their procedures for dealing with requests for information, particularly since this duty extends to prospective applicants.

12.6.5 Exceptions to disclosure

The Regulations allow for certain categories of information to be excluded from the duty of disclosure; these are referred to as exceptions. The exceptions to the duty to disclose environmental information are contained in Part 3 of the EIR 2004 in regs 12–15. The EIR includes an expressly worded presumption in favour of disclosure.[88] Additionally the Access to Environmental Information Directive[89] explicitly states that the grounds for refusal shall be interpreted in a restrictive way, taking into account for the particular case the public interest served by disclosure. In every particular case, the public interest served by disclosure shall be weighed against the interest served by the refusal. The public interest test is considered more fully at 12.6.6.

Regulation 12 EIR provides that a public authority may refuse to disclose environmental information requested if:

(a)   an exception to disclosure applies under paras (4) or (5); and

(b)   in all the circumstances of the case, the public interest in maintaining the exception outweighs the public interest in disclosing the information.

The exceptions may be categorised into three groups, as follows.

12.6.5.1 Refusals based upon procedural grounds—reg 12(4)(a)–(c)

Regulation 12(4)(a) permits a public authority to refuse to disclose information to the extent that it does not hold that information when an applicant's request is received. A public authority is only

---

84 See R (on the application of Rockware Glass Ltd) v Chester City Council, [2005] EWHC 2250; [2006] Env LR 30; [2006] JPL 699; [2006] ACD 11; [2005] NPC 120; 2005 WL 3048992 (QBD (Admin)).

85 Reg 9.

86 As soon as possible and within the 20 working days limit.

87 Defra, (2005) Code of Practice on the discharge of the obligations of public authorities under the Environmental Information Regulations 2004 SI 2004/3391.

88 Reg 12(2) EIR 2004.

89 Directive 2003/4/EC of the European Parliament and of the Council of 28 January 2003 on public access to environmental information and repealing Council Directive 90/313/EEC OJ L 41, 14/2/2003, pp 26–32.

obliged to disclose the information it holds at the time the request is made. However, where a public authority does not hold the requested information but believes that another public authority does, it may either transfer the request to the other public authority, or supply the applicant with the name and address of that authority. Although all of the exceptions are subject to the public interest test, it is fairly self-evident that if a public authority doesn't hold the information it simply cannot disclose it, irrespective of any public interest arguments. This was recognised by Advocate General Kokott in her Opinion in Case C-71/10 *Office of Communications v Information Commissioner*.[90]

Information may also be withheld under reg 12(4)(b) if the request is manifestly unreasonable. The emphasis in the EIR guidance, in respect of this exception, is on whether the request could place a *substantial and unreasonable burden on the resources of the public authority*, particularly where, for example, the request involves extensive scans of historic files or searching large databases, or where extensive redaction is necessary. Central is the notion that the retrieval would result in an unreasonable diversion of resources from the provision of essential public services.[91] Finally in this category the request can be refused if the request is formulated in too general a manner and the public authority has complied with reg 9, which places a duty on the authority to provide advice and assistance to the applicant. All of the procedural exceptions are subject to the application of a public interest test (subject to the note above re information not held).[92] Accordingly if a public authority seeks to rely on one of these exceptions it must be shown that in all the circumstances of the case the public interest in maintaining the exception outweighs the public interest in disclosure.

12.6.5.2 Class-based exceptions

The EIR contains the following three class-based exceptions:

(a) *The information includes personal data of which the applicant is not the data subject.* To the extent that information requested includes personal data of which the applicant is not the data subject, the personal data must not be disclosed except in accordance with the requirements of reg 13. Essentially, disclosure is not permitted if it would result in a breach of the eight principles set out in the Data Protection Act 1988.

(b) *The request relates to material which is still in the course of completion, to unfinished documents or to incomplete data*—reg 12(4)(d). This exception permits a public authority to refuse to disclose any unfinished material. However, the guidance is clear that this exception is not designed to enable a public authority to evade its obligation to make environmental information available merely by labelling documents as 'draft' and in fact the public authority is required[93] to tell the applicant (if it knows) the name of any other public authority preparing the information and when it is likely to be completed or finished.

(c) *The request involves the disclosure of internal communications.* This is a widely drafted exception and does not sit well or comfortably with the overall approach of the Convention or Directive particularly since most information held by a public authority will be an internal communication of some sort or another. Jones and Rees (2006) state that 'Internal communications' could not be said to be one of the exceptions that is 'more narrowly drawn under the EIR than under the FOIA'.[94] The aim of this exception is to provide public authorities with the necessary space to think in private. Arguments about this exception have been well rehearsed before the Information Rights Tribunal and indeed now before the High Court.[95] The exception is,

---

90 Case C–71/10 *Office of Communications v Information Commissioner* [2011] PTSR 1676 [2012] 1 CMLR 7 [2012] Env LR 7.
91 See *Carpenter v Information Commissioner and Stevenage Borough Council*, 17/11/08, EA/2008/0046.
92 See below at 12.6.6.
93 By reg 14(4).
94 Jones, B, Rees, C et al, 'The Environmental Information Regulations 2004', *Freedom of Information Handbook*, (2006) p 229.
95 *Export Credits Guarantee Department v Friends of the Earth* [2008] EWHC 638 (Admin).

however, subject to the public interest test and an authority wishing to withhold information under this limb would need to provide clear reasons (as opposed to generic assertions) that the public interest in maintaining thinking space etc outweighed the public interest in disclosure. In *Export Credits Guarantee Department v Friends of the Earth* (2008) the High Court upheld the Tribunal's conclusion that the disclosure of advice between government departments could improve the quality of the deliberative process.

12.6.5.3 Refusals where disclosure of the information would adversely affect one of the matters specified in reg 12(5)

The final category of exception allows a public authority to withhold information where disclosure would adversely affect one of the interests listed in reg 12(5):

1. international relations, defence, national security or public safety;
2. the course of justice, ability of a person to receive a fair trial or ability of a public authority to conduct a criminal or disciplinary inquiry;
3. intellectual property rights;
4. the confidentiality or proceedings of any public authority where such confidentiality is protected by law;
5. the confidentiality of commercial or industrial information where such confidentiality is provided by law to protect a legitimate economic interest;
6. the interests of the person providing the information where that person:

   i. was not under (and could not have been put under) a legal obligation to supply it to that or another public authority;
   ii. did not supply it in circumstances such that that or another public authority was entitled apart from the EIR to disclose it; and
   iii. has not consented to its disclosure;

7. the protection of the environment to which the information relates.

The Information Rights Tribunal has concluded in respect of these exceptions that the effect must be adverse and that refusal to disclose is only permitted to the extent of the adverse effect. Additionally it is necessary to show that the disclosure 'would' have an adverse effect, not that it could or might have such effect. In this context 'would' means 'more likely than not'.[96] A civil standard of proof applies.[97] The threshold for engaging these exceptions is higher than the prejudice-based exemptions under FOIA where it is sufficient to prove that disclosure 'would or would be likely' to prejudice the protected interest and where there is no explicitly stated requirement to interpret the exceptions in a restrictive manner.

Even in the event that a public authority determines that disclosure would adversely affect one of the above interests, the information must still be disclosed unless 'in all the circumstances of the case the public interest in maintaining the exception outweighs the public interest in disclosing the information'.

12.6.6 The public interest test

All of the exceptions listed in reg 12(4) and (5) are subject to the application of a public interest test.[98] In other words, it is not sufficient that information falls within one of the exceptions.

---

96 *Burgess v Information Commissioner and Stafford Borough Council*, 07/06/07, EA/2006/0091.
97 The public authority must be satisfied on the balance of probabilities that the relevant harm would be suffered.
98 However, if the environmental information includes personal data of which the applicant is not the data subject (reg 12(3)) the public interest test does not apply. This is an absolute exception.

In addition it must also be shown that in all the circumstances of the case the public interest in maintaining the exception outweighs the public interest in disclosing the information. This necessarily requires the public authority to carry out a balancing act between the 'competing' public interests. When considering the public interest test public authorities should also bear in mind the presumption in favour of disclosure in reg 12(2). If arguments are evenly balanced for witholding or disclosing information, the information must be disclosed.

The public interest in maintaining the exception rests with the exception itself and this must be weighed against the general public interest in disclosure. The Information Commissioner's Office has produced guidance on the public interest test and it includes the factors that one would expect to see: promoting government accountability and transparency and enabling individuals to understand how decisions have been taken. However, the public interest in disclosure must be considered in the light of the broader aims of the Convention, namely providing the public with the information they need to enable them to participate in environmental decision-making and the enforcement of environmental law.

In *Office of Communications (Ofcom) v The Information Commissioner* (2010)[99] the Supreme Court was asked to reach a judgment on the correct approach in law to a request for environmental information when the public authority holding the information relies upon more than one of the exceptions to the duty to disclose such information. The question that the SCA had to address was whether each exception had to be addressed separately, by considering whether the interest served by it is outweighed by the public interest in disclosure or whether the interests served by different exceptions had to be combined and then weighed against the public interest in disclosure. The Information Commissioner and Tribunal favoured the former approach and Ofcom favoured the latter. The Court of Appeal, taking a particularly literal approach to the interpretation, held that the public interests in the exception had to be aggregated. The SCA was divided but in any event considered that the question raised required a preliminary ruling from the European Court of Justice and accordingly sought a ruling on the interpretation of the EU Directive. The preliminary ruling handed down by the Court of Justice in Case C-71/10 was somewhat surprising particularly to information rights practitioners.[100] The ECJ held that the directive was open to an interpretation which would allow public authorities to evaluate cumulatively the grounds for refusal to disclose. The fact that those interests were referred to separately in the directive did not preclude the cumulation of those exceptions to the general rule of disclosure, given that the interests served by refusal to disclose might sometimes overlap in the same situation or the same circumstances. Significantly the Court of Justice held that the use of a cumulative approach is not likely to introduce another exception in addition to those laid down in the directive. The ruling did not say that the directive requires this cumulation of public interests in non-disclosure, merely that public authorities may undertake this further cumulative exercise. This would appear to suggest that Member States may adopt different approaches to the operation of the public interest test.

12.6.7 Proactive dissemination of environmental information

The EIR 2004 requires, in reg 4, that public authorities progressively make the environmental information they hold available to the public by electronic means and such means should be easily accessible. Additionally reg 4 requires public authorities to take reasonable steps to organise the information relevant to its functions with a view to the active and systematic dissemination to the public of the information. Although of course this does not include information that would

---

99 *Communications (Ofcom) v The Information Commissioner* [2010] UKSC 3 (on appeal from: [2009] EWCA Civ 90).
100 Case C-71/10 *Office of Communications v Information Commissioner* [2011] PTSR 1676 [2012] 1 CMLR 7 [2012] Env LR 7.

otherwise be exempt under the EIR 2004 it is also not required in relation to information collected before 1 January 2005 by non-electronic means. Defra guidance[101] suggests that public authorities, in fulfilling this obligation, should prioritise the identification and dissemination of information which is most likely to be of interest to the public, such as information on emissions and waste streams. The EIR 2004 prescribe, as a minimal requirement, that the information covered by reg 4 must include certain information referred to in Art 7(2) of the Directive and also the facts and analyses of facts which the public authority considers relevant and important in framing major environmental policy proposals.

In practice it means that public authorities subject to the EIR 2004 who hold information in an electronic form should progressively make it available via a website, which is easily accessible to the public. Those public authorities which are already subject to FOIA 2000 are required to produce publication schemes which include environmental information should be compliant with this aspect of the EIR 2004. The greater difficulty is for those bodies that are not subject to FOIA but are still required to comply with reg 4 EIR 2004. These bodies will need to consider what steps they need to take to proactively disseminate the environmental information they hold, whether on websites, through annual reports or other literature.

12.6.8 Rights of appeal

The principal problem with the EIR 1992 was that they failed to provide applicants with any right of appeal against a refusal to supply information, although it was possible for an applicant to judicially review a decision of a public authority. Clearly, this was a very expensive and litigious solution to a problem and likely to deter all but the most committed applicant. However, Art 9(1) of the Aarhus Convention requires that any persons whose request is wrongfully refused or not dealt with in accordance with the Convention should, in addition to judicial review procedures, have the right to have the decision reconsidered by the public authority or a review by an independent impartial body, such review being free or inexpensive and also expeditious. The EIR 2004 have made provision for this by importing the enforcement provisions of the Freedom of Information Act 2000 into the EIR 2004. Accordingly a person who has made a request for information and has been refused or who has a complaint about the way in which his/her request was handled may:

- request the relevant public authority to reconsider its decision or review its handling via the internal review procedure (reg 11 EIR 2004); after which
- complain to the Information Commissioner:
  - the Information Commissioner is not obliged to investigate all complaints and the complainant must have exhausted the internal review procedure; he can also decline to investigate out of time, frivolous or vexatious complaints;
  - the Information Commissioner may seek further information from the public authority by serving an Information Notice or may serve an Enforcement Notice;
  - the Information Commissioner has powers of entry, search and seizure;
  - it is a criminal offence to obstruct the Information Commissioner in the exercise of his functions;
  - the Information Commissioner will serve a Decision Notice which gives his decision in relation to the complaint. This may, for example, uphold the public authority's decision or require it to disclose all or some of the information;

---

101 Defra (2005) Guidance on Proactive Dissemination.

- make an appeal against the Information Commissioner's decision (and relevant public authority) to the First-tier (Information Rights) Tribunal.

The public authority also has a right of appeal against the Information Commissioner's decision, to the tribunal. There are only two grounds for appeal: either the notice is not in accordance with the law, or the notice involves the exercise of discretion and the Commissioner ought to have exercised his discretion differently. This latter usually relates to decisions regarding the public interest. A further right of appeal exists to the Administrative Appeals Chamber (AAC) of the Upper Tribunal, which is a Superior Court of Record. Prior to the Tribunals Courts and Enforcement Act 2007, appeals were to the High Court. The right of appeal is granted to any of the parties to the Information Rights Tribunal decision, but only on a point of law and subject to permission to appeal.

The decisions of the Information Commissioner and Information Rights Tribunal must be in writing and are legally binding. They are published on the respective websites.[102]

12.6.9 Using environmental information

NGOs (for example, Friends of the Earth and Greenpeace) and individuals do not have to provide any reasons or justifications for accessing the public registers or information via the EIR 2004. To that extent both access regimes are applicant and purpose blind. The information gained from the public registers and via the EIR 2004 can be 'used' by NGOs and individuals for a wide variety of reasons including:

- lobbying regulators and/or government departments with regard to policy changes and licensing/siting decisions;
- as evidence of breach of the law in civil compensation claims;
- as the basis of a private prosecution or in support of a judicial review action, for example challenging government policy or regulatory decision-making;
- environmental consultants use information to target customers regarding sales of pollution abatement technology and environmental services;
- industry and commerce may attempt to use register data to gain insight into a competitor's process and products (so-called 'reverse technology');
- the finance sector may use registers in order to assess the level of their clients' environmental risk exposure (for example, contaminated land) with regard to current landholdings and proposed acquisitions.

12.7 Public participation in environmental decision-making

12.7.1 The Aarhus Convention and EU implementation

The second pillar of the Aarhus Convention (Arts 6–8) is concerned with public participation in environmental decision-making. Article 6 deals with public participation in decisions for specific activities listed in Annex 1 and to other activities which may have a significant effect on the environment. Article 6 requires that 'the public concerned' should be informed early in the decision-making procedure about the proposed activity and the nature of the decision that may be taken. The public concerned is defined as the public affected or likely to be affected by, or having an interest in, the environmental decision-making. However, the Convention also explicitly states that for the

---

102 See end of chapter for website details.

purposes of this definition, non-governmental organisations promoting environmental protection and meeting any requirements under national law shall be deemed to have an interest.

The procedures adopted must allow opportunities for the public to participate, for example by submitting their views and attending any planned public hearing. The public must be given this information in a timely and effective manner and must be given reasonable time frames for participation. Essentially this must be done at an early stage, when all options are open and effective participation can take place. In order to comply with Art 6 it was necessary for the EU to amend the existing Environmental Impact Assessment Directive 85/337/EEC[103] and the Integrated Pollution and Prevention Control Directive.[104] The EIA Directive relates to projects that are likely to have a significant effect on the environment. The IPPC Directive requires regulation in respect of certain industrial activities. The amendments brought both directives in line with the public participation requirements of the Convention. It should be noted that since then both the EIA Directive and the IPPC Directive have been repealed and replaced by codifying legislation. The public participation requirements are now to be found in Art 6 of the new EIA Directive 2011/92/EU [105] and Art 15 of the new IPPC Directive 2008/1/EC.[106] For example, Art 15 of the 2008 IPPC Directive provides that Member States must (shall) ensure that the public concerned is given early and effective opportunities to participate in the procedure for:

See Chapter ◄ 5

(a)   issuing a permit for new installations;
(b)   issuing a permit for any substantial change;
(c)   updating of a permit or permit conditions for an installation.

Annex V of the IPPC Directive sets out the procedures that are to be followed as regards public participation. The procedure set out in Annex V shall apply for the purposes of such participation. Once the decision-maker (which will be the relevant local authority or the Environment Agency) has taken its decision with regard to the permit, it must inform the public about the content of the decision, including a copy of the permit and of any conditions and any subsequent updates; and having examined the concerns and opinions expressed by the public concerned, the reasons and considerations on which the decision is based, including information on the public participation process. A failure to comply with the prescribed procedures will amount to a breach of the directive and will constitute grounds for legal challenge by members of the public.

Article 7 of the Convention extends the rights of the public to participate during the preparation of plans and programmes relating to the environment. Each party to the Convention is required to make appropriate practical and/or other provisions for the public to participate during the preparation of such plans and programmes within a transparent and fair framework, having provided the necessary information to the public. The relevant public authority is required to identify the public which may participate and in doing this they are required to take into account the objectives of this Convention. As with Art 6, the procedures adopted must include reasonable timeframes for the different phases, allowing sufficient time for informing the public in and allowing the public to prepare and participate effectively during the plan/programme decision-making. Similarly the public participation stages should take place at an early stage when all options are

103 Council Directive 85/337/EEC of 27 June 1985 on the assessment of the effects of certain public and private projects on the environment OJ L 175, 5/7/1985, pp 40–48, as amended by Directive 2003/35/EC.
104 Directive 2008/1/EC of the European Parliament and of the Council of 15 January 2008 concerning integrated pollution prevention and control (Codified version) (text with EEA relevance) OJ L 24, 29/1/2008, pp 8–29.
105 Directive 2011/92/EU of the European Parliament and of the Council of 13 December 2011 on the assessment of the effects of certain public and private projects on the environment, OJ L 026, 28/01/2012 pp 1–21.
106 2008/1/EC of the European Parliament and of the Council of 15 January 2008 concerning integrated pollution prevention and control (Codified version) OJ L 24, 29/1/2008, pp 8–29.

open and effective public participation can take place. This part of Art 7 has been incorporated in EU law by Directive 2003/35/EC,[107] Directive 2001/42/EC[108] and also the Water Framework Directive 2000/60/EC.[109]

In addition it should be noted that Art 7 of the Convention also includes a non-binding provision which 'encourages' each party, to the extent appropriate, to provide opportunities for the public to participate in the preparation of policies relating to the environment. This has not been translated into any legally binding directive and therefore it remains a matter for each Member State to determine the extent they consider to be appropriate. In *R (on the application of Greenpeace Ltd) v Secretary of State for Trade and Industry (2007)*[110] Greenpeace successfully challenged the government's decision in relation to new nuclear build. Sullivan J was unequivocal about the impact of the Aarhus Convention on public participation in relation to the formulation of government policy in relation to the environment:

> Whatever the position may be in other policy areas, in the development of policy in the environmental field consultation is no longer a privilege to be granted or withheld at will by the executive. The United Kingdom Government is a signatory to the Convention on Access to Information, Public Participation in Decision-making and Access to Justice in Environmental Matters (the Aarhus Convention). The Preamble records the parties to the Convention.[111]

However, see also *Bard Campaign v Secretary of State for Communities and Local Government (2009)*[112] in relation to the government's consultation exercise regarding Eco-towns in which the court held the consultation process was lawful. The case demonstrates the difficulties that litigants face mounting this type of challenge.

Finally, Art 8 of the Convention is concerned with public participation during the preparation of executive regulations and/or generally applicable legally binding normative instruments that may have a significant effect on the environment. This would include, for example, environmental protection statutes and statutory instruments. According to Art 8 each party shall strive to promote effective public participation at an appropriate stage during the preparation of such rules/legal measures and while options are still open.

12.8 Access to justice in environmental matters—the Aarhus Convention and EU legislation

12.8.1 The Aarhus Convention—Article 9

The third pillar, Art 9, concerns access to justice in environmental matters. The article is based on the premise that it is not sufficient to afford members of the public rights to access information and participate in decision-making if they cannot enforce those rights. Hence Arts 9(1) and 9(2) lay

---

107 Directive 2003/35/EC of the European Parliament and of the Council of 26 May 2003 providing for public participation in respect of the drawing up of certain plans and programmes relating to the environment and amending with regard to public participation and access to justice Council Directives 85/337/EEC and 96/61/EC – Statement by the Commission OJ L 156, 25/6/2003, pp 17–25.
108 Directive 2001/42/EC of the European Parliament and of the Council of 27 June 2001 on the assessment of the effects of certain plans and programmes on the environment OJ L 197, 21/7/2001, pp 30–37.
109 Directive 2000/60/EC of the European Parliament and of the Council of 23 October 2000 establishing a framework for Community action in the field of water policy OJ L 327, 22/12/2000, pp 1–73.
110 *R (on the application of Greenpeace Ltd) v Secretary of State for Trade and Industry* [2007] EWHC 311 (Admin); [2007] Env LR 29; [2007] JPL 1314; [2007] NPC 21.
111 Ibid at para 49.
112 *Bard Campaign v Secretary of State for Communities and Local Government* [2009] EWHC 308 (Admin).

down minimum procedures for ensuring that the rights provided in the first two pillars are protected and upheld. However, Art 9 is more ambitious in its scope. Article 9(3) seeks to ensure that members of the public have access to judicial proceedings which enable them to challenge both public and private organisations that contravene national environmental law. This is followed by Art 9(4), which lays down certain overriding conditions that should apply to all of the procedures. Finally Art 9(5) includes additional provisions which seek to further the overall effectiveness of Art 9:

- Art 9(1) relates specifically to the access to information pillar;
- Art 9(2) relates specifically to the public participation pillar;
- Art 9(3) relates to access to administrative or judicial procedures to challenge acts and omissions by private persons and public authorities which contravene provisions of national law relating to the environment;
- Art 9(4) stipulates certain important overriding conditions which apply to the above;
- Art 9(5) requires the parties to take steps to further the effectiveness of all of the above.

Article 9 is proving to be fertile ground for debate and litigation and the consensus is that the UK is in breach of its obligations under Art 9. In 2011 the European Commission commenced infringement proceedings against the UK in respect of its obligation to remove financial barriers to access to justice in environmental matters.[113] The case will be considered later at 12.9.4.

12.8.2 EU legislation on access to justice

The position regarding EU implementation of this limb is slightly more complex than in relation to the other two limbs in that the access to justice provisions are integrated into the directives that have been discussed so far. As far as Art 9(1) is concerned, Directive 2003/4/EC on public access to environmental information includes provisions relating to access to justice at Art 6.[114] The provisions of Art 6 comply with the requirements of Art 9(1) of the Convention.

With respect to the public participation limb it was explained above that the EU used Directive 2003/35/EC to amend the Environmental Impact Assessment Directive 85/337/EEC and the IPPC Directive 96/61/EC to ensure compliance with the requirements of Art 6 of the Convention. Directive 2003/35/EC also incorporated the access to justice provisions of Art 9 into these directives. As far as the EIA Directive was concerned the access to justice provisions were incorporated into Art 10A but they are now to be found in Art 11 of the current EIA Directive 2011/92/EU.[115] Similarly the access to justice provisions relating to the IPPC Directive are now to be found in Art 16 of Directive 2008/1/EC.[116] It should be noted that with effect from 7 January 2014 the 2008 Directive will be repealed and replaced by Directive 2010/75/EU.[117] It is not necessary here to include the text of both provisions; although they are structured slightly differently both Art 11 and Art 16 are substantively the same and accord with the requirements of Art 9(2) of the Convention. They both provide that Member States are required to ensure that members of the 'public concerned' have access to a review procedure before a court of law or another independent and impartial body

---

113 Case C-530/11 Commission v United Kingdom (case pending).
114 Directive 2003/4/EC of the European Parliament and of the Council of 28 January 2003 on public access to environmental information and repealing Council Directive 90/313/EEC OJ L 41, 14/2/2003, pp 26–32.
115 Directive 2011/92/EU of the European Parliament and of the Council of 13 December 2011 on the assessment of the effects of certain public and private projects on the environment, OJ L 026, 28/01/2012, pp 1–21.
116 Directive 2008/1/EC of the European Parliament and of the Council of 15 January 2008 concerning integrated pollution prevention and control (Codified version) OJ L 24, 29/1/2008, pp 8–29.
117 Directive 2010/75/EU of the European Parliament and of the Council of 24 November 2010 on industrial emissions (integrated pollution prevention and control) OJ L 334, 17/12/2010, pp 17–119.

established by law to challenge the substantive or procedural legality of decisions, acts or omissions subject to the public participation provisions of the relevant directive. The public concerned are defined, in accordance with the Convention, as those members of the public who have a sufficient interest or are maintaining the impairment of a right, where administrative procedural law of a Member State requires this as a precondition. What constitutes a sufficient interest and impairment of a right is to be determined by the Member States, consistently with the objective of giving the public concerned wide access to justice. To that end, the interest of any non-governmental organisation meeting certain requirements shall be deemed sufficient. In both directives the Member State has discretion to determine at what stage the decisions, acts or omissions may be challenged.

However, as is noted above the scope of Art 9 extends beyond access to justice relating to the first two pillars. In particular Art 9(3), which is discussed more fully below, relates to access to administrative or judicial procedures to challenge acts and omissions by private persons and public authorities which contravene provisions of national law relating to the environment. This extends the material scope of the access to justice limb well beyond the directives that have been discussed above. This therefore would have required the EU to adopt further legislation to implement the provisions of Art 9(3), or to leave it to the Member States to determine how they would comply. Although the Commission presented a proposal for a directive on access to justice in October 2003, the Directive has yet to be agreed by the institutions and is unlikely to in the near future.[118]

12.8.3 Access to justice in relation to the access to information pillar

Article 9(1) relates to the access to information pillar. Essentially it requires the parties to establish independent review proceedings to enable any person to challenge the way in which their request for environmental information has been handled or any decision to withhold any information requested. In the circumstances where a party provides for such a review by a court of law, it must also ensure that such a person also has access to an expeditious procedure established by law that is free of charge or inexpensive for reconsideration by a public authority or review by an independent and impartial body other than a court of law. It was noted above that Art 9(1) was transposed into the requirements of the Environmental Information Directive 2003/4/EC at Art 6, and that the provisions of Art 6 comply with the requirements of Art 9(1) of the Convention.

The UK has substantially complied with its obligations under the Directive and therefore the Convention, although as noted below there are some concerns about whether the procedures are expeditious. Under EIR reg 11, anyone who considers that his/her request for environmental information has been wrongly refused or not dealt with properly can ask the public authority concerned to internally review its decision. This gives the public authority the opportunity to reconsider its decision. If the internal review does not resolve the issue to the satisfaction of the applicant then they can make a complaint to the Information Commissioner's Office (ICO). The ICO is an independent regulator with responsibility for ensuring public authorities comply with their obligations under the Freedom of Information Act 2000, the EIR 2004 and the Data Protection Act 1998. The ICO can investigate the complaint and can take a decision that is binding. The Commissioner can decide that information must be disclosed or can uphold a public authority's decision to withhold it from the public. Both the applicant and the public authority have a right of appeal against the Commissioner's decision. Appeals are considered by the First-tier Information Rights Tribunal and beyond that, on a point of law, to the Upper Tribunal of the Administrative Chamber. (See above at 12.6.7.)

---

118 Proposal for a Directive of the European Parliament and of the Council on Access to Justice in Environmental Matters COM (2003) 624 final.

Complaining to the ICO is free of charge. However, it has been known in some cases to take as long as two years for the ICO to investigate and issue a decision. This actually raises some concerns in terms of Aarhus compliance since the Convention requires that the review procedure be 'expeditious', and with the best will in the world waiting for two years for a decision from the ICO cannot be described as expeditious. Similarly an appeal to the Information Rights Tribunal costs nothing unless of course the appellant instructs lawyers. The Tribunal is accustomed to applicants who are unrepresented, as legal aid for representation is not available for first instance appeals before the Information Rights Tribunal. In a number of instances NGOs have supported appellants where the case raises issues of general importance.

12.8.4 Access to justice in relation to public participation in environmental decision-making

Article 9(2) deals specifically with the environmental decisions taken by public authorities under Art 6 of the Convention. (See above at 12.7.1.) Recalling Art 6, the Convention provides that the public concerned should have a right to participate in decision-making relating to certain activities likely to have significant effects on the environment. These decisions are taken largely by local planning authorities, the Secretary of State and the Environment Agency. In the event that members of the public are denied these rights (either at all or due to some procedural irregularity), Art 9(2) provides that

> members of the public concerned who have sufficient interest must have access to a review procedure before a court of law and/or another independent and impartial body established by law, to challenge the substantive and procedural legality of any decision, act or omission subject to the provisions of Article 6.

In short, Art 9(2) requires that members of the public concerned should have access to judicial review procedures which enable a court to review the legality of any public authority decision, act or omission that breaches Art 6. Article 9(2) deals with the issue of who can bring such proceedings. It states that actions may be brought by the public concerned, which means the public affected or likely to be affected by, or having an interest in, the environmental decision-making.[119] The Convention does not afford a general right to anybody to commence a judicial review, and to that extent is in keeping with the requirements of domestic law which requires that applicants have a sufficient interest in the challenged decision. Neither does the Convention seek to import into national law a definition of sufficient interest. However, the question of what constitutes sufficient interest must be determined 'consistently with the objective of giving the public concerned wide access to justice within the scope of this Convention'. The Convention does, however, address the issue of standing of non-governmental organisations (NGOs) in the field of environmental protection and provides that such an NGO, which meets the requirements of national law, shall be deemed to have sufficient interest. Article 9(2) also states that the procedure should enable the applicant to challenge both the substantive and procedural legality of a decision. This too is proving to be a contentious issue and in 12.9 below we shall consider the extent to which judicial review in England provides for both a procedural and substantive review of legality.

In order to ensure that EU law complied with Art 9(2) of the Convention it was necessary for the EU to amend the EIA and IPPC Directives. The EU measures were discussed at 12.8.2 above.

---

119 Art 2(5) Aarhus Convention.

12.8.5 General provisions relating to access to justice in environmental matters

Although Arts 9(1) and (2) are linked to the other pillars of the Convention, Art 9(3) has a much wider scope of application. Art 9(3) provides that in addition to the review procedures in 9(1) and (2) each party to the Convention must ensure

> that, where they meet the criteria, if any, laid down in its national law, members of the public have access to administrative or judicial procedures to challenge acts and omissions by private persons and public authorities which contravene provisions of its national law relating to the environment.

This affords the public the right to judicial review proceedings to challenge the acts or omissions of public authorities where such acts/omissions breach any other national law relating to the environment.[120] Of course such review has always been available in England and Wales if the applicant has sufficient interest (and financial resources—see below). Additionally Art 9(3) also refers to challenges to acts/omissions of private persons which breach national environmental law. This of course does not concern judicial review but could include civil claims arising from a breach of national environmental law or private prosecutions against companies acting in breach of an environmental permit. Article 9(3) would also appear to include the possibility of an individual commencing a private prosecution against a regulatory body if the regulatory body commits an environmental crime. The capacity of individuals and NGOs to commence judicial review actions and private prosecution are considered later in this chapter.

It has already been noted above at 12.8.2 that the Commission proposed a directive on access to justice in October 2003. The purpose of this directive was to ensure Member States complied with the requirements of Art 9(3) of the Convention. The directive, however, failed to be agreed by the EU institutions and therefore there is something of a lacuna in the portfolio of EU legislation implementing the Convention. This therefore begs a very important question, namely whether rights and obligations created by Art 9(3) have effect in the domestic legal system. According to Defra,

> The rights and obligations created by international treaties have no effect in UK domestic law unless legislation is in force to give effect to them, i.e. they have been 'incorporated'. The provisions of the Aarhus Convention cannot therefore be said to apply directly in English law to any particular procedure or remedy.

In the absence of an EU directive that specifically requires Member States to comply with Art 9(3) and by extension the conditions laid down in Art 9(4) the question is to what extent the provisions of Art 9(3) can be directly enforced by members of the public. This question was addressed by the European Court of justice in a preliminary ruling from the Slovakian Court in *Lesoochranarske Zoskupenie VLK v Ministerstvo Zivotneho Prostredia Slovenskej Republiky* (C-240-09) (or the *Brown Bears* case).[121] The case concerned a Slovak environmental protection group (LZ) which had asked the defendant Slovak Ministry of Environment (M) to inform it of any administrative decision-making procedure which might potentially affect the protection of nature and the environment, or which concerned granting derogations to the protection of certain species or areas, in particular brown bears. In early 2008 LZ was informed of a number of pending administrative proceedings brought by various hunting

---

120 I.e. not just access to information or those decisions within the scope of Art 6.
121 *Lesoochranarske Zoskupenie VLK v Ministerstvo Zivotneho Prostredia Slovenskej Republiky* (C-240/09).

associations. On 21 April 2008 the Ministry took a decision granting a hunting association's application for permission to derogate from the protective conditions accorded to the brown bear. In the course of that procedure, and in subsequent ones, LZ notified the Ministry that it wished to participate in the decision-making. The Ministry refused and said that LZ did not have the status of a party which could appeal against its decision of April 2008. The Ministry considered that Art 9(3) of the Convention needed to be implemented into national law before it could take effect. LZ argued that the proceedings in question directly affected its rights and legally protected interests arising from the Aarhus Convention. It also considered that Convention to have direct effect. The Slovakian Court requested a preliminary ruling on whether an organisation such as LZ, wishing to challenge a decision to derogate from a system of environmental protection, was entitled to bring proceedings under EU law, having particular regard to the provisions of Art 9(3) of the Aarhus Convention on direct effect.

The first question was whether the ECJ had jurisdiction to rule on this given that Art 9(3) has not been implemented into any EU directive. The Court said it had. Under Art 218 TFEU, agreements concluded by the Union were binding on the Union's institutions and the Member States. Given that the Aarhus Convention had been concluded by the Union in 2005 it now formed an integral part of the legal order of the European Union and therefore the ECJ had jurisdiction to interpret Art 9(3) of the Convention. The ECJ then said that it was necessary to determine whether the EU had exercised its powers and adopted provisions to implement Art 9(3), because if it hadn't, the obligations arising from Art 9(3) would continue to be covered by the national law of the Member States and not EU law. In those circumstances, it would be for the courts of those Member States to determine, on the basis of national law, whether individuals could rely directly on the rules of that international agreement relevant to that field. However, if it were to be held that the European Union had exercised its powers and adopted provisions in the field covered by Art 9(3), it would be for the Court of Justice to determine whether the provision of the international agreement in question had direct effect. The reasoning of the Court thereafter is interesting and creative. It has already been noted above that the EU has failed to implement Art 9(3) into a directive. However, the ECJ held that a specific issue which had not yet been the subject of EU legislation was part of EU law, where that issue was regulated in agreements concluded by the European Union and the Member State and it concerned a field 'in large measure' covered by it. In the present case, the dispute in the main proceedings concerned whether an environmental protection association might be a party to administrative proceedings concerning, in particular, the grant of derogations to the system of protection for species such as the brown bear. That species was mentioned in Annex IV of the Habitats Directive (Directive 92/43/EC), so that under Art 12 of the Habitats Directive it was subject to a system of strict protection from which derogations might be granted only under the conditions laid down in Art 16 of that directive. It followed that the dispute in the main proceedings fell within the scope of EU law. Having established this, the Court was then faced with the question of the direct effect of Art 9(3) within the domestic legal order of the Member States. The ECJ concluded that Art 9(3) was not sufficiently clear and precise and was therefore not capable of direct effect. Since only members of the public who met the criteria, if any, laid down by national law were entitled to exercise the rights provided for in Art 9(3), that provision was subject, in its implementation or effects, to the adoption of a subsequent measure. However the ECJ did not leave the matter there. The ECJ resumed its analysis of the Habitats Directive and held that whilst this did not prescribe detailed procedural rules on access to justice, the Member States were responsible for ensuring that the rights provided by the directive were effectively protected and the national rules governing actions for safeguarding an individual's rights under EU law had to be no less favourable than those governing similar domestic actions (principle of equivalence) and must not make it in practice impossible or excessively difficult to exercise rights conferred by EU law (principle of effectiveness). Therefore, if the effective protection of EU environmental law was not to be undermined,

See Chapter 3

it was inconceivable that Art 9(3) of the Convention be interpreted in such a way as to make it in practice impossible or excessively difficult to exercise rights conferred by EU law. It followed that, insofar as concerned a species protected by EU law, and in particular the Habitats Directive, it was for the national court, in order to ensure effective judicial protection in the fields covered by EU environmental law, to interpret its national law in a way which, to the fullest extent possible, was consistent with the objectives laid down in Art 9(3).

Whilst this decision is welcome it is important to point out that this duty of sympathetic interpretation will only apply where the case concerns an environmental protection issue that falls within EU law. Given the very broad scope and range of EU environmental protection legislation this should not usually be a problem. However, see, for example, R (on the application of Macrae) v Herefordshire DC (2011),[122] where the Divisional Court held that the decision in the Brown Bears case was not relevant to the application of non-EU rights.

12.8.6 Article 9(4) overriding conditions and Article 9(5)

In addition to the procedures referred to in Arts 9(1)–(3), Art 9(4) requires that the parties:

> shall provide adequate and effective remedies, including injunctive relief as appropriate, and be fair, equitable, timely and not prohibitively expensive.

This is an overriding requirement; any environmental litigation that falls within the scope of the Aarhus Convention must meet the requirements of Art 9(4). It has been argued strongly that the UK's heavy reliance on judicial review and in particular the costs associated with judicial review claims means that the UK is not fulfilling its obligations under Art 9(4) of the Convention. In short, judicial review is not guaranteed to secure an adequate and effective remedy, injunctive relief is almost impossible to secure in practice and the costs of judicial review amount to the biggest stumbling block of all, meaning that in reality, access to judicial review may be limited to the very rich or the very poor. As Sir Robert Carnwath remarked in 1990:

> Litigation through the courts is prohibitively expensive for most people, unless they are either poor enough to qualify for legal aid, or rich enough to be able to undertake an open-ended commitment to expenditure running into tens or hundreds of thousands of pounds.[123]

It has already been noted that the requirements of Arts 9(1) and (2) have been implemented into the respective directives that relate to access to environmental information and public participation. These have sought to incorporate the conditions listed in Art 9(4) although none of the directives refer to injunctive remedies. The conditions in Art 9(4) also apply to litigation falling within Art 9(3). This is important to bear in mind because Art 9(3) of the Convention has not been implemented by an EU law measure and is not capable of direct effect. It therefore falls to the national courts to consider the extent to which they will construe national procedural rules sympathetically in the light of the Convention. Perhaps this is best illustrated in the case of Morgan v Hinton Organics (Wessex) Ltd (2009).[124] The case involved a private nuisance action brought by Morgan (M) against H, which operated a composting site near to M's home. M complained about the smells and sought an injunction and damages. An interim injunction was granted during the trial but was later discharged, and M was ordered to pay H's costs. In total M was left with a potential cost bill of

---

122 R (on the application of Macrae) v Herefordshire DC [2011] EWHC 2810 (Admin); [2012] 1 CMLR 28.
123 Sir Robert Carnwath, 'Environmental Litigation – A way through the Maze?' (1999) Journal of Environmental Law 11(1).
124 Morgan v Hinton Organics (Wessex) Ltd [2009] EWCA Civ 107; [2009] Env LR 30.

£25,000. M argued that the costs order contravened the principle of the Aarhus Convention, that costs in environmental proceedings should not be prohibitively expensive, and that the requirement to comply with the Convention was an obligation of the court which should have been considered by the judge of his own motion. The Court of Appeal was required to consider whether the case fell within the broad sweep of Art 9(3) and in which case whether it was bound to give effect to the conditions of Art 9(4) of the Convention, namely that the litigation should not be prohibitively expensive. Counsel for H sought to argue that a private nuisance claim could not fall within Art 9(3), which was concerned with actions to vindicate general public rights to a clean environment (as opposed to private nuisance, which was designed to protect private property rights). The court rejected this distinction and held that the 'public' as defined may be a single natural person, and the proceedings may be in respect of acts or omissions of 'private persons'. Although in the present case, the claimants' action was primarily directed to the protection of their own private rights, if the nuisance existed it was capable of affecting the whole locality. The public aspect is underlined by the interest of the Agency and the Council. The Court also rejected the argument that although the EU had integrated Aarhus rights into Directives on public law matters of environmental assessment and pollution control, it had not ventured into the field of private law claims for environmental harm. In its decision the Court of Appeal was content to proceed on the basis that the Convention is capable of applying to private nuisance proceedings. However, in the absence of any rule of the EU the Court concluded that the principles of the Convention were at the most 'something to be taken into account in resolving ambiguities or exercising discretion'.

12.8.7 Article 9(5)

In addition it should be noted that the Convention goes further, requiring in Art 9(5) that parties ensure that information is provided to the public about access to the administrative and judicial review procedures. Moreover the parties are required to *consider* the establishment of appropriate assistance mechanisms to remove or reduce financial and other barriers to access to justice. Given the current economic climate in most of the EU Member States, this is unlikely to be rigorously enforced by the EU, and in any event states are only required to consider making such arrangements. As from 1 April 2013 public funding to the Advice Services Alliance, Law Centres Network and the Royal Courts of Justice CAB ceased.

12.9 Judicial review in English law

The Command and Control regulatory regimes examined in this text contain provisions enabling an applicant to appeal to either the magistrates' court or the Secretary of State against a number of regulatory decisions addressed to them. For example, a person who has been refused an environmental permit or objects to the conditions attached to it can appeal to the Secretary of State. Where a regulatory body serves an administrative notice on a person, such as an enforcement notice on the operator of a regulated facility[125] or a remediation notice on an appropriate person,[126] that person gains a right of appeal to the Secretary of State. However, these rights of statutory appeal are limited; they do not extend to third parties such as members of the public who may object to the grant of a permit or the grant of a planning permission. In short the statutory appeals mechanisms discussed in this book provide no equivalent right of appeal for aggrieved citizens. Short of other non-legal actions such as protest and campaigning, the only way

See Chapters

5

7

---

125 Under the Environmental Permitting Regulations 2010.
126 Under Part 2A EPA 1990.

in which an aggrieved person can challenge a public authority decision is by way of judicial review. Judicial review is available with regard to actions of state or public authorities exercising the powers granted by statute. Given that almost all of the environmental law discussed in this book involves public authorities exercising statutory powers and taking decisions, it is self-evident that judicial review is an extremely important tool. It is the principal means by which members of the public can challenge a range of environmental decisions ranging from policy decisions to individual decisions relating to the grant of an environmental permit or a planning permission. In short judicial review is a very important tool in the enforcement armoury of the private person. This raises a very important question: do the rules of judicial review comply with the requirements of the Convention?

In 2004 the Environmental Justice Project (EJP) published their review of the operation of environmental law in England and Wales.[127] The purpose of the review was to identify any inadequacies with regard to access to environmental justice and to make any recommendations for change. The report considered both the adequacy of the civil and criminal law systems in providing access to justice and in particular examined the extent to which the current reliance on judicial review in environmental law fully meets the requirements of the Convention. The report makes interesting reading and includes a variety of statistics, case studies and examples and also makes certain recommendations for change. The review was based heavily on the experience of practitioners within the field of environmental law and a number of environmental protection NGOs. In particular, the report commences with a worrying claim: 'Ninety seven per cent of leading practitioners and NGOs questioned in England and Wales believe the civil law system fails to provide environmental justice.' [128]

Essentially the criticisms of the current system are:

1. The rules on standing have evolved and are currently generous but they are not enshrined in legislation and so applicants have to first establish that they have standing.
2. Judicial review does not meet the requirements of the Convention since it only provides for review on procedural legality and not substantive legality.
3. The costs of bringing actions before the courts in JR proceedings are so high as to be prohibitively expensive. In particular because the cost rules are based on the loser pays, this could have a substantial deterrent effect on would-be litigants daunted by the possibility of facing the other side's costs.
4. The lack of public funding. This raises an access to justice issue as either only the very rich or the very poor.
5. The judiciary lacks the necessary understanding of difficult and scientific issue raised in environmental cases.

There is not scope within this chapter to examine all of the issues raised in any depth, but the arguments and recommendations are well documented and there is a list of suggested reading at the end of the chapter. Instead, the following commentary will pick out a few of the key issues and recommendations as they relate to judicial review.

12.9.1 Judicial review: the requirement for standing

As a matter of English law in order to challenge administrative decisions, it is necessary for the person, persons or group seeking judicial review to demonstrate the requisite standing, or *locus*

---

127 The Environmental Justice Project (UKELA, 2004).
128 Ibid.

standi. The test for standing is contained in s 31(3) of the Senior Courts Act (SCA) 1981 and Part 54 of the Civil Procedure Rules. The SCA 1981 requires a person or group to have 'sufficient interest' in the matter to which his or her application for judicial review relates. The courts have developed rules on what amounts to sufficient interest, but each case is considered on its own facts.

It will be recalled that the Convention requires that in relation to decisions that fall within the scope of the Convention judicial review actions may be brought by the 'public concerned' and this is further defined as members of the public who are affected or likely to be affected by, or having an interest in, the environmental decision-making.[129] This can be broken down into (a) a person affected or likely to be affected by a decision; and (b) a person having an interest in the environmental decision-making. The Convention doesn't define the latter part of this, but nor does it limit it to a property or legal interest. Therefore the term 'interest' may arguably include, for example, people who have an interest in environmental protection. A person affected or likely to be affected by a decision would, for instance, include a person whose property, person or social rights are affected by a decision, for example a person who lives close to a proposed landfill site. However, the question of what constitutes sufficient interest must be determined 'consistently with the objective of giving the public concerned wide access to justice within the scope of this Convention'.[130]

As a general rule, individuals who are geographically proximate to the subject matter of the relevant proceedings, or who are personally affected by them, will have a sufficient interest providing them with standing. Unfortunately in the not so recent past a number of judicial decisions on standing in an environmental context send rather mixed messages on the degree of interest which will suffice.[131] The more liberal approach to standing evident in *ex p Dixon* is to be preferred, since the question of standing should operate as a filter to eliminate vexatious or unmeritorious claims. In contrast, the *ex p Garnett* decision supports the view that the question of standing can only be determined by analysing the relevant statutory regime to assess whether the legislation expressly or impliedly provides the applicant with standing. The later case of *North West Leicestershire ex p Moses* (2000)[132] supports this restrictive approach. In this case the applicant was held not to have standing, because at the date of her application for permission she had moved to a town six miles away from the location of the end of the runway which formed the matter of her judicial review challenge.

12.9.1.1 NGOs and standing

Article 2 of the Convention explicitly provides that an NGO promoting environmental protection and meeting any requirements under national law shall be deemed to have an interest. This wording suggests that environmental protection groups that meet any requirements of national law (the Convention does not define these) will automatically have sufficient interest in a challenge that falls within the scope of the Convention. In some countries the standing of NGOs is enshrined by statute but in England this is not the case and it falls to the court to decide, in each case, whether the NGO has a sufficient interest in the matter. The concept of a group action is one which presumes that citizens generally should be able to bring judicial review actions in the public interest without having to show any individual harm over and above that suffered by the general community. Although no such right of action exists in English public law, it has received some judicial support. In particular, Lord Diplock in *R v Inland Revenue Comrs ex p National Federation of the Self-Employed and Small Businesses Ltd* (1982)[133] asserted that:

---

129 Art 2(5) Aarhus Convention.
130 Art 9(2) Aarhus Convention.
131 See *R v North Somerset DC ex p Garnett* [1998] Env LR 91; [1997] JPL 1015 and *R v Somerset DC ex p Dixon* [1998] Env LR 111.
132 *North West Leicestershire ex p Moses* (No 1) [2000] JPL 733.
133 *R v Inland Revenue Comrs ex p National Federation of the Self-Employed and Small Businesses Ltd* [1982] AC 617; [1981] 2 WLR 722; [1981] 2 All ER 93.

> It would, in my view, be a grave lacuna in our system of public law if a pressure group, like the federation, or even a single public-spirited taxpayer, were prevented by outdated technical rules of *locus standi* from bringing the matter to the attention of the court to vindicate the rule of law and get the unlawful matter stopped.

The position of the courts regarding environmental protection NGOs is currently quite liberal, but that has not always been the case. The case of *R v Secretary of State for the Environment ex p Rose Theatre Trust* (1990)[134] illustrates the restrictive approach to standing. Developers had been granted planning permission to build an office block on the site of an Elizabethan theatre (the Rose Theatre) in London. A trust company was set up by numerous campaigners to preserve the remains of the theatre, which was of particular historical importance because it claimed to be the venue of two first performances of Shakespeare's plays. The Rose Theatre Trust sought to persuade the Secretary of State to designate the site as one of national importance and include it in the list of monuments under the Ancient Monuments and Archaeological Areas Act 1979. If the Secretary of State had so listed the site, it would have meant that no work could begin on the site without his consent. The Secretary of State agreed that the site was of national importance, but decided that it did not fall within the relevant legislation. The Theatre Trust brought the action for judicial review, alleging that the Secretary of State's decision was unlawful. The question was whether or not the Trust had 'sufficient interest' to bring such an action. Members of the Trust argued that since they had entered into correspondence with the Secretary of State, they had the necessary interest. However, the court found that the Trust did not have *locus standi*. Schiemann J stated that it was necessary to consider the statute to determine whether it afforded standing to these individuals in this instance. On the facts of the case, the court held that no individual could point to anything in the statute that would serve to give him or her a greater right or interest than any other person that the decision would be taken lawfully. The case resulted in a great deal of criticism and was a blow to the notion of public interest litigation. Among other things, it appeared that the court was not concerned that no one could sue in such a situation, leaving the decision of the Secretary of State beyond challenge.

However, a more liberal approach can be seen in *R v Her Majesty's Inspectorate of Pollution ex p Greenpeace* (No 2) (1994).[135] Greenpeace applied for a judicial review of the decision by HMIP to allow testing at British Nuclear Fuels Thermal Oxide Reprocessing Plant (THORP) at Sellafield. British Nuclear Fuels Ltd (BNFL) argued that Greenpeace had failed to establish a sufficient interest and that its application should be set aside. However, this argument was rejected by the court. Otton J held that Greenpeace was an eminently respectable and responsible organisation and that its genuine interest in the matter was sufficient for it to be granted *locus standi*. In reaching this welcome decision, the court took into account the following factors:

(a) Greenpeace's genuine concern relating to the health of the 2,500 Greenpeace supporters in the Cumbria region;
(b) the nature of Greenpeace ('guardians of the environment') as a campaigning group whose prime objective was the protection of the environment;
(c) the fact that Greenpeace as a responsible and respected environmental organisation had been accredited by the United Nations (UN) and several other international bodies.

Otton J stated that a denial of standing would mean that the people represented by Greenpeace would not have 'an effective way to bring the issues before the court'. Otton J declined to follow the decision in *Rose Theatre Trust* and stated that a denial of standing to Greenpeace would have meant

---

134 *R v Secretary of State for the Environment ex p Rose Theatre Trust* [1990] 1 QB 504; [1990] 2 WLR 186; [1990] 1 All ER 754.
135 *R v Her Majesty's Inspectorate of Pollution ex p Greenpeace* (No 2) [1994] 4 All ER 329; [1994] 2 CMLR 548; [1994] Env LR 76.

that an application for judicial review would have had to be brought either by an individual employee of BNFL or a near neighbour. Neither would have had the resources or the expertise to bring such an action and this would have resulted in a less well informed challenge which would have stretched the court's resources.

The decision in this case is greatly welcomed. With a less restrictive view of standing, environmental pressure groups such as Greenpeace, which represent people who are directly affected by the challenged decision or action, are more likely to succeed in achieving *locus standi*. However, a note of caution: in the judgment, the court referred to the advantages of an application from Greenpeace which, with its particular experience in environmental matters and its access to experts in the realms of science, technology and law, could bring a focused, relevant and well-argued challenge. It seems, therefore, that the larger national or international NGOs are more likely to satisfy the test than small *ad hoc* or localised groups without the benefit of a 'deep pocket' and expert back-up.

The trend towards recognising the standing of pressure groups was given further support in *R v Secretary of State for Foreign Affairs ex p World Development Movement Ltd* (1995).[136] The World Development Movement (WDM) was an NGO whose main objective was to bring about improvements in the provision of overseas aid. WDM applied for a judicial review of the Foreign Secretary's decision to provide aid to construct the Pergau Dam against the advice of the Overseas Development Administration. Rose LJ held that the WDM had sufficient interest to challenge the government's decision to provide aid for the Pergau Dam scheme, on the basis: (a) that there were few other parties that could challenge the decision; and (b) of the prominence of the WDM in the protection of aid to under-developed countries. The WDM was granted standing even though its members had no direct personal interest in the issue before the court. The Court of Appeal's decision in this case is important not least because it drew attention to the growing willingness of the courts to grant 'surrogate' standing to interest groups. Rose LJ observed that the real question 'is whether the applicant can show some substantial default or abuse, and not whether his personal rights or interests are involved'. In contrast to the *Rose Theatre Trust* decision, the Court made it clear that if standing were not granted, then a clear illegality would not be subject to challenge.

In *R v Secretary of State for the Environment ex p Friends of the Earth and Andrew Lees* (1994),[137] Friends of the Earth (FoE) and Andrew Lees (who was FoE's campaign director, before his tragic death) challenged the decision of the Secretary of State to accept undertakings from water companies which were in breach of the EU Drinking Water Directive (80/778/EEC)[138] rather than take enforcement action. In this case, Andrew Lees was a resident in the area supplied by one of the water companies, Thames Water, and clearly had a direct health interest in the decision. Like the *Greenpeace* case, the fact that local people who had a local interest (in both cases the interest was in health rather than the protection of the environment per se) in the issue and were joined in the action with a pressure group appears to have been relevant. When the *Friends of the Earth* case was considered by the Court of Appeal, it was merely noted that the High Court had granted standing and there was no further discussion of the point.

Standing will normally be granted in cases where a pressure group or individual expects to be consulted in relation to a decision and is not. For example, in *R v Poole BC ex p Beebee and Others* (1991),[139] the applicants represented the Worldwide Fund for Nature and the British Herpetological Society (BHS). They sought to challenge the refusal of the Secretary of State for the Environment to 'call in' a decision of Poole Borough Council to grant planning permission for a new housing development on land which was part of a Site of Special Scientific Interest (SSSI). The applicants had

136 *R v Secretary of State for Foreign Affairs ex p World Development Movement Ltd* [1995] 1 WLR 386; [1995] 1 All ER 611.
137 *R v Secretary of State for the Environment ex p Friends of the Earth and Andrew Lees* [1996] 1 CMLR 117; [1996] Env LR 198.
138 Council Directive 80/778/EEC of 15 July 1980 relating to the quality of water intended for human consumption OJ L 229, 30/8/1980, pp 11–29.
139 *R v Poole BC ex p Beebee and Others* [1991] 2 PLR 27; [1991] JPL 643.

no legal interest in the land in question, but the High Court decided that they did have sufficient interest because one of the conditions of planning permission was that the developers would inform the BHS in advance of any development in order that the BHS could take steps to protect and relocate any protected species. The fact that the applicants had been given the right to be informed in these circumstances was enough to give them the necessary *locus standi*. Similarly, in *R v Swale BC and Medway Ports Authority ex p the Royal Society for the Protection of Birds (RSPB)* (1991),[140] the RSPB was granted standing in a judicial review action. The RSPB sought to challenge a decision by Swale Borough Council to grant planning permission to the Medway Ports Authority to reclaim and develop 125 acres of mud flats known as the Lappel Bank. The RSPB was granted standing on the basis that it had a legitimate expectation, based on correspondence from the Borough Council, that it would be consulted as an interested party before planning permission was granted and that the Borough Council had failed to consult it.

One possibility for a group of individuals is to form a limited company for the purposes of mounting a judicial review action. The courts have been willing to accept this. This has the particular advantage of reducing the potential cost liability for individual members. However, it would be usual in such cases for the defendant to press for an order for advance security of costs should the case fail. The Sullivan Report 2008[141] suggests that:

> for environmental cases to which Aarhus applies, the level at which security is set should reflect the requirements of Aarhus that the procedures are not prohibitively expensive.

Law in Action

A group of residents in Lancashire formed a limited company, Residents against Waste Site Ltd, to bring a judicial review action to challenge the legality of a planning permission granted by Lancashire County Council to itself for a waste facility.[142] The High Court considered that although the company had been formed after the planning permission it had sufficient interest in the matter, 'Technically it may be said that the company does not have a relevant interest of its own; but in substance it represents the interests of local residents, many of whom do have a relevant interest.' One reason for forming a company in these circumstances is to attempt to limit the personal liability of individuals should they face an adverse costs order.[143]

12.9.1.2 Are the current rules on standing Convention-compliant?

In 2004 the Environmental Justice Project noted that whilst the courts have shown a more relaxed and liberal approach to standing for NGOs, it is possible that they could revert to a more conservative phase.[144] Thirteen per cent of the respondents to the EJP review considered that the lack of an assured position on standing was unsatisfactory. Moreover, the fact that an individual or NGO bringing an environmental case has to establish standing could prove to be an added deterrent, given that the situation on standing is by no means certain. As the report notes,

---

140 *R v Swale BC and Medway Ports Authority ex p the Royal Society for the Protection of Birds (RSPB)* (1990) 2 Admin LR 790; [1991] 1 PLR 6; [1991] JPL 39.
141 See below.
142 See *Residents against Waste Site Ltd v Lancashire County Council* [2007] EWHC 2558 (Admin); [2008] Env LR 27; [2008] JPL 644.
143 See ENDS Report 395, December 2007, pp 60–61, Judicial review and standing against waste facility planning consent.
144 The Environmental Justice Project (UKELA, 2004).

Environmental NGOs often face an uphill battle on standing before the merits of the action are even considered, especially when there is an aggressive third party whose commercial interests are at stake.[145]

Although the report concludes that the issue of standing does not constitute a formidable barrier to bringing a case, it is still a cause for concern amongst practitioners, particularly in relation to NGOs. In some Member States of the EU, environmental protection NGOs have been granted automatic rights to bring judicial review actions before the national courts. One suggestion would be to amend the Senior Courts Act 1981 or to introduce new legislation which enshrines the rights of environmental NGOs on a statutory footing.

12.9.2 Substantial and procedural legality

Article 9(2) of the Aarhus Convention gives the public concerned the right to challenge both the substantive and procedural legality of decisions. In England the standard of review applicable in judicial review procedures is largely governed by common law, and three grounds are generally recognised as providing the standards for judicial review: illegality, irrationality (*Wednesbury* test[146]) and procedural impropriety. The question is whether these grounds provide for a review of substantive legality. It has been argued that the *Wednesbury* test allows for a review of substantive legality because it requires the courts to examine whether public authorities 'have taken into account matters which they ought not to have taken into account or conversely have refused . . . or neglected to take into account matters which they ought to have taken into account.' However, the *Wednesbury* test has been widely criticised as setting the bar too high.[147] For example in 2001 Lord Cooke in R v *Secretary of State for the Home Department, ex parte Daly* [2001] UKHL 26, [2001] 2 AC 532 held:

> And I think that the day will come when it will be more widely recognised that [*Wednesbury*] was an unfortunately retrogressive decision in English administrative law, insofar as it suggested that there are degrees of unreasonableness and that only a very extreme degree can bring an administrative decision within the legitimate scope of judicial invalidation.[148]

In September 2010 the Aarhus Compliance Committee issued its findings in response to a complaint by Clientearth. The Committee found that despite the fact that judicial review in England allows for challenges of substantive legality on the basis of material error of fact, error of law, regard to irrelevant considerations and failure to have regard to relevant considerations, jurisdictional error, and on the grounds of *Wednesbury* unreasonableness, it was not satisfied that these meet the standards for review required by the Convention as regards substantive legality. To resolve this, the Committee recommended that for cases falling within the scope of the Convention, the application of a 'proportionality principle' could provide an adequate standard of review. A proportionality test requires a public authority to provide evidence that the act or decision pursued justifies the limitation of the right at stake, is connected to the aims which that act or decision seeks to achieve and that the means used to limit the right at stake are no more than necessary to attain those aims.[149] Having said that, the Committee did not go so far as to say that the UK had failed to comply with Art 9(4) in this respect. In R (*on the application of Evans*) v *Secretary of State for Communities and Local Government*

---

145 Gerry Facenna of Monkton Chambers, as cited in the Environmental Justice Project at para 47, ibid.
146 *Associated Provincial Picture Houses Limited v Wednesbury Corporation* [1948] 1 KB 223.
147 See e.g. the Environmental Justice Project.
148 R v *Secretary of State for the Home Department, ex p Daly* [2001] UKHL 26, [2001] 2 AC 532 at para 32.
149 Findings and recommendations with regard to communication ACCC/C/2008/33 concerning compliance by the United Kingdom of Great Britain and Northern Ireland.

(2013)[150] the Court of Appeal was not persuaded by arguments relating to the Compliance Committee's recommendations. In this case Evans argued that the *Wednesbury* grounds were insufficient to review the legality of the Secretary of State's decision not to require an Environmental Impact Assessment. The Court of Appeal stated that first the Aarhus Convention and the views of the Aarhus Convention Compliance Committee were not relevant in so far as the Convention is not part of domestic law or EU law, and second the Compliance Committee had not concluded that the *Wednesbury* approach is impermissible. See also the Supreme Court's decision in *Walton v Scottish Ministers* (2012).[151]

12.9.3 Prohibitively expensive

Judicial review is an expensive form of litigation. However, Art 9(4) mandates that the judicial review procedures provided for by Arts 9(2) and (3) must not be prohibitively expensive. When Defra published its Aarhus Implementation Report it noted in relation to Art 9(4) that 'any legal person has equal opportunity to access the courts throughout the UK, subject to the requirements laid down by national law' and that court fees are reasonable.[152] The report further states: 'Certain applicants will be exempted from court fees; others will have court fees remitted on grounds of hardship, or will receive public funding.' This appears to suggest that as far as Defra is concerned, judicial review actions are not prohibitively expensive because (a) the court fees are relatively modest and (b) some litigants may obtain public funding. Such a positive spin fails to take into account at least two fundamentally important points. First, the cost of litigation is not confined to the court fee. Such a suggestion is in this author's view at best disingenuous. Secondly the availability of public funding is extremely limited. In relation to the first point the Defra assertion fails to take account of the fact that difficult and complex judicial review cases require experienced counsel, who will frequently command extremely high fees in difficult specialist environmental litigation. As the Court of Appeal noted in an addendum to its order for costs in *R (on the application of Burkett) v Hammersmith, Fulham LBC (Costs)* (2004):

> If the figures revealed by this case were in any sense typical of the costs reasonably incurred in litigating such cases up to the highest level, very serious questions would be raised as to the possibility of ever living up to the Aarhus ideals within our present legal system. And if these costs were upheld on detailed assessment, the outcome would cast serious doubts on the cost-effectiveness of the courts as a means of resolving environmental disputes.[153]

The *Burkett* case fell squarely within the scope of the Convention involving an unsuccessful and protracted challenge of a planning decision. Although there is little doubt that the costs of embarking on such litigation are high, the principal concern stems from the degree of uncertainty faced by litigants because of the general principle that costs follow the event. Under CPR r 43, an unsuccessful applicant can expect ordinarily to have to pay the other side's legal costs, and as Brooke LJ also observes in *Burkett*:

> an unprotected claimant . . . if unsuccessful in a public interest challenge, may have to pay very heavy legal costs to the successful defendant, and that this may be a potent factor in deterring litigation directed towards protecting the environment from harm.

---

150 *R (on the application of Evans) v Secretary of State for Communities and Local Government* [2013] EWCA Civ 115.
151 *Walton v Scottish Ministers* [2012] UKSC 44; [2013] 1 CMLR 28 at para 100.
152 Defra, Implementing Measures to achieve compliance with the UNECE Aarhus Convention. Available at http://www.defra.gov.uk/environment/policy/international/aarhus/pdf/compliance-summary.pdf. Accessed 10 March 2010.
153 *R (on the application of Burkett) v Hammersmith, Fulham LBC (Costs)* [2004] EWCA Civ 1342; [2005] CP Rep 11.

At the beginning of a case it is practically impossible for a litigant, be they an individual or an NGO, to know how much money they will need to pay if they lose. The prospect of facing unpredictably high costs is likely to deter all but the wealthiest of litigants or those very few who may benefit from public funding. In the worst-case scenario this can even happen where the application for judicial review has been refused. In 2008 the Sullivan Report on Access to Justice echoed these views in unequivocal terms:[154]

> Our overall view is that the key issue limiting access to environmental justice and inhibiting compliance with Article 9(4) of Aarhus is that of costs and the potential exposure to costs. What is notable about the problem is that, by and large, it flows from the application of ordinary costs principles of private law to judicial review and, within that, of ordinary principles of judicial review to environmental judicial review. We consider that the first of those does not take proper account of the particular features of public law. And that the latter is only acceptable in so far as it maintains compliance with Aarhus.

Law in Action

In August 2011 Greenpeace submitted a claim for Judicial Review of the designation by the Secretary of State for Energy and Climate Change of the National Policy Statement for Nuclear Power Generation in the United Kingdom. The case clearly falls within the scope of the Aarhus Convention. In December Greenpeace was informed that its application permission to apply for Judicial Review had been refused. Costs of £11,813.00 were awarded against Greenpeace to be paid to the Secretary of State. This represents the costs incurred by the Secretary of State in preparing the Acknowledgement of Service to the Judicial Review claim submitted. The Secretary of State had instructed two QCs and an experienced junior with ten years' call, specialising in planning and environmental law. Greenpeace has lodged a complaint with the Aarhus Compliance Committee claiming that the costs are manifestly far beyond the costs/ effort which a defendant was required to go to to file an acknowledgment of service. The Compliance Committee has accepted the complaint as admissible and will report later in 2013.[155]

It should be noted that it is always open to a court to order that an unsuccessful applicant is not required to pay the other side's costs but this is both rare and doesn't address the uncertainty issue since the court will not normally do this until the case has been concluded. See, for example, *Belize Alliance of Conservation Non-Governmental Organisations v Department of the Environment* (2004)[156] and *Greenpeace Ltd v SS for the Environment, Food and Rural Affairs* (2005).[157]

One way of addressing the uncertainty inherent in the loser pays rule is to dissaply the rule in environmental cases which fall within the scope of the Convention. The 2008 Sullivan Report rejected this on the basis that the Aarhus Convention does not require that legal actions are free or cheap, just that exposure to the other side's costs does not make the litigation prohibitively

---

154 The Working Group on Access to Environmental Justice, 'Ensuring access to environmental justice in England and Wales' (2008) (Sullivan Report).
155 UK ACC/C/2012/77.
156 *Belize Alliance of Conservation Non-Governmental Organisations v Department of the Environment* [2004] UKPC 6.
157 *Greenpeace Ltd v SS for the Environment, Food and Rural Affairs* [2005] EWHC 2144 (Admin).

expensive.[158] On the contrary, the report considered that some exposure to the 'winner's costs' is a positive thing because it discourages frivolous actions and ensures a 'degree of engagement and commitment' with the challenge. The principal procedural mechanisms that can be used to remove uncertainties from the outset is a protective costs order (PCO).

12.9.4 Protective costs orders

An alternative approach to limiting an applicant's liability for costs in public interest litigation comes in the shape of a protective costs order (PCO), and these have been subject to considerable judicial attention in what might be called 'Aarhus' cases. A PCO is an order which applicants can seek before a full hearing to determine the applicant's exposure to costs. A PCO is an order of the court by which the court specifies or constrains at an early stage what the costs outcome of the case will be. A PCO may render the applicant free of liability for paying the other side's costs or capping their liability to a specified limit in the event that the action is unsuccessful. A PCO therefore gives the litigant some degree of certainty about the costs they are likely to be exposed to in the event they lose their case. The guidelines for granting a PCO were developed by the Court of Appeal in the seminal case of *R v Cornerhouse Research v Secretary of State for Trade and Industry*.[159] According to the Court of Appeal a PCO could be made by the court if it saw fit to do so at any stage of the proceedings. However, the Court of Appeal made it clear that PCOs should be used exceptionally. To enable the court to make a decision whether to award a PCO, Lord Phillips MR laid down five guiding principles. Before granting a PCO, the court must be satisfied that:

- the issues raised are of general public importance;
- the public interest requires that those issues should be resolved;
- the claimant has no private interest in the outcome of the case;
- having regard to the financial resources of the claimant and the respondent(s) and to the amount of costs that are likely to be involved it is fair and just to make the order;
- if the order is not made the claimant will probably discontinue the proceedings and will be acting reasonably in doing so.

In addition it was noted that if the applicant's lawyers were acting on a pro bono basis this might enhance the prospects of granting a PCO. The problems arise from the fact that the *Cornerhouse* rules were developed in a case that was not concerned with environmental protection issues and the Court of Appeal made no reference to the Aarhus Convention. In 2008 the Sullivan Report observed a number of problems with the *Cornerhouse* rules as they applied in an environmental context. In particular, two of the core conditions stood out as posing problems. The first concerns the condition that the issues raised must be of general public importance. The report noted that many environmental challenges would not cross that threshold if that is interpreted as meaning that the case must either decide a new point of law or be of widescale importance, or affect people over a wide geographical area. The Sullivan Report considered that the obligation to ensure that procedures are not prohibitively expensive was not limited to cases of general public importance. In any event, the upholding of environmental law is of itself a matter of general public interest. The second core condition relates to the requirement that the applicant has no private interest in the matter. On the one hand, this fails to take account of the fact that an application for judicial review for the purposes of protecting the environment is inherently in the public interest. However, litigants may well have

---

158 The Working Group on Access to Environmental Justice, 'Ensuring access to environmental justice in England and Wales' (2008) (Sullivan Report).
159 *R (Corner House Research) v Secretary of State for Trade & Industry* [2005] 1 WLR 2600.

a vested private interest (for example if they are seeking to protect their locality from a polluting development) but this should not be a bar to awarding a PCO. It could, however, be a factor to take into account in determining the level of the PCO. Third, the Report also observed that this requirement sits uncomfortably with the standing requirement where the applicant is required to demonstrate they have sufficient interest in the matter. Moreover, the Aarhus Convention contains no exclusion on cases involving private interests. Overall the 2008 Sullivan Report did not consider it necessary to reformulate the rules; rather it favoured that specific principles should be applied to those judicial review cases to which the Convention applies. In particular the report recommended that if the individual Aarhus claimant, acting reasonably in the circumstances, would be prohibited by the level of costs or cost risks from bringing the case then the court must make some form of PCO. The case law in this area demonstrates some of the difficulties litigants have faced in obtaining PCOs, even to the extent that it has been suggested that there is a growing costs litigation industry.[160] See, for example, R (on the application of Buglife: The Invertebrate Conservation Trust) v Thurrock Thames Gateway Development Corp (2008),[161] where the Court of Appeal held that the courts should do their utmost to dissuade the parties from engaging in expensive satellite litigation on the question of whether PCOs and costs capping orders should be made.

The case of R (on the application of Garner) v Elmbridge Council & Gladedale Group Ltd & Network Rail (2010)[162] neatly demonstrates some of the problems that litigants face in trying to obtain a PCO. In March 2010 the Divisional Court refused to grant a PCO to Garner in respect of judicial review proceedings he brought against Elmbridge Council (E). The council had granted planning permission for the development of site opposite Hampton Court Palace, a scheduled ancient monument and Grade I listed building.

G was an employee of a group called Historic Royal Palaces, which had made objections to the development. The Divisional Court refused the PCO on the basis that the issues raised were not of general public importance and there was insufficient evidence of the applicant's resources. The decision was controversial, not least because many would regard Hampton Court as being a significant part of the country's heritage. However, Garner successfully appealed this decision in R (on the application of Garner) v Elmbridge Council & Gladedale Group Ltd & Network Rail (2010). The Court of Appeal held the particular project was subject to the requirements of Art 10A of the Environmental Impact Assessment Directive (see above at 12.7). In deciding whether to grant a PO in cases involving Art 10A of the EIA Directive, the Court decided there was no justification for the application of the issues of 'general public importance' or 'public interest requiring resolution of those issues' in the Corner House conditions. Both the Convention and the EIA Directive were based on the premise that it was in the public interest that there should be effective public participation in the decision-making process in significant environmental cases. Consequently the Court of Appeal ruled that the Divisional Court had not been entitled to reject the appellant's application for a PCO on the basis that the issues raised were not of general public importance which the public interest required to be resolved. This judicial willingness to apply the Corner House rules flexibly in Aarhus cases, however, does not extend to cases that fall outside the scope of the EIA or IPPC Directives. It will be recalled that the case of Morgan v Hinton Organics (Wessex) Ltd (2009)[163] concerned a private nuisance claim (see earlier discussion at 12.8.6). Here, the court accepted that although the principle that costs should not be prohibitively expensive was capable of applying to private nuisance proceedings, it was, at most, a matter to which the court might have regard in exercising its discretion. There was no legal principle which would enable the court to treat a pure treaty

---

160 Zuckerman, A, 'Protective costs orders—a growing costs litigation industry' [2009] 28(2)CJQ 161.
161 R (on the application of Buglife: The Invertebrate Conservation Trust) v Thurrock Thames Gateway Development Corp [2008] EWCA Civ 1209; [2009] 1 Costs LR 80; [2009] Env LR 18.
162 R (on the application of Garner) v Elmbridge Council & Gladedale Group Ltd & Network Rail LTL 3/3/20 EXTEMPRE (not yet reported).
163 Morgan v Hinton Organics (Wessex) Ltd 2009] EWCA Civ 107; [2009] Env LR 30; [2009] JPL 1335.

obligation, even one adopted by the EU, as converted into a rule of law directly binding on the English court.

In the *Garner* case also, G argued that Art 10A placed the UK under an obligation to ensure that the procedure for challenging the lawfulness of the planning permission was not prohibitively expensive and this had to be taken into account in assessing the level of the PCO. This raised an important question as to whether the assessment of what is prohibitively expensive should be decided on an 'objective' basis by reference to the ability of an 'ordinary' member of the public to meet the potential liability for costs, or on a 'subjective' basis by reference to the means of the particular claimant, or upon some combination of the two bases. In the Divisional Court the judge had refused to grant a PCO, because he was of the view that it was impossible to tell whether the proceedings would be prohibitively expensive unless there was detailed information about Garner's financial resources. In the Court of Appeal Sullivan LJ thought that this raised an important issue of principle:

> Should the question whether the procedure is or is not prohibitively expensive be decided on an 'objective' basis by reference to the ability of an 'ordinary' member of the public to meet the potential liability for costs, or should it be decided on a 'subjective' basis by reference to the means of the particular claimant, or upon some combination of the two bases?

Sullivan LJ said that he would have preferred to have deferred answering that question until the Aarhus Compliance Committee had issued its findings, and until it was known whether the European Commission had accepted the UK's response in relation to the Commission's reasoned opinion that the UK was in breach of Art 10A of the EIA Directive.[164] However, in ruling on the case before it, Sullivan LJ stated that:

> Whether or not the proper approach to the 'not prohibitively expensive requirement under article 10a' should be a wholly objective one, I am satisfied that a purely *subjective* approach, as was applied by Nicol J, is not consistent with the objectives underlying the Directive. Even if it is either permissible or necessary to have some regard to the financial circumstances of the individual claimant, the underlying purpose of the Directive to ensure that members of the public concerned having a sufficient interest should have access to a review procedure which is not prohibitively expensive would be frustrated if the court were entitled to consider the matter solely by reference to the means of the claimant who happened to come forward, without having to consider whether the potential costs would be prohibitively expensive for an ordinary member of 'the public concerned'.

The question was unresolved but raised its head again in the case of R (*Edwards and another*) v *Environment Agency and others* (No 2).[165] In this case Edwards sought judicial review of the Environment Agency's decision to grant an environmental permit for a cement works in Rugby. During the hearing before the Court of Appeal Mr Edwards withdrew his claim, but a second claimant, Mrs P, who had been closely involved in the campaign against the permit, was added to the proceedings. Her liability for costs was capped at £2,000, which was awarded against her when the Court of Appeal dismissed the claim. Mrs P sought leave to appeal to the House of Lords and she applied for a PCO, relying on Art 10A of the EIA Directive and Art 15 of the IPPC Directive 96/61/EEC. Her application was rejected, but she continued with the appeal and was unsuccessful. The House of Lords ordered that she pay the costs. The case then involved issues regarding the jurisdiction of the costs officers, which in itself is interesting because the costs officers were clearly willing to take into account the requirements of the directive in assessing the level of costs. The

---

164 The Commission announced its reasoned opinion by press release on 18 March 2010. The Commission has now commenced proceedings against the UK in Case C-530/11 *Commission v United Kingdom*.
165 [2010] UKSC 57; [2011] 1 WLR 79.

Supreme Court (by this stage the House of Lords had become the Supreme Court) held that the costs officers did not have this jurisdiction as this was exclusively a matter for the Court. It therefore fell to the Court to determine the correct approach to assessing whether costs were prohibitively expensive. The Supreme Court considered that the observations made by Sullivan J in *Garner* had gathered strength when viewed in the light of subsequent developments. (The 2009 Jackson Review of Civil Litigation Costs had proposed, in relation to environmental judicial review cases that the costs ordered against the claimant should not exceed the amount (if any) which is a reasonable one for him to pay having regard to all the circumstances. The Sullivan Update Report of 2010 proposed that an unsuccessful claimant in a claim for judicial review should not be ordered to pay the costs of any other party other than where the claimant has acted unreasonably in bringing or conducting the proceedings.) The Supreme Court also said the question had to be considered in the light of the conclusion of the Aarhus Convention Compliance Committee of October 2010. The Committee stated that, in legal proceedings in the UK the public interest nature of the environmental claims under consideration did not seem to have been given sufficient consideration in the apportioning of costs by the courts. Further the Committee stated that despite the various measures available to address prohibitive costs, taken together they failed to ensure that the costs remain at a level which meets the requirements of the Convention.[166] In view of this the Supreme Court considered that although the balance seemed to favour an objective approach the question of how it should assess whether costs are prohibitively expensive was still uncertain. Accordingly the Supreme Court made a request for a preliminary ruling from the Court of Justice on what should be the correct test was for determining whether proceedings were 'prohibitively expensive' within the meaning of the Directives. At the time of writing this request is still pending although the Advocate General has published his opinion.[167]

12.9.5 Are the English rules on cost Convention-compliant?

As the above discussion demonstrates, a litigant who chooses to commence a judicial review action faces real uncertainties about the possible costs outcome, unless they can successfully secure a PCO at the outset which sets the cap on their potential liability at a reasonable level. The fact remains though that the wealth of evidence to date is that the current rules on costs in judicial review litigation represent the single largest barrier to access to justice. In 2004, 82 per cent of respondents to the Environmental Justice Project reported that they were 'not satisfied' with the current rules on costs. In his foreword to the report 'Ensuring Access to Justice'[168] Sullivan J (as he was then), with apparent clairvoyance, asserted that 'Unless more is done, and the Court's approach to costs is altered so as to recognise that there is a public interest in securing compliance with environmental law, it will only be a matter of time before the United Kingdom is taken to task for failing to live up to its obligations under Aarhus'. It was therefore no surprise when, in September 2010, the Aarhus Compliance Committee ruled that:

> By failing to ensure that the costs for all court procedures subject to Art 9 are not prohibitively expensive, and in particular by the absence of any clear legally binding directions from the legislature or judiciary to this effect, the Party concerned fails to comply with article 9, paragraph 4, of the Convention.[169]

The Committee also found that the system as a whole is not such as 'to remove or reduce financial. . . barriers to access to justice', as required by Art 9, para 5. In consequence of this the

---

166 See documents relating to ACC/C/2008/27.
167 Case C-260/11 R (on the applications of David Edwards and Lilian Pallikaropoulos) v The Environment Agency and others (pending).
168 'Ensuring Access to Justice in Environmental Matters', May 2008—Report of the Working Group on Access to Environmental Justice.
169 Findings and recommendations with regard to communication ACCC/C/2008/33 concerning compliance by the United Kingdom of Great Britain and Northern Ireland Adopted by the Compliance Committee on 24 September 2010.

Committee recommended that the UK review its system for allocating costs in environmental cases within the scope of the Convention and to undertake practical and legislative measures to ensure that such procedures (a) were fair and equitable and not prohibitively expensive; and (b) provided a clear and transparent framework. In response to these recommendations the Ministry of Justice undertook a consultation exercise in relation to amendments to the Civil Procedure Rules in respect of cases falling within the scope of the Convention. Consequently the CPR rules were amended (with effect from April 2013) to make specific provision for cost orders which are to be recoverable between the parties in Aarhus Convention claims. (CPR Rule 45.41–44). Then new rules refer to Practice Direction 45 for the maximum amount of costs that the court can order a party to pay. The recoverable costs under the PCO regime will be fixed at £5,000 for an individual claimant, £10,000 for an organisation and there will be a cross-cap on the claimant's recoverable costs of £35,000. In order to benefit from these provisions the claimant must state that the cost order claim falls within the scope of the Aarhus Convention. It is open to the defendant to argue that the claim does not fall within the scope of the Convention and if this happens then the Court will make the necessary determination. If the court holds that the claim is an Aarhus Convention claim, it will normally order the defendant to pay the claimant's costs of those proceedings on the indemnity basis, and that order may be enforced notwithstanding that this would increase the costs payable by the defendant beyond the amount prescribed in Practice Direction 45. For a further discussion of the likely impact of the new rules see http://www.6pumpcourt.co.uk/files/articles/The_Aarhus_convention_after_jackson.pdf.[170]

In 2011 the European Commission also commenced infringement proceedings against the UK in respect of costs associated with judicial review claims falling within the scope of the public participation limb.[171] The case was still pending at the time of writing, but will be discussed further below.

12.10 Private prosecutions

The enforcement of environmental law is not the monopoly of the pollution control authorities. Neither the Environment Agency nor the local authorities exercising their respective pollution control functions have the financial resources or personnel to ensure full enforcement of the environmental controls laid down in statute or in the permissive authorisations (environmental permits) granted. It is for these reasons that the individuals and pressure groups can play a role in the enforcement of environmental law by bringing private criminal prosecutions. The environmental legislation considered in this book contains a number of provisions which enable citizens to bring their own prosecutions against those who commit offences under specific pollution control legislation. The Environmental Protection Act (EPA) 1990, for example, provides considerable scope for citizens to bring private prosecutions.[172] Other examples of the restricted right to bring a private prosecution include s 211 of the WIA 1991 and s 38 of the Radioactive Substances Act 1993. However, it appears that these rights have not been widely recognised or taken up. There are several reasons why this might be the case and these are considered below.

12.10.1 The right to bring a private prosecution

At common law, it is a well established rule that a citizen has the right to bring a private prosecution under an Act of Parliament. In *R v Stewart* (1896),[173] the High Court allowed a private prosecution to be brought by the Royal Society for the Prevention of Cruelty to Animals under the Diseases of

---

170 The Working Group on Access to Environmental Justice, 'Ensuring access to environmental justice in England and Wales' (2008) (Sullivan Report).
171 Case C 530/11 *Commission v United Kingdom* (still pending).
172 Except in the case of Pt IV, s 118(10), which deals with genetically modified organisms.
173 *R v Stewart* [1896] 1 QB 300.

Animals Act 1894. The Court held that a citizen has a right to prosecute under any statute unless an Act specifically precludes that right in clear words. Various statutes contain provisions which explicitly give individuals the right to enforce the statutory provisions by means of private prosecutions and clearly these rights are of particular importance for environmental pressure groups. But even in the absence of a specific statutory provision, an individual or pressure group can still bring a private prosecution under an Act of Parliament, providing that the Act does not expressly and clearly preclude such a right and providing the prosecution is not vexatious. In the context of environmental protection where most businesses have statutory authority to pollute,[174] it is necessary to establish whether an offence has been committed. Access to information about polluting activities is essential and the public registers and the EIR 2004 described earlier may provide the information necessary in order to assist people in identifying the firms or businesses that are committing offences. From the information on the public registers, it should be possible, for example, to ascertain who is responsible for a particular discharge into a river, what the environmental permit conditions are, whether any monitoring data has been collected revealing breach of permit, any notices served, or previous offences recorded. Where a person or group of persons believes that an offence has been committed, is being committed or is likely to be committed, the easiest and cheapest course of action will be to complain to the regulatory authority and ask it to take enforcement action. It has already been stated that the pollution control authorities do not have the resources to monitor every discharge or emission all the time and they therefore rely on reports and complaints brought by people in this respect. For instance, the anglers' associations were often the first to draw the National River Authority's (NRA) attention to pollution incidents and fish kills. The Environment Agency operates a 24-hour hotline telephone number enabling the public to report incidents to it.

However, the alternative course of action is for an individual or pressure group to bring a private prosecution.[175] An example of a statutory right to bring a private prosecution is s 82 of the EPA 1990 where the aggrieved citizen is given the right to prosecute statutory nuisances. This is one of the better-known 'rights' and is covered in Chapter 9.

See Chapter 9

12.10.2 Problems for private prosecutors

The reality is that private prosecutions are not commonplace; they are relatively rare. In relation to water offences anglers have brought a number of prosecutions where pollution has affected their fishing rights. Similarly the NGOs have been willing to commence criminal proceedings in situations where the regulatory body has failed to act. Greenpeace brought the first private prosecution under the Water Resources Act 1991 in *Greenpeace v Albright and Wilson*.[176] Greenpeace brought the action in respect of an alleged breach of the terms of a Water Discharge Consent under the WRA 1991. Parpworth[177] notes that Greenpeace was critical of the NRA's decision not to prosecute. The prosecution was successful, however, and the company was fined £2,000. An NGO may commence a criminal case where the regulator delays bringing a case or seemingly demonstrates some inertia or unwillingness to proceed. Parpworth also refers to the case of *Environment Agency v Milford Haven Port Authority* (2000).[178] Although the Agency eventually prosecuted the port authority for its part in the pollution of the port as a result of the *Sea Empress* running aground, it did so over a year after the incident. In a statement issued by Friends of the Earth, the NGO warned that if the Agency failed to prosecute then the NGO would.[179]

174 E.g., in accordance with the conditions imposed in environmental permits.
175 Often using the information obtained from the public registers.
176 *Greenpeace v Albright and Wilson* [1991] 3 LMELR 170.
177 Parpworth, N, 'Enforcing environmental laws: the role of the private prosecution' [2007] JPL 327.
178 *Environment Agency v Milford Haven Port Authority* [2000] Env LR 632.
179 Parpworth, N, 'Enforcing environmental laws: the role of the private prosecution' [2007] JPL 327.

Law in Action

In *R v Anglian Water Services Ltd, Hart v Anglian Water Services Ltd*[180] the Court of Appeal reduced a fine of £200,000 imposed by the Crown Court in relation to a criminal prosecution brought initially by a private individual. In this case a Mr Hart saw condoms and sewage floating down the River Crouch and he reported this immediately to the Environment Agency. The pollution was caused by a discharge from a sewage treatment works operated by Anglian Water. H commenced a private prosecution against AW in which the company pleaded guilty; the magistrates remitted the case to the Crown Court for sentencing, given the seriousness of the pollution and because the maximum penalty they could impose was £20,000. The Crown Court imposed a fine of £200,000 but on appeal the Court of Appeal held the fine was manifestly excessive for a single offence, and reduced it to £60,000. Although it is not entirely clear why H brought the prosecution rather than the Agency (seemingly they had different views on this [181]), the Court of Appeal did observe:

> The Environment Agency offered to take over the case but this offer was rejected by Mr Hart. This case, and others like it, should be prosecuted by the Environment Agency rather than by an individual member of the public and it is unfortunate that it was not. We have not explored the reason in any detail. Suffice it to say Mr Hart thought the Agency was dragging its feet, whereas the Agency said it was gathering evidence.[182]

In the case above it is not entirely clear why the Court made the observation that it was 'unfortunate' that the prosecution was brought by Mr Hart. Whatever the reasons, without further clarification, this type of remark could put people off bringing such actions. This would seem to run counter to the objectives of Art 9(3) of the Convention.

Undoubtedly there are a number of problems associated with starting such litigation. It may not always be necessary to commence a legal action; it is possible that the threat of litigation will produce the desired results, or as noted above, will prompt the regulatory body to act. However, if an individual is serious about commencing a private prosecution he/she will need to consider the financial cost of commencing a criminal prosecution. There is no public funding to assist a person with a private prosecution, and so the individual will have to bear the costs without any public support. Additionally it is always possible that well-heeled defendants in civil and criminal litigation may be tempted to use their financial muscle to restrict and stifle tactically civil claims and private prosecutions by increasing the length, complexity and costs of the litigation with the intention of exhausting the claimant's limited financial resources. In addition, a defendant could resort to a 'SLAPP' (strategic lawsuit against public participation) to head off unwelcome interest in its activities by environmental groups and others.

Problems also arise in relation to admissible evidence. Private prosecutors are not entitled, like the regulatory authorities, to enter premises and take samples, records, etc. They therefore have to rely on other evidence, such as samples taken by themselves without trespassing on the defendants' property and information entered on the public registers. This is where NGOs are probably better placed than individuals since they will have access to scientific advice and testing facilities.

---

180 R v Anglian Water Services Ltd, Hart v Anglian Water Services Ltd [2003] EWCA Crim 2243; [2004] 1 Cr App R (S) 62; [2004] Env LR 10.
181 Parpworth, N, 'Enforcing environmental laws: the role of the private prosecution' [2007] JPL 327.
182 At para 3.

Evidential problems could conceivably arise in a private prosecution involving the use of self-monitoring data entered on the public register. A defendant's privilege against self-incrimination enables a criminal court to decline to hear such evidence.[183] The privilege against self-incrimination and the use of a challenge under Art 6 of the European Convention on Human Rights in an environmental context has been restricted following the decision in *R v Hertfordshire CC ex p Green Environmental Industries Ltd and Another* (2001).[184]

12.11 Human rights

Human rights represents an emerging area in which individuals and environmental groups may use rights-based arguments to challenge the decisions of public authorities. The courts, as well as regulatory agencies, are public bodies for the purposes of the Human Rights Act (HRA) 1998 and are therefore constrained to act in a way which is compatible with the rights enshrined in the European Convention on Human Rights (ECHR). The HRA 1998 requires the courts to take into account, in their decisions, not only the rights granted to citizens by the Convention, but also the judgments and opinions of the European Court of Human Rights and the Commission. National legislation must, as far as possible, be read so as to give effect to the Convention rights, even if this means that the court will depart from a previous decision which would otherwise have been binding on it. It will be unlawful for the courts, and other public bodies, to act in ways which are incompatible with Convention rights (unless the public authority could not have acted differently because of the existence of incompatible legislation). National courts are empowered to grant such remedies which they consider 'just and appropriate'. This power will enable the courts both to award damages for breach of human rights and, in appropriate cases, quash incompatible subordinate legislation.

Debate as to the potential impact of the ECHR and HRA 1998 centres upon two issues: (a) to what extent the ECHR and the HRA 1998 guarantee substantive environmental human rights; and (b) to what extent the ECHR and the HRA 1998 guarantee procedural environmental human rights. Interestingly the debate about the impact of the ECHR has also extended to the relationship between the common law duties of public bodies and their obligations under the ECHR. Certainly in some of the cases discussed below it is clear that claimants are attempting to assert their rights under the two 'regimes' (for want of a better word). This has been particularly the case in relation to Art 8 claims. The case that raises this issue at its most extreme is *Marcic v Thames Water Utilities Ltd* (2004),[185] which is discussed below.

The ECHR does not directly address the question of whether an individual has a right to a healthy environment. Early ECHR environmental litigation supported the view that the Convention did not provide a right to environmental protection or standards of environmental quality. Nevertheless, the ECHR has been used by litigants as the basis of a number of claims the objective of which was to secure an acceptable level of environmental quality.

12.11.1 The right to life: Article 2

Article 2 of the ECHR provides that 'Everyone's right to life shall be protected by law.' At first sight, it seems unlikely that such a right could serve the interests of environmental protection, but it would appear that breaches of Art 2 are not restricted to the protection of physical life. Both significant interference with the quality of life and a threat to life caused by the activities of a public

---

183 S 78 of PACE 1984 and *R v Director of Serious Fraud Office ex p Smith* [1993] AC 1; [1992] 3 WLR 66; [1992] 3 All ER 456.
184 *R v Hertfordshire CC ex p Green Environmental Industries Ltd and Another* [2000] 2 AC 412; [2000] 2 WLR 373; [2000] 1 All ER 773; [2000] Env LR 414; [2000] Env LR 426.
185 *Marcic v Thames Water Utilities Ltd* [2003] UKHL 66; [2004] 2 AC 42; [2003] 3 WLR 1603; [2004] 1 All ER 135; [2004] Env LR 25.

authority could form the basis of an Art 2 action. For example, in Guerra v Italy (1998),[186] two members of the European Court of Human Rights were of the opinion that a government which withheld information about circumstances which created a foreseeable and substantial risk of damage to physical health and physical integrity could amount to a breach of Art 2. In the Guerra case, the applicants lived only 1 km from a chemical plant which was discharging large quantities of inflammable gases into the environment. It was argued that the gases could cause chemical reactions leading to the release of highly toxic substances. The chemical plant had a chequered operational history. Various accidents had occurred, including an incident in 1976 when 150 people had been hospitalised with serious arsenic poisoning. The applicants complained that the 'Seveso' Directive on the Control of Major Accident Hazards had not been complied with. The Directive required local authorities to advise the local population with regard to the relevant hazards from the plant and the procedures and plans in place to safeguard the local population, but this had not been done. Although the Court ruled that the claim under Art 2 was inadmissible, since it had already decided the case on the basis of Art 8, the comments of the two concurring members of the Court are significant because they indicate that in certain circumstances, public authorities have a positive obligation to safeguard a citizen's right to life.

Guerra is also significant in that Jamboek J called for the development of implied human rights, such as the right to an environment free from health-threatening pollution. The question of liability for failing to warn the public also arose in LCB v UK (1998).[187] This case concerned the UK's alleged failure (a) to warn LCB's parents that LCB might develop leukaemia due to her father's exposure to radiation whilst serving on Christmas Island during nuclear weapon testing; and (b) to monitor LCB's health. Whilst LCB's action failed, the case confirmed that a state is under a duty to take positive action to safeguard the lives of people within its territory, although what action, if any, a state is obliged to take will vary with the circumstances.

The action which a state takes in response to hazards has been the subject of further judicial consideration in McGinley and Egan v UK (1998).[188] In this case, it was the government itself which undertook hazardous activities, rather than a private company, as in Guerra. Where such activities could pose hidden health risks for workers or others (that is, pollution victims), the duty to provide information to the potential victims includes both the provision of documents and effective procedures to access that information. The decision in McGinley was applied by the Divisional Court in R (on the application of Hardy) v Milford Haven Port Authority (2007).[189]

Law in Action

In R (on the application of Hardy) v Milford Haven Port Authority (2007) the port authority (M) had been granted both planning permission and a hazardous substance consent for the construction of two liquefied gas port terminals. H requested a copy of the risk assessment that the port authority had supplied to the planning authority. She made the request under the Environmental Information Regulations (EIR) 2004. M refused to supply the information and this was subsequently considered by the Information Commissioner and Tribunal. However, H sought to rely on McGinley and argued that M was under a duty to supply the information as

---

186 Guerra v Italy (1998) 26 EHRR 357.
187 LCB v UK (1999) 27 EHRR 212; 4 BHRC 447.
188 McGinley and Egan v UK (1999) 27 EHRR 1; 4 BHRC 421.
189 R (on the application of Hardy) v Milford Haven Port Authority [2007] EWHC 1883 (Admin); [2008] JPL 702.

part of its obligations under the Art 8 and Art 2 ECHR. The Divisional Court held that, to the extent that the information fell outside the scope of the EIR 2004, H had failed to show that either Art 8 or Art 2 ECHR was engaged. The planning process constituted a sufficient legal and administrative procedure to prevent breaches of Arts 2 and 8 and the planning authority had concluded that the risks presented by the terminals was so low as not to warrant a refusal of either the planning permission or the hazardous substances consent. Interestingly the Information Commissioner had decided that M should disclose the information under the EIR 2004. The port had been set to appeal this decision, but withdrew the appeal and disclosed the disputed information.[190]

Whilst decision-makers in public authorities must be mindful of the need to protect the health and well being of the authority's citizens, Art 2 does not oblige a public authority to provide a healthy environment for its population. Article 2 actions are therefore only likely to stand a reasonable prospect of success where the relevant claim relates to allegations of unreasonable exposure to pollution risks. Even then the Court will be wary of imposing unreasonable burdens upon public authorities. Thus, in *Osman v UK* (1998),[191] an Art 2 claim based on negligent policing, the Court stated that the right to life 'must be interpreted in a way that does not impose an impossible or disproportionate burden on the authorities. Accordingly, not every risk to life can entail for the authorities a Convention requirement to take operational measures to prevent the risk from arising'. In view of this decision, it remains to be seen whether the suggested link between traffic pollution and asthma could form the basis of a successful Art 2 action. Nevertheless, it is conceivable, following *Osman v UK*, that any public authority (for example, the Environment Agency, local authority, etc) which in full knowledge of the existence of a serious risk to public health (or in circumstances in which it ought to have known of the risk) fails to take reasonable preventive measures (such as closing down a risky activity or at least warning the public of the relevant risks) which results in injury to an identifiable member or section of the public will be liable for breach of Art 2.

12.11.2 The right to privacy and family life: Article 8

Article 8 provides that:

(1) Everyone has the right to respect for his private and family life, his home and his correspondence;

(2) There shall be no interference by a public authority with the exercise of this right except such as is in accordance with the law and is necessary in a democratic society in the interests of national security, public safety or the economic wellbeing of the country, for the prevention of disorder or crime, for the protection of health or morals, or for the protection of the rights and freedoms of others.

Article 8 imposes a positive obligation on states to take reasonable and appropriate measures to secure the rights of applicants and a negative obligation not to interfere with Art 8 rights unless these are justified by Art 8(2). Article 8 has been cited in a number of cases concerning aircraft noise, an issue that continues to cause a great deal of public disquiet with plans to extend airports

---

190 See *Milford Haven Port Authority v Information Commissioner*. Information Tribunal Appeal No: EA/2007/0036; Information Commissioner's Ref: FER0072936.
191 *Osman v UK* [1999] 1 FLR 193; (2000) 29 EHRR 245; 5 BHRC 293.

such as London Heathrow. The cases demonstrate the difficulties claimants face in establishing a breach of their Art 8 rights, given that the right is 'qualified' and interference can be justified on a number of grounds, including that of the economic wellbeing of the country.

In *Powell and Rayner v UK* (1990),[192] the applicants, who lived close to Heathrow Airport, based their action on Art 8. The applicants alleged that the noise from the airport adversely affected the quality of their private lives and the scope for enjoying the amenities of their homes and so breached their Art 8 rights. The applicants, along with approximately 6,500 other residents, lived in an area considered to be one of high noise annoyance. The Court rejected the applicants' action because of the qualification, in Art 8(2), to strike a balance between the competing interests of the applicants and the wider community. In balancing the relevant interests, the Court had regard to (a) the fact that residents had received compensation for noise disturbance, (b) the noise abatement measures which had been taken by the airport, (c) the economic importance of Heathrow Airport to the country,[193] and (d) the use, by the UK government, of a regulatory regime to control noise pollution, rather than favouring the use of civil actions to resolve noise disputes. Whilst the Court found that aircraft noise was interfering with the applicants' use of their homes, the interference was justified in the particular circumstances. The measures taken by the UK government to address the problem were held to be within the UK's margin of appreciation.

The issue of airport noise was raised once again in the later case of *Hatton v UK* (2003),[194] albeit this time the case focused specifically on noise caused during the night in consequence of the government's night-time flying policy. H, who lived near Heathrow Airport, complained that the policy violated her rights under Arts 8 and 13. In 1993, a noise quota system was introduced for each airline operator at Heathrow Airport, permitting a greater number of take-offs and landings of quieter aircraft, or of a smaller number of noisier aeroplanes, providing the overall noise quota was not exceeded. Following two successful judicial reviews the scheme was amended by imposing an upper limit on the number of aircraft that could be operated, whilst retaining the noise quota scheme. Initially the Commission found that the UK had breached the applicant's Art 8 rights, and awarded compensation, but this decision was appealed and overturned by the Grand Chamber. The government argued that when determining its policy it should be accorded a wide margin of appreciation because it had to balance a number of competing rights of varying levels of importance and sensitivity and that the decision-making process was a matter for the national government. The Grand Chamber of the ECHR held that although a person who was significantly affected by noise pollution could bring a claim under Art 8, states had a wide margin of appreciation that required them to weigh all the competing interests involved.[195] The extent or 'width' of the margin depended on the facts of each case, and the question as to whether the appropriate balance had been struck depended upon the weight given to the different rights and interests involved. The Court stated that when assessing the appropriateness of the balance, the measures available to mitigate the effect of interference with those rights had to be considered. On the facts, the Court held that the UK had not exceeded the margin of appreciation.

In *Andrews v Reading Borough Council*[196] Andrews installed noise insulation in his home at a cost of just over £4,000 because of what he claimed was excessive traffic noise which had been created by a traffic regulation order made by the local authority (R). A claimed that the noise seriously interfered with his family's sleep and that to impose the increased level of traffic noise on his family,

192 *Powell and Rayner v UK* (1990) 12 EHRR 355.
193 E.g., in 1998, Heathrow handled cargo to the value of £26.3 billion, contributed £16 million in local rents and rates, generated £200 million to the UK's balance of payments, and provided over 48,000 jobs.
194 *Hatton v UK* (2003) 37 EHRR 28; 15 BHRC 259.
195 The interests of those affected by noise, the interests of the state in maintaining an international airport and the economic benefits of the airport.
196 *Andrews v Reading Borough Council* [2004] EWHC 970 (Admin); [2005] Env LR 2; [2004] UKHRR 599.

without any noise mitigation steps or financial assistance, breached his Art 8 rights. There was no grant scheme available to assist A to install the noise insulation, and so he claimed the costs from the local authority, arguing that as there was no possibility of compensation, the interference with his Art 8 rights was disproportionate. In response, R argued that any adverse affects were outweighed by the public benefits of the scheme, including quicker traffic flows and shorter bus journeys and therefore any interference was proportionate. The action was stayed pending the decision of the Grand Chamber in the *Hatton* case, following which R applied to have the claim struck out on the basis that it had no real prospect of success. The Divisional Court refused the council's application, stating:

> Aircraft noise is undoubtedly often more intensive than traffic noise, but I have no doubt that an increase in traffic noise which seriously affects an individual may engage Art 8 . . . It cannot be said at this stage that there is no real prospect that such a breach will be established.

Turning to the margin of appreciation question, Collins J reiterated that a fair balance has to be struck between the competing interests of the individual and of the community as a whole. The Court distinguished the decision in *Marcic*;[197] a relevant factor in assessing whether the right balance has been struck is the availability of measures to mitigate the effects of noise; the absence of any possibility of a grant scheme to mitigate the effect of the noise or consideration of whether such a possibility should exist was a relevant factor to take into account.

In *Lopez Ostra v Spain* (1995),[198] waste treatment plants were constructed on municipal land just 12 metres from the applicant's home. The operators omitted to acquire a licence authorising their 'nuisance causing' activities. The applicant alleged that odour and noise emissions from the waste treatment plants were causing health problems and were disrupting home life. The Court found that as the emissions exceeded permitted limits, they could endanger the health of citizens living nearby. The Court stated that 'severe environmental pollution may affect individuals' wellbeing and prevent them from enjoying their private and family life adversely without, however, seriously endangering their health'. The Court found in favour of the applicant and awarded 4 million pesetas' compensation. There had been an interference with the applicant's Art 8 rights and the interference was not justified by the Art 8(2) qualification. The Court noted that whilst the key objective of Art 8 was to protect citizens against arbitrary interference by public authorities, a public body's duty under Art 8 included a positive obligation to ensure effective respect for private and family life. The court concluded that the economic benefit of the treatment plants to the local community did not outweigh the applicant's right to respect for her home and home life. Article 8 could therefore be a fertile source of human rights litigation in circumstances where inaction by a public body exposes citizens to the adverse impacts of environmental pollution. For example, a judicial review action against a regulator is possible in circumstances where the regulator refuses to take enforcement action against a person, such as an IPPC-licensed facility, whose emissions are interfering with the Art 8 rights of citizens living close to the polluter.

There is an interesting contrast between the decisions in *Lopez Ostra* and *Powell and Rayner/Hatton*. In the successful *Lopez Ostra* case, the economic interests were relatively narrow economic interests comprising the private tanneries who used the waste treatment plants and the level/nature of the harm suffered. In *Powell and Rayner* and *Hatton*, the relevant economic interests at Heathrow Airport were of a different order of magnitude altogether and were not confined to a narrow range of private interests.

---

197 See below.
198 *Lopez Ostra v Spain* (1995) 20 EHRR 277.

In *Khatun and Others v UK* (1998),[199] a complaint was made to the European Commission of Human Rights arising out of the disturbance caused by the Canary Wharf development. Residents living close to the development were affected by construction dust, could not use their gardens and were forced to close their windows in the height of summer, resulting in excessive heat levels in their homes. The Court rejected the claims and accepted the developer's submissions relating to the public benefit arising from the regeneration of Docklands. The Court recognised the 'pressing social need' of the project and concluded that a fair balance had been struck between the interference with the applicants' home and private life and the wider public benefit. The *Khatun* case provides an example of the private interests of a developer winning out, as a result of a public decision, over the adverse impacts of the development on the applicants. In this case, the Court was able to identify a public economic benefit which justified the interference complained of.

In *McKenna and Others v British Aluminium Ltd* (2002),[200] the Birmingham District Registry of the High Court heard an application to strike out a claim by claimants (miners) relating to alleged mental distress and physical harm caused by the operation (environmental emissions, noise and invasion of privacy) of the defendant's factory in the context of the claimants' occupation and/or enjoyment of their homes. The defendant sought to strike out the relevant claims in nuisance and *Rylands v Fletcher*[202] on the basis that the claimants had no proprietary interest in their homes[201] and therefore had no reasonable prospect of winning their case. The claimants argued that their claim should not be struck out on human rights grounds because of: (a) the existence of their Art 8 right to respect for private and family life; and (b) s 6 of the Human Rights Act 1998, which required public authorities (including courts) not to act incompatibly with their ECHR rights. The claimants also relied on *Douglas v Hello! Ltd* (2001)[203] as authority requiring the courts to develop the common law so that it accorded with their ECHR rights.

The Court refused to strike out the claim. Although the Court thought that an interest in land was probably necessary to found a claim in *Rylands v Fletcher*,[204] the case ought to proceed to trial, as the Court should develop the common law so as to be compliant with the ECHR. There was a powerful argument that the claimant's Art 8 rights would not have been properly given effect to if the claimant (with no proprietary interest in his or her home) could not bring an action himself or herself and was therefore at the mercy of the owner of his or her home as the only person allowed to bring proceedings.

It was noted earlier, in relation to the *Hatton* decision, that one of the considerations of the Grand Chamber, in deciding whether the UK had breached the claimant's Art 8 rights, was the availability of alternative mitigating measures. However, in the *Marcic* case discussed below it appears that the House of Lords was not swayed by the fact that the effect of its ruling was effectively to deny the claimant any remedy to what was a very unpleasant impact on his family life. The case also raises important points about the relationship between the common law of nuisance and the Human Rights Act 1998.

In *Marcic v Thames Water Utilities Ltd* (2003)[205] the claimant sued his sewerage services provider (TWU) in (a) nuisance, (b) breach of statutory duty, and (c) breach of Art 8 and Protocol 1, Art 1. M brought the action in response to continued overflow of the sewage treatment system flooding his garden (the sewage never flooded his house, however). The sewers, although adequate when they had been laid in the 1930s, were now overburdened by substantial residential development

---

199 *Khatun and Others v UK* (1998) 26 EHRR CD212.
200 *McKenna and Others v British Aluminium Ltd* [2002] Env LR 30.
201 *Rylands v Fletcher* (1868) LR 3 HL 330.
202 See *Hunter v Canary Wharf Ltd* [1997] 2 WLR 684; (1995) 139 SJ LB 214 and *Cambridge Water Co v Eastern Counties Leather plc* [1994] 2 AC 264; [1994] 2 WLR 53; [1994] 1 All ER 53.
203 *Douglas v Hello! Ltd* [2001] 2 WLR 992 485.
204 On the basis of the reasoning in *Cambridge Water* that the *Rylands v Fletcher* principle was an extension of the law of nuisance.
205 *Marcic v Thames Water Utilities Ltd* [2003] UKHL 66; [2004] 2 AC 42; [2003] 3 WLR 1603; [2004] 1 All ER 135; [2004] Env LR 25.

since that date and when there was heavy rain the system became overburdened, which resulted in the flooding of M's garden. The only real solution to the problem was to enlarge the public sewerage system, which was controlled by TWU. M asked TWU to do something about the problem but TWU refused, citing costs; the company gave a higher priority to projects aimed at combating internal flooding. The Court of Appeal held (a) that the inadequacy of the sewage treatment system constituted a nuisance, and (b) that the defendant had infringed the claimant's human rights. The Appeal Court's decision was overruled by the House of Lords, who first considered that the right to bring an action in nuisance was incompatible with the statutory scheme of the Water Industry Act 1991; a sewerage undertaker's duty to provide an adequate system of public sewers under s 94(1) WIA 1991[206] is enforceable by the Director General of Water Services under s 18 WIA 1991. The Lords said that the remedy in respect of a contravention of the sewerage undertaker's general drainage obligation lies solely in the enforcement procedure set out in s 18, which stated that any person affected by a breach of s 94 could seek an enforcement notice against the sewerage undertaker from the Director of Water Services at Ofwat.

The Law Lords also held that the claim under the HRA failed. Following the Grand Chamber's decision in *Hatton*, Lord Nicholls held that it was necessary to consider whether the statutory scheme established by Parliament struck a fair balance between the interests of the individual and the community and in assessing this the role of domestic policy maker should be given special weight. The Lords accepted that under the statutory scheme the water company had to deal with competing priorities:

> The need to adopt some system of priorities for building more sewers is self-evident. So is the need for the system to be fair. A fair system of priorities necessarily involves balancing many intangible factors. Whether the system adopted by a sewerage undertaker is fair is a matter inherently more suited for decision by the industry regulator than by a court.

Additionally, the scheme under the Water Industry Act provided a mechanism for the Director General to deal with water companies that are not discharging their functions and 'Parliament entrusted this decision to the Director, not the courts'.

The *Marcic* decision, although no doubt correct, raises some very difficult issues. The consequences of it are that Mr Marcic was left with no remedy; it appears to have effectively closed the door to private claims in nuisance and under the HRA 1998 where there is a statutory framework for dealing with it. It also demonstrates the reluctance of the courts to interfere with the way in which a public body prioritises its investments. However, it should be recalled that TWU is a private sector company and makes enormous profits for the benefit of its shareholders; seemingly such consideration is outwith the jurisdiction of the court when assessing the margin of appreciation afforded to this semi-public/private body.

Another case that concerned the same sewerage undertaker is *Dobson v Thames Water Utilities Ltd* (2007).[207] A large group of residents brought a group action against the sewerage undertaker because of the odours and mosquitoes from the sewage works near their properties. The claimants were divided into two categories: those who occupied properties as owners or lessees and those who occupied without any legal interest in the properties. The residents alleged that the smell nuisance/mosquitoes was caused by the TWU's negligence in failing to treat the sewage properly. In addition their claims in nuisance and negligence were coupled with a claim for damages under the Human Rights Act for breach of their rights under Art 8 (and Art 1 of Protocol 1). The case is

---

206 S 94(1)(a) imposes a specific statutory duty on Thames Water to 'improve and extend its sewerage system, so as to ensure that the local area is effectively drained'.
207 *Dobson v Thames Water Utilities Ltd* [2009] EWCA Civ 28; [2009] 3 All ER 319.

still at its preliminary stages and the Court of Appeal's decision in 2009 was an appeal from the High Court on three preliminary issues. On appeal TWU was largely concerned with the way in which damages should be assessed where there were claims in both nuisance and the HRA 1998. The Appeal Court held that an award of damages in nuisance to a person or persons with a proprietary interest in a property would be relevant to the question whether an award of damages was necessary to afford just satisfaction under Art 8 to a person who lived in the same household but had no proprietary interest in the property. The availability of other remedies was relevant to the issue of whether damages were necessary to afford just satisfaction under s 8(3) of the 1998 Act and that required all circumstances to be taken into account. Despite the fact that damages for private nuisance were awarded as damage to 'land', it was highly improbable, if not inconceivable, that the ECtHR would think it appropriate or just or necessary to award a further sum on top for breach of Art 8. Accordingly, the award of damages at common law to a property owner would normally constitute just satisfaction to the owner for the purposes of s 8(3) of the 1998 Act, and no additional award of compensation under that Act would normally be necessary.

Law in Action

The significance of the HRA 1998 in the context of Art 8 rights is illustrated by the planning case involving the Kings Hill Collective (a group of people who believe in pursuing a sustainable lifestyle). The Collective constructed a number of low-impact dwellings known as 'benders' (wooden and canvas shelters) on land near Shepton Mallet without the benefit of planning permission. A planning enforcement notice was served on the Collective requiring the removal of the benders. The Collective appealed unsuccessfully to the Secretary of State for the Environment against the enforcement notice. Subsequently, the Collective made an application to the High Court to have the Secretary of State's decision judicially reviewed. On appeal, the Court of Appeal confirmed the decision of the High Court that the Secretary of State had erred in not considering whether or not a decision adverse to the Collective would breach Art 8. The decision was remitted to the Secretary of State for reconsideration and the original decision was reversed. Although the erection of the benders was a development which was contrary to the planning policies in the relevant development plan,[208] the appellants' human rights were material considerations of significant weight. Upholding the enforcement notice was a serious interference with the appellants' Art 8 rights. Breach of the right to a private and home life had to be balanced against the wider public interest issues comprising the effect of the benders on the surrounding landscape, traffic generation and the potential precedent effect of the bender development. The Secretary of State concluded that the development would not have a significant adverse impact on the public interest and, after taking Art 8 into account, he concluded that these factors outweighed the planning presumption in favour of development which accords with the development plan. Accordingly, the enforcement notice appeal was upheld and retrospective planning permission was granted. The *Kings Hill Collective* case runs somewhat contrary to the general run of similar UK planning cases in which human rights issues have arisen. For example, in *Buckley v UK* (1996),[209] the applicant, a gypsy who purchased land on which she parked her caravans, did not obtain planning

---

208 And therefore the presumption was that the outcome of the appeal would be in accordance with the development plan—see s 54(A) of the Town and Country Planning Act 1990.
209 *Buckley v UK* (1996) (1997) 23 EHRR 101; [1997] 2 PLR 10.

approval for the use of her land, which resulted in the local planning authority taking enforcement action for breach of planning control. Mrs Buckley argued that the enforcement proceedings prevented her from living a gypsy lifestyle, contrary to Art 8. Whilst the court held that Art 8 could apply in such cases, it concluded that the interference with the applicant's Art 8 rights was justified on road safety and public health grounds.[210]

12.11.3 The right to property: Article 1 of Protocol 1

Article 1 of Protocol 1 states that:

Every natural or legal person is entitled to the peaceful enjoyment of his possessions. No one shall be deprived of his possessions except in the general public interest and subject to the conditions provided for by law and by the general principles of international law.

The preceding provisions shall not, however, in any way impair the right of a state to enforce such laws as it deems necessary to control the use of property in accordance with the general interest or to secure the payment of other taxes or contributions or penalties.

In *Powell and Rayner v UK*,[211] it was stated that Art 1 of Protocol 1 does not, in principle, guarantee a right to the peaceful enjoyment of possessions in a pleasant environment. It is unlikely that the article will be capable of forming the basis of an action relating to loss of amenity, such as a pleasant view. Any person (including a company) may be able to rely on the Art 1 right to challenge the decisions of public bodies which, although taken with the object of protecting the natural environment for the general benefit of society (the general public interest), interfere with his or her right to peaceful enjoyment of his or her possessions. In *Fredin v Sweden* (1991),[212] the applicant's licence to extract gravel from his land was revoked (by a public body) following changes in Swedish nature conservation law. In rejecting the applicant's claim, the European Court of Human Rights took note of the following factors: (a) the revocation decision was a property-related control; (b) the Swedish authorities had a legitimate objective in revoking the permission—environmental protection; and (c) the applicant had no legitimate expectation that the permission would not be revoked. It seems that interference with the right to property will be justified where the interference is in conformity with planning laws and is designed to protect the environment.

The European Court of Human Rights has so far adopted a liberal interpretation of the term 'possessions' in Art 1 of Protocol 1. Licences authorising the development of land,[213] mineral extraction,[214] waste management[215] and public entertainment[216] are all possessions with significant economic values. Article 1 has also been used as the basis of an action to recover the cost of salmon destroyed without payment of compensation under a Fish Health Regulation Order.[217]

---

210 See also *Brazil v Secretary of State for Transport, Local Government and the Regions* [2009] EWHC 424 (Admin), *Chapman v UK* (2001) 33 EHRR 18; 10 BHRC 48, *Clarke v Secretary of State for Transport, Local Government and the Regions* [2002] EWCA Civ 819; [2002] JPL 1365 and *South Bucks District Council v Porter* [2001] EWCA Civ 1549.
211 *Powell and Rayner v UK* (1990) 12 EHRR 355.
212 *Fredin v Sweden* 1993) 15 EHRR CD58.
213 Ibid.
214 Ibid.
215 R v *Leicestershire County Council ex p Blackfordby and Boothorpe Action Group Ltd* [2001] Env LR 2; [2000] EHLR 215; [2000] JPL 1266.
216 *Catscratch Ltd and Lettuce Holdings Ltd v Glasgow Licensing Board* 2002 SLT 503; 2001 SCLR 817; [2001] UKHRR 1309.
217 *Booker Aquaculture Ltd v Secretary of State for Scotland* [1999] 1 CMLR 35 Outer House.

Similarly, any state or public authority decision to deprive (or refuse to license) an individual of a possession (for example, planning permission) can be challenged on the basis that the state or public authority has failed to strike a fair balance between the individual's Convention rights and the rights of the wider community. The aims of the state or public authorities must be legitimate and actions in furtherance of the relevant aims must be necessary, proportionate and fair. Human rights-based challenges may not only arise in relation to refusal of planning permission and enforcement of planning control, but also in regard to restrictive policies included in development plans which are alleged to breach Art 1 of Protocol 1.[218]

In addition to the substantive rights discussed above, the ECHR confers a number of procedural rights which have been used in planning and environmental litigation.

12.11.4 The right to a fair trial: Article 6

Article 6(1) states:

> In the determination of his civil rights and obligations or of any criminal charge against him everyone is entitled to a fair and public hearing within a reasonable time by an independent and impartial tribunal established by law.

The European Court of Human Rights has liberally construed the reference in Art 6 to a person's 'civil rights and obligations'. These include a range of property-related rights benefiting both the private and commercial sectors.[219] If a person's property is affected by a State or public authority decision and that person has no effective means of challenge, then it is probable that the person's right to a fair hearing by an independent and impartial tribunal will have been breached (Art 6).

Article 6 may be subdivided into the following rights: access to a tribunal (impartial, independent and lawfully constituted); a fair hearing; a prompt hearing; a public hearing; and a public judgment.

In *Benthem v Netherlands* (1985),[220] the applicant was granted a licence to operate a liquid petroleum gas plant by a local authority, but this was later revoked by a central government decree. The European Court of Human Rights held that the applicant's Art 6 rights had been breached because the rights had not been subjected to an adjudication by an independent tribunal. In *Ortenberg v Austria* (1994),[221] the applicant's property adjoined a new housing development and she feared that her right to the enjoyment of the amenities of her property would be infringed by the construction works. She also feared that the value of her property would be adversely affected by the adjoining development. She unsuccessfully attempted to challenge the grant of planning permission in the Austrian Administrative Court. Ultimately, the matter came before the European Court of Human Rights, at which juncture it was held that Art 6 did apply to the circumstances of the applicant's case and although the applicant was attempting to protect her own private pecuniary interests, nevertheless, her Art 6 rights should have been considered by an appropriate tribunal.

Only 'victims' may rely upon Art 6—those persons whose civil rights and obligations are in issue. NGOs such as Greenpeace will generally not have sufficient standing to mount Art 6 challenges.[222]

---

218 *Katte Klitsche de la Grange v Italy* (1994) 19 EHRR 368.
219 E.g., planning permission, revocation of permission and compulsory purchase.
220 *Benthem v Netherlands* (1985) 8 EHRR 1.
221 *Ortenberg v Austria* (1994) EHRR 524.
222 See *R (on the Application of Vetterlein) v Hampshire CC* [2001] EWHC (Admin) 560; [2001] All ER(D) 146.

Article 6 challenges may be based not only on allegations concerning failures in access to, impartiality and independence of tribunals, but also with regard to procedural failures such as timely access to information, the giving of adequate reasons for a decision, the imposition of inadequate time limits or the lack of proper notice that a tribunal's decision was pending.

The *Alconbury* case (2001)[223] concerned a planning application to develop a redundant Ministry of Defence airfield (government property) as a distribution centre. Planning permission had been refused by the planning committee of the local planning authority and an appeal against the refusal followed. The Secretary of State used his 'call-in' power[224] to recover jurisdiction in the case at the appeal stage. This was a case in which the government stood to gain from a decision to allow the development to proceed. A legal challenge was launched against the Secretary of State's action based on Art 6.[225] The High Court ruled in favour of the applicants and held that the Secretary of State's role as both policy-maker and decision-maker on the 'called-in' planning application was incompatible with Art 6 of the ECHR. In effect, the Secretary of State was judge in his own cause. The Court went on to state that, in its opinion, the inquiry system provided an adequate safeguard for the public where a planning inspector took a decision with regard to a planning appeal, but not where the Secretary of State took the decision. An appeal to the House of Lords followed swiftly. The House of Lords reversed the High Court's ruling and held that the Secretary of State's powers are not incompatible with the Human Rights Act 1998. The Court held that whilst the Secretary of State's consideration of the case, using his 'call-in' power, was not an impartial hearing, nevertheless, this was not the decisive factor. It was enough that the Secretary of State's decision was subject to a judicial body which did provide the Art 6 guarantees.[226] Importantly, the judicial control over the Secretary of State's hearing of the matter did not require a rehearing of the merits of the case in order for the current process to amount to a sufficient review of the legality of the decision and the procedures which were followed in reaching that decision. The courts' judicial review powers and the accountability of the Secretary of State to Parliament were adequate safeguards under the Human Rights Act 1998.

The right to a fair hearing may also be the subject of legal challenge relating to the use of the administrative powers of regulatory bodies. Regulators such as the Environment Agency often have legal powers which may be used to elicit information which causes defendants to incriminate themselves. In *Hertfordshire CC ex p Green Environmental Industries Ltd and John Moynihan* (2000),[227] the county council in its capacity as WRA conducted an investigation into allegations of illegal fly-tipping of waste by Mr Moynihan contrary to s 33(1) of the EPA 1990. The council used its powers (under s 71(2) of the EPA 1990) to require Mr Moynihan to assist the council with its inquiries into alleged waste offences. Mr Moynihan challenged the use of the council's powers on the grounds that their use infringed the rule against self-incrimination and the right to remain silent which is implied in the Art 6(1) right to a fair trial/hearing. Both the Court of Appeal and House of Lords rejected these arguments and dismissed the case. The House of Lords approached this issue by reference to EC law,[228] UK law,[229] and the principles and case law of the European Court of Human Rights, which form part of EC jurisprudence. The Court relied on the cases of *Saunders v UK* (1996),[230] in which the European Court held that the privilege against self-incrimination did not apply to

223 R (On the Application of Holding & Barnes Plc and Others) v Secretary of State for the Environment, Transport and the Regions [2001] UKHL 23; [2003] 2 AC 295; [2001] 2 WLR 1389; [2001] 2 All ER 929; [2002] Env LR 12.
224 S 77 of the TCPA 1990.
225 The right to a hearing before an 'independent and impartial tribunal'.
226 In such cases, a right exists enabling the applicant to apply to the higher courts against the decision of the Secretary of State on a point of law.
227 Hertfordshire CC ex p Green Environmental Industries Ltd and John Moynihan [2000] 1 All ER 773; [1998] Env LR 153.
228 The Waste Framework Directive (91/156/EEC).
229 Pt II of the EPA 1990 and the Waste Management Regulations 1994 SI 1994/1056.
230 Saunders v UK (1997) 23 EHRR 313.

extra-judicial inquiries, and Case 374/87, *Orkem v Commission* (1989),[231] in which the applicant received a questionnaire from a regulator containing a request for information which, when completed, would amount to an admission of guilt. The questionnaire was held by the European Court to breach the Art 6 privilege against self-incrimination. The House of Lords in *Saunders* held that as the s 71(2) EPA 1990 notice was a request for purely factual information, the notice did not breach Art 6, even though the answers provided might be incriminating. Thus, compulsory questioning does not automatically result in a breach of Art 6. Even if a subsequent case were to hold that such a practice breached the information provider's Art 6 rights, there appears to be no bar to a regulator (public authority) issuing multiple requests for information to several individuals on a site where illegal activity is suspected. The information provided by one individual might incriminate another person and vice versa. In these circumstances, there seems to be no breach of Art 6.

In considering the evidence in a criminal prosecution,[232] a judge is entitled to exclude evidence obtained via the exercise of a s 71 of the EPA 1990 notice if: (a) the questions are designed to extract an admission of guilt; or (b) the information was unfairly obtained, or was obtained without proper regard to due process. Section 71 of the EPA 1990 or similar information-gathering interview powers are not subject to the same strict requirements as interviews conducted by the police under the Police and Criminal Evidence Act 1984.

What happens if information provided via a s 71 or similar information-gathering power is subsequently relied upon as evidence in a later criminal trial? Does a breach of Art 6 occur? This issue was considered in *Stott (Procurator Fiscal Dunfermline) v Brown* (2001),[233] not in an environmental context, but with regard to the power to obtain information under s 172 of the Road Traffic Act 1972. In reaching the conclusion that the use of the s 172 power was not a breach of Art 6, the court drew attention to the following factors: (a) the ECHR did not expressly guarantee that a defendant had a right not to incriminate himself or herself; (b) the scope of the privilege against self-incrimination is not set out in detail; and (c) none of the Art 6 rights, express or implied, was absolute. The court went on to hold that a state may limit Art 6 rights, provided (a) in restricting Art 6, the state's objectives were clear and proper; and (b) the limitation of Art 6 was the minimum necessary to enable the state to achieve its objectives. In view of the widespread problem of motor accidents and consequent injuries and deaths, some form of regulation was necessary. Section 172 required the provision of information only with regard to the identity of the driver of a motor vehicle and that information of itself did not incriminate anyone. The penalty for refusing to respond to s 172 was a moderate fine (with no custodial option) and there was no suggestion that the defendant had been coerced into responding to the s 172 request. As s 172 applied equally to all motorists, the restriction on Art 6 was not disproportionate to the objective of the legislation—to improve road safety through identifying and punishing motorists who broke the relevant law.

Compulsory questioning does not breach Art 6 provided: (a) there is a good reason for restricting Art 6; (b) questions are clear and are not designed to extract an admission of guilt; and (c) the information provider is not coerced to supply the information. Any threat relating to the penalties for failure to supply information is likely to amount to coercion and breach of the article.[234]

---

231 *Orkem v Commission* (Case 374/87) [1989] ECR 3283.
232 E.g., s 33 of the EPA 1990.
233 *Stott (Procurator Fiscal Dunfermline) v Brown* [2001] 2 WLR 817; [2001] 2 All ER 97.
234 *Heaney and McGuinness v Ireland* [2001] Crim LR 481.

12.11.5 The right to freedom of expression: Article 10

Article 10 provides:

1 Everyone has the right to freedom of expression. This right shall include freedom to hold opinions and to receive and impart information and ideas without interference by public authority and regardless of frontiers . . .

2 The exercise of these freedoms, since it carries with it duties and responsibilities, may be subject to such formalities, conditions, restrictions, or penalties as are prescribed by law and are necessary in a democratic society.

In *Guerra v Italy*,[235] the application of Art 10 to the facts of the case was considered. Both the Commission and the European Court had interesting remarks to make concerning the relevance of Art 10 rights in circumstances in which state inaction exposes citizens to environmental risks. The failure of the Italian authorities to inform the applicant about the pollution risks generated by the waste treatment plants and the failure to provide information, as required by the Control of Major Accident Hazards Directive, infringed Art 10. The Commission was of the opinion that the provision of information to the public was an essential means to protect the health and well being of the population. Article 10 conferred on the local population who had been affected, or who might be affected, by the activity representing a threat to the environment, a right to receive such information. The court agreed with the Commission but found, in the particular circumstances, that there was no positive obligation on the state to collect and disseminate such information.

12.12 Online resource centre

We recommend that the reader regularly refers to the section of the online resources corresponding to this chapter for information relating to updates, amendments and corrections.

12.13 Summary of key points

Chapter 12 has covered the following topics and issues:

- the reasons why public participation in environmental matters is so important and the different ways in which the public, either individually or through group action, have a role to play in protecting the environment;
- the inextricable relationship between access to environmental information and public participation and access to justice in environmental matters, and the significance of the Aarhus Convention in securing these three 'rights';
- the fact that neither the Aarhus Convention or the European Convention on Human Rights confer a 'right' to a clean environment but how both provide a range of procedural and substantive rights that are increasingly being used by the public in an attempt to secure better protection of the environment;
- the information 'rights' that have been conferred on the public by the Environmental Information Directive and Environmental Information Regulations 2004;
- the role of judicial review in environmental protection and the rights that it affords the public to challenge decisions taken by public authorities; coupled with an understanding of some of the difficulties that individuals and NGOs face in mounting successful judicial review cases;

---

235 See 12.7.1.1 above.

- the Access to Justice pillar of the Aarhus Convention and the extent to which the judicial system in England and Wales is not necessarily 'Convention compliant', particularly in relation to the requirements that environmental litigation within the scope of the Convention should not be 'prohibitively expensive';
- a knowledge and understanding of the emerging role of the Human Rights Act 1998 in the armoury of litigants seeking to enforce environmental laws.

12.14 Further reading

Books

See Chapter 7 of *Sourcebook on Environmental Law* (Cavendish Publishing, 2001, 2nd edn), which covers *Guerra v Italy, Booker Aquaculture Ltd v Secretary of State for the Environment, Powell and Rayner v UK* and extracts from the ECHR.

Adams, J, *Risk* (UCL Press, 1995).

Alston, P (ed), *The EU and Human Rights* (Clarendon, 1999).

Beck, U, *Risk Society* (Sage, 1992).

Boyle, A and Anderson, M (eds), *Human Rights Approaches to Environmental Protection* (Clarendon, 1996).

Brinkman, R, Jasonoff, S and Ilgen, T, *Controlling Chemicals* (Cornell UP, 1985).

English, R and Havers, P (eds), *An Introduction to Human Rights and the Common Law* (Hart, 2000).

Furedi, F, *Culture of Fear* (Cassell, 1997).

Grant, W, *Pressure Groups, Politics and Democracy in Great Britain* (Harvester Wheatsheaf, 1995, 2nd edn).

Hadfield, B, *Judicial Review: A Thematic Approach* (Macmillan, 1995).

Hallo, R, *Access to Environmental Information in Europe: The Implementation and Implications of Directive 90/313/EEC* (Kluwer, 1996).

Jewell, T and Steele, J (eds), *Law in Environmental Decision-Making* (Clarendon, 1998).

Miller, C, *Environmental Rights: Critical Perspectives* (Routledge, 1998).

Pugh, C and Day, M, *Pollution and Personal Injury: Toxic Torts II* (Cameron and May, 1995).

Ridley, F and Jordan, G, *Protest Politics: Cause Groups and Campaigns* (OUP, 1998).

Robinson, D and Dunkley, J (eds), *Public Interest Perspectives in Environmental Law* (Wiley, 1995).

Rowell, A, *Green Backlash: Global Subversion of the Environmental Movement* (Routledge, 1996).

Royal Commission on Environmental Pollution, *Tackling Pollution: Experience and Prospects*, 10th Report, Cmnd 9149 (HMSO, 1984).

The Royal Society, *Risk: Analysis, Perception, and Management* (1992).

Sandman, P, *Responding to Community Outrage: Strategies for Effective Risk Communication* (American Industrial Hygiene Association, 1993).

Simpson, D, *Pressure Groups* (Hodder & Stoughton, 1999).

Symonides, J (ed), *Human Rights—New Dimensions and Challenges* (Ashgate, 1998).

Vogler, J, *The Global Commons: A Regime Analysis* (Wiley, 1995).

Wilson, D, *The Secrets File* (Heinemann, 1984).

Articles

Birtles, W, 'A right to know: the Environmental Information Regulations 1992' [1993] JPL 615.

Cane, P, 'Standing up for the public' [1995] PL 276.

De Merieux, M, 'Deriving environmental rights from the ECHR' (2001) OJLS 521.

Etemire, U, 'Public Access to Environmental Information Held by Private Companies' [2012] 14(1) *Environmental Law Review* 7.

Feldman, D, 'Public interest litigation and constitutional theory in comparative perspective' [1992] MLR 44.

Hart, D, 'The impact of the European Convention on planning and environmental law' [2000] JPL 117.

Hilson, C and Cram, I, 'Judicial review and environmental law: is there a coherent view of standing?' (1996) *Legal Studies* 1.

Jendroska, J and Stec, S, 'The Aarhus Convention: towards a new era in environmental democracy' (2001) Env Liability 140.

Klamert, M, 'Dark matter: competence, jurisdiction and 'the area largely covered by EU law' – comment on *Lesoochranarske* (2012) 3 EuL Rev 340.

Mowbray, A, '*Guerra v Italy:* the right to environmental information under the ECHR' (1998) Env Liability 81.

Rowan-Robinson, J, 'Public access to environmental information: a means to what end?' [1996] JEL 19.

Schiemann, K, '*Locus standi*' (1990) PL 342.

Stanley, N, 'Public concern: the decision-maker's dilemma' [1998] JPL 919.

Stanley, N, 'Contentious planning disputes: an insoluble problem?' [2000] JPL 1226.

Steele, J, 'Participation and deliberation in environmental law: exploring a problem-solving approach' (2001) OJLS 415.

Thornton, J and Tromans, S, 'Human rights and environmental wrongs incorporating the ECHR; some thoughts on the consequences for UK environmental law' [1999] JEL 35.

Vick, D and Campbell, K, 'Public protests, private lawsuits and the market: the investor response to the McLibel case' (2001) *Journal of Law and Society* 204.

Zuckerman, A, 'Protective Costs Orders—a growing costs litigation industry' (2009) 28(2) CJQ 161.

Appendix

Legal resources: a basic guide for non-lawyers

Non-law students embarking upon the study of environmental law for the first time may be intimidated at first by the materials which are the stock-in-trade of the lawyer: textbooks packed full of information, reports of court cases contained in a variety of law reports, legislation (both primary—Acts of Parliament—and secondary—regulations) and academic/professional journal articles. However, based on our own experience of teaching a variety of environmental courses to both law and non-law students, we can state with confidence that non-lawyers find, after an initial period of familiarisation, that they can perform just as well as law students.

This appendix introduces non-law students to the most important sources of information on environmental law.

Cases

You will find reports of legal cases in law reports which are to be found in most university libraries (provided the relevant university has a law school).

There are a wide range of law reports to access, for example, the All England Reports, and these are arranged by year. Your course textbooks and case reports will cite (refer to) previously decided cases as authority for the statements made in the chapters of each text. The relevant case citation may look something like this: *Alphacell Ltd v Woodward* [1972] 2 WLR 1320. This means that this case is reported in the Weekly Law Reports, for the year 1972, in the second volume for that year, commencing on page 1320. Often, a case is reported in more than one report and you will therefore have a choice of reports to refer to. The abbreviations used to describe the relevant reports are often explained in a pamphlet which your university library will make available. Alternatively, there should be a notice or board in the law library which explains which reports are stocked and where they are to be found. Law libraries should stock the British Libraries Legal Index. This is a publication which records academic journal articles published on a year-by-year basis. At the front of each part of the Index, you will find an explanation of the abbreviations (for example, JEL—Journal of Environmental Law) used in the Index. Students will also be able to search the library's online catalogue.

When you have successfully located the case which you have been looking for, you will usually find the case report divided up into (a) a summary of the main facts of the case, (b) a note of what the case actually decided (look for the heading 'Held'), (c) the cases and legislation which were referred to by the advocates in the case, and (d) the individual judgments of the judges making up the court. Cases decided in the Court of Appeal and the House of Lords (now the Supreme Court) will each contain a series of judgments, whereas cases decided in the High Court will usually be decided by a single judge.

Currently, there is only one series of reports which focuses on reporting environmental cases decided in the UK or decisions of the ECJ which will have a bearing on future cases in the UK (the Environmental Law Reports—cited as Env LR and published by Sweet & Maxwell).

Textbooks

There are several books which cover environmental law in England and Wales (see the texts and other materials listed at the end of each chapter or listed in the online resource which correspond to each chapter in this text). Non-lawyers will quickly come to realise that the information in legal textbooks cannot be absorbed by a cursory browse through the chapters which correspond to the topics on your module. The contents of textbooks have to be read and re-read until the reader understands the points which are being made. Your course or module handouts will almost certainly not provide you with all the information you must know and be able to apply to enable you to answer examination questions and assessed essays successfully. Your course handouts provide you with a framework for your studies. That framework must be supplemented by studying your textbook(s), case reports, relevant extracts from legislation, journal articles and other materials. If you are prepared to devote an appropriate amount of time to your studies, you should do well. If for any reason you encounter problems understanding the course material, the onus is on you to discuss the matter with your environmental law tutor.

Journals

The main environmental law journals are referred to in the materials in the online resource relating to Chapter 1.

Legal dictionaries

The law section of your library should contain copies of legal dictionaries. Non-law students often find legal terminology a little alien at first, but being aware of where to find a legal dictionary ought to soothe any concerns you may have that you will not understand 'legal language'.

The library catalogue

It is highly likely that your university will have a catalogue of contents which can be searched electronically. Provided you have a password (often this is not necessary), you may even be able to search the catalogue from your own PC rather than attending the library in person. The most common searches are: author searches, title searches and key word searches. Students (whose university has a law school) will probably be able to access WESTLAW, Lexis/Nexis, Lawtel and other databases of legal information online through their university library home page. These databases contain reported cases (UK and other jurisdictions), legislation, journal articles and other resources (refer to your library for full details of the extent of these resources).

Websites

At the end of most chapters in this text we have included a number of website addresses which will enable you to access a wide range of materials relating to environmental law and policy.

Inter-library loan system

Your university will be able to obtain for you via this system a book, article, report, etc, which is not held in your own library collection (a fee is payable for this service).

Public libraries

Public libraries in major cities in the UK will often have a legal section both in the reference section and the lending library. As might be expected, the range of materials is limited when compared with university collections. Public libraries operate a similar system of inter-library loans to that used by university libraries (a fee is payable).

The court systems

Non-lawyers should note the basic division of our legal system into criminal law and civil law. We set out below a simple diagram distinguishing between the criminal and civil court systems.

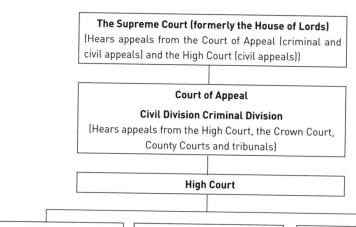

Index